Along Interstate 75

Year 2000
(8th edition)

by Dave Hunter

The ***Local Knowledge*** Driving Guide
for interstate travelers between
Detroit and the Florida Border

Along Interstate-75 is updated annually and available from **most bookstores** in the USA and Canada, from **selected AAA offices** (CAA in Ontario) and at **our website.**

The International Standard Book Order Number (ISBN) is **1-896819-109**

"Best Before" date - Nov., 2000
Travel guide information is very perishable - we work hard to make our travel information as fresh as possible for you.

Mile Oak Publishing Inc.
Suite 81, 20 Mineola Road East,
Mississauga, ON Canada L5G 4N9

e.mail: mile_oak@compuserve.com
Phone: 905-274-4356
Fax: 905-274-8656

Cover design by Margrie Wallace
Cover photograph by Akis Sofroniou

Research assistance and proofing – Kathy Hunter and Joan Gingras.

COPYRIGHT ©2000 by Mile Oak Publishing Inc.
All Rights Reserved which include but are not limited to the Rights to reproduce or record this book or portions thereof in any form whatsoever, or use the book's data for any commercial purposes without the express written permission of the Publisher.

Please note - every effort has been taken to ensure the accuracy of the contents of this book which is based on data sources believed to be reliable. The publisher and/or author assume no liability for the consequences of the accuracy or inaccuracy of the information contained herein or error or omission.

Cataloging in Publication Data

Hunter, Dave, 1941 -
Along Interstate-75, Local knowledge for the I-75 between Detroit & the Florida Border
2000 Edition
ISBN 1-896819-10-9
1. Interstate-75 - Guidebooks. 2. United States - Guidebooks
3. Automobile Travel - United States - Guidebooks
I. Title II. Series

Printing History

Original (1993) edition -printed Oct., 1992; updated annually and released each October. Current (8th) edition released October, 1999.

Artwork courtesy of Softkey Clipmaster Pro and Corel Corporation's Gallery, Gallery 2, Mega Gallery and IMSI USA including:
Image Club Graphics Inc., One Mile Up Inc.,
Techpool Studios Inc. and Totem Graphics Inc.

A Word About the Production of this Book . . .

A highly detailed book such as *"Along Interstate-75"* could not be written without the aid of very powerful computers and graphics/publishing software. For those interested in such matters, we use Corel Draw 5 & 8 for all our maps and then transfer these to QuarkXPress - our publishing software. Many of the small pieces of art throughout the book are either drawn or adapted by myself, or are courtesy of Corel's wonderful gallery collections of clipart - Gallery, Gallery 2 and Mega Gallery. Several pieces are also courtesy of Softkey's ClipMaster Pro collection.

All of this comes together on a Pentium II 300mhz computer with all sorts of additional bells and whistles to make the job just a little easier. The entire process is driven by one person — myself — who within five weeks takes all of your ideas, letters and our field notes — and melds them into a brand new edition of *"Along Interstate-75"* — ready for the forthcoming season.

The resulting computer files are then, through the electronic pre-press magic of Toronto's ***PC Imaging Inc.***, turned into sheets of printing media (each containing 16 pages) from which our printer produces the shiny finished book now in your hands.

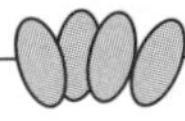

Printed in Canada by Gerrie-Young
Lithography, Mississauga, Ontario

Contents at a Glance . . .

Plus, **many *$avings hint$* and *"Insider Tips"* . . .**
. . . to help you save money and enjoy your trip.

Contents

Revised: Aug 20, 1999

Page

MISCELLANEOUS

. . . and ***tips, tips and more tips*** — throughout the section

I-75 LODGING

NORTHBOUND I-75 DETAIL MAPS (1 page = 25 miles)

BYPASS STRATEGY

Revised: Aug 20, 1999

Hello and Welcome to the 2000 Edition of Along Interstate-75

Hello to all my I-75 friends,

I just returned from a ten day journey up and down Interstate-75 and let me tell you, there are many new and exciting things happening. The big one you'll experience in year 2000 is the statewide change of all the Georgia exit numbers (see page 101). New signage will start to go up in Georgia in January, 2000, and all will be completed by July. I suspect that I-75 will be one of the first Georgia interstates to be completed since it's the state's major north-south corridor.

If you're heading south before the new year, you'll not see this change but when you come back in the spring, you probably will. I therefore decided to change to the new exit numbers throughout this book, but keep the old numbers alongside - so you'll have the best of both worlds!

Many more new motels and inns have recently been built, particularly in the mid scale market range. New Jamesons and Wingates are rapidly appearing along I-75 but because much of the prime real estate has already been taken, some of these are being built on the east/west service roads which parallel the interstate. Because of this, people don't always know how to reach them - but let me tell you, there are good rates to be had as these properties need to be "discovered." All are on our maps.

A hint here - always drive around a motel before going to the front counter to negotiate for a room. If it's 5 o'clock and there are only a few cars in the back - then they definitely need your business. For your interest, we recorded 532 changes to the exit information (gas, food, lodging) between last year's book and this one.

I keep reading about I-75 construction, but quite frankly, my drives in the last two years have been excellent (now the Toledo project is complete) with hardly any slow stretches. What is going on here? I've given you my answer on page 144.

My maps have been redrawn this year with even more information to help you - 24 hour superstores, vet/animal clinics, rest area hours - you'll find these included on our maps now which should be more convenient for you. Also included are gas stations with mechanics, food places with playgrounds, and motels accepting pets. You'll also note that I have colored the book's pages to help you find the various section much more easily this year. We wanted to add tabs but found the cost to be too prohibitive (did you know the price for *"Along I-75"* has been the same since 1996?).

Finally, I recognize that many of my readers now have computer Internet access so I'll be introducing a new free service in the late fall. I have opened a website - *www.i75online.com* - and you will be able to get information such as the latest I-75 road construction, new I-75 speedtraps, state-by-state gas prices, and much more, from it. It'll only be for people such as you, my I-75 friends. To ensure this, I have hidden a secret password in this book and when you sign on for the first time, I'll tell you how to find it.

Have a great and safe trip.

Dave

Quick Start Hints - Getting the most from this book

Along Interstate-75 is quite different from other travel books you may have read. Between its covers we have included an interstate exit guide, an "arm-chair" travel book, a tour book, a driving guide and much more. So let's take a few minutes before you hit the road to explore its pages . . . that way, you'll get the maximum benefit from it on your I-75 journey.

By now, you will have noticed that the book is divided into a number of colorful sections. The orange and blue pages are the 25 mile-per-page southbound and northbound maps - we'll come back to those in a minute.

The first white section is the unfolding story of the country around you, told milepost by milepost as you proceed on your journey. Everything is here - things you see along the way, roadside history, local knowledge, special money saving tips, notes about the countryside and personal recommendations for the best places to eat and stay - our Insider Tips - we've gathered over the years. This section and the maps are the pages you'll probably use most on your journey.

The gray section contains useful information and phone numbers - we give you local radio stations which broadcast your favorite type of music or other programs, campgrounds for RVers and even information to help you should the weather become nasty.

The next section (white) is full of miscellaneous information which wouldn't fit anywhere else. Presented for general interest, you might want to browse through this before you leave.

The yellow section will help you with I-75 lodgings, including how to get the best bargain rate at the front desk. If you travel with a pet, you'll also find valuable advice here.

The pink section gives you all the radio stations (and personalities) for the best traffic reports in urban areas. Rush hour information and bypass route maps are also included.

The last white section contains "housekeeping" items. Additional resources, index to abbreviations, daily log sheet and other bits and pieces.

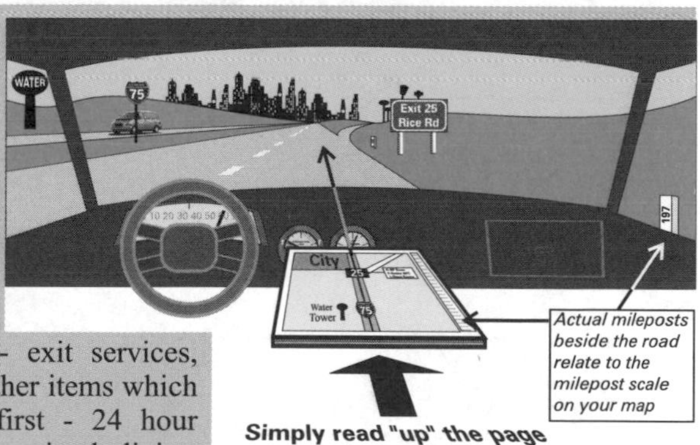

And now back to the maps: They are quite unique and very easy to use. As you can see from this diagram, they are printed in the direction you travel so that things drawn on the right side of the map pass you on the right side of your car, and vice-versa. They include all the usual things - exit services, landmarks, etc., but there are other items which may not be as apparent at first - 24 hour superstores, pharmacies, vets & animal clinics, "dry" counties, radar traps, rest area information and hours, color coded road speeds . . . even when you should change lane and which is the best lane to use so you don't interfere with local traffic.

Simply read "up" the page as the book sits in your lap — the road outside your car appears exactly as drawn on the map.

I think you'll agree they are like no other maps you've ever seen. Study them before you go - they'll ensure you have a fun yet safe journey.

Interstate-75 between Detroit and the Florida Border

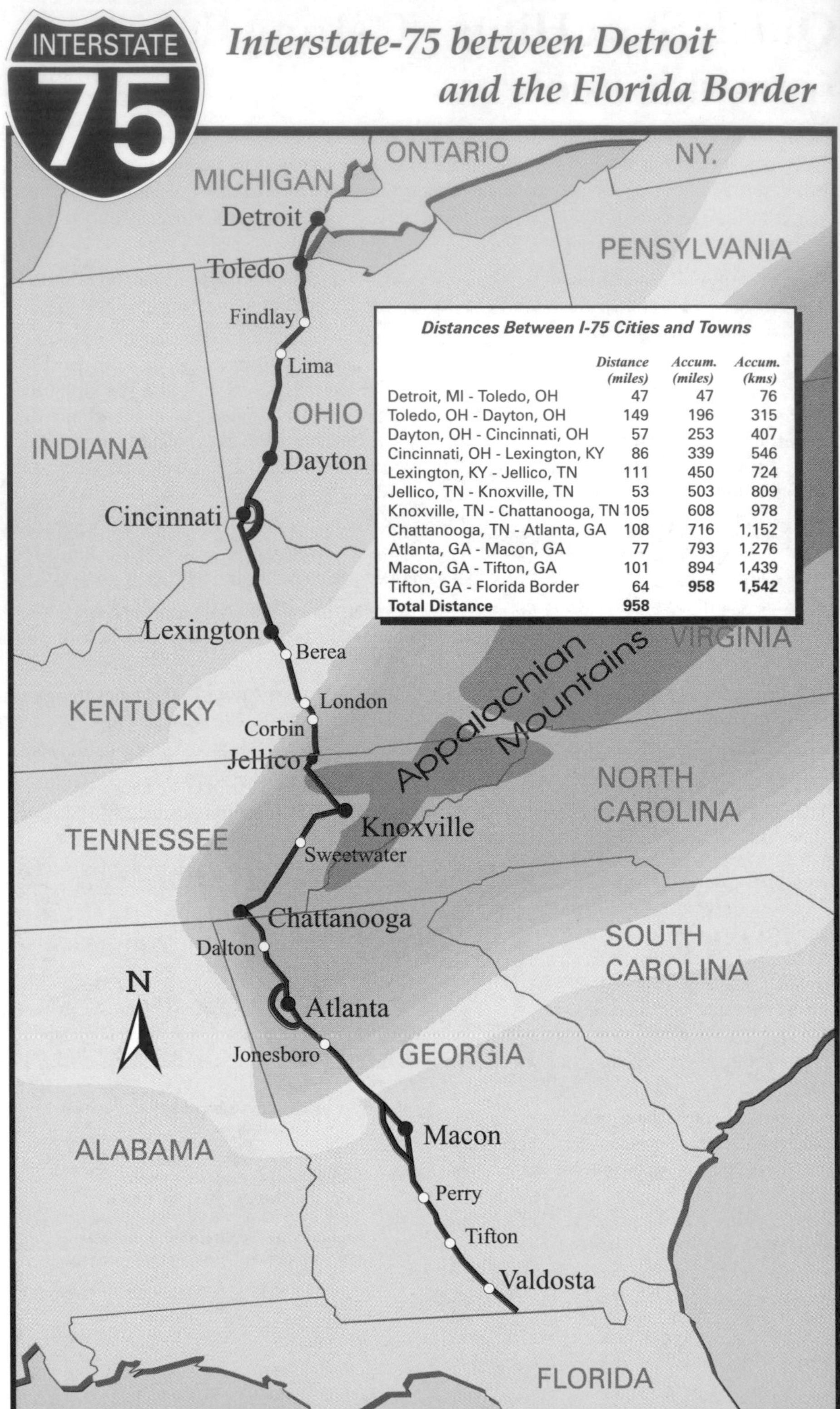

Distances Between I-75 Cities and Towns

	Distance (miles)	*Accum. (miles)*	*Accum. (kms)*
Detroit, MI - Toledo, OH	47	47	76
Toledo, OH - Dayton, OH	149	196	315
Dayton, OH - Cincinnati, OH	57	253	407
Cincinnati, OH - Lexington, KY	86	339	546
Lexington, KY - Jellico, TN	111	450	724
Jellico, TN - Knoxville, TN	53	503	809
Knoxville, TN - Chattanooga, TN	105	608	978
Chattanooga, TN - Atlanta, GA	108	716	1,152
Atlanta, GA - Macon, GA	77	793	1,276
Macon, GA - Tifton, GA	101	894	1,439
Tifton, GA - Florida Border	64	**958**	**1,542**
Total Distance	**958**		

Southbound Route

From Detroit to the Florida Border

Insider Tip for Southbound Travelers
Avoiding "Drive South" Sunburn

Did you know that you can get a sunburn and dangerous overload of cancer causing ultraviolet (UV) light while driving south, especially if you are not used to being outdoors for long periods of time? Three days of driving into the sun - the average run from Michigan to Florida on I-75 - can create a very high exposure to UV light on the face and arms, even on cloudy days.

The thick glass and plastic laminate of car windshields helps filter UV light so that only about 15% of UVA* and virtually no UVB* reach the car's interior, but the extra long hours of constant exposure and UV light coming through the thinner, non-laminated side windows can mean that you are receiving too much higher UV radiation than under normal circumstances.

To protect yourself from these harmful rays, wear long sleeves and use a sunscreen with protection factor of at least SPF15 on your face - and of course, keep your side windows rolled up.

Note: UVA ages the skin and can cause skin cancer; UVB causes burning.

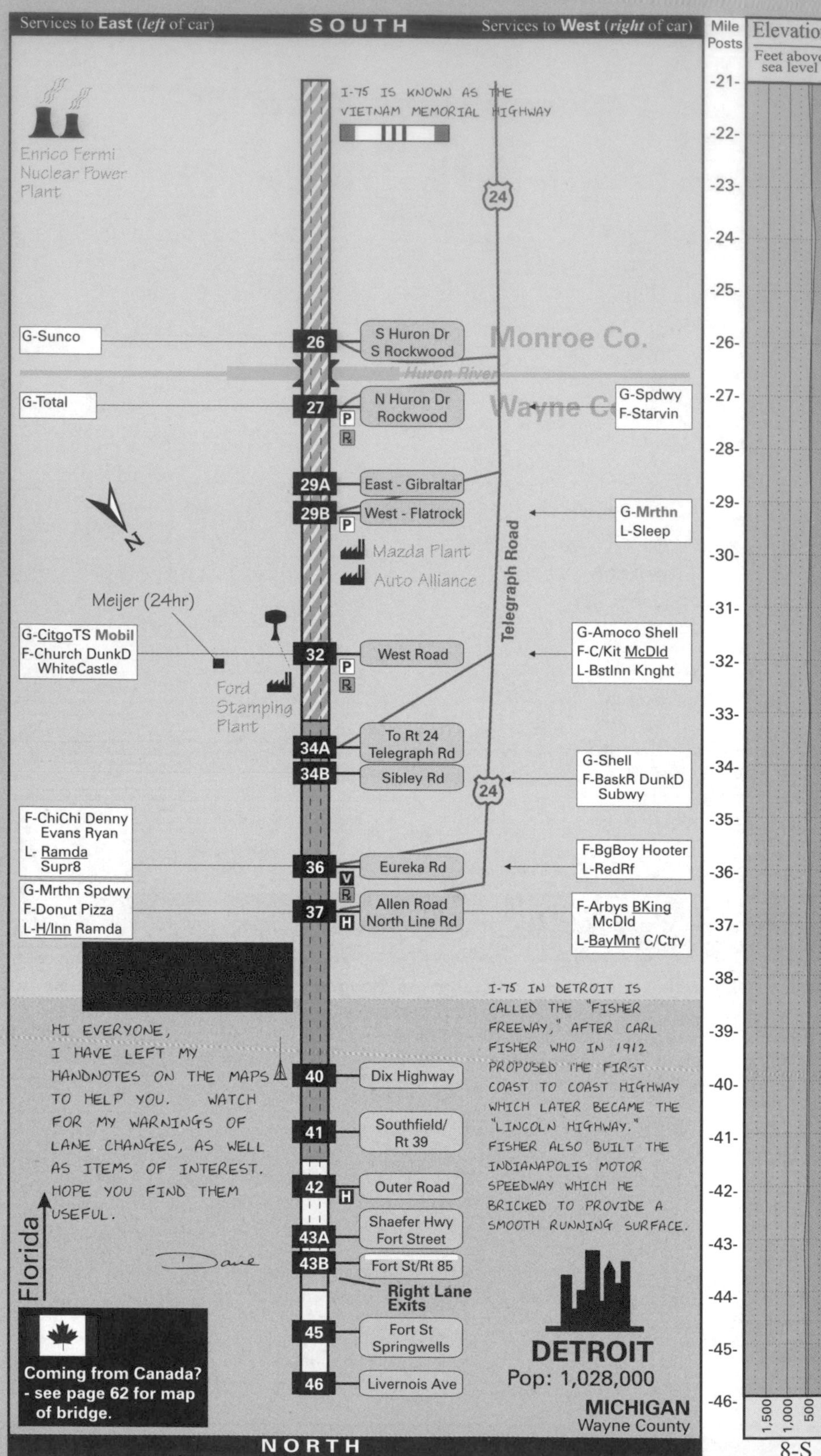

Services to East (left of car)
SOUTH
Services to West (right of car)
Mile Posts
Elevation
Feet above sea level
I-75 IS KNOWN AS THE VIETNAM MEMORIAL HIGHWAY
Enrico Fermi Nuclear Power Plant
24
G-Sunco
26
S Huron Dr
S Rockwood
Monroe Co.
Huron River
G-Total
27
N Huron Dr
Rockwood
Wayne Co
G-Spdwy
F-Starvin
29A
East - Gibraltar
29B
West - Flatrock
G-Mrthn
L-Sleep
N
Mazda Plant
Auto Alliance
Telegraph Road
Meijer (24hr)
G-CitgoTS Mobil
F-Church DunkD
WhiteCastle
32
West Road
G-Amoco Shell
F-C/Kit McDld
L-BstInn Knght
Ford Stamping Plant
34A
To Rt 24
Telegraph Rd
34B
Sibley Rd
24
G-Shell
F-BaskR DunkD
Subwy
F-ChiChi Denny
Evans Ryan
L- Ramda
Supr8
36
Eureka Rd
F-BgBoy Hooter
L-RedRf
G-Mrthn Spdwy
F-Donut Pizza
L-H/Inn Ramda
37
Allen Road
North Line Rd
F-Arbys BKing
McDld
L-BayMnt C/Ctry
HI EVERYONE,
I HAVE LEFT MY HANDNOTES ON THE MAPS TO HELP YOU. WATCH FOR MY WARNINGS OF LANE CHANGES, AS WELL AS ITEMS OF INTEREST. HOPE YOU FIND THEM USEFUL.
Dave
I-75 IN DETROIT IS CALLED THE "FISHER FREEWAY," AFTER CARL FISHER WHO IN 1912 PROPOSED THE FIRST COAST TO COAST HIGHWAY WHICH LATER BECAME THE "LINCOLN HIGHWAY." FISHER ALSO BUILT THE INDIANAPOLIS MOTOR SPEEDWAY WHICH HE BRICKED TO PROVIDE A SMOOTH RUNNING SURFACE.
40
Dix Highway
41
Southfield/
Rt 39
42
Outer Road
43A
Shaefer Hwy
Fort Street
43B
Fort St/Rt 85
Right Lane Exits
Florida
45
Fort St
Springwells
46
Livernois Ave
Coming from Canada?
- see page 62 for map of bridge.
DETROIT
Pop: 1,028,000
MICHIGAN
Wayne County
NORTH
-21- -22- -23- -24- -25- -26- -27- -28- -29- -30- -31- -32- -33- -34- -35- -36- -37- -38- -39- -40- -41- -42- -43- -44- -45- -46-
1,500 1,000 500
8-S

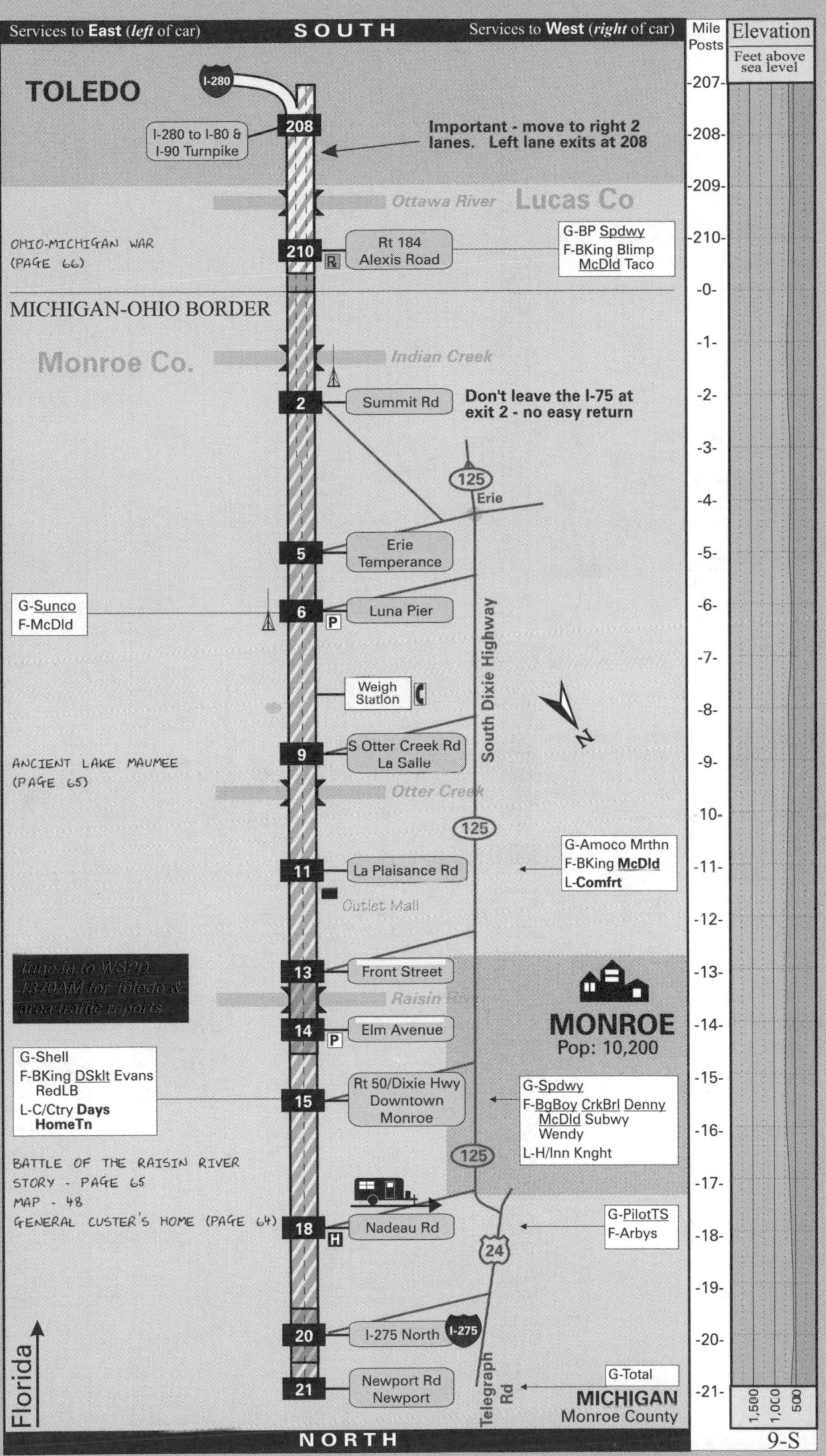

Services to East (left of car)
SOUTH
Services to West (right of car)
Mile Posts
Elevation
Feet above sea level
TOLEDO
I-280
208
I-280 to I-80 & I-90 Turnpike
Important - move to right 2 lanes. Left lane exits at 208
Ottawa River
Lucas Co
OHIO-MICHIGAN WAR (PAGE 66)
210
Rt 184 Alexis Road
G-BP Spdwy
F-BKing Blimp McDld Taco
MICHIGAN-OHIO BORDER
Monroe Co.
Indian Creek
2
Summit Rd
Don't leave the I-75 at exit 2 - no easy return
125
Erie
5
Erie Temperance
G-Sunco
F-McDld
6
Luna Pier
South Dixie Highway
Weigh Station
N
ANCIENT LAKE MAUMEE (PAGE 65)
9
S Otter Creek Rd La Salle
Otter Creek
125
11
La Plaisance Rd
G-Amoco Mrthn
F-BKing McDld
L-Comfrt
Outlet Mall
Tune in to WSPD 1370AM for Toledo & area traffic reports
13
Front Street
Raisin River
MONROE
Pop: 10,200
14
Elm Avenue
G-Shell
F-BKing DSklt Evans RedLB
L-C/Ctry Days HomeTn
15
Rt 50/Dixie Hwy Downtown Monroe
G-Spdwy
F-BgBoy CrkBrl Denny McDld Subwy Wendy
L-H/Inn Knght
125
BATTLE OF THE RAISIN RIVER
STORY - PAGE 65
MAP - 48
GENERAL CUSTER'S HOME (PAGE 64)
18
Nadeau Rd
G-PilotTS
F-Arbys
24
20
I-275 North
I-275
Florida
21
Newport Rd Newport
Telegraph Rd
G-Total
MICHIGAN
Monroe County
NORTH
-207- -208- -209- -210- -0- -1- -2- -3- -4- -5- -6- -7- -8- -9- -10- -11- -12- -13- -14- -15- -16- -17- -18- -19- -20- -21-
1,500 1,000 500

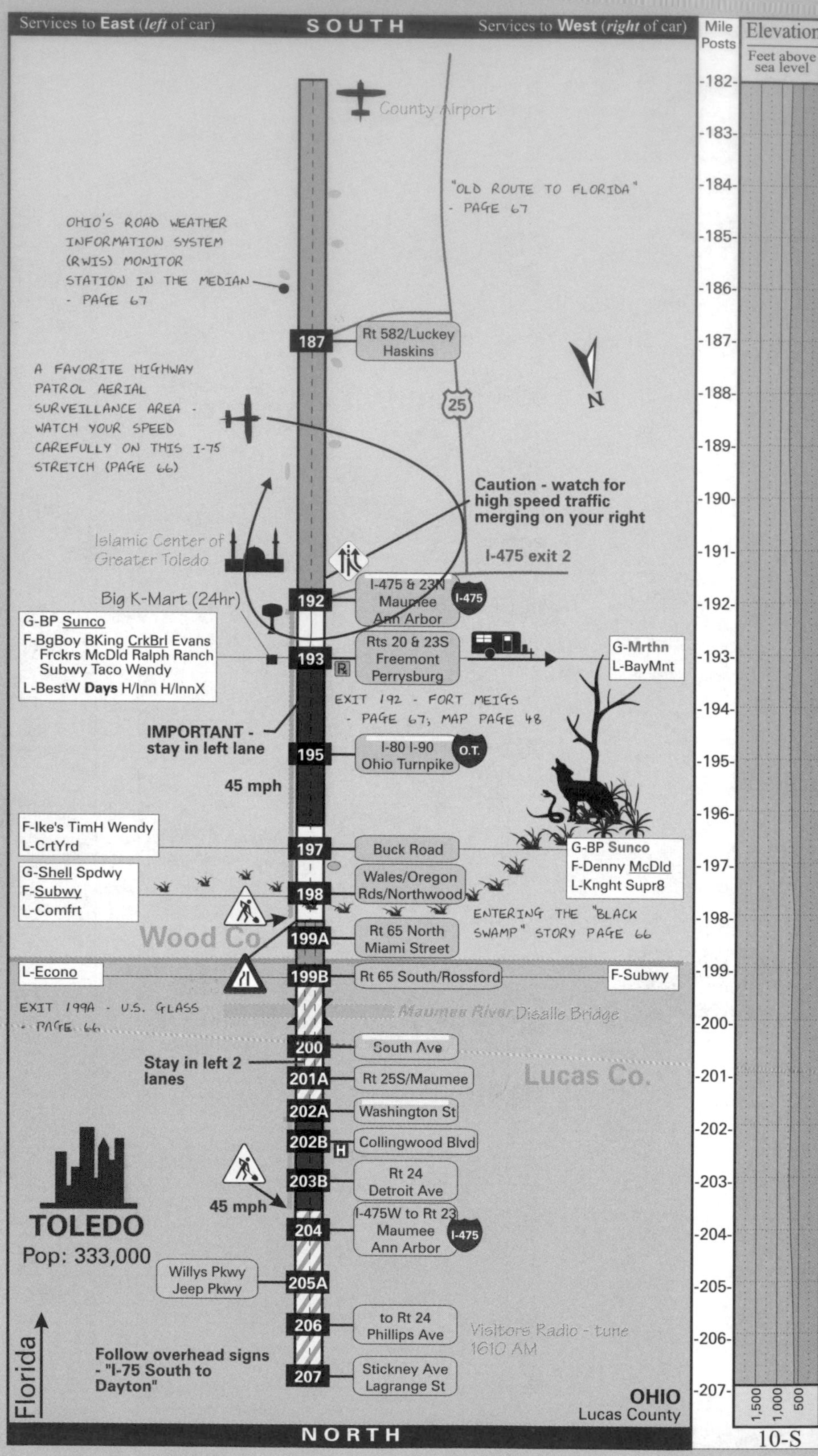
Services to East (left of car)
SOUTH
Services to West (right of car)
Mile Posts
Elevation
Feet above sea level
County Airport
"OLD ROUTE TO FLORIDA" - PAGE 67
OHIO'S ROAD WEATHER INFORMATION SYSTEM (RWIS) MONITOR STATION IN THE MEDIAN - PAGE 67
187
Rt 582/Luckey
Haskins
A FAVORITE HIGHWAY PATROL AERIAL SURVEILLANCE AREA - WATCH YOUR SPEED CAREFULLY ON THIS I-75 STRETCH (PAGE 66)
25
N
Caution - watch for high speed traffic merging on your right
Islamic Center of Greater Toledo
I-475 exit 2
Big K-Mart (24hr)
192
I-475 & 23N
Maumee
Ann Arbor
I-475
G-BP Sunco
F-BgBoy BKing CrkBrl Evans Frckrs McDld Ralph Ranch Subwy Taco Wendy
L-BestW Days H/Inn H/InnX
193
Rts 20 & 23S
Freemont
Perrysburg
G-Mrthn
L-BayMnt
EXIT 192 - FORT MEIGS - PAGE 67; MAP PAGE 48
IMPORTANT - stay in left lane
195
I-80 I-90
Ohio Turnpike
O.T.
45 mph
F-Ike's TimH Wendy
L-CrtYrd
197
Buck Road
G-BP Sunco
F-Denny McDld
L-Knght Supr8
G-Shell Spdwy
F-Subwy
L-Comfrt
198
Wales/Oregon
Rds/Northwood
ENTERING THE "BLACK SWAMP" STORY PAGE 66
Wood Co
199A
Rt 65 North
Miami Street
L-Econo
199B
Rt 65 South/Rossford
F-Subwy
EXIT 199A - U.S. GLASS - PAGE 66
Maumee River Disalle Bridge
200
South Ave
Stay in left 2 lanes
201A
Rt 25S/Maumee
Lucas Co.
202A
Washington St
202B
Collingwood Blvd
203B
Rt 24
Detroit Ave
45 mph
204
I-475W to Rt 23
Maumee
Ann Arbor
I-475
TOLEDO
Pop: 333,000
Willys Pkwy
Jeep Pkwy
205A
206
to Rt 24
Phillips Ave
Visitors Radio - tune 1610 AM
Follow overhead signs - "I-75 South to Dayton"
207
Stickney Ave
Lagrange St
Florida
OHIO
Lucas County
NORTH
-182- -183- -184- -185- -186- -187- -188- -189- -190- -191- -192- -193- -194- -195- -196- -197- -198- -199- -200- -201- -202- -203- -204- -205- -206- -207-
1,500 1,000 500

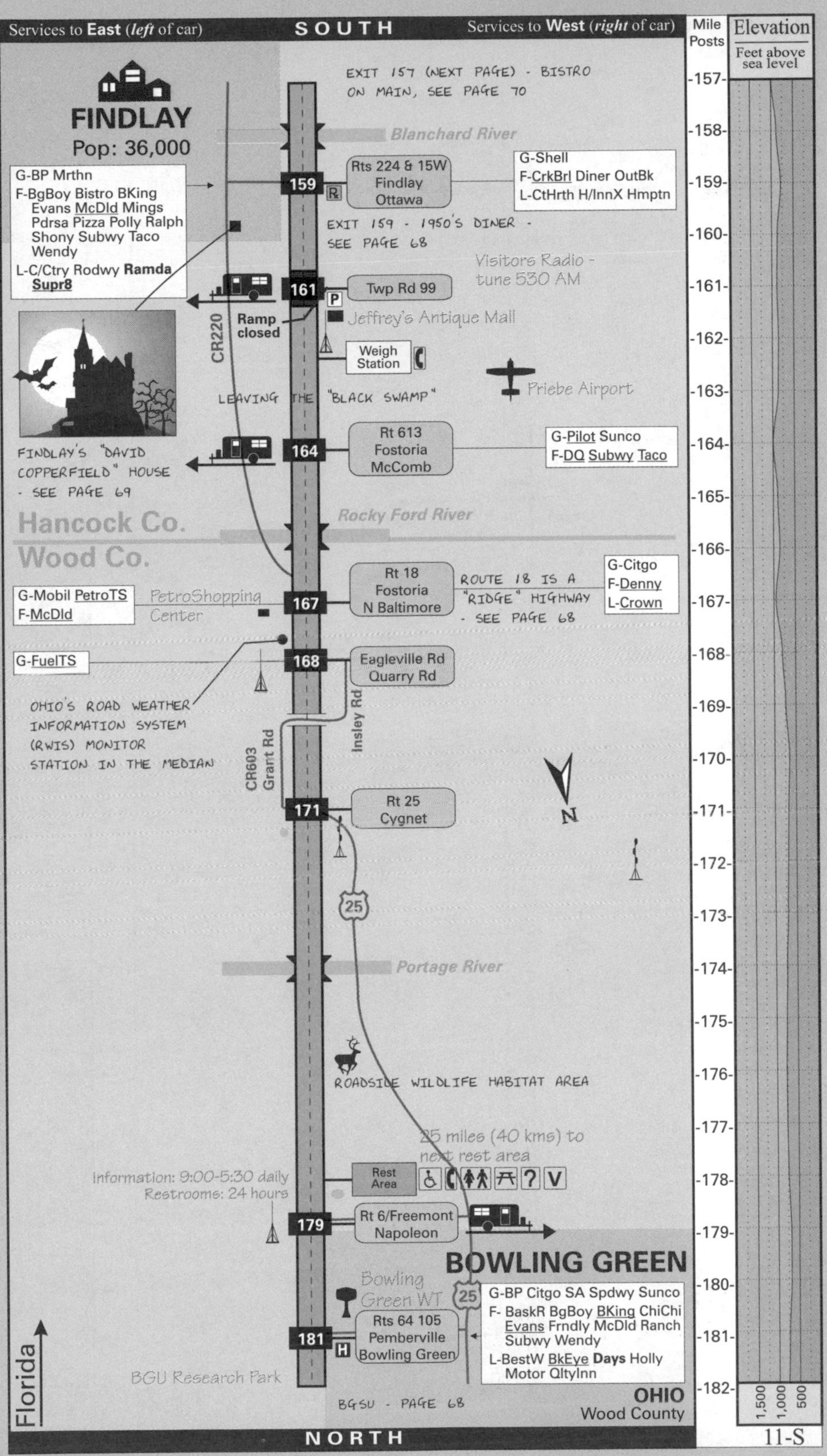
Services to East (left of car)
SOUTH
Services to West (right of car)
Mile Posts
Elevation
Feet above sea level
FINDLAY
Pop: 36,000
EXIT 157 (NEXT PAGE) - BISTRO ON MAIN, SEE PAGE 70
Blanchard River
G-BP Mrthn
F-BgBoy Bistro BKing Evans McDld Mings Pdrsa Pizza Polly Ralph Shony Subwy Taco Wendy
L-C/Ctry Rodwy Ramda Supr8
159
Rts 224 & 15W Findlay Ottawa
G-Shell
F-CrkBrl Diner OutBk
L-CtHrth H/InnX Hmptn
EXIT 159 - 1950'S DINER - SEE PAGE 68
Visitors Radio - tune 530 AM
161
Twp Rd 99
Ramp closed
Jeffrey's Antique Mall
CR220
Weigh Station
LEAVING THE "BLACK SWAMP"
Priebe Airport
164
Rt 613 Fostoria McComb
G-Pilot Sunco
F-DQ Subwy Taco
FINDLAY'S "DAVID COPPERFIELD" HOUSE - SEE PAGE 69
Hancock Co.
Rocky Ford River
Wood Co.
167
Rt 18 Fostoria N Baltimore
ROUTE 18 IS A "RIDGE" HIGHWAY - SEE PAGE 68
G-Citgo
F-Denny
L-Crown
G-Mobil PetroTS
F-McDld
PetroShopping Center
168
G-FuelTS
Eagleville Rd Quarry Rd
OHIO'S ROAD WEATHER INFORMATION SYSTEM (RWIS) MONITOR STATION IN THE MEDIAN
Insley Rd
CR603 Grant Rd
171
Rt 25 Cygnet
N
25
Portage River
ROADSIDE WILDLIFE HABITAT AREA
25 miles (40 kms) to next rest area
Information: 9:00-5:30 daily
Restrooms: 24 hours
Rest Area
179
Rt 6/Freemont Napoleon
BOWLING GREEN
Bowling Green WT
25
G-BP Citgo SA Spdwy Sunco
F- BaskR BgBoy BKing ChiChi Evans Frndly McDld Ranch Subwy Wendy
L-BestW BkEye Days Holly Motor QltyInn
181
Rts 64 105 Pemberville Bowling Green
BGU Research Park
BGSU - PAGE 68
OHIO
Wood County
Florida
NORTH
-157- -158- -159- -160- -161- -162- -163- -164- -165- -166- -167- -168- -169- -170- -171- -172- -173- -174- -175- -176- -177- -178- -179- -180- -181- -182-
1,500 1,000 500

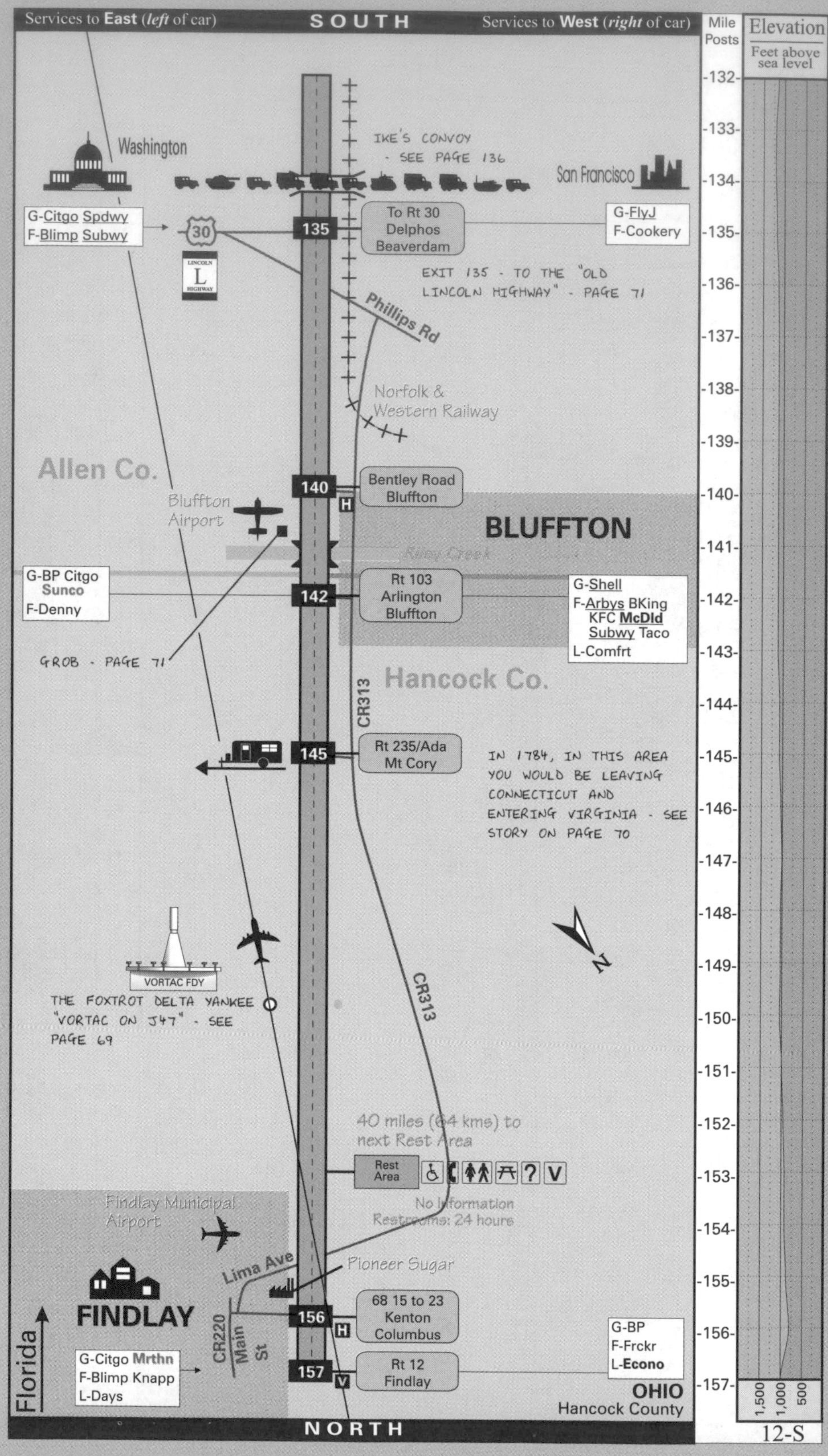
Services to East (left of car)
SOUTH
Services to West (right of car)
Mile Posts
Elevation
Feet above sea level
Washington
IKE'S CONVOY - SEE PAGE 136
San Francisco
G-Citgo Spdwy
F-Blimp Subwy
30
LINCOLN L HIGHWAY
135
To Rt 30 Delphos Beaverdam
G-FlyJ
F-Cookery
EXIT 135 - TO THE "OLD LINCOLN HIGHWAY" - PAGE 71
Phillips Rd
Norfolk & Western Railway
Allen Co.
140
Bentley Road Bluffton
H
Bluffton Airport
BLUFFTON
Riley Creek
G-BP Citgo
Sunco
F-Denny
142
Rt 103 Arlington Bluffton
G-Shell
F-Arbys BKing KFC McDld Subwy Taco
L-Comfrt
GROB - PAGE 71
Hancock Co.
CR313
145
Rt 235/Ada Mt Cory
IN 1784, IN THIS AREA YOU WOULD BE LEAVING CONNECTICUT AND ENTERING VIRGINIA - SEE STORY ON PAGE 70
N
VORTAC FDY
THE FOXTROT DELTA YANKEE "VORTAC ON J47" - SEE PAGE 69
CR313
40 miles (64 kms) to next Rest Area
Rest Area
No Information
Restrooms: 24 hours
Findlay Municipal Airport
Lima Ave
Pioneer Sugar
FINDLAY
CR220
Main St
156
68 15 to 23 Kenton Columbus
G-Citgo Mrthn
F-Blimp Knapp
L-Days
157
Rt 12 Findlay
G-BP
F-Frckr
L-Econo
OHIO
Hancock County
Florida
NORTH
-132- -133- -134- -135- -136- -137- -138- -139- -140- -141- -142- -143- -144- -145- -146- -147- -148- -149- -150- -151- -152- -153- -154- -155- -156- -157-
1,500 1,000 500

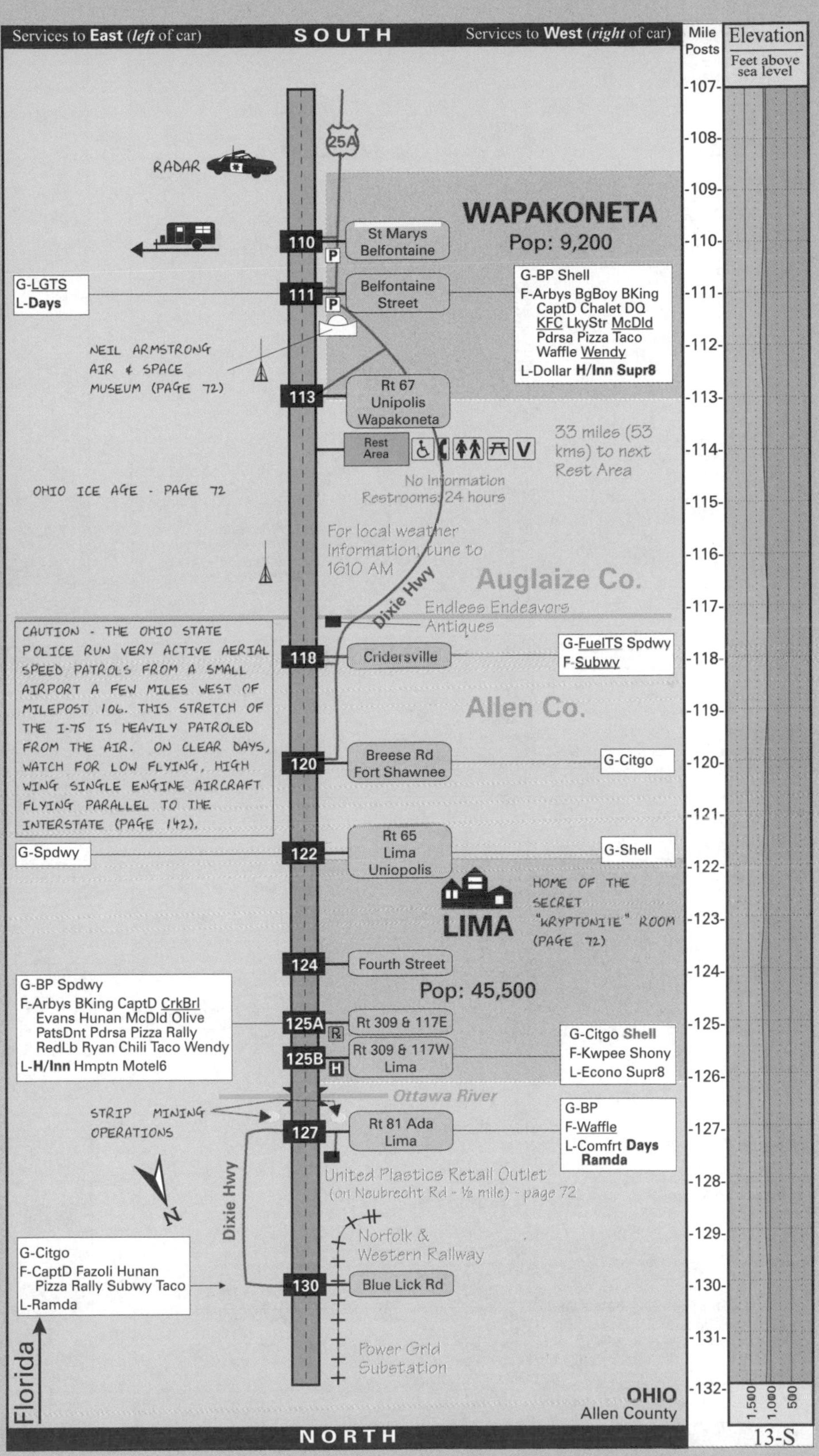

Services to East (left of car)
SOUTH
Services to West (right of car)
Mile Posts
Elevation
Feet above sea level
25A
RADAR
WAPAKONETA
Pop: 9,200
110
St Marys Belfontaine
G-LGTS
L-Days
111
Belfontaine Street
G-BP Shell
F-Arbys BgBoy BKing CaptD Chalet DQ KFC LkyStr McDld Pdrsa Pizza Taco Waffle Wendy
L-Dollar H/Inn Supr8
NEIL ARMSTRONG AIR & SPACE MUSEUM (PAGE 72)
113
Rt 67 Unipolis Wapakoneta
Rest Area
33 miles (53 kms) to next Rest Area
No Information
Restrooms: 24 hours
OHIO ICE AGE - PAGE 72
For local weather information, tune to 1610 AM
Dixie Hwy
Auglaize Co.
Endless Endeavors Antiques
CAUTION - THE OHIO STATE POLICE RUN VERY ACTIVE AERIAL SPEED PATROLS FROM A SMALL AIRPORT A FEW MILES WEST OF MILEPOST 106. THIS STRETCH OF THE I-75 IS HEAVILY PATROLED FROM THE AIR. ON CLEAR DAYS, WATCH FOR LOW FLYING, HIGH WING SINGLE ENGINE AIRCRAFT FLYING PARALLEL TO THE INTERSTATE (PAGE 142).
118
Cridersville
G-FuelTS Spdwy
F-Subwy
Allen Co.
120
Breese Rd Fort Shawnee
G-Citgo
G-Spdwy
122
Rt 65 Lima Uniopolis
G-Shell
LIMA
HOME OF THE SECRET "KRYPTONITE" ROOM (PAGE 72)
124
Fourth Street
Pop: 45,500
G-BP Spdwy
F-Arbys BKing CaptD CrkBrl Evans Hunan McDld Olive PatsDnt Pdrsa Pizza Rally RedLb Ryan Chili Taco Wendy
L-H/Inn Hmptn Motel6
125A
Rt 309 & 117E
125B
Rt 309 & 117W Lima
G-Citgo Shell
F-Kwpee Shony
L-Econo Supr8
Ottawa River
STRIP MINING OPERATIONS
127
Rt 81 Ada Lima
G-BP
F-Waffle
L-Comfrt Days Ramda
United Plastics Retail Outlet
(on Neubrecht Rd - ½ mile) - page 72
Dixie Hwy
N
Norfolk & Western Railway
G-Citgo
F-CaptD Fazoli Hunan Pizza Rally Subwy Taco
L-Ramda
130
Blue Lick Rd
Power Grid Substation
Florida
OHIO
Allen County
NORTH
-107- -108- -109- -110- -111- -112- -113- -114- -115- -116- -117- -118- -119- -120- -121- -122- -123- -124- -125- -126- -127- -128- -129- -130- -131- -132-
1,500 1,000 500

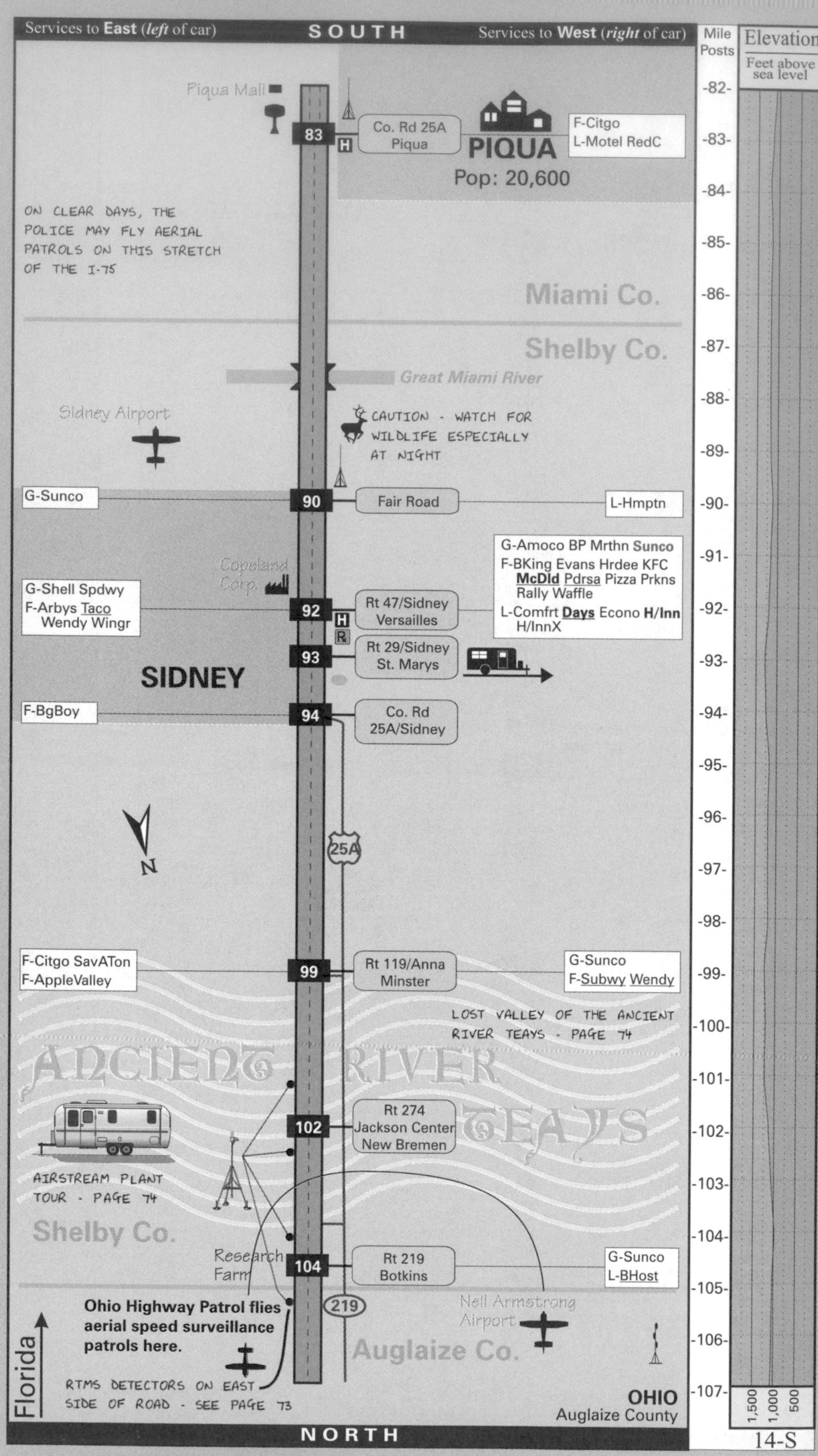

Services to East (left of car)
SOUTH
Services to West (right of car)
Mile Posts
Elevation
Feet above sea level
Piqua Mall
83
Co. Rd 25A Piqua
PIQUA
Pop: 20,600
F-Citgo
L-Motel RedC
ON CLEAR DAYS, THE POLICE MAY FLY AERIAL PATROLS ON THIS STRETCH OF THE I-75
Miami Co.
Shelby Co.
Great Miami River
Sidney Airport
CAUTION - WATCH FOR WILDLIFE ESPECIALLY AT NIGHT
G-Sunco
90
Fair Road
L-Hmptn
G-Amoco BP Mrthn Sunco
F-BKing Evans Hrdee KFC McDld Pdrsa Pizza Prkns Rally Waffle
L-Comfrt Days Econo H/Inn H/InnX
Copeland Corp.
G-Shell Spdwy
F-Arbys Taco Wendy Wingr
92
Rt 47/Sidney Versailles
93
Rt 29/Sidney St. Marys
SIDNEY
F-BgBoy
94
Co. Rd 25A/Sidney
N
25A
F-Citgo SavATon
F-AppleValley
99
Rt 119/Anna Minster
G-Sunco
F-Subwy Wendy
LOST VALLEY OF THE ANCIENT RIVER TEAYS - PAGE 74
ANCIENT RIVER TEAYS
102
Rt 274 Jackson Center New Bremen
AIRSTREAM PLANT TOUR - PAGE 74
Shelby Co.
Research Farm
104
Rt 219 Botkins
G-Sunco
L-BHost
219
Neil Armstrong Airport
Ohio Highway Patrol flies aerial speed surveillance patrols here.
Auglaize Co.
Florida
RTMS DETECTORS ON EAST SIDE OF ROAD - SEE PAGE 73
OHIO
Auglaize County
NORTH
-82- -83- -84- -85- -86- -87- -88- -89- -90- -91- -92- -93- -94- -95- -96- -97- -98- -99- -100- -101- -102- -103- -104- -105- -106- -107-
1,500 1,000 500

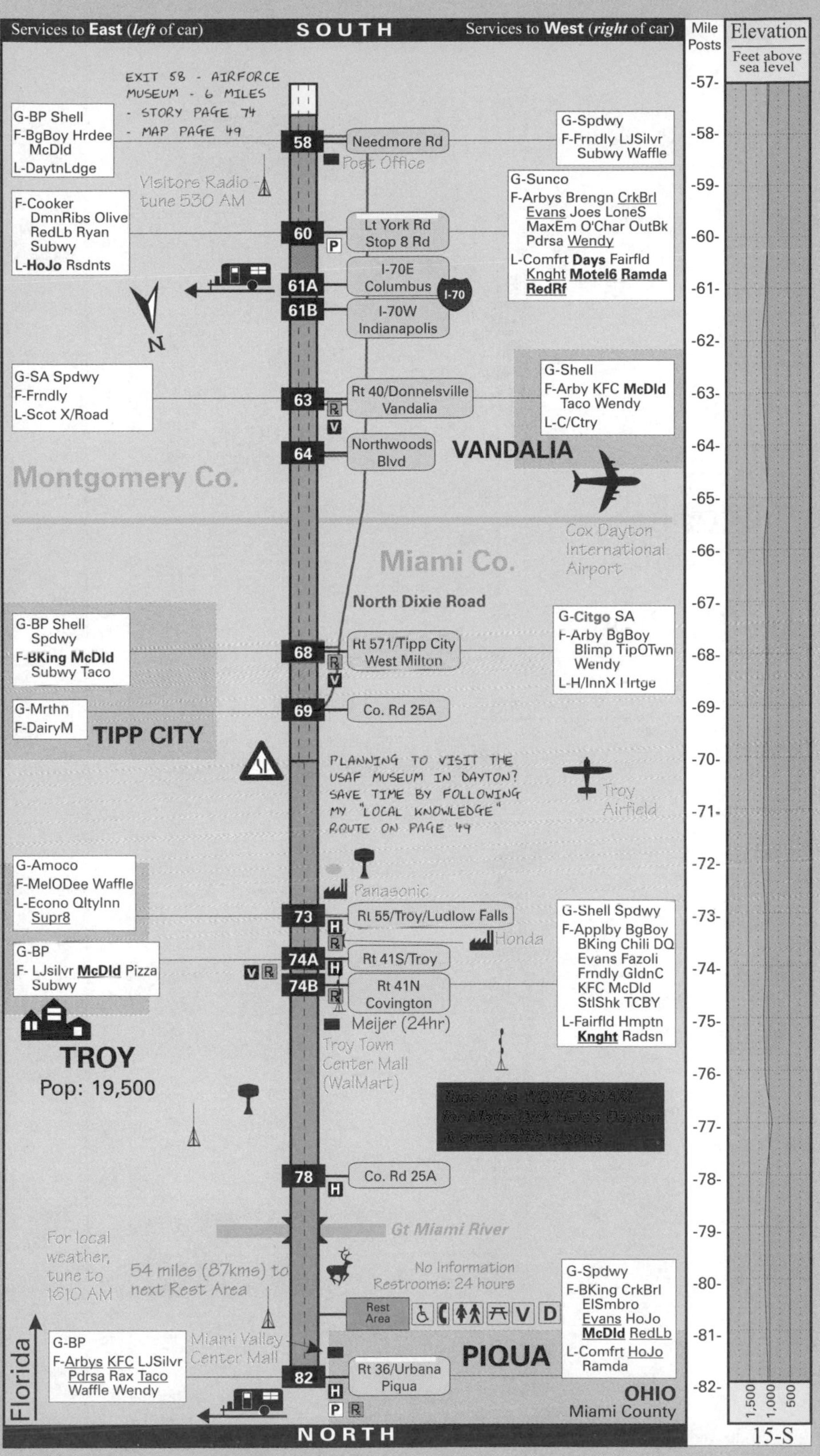
Services to East (left of car)
SOUTH
Services to West (right of car)
Mile Posts
Elevation
Feet above sea level
EXIT 58 - AIRFORCE MUSEUM - 6 MILES
- STORY PAGE 74
- MAP PAGE 49
G-BP Shell
F-BgBoy Hrdee McDld
L-DaytnLdge
58
Needmore Rd
Post Office
G-Spdwy
F-Frndly LJSilvr Subwy Waffle
Visitors Radio - tune 530 AM
G-Sunco
F-Arbys Brengn CrkBrl Evans Joes LoneS MaxEm O'Char OutBk Pdrsa Wendy
L-Comfrt Days Fairfld Knght Motel6 Ramda RedRf
F-Cooker DmnRibs Olive RedLb Ryan Subwy
L-HoJo Rsdnts
60
Lt York Rd Stop 8 Rd
P
61A
I-70E Columbus
I-70
61B
I-70W Indianapolis
N
G-SA Spdwy
F-Frndly
L-Scot X/Road
63
Rt 40/Donnelsville Vandalia
V
G-Shell
F-Arby KFC McDld Taco Wendy
L-C/Ctry
64
Northwoods Blvd
VANDALIA
Montgomery Co.
Cox Dayton International Airport
Miami Co.
North Dixie Road
G-BP Shell Spdwy
F-BKing McDld Subwy Taco
68
Rt 571/Tipp City West Milton
V
G-Citgo SA
F-Arby BgBoy Blimp TipOTwn Wendy
L-H/InnX Hrtge
G-Mrthn
F-DairyM
69
Co. Rd 25A
TIPP CITY
PLANNING TO VISIT THE USAF MUSEUM IN DAYTON? SAVE TIME BY FOLLOWING MY "LOCAL KNOWLEDGE" ROUTE ON PAGE 49
Troy Airfield
Panasonic
G-Amoco
F-MelODee Waffle
L-Econo QltyInn Supr8
73
Rt 55/Troy/Ludlow Falls
H
Honda
G-Shell Spdwy
F-Applby BgBoy BKing Chili DQ Evans Fazoli Frndly GldnC KFC McDld StlShk TCBY
L-Fairfld Hmptn Knght Radsn
G-BP
F- LJsilvr McDld Pizza Subwy
V
74A
Rt 41S/Troy
H
74B
Rt 41N Covington
Meijer (24hr)
Troy Town Center Mall (WalMart)
TROY
Pop: 19,500
78
Co. Rd 25A
H
Gt Miami River
For local weather, tune to 1610 AM
54 miles (87kms) to next Rest Area
No Information
Restrooms: 24 hours
Rest Area
V
D
G-Spdwy
F-BKing CrkBrl ElSmbro Evans HoJo McDld RedLb
L-Comfrt HoJo Ramda
Miami Valley Center Mall
PIQUA
G-BP
F-Arbys KFC LJSilvr Pdrsa Rax Taco Waffle Wendy
82
Rt 36/Urbana Piqua
H
P
OHIO
Miami County
Florida
NORTH
-57- -58- -59- -60- -61- -62- -63- -64- -65- -66- -67- -68- -69- -70- -71- -72- -73- -74- -75- -76- -77- -78- -79- -80- -81- -82-
1,500 1,000 500
15-S

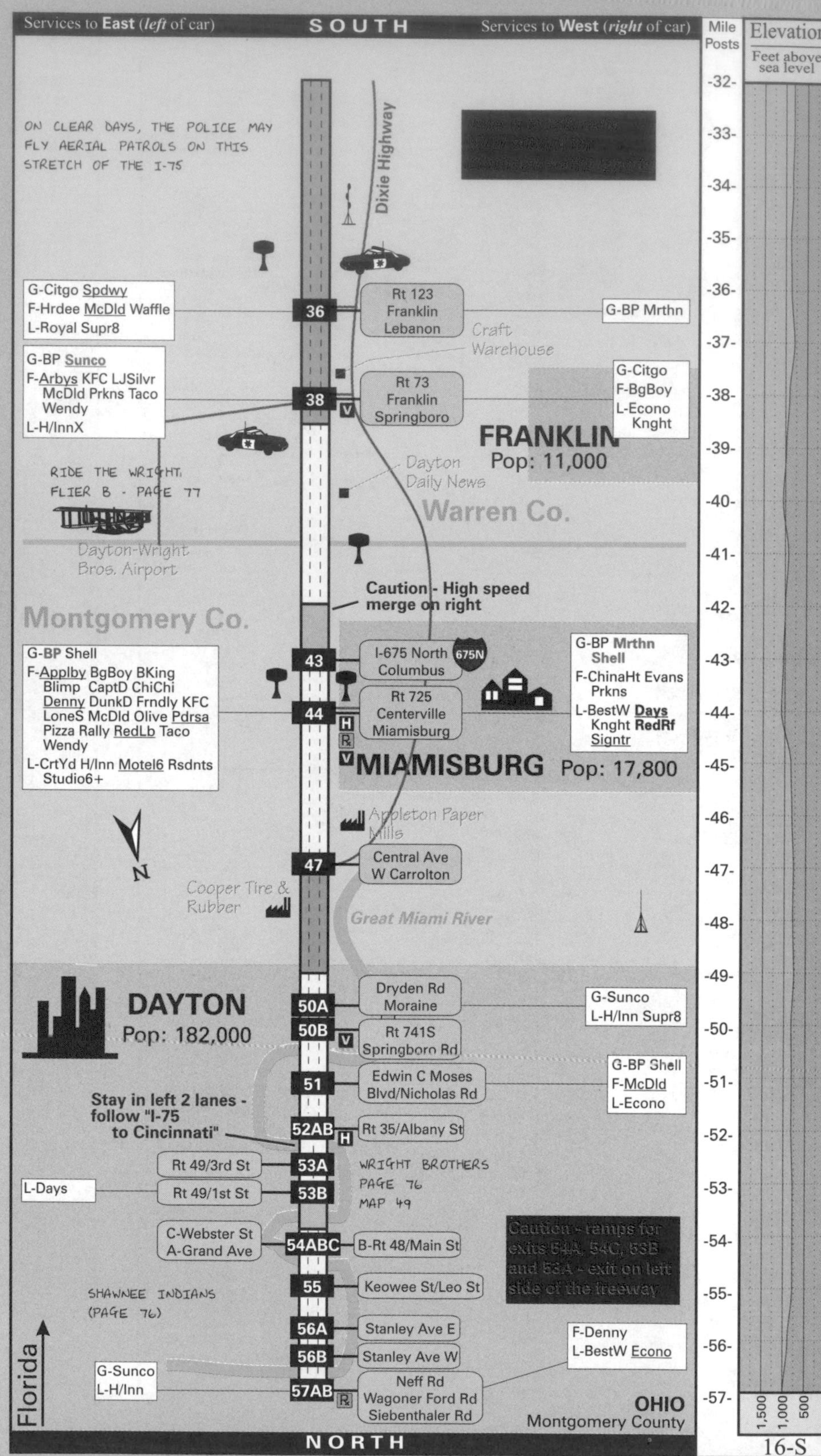

Services to East (left of car)
SOUTH
Services to West (right of car)
Mile Posts
Elevation
Feet above sea level
ON CLEAR DAYS, THE POLICE MAY FLY AERIAL PATROLS ON THIS STRETCH OF THE I-75
Dixie Highway
-32-
-33-
-34-
-35-
G-Citgo Spdwy
F-Hrdee McDld Waffle
L-Royal Supr8
36
Rt 123 Franklin Lebanon
G-BP Mrthn
-36-
Craft Warehouse
-37-
G-BP Sunco
F-Arbys KFC LJSilvr McDld Prkns Taco Wendy
L-H/InnX
38
V
Rt 73 Franklin Springboro
G-Citgo
F-BgBoy
L-Econo Knght
-38-
FRANKLIN
Pop: 11,000
-39-
RIDE THE WRIGHT FLIER B - PAGE 77
Dayton Daily News
Warren Co.
-40-
Dayton-Wright Bros. Airport
-41-
Caution - High speed merge on right
Montgomery Co.
-42-
G-BP Shell
F-Applby BgBoy BKing Blimp CaptD ChiChi Denny DunkD Frndly KFC LoneS McDld Olive Pdrsa Pizza Rally RedLb Taco Wendy
L-CrtYd H/Inn Motel6 Rsdnts Studio6+
43
I-675 North Columbus
675N
G-BP Mrthn Shell
F-ChinaHt Evans Prkns
L-BestW Days Knght RedRf Signtr
-43-
44
H
Rx
V
Rt 725 Centerville Miamisburg
-44-
MIAMISBURG
Pop: 17,800
-45-
Appleton Paper Mills
-46-
N
47
Central Ave W Carrolton
-47-
Cooper Tire & Rubber
Great Miami River
-48-
-49-
DAYTON
Pop: 182,000
50A
Dryden Rd Moraine
G-Sunco
L-H/Inn Supr8
50B
V
Rt 741S Springboro Rd
-50-
51
Edwin C Moses Blvd/Nicholas Rd
G-BP Shell
F-McDld
L-Econo
-51-
Stay in left 2 lanes - follow "I-75 to Cincinnati"
52AB
H
Rt 35/Albany St
-52-
Rt 49/3rd St
53A
WRIGHT BROTHERS PAGE 76 MAP 49
L-Days
Rt 49/1st St
53B
-53-
C-Webster St
A-Grand Ave
54ABC
B-Rt 48/Main St
Caution - ramps for exits 54A, 54C, 53B and 53A - exit on left side of the freeway
-54-
SHAWNEE INDIANS (PAGE 76)
55
Keowee St/Leo St
-55-
56A
Stanley Ave E
F-Denny
L-BestW Econo
-56-
Florida
56B
Stanley Ave W
G-Sunco
L-H/Inn
57AB
Rx
Neff Rd Wagoner Ford Rd Siebenthaler Rd
-57-
1,500
1,000
500
OHIO
Montgomery County
NORTH
16-S

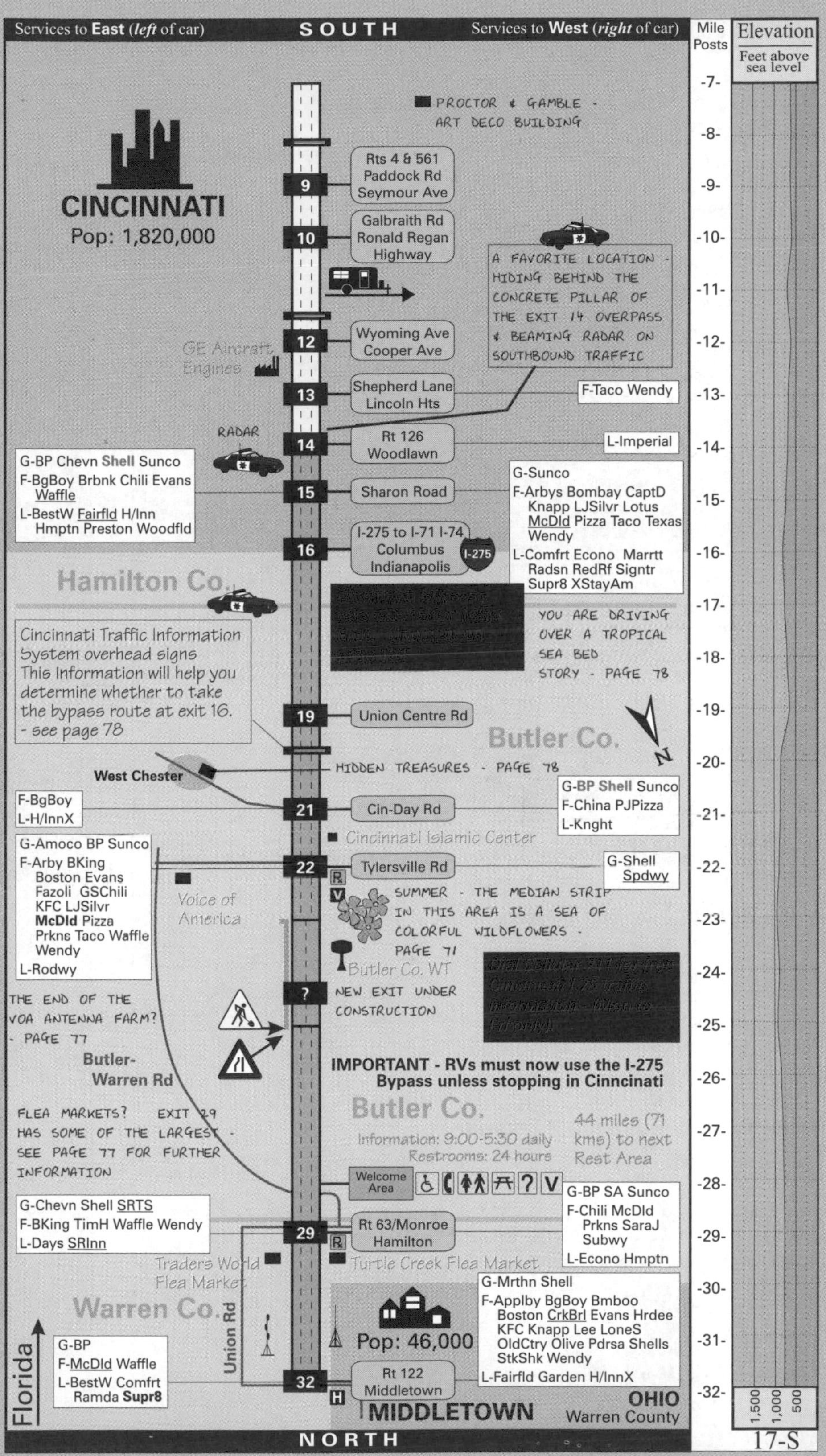

Services to East (left of car)
SOUTH
Services to West (right of car)
Mile Posts
Elevation
Feet above sea level
PROCTOR & GAMBLE - ART DECO BUILDING
CINCINNATI
Pop: 1,820,000
9
Rts 4 & 561 Paddock Rd Seymour Ave
10
Galbraith Rd Ronald Regan Highway
A FAVORITE LOCATION - HIDING BEHIND THE CONCRETE PILLAR OF THE EXIT 14 OVERPASS & BEAMING RADAR ON SOUTHBOUND TRAFFIC
12
Wyoming Ave Cooper Ave
GE Aircraft Engines
13
Shepherd Lane Lincoln Hts
F-Taco Wendy
RADAR
14
Rt 126 Woodlawn
L-Imperial
G-BP Chevn Shell Sunco
F-BgBoy Brbnk Chili Evans Waffle
L-BestW Fairfld H/Inn Hmptn Preston Woodfld
15
Sharon Road
G-Sunco
F-Arbys Bombay CaptD Knapp LJSilvr Lotus McDld Pizza Taco Texas Wendy
L-Comfrt Econo Marrtt Radsn RedRf Signtr Supr8 XStayAm
16
I-275 to I-71 I-74 Columbus Indianapolis
I-275
Hamilton Co.
YOU ARE DRIVING OVER A TROPICAL SEA BED STORY - PAGE 78
Cincinnati Traffic Information System overhead signs This information will help you determine whether to take the bypass route at exit 16. - see page 78
19
Union Centre Rd
Butler Co.
N
HIDDEN TREASURES - PAGE 78
West Chester
F-BgBoy
L-H/InnX
21
Cin-Day Rd
G-BP Shell Sunco
F-China PJPizza
L-Knght
Cincinnati Islamic Center
G-Amoco BP Sunco
F-Arby BKing Boston Evans Fazoli GSChili KFC LJSilvr McDld Pizza Prkns Taco Waffle Wendy
L-Rodwy
22
Tylersville Rd
G-Shell Spdwy
R
V
Voice of America
SUMMER - THE MEDIAN STRIP IN THIS AREA IS A SEA OF COLORFUL WILDFLOWERS - PAGE 71
Butler Co. WT
THE END OF THE VOA ANTENNA FARM? - PAGE 77
?
NEW EXIT UNDER CONSTRUCTION
Butler-Warren Rd
IMPORTANT - RVs must now use the I-275 Bypass unless stopping in Cinncinati
Butler Co.
FLEA MARKETS? EXIT 29 HAS SOME OF THE LARGEST - SEE PAGE 77 FOR FURTHER INFORMATION
Information: 9:00-5:30 daily
Restrooms: 24 hours
44 miles (71 kms) to next Rest Area
Welcome Area
?
V
G-BP SA Sunco
F-Chili McDld Prkns SaraJ Subwy
L-Econo Hmptn
G-Chevn Shell SRTS
F-BKing TimH Waffle Wendy
L-Days SRInn
29
Rt 63/Monroe Hamilton
R
Traders World Flea Market
Turtle Creek Flea Market
G-Mrthn Shell
F-Applby BgBoy Bmboo Boston CrkBrl Evans Hrdee KFC Knapp Lee LoneS OldCtry Olive Pdrsa Shells StkShk Wendy
L-Fairfld Garden H/InnX
Warren Co.
Pop: 46,000
Union Rd
Florida
G-BP
F-McDld Waffle
L-BestW Comfrt Ramda Supr8
32
Rt 122 Middletown
H
MIDDLETOWN
OHIO
Warren County
NORTH
-7- -8- -9- -10- -11- -12- -13- -14- -15- -16- -17- -18- -19- -20- -21- -22- -23- -24- -25- -26- -27- -28- -29- -30- -31- -32-
1,500 1,000 500
17-S

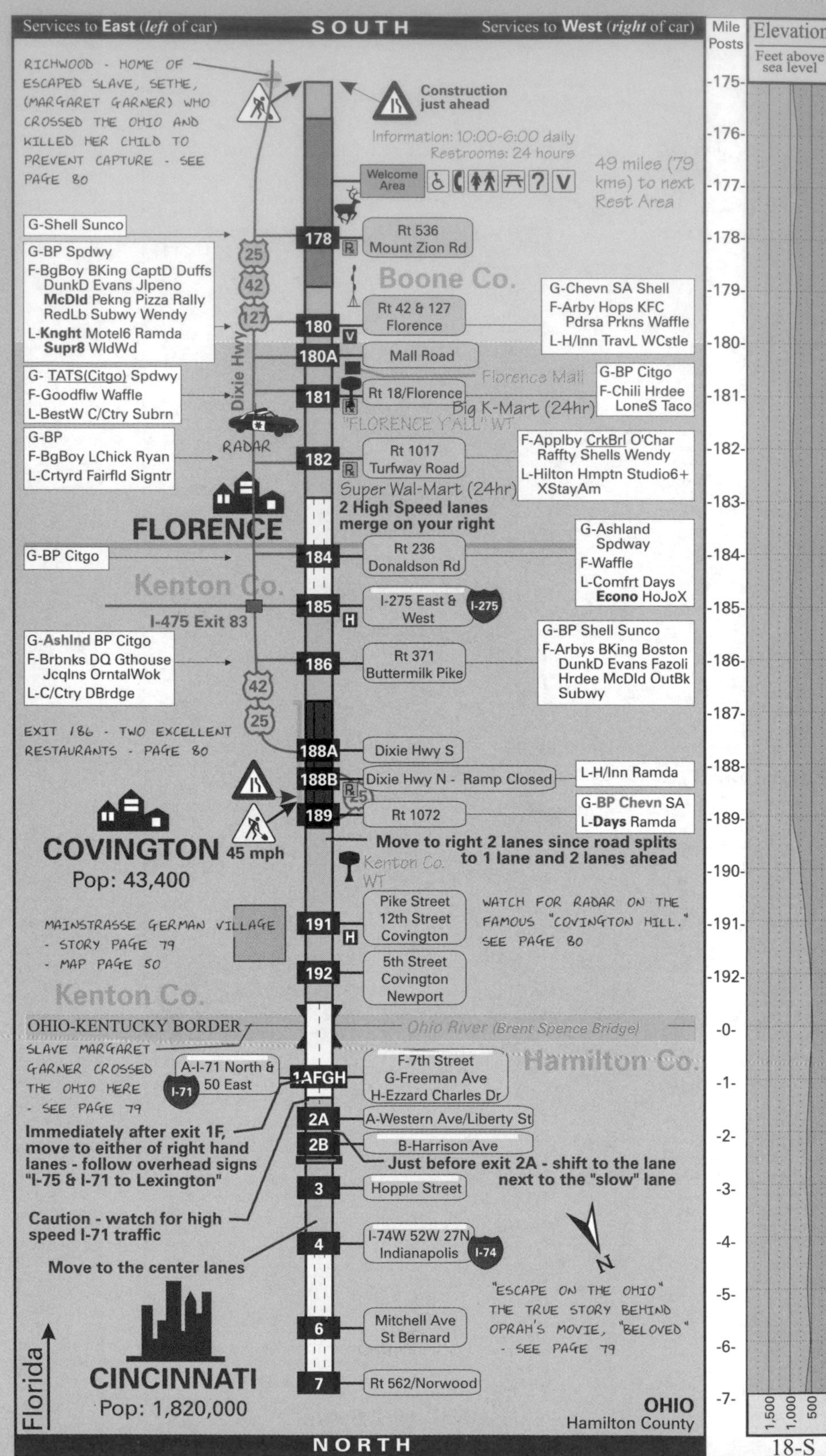

Services to East (left of car)
SOUTH
Services to West (right of car)
Mile Posts
Elevation
Feet above sea level
RICHWOOD - HOME OF ESCAPED SLAVE, SETHE, (MARGARET GARNER) WHO CROSSED THE OHIO AND KILLED HER CHILD TO PREVENT CAPTURE - SEE PAGE 80
Construction just ahead
Information: 10:00-6:00 daily
Restrooms: 24 hours
Welcome Area
49 miles (79 kms) to next Rest Area
G-Shell Sunco
178
Rt 536 Mount Zion Rd
G-BP Spdwy
F-BgBoy BKing CaptD Duffs DunkD Evans Jlpeno McDld Pekng Pizza Rally RedLb Subwy Wendy
L-Knght Motel6 Ramda Supr8 WldWd
Boone Co.
G-Chevn SA Shell
F-Arby Hops KFC Pdrsa Prkns Waffle
L-H/Inn TravL WCstle
180
Rt 42 & 127 Florence
180A
Mall Road
Florence Mall
G- TATS(Citgo) Spdwy
F-Goodflw Waffle
L-BestW C/Ctry Subrn
Dixie Hwy
181
Rt 18/Florence
G-BP Citgo
F-Chili Hrdee LoneS Taco
Big K-Mart (24hr)
"FLORENCE Y'ALL" WT
G-BP
F-BgBoy LChick Ryan
L-Crtyrd Fairfld Signtr
RADAR
182
Rt 1017 Turfway Road
F-Applby CrkBrl O'Char Raffty Shells Wendy
L-Hilton Hmptn Studio6+ XStayAm
Super Wal-Mart (24hr)
2 High Speed lanes merge on your right
FLORENCE
G-BP Citgo
184
Rt 236 Donaldson Rd
G-Ashland Spdway
F-Waffle
L-Comfrt Days Econo HoJoX
Kenton Co.
185
I-275 East & West
I-475 Exit 83
G-Ashlnd BP Citgo
F-Brbnks DQ Gthouse Jcqlns OrntalWok
L-C/Ctry DBrdge
186
Rt 371 Buttermilk Pike
G-BP Shell Sunco
F-Arbys BKing Boston DunkD Evans Fazoli Hrdee McDld OutBk Subwy
EXIT 186 - TWO EXCELLENT RESTAURANTS - PAGE 80
188A
Dixie Hwy S
188B
Dixie Hwy N - Ramp Closed
L-H/Inn Ramda
189
Rt 1072
G-BP Chevn SA
L-Days Ramda
COVINGTON
45 mph
Pop: 43,400
Move to right 2 lanes since road splits to 1 lane and 2 lanes ahead
Kenton Co. WT
MAINSTRASSE GERMAN VILLAGE
- STORY PAGE 79
- MAP PAGE 50
191
Pike Street 12th Street Covington
WATCH FOR RADAR ON THE FAMOUS "COVINGTON HILL." SEE PAGE 80
192
5th Street Covington Newport
Kenton Co.
OHIO-KENTUCKY BORDER
Ohio River (Brent Spence Bridge)
SLAVE MARGARET GARNER CROSSED THE OHIO HERE - SEE PAGE 79
Hamilton Co.
A-I-71 North & 50 East
1AFGH
F-7th Street G-Freeman Ave H-Ezzard Charles Dr
2A
A-Western Ave/Liberty St
Immediately after exit 1F, move to either of right hand lanes - follow overhead signs "I-75 & I-71 to Lexington"
2B
B-Harrison Ave
Just before exit 2A - shift to the lane next to the "slow" lane
3
Hopple Street
Caution - watch for high speed I-71 traffic
4
I-74W 52W 27N Indianapolis
Move to the center lanes
N
"ESCAPE ON THE OHIO" THE TRUE STORY BEHIND OPRAH'S MOVIE, "BELOVED" - SEE PAGE 79
6
Mitchell Ave St Bernard
CINCINNATI
Pop: 1,820,000
7
Rt 562/Norwood
Florida
OHIO
Hamilton County
NORTH
-175- -176- -177- -178- -179- -180- -181- -182- -183- -184- -185- -186- -187- -188- -189- -190- -191- -192- -0- -1- -2- -3- -4- -5- -6- -7-
1,500 1,000 500

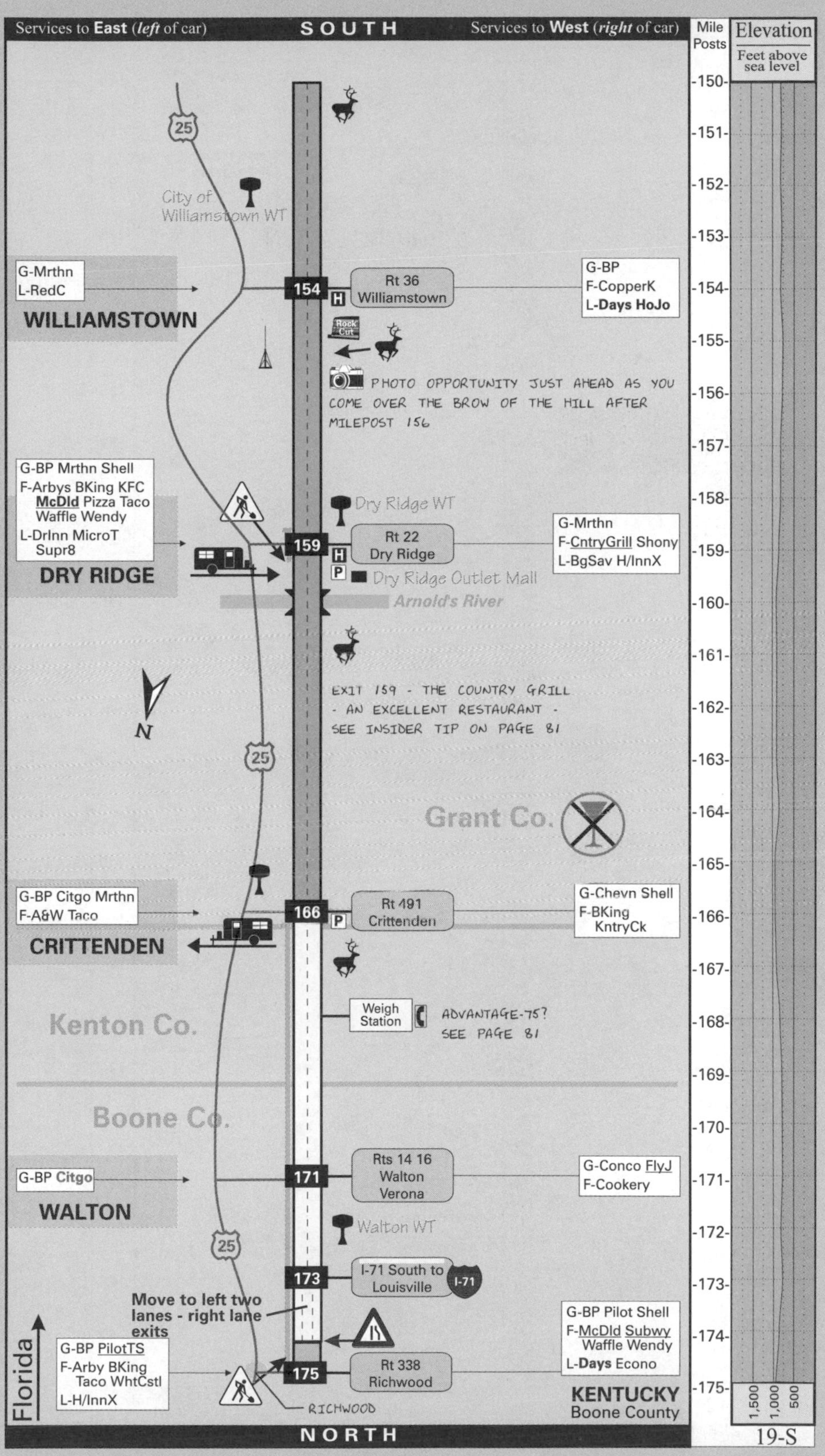

Services to East (left of car)
SOUTH
Services to West (right of car)
Mile Posts
Elevation
Feet above sea level
25
City of Williamstown WT
G-Mrthn
L-RedC
WILLIAMSTOWN
154
Rt 36 Williamstown
G-BP
F-CopperK
L-Days HoJo
Rock Cut
PHOTO OPPORTUNITY JUST AHEAD AS YOU COME OVER THE BROW OF THE HILL AFTER MILEPOST 156
G-BP Mrthn Shell
F-Arbys BKing KFC McDld Pizza Taco Waffle Wendy
L-DrInn MicroT Supr8
DRY RIDGE
Dry Ridge WT
159
Rt 22 Dry Ridge
G-Mrthn
F-CntryGrill Shony
L-BgSav H/InnX
Dry Ridge Outlet Mall
Arnold's River
N
EXIT 159 - THE COUNTRY GRILL - AN EXCELLENT RESTAURANT - SEE INSIDER TIP ON PAGE 81
Grant Co.
G-BP Citgo Mrthn
F-A&W Taco
CRITTENDEN
166
Rt 491 Crittenden
G-Chevn Shell
F-BKing KntryCk
Weigh Station
ADVANTAGE-75? SEE PAGE 81
Kenton Co.
Boone Co.
G-BP Citgo
WALTON
171
Rts 14 16 Walton Verona
G-Conco FlyJ
F-Cookery
Walton WT
173
I-71 South to Louisville
I-71
Move to left two lanes - right lane exits
G-BP Pilot Shell
F-McDld Subwy Waffle Wendy
L-Days Econo
Florida
G-BP PilotTS
F-Arby BKing Taco WhtCstl
L-H/InnX
175
Rt 338 Richwood
RICHWOOD
KENTUCKY
Boone County
NORTH
-150- -151- -152- -153- -154- -155- -156- -157- -158- -159- -160- -161- -162- -163- -164- -165- -166- -167- -168- -169- -170- -171- -172- -173- -174- -175-
1,500 1,000 500

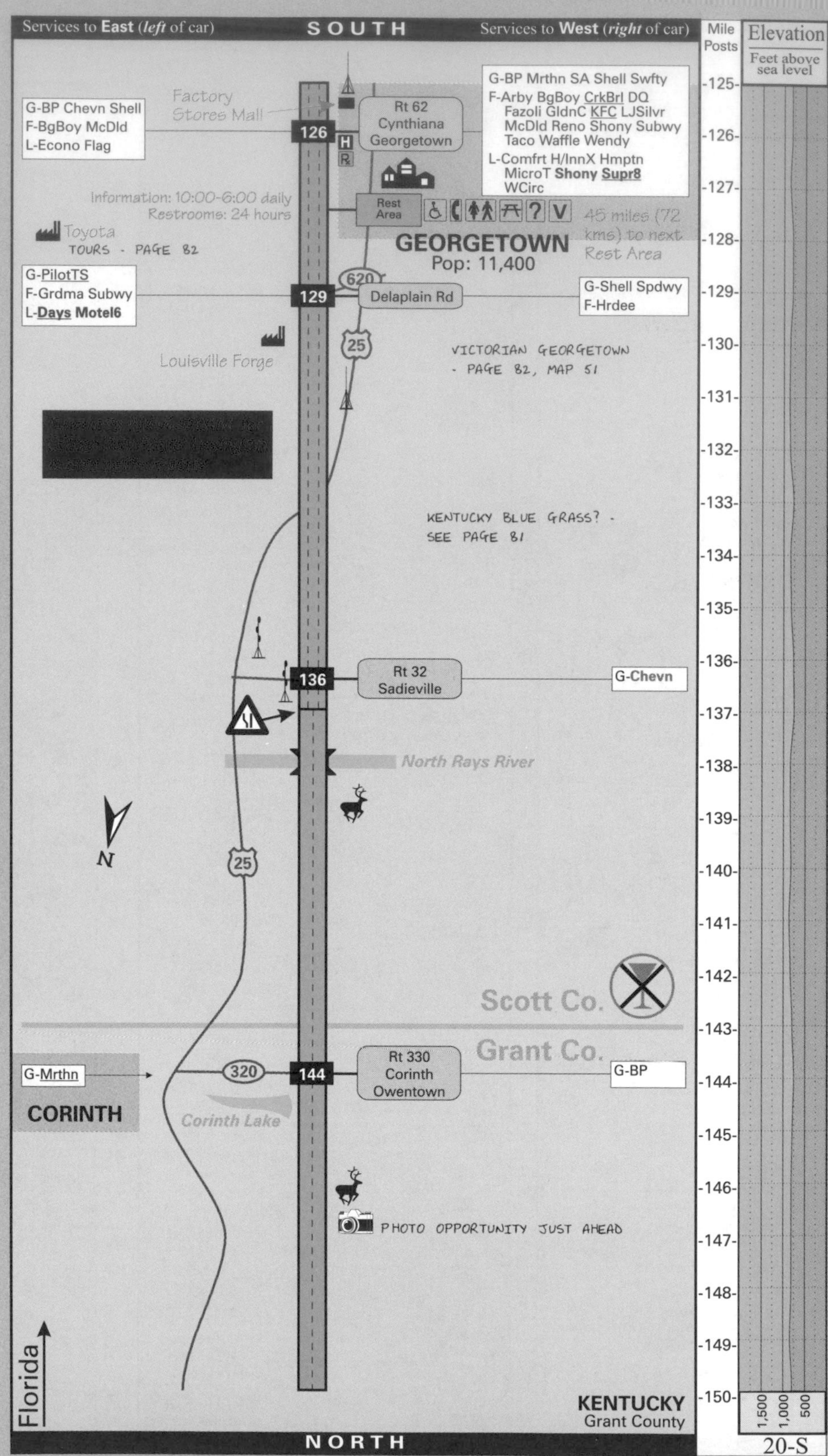

Services to East (left of car)
SOUTH
Services to West (right of car)
Mile Posts
Elevation
Feet above sea level
G-BP Chevn Shell
F-BgBoy McDld
L-Econo Flag
Factory Stores Mall
126
Rt 62
Cynthiana
Georgetown
G-BP Mrthn SA Shell Swfty
F-Arby BgBoy CrkBrl DQ
Fazoli GldnC KFC LJSilvr
McDld Reno Shony Subwy
Taco Waffle Wendy
L-Comfrt H/InnX Hmptn
MicroT Shony Supr8
WCirc
Information: 10:00-6:00 daily
Restrooms: 24 hours
Rest Area
45 miles (72 kms) to next Rest Area
Toyota
TOURS - PAGE 82
GEORGETOWN
Pop: 11,400
G-PilotTS
F-Grdma Subwy
L-Days Motel6
620
129
Delaplain Rd
G-Shell Spdwy
F-Hrdee
25
Louisville Forge
VICTORIAN GEORGETOWN - PAGE 82, MAP 51
KENTUCKY BLUE GRASS? - SEE PAGE 81
136
Rt 32
Sadieville
G-Chevn
North Rays River
N
25
Scott Co.
Grant Co.
G-Mrthn
320
144
Rt 330
Corinth
Owentown
G-BP
CORINTH
Corinth Lake
PHOTO OPPORTUNITY JUST AHEAD
Florida
KENTUCKY
Grant County
NORTH
-125-
-126-
-127-
-128-
-129-
-130-
-131-
-132-
-133-
-134-
-135-
-136-
-137-
-138-
-139-
-140-
-141-
-142-
-143-
-144-
-145-
-146-
-147-
-148-
-149-
-150-
1,500
1,000
500
20-S

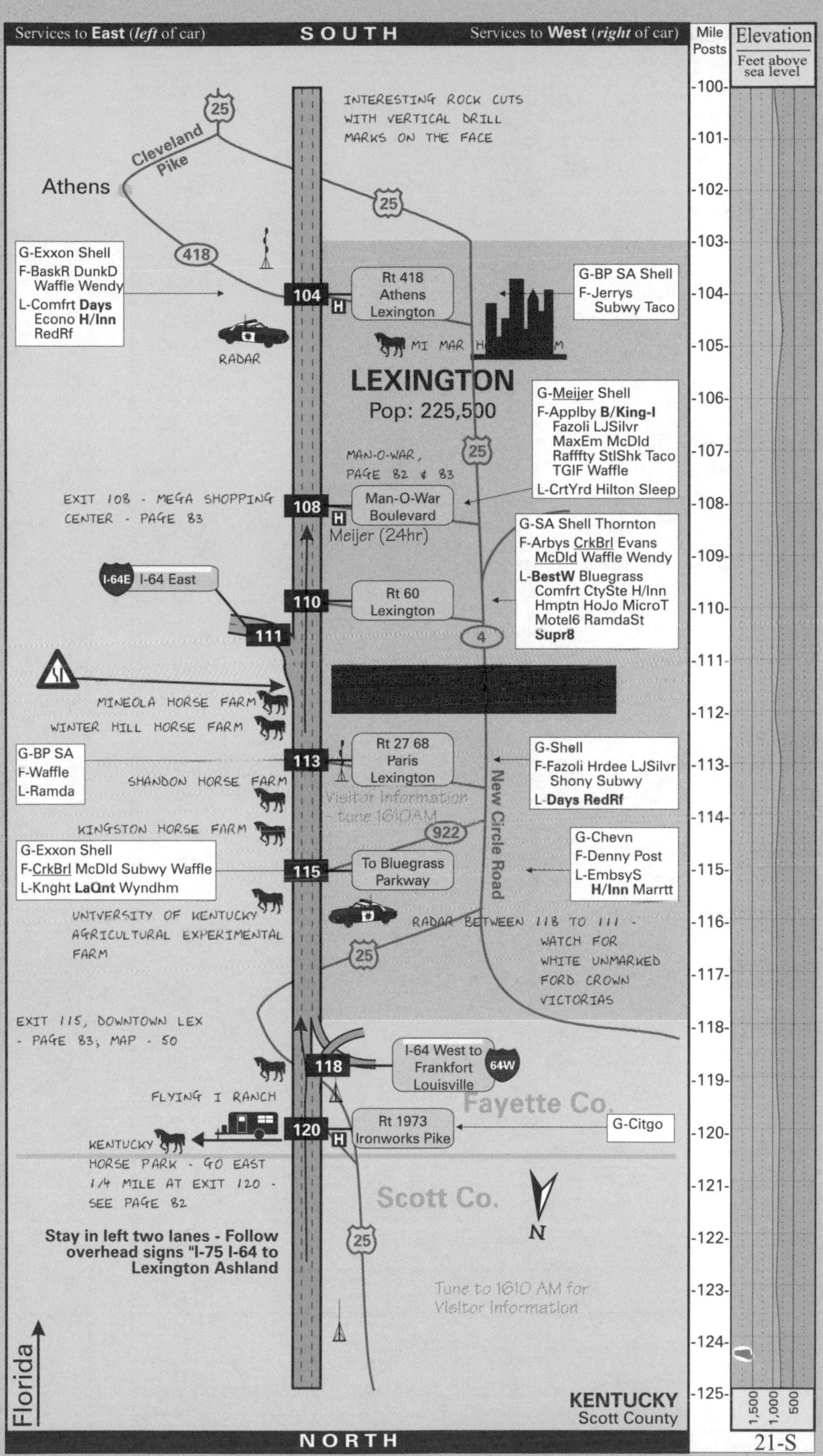
Services to East (left of car)
SOUTH
Services to West (right of car)
Mile Posts
Elevation
Feet above sea level
-100-
-101-
-102-
-103-
-104-
-105-
-106-
-107-
-108-
-109-
-110-
-111-
-112-
-113-
-114-
-115-
-116-
-117-
-118-
-119-
-120-
-121-
-122-
-123-
-124-
-125-
1,500
1,000
500
INTERESTING ROCK CUTS WITH VERTICAL DRILL MARKS ON THE FACE
25
Cleveland Pike
Athens
418
G-Exxon Shell
F-BaskR DunkD Waffle Wendy
L-Comfrt Days Econo H/Inn RedRf
104
H
Rt 418 Athens Lexington
G-BP SA Shell
F-Jerrys Subwy Taco
RADAR
MI MAR
LEXINGTON
Pop: 225,500
G-Meijer Shell
F-Applby B/King-I Fazoli LJSilvr MaxEm McDld Rafffty StlShk Taco TGIF Waffle
L-CrtYrd Hilton Sleep
MAN-O-WAR, PAGE 82 & 83
EXIT 108 - MEGA SHOPPING CENTER - PAGE 83
108
Man-O-War Boulevard
Meijer (24hr)
G-SA Shell Thornton
F-Arbys CrkBrl Evans McDld Waffle Wendy
L-BestW Bluegrass Comfrt CtySte H/Inn Hmptn HoJo MicroT Motel6 RamdaSt Supr8
I-64E
I-64 East
110
Rt 60 Lexington
111
4
MINEOLA HORSE FARM
WINTER HILL HORSE FARM
G-BP SA
F-Waffle
L-Ramda
113
Rt 27 68 Paris Lexington
G-Shell
F-Fazoli Hrdee LJSilvr Shony Subwy
L-Days RedRf
SHANDON HORSE FARM
Visitor Information - tune 1610AM
New Circle Road
KINGSTON HORSE FARM
922
G-Exxon Shell
F-CrkBrl McDld Subwy Waffle
L-Knght LaQnt Wyndhm
115
To Bluegrass Parkway
G-Chevn
F-Denny Post
L-EmbsyS H/Inn Marrtt
UNIVERSITY OF KENTUCKY AGRICULTURAL EXPERIMENTAL FARM
RADAR BETWEEN 118 TO 111 - WATCH FOR WHITE UNMARKED FORD CROWN VICTORIAS
EXIT 115, DOWNTOWN LEX - PAGE 83; MAP - 50
118
I-64 West to Frankfort Louisville
64W
FLYING I RANCH
Fayette Co.
120
Rt 1973 Ironworks Pike
G-Citgo
KENTUCKY HORSE PARK - GO EAST 1/4 MILE AT EXIT 120 - SEE PAGE 82
Scott Co.
N
Stay in left two lanes - Follow overhead signs "I-75 I-64 to Lexington Ashland
Tune to 1610 AM for Visitor Information
Florida
KENTUCKY
Scott County
NORTH
21-S

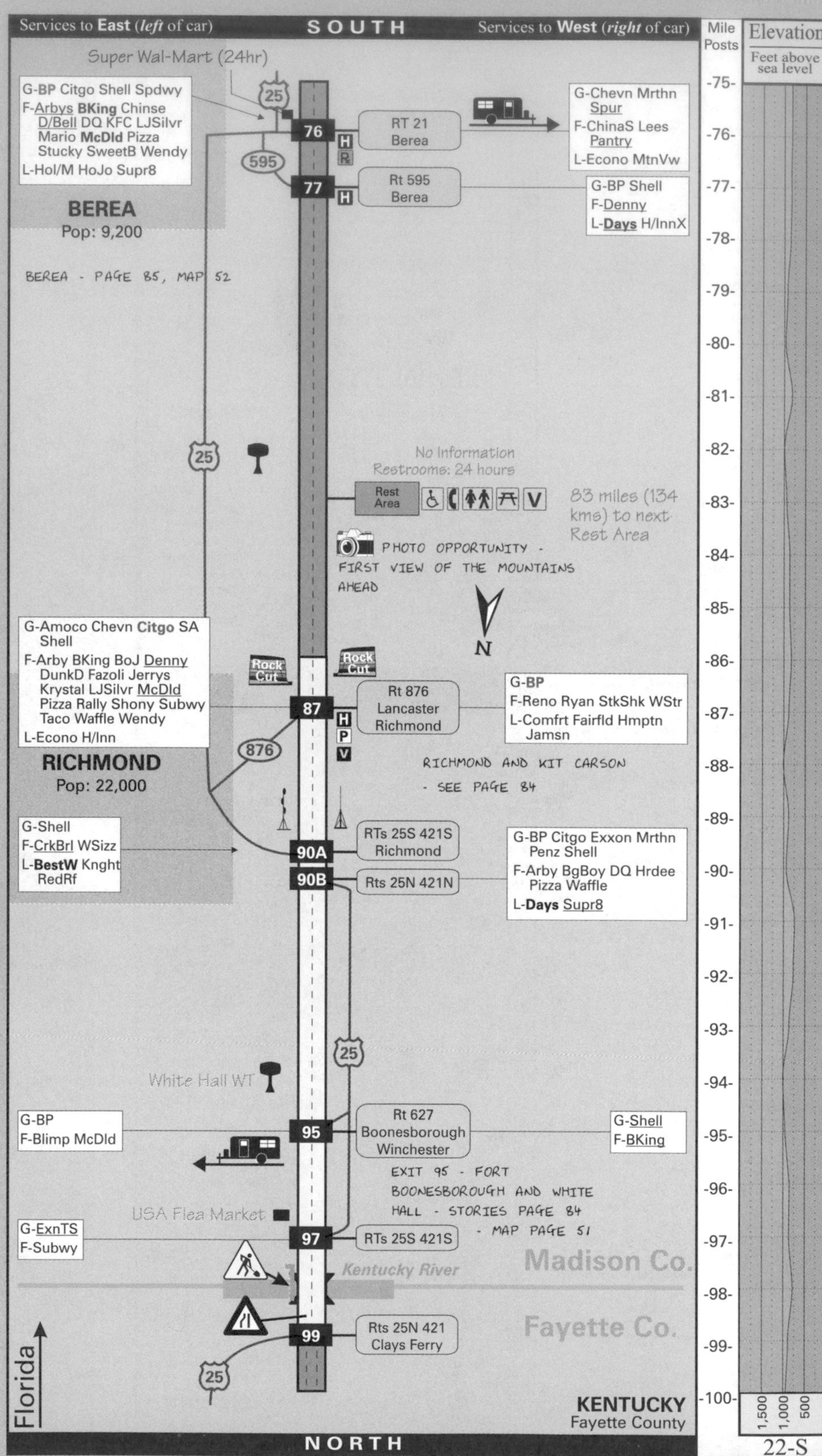
Services to East (left of car)
SOUTH
Services to West (right of car)
Mile Posts
Elevation
Feet above sea level
Super Wal-Mart (24hr)
G-BP Citgo Shell Spdwy
F-Arbys BKing Chinse D/Bell DQ KFC LJSilvr Mario McDld Pizza Stucky SweetB Wendy
L-Hol/M HoJo Supr8
BEREA
Pop: 9,200
BEREA - PAGE 85, MAP 52
76
RT 21 Berea
G-Chevn Mrthn Spur
F-ChinaS Lees Pantry
L-Econo MtnVw
595
77
Rt 595 Berea
G-BP Shell
F-Denny
L-Days H/InnX
No Information
Restrooms: 24 hours
Rest Area
83 miles (134 kms) to next Rest Area
PHOTO OPPORTUNITY - FIRST VIEW OF THE MOUNTAINS AHEAD
N
Rock Cut
Rock Cut
G-Amoco Chevn Citgo SA Shell
F-Arby BKing BoJ Denny DunkD Fazoli Jerrys Krystal LJSilvr McDld Pizza Rally Shony Subwy Taco Waffle Wendy
L-Econo H/Inn
87
Rt 876 Lancaster Richmond
G-BP
F-Reno Ryan StkShk WStr
L-Comfrt Fairfld Hmptn Jamsn
876
RICHMOND
Pop: 22,000
RICHMOND AND KIT CARSON - SEE PAGE 84
G-Shell
F-CrkBrl WSizz
L-BestW Knght RedRf
90A
RTs 25S 421S Richmond
90B
Rts 25N 421N
G-BP Citgo Exxon Mrthn Penz Shell
F-Arby BgBoy DQ Hrdee Pizza Waffle
L-Days Supr8
25
White Hall WT
G-BP
F-Blimp McDld
95
Rt 627 Boonesborough Winchester
G-Shell
F-BKing
EXIT 95 - FORT BOONESBOROUGH AND WHITE HALL - STORIES PAGE 84 - MAP PAGE 51
USA Flea Market
G-ExnTS
F-Subwy
97
RTs 25S 421S
Kentucky River
Madison Co.
Fayette Co.
99
Rts 25N 421 Clays Ferry
Florida
KENTUCKY
Fayette County
NORTH
-75- -76- -77- -78- -79- -80- -81- -82- -83- -84- -85- -86- -87- -88- -89- -90- -91- -92- -93- -94- -95- -96- -97- -98- -99- -100-
1,500 1,000 500

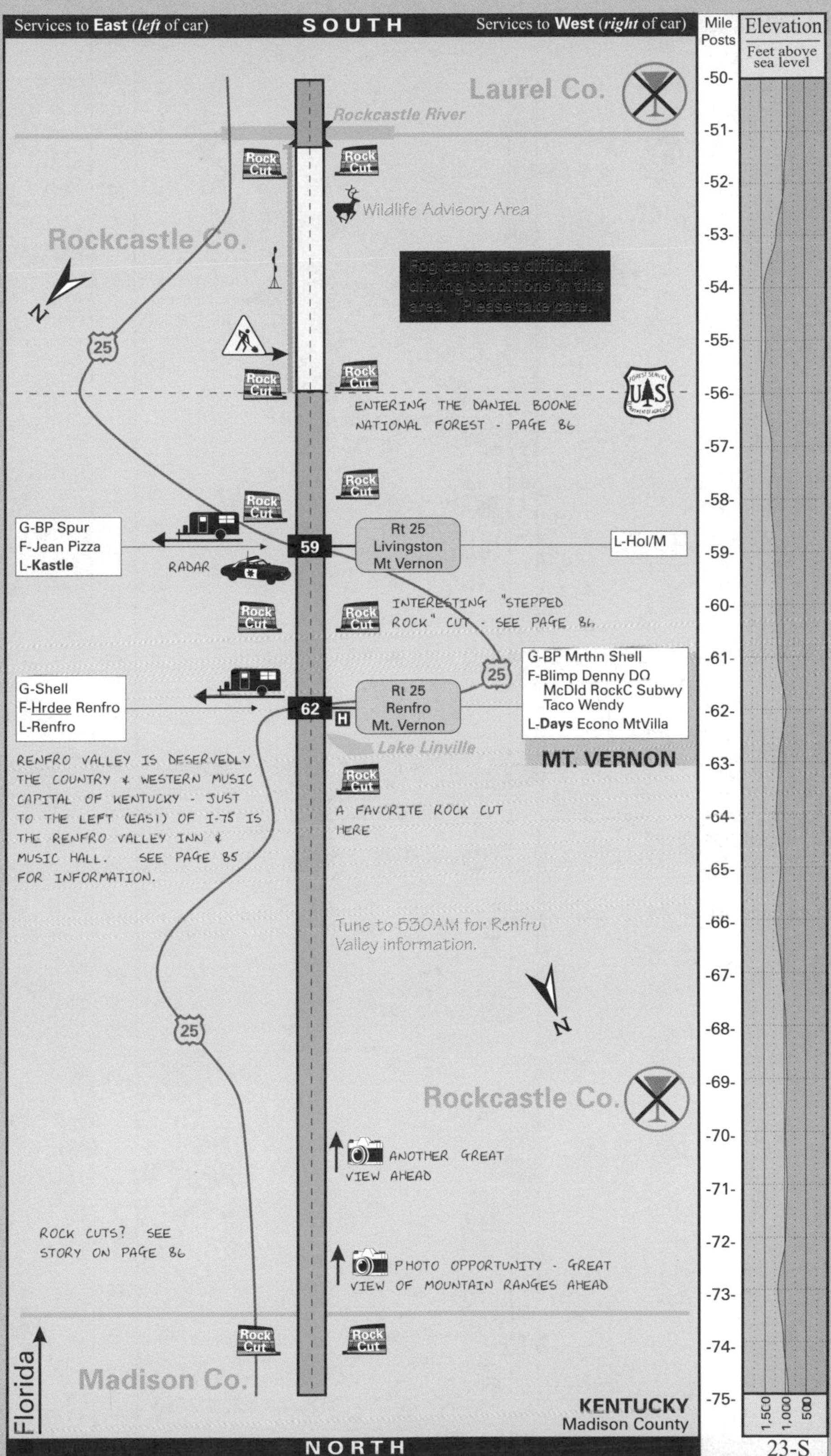

Services to East (left of car)
SOUTH
Services to West (right of car)
Mile Posts
Elevation
Feet above sea level
Laurel Co.
Rockcastle River
Rock Cut
Wildlife Advisory Area
Rockcastle Co.
Fog can cause difficult driving conditions in this area. Please take care.
N
25
ENTERING THE DANIEL BOONE NATIONAL FOREST - PAGE 86
G-BP Spur
F-Jean Pizza
L-Kastle
59
Rt 25
Livingston
Mt Vernon
L-Hol/M
RADAR
INTERESTING "STEPPED ROCK" CUT - SEE PAGE 86
G-BP Mrthn Shell
F-Blimp Denny DQ
McDld RockC Subwy
Taco Wendy
L-Days Econo MtVilla
G-Shell
F-Hrdee Renfro
L-Renfro
62
H
Rt 25
Renfro
Mt. Vernon
Lake Linville
MT. VERNON
RENFRO VALLEY IS DESERVEDLY THE COUNTRY & WESTERN MUSIC CAPITAL OF KENTUCKY - JUST TO THE LEFT (EAST) OF I-75 IS THE RENFRO VALLEY INN & MUSIC HALL. SEE PAGE 85 FOR INFORMATION.
A FAVORITE ROCK CUT HERE
Tune to 530AM for Renfru Valley information.
Rockcastle Co.
ANOTHER GREAT VIEW AHEAD
ROCK CUTS? SEE STORY ON PAGE 86
PHOTO OPPORTUNITY - GREAT VIEW OF MOUNTAIN RANGES AHEAD
Madison Co.
Florida
KENTUCKY
Madison County
NORTH
-50-
-51-
-52-
-53-
-54-
-55-
-56-
-57-
-58-
-59-
-60-
-61-
-62-
-63-
-64-
-65-
-66-
-67-
-68-
-69-
-70-
-71-
-72-
-73-
-74-
-75-
1,500
1,000
500

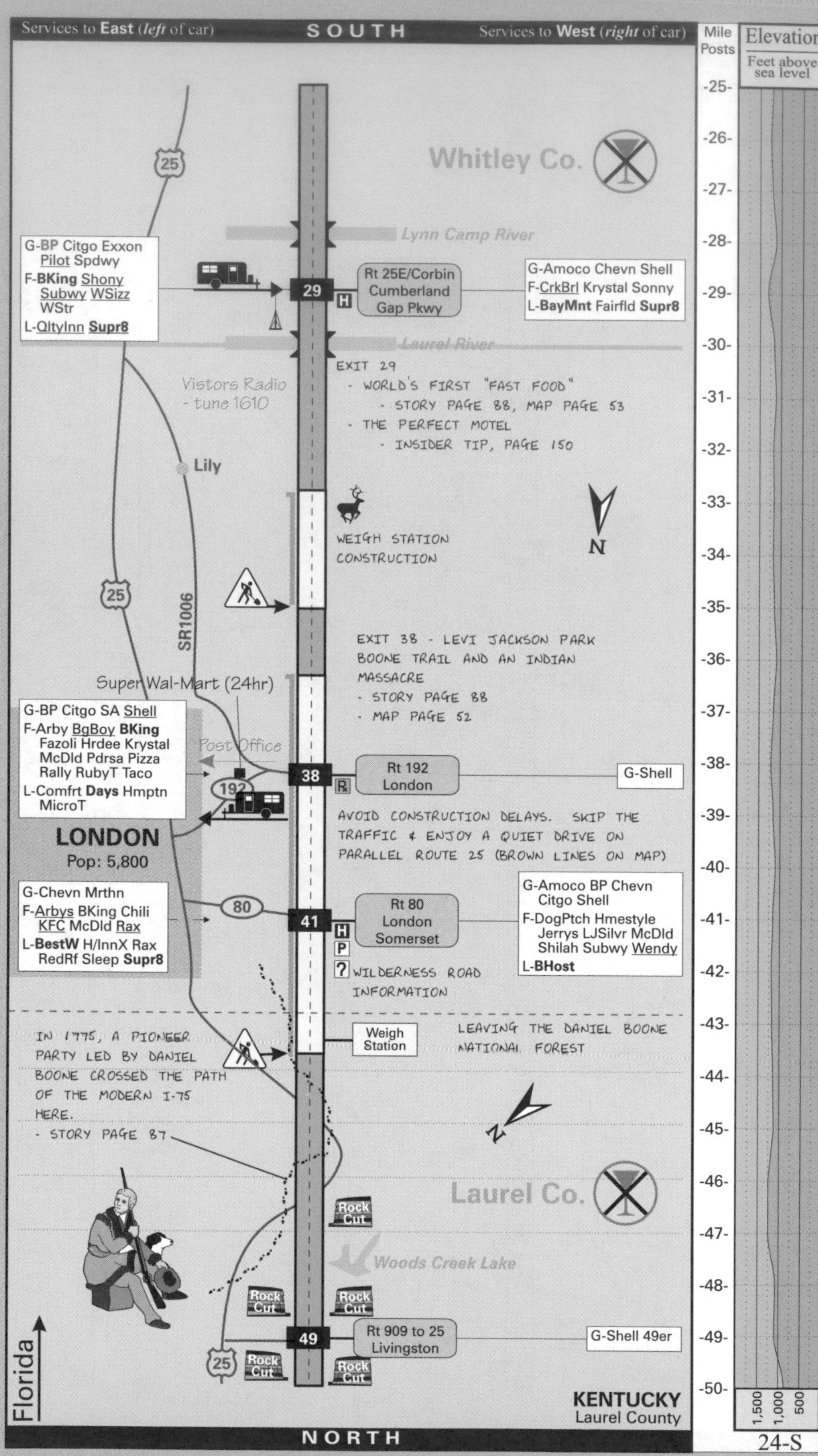

Services to East (left of car)
SOUTH
Services to West (right of car)
Mile Posts
Elevation
Feet above sea level
-25-
-26-
-27-
-28-
-29-
-30-
-31-
-32-
-33-
-34-
-35-
-36-
-37-
-38-
-39-
-40-
-41-
-42-
-43-
-44-
-45-
-46-
-47-
-48-
-49-
-50-
25
Whitley Co.
Lynn Camp River
G-BP Citgo Exxon Pilot Spdwy
F-BKing Shony Subwy WSizz WStr
L-QltyInn Supr8
29
H
Rt 25E/Corbin Cumberland Gap Pkwy
G-Amoco Chevn Shell
F-CrkBrl Krystal Sonny
L-BayMnt Fairfld Supr8
Laurel River
EXIT 29
- WORLD'S FIRST "FAST FOOD"
- STORY PAGE 88, MAP PAGE 53
- THE PERFECT MOTEL
- INSIDER TIP, PAGE 150
Vistors Radio
- tune 1610
Lily
WEIGH STATION
CONSTRUCTION
N
25
SR1006
EXIT 38 - LEVI JACKSON PARK
BOONE TRAIL AND AN INDIAN
MASSACRE
- STORY PAGE 88
- MAP PAGE 52
Super Wal-Mart (24hr)
G-BP Citgo SA Shell
F-Arby BgBoy BKing Fazoli Hrdee Krystal McDld Pdrsa Pizza Rally RubyT Taco
L-Comfrt Days Hmptn MicroT
Post Office
192
38
R
Rt 192 London
G-Shell
LONDON
Pop: 5,800
AVOID CONSTRUCTION DELAYS. SKIP THE
TRAFFIC & ENJOY A QUIET DRIVE ON
PARALLEL ROUTE 25 (BROWN LINES ON MAP)
G-Chevn Mrthn
F-Arbys BKing Chili KFC McDld Rax
L-BestW H/InnX Rax RedRf Sleep Supr8
80
41
H
P
?
Rt 80 London Somerset
G-Amoco BP Chevn Citgo Shell
F-DogPtch Hmestyle Jerrys LJSilvr McDld Shilah Subwy Wendy
L-BHost
WILDERNESS ROAD
INFORMATION
IN 1775, A PIONEER
PARTY LED BY DANIEL
BOONE CROSSED THE PATH
OF THE MODERN I-75
HERE.
- STORY PAGE 87
Weigh Station
LEAVING THE DANIEL BOONE
NATIONAL FOREST
N
Laurel Co.
Rock Cut
Woods Creek Lake
Rock Cut
Rock Cut
49
Rt 909 to 25 Livingston
G-Shell 49er
25
Rock Cut
Rock Cut
Florida
KENTUCKY
Laurel County
NORTH
1,500
1,000
500
24-S

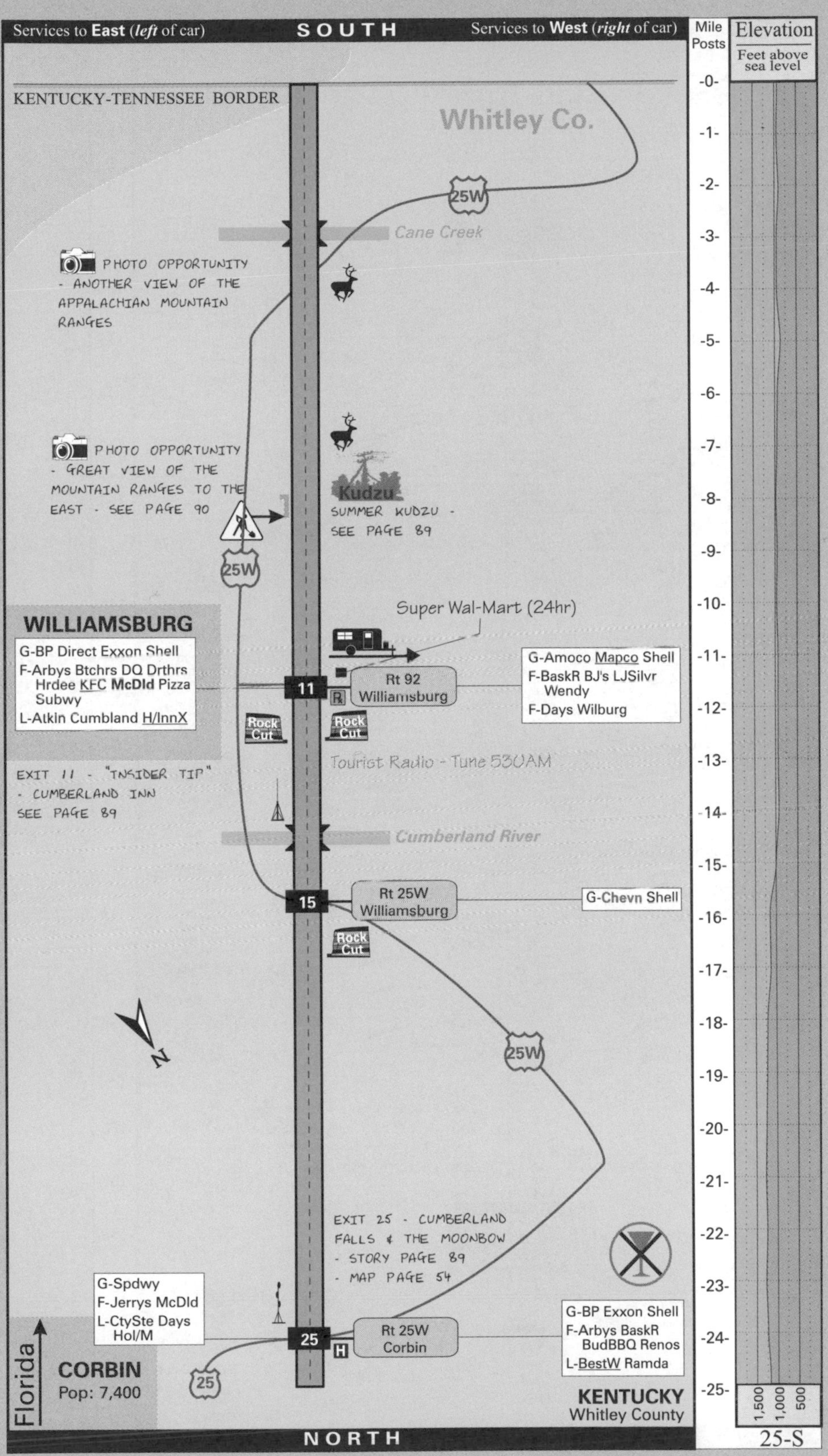
Services to East (left of car)
SOUTH
Services to West (right of car)
Mile Posts
Elevation
Feet above sea level
KENTUCKY-TENNESSEE BORDER
Whitley Co.
25W
Cane Creek
PHOTO OPPORTUNITY - ANOTHER VIEW OF THE APPALACHIAN MOUNTAIN RANGES
PHOTO OPPORTUNITY - GREAT VIEW OF THE MOUNTAIN RANGES TO THE EAST - SEE PAGE 90
Kudzu
SUMMER KUDZU - SEE PAGE 89
Super Wal-Mart (24hr)
WILLIAMSBURG
G-BP Direct Exxon Shell
F-Arbys Btchrs DQ Drthrs Hrdee KFC McDld Pizza Subwy
L-Atkin Cumbland H/InnX
11
Rt 92 Williamsburg
G-Amoco Mapco Shell
F-BaskR BJ's LJSilvr Wendy
F-Days Wilburg
Rock Cut
Rock Cut
Tourist Radio - Tune 530AM
EXIT 11 - "INSIDER TIP" - CUMBERLAND INN SEE PAGE 89
Cumberland River
15
Rt 25W Williamsburg
G-Chevn Shell
Rock Cut
N
EXIT 25 - CUMBERLAND FALLS & THE MOONBOW - STORY PAGE 89 - MAP PAGE 54
G-Spdwy
F-Jerrys McDld
L-CtySte Days Hol/M
25
Rt 25W Corbin
G-BP Exxon Shell
F-Arbys BaskR BudBBQ Renos
L-BestW Ramda
Florida
CORBIN
Pop: 7,400
KENTUCKY
Whitley County
NORTH
-0- -1- -2- -3- -4- -5- -6- -7- -8- -9- -10- -11- -12- -13- -14- -15- -16- -17- -18- -19- -20- -21- -22- -23- -24- -25-
1,500 1,000 500
25-S

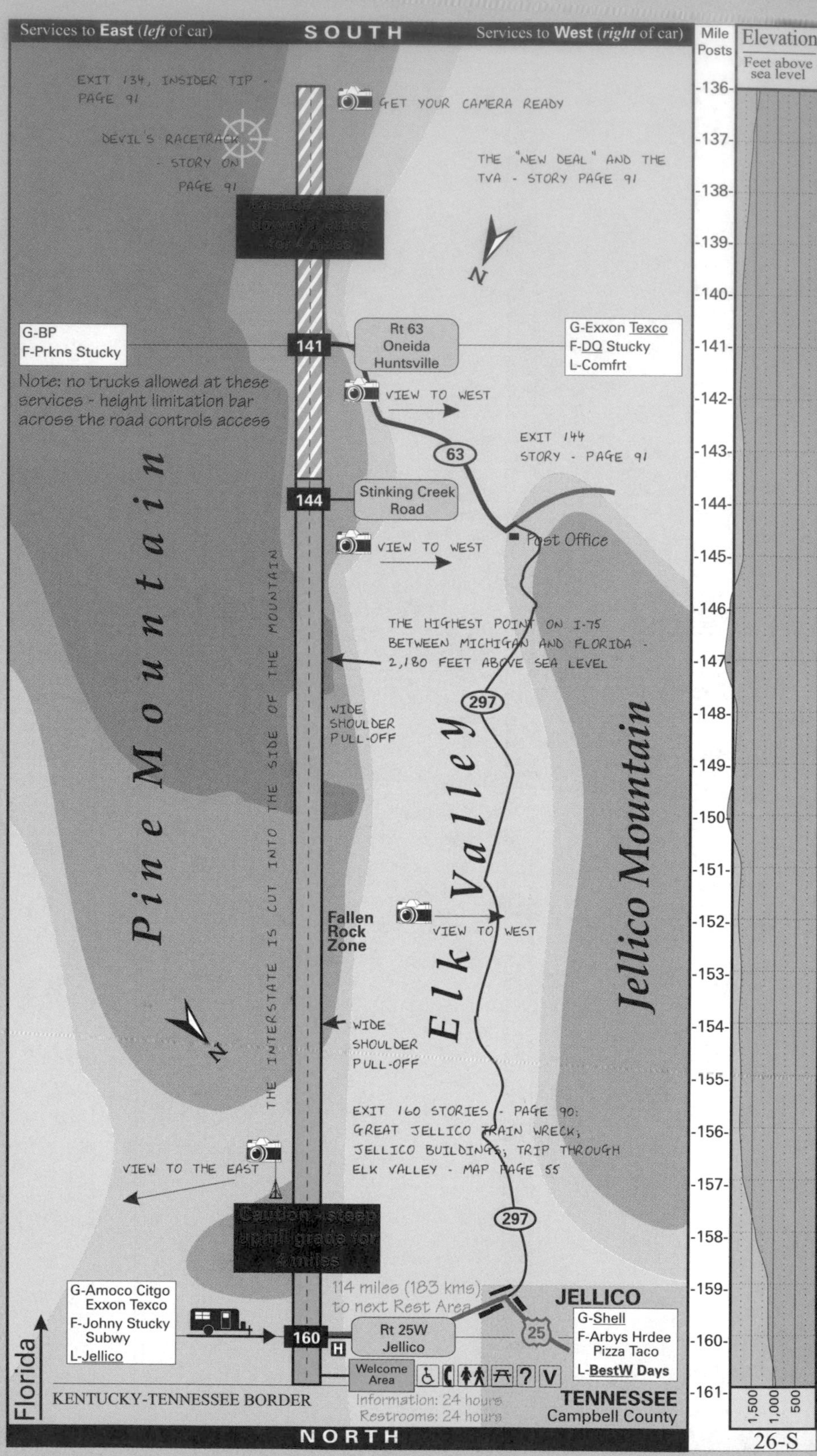
Services to East (left of car)
SOUTH
Services to West (right of car)
Mile Posts
Elevation
Feet above sea level
EXIT 134, INSIDER TIP - PAGE 91
GET YOUR CAMERA READY
DEVIL'S RACETRACK - STORY ON PAGE 91
THE "NEW DEAL" AND THE TVA - STORY PAGE 91
Caution - steep downhill grade for 4 miles
N
G-BP
F-Prkns Stucky
141
Rt 63
Oneida
Huntsville
G-Exxon Texco
F-DQ Stucky
L-Comfrt
Note: no trucks allowed at these services - height limitation bar across the road controls access
VIEW TO WEST
63
EXIT 144
STORY - PAGE 91
144
Stinking Creek Road
VIEW TO WEST
Post Office
Pine Mountain
THE INTERSTATE IS CUT INTO THE SIDE OF THE MOUNTAIN
THE HIGHEST POINT ON I-75 BETWEEN MICHIGAN AND FLORIDA - 2,180 FEET ABOVE SEA LEVEL
297
WIDE SHOULDER PULL-OFF
Elk Valley
Jellico Mountain
Fallen Rock Zone
VIEW TO WEST
N
WIDE SHOULDER PULL-OFF
EXIT 160 STORIES - PAGE 90: GREAT JELLICO TRAIN WRECK; JELLICO BUILDINGS; TRIP THROUGH ELK VALLEY - MAP PAGE 55
VIEW TO THE EAST
Caution - steep uphill grade for 4 miles
297
114 miles (183 kms) to next Rest Area
JELLICO
G-Amoco Citgo Exxon Texco
F-Johny Stucky Subwy
L-Jellico
160
H
Rt 25W
Jellico
25
G-Shell
F-Arbys Hrdee Pizza Taco
L-BestW Days
Welcome Area
Florida
KENTUCKY-TENNESSEE BORDER
Information: 24 hours
Restrooms: 24 hours
TENNESSEE
Campbell County
NORTH
-136-
-137-
-138-
-139-
-140-
-141-
-142-
-143-
-144-
-145-
-146-
-147-
-148-
-149-
-150-
-151-
-152-
-153-
-154-
-155-
-156-
-157-
-158-
-159-
-160-
-161-
1,500
1,000
500

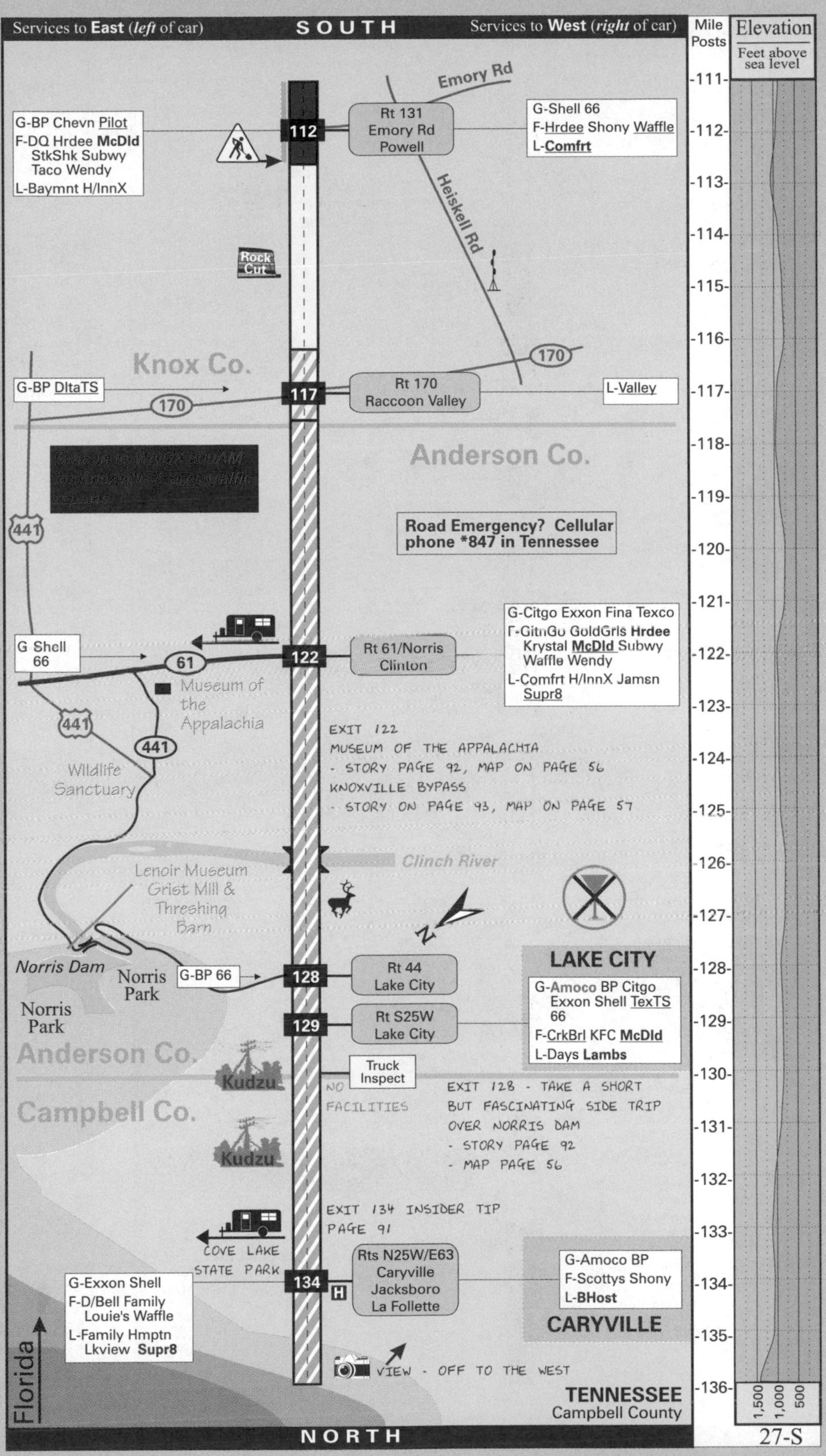

Services to East (left of car)
SOUTH
Services to West (right of car)
Mile Posts
Elevation
Feet above sea level
-111-
-112-
-113-
-114-
-115-
-116-
-117-
-118-
-119-
-120-
-121-
-122-
-123-
-124-
-125-
-126-
-127-
-128-
-129-
-130-
-131-
-132-
-133-
-134-
-135-
-136-
1,500
1,000
500
Emory Rd
G-BP Chevn Pilot
F-DQ Hrdee McDld StkShk Subwy Taco Wendy
L-Baymnt H/InnX
112
Rt 131 Emory Rd Powell
G-Shell 66
F-Hrdee Shony Waffle
L-Comfrt
Heiskell Rd
Rock Cut
Knox Co.
170
G-BP DltaTS
117
Rt 170 Raccoon Valley
L-Valley
Anderson Co.
441
Road Emergency? Cellular phone *847 in Tennessee
G-Citgo Exxon Fina Texco
F-GitnGo GoldGrls Hrdee Krystal McDld Subwy Waffle Wendy
L-Comfrt H/InnX Jamsn Supr8
G Shell 66
61
122
Rt 61/Norris Clinton
Museum of the Appalachia
EXIT 122
MUSEUM OF THE APPALACHIA
- STORY PAGE 92, MAP ON PAGE 56
KNOXVILLE BYPASS
- STORY ON PAGE 93, MAP ON PAGE 57
Wildlife Sanctuary
Clinch River
Lenoir Museum Grist Mill & Threshing Barn
N
LAKE CITY
Norris Dam
Norris Park
G-BP 66
128
Rt 44 Lake City
G-Amoco BP Citgo Exxon Shell TexTS 66
F-CrkBrl KFC McDld
L-Days Lambs
Norris Park
129
Rt S25W Lake City
Anderson Co.
Kudzu
Truck Inspect
NO FACILITIES
EXIT 128 - TAKE A SHORT BUT FASCINATING SIDE TRIP OVER NORRIS DAM
- STORY PAGE 92
- MAP PAGE 56
Campbell Co.
Kudzu
EXIT 134 INSIDER TIP PAGE 91
COVE LAKE STATE PARK
Rts N25W/E63 Caryville Jacksboro La Follette
G-Amoco BP
F-Scottys Shony
L-BHost
134
H
G-Exxon Shell
F-D/Bell Family Louie's Waffle
L-Family Hmptn Lkview Supr8
CARYVILLE
VIEW - OFF TO THE WEST
Florida
TENNESSEE
Campbell County
NORTH

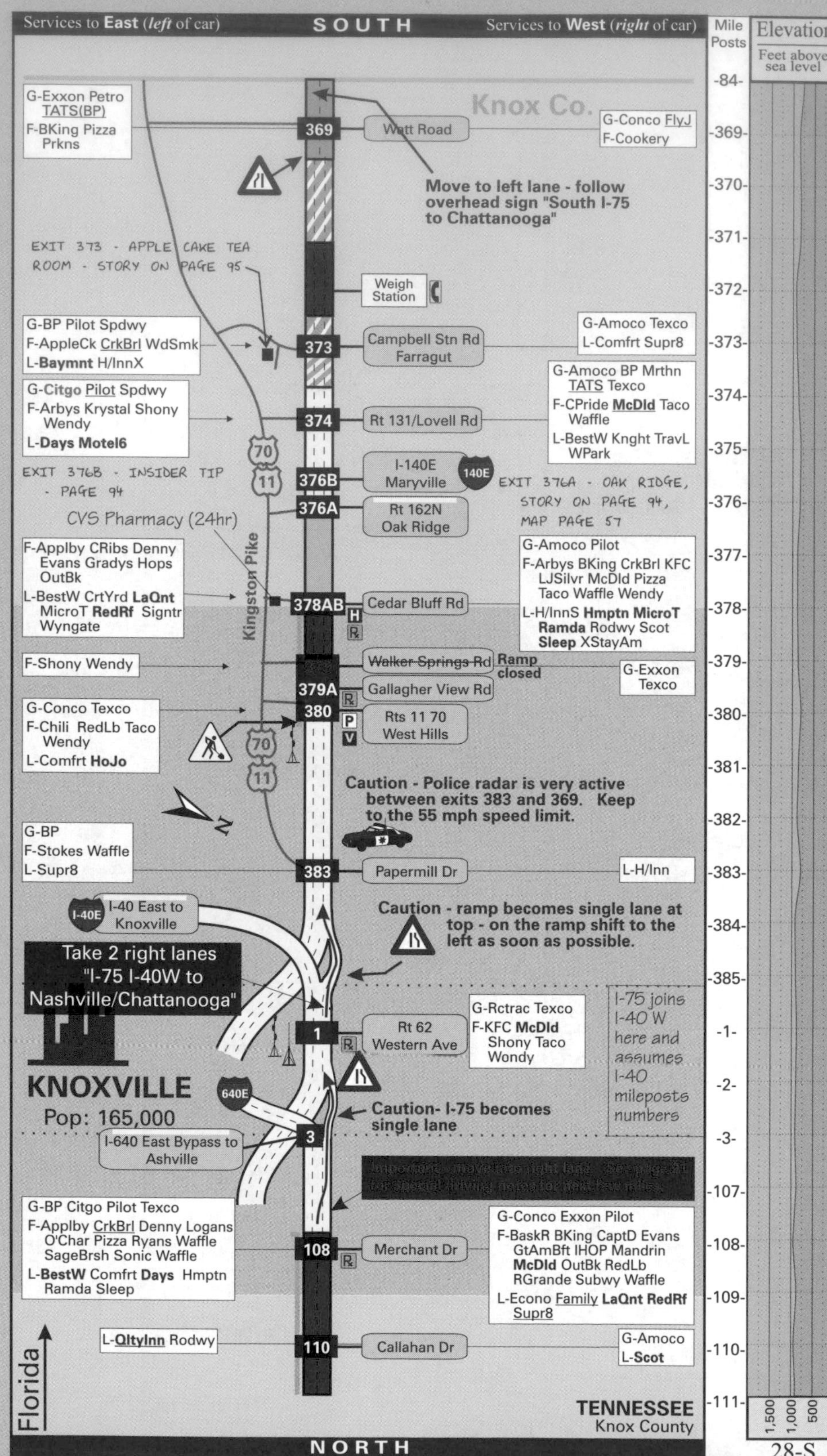

Services to East (left of car)
SOUTH
Services to West (right of car)
Mile Posts
Elevation
Feet above sea level
-84-
Knox Co.
G-Exxon Petro TATS(BP)
F-BKing Pizza Prkns
369
Watt Road
G-Conco FlyJ
F-Cookery
-369-
Move to left lane - follow overhead sign "South I-75 to Chattanooga"
-370-
-371-
EXIT 373 - APPLE CAKE TEA ROOM - STORY ON PAGE 95
Weigh Station
-372-
G-BP Pilot Spdwy
F-AppleCk CrkBrl WdSmk
L-Baymnt H/InnX
373
Campbell Stn Rd Farragut
G-Amoco Texco
L-Comfrt Supr8
-373-
G-Amoco BP Mrthn TATS Texco
F-CPride McDld Taco Waffle
L-BestW Knght TravL WPark
-374-
G-Citgo Pilot Spdwy
F-Arbys Krystal Shony Wendy
L-Days Motel6
374
Rt 131/Lovell Rd
-375-
70
11
EXIT 376B - INSIDER TIP - PAGE 94
376B
I-140E Maryville
140E
EXIT 376A - OAK RIDGE, STORY ON PAGE 94, MAP PAGE 57
376A
Rt 162N Oak Ridge
-376-
CVS Pharmacy (24hr)
F-Applby CRibs Denny Evans Gradys Hops OutBk
L-BestW CrtYrd LaQnt MicroT RedRf Signtr Wyngate
Kingston Pike
G-Amoco Pilot
F-Arbys BKing CrkBrl KFC LJSilvr McDld Pizza Taco Waffle Wendy
L-H/InnS Hmptn MicroT Ramda Rodwy Scot Sleep XStayAm
-377-
378AB
Cedar Bluff Rd
H
-378-
F-Shony Wendy
Walker Springs Rd
Ramp closed
G-Exxon Texco
-379-
379A
Gallagher View Rd
G-Conco Texco
F-Chili RedLb Taco Wendy
L-Comfrt HoJo
380
Rts 11 70 West Hills
P
V
-380-
70
11
-381-
Caution - Police radar is very active between exits 383 and 369. Keep to the 55 mph speed limit.
N
-382-
G-BP
F-Stokes Waffle
L-Supr8
383
Papermill Dr
L-H/Inn
-383-
I-40E
I-40 East to Knoxville
Caution - ramp becomes single lane at top - on the ramp shift to the left as soon as possible.
-384-
Take 2 right lanes "I-75 I-40W to Nashville/Chattanooga"
-385-
G-Rctrac Texco
F-KFC McDld Shony Taco Wndy
I-75 joins I-40 W here and assumes I-40 mileposts numbers
1
Rt 62 Western Ave
-1-
KNOXVILLE
Pop: 165,000
640E
Caution- I-75 becomes single lane
-2-
I-640 East Bypass to Ashville
3
-3-
-107-
G-BP Citgo Pilot Texco
F-Applby CrkBrl Denny Logans O'Char Pizza Ryans Waffle SageBrsh Sonic Waffle
L-BestW Comfrt Days Hmptn Ramda Sleep
108
Merchant Dr
G-Conco Exxon Pilot
F-BaskR BKing CaptD Evans GtAmBft IHOP Mandrin McDld OutBk RedLb RGrande Subwy Waffle
L-Econo Family LaQnt RedRf Supr8
-108-
-109-
L-QltyInn Rodwy
110
Callahan Dr
G-Amoco
L-Scot
-110-
Florida
TENNESSEE
Knox County
-111-
1,500
1,000
500
NORTH
28-S

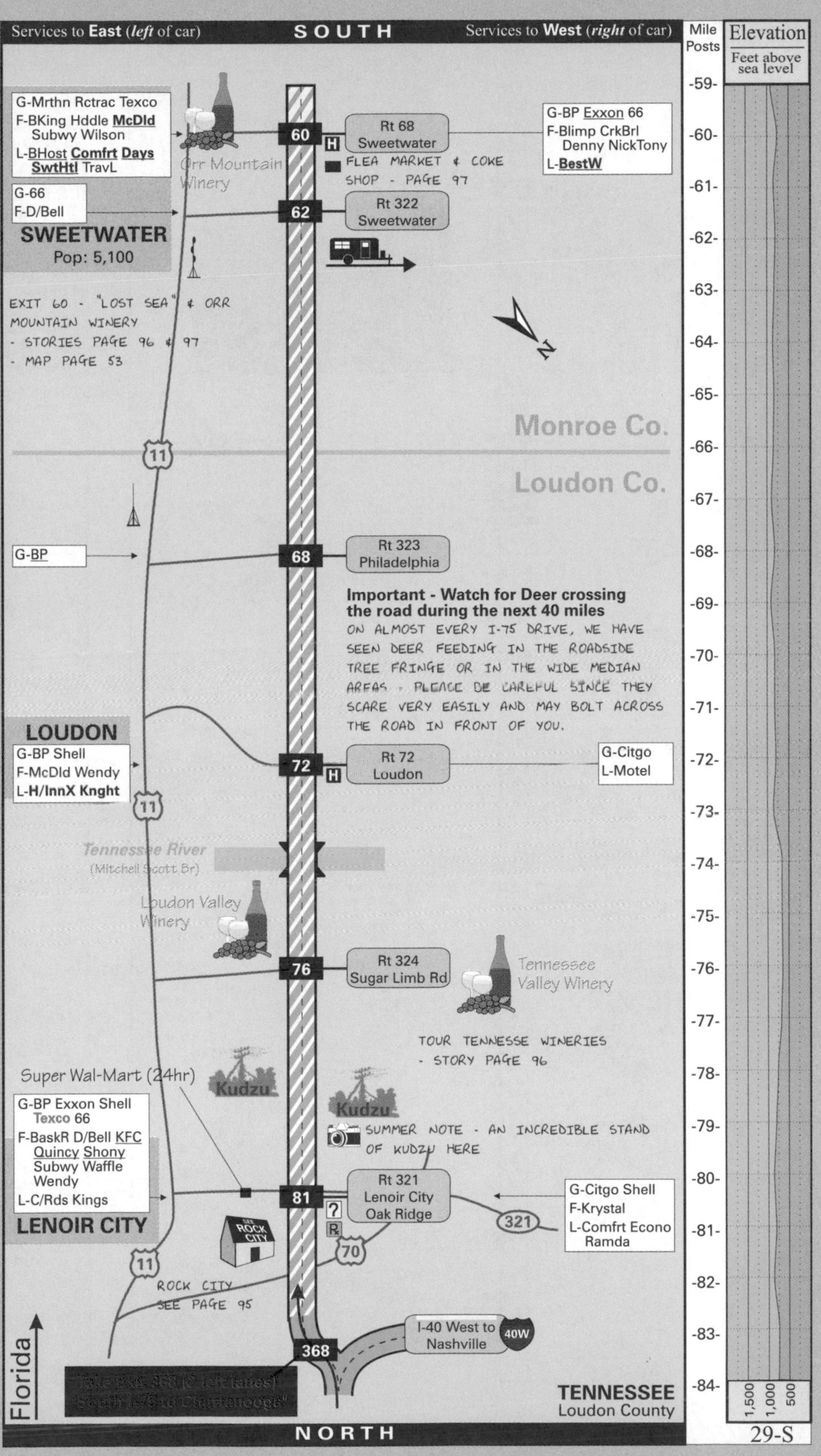

Services to East (left of car)
SOUTH
Services to West (right of car)
Mile Posts
Elevation
Feet above sea level
G-Mrthn Rctrac Texco
F-BKing Hddle McDld Subwy Wilson
L-BHost Comfrt Days SwtHtl TravL
Orr Mountain Winery
60
Rt 68 Sweetwater
FLEA MARKET & COKE SHOP - PAGE 97
G-BP Exxon 66
F-Blimp CrkBrl Denny NickTony
L-BestW
G-66
F-D/Bell
SWEETWATER
Pop: 5,100
62
Rt 322 Sweetwater
EXIT 60 - "LOST SEA" & ORR MOUNTAIN WINERY
- STORIES PAGE 96 & 97
- MAP PAGE 53
N
Monroe Co.
Loudon Co.
11
G-BP
68
Rt 323 Philadelphia
Important - Watch for Deer crossing the road during the next 40 miles
ON ALMOST EVERY I-75 DRIVE, WE HAVE SEEN DEER FEEDING IN THE ROADSIDE TREE FRINGE OR IN THE WIDE MEDIAN AREAS. PLEASE BE CAREFUL SINCE THEY SCARE VERY EASILY AND MAY BOLT ACROSS THE ROAD IN FRONT OF YOU.
LOUDON
G-BP Shell
F-McDld Wendy
L-H/InnX Knght
72
Rt 72 Loudon
G-Citgo
L-Motel
11
Tennessee River
(Mitchell Scott Br)
Loudon Valley Winery
76
Rt 324 Sugar Limb Rd
Tennessee Valley Winery
TOUR TENNESSE WINERIES - STORY PAGE 96
Super Wal-Mart (24hr)
Kudzu
Kudzu
SUMMER NOTE - AN INCREDIBLE STAND OF KUDZU HERE
G-BP Exxon Shell Texco 66
F-BaskR D/Bell KFC Quincy Shony Subwy Waffle Wendy
L-C/Rds Kings
LENOIR CITY
81
Rt 321 Lenoir City Oak Ridge
G-Citgo Shell
F-Krystal
L-Comfrt Econo Ramda
321
70
SEE ROCK CITY
11
ROCK CITY SEE PAGE 95
368
I-40 West to Nashville
40W
Florida
TENNESSEE
Loudon County
NORTH
-59-
-60-
-61-
-62-
-63-
-64-
-65-
-66-
-67-
-68-
-69-
-70-
-71-
-72-
-73-
-74-
-75-
-76-
-77-
-78-
-79-
-80-
-81-
-82-
-83-
-84-
1,500
1,000
500

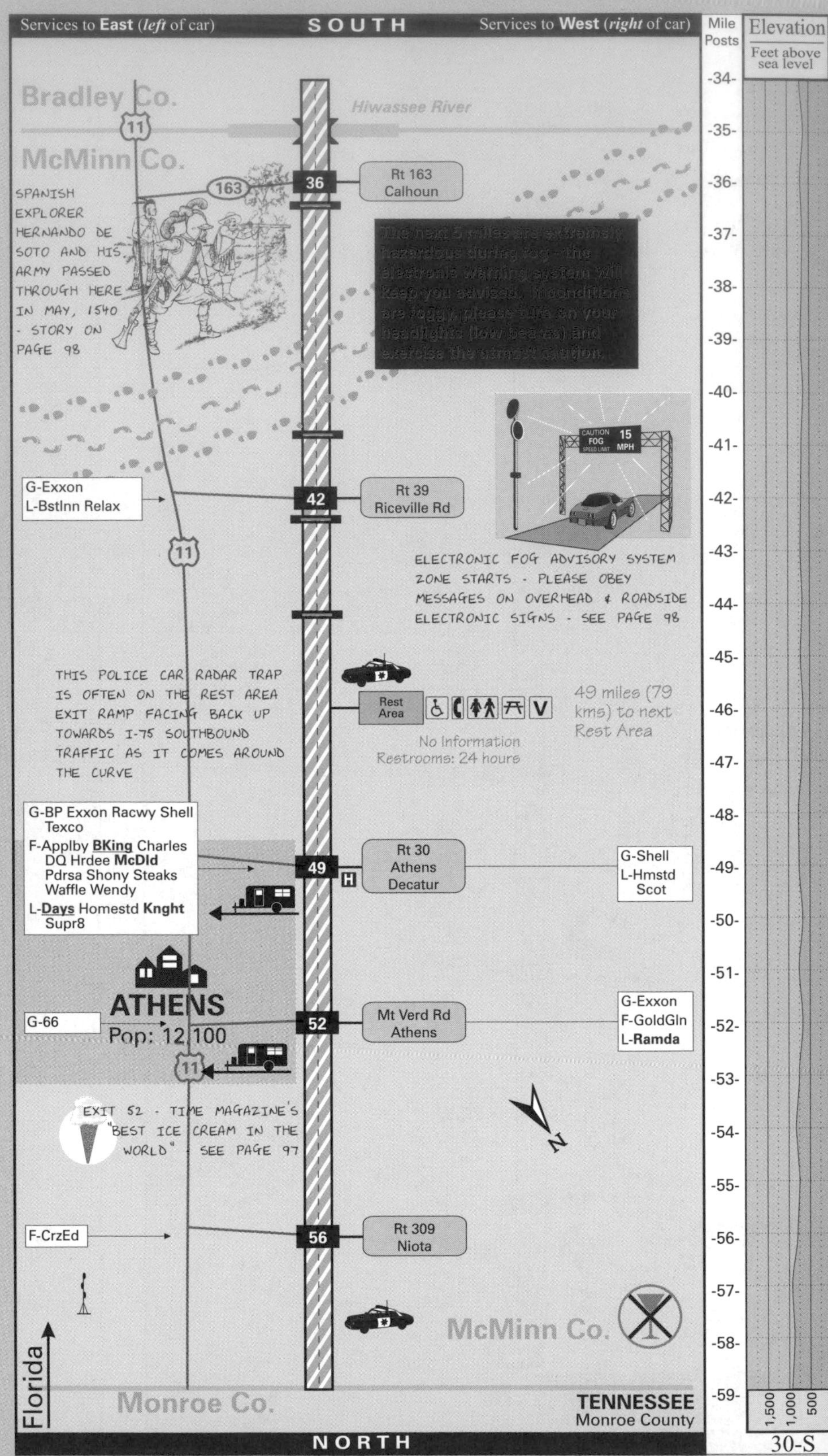
Services to East (left of car)
SOUTH
Services to West (right of car)
Mile Posts
Elevation
Feet above sea level
Bradley Co.
Hiwassee River
11
McMinn Co.
163
SPANISH EXPLORER HERNANDO DE SOTO AND HIS ARMY PASSED THROUGH HERE IN MAY, 1540 - STORY ON PAGE 98
36
Rt 163
Calhoun
The next 5 miles are extremely hazardous during fog - the electronic warning system will keep you advised. If conditions are foggy, please turn on your headlights (low beams) and exercise the utmost caution.
CAUTION FOG SPEED LIMIT 15 MPH
G-Exxon
L-BstInn Relax
42
Rt 39
Riceville Rd
11
ELECTRONIC FOG ADVISORY SYSTEM ZONE STARTS - PLEASE OBEY MESSAGES ON OVERHEAD & ROADSIDE ELECTRONIC SIGNS - SEE PAGE 98
THIS POLICE CAR RADAR TRAP IS OFTEN ON THE REST AREA EXIT RAMP FACING BACK UP TOWARDS I-75 SOUTHBOUND TRAFFIC AS IT COMES AROUND THE CURVE
Rest Area
V
No Information
Restrooms: 24 hours
49 miles (79 kms) to next Rest Area
G-BP Exxon Racwy Shell Texco
F-Applby BKing Charles DQ Hrdee McDld Pdrsa Shony Steaks Waffle Wendy
L-Days Homestd Knght Supr8
49
H
Rt 30
Athens
Decatur
G-Shell
L-Hmstd Scot
ATHENS
Pop: 12,100
G-66
52
Mt Verd Rd
Athens
G-Exxon
F-GoldGln
L-Ramda
11
EXIT 52 - TIME MAGAZINE'S "BEST ICE CREAM IN THE WORLD" - SEE PAGE 97
N
F-CrzEd
56
Rt 309
Niota
McMinn Co.
Florida
Monroe Co.
TENNESSEE
Monroe County
NORTH
-34-
-35-
-36-
-37-
-38-
-39-
-40-
-41-
-42-
-43-
-44-
-45-
-46-
-47-
-48-
-49-
-50-
-51-
-52-
-53-
-54-
-55-
-56-
-57-
-58-
-59-
1,500
1,000
500

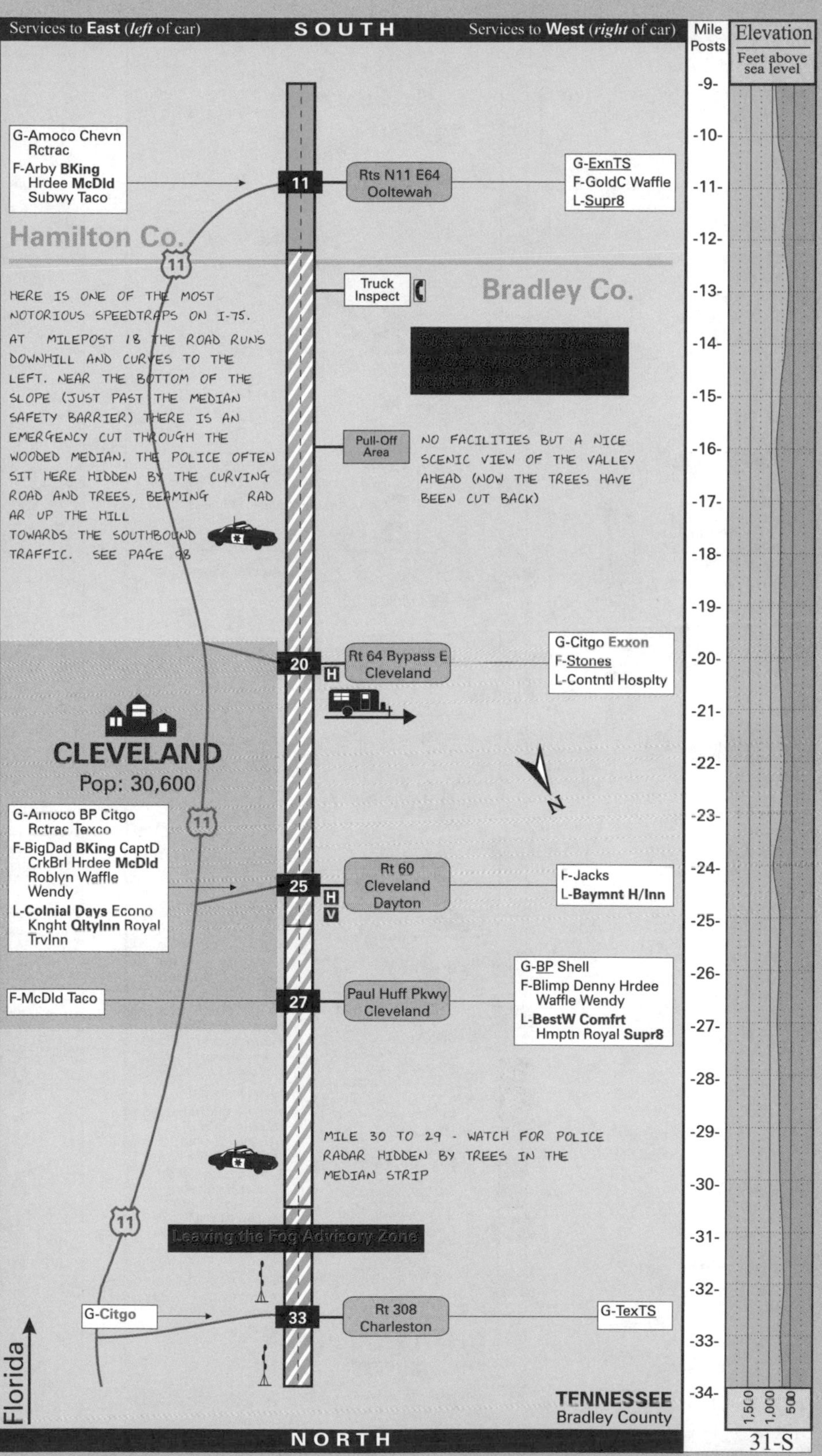
Services to East (left of car)
SOUTH
Services to West (right of car)
Mile Posts
Elevation
Feet above sea level
G-Amoco Chevn Rctrac
F-Arby BKing Hrdee McDld Subwy Taco
11
Rts N11 E64 Ooltewah
G-ExnTS
F-GoldC Waffle
L-Supr8
Hamilton Co.
11
Truck Inspect
Bradley Co.
HERE IS ONE OF THE MOST NOTORIOUS SPEEDTRAPS ON I-75.
AT MILEPOST 18 THE ROAD RUNS DOWNHILL AND CURVES TO THE LEFT. NEAR THE BOTTOM OF THE SLOPE (JUST PAST THE MEDIAN SAFETY BARRIER) THERE IS AN EMERGENCY CUT THROUGH THE WOODED MEDIAN. THE POLICE OFTEN SIT HERE HIDDEN BY THE CURVING ROAD AND TREES, BEAMING RADAR UP THE HILL TOWARDS THE SOUTHBOUND TRAFFIC. SEE PAGE 98
Pull-Off Area
NO FACILITIES BUT A NICE SCENIC VIEW OF THE VALLEY AHEAD (NOW THE TREES HAVE BEEN CUT BACK)
20
Rt 64 Bypass E Cleveland
G-Citgo Exxon
F-Stones
L-Contntl Hosplty
CLEVELAND
Pop: 30,600
N
G-Amoco BP Citgo Rctrac Texco
F-BigDad BKing CaptD CrkBrl Hrdee McDld Roblyn Waffle Wendy
L-Colnial Days Econo Knght QltyInn Royal TrvInn
11
25
Rt 60 Cleveland Dayton
F-Jacks
L-Baymnt H/Inn
G-BP Shell
F-Blimp Denny Hrdee Waffle Wendy
L-BestW Comfrt Hmptn Royal Supr8
F-McDld Taco
27
Paul Huff Pkwy Cleveland
MILE 30 TO 29 - WATCH FOR POLICE RADAR HIDDEN BY TREES IN THE MEDIAN STRIP
11
Leaving the Fog Advisory Zone
G-Citgo
33
Rt 308 Charleston
G-TexTS
Florida
TENNESSEE
Bradley County
NORTH
-9-
-10-
-11-
-12-
-13-
-14-
-15-
-16-
-17-
-18-
-19-
-20-
-21-
-22-
-23-
-24-
-25-
-26-
-27-
-28-
-29-
-30-
-31-
-32-
-33-
-34-
1,500
1,000
500
31-S

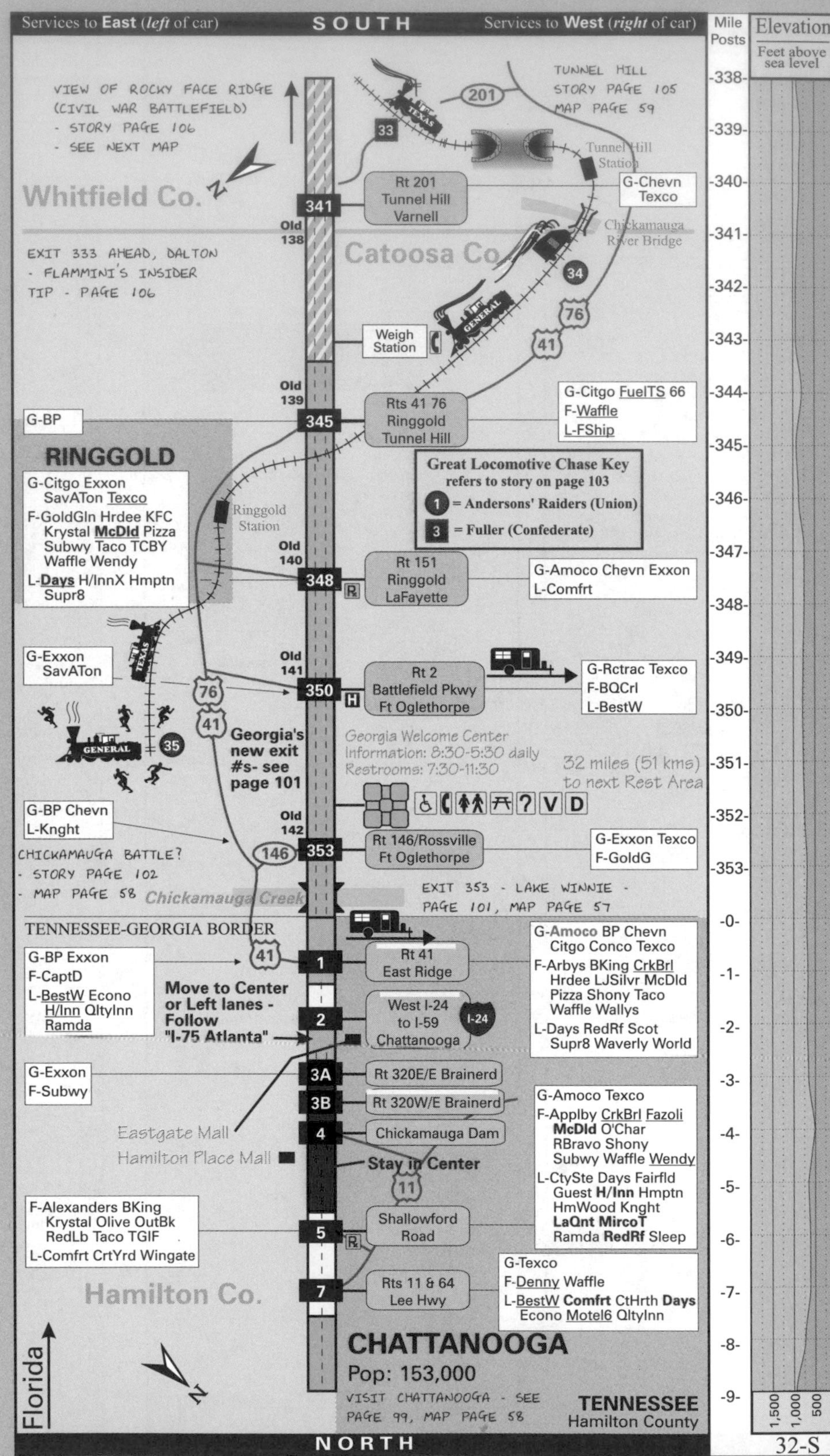

Services to East (left of car)
SOUTH
Services to West (right of car)
Mile Posts
Elevation
Feet above sea level
VIEW OF ROCKY FACE RIDGE (CIVIL WAR BATTLEFIELD)
- STORY PAGE 106
- SEE NEXT MAP
TUNNEL HILL
STORY PAGE 105
MAP PAGE 59
201
33
TEXAS
Tunnel Hill Station
Whitfield Co.
N
341
Rt 201
Tunnel Hill
Varnell
G-Chevn
Texco
Old 138
Chickamauga River Bridge
Catoosa Co.
34
EXIT 333 AHEAD, DALTON
- FLAMMINI'S INSIDER TIP - PAGE 106
GENERAL
76
41
Weigh Station
Old 139
345
Rts 41 76
Ringgold
Tunnel Hill
G-BP
G-Citgo FuelTS 66
F-Waffle
L-FShip
RINGGOLD
G-Citgo Exxon
SavATon Texco
F-GoldGln Hrdee KFC
Krystal McDld Pizza
Subwy Taco TCBY
Waffle Wendy
L-Days H/InnX Hmptn
Supr8
Great Locomotive Chase Key
refers to story on page 103
1 = Andersons' Raiders (Union)
3 = Fuller (Confederate)
Ringgold Station
Old 140
348
Rt 151
Ringgold
LaFayette
G-Amoco Chevn Exxon
L-Comfrt
G-Exxon
SavATon
TEXAS
Old 141
350
Rt 2
Battlefield Pkwy
Ft Oglethorpe
G-Rctrac Texco
F-BQCrl
L-BestW
76
41
35
GENERAL
Georgia's new exit #s- see page 101
Georgia Welcome Center
Information: 8:30-5:30 daily
Restrooms: 7:30-11:30
32 miles (51 kms) to next Rest Area
G-BP Chevn
L-Knght
Old 142
146
353
Rt 146/Rossville
Ft Oglethorpe
G-Exxon Texco
F-GoldG
CHICKAMAUGA BATTLE?
- STORY PAGE 102
- MAP PAGE 58
Chickamauga Creek
EXIT 353 - LAKE WINNIE - PAGE 101, MAP PAGE 57
TENNESSEE-GEORGIA BORDER
G-BP Exxon
F-CaptD
L-BestW Econo
H/Inn QltyInn
Ramda
41
1
Rt 41
East Ridge
G-Amoco BP Chevn
Citgo Conco Texco
F-Arbys BKing CrkBrl
Hrdee LJSilvr McDld
Pizza Shony Taco
Waffle Wallys
L-Days RedRf Scot
Supr8 Waverly World
Move to Center or Left lanes - Follow "I-75 Atlanta"
2
West I-24
to I-59
Chattanooga
I-24
G-Exxon
F-Subwy
3A
Rt 320E/E Brainerd
3B
Rt 320W/E Brainerd
G-Amoco Texco
F-Applby CrkBrl Fazoli
McDld O'Char
RBravo Shony
Subwy Waffle Wendy
L-CtySte Days Fairfld
Guest H/Inn Hmptn
HmWood Knght
LaQnt MircoT
Ramda RedRf Sleep
Eastgate Mall
Hamilton Place Mall
4
Chickamauga Dam
Stay in Center
11
F-Alexanders BKing
Krystal Olive OutBk
RedLb Taco TGIF
L-Comfrt CrtYrd Wingate
5
Shallowford Road
G-Texco
F-Denny Waffle
L-BestW Comfrt CtHrth Days
Econo Motel6 QltyInn
Hamilton Co.
7
Rts 11 & 64
Lee Hwy
CHATTANOOGA
Pop: 153,000
VISIT CHATTANOOGA - SEE PAGE 99, MAP PAGE 58
TENNESSEE
Hamilton County
Florida
N
NORTH
-338- -339- -340- -341- -342- -343- -344- -345- -346- -347- -348- -349- -350- -351- -352- -353-
-0- -1- -2- -3- -4- -5- -6- -7- -8- -9-
1,500 1,000 500

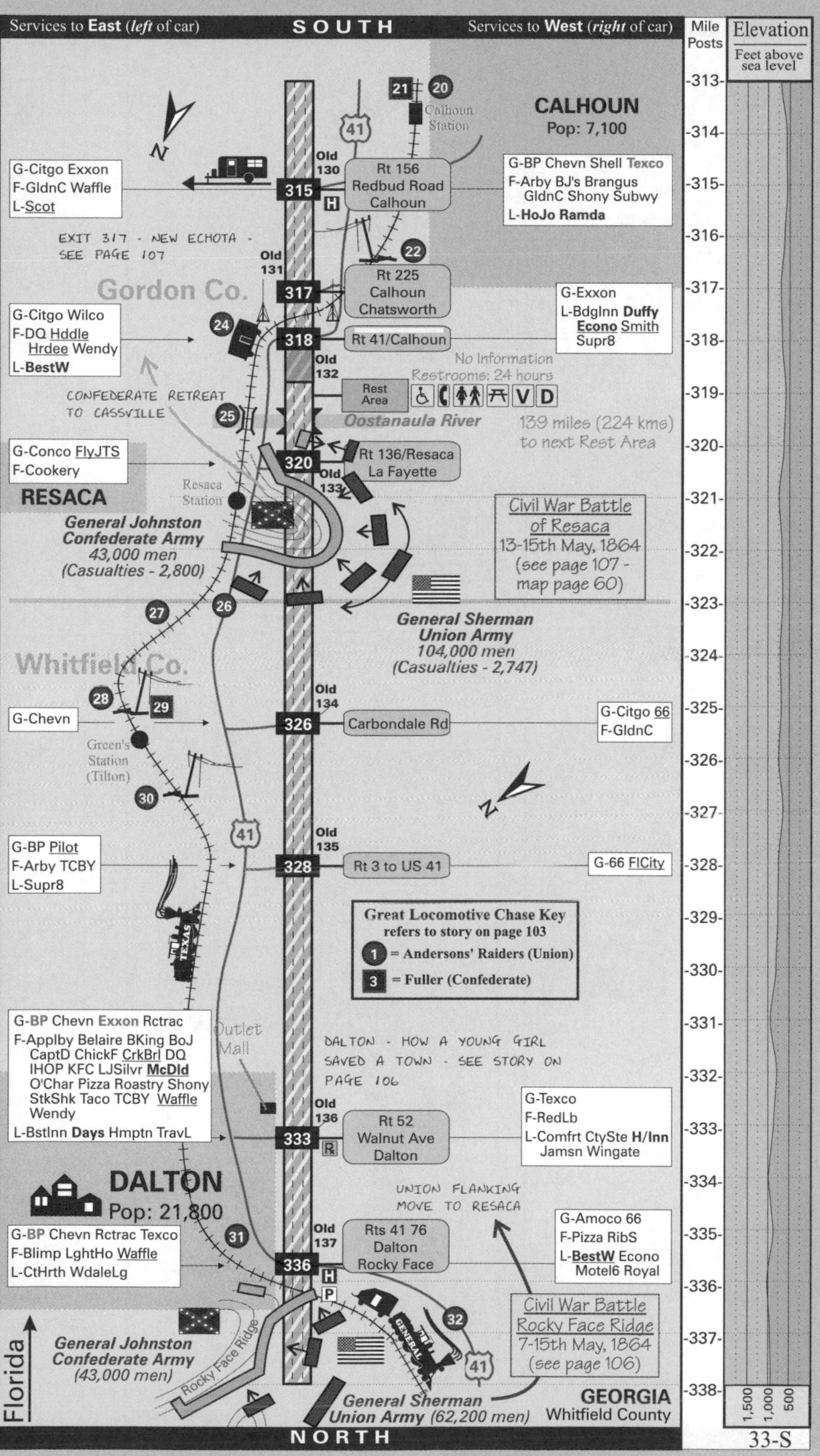

Services to East (left of car)
SOUTH
Services to West (right of car)
Mile Posts
Elevation
Feet above sea level
CALHOUN
Pop: 7,100
21
20
Calhoun Station
41
Old 130
315
H
Rt 156 Redbud Road Calhoun
G-Citgo Exxon
F-GldnC Waffle
L-Scot
G-BP Chevn Shell Texco
F-Arby BJ's Brangus GldnC Shony Subwy
L-HoJo Ramda
EXIT 317 - NEW ECHOTA - SEE PAGE 107
22
Old 131
Gordon Co.
317
Rt 225 Calhoun Chatsworth
G-Exxon
L-BdgInn Duffy Econo Smith Supr8
G-Citgo Wilco
F-DQ Hddle Hrdee Wendy
L-BestW
24
318
Rt 41/Calhoun
Old 132
No Information
Restrooms: 24 hours
Rest Area
V D
CONFEDERATE RETREAT TO CASSVILLE
25
Oostanaula River
139 miles (224 kms) to next Rest Area
G-Conco FlyJTS
F-Cookery
320
Rt 136/Resaca La Fayette
Old 133
RESACA
Resaca Station
General Johnston Confederate Army
43,000 men
(Casualties - 2,800)
Civil War Battle of Resaca
13-15th May, 1864
(see page 107 - map page 60)
27
26
General Sherman Union Army
104,000 men
(Casualties - 2,747)
Whitfield Co.
28
29
Old 134
G-Chevn
326
Carbondale Rd
G-Citgo 66
F-GldnC
Green's Station (Tilton)
30
N
41
Old 135
G-BP Pilot
F-Arby TCBY
L-Supr8
328
Rt 3 to US 41
G-66 FlCity
TEXAS
Great Locomotive Chase Key
refers to story on page 103
1 = Andersons' Raiders (Union)
3 = Fuller (Confederate)
G-BP Chevn Exxon Rctrac
F-Applby Belaire BKing BoJ CaptD ChickF CrkBrl DQ IHOP KFC LJSilvr McDld O'Char Pizza Roastry Shony StkShk Taco TCBY Waffle Wendy
L-BstInn Days Hmptn TravL
Outlet Mall
DALTON - HOW A YOUNG GIRL SAVED A TOWN - SEE STORY ON PAGE 106
Old 136
333
Rx
Rt 52 Walnut Ave Dalton
G-Texco
F-RedLb
L-Comfrt CtySte H/Inn Jamsn Wingate
DALTON
Pop: 21,800
UNION FLANKING MOVE TO RESACA
G-BP Chevn Rctrac Texco
F-Blimp LghtHo Waffle
L-CtHrth WdaleLg
31
Old 137
336
H
P
Rts 41 76 Dalton Rocky Face
G-Amoco 66
F-Pizza RibS
L-BestW Econo Motel6 Royal
32
GENERAL
Civil War Battle Rocky Face Ridge
7-15th May, 1864
(see page 106)
Rocky Face Ridge
General Johnston Confederate Army
(43,000 men)
Florida
41
General Sherman Union Army (62,200 men)
GEORGIA
Whitfield County
NORTH
-313- -314- -315- -316- -317- -318- -319- -320- -321- -322- -323- -324- -325- -326- -327- -328- -329- -330- -331- -332- -333- -334- -335- -336- -337- -338-
1,500 1,000 500
33-S

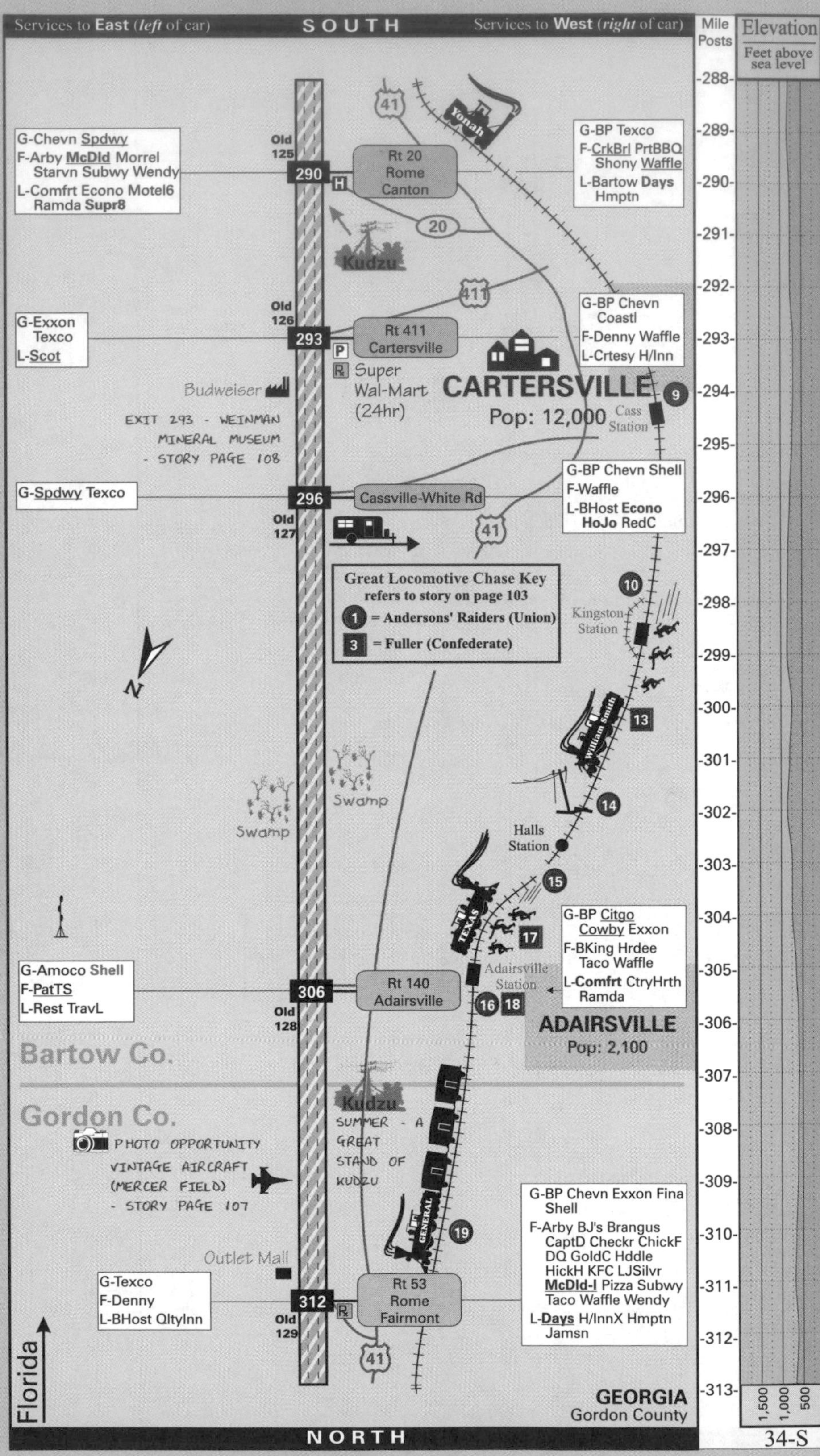

Services to East (left of car)
SOUTH
Services to West (right of car)
Mile Posts
Elevation
Feet above sea level
G-Chevn Spdwy
F-Arby McDld Morrel Starvn Subwy Wendy
L-Comfrt Econo Motel6 Ramda Supr8
Old 125
290
Rt 20 Rome Canton
20
41
Yonah
Kudzu
G-BP Texco
F-CrkBrl PrtBBQ Shony Waffle
L-Bartow Days Hmptn
G-Exxon Texco
L-Scot
Old 126
293
Rt 411 Cartersville
411
Super Wal-Mart (24hr)
Budweiser
EXIT 293 - WEINMAN MINERAL MUSEUM - STORY PAGE 108
CARTERSVILLE
Pop: 12,000
Cass Station
G-BP Chevn Coastl
F-Denny Waffle
L-Crtesy H/Inn
G-Spdwy Texco
296
Old 127
Cassville-White Rd
41
G-BP Chevn Shell
F-Waffle
L-BHost Econo HoJo RedC
Great Locomotive Chase Key refers to story on page 103
1 = Andersons' Raiders (Union)
3 = Fuller (Confederate)
N
Kingston Station
William Smith
Swamp
Swamp
Halls Station
TEXAS
G-BP Citgo Cowby Exxon
F-BKing Hrdee Taco Waffle
L-Comfrt CtryHrth Ramda
G-Amoco Shell
F-PatTS
L-Rest TravL
306
Old 128
Rt 140 Adairsville
Adairsville Station
ADAIRSVILLE
Pop: 2,100
Bartow Co.
Gordon Co.
Kudzu
SUMMER - A GREAT STAND OF KUDZU
PHOTO OPPORTUNITY VINTAGE AIRCRAFT (MERCER FIELD) - STORY PAGE 107
GENERAL
Outlet Mall
G-Texco
F-Denny
L-BHost QltyInn
312
Old 129
Rt 53 Rome Fairmont
41
G-BP Chevn Exxon Fina Shell
F-Arby BJ's Brangus CaptD Checkr ChickF DQ GoldC Hddle HickH KFC LJSilvr McDld-I Pizza Subwy Taco Waffle Wendy
L-Days H/InnX Hmptn Jamsn
Florida
GEORGIA
Gordon County
NORTH
-288- -289- -290- -291- -292- -293- -294- -295- -296- -297- -298- -299- -300- -301- -302- -303- -304- -305- -306- -307- -308- -309- -310- -311- -312- -313-
1,500 1,000 500

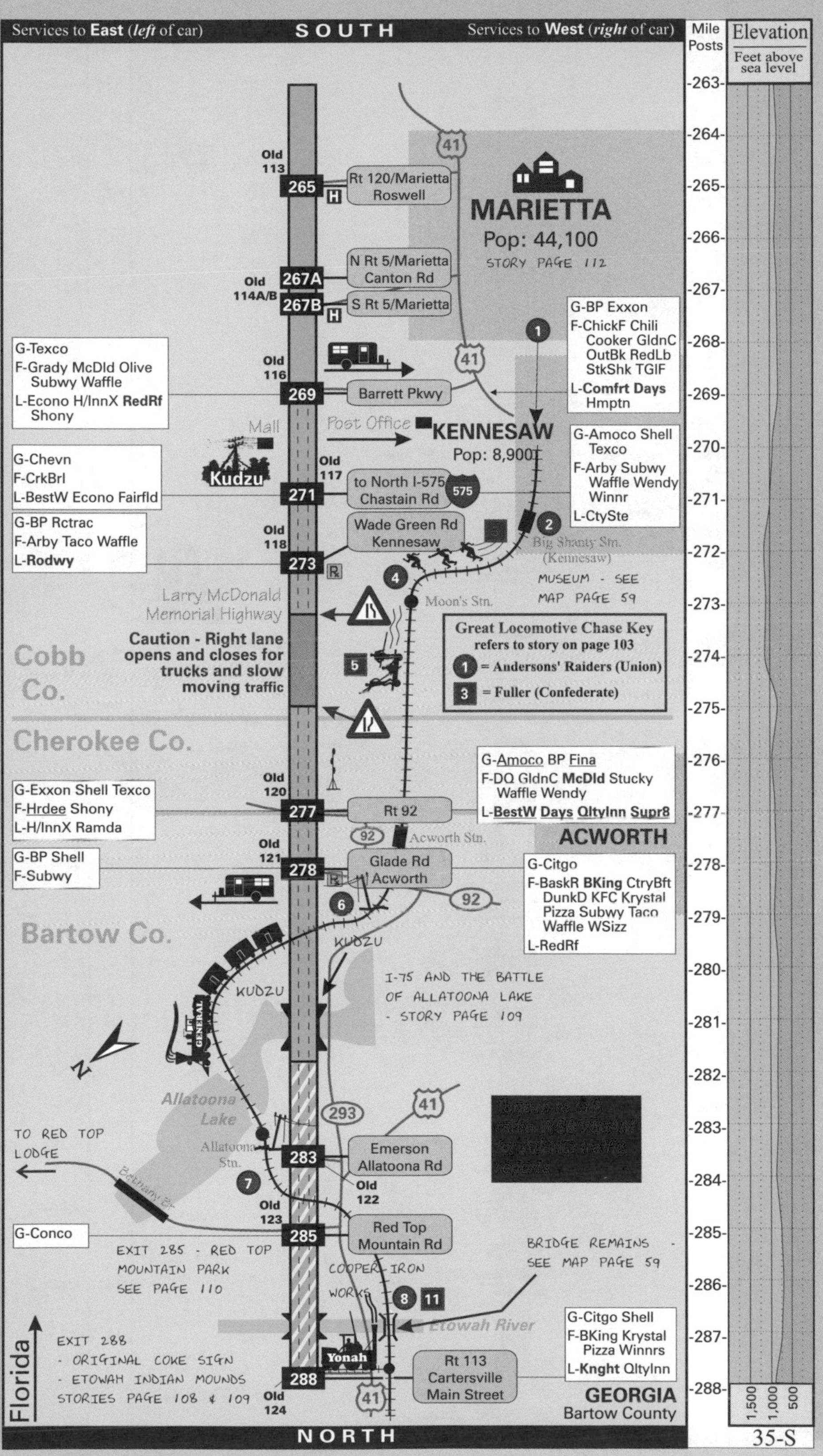

Services to East (left of car)
SOUTH
Services to West (right of car)
Mile Posts
Elevation
Feet above sea level
-263-
-264-
-265-
-266-
-267-
-268-
-269-
-270-
-271-
-272-
-273-
-274-
-275-
-276-
-277-
-278-
-279-
-280-
-281-
-282-
-283-
-284-
-285-
-286-
-287-
-288-
1,500
1,000
500
41
Old 113
265
Rt 120/Marietta Roswell
MARIETTA
Pop: 44,100
STORY PAGE 112
Old 114A/B
267A
N Rt 5/Marietta Canton Rd
267B
S Rt 5/Marietta
G-BP Exxon
F-ChickF Chili Cooker GldnC OutBk RedLb StkShk TGIF
L-Comfrt Days Hmptn
G-Texco
F-Grady McDld Olive Subwy Waffle
L-Econo H/InnX RedRf Shony
Old 116
269
Barrett Pkwy
Mall
Post Office
KENNESAW
Pop: 8,900
G-Amoco Shell Texco
F-Arby Subwy Waffle Wendy Winnr
L-CtySte
G-Chevn
F-CrkBrl
L-BestW Econo Fairfld
Kudzu
Old 117
271
to North I-575 Chastain Rd
575
G-BP Rctrac
F-Arby Taco Waffle
L-Rodwy
Old 118
273
Wade Green Rd Kennesaw
Big Shanty Stn. (Kennesaw)
MUSEUM - SEE MAP PAGE 59
Larry McDonald Memorial Highway
Moon's Stn.
Great Locomotive Chase Key
refers to story on page 103
1 = Andersons' Raiders (Union)
3 = Fuller (Confederate)
Caution - Right lane opens and closes for trucks and slow moving traffic
Cobb Co.
Cherokee Co.
G-Amoco BP Fina
F-DQ GldnC McDld Stucky Waffle Wendy
L-BestW Days QltyInn Supr8
G-Exxon Shell Texco
F-Hrdee Shony
L-H/InnX Ramda
Old 120
277
Rt 92
92
Acworth Stn.
ACWORTH
G-BP Shell
F-Subwy
Old 121
278
Glade Rd Acworth
G-Citgo
F-BaskR BKing CtryBft DunkD KFC Krystal Pizza Subwy Taco Waffle WSizz
L-RedRf
Bartow Co.
KUDZU
KUDZU
I-75 AND THE BATTLE OF ALLATOONA LAKE - STORY PAGE 109
GENERAL
N
Allatoona Lake
293
41
TO RED TOP LODGE
Allatoona Stn.
283
Emerson Allatoona Rd
Old 122
Bethany Br.
Old 123
G-Conco
285
Red Top Mountain Rd
EXIT 285 - RED TOP MOUNTAIN PARK SEE PAGE 110
COOPER IRON WORKS
BRIDGE REMAINS - SEE MAP PAGE 59
Etowah River
G-Citgo Shell
F-BKing Krystal Pizza Winnrs
L-Knght QltyInn
Florida
EXIT 288
- ORIGINAL COKE SIGN
- ETOWAH INDIAN MOUNDS
STORIES PAGE 108 & 109
Yonah
288
Old 124
41
Rt 113 Cartersville Main Street
GEORGIA
Bartow County
NORTH
35-S

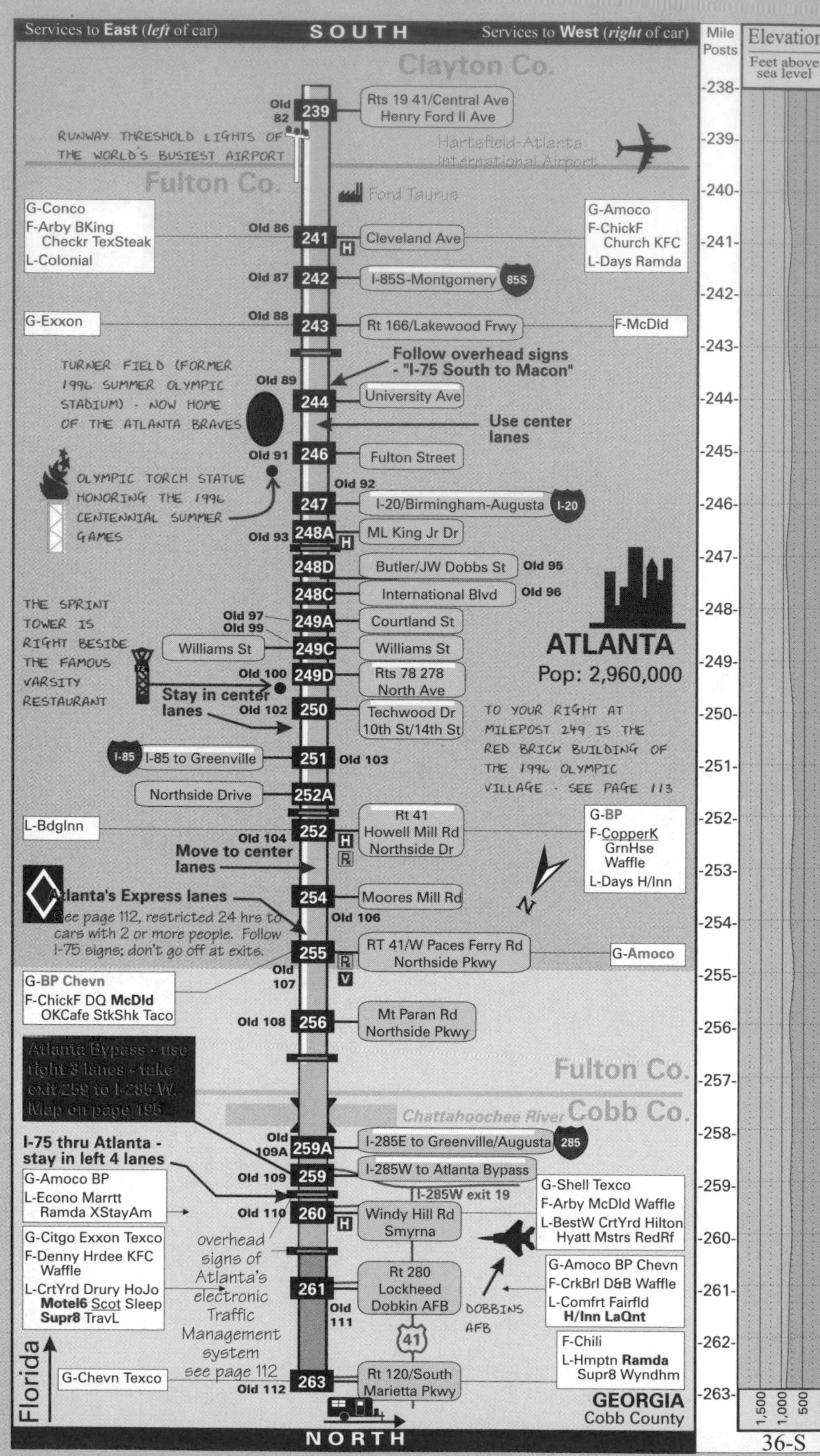

Services to East (left of car)
SOUTH
Services to West (right of car)
Mile Posts
Elevation
Feet above sea level
Clayton Co.
Old 82
239
Rts 19 41/Central Ave
Henry Ford II Ave
RUNWAY THRESHOLD LIGHTS OF THE WORLD'S BUSIEST AIRPORT
Hartsfield-Atlanta International Airport
Fulton Co.
Ford Taurus
G-Conco
F-Arby BKing Checkr TexSteak
L-Colonial
Old 86
241
Cleveland Ave
G-Amoco
F-ChickF Church KFC
L-Days Ramda
Old 87
242
I-85S-Montgomery
85S
G-Exxon
Old 88
243
Rt 166/Lakewood Frwy
F-McDld
Follow overhead signs - "I-75 South to Macon"
TURNER FIELD (FORMER 1996 SUMMER OLYMPIC STADIUM) - NOW HOME OF THE ATLANTA BRAVES
Old 89
244
University Ave
Use center lanes
Old 91
246
Fulton Street
OLYMPIC TORCH STATUE HONORING THE 1996 CENTENNIAL SUMMER GAMES
Old 92
247
I-20/Birmingham-Augusta
I-20
Old 93
248A
ML King Jr Dr
248D
Butler/JW Dobbs St
Old 95
248C
International Blvd
Old 96
THE SPRINT TOWER IS RIGHT BESIDE THE FAMOUS VARSITY RESTAURANT
Old 97
Old 99
249A
Courtland St
Williams St
249C
Williams St
ATLANTA
Pop: 2,960,000
Old 100
249D
Rts 78 278 North Ave
Stay in center lanes
Old 102
250
Techwood Dr 10th St/14th St
TO YOUR RIGHT AT MILEPOST 249 IS THE RED BRICK BUILDING OF THE 1996 OLYMPIC VILLAGE - SEE PAGE 113
I-85
I-85 to Greenville
251
Old 103
Northside Drive
252A
L-BdgInn
Old 104
252
Rt 41 Howell Mill Rd Northside Dr
G-BP
F-CopperK GrnHse Waffle
L-Days H/Inn
Move to center lanes
Atlanta's Express lanes
See page 112, restricted 24 hrs to cars with 2 or more people. Follow I-75 signs; don't go off at exits.
254
Moores Mill Rd
Old 106
N
255
RT 41/W Paces Ferry Rd Northside Pkwy
G-Amoco
Old 107
G-BP Chevn
F-ChickF DQ McDld OKCafe StkShk Taco
Old 108
256
Mt Paran Rd Northside Pkwy
Atlanta Bypass - use right 3 lanes - take exit 259 to I-285 W. Map on page 195
Fulton Co.
Chattahoochee River
Cobb Co.
I-75 thru Atlanta - stay in left 4 lanes
Old 109A
259A
I-285E to Greenville/Augusta
285
G-Amoco BP
L-Econo Marrtt Ramda XStayAm
Old 109
259
I-285W to Atlanta Bypass
I-285W exit 19
G-Shell Texco
F-Arby McDld Waffle
L-BestW CrtYrd Hilton Hyatt Mstrs RedRf
Old 110
260
Windy Hill Rd Smyrna
G-Citgo Exxon Texco
F-Denny Hrdee KFC Waffle
L-CrtYrd Drury HoJo Motel6 Scot Sleep Supr8 TravL
overhead signs of Atlanta's electronic Traffic Management system see page 112
261
Rt 280 Lockheed Dobkin AFB
Old 111
DOBBINS AFB
G-Amoco BP Chevn
F-CrkBrl D&B Waffle
L-Comfrt Fairfld H/Inn LaQnt
41
F-Chili
L-Hmptn Ramda Supr8 Wyndhm
Florida
G-Chevn Texco
263
Old 112
Rt 120/South Marietta Pkwy
GEORGIA
Cobb County
NORTH
-238- -239- -240- -241- -242- -243- -244- -245- -246- -247- -248- -249- -250- -251- -252- -253- -254- -255- -256- -257- -258- -259- -260- -261- -262- -263-
1,500 1,000 500

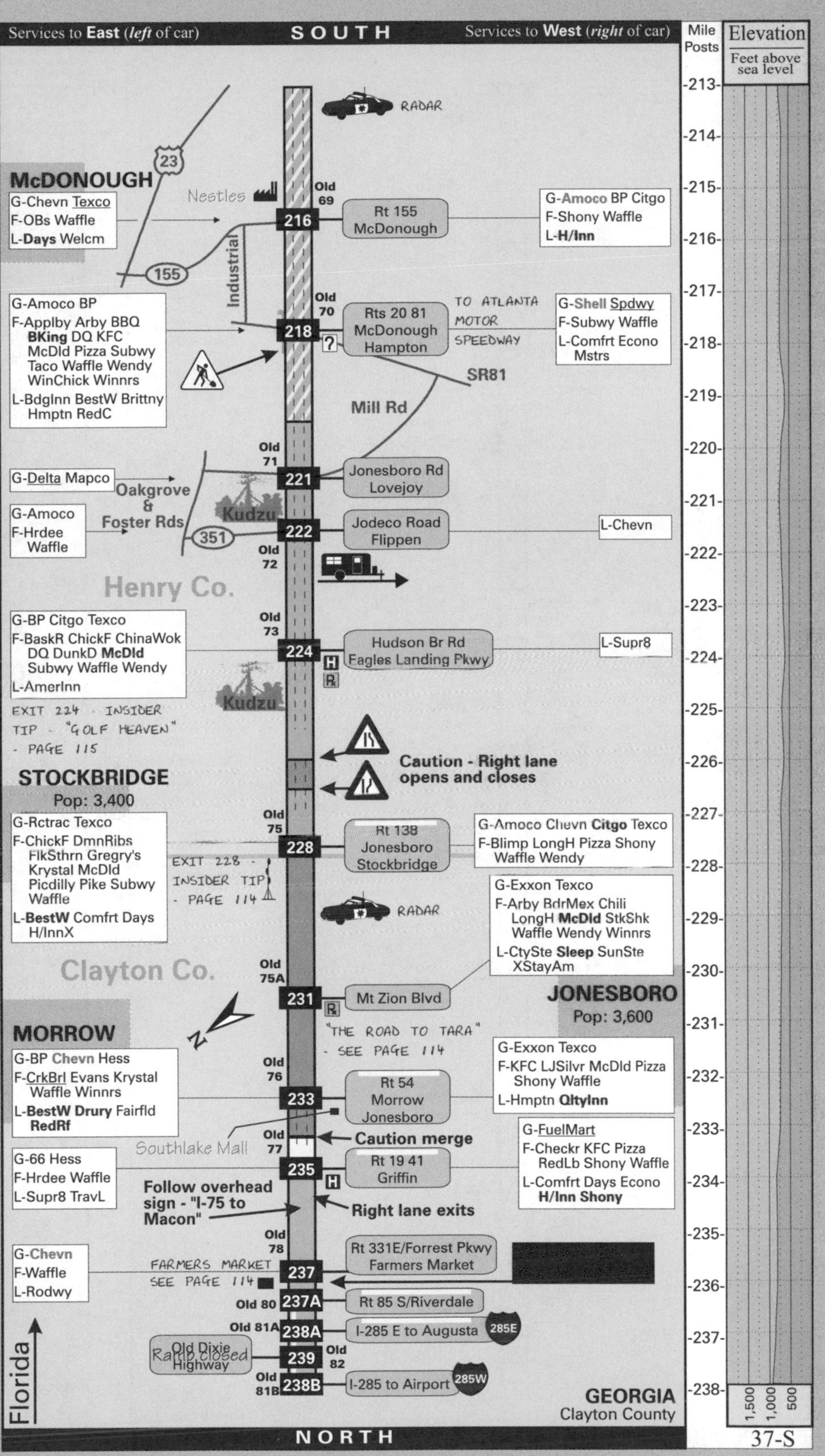

Services to East (left of car)
SOUTH
Services to West (right of car)
Mile Posts
Elevation
Feet above sea level
RADAR
23
McDONOUGH
G-Chevn Texco
F-OBs Waffle
L-Days Welcm
Nestles
Old 69
216
Rt 155 McDonough
G-Amoco BP Citgo
F-Shony Waffle
L-H/Inn
155
Industrial
G-Amoco BP
F-Applby Arby BBQ
BKing DQ KFC
McDld Pizza Subwy
Taco Waffle Wendy
WinChick Winnrs
L-BdgInn BestW Brittny
Hmptn RedC
Old 70
218
Rts 20 81 McDonough Hampton
TO ATLANTA MOTOR SPEEDWAY
G-Shell Spdwy
F-Subwy Waffle
L-Comfrt Econo
Mstrs
SR81
Mill Rd
Old 71
G-Delta Mapco
221
Jonesboro Rd Lovejoy
Oakgrove & Foster Rds
Kudzu
G-Amoco
F-Hrdee
Waffle
351
222
Jodeco Road Flippen
L-Chevn
Old 72
Henry Co.
G-BP Citgo Texco
F-BaskR ChickF ChinaWok
DQ DunkD McDld
Subwy Waffle Wendy
L-AmerInn
Old 73
224
Hudson Br Rd Eagles Landing Pkwy
L-Supr8
Kudzu
EXIT 224 - INSIDER TIP - "GOLF HEAVEN" - PAGE 115
Caution - Right lane opens and closes
STOCKBRIDGE
Pop: 3,400
G-Rctrac Texco
F-ChickF DmnRibs
FlkSthrn Gregry's
Krystal McDld
Picdilly Pike Subwy
Waffle
L-BestW Comfrt Days
H/InnX
Old 75
228
Rt 138 Jonesboro Stockbridge
G-Amoco Chevn Citgo Texco
F-Blimp LongH Pizza Shony
Waffle Wendy
EXIT 228 - INSIDER TIP - PAGE 114
RADAR
G-Exxon Texco
F-Arby BdrMex Chili
LongH McDld StkShk
Waffle Wendy Winnrs
L-CtySte Sleep SunSte
XStayAm
Clayton Co.
Old 75A
231
Mt Zion Blvd
JONESBORO
Pop: 3,600
N
"THE ROAD TO TARA" - SEE PAGE 114
MORROW
G-BP Chevn Hess
F-CrkBrl Evans Krystal
Waffle Winnrs
L-BestW Drury Fairfld
RedRf
Old 76
233
Rt 54 Morrow Jonesboro
G-Exxon Texco
F-KFC LJSilvr McDld Pizza
Shony Waffle
L-Hmptn QltyInn
Southlake Mall
Old 77
Caution merge
G-66 Hess
F-Hrdee Waffle
L-Supr8 TravL
235
Rt 19 41 Griffin
G-FuelMart
F-Checkr KFC Pizza
RedLb Shony Waffle
L-Comfrt Days Econo
H/Inn Shony
Follow overhead sign - "I-75 to Macon"
Right lane exits
Old 78
G-Chevn
F-Waffle
L-Rodwy
FARMERS MARKET SEE PAGE 114
237
Rt 331E/Forrest Pkwy Farmers Market
Old 80
237A
Rt 85 S/Riverdale
Old 81A
238A
I-285 E to Augusta
285E
Old Dixie Highway
Ramp closed
239
Old 82
Old 81B
238B
I-285 to Airport
285W
Florida
GEORGIA
Clayton County
NORTH
-213-
-214-
-215-
-216-
-217-
-218-
-219-
-220-
-221-
-222-
-223-
-224-
-225-
-226-
-227-
-228-
-229-
-230-
-231-
-232-
-233-
-234-
-235-
-236-
-237-
-238-
1,500
1,000
500

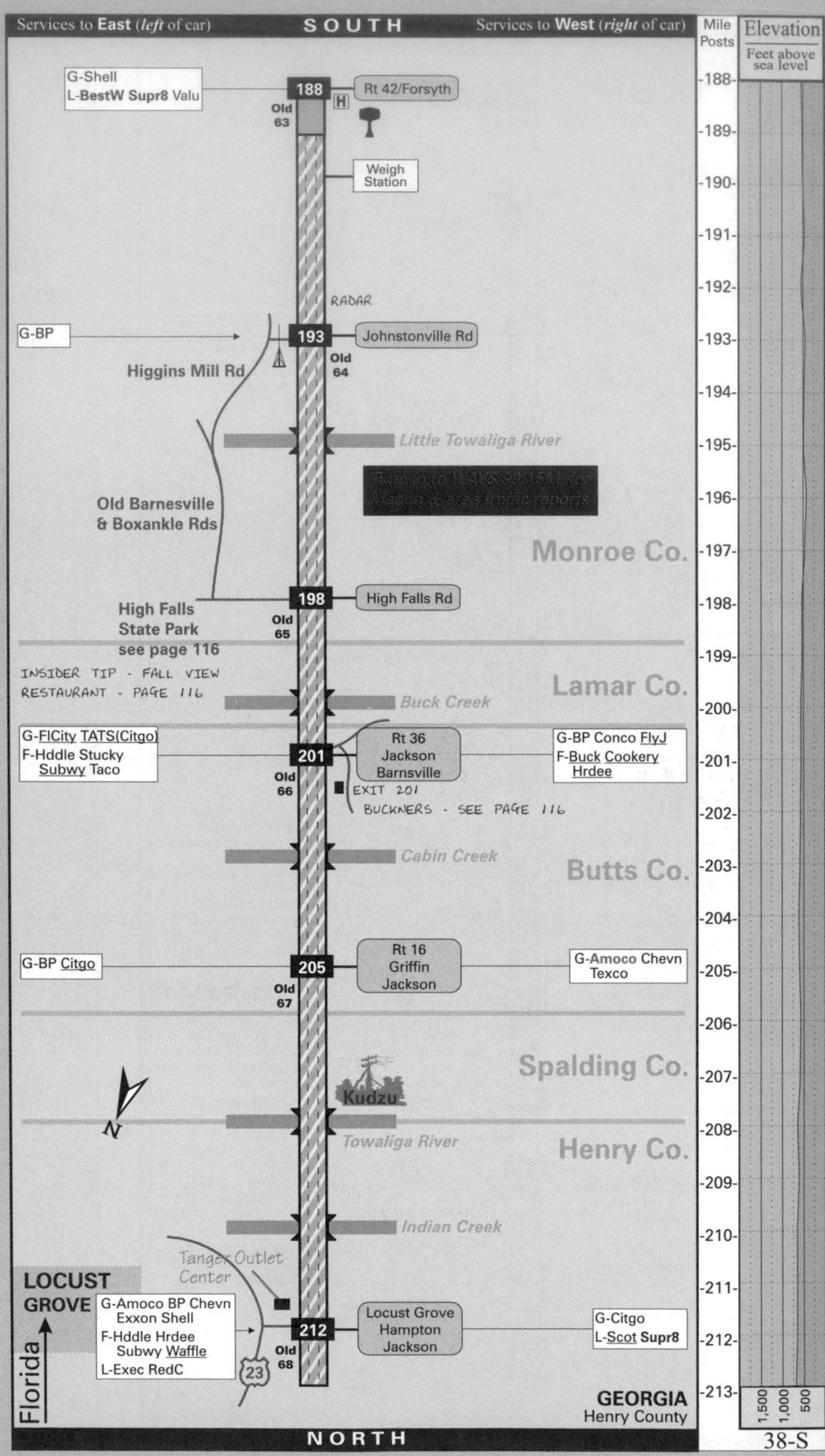

Services to East (left of car)
SOUTH
Services to West (right of car)
Mile Posts
Elevation
Feet above sea level
G-Shell
L-BestW Supr8 Valu
188
Old 63
Rt 42/Forsyth
H
Weigh Station
RADAR
G-BP
193
Johnstonville Rd
Old 64
Higgins Mill Rd
Little Towaliga River
Old Barnesville & Boxankle Rds
Monroe Co.
198
High Falls Rd
Old 65
High Falls State Park see page 116
INSIDER TIP - FALL VIEW RESTAURANT - PAGE 116
Lamar Co.
Buck Creek
G-FlCity TATS(Citgo)
F-Hddle Stucky Subwy Taco
201
Old 66
Rt 36 Jackson Barnsville
G-BP Conco FlyJ
F-Buck Cookery Hrdee
EXIT 201
BUCKNERS - SEE PAGE 116
Cabin Creek
Butts Co.
G-BP Citgo
205
Old 67
Rt 16 Griffin Jackson
G-Amoco Chevn Texco
Spalding Co.
Kudzu
N
Towaliga River
Henry Co.
Indian Creek
Tanger Outlet Center
LOCUST GROVE
G-Amoco BP Chevn Exxon Shell
F-Hddle Hrdee Subwy Waffle
L-Exec RedC
212
Old 68
23
Locust Grove Hampton Jackson
G-Citgo
L-Scot Supr8
Florida
GEORGIA
Henry County
NORTH
-188-
-189-
-190-
-191-
-192-
-193-
-194-
-195-
-196-
-197-
-198-
-199-
-200-
-201-
-202-
-203-
-204-
-205-
-206-
-207-
-208-
-209-
-210-
-211-
-212-
-213-
1,500
1,000
500

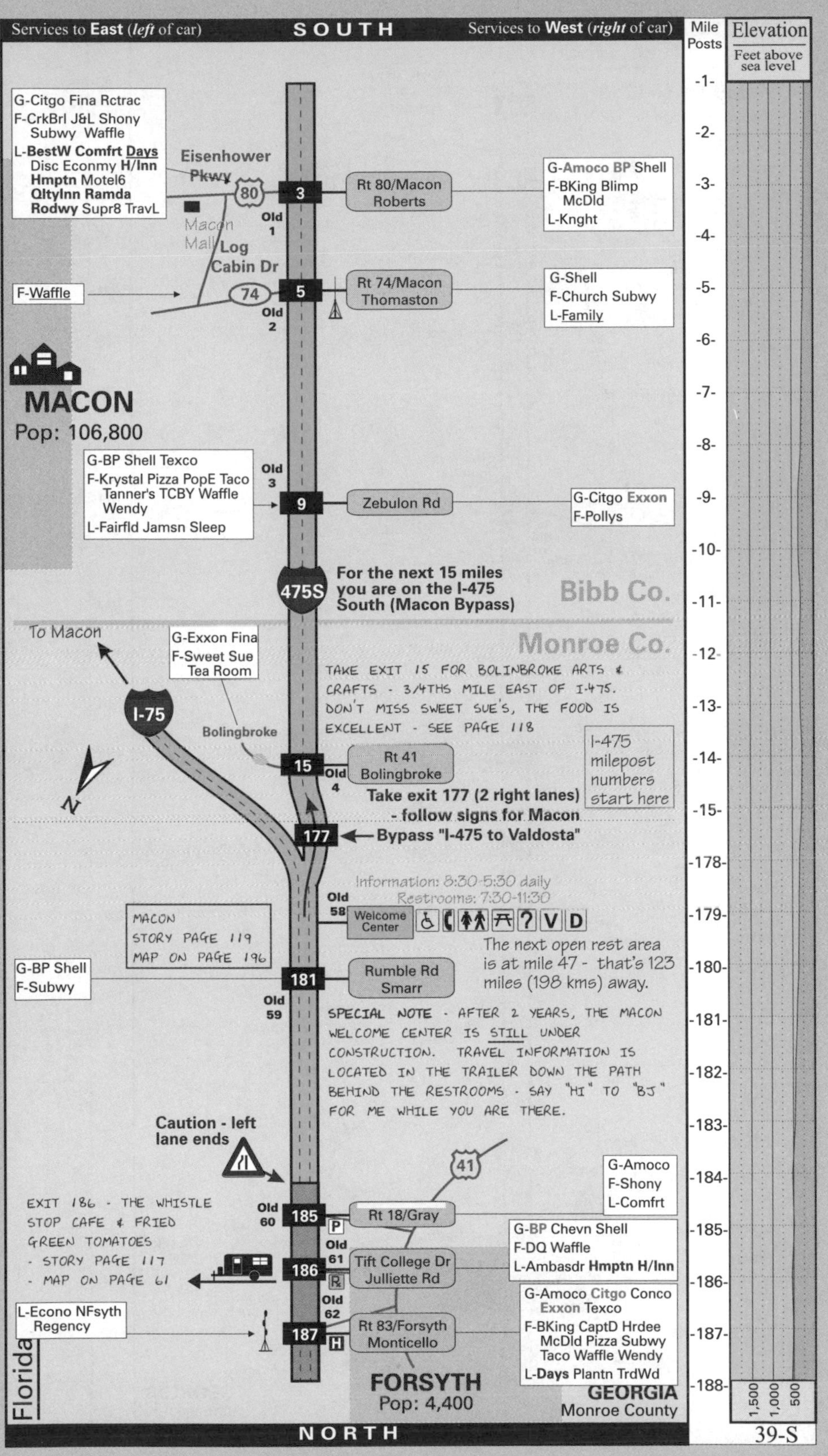

Services to East (left of car)
SOUTH
Services to West (right of car)
Mile Posts
Elevation
Feet above sea level
G-Citgo Fina Rctrac
F-CrkBrl J&L Shony Subwy Waffle
L-BestW Comfrt Days Disc Econmy H/Inn Hmptn Motel6 QltyInn Ramda Rodwy Supr8 TravL
Eisenhower Pkwy
80
3
Old 1
Rt 80/Macon Roberts
G-Amoco BP Shell
F-BKing Blimp McDld
L-Knght
Macon Mall
Log Cabin Dr
F-Waffle
74
5
Old 2
Rt 74/Macon Thomaston
G-Shell
F-Church Subwy
L-Family
MACON
Pop: 106,800
G-BP Shell Texco
F-Krystal Pizza PopE Taco Tanner's TCBY Waffle Wendy
L-Fairfld Jamsn Sleep
Old 3
9
Zebulon Rd
G-Citgo Exxon
F-Pollys
475S
For the next 15 miles you are on the I-475 South (Macon Bypass)
Bibb Co.
Monroe Co.
To Macon
G-Exxon Fina
F-Sweet Sue Tea Room
TAKE EXIT 15 FOR BOLINBROKE ARTS & CRAFTS - 3/4THS MILE EAST OF I-475. DON'T MISS SWEET SUE'S, THE FOOD IS EXCELLENT - SEE PAGE 118
I-75
Bolingbroke
15
Old 4
Rt 41 Bolingbroke
I-475 milepost numbers start here
N
Take exit 177 (2 right lanes) - follow signs for Macon
177
Bypass "I-475 to Valdosta"
Information: 8:30-5:30 daily
Restrooms: 7:30-11:30
Old 58
Welcome Center
V D
MACON STORY PAGE 119 MAP ON PAGE 196
The next open rest area is at mile 47 - that's 123 miles (198 kms) away.
G-BP Shell
F-Subwy
181
Old 59
Rumble Rd Smarr
SPECIAL NOTE - AFTER 2 YEARS, THE MACON WELCOME CENTER IS STILL UNDER CONSTRUCTION. TRAVEL INFORMATION IS LOCATED IN THE TRAILER DOWN THE PATH BEHIND THE RESTROOMS - SAY "HI" TO "BJ" FOR ME WHILE YOU ARE THERE.
Caution - left lane ends
41
G-Amoco
F-Shony
L-Comfrt
EXIT 186 - THE WHISTLE STOP CAFE & FRIED GREEN TOMATOES - STORY PAGE 117 - MAP ON PAGE 61
Old 60
185
P
Rt 18/Gray
G-BP Chevn Shell
F-DQ Waffle
L-Ambasdr Hmptn H/Inn
Old 61
186
R
Tift College Dr Juliette Rd
L-Econo NFsyth Regency
Old 62
187
H
Rt 83/Forsyth Monticello
G-Amoco Citgo Conco Exxon Texco
F-BKing CaptD Hrdee McDld Pizza Subwy Taco Waffle Wendy
L-Days Plantn TrdWd
FORSYTH
Pop: 4,400
GEORGIA
Monroe County
Florida
NORTH
-1- -2- -3- -4- -5- -6- -7- -8- -9- -10- -11- -12- -13- -14- -15- -178- -179- -180- -181- -182- -183- -184- -185- -186- -187- -188-
1,500 1,000 500

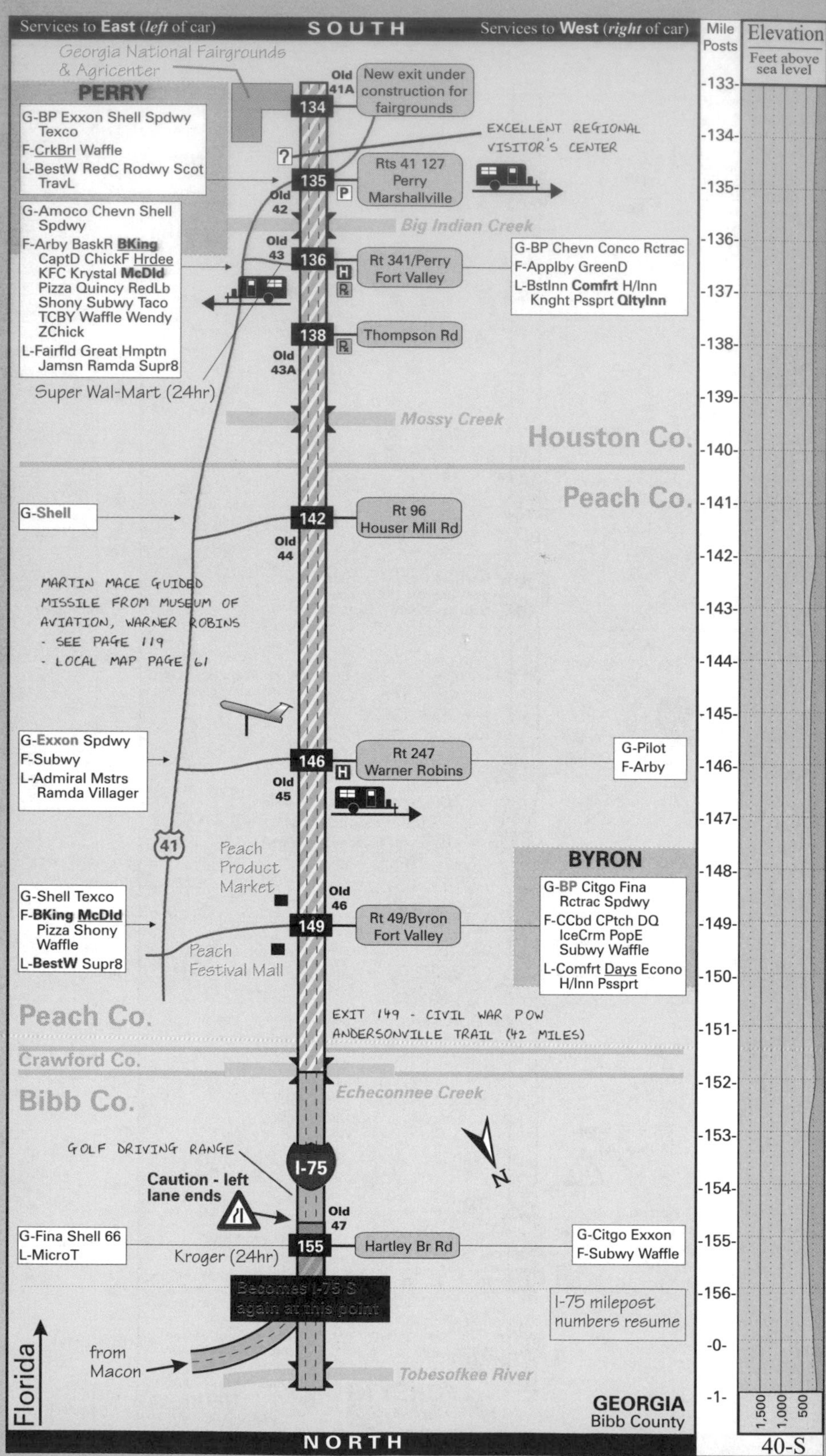

Services to East (left of car)
SOUTH
Services to West (right of car)
Mile Posts
Elevation
Feet above sea level
Georgia National Fairgrounds & Agricenter
PERRY
Old 41A
New exit under construction for fairgrounds
134
G-BP Exxon Shell Spdwy Texco
F-CrkBrl Waffle
L-BestW RedC Rodwy Scot TravL
EXCELLENT REGIONAL VISITOR'S CENTER
135
Old 42
Rts 41 127 Perry Marshallville
G-Amoco Chevn Shell Spdwy
F-Arby BaskR BKing CaptD ChickF Hrdee KFC Krystal McDld Pizza Quincy RedLb Shony Subwy Taco TCBY Waffle Wendy ZChick
L-Fairfld Great Hmptn Jamsn Ramda Supr8
Big Indian Creek
Old 43
136
Rt 341/Perry Fort Valley
G-BP Chevn Conco Rctrac
F-Applby GreenD
L-BstInn Comfrt H/Inn Knght Pssprt QltyInn
138
Thompson Rd
Old 43A
Super Wal-Mart (24hr)
Mossy Creek
Houston Co.
Peach Co.
G-Shell
142
Old 44
Rt 96 Houser Mill Rd
MARTIN MACE GUIDED MISSILE FROM MUSEUM OF AVIATION, WARNER ROBINS
- SEE PAGE 119
- LOCAL MAP PAGE 61
G-Exxon Spdwy
F-Subwy
L-Admiral Mstrs Ramda Villager
146
Old 45
Rt 247 Warner Robins
G-Pilot
F-Arby
41
Peach Product Market
BYRON
G-Shell Texco
F-BKing McDld Pizza Shony Waffle
L-BestW Supr8
Old 46
149
Rt 49/Byron Fort Valley
G-BP Citgo Fina Rctrac Spdwy
F-CCbd CPtch DQ IceCrm PopE Subwy Waffle
L-Comfrt Days Econo H/Inn Pssprt
Peach Festival Mall
Peach Co.
EXIT 149 - CIVIL WAR POW ANDERSONVILLE TRAIL (42 MILES)
Crawford Co.
Bibb Co.
Echeconnee Creek
GOLF DRIVING RANGE
I-75
N
Caution - left lane ends
Old 47
G-Fina Shell 66
L-MicroT
155
Kroger (24hr)
Hartley Br Rd
G-Citgo Exxon
F-Subwy Waffle
Becomes I-75 S again at this point
I-75 milepost numbers resume
Florida
from Macon
Tobesofkee River
GEORGIA
Bibb County
NORTH
-133- -134- -135- -136- -137- -138- -139- -140- -141- -142- -143- -144- -145- -146- -147- -148- -149- -150- -151- -152- -153- -154- -155- -156- -0- -1-
1,500 1,000 500

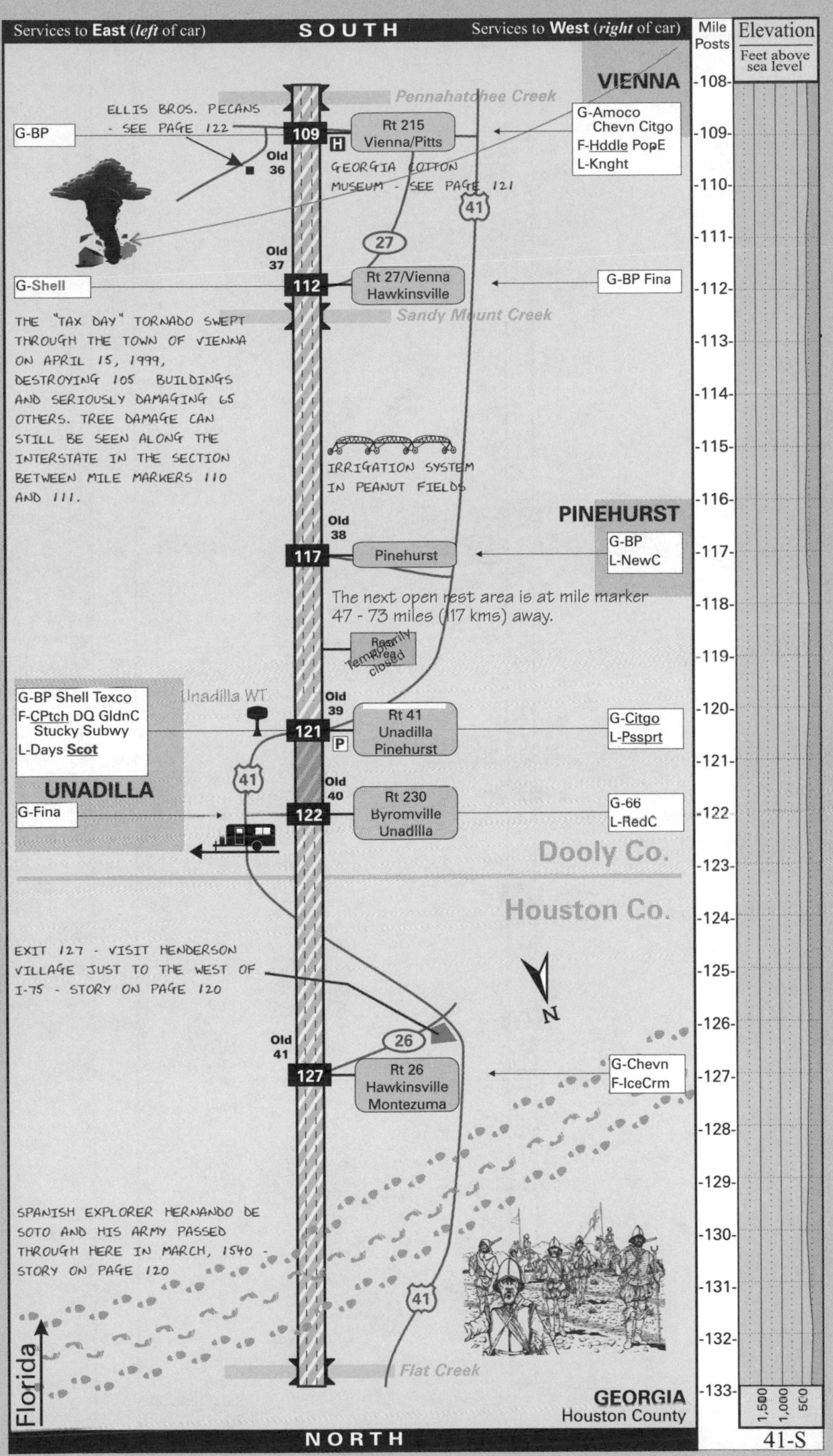

Services to East (left of car)
SOUTH
Services to West (right of car)
Mile Posts
Elevation
Feet above sea level
VIENNA
Pennahatchee Creek
ELLIS BROS. PECANS - SEE PAGE 122
G-BP
109
H
Old 36
Rt 215 Vienna/Pitts
G-Amoco Chevn Citgo
F-Hddle PopE
L-Knght
GEORGIA COTTON MUSEUM - SEE PAGE 121
41
27
Old 37
G-Shell
112
Rt 27/Vienna Hawkinsville
G-BP Fina
Sandy Mount Creek
THE "TAX DAY" TORNADO SWEPT THROUGH THE TOWN OF VIENNA ON APRIL 15, 1999, DESTROYING 105 BUILDINGS AND SERIOUSLY DAMAGING 65 OTHERS. TREE DAMAGE CAN STILL BE SEEN ALONG THE INTERSTATE IN THE SECTION BETWEEN MILE MARKERS 110 AND 111.
IRRIGATION SYSTEM IN PEANUT FIELDS
PINEHURST
Old 38
117
Pinehurst
G-BP
L-NewC
The next open rest area is at mile marker 47 - 73 miles (117 kms) away.
Rest Area Temporarily closed
G-BP Shell Texco
F-CPtch DQ GldnC Stucky Subwy
L-Days Scot
Unadilla WT
Old 39
121
P
Rt 41 Unadilla Pinehurst
G-Citgo
L-Psspt
41
UNADILLA
Old 40
G-Fina
122
Rt 230 Byromville Unadilla
G-66
L-RedC
Dooly Co.
Houston Co.
EXIT 127 - VISIT HENDERSON VILLAGE JUST TO THE WEST OF I-75 - STORY ON PAGE 120
N
26
Old 41
127
Rt 26 Hawkinsville Montezuma
G-Chevn
F-IceCrm
SPANISH EXPLORER HERNANDO DE SOTO AND HIS ARMY PASSED THROUGH HERE IN MARCH, 1540 - STORY ON PAGE 120
41
Flat Creek
Florida
GEORGIA
Houston County
NORTH
-108-
-109-
-110-
-111-
-112-
-113-
-114-
-115-
-116-
-117-
-118-
-119-
-120-
-121-
-122-
-123-
-124-
-125-
-126-
-127-
-128-
-129-
-130-
-131-
-132-
-133-
1,500
1,000
500

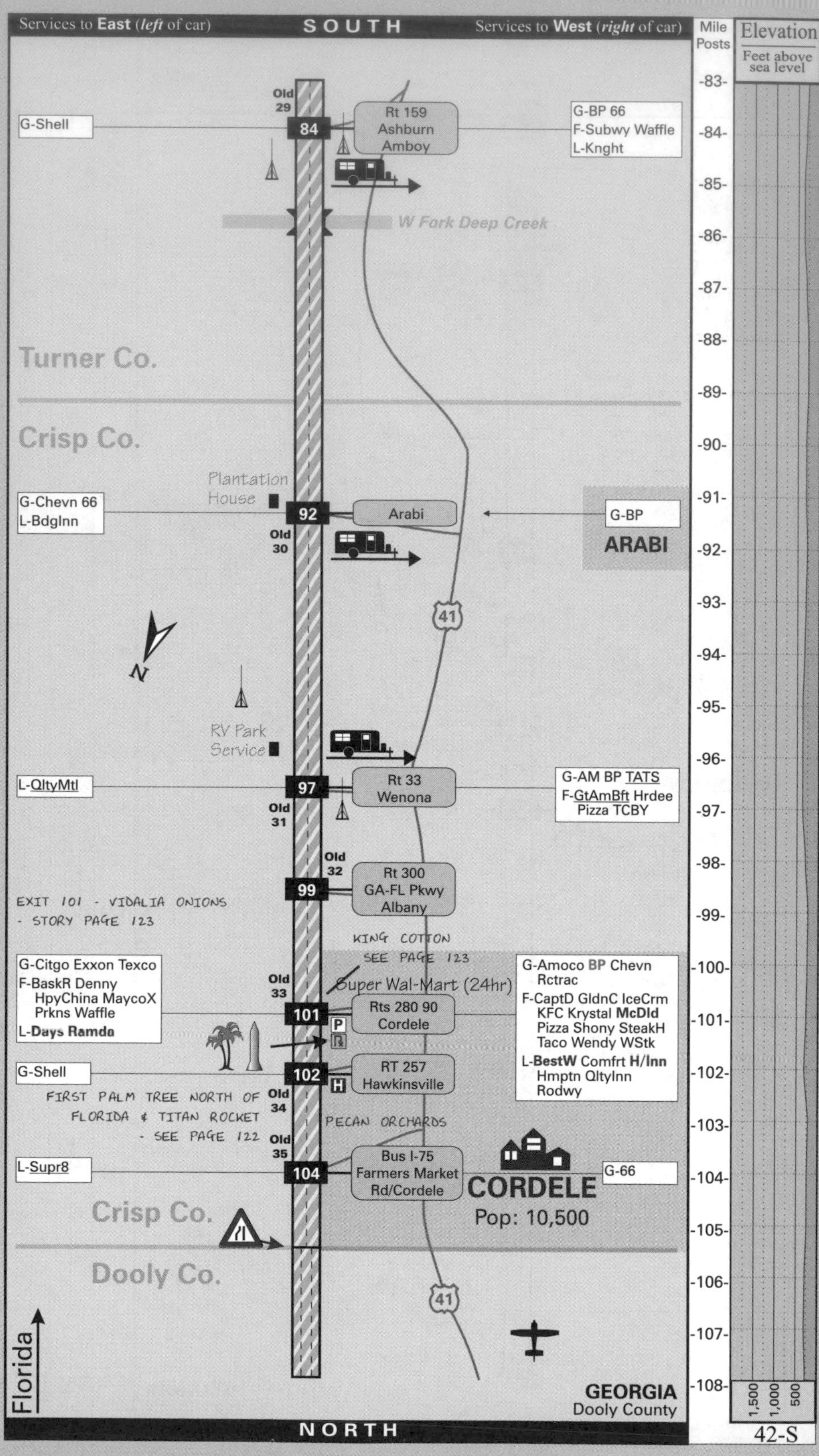

Services to East (left of car)
SOUTH
Services to West (right of car)
Mile Posts
Elevation
Feet above sea level
Old 29
84
Rt 159
Ashburn
Amboy
G-Shell
G-BP 66
F-Subwy Waffle
L-Knght
W Fork Deep Creek
Turner Co.
Crisp Co.
Plantation House
G-Chevn 66
L-BdgInn
92
Arabi
Old 30
G-BP
ARABI
41
N
RV Park Service
L-QltyMtl
97
Rt 33
Wenona
Old 31
G-AM BP TATS
F-GtAmBft Hrdee
Pizza TCBY
Old 32
99
Rt 300
GA-FL Pkwy
Albany
EXIT 101 - VIDALIA ONIONS
- STORY PAGE 123
KING COTTON
SEE PAGE 123
G-Citgo Exxon Texco
F-BaskR Denny
HpyChina MaycoX
Prkns Waffle
L-Days Ramda
Old 33
Super Wal-Mart (24hr)
101
Rts 280 90
Cordele
G-Amoco BP Chevn
Rctrac
F-CaptD GldnC IceCrm
KFC Krystal McDld
Pizza Shony SteakH
Taco Wendy WStk
L-BestW Comfrt H/Inn
Hmptn QltyInn
Rodwy
G-Shell
102
RT 257
Hawkinsville
FIRST PALM TREE NORTH OF
FLORIDA & TITAN ROCKET
- SEE PAGE 122
Old 34
PECAN ORCHARDS
Old 35
L-Supr8
104
Bus I-75
Farmers Market
Rd/Cordele
CORDELE
Pop: 10,500
G-66
Crisp Co.
Dooly Co.
41
Florida
GEORGIA
Dooly County
NORTH
-83- -84- -85- -86- -87- -88- -89- -90- -91- -92- -93- -94- -95- -96- -97- -98- -99- -100- -101- -102- -103- -104- -105- -106- -107- -108-
1,500
1,000
500

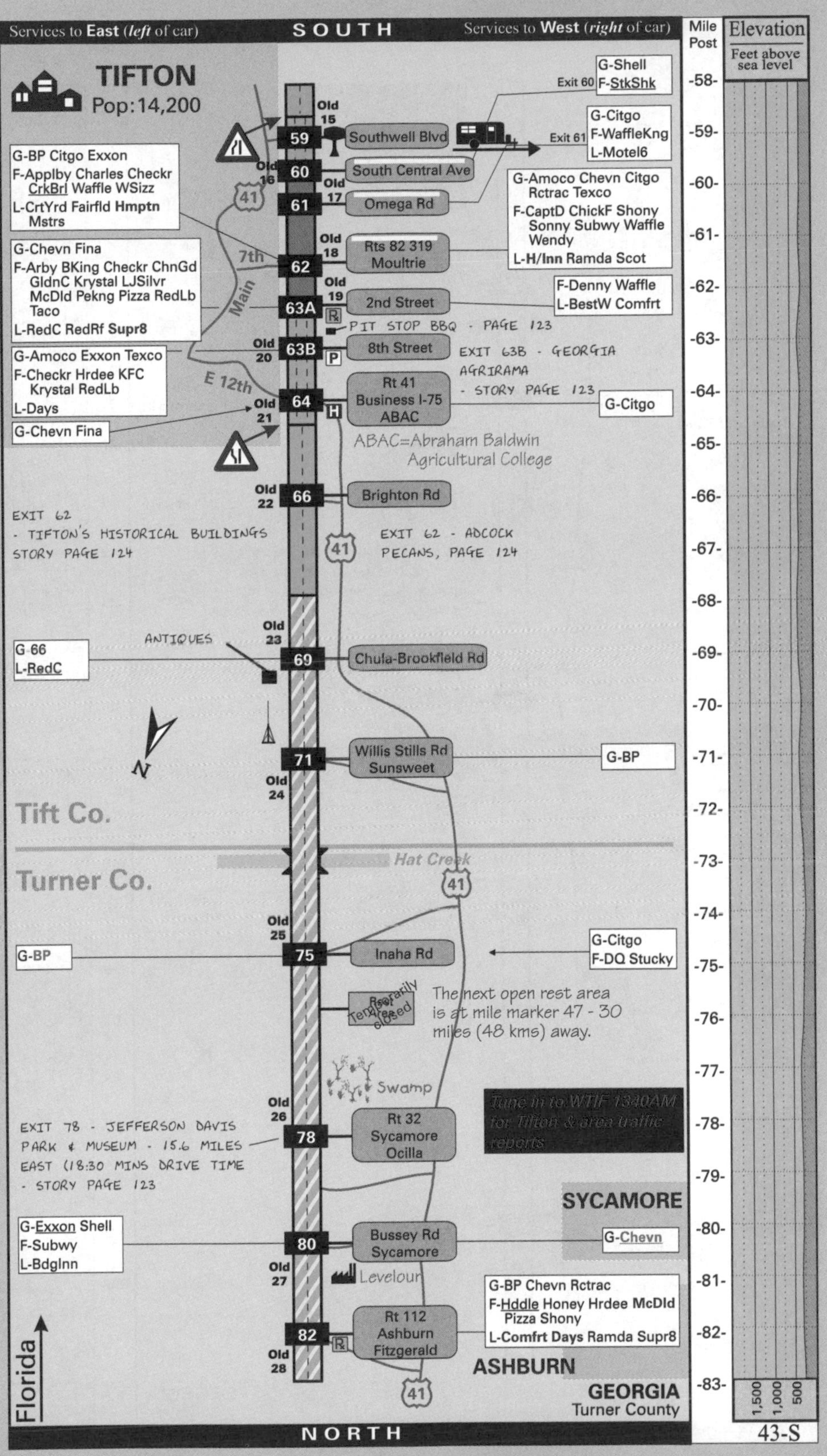
Services to East (left of car)
SOUTH
Services to West (right of car)
Mile Post
Elevation
Feet above sea level
TIFTON
Pop:14,200
G-BP Citgo Exxon
F-Applby Charles Checkr CrkBrl Waffle WSizz
L-CrtYrd Fairfld Hmptn Mstrs
G-Chevn Fina
F-Arby BKing Checkr ChnGd GldnC Krystal LJSilvr McDld Pekng Pizza RedLb Taco
L-RedC RedRf Supr8
G-Amoco Exxon Texco
F-Checkr Hrdee KFC Krystal RedLb
L-Days
G-Chevn Fina
Exit 60
G-Shell
F-StkShk
Exit 61
G-Citgo
F-WaffleKng
L-Motel6
G-Amoco Chevn Citgo Rctrac Texco
F-CaptD ChickF Shony Sonny Subwy Waffle Wendy
L-H/Inn Ramda Scot
F-Denny Waffle
L-BestW Comfrt
G-Citgo
Old 15
59
Southwell Blvd
Old 16
60
South Central Ave
Old 17
61
Omega Rd
Old 18
62
Rts 82 319 Moultrie
Old 19
63A
2nd Street
PIT STOP BBQ - PAGE 123
Old 20
63B
8th Street
EXIT 63B - GEORGIA AGRIRAMA - STORY PAGE 123
Old 21
64
Rt 41 Business I-75 ABAC
ABAC=Abraham Baldwin Agricultural College
7th
Main
E 12th
41
Old 22
66
Brighton Rd
EXIT 62 - TIFTON'S HISTORICAL BUILDINGS STORY PAGE 124
EXIT 62 - ADCOCK PECANS, PAGE 124
Old 23
69
Chula-Brookfield Rd
ANTIQUES
G-66
L-RedC
N
Old 24
71
Willis Stills Rd Sunsweet
G-BP
Tift Co.
Turner Co.
Hat Creek
Old 25
75
Inaha Rd
G-BP
G-Citgo
F-DQ Stucky
Rest Area Temporarily closed
The next open rest area is at mile marker 47 - 30 miles (48 kms) away.
Swamp
Tune in to WTIF 1340AM for Tifton & area traffic reports
Old 26
78
Rt 32 Sycamore Ocilla
EXIT 78 - JEFFERSON DAVIS PARK & MUSEUM - 15.6 MILES EAST (18:30 MINS DRIVE TIME - STORY PAGE 123
SYCAMORE
G-Exxon Shell
F-Subwy
L-BdgInn
80
Bussey Rd Sycamore
G-Chevn
Old 27
Levelour
G-BP Chevn Rctrac
F-Hddle Honey Hrdee McDld Pizza Shony
L-Comfrt Days Ramda Supr8
82
Old 28
Rt 112 Ashburn Fitzgerald
ASHBURN
GEORGIA
Turner County
Florida
NORTH
-58-
-59-
-60-
-61-
-62-
-63-
-64-
-65-
-66-
-67-
-68-
-69-
-70-
-71-
-72-
-73-
-74-
-75-
-76-
-77-
-78-
-79-
-80-
-81-
-82-
-83-
1,500
1,000
500

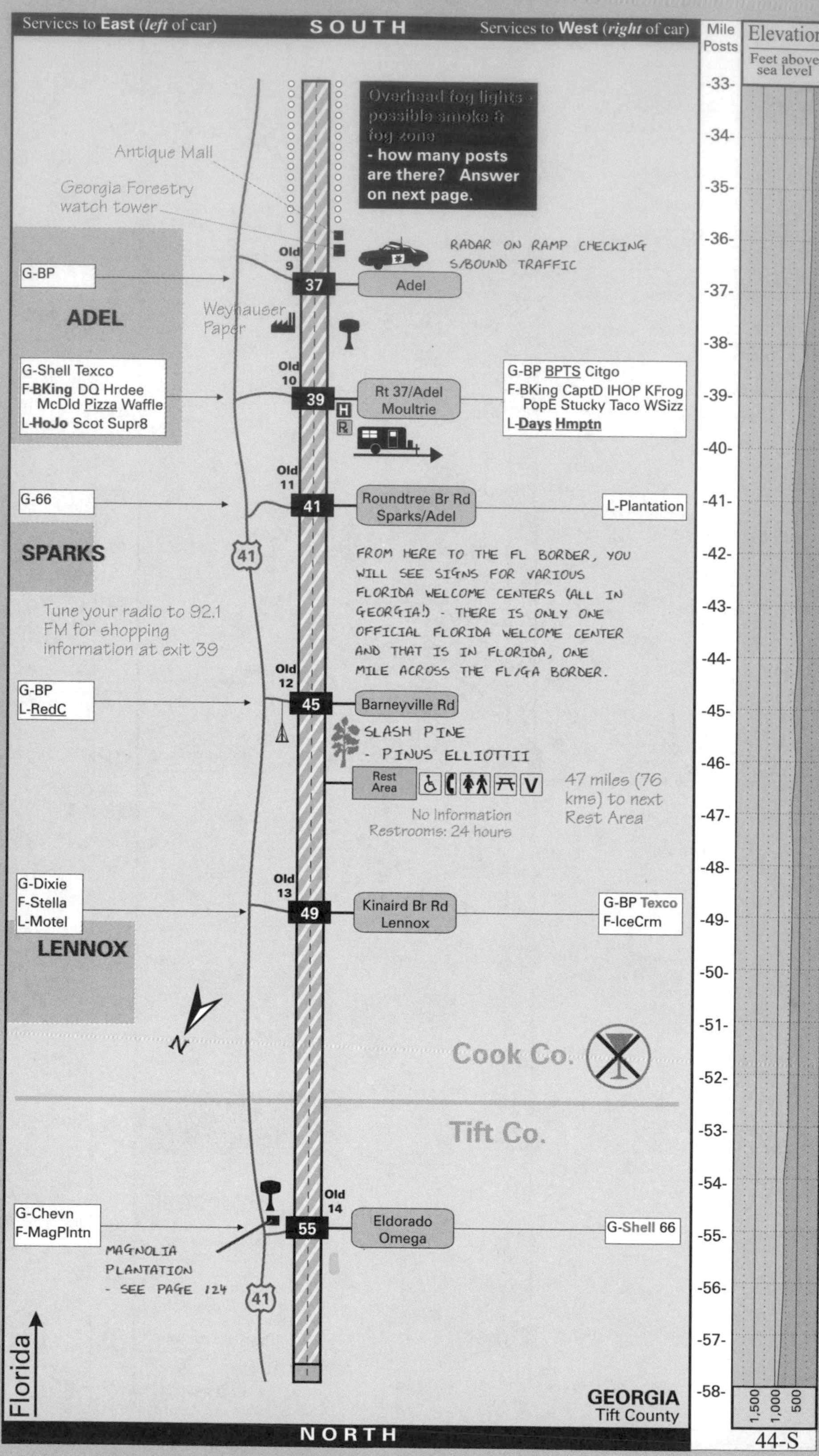

Services to East (left of car)
SOUTH
Services to West (right of car)
Mile Posts
Elevation
Feet above sea level
Overhead fog lights - possible smoke & fog zone
- how many posts are there? Answer on next page.
Antique Mall
Georgia Forestry watch tower
RADAR ON RAMP CHECKING S/BOUND TRAFFIC
Old 9
37
Adel
G-BP
ADEL
Weyhauser Paper
Old 10
39
Rt 37/Adel Moultrie
G-Shell Texco
F-BKing DQ Hrdee McDld Pizza Waffle
L-HoJo Scot Supr8
G-BP BPTS Citgo
F-BKing CaptD IHOP KFrog PopE Stucky Taco WSizz
L-Days Hmptn
Old 11
41
Roundtree Br Rd Sparks/Adel
G-66
L-Plantation
SPARKS
41
FROM HERE TO THE FL BORDER, YOU WILL SEE SIGNS FOR VARIOUS FLORIDA WELCOME CENTERS (ALL IN GEORGIA!) - THERE IS ONLY ONE OFFICIAL FLORIDA WELCOME CENTER AND THAT IS IN FLORIDA, ONE MILE ACROSS THE FL/GA BORDER.
Tune your radio to 92.1 FM for shopping information at exit 39
Old 12
45
Barneyville Rd
G-BP
L-RedC
SLASH PINE - PINUS ELLIOTTII
Rest Area
No Information
Restrooms: 24 hours
47 miles (76 kms) to next Rest Area
Old 13
49
Kinaird Br Rd Lennox
G-Dixie
F-Stella
L-Motel
G-BP Texco
F-IceCrm
LENNOX
N
Cook Co.
Tift Co.
Old 14
55
Eldorado Omega
G-Chevn
F-MagPlntn
G-Shell 66
MAGNOLIA PLANTATION - SEE PAGE 124
41
Florida
GEORGIA
Tift County
NORTH
-33- -34- -35- -36- -37- -38- -39- -40- -41- -42- -43- -44- -45- -46- -47- -48- -49- -50- -51- -52- -53- -54- -55- -56- -57- -58-
1,500
1,000
500

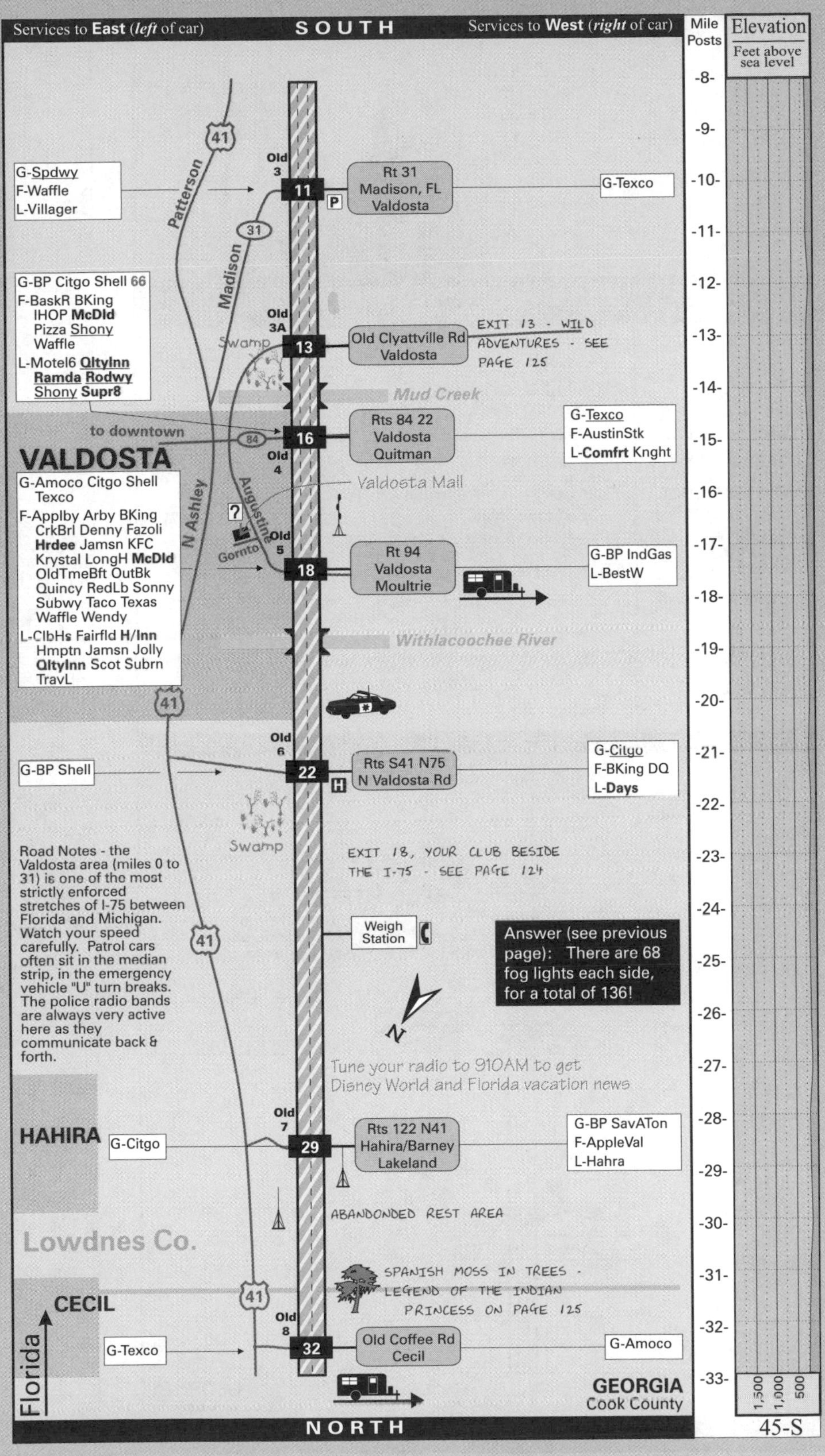

Services to East (left of car)
SOUTH
Services to West (right of car)
Mile Posts
Elevation
Feet above sea level
-8-
-9-
-10-
-11-
-12-
-13-
-14-
-15-
-16-
-17-
-18-
-19-
-20-
-21-
-22-
-23-
-24-
-25-
-26-
-27-
-28-
-29-
-30-
-31-
-32-
-33-
G-Spdwy
F-Waffle
L-Villager
41
Patterson
Old 3
11
P
Rt 31
Madison, FL
Valdosta
G-Texco
31
Madison
G-BP Citgo Shell 66
F-BaskR BKing
IHOP McDld
Pizza Shony
Waffle
L-Motel6 QltyInn
Ramda Rodwy
Shony Supr8
Old 3A
Swamp
13
Old Clyattville Rd
Valdosta
EXIT 13 - WILD ADVENTURES - SEE PAGE 125
Mud Creek
to downtown
84
16
Rts 84 22
Valdosta
Quitman
G-Texco
F-AustinStk
L-Comfrt Knght
VALDOSTA
Old 4
G-Amoco Citgo Shell
Texco
F-Applby Arby BKing
CrkBrl Denny Fazoli
Hrdee Jamsn KFC
Krystal LongH McDld
OldTmeBft OutBk
Quincy RedLb Sonny
Subwy Taco Texas
Waffle Wendy
L-ClbHs Fairfld H/Inn
Hmptn Jamsn Jolly
QltyInn Scot Subrn
TravL
N Ashley
Augustine
Valdosta Mall
?
Gornto
Old 5
18
Rt 94
Valdosta
Moultrie
G-BP IndGas
L-BestW
Withlacoochee River
41
Old 6
G-BP Shell
22
H
Rts S41 N75
N Valdosta Rd
G-Citgo
F-BKing DQ
L-Days
Swamp
EXIT 18, YOUR CLUB BESIDE THE I-75 - SEE PAGE 124
Road Notes - the Valdosta area (miles 0 to 31) is one of the most strictly enforced stretches of I-75 between Florida and Michigan. Watch your speed carefully. Patrol cars often sit in the median strip, in the emergency vehicle "U" turn breaks. The police radio bands are always very active here as they communicate back & forth.
41
Weigh Station
Answer (see previous page): There are 68 fog lights each side, for a total of 136!
N
Tune your radio to 910AM to get Disney World and Florida vacation news
HAHIRA
G-Citgo
Old 7
29
Rts 122 N41
Hahira/Barney
Lakeland
G-BP SavATon
F-AppleVal
L-Hahra
ABANDONDED REST AREA
Lowdnes Co.
SPANISH MOSS IN TREES - LEGEND OF THE INDIAN PRINCESS ON PAGE 125
CECIL
41
Old 8
G-Texco
32
Old Coffee Rd
Cecil
G-Amoco
Florida
GEORGIA
Cook County
1,500
1,000
500
NORTH
45-S

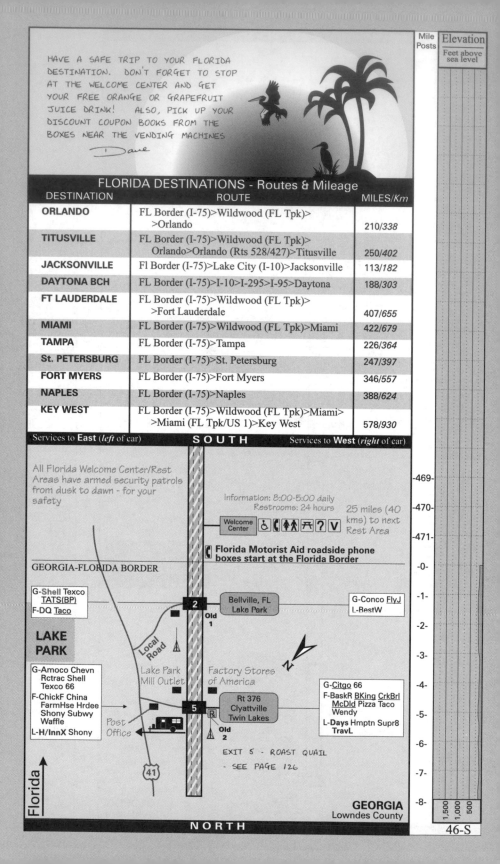

HAVE A SAFE TRIP TO YOUR FLORIDA DESTINATION. DON'T FORGET TO STOP AT THE WELCOME CENTER AND GET YOUR FREE ORANGE OR GRAPEFRUIT JUICE DRINK! ALSO, PICK UP YOUR DISCOUNT COUPON BOOKS FROM THE BOXES NEAR THE VENDING MACHINES
Dave

FLORIDA DESTINATIONS - Routes & Mileage

DESTINATION	ROUTE	MILES/*Km*
ORLANDO	FL Border (I-75)>Wildwood (FL Tpk)> >Orlando	210/*338*
TITUSVILLE	FL Border (I-75)>Wildwood (FL Tpk)> Orlando>Orlando (Rts 528/427)>Titusville	250/*402*
JACKSONVILLE	Fl Border (I-75)>Lake City (I-10)>Jacksonville	113/*182*
DAYTONA BCH	FL Border (I-75)>I-10>I-295>I-95>Daytona	188/*303*
FT LAUDERDALE	FL Border (I-75)>Wildwood (FL Tpk)> >Fort Lauderdale	407/*655*
MIAMI	FL Border (I-75)>Wildwood (FL Tpk)>Miami	422/*679*
TAMPA	FL Border (I-75)>Tampa	226/*364*
St. PETERSBURG	FL Border (I-75)>St. Petersburg	247/*397*
FORT MYERS	FL Border (I-75)>Fort Myers	346/*557*
NAPLES	FL Border (I-75)>Naples	388/*624*
KEY WEST	FL Border (I-75)>Wildwood (FL Tpk)>Miami> >Miami (FL Tpk/US 1)>Key West	578/*930*

Services to **East** (*left* of car) **SOUTH** Services to **West** (*right* of car)

All Florida Welcome Center/Rest Areas have armed security patrols from dusk to dawn - for your safety

Information: 8:00-5:00 daily
Restrooms: 24 hours

Welcome Center

25 miles (40 kms) to next Rest Area

Florida Motorist Aid roadside phone boxes start at the Florida Border

GEORGIA-FLORIDA BORDER

2 — Bellville, FL / Lake Park — Old 1

East: G-Shell Texco TATS(BP); F-DQ Taco

West: G-Conco FlyJ; L-BestW

LAKE PARK

Local Road

Lake Park Mill Outlet

Factory Stores of America

5 — Rt 376 / Clyattville / Twin Lakes — Old 2

East: G-Amoco Chevn Rctrac Shell Texco 66; F-ChickF China FarmHse Hrdee Shony Subwy Waffle; L-**H/InnX** Shony

Post Office

West: G-Citgo 66; F-BaskR BKing CrkBrl McDld Pizza Taco Wendy; L-**Days** Hmptn Supr8 **TravL**

EXIT 5 - ROAST QUAIL
- SEE PAGE 126

41

Florida

GEORGIA
Lowndes County

NORTH

Mile Posts: -469- -470- -471- -0- -1- -2- -3- -4- -5- -6- -7- -8-

Elevation — Feet above sea level: 1,500 1,000 500

Off The Beaten Path

One of the enjoyable aspects of a journey along I-75 is the abundance of interesting places you can visit within just a few minutes of an interstate exit. Yet many travelers don't take advantage of this because of the fear of becoming lost in unfamiliar territory.

On the following pages we provide you with some short side trips you can take - perhaps as a brief evening tour after checking into your motel, or as a short excursion in your day's drive. Enjoy!

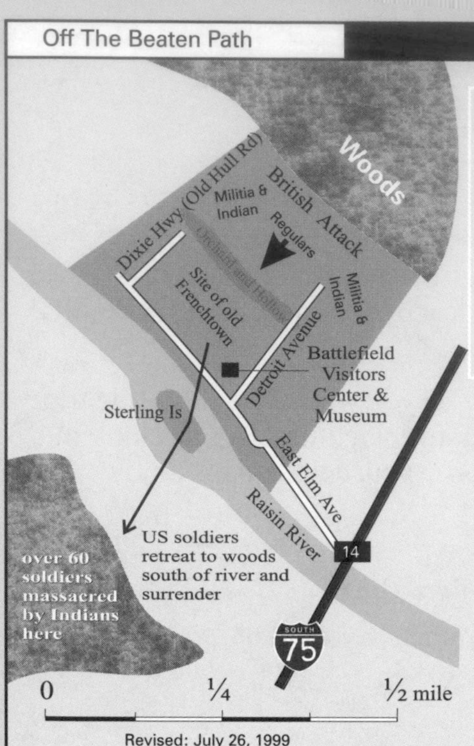

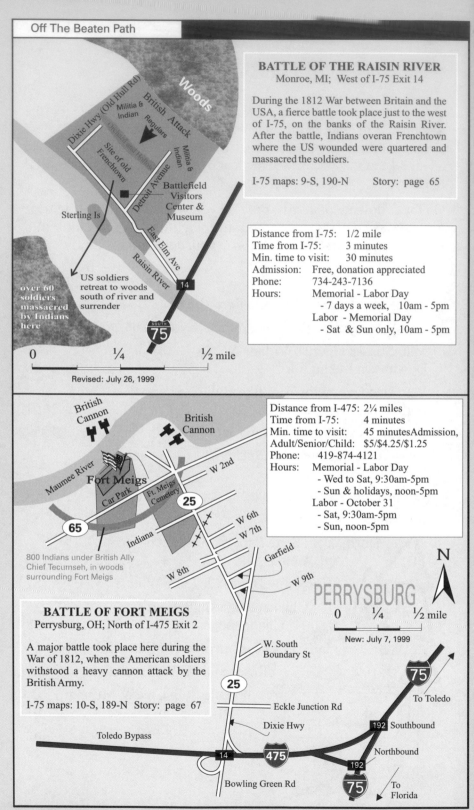

BATTLE OF THE RAISIN RIVER

Monroe, MI; West of I-75 Exit 14

During the 1812 War between Britain and the USA, a fierce battle took place just to the west of I-75, on the banks of the Raisin River. After the battle, Indians overan Frenchtown where the US wounded were quartered and massacred the soldiers.

I-75 maps: 9-S, 190-N Story: page 65

Distance from I-75: 1/2 mile
Time from I-75: 3 minutes
Min. time to visit: 30 minutes
Admission: Free, donation appreciated
Phone: 734-243-7136
Hours: Memorial - Labor Day
- 7 days a week, 10am - 5pm
Labor - Memorial Day
- Sat & Sun only, 10am - 5pm

British Cannon
British Cannon
Maumee River
Fort Meigs
Car Park
Ft. Meigs Cemetery
W 2nd
25
65
Indiana
W 6th
W 7th
800 Indians under British Ally Chief Tecumseh, in woods surrounding Fort Meigs
W 8th
Garfield
W 9th
PERRYSBURG
N
0 ¼ ½ mile
New: July 7, 1999
W. South Boundary St
25
Eckle Junction Rd
Dixie Hwy
Toledo Bypass
14
475
192 Southbound
192 Northbound
75
To Toledo
75
Bowling Green Rd
To Florida

Distance from I-475: 2¼ miles
Time from I-75: 4 minutes
Min. time to visit: 45 minutesAdmission,
Adult/Senior/Child: $5/$4.25/$1.25
Phone: 419-874-4121
Hours: Memorial - Labor Day
- Wed to Sat, 9:30am-5pm
- Sun & holidays, noon-5pm
Labor - October 31
- Sat, 9:30am-5pm
- Sun, noon-5pm

BATTLE OF FORT MEIGS

Perrysburg, OH; North of I-475 Exit 2

A major battle took place here during the War of 1812, when the American soldiers withstood a heavy cannon attack by the British Army.

I-75 maps: 10-S, 189-N Story: page 67

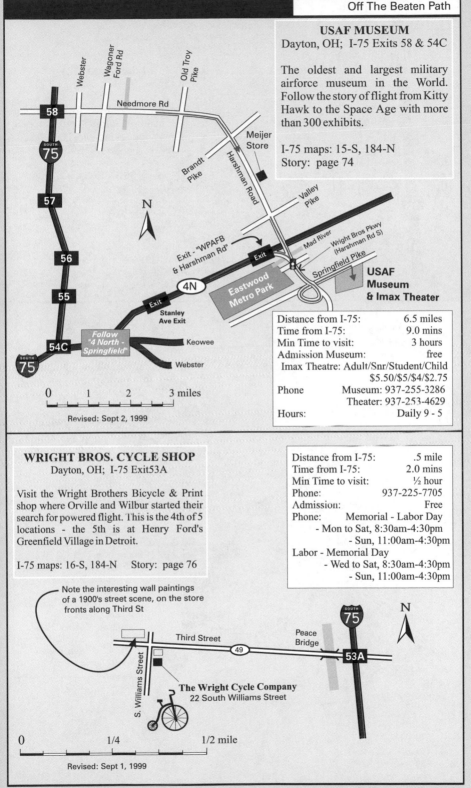

USAF MUSEUM

Dayton, OH; I-75 Exits 58 & 54C

The oldest and largest military airforce museum in the World. Follow the story of flight from Kitty Hawk to the Space Age with more than 300 exhibits.

I-75 maps: 15-S, 184-N
Story: page 74

Webster
Wagoner Ford Rd
Old Troy Pike
Needmore Rd
58
75
Meijer Store
Brandt Pike
Harshman Road
57
Valley Pike
N
Mad River
Wright Bros Pkwy (Harshman Rd S)
Exit - "WPAFB & Harshman Rd"
Exit
56
Springfield Pike
USAF Museum & Imax Theater
Eastwood Metro Park
4N
55
Exit
Stanley Ave Exit
Follow "4 North - Springfield"
Keowee
54C
75
Webster
0 1 2 3 miles
Revised: Sept 2, 1999

Distance from I-75:	6.5 miles
Time from I-75:	9.0 mins
Min Time to visit:	3 hours
Admission Museum:	free
Imax Theatre: Adult/Snr/Student/Child	$5.50/$5/$4/$2.75
Phone	Museum: 937-255-3286 Theater: 937-253-4629
Hours:	Daily 9 - 5

WRIGHT BROS. CYCLE SHOP

Dayton, OH; I-75 Exit53A

Visit the Wright Brothers Bicycle & Print shop where Orville and Wilbur started their search for powered flight. This is the 4th of 5 locations - the 5th is at Henry Ford's Greenfield Village in Detroit.

I-75 maps: 16-S, 184-N Story: page 76

Distance from I-75:	.5 mile
Time from I-75:	2.0 mins
Min Time to visit:	½ hour
Phone:	937-225-7705
Admission:	Free
Phone:	Memorial - Labor Day - Mon to Sat, 8:30am-4:30pm - Sun, 11:00am-4:30pm
Labor - Memorial Day	- Wed to Sat, 8:30am-4:30pm - Sun, 11:00am-4:30pm

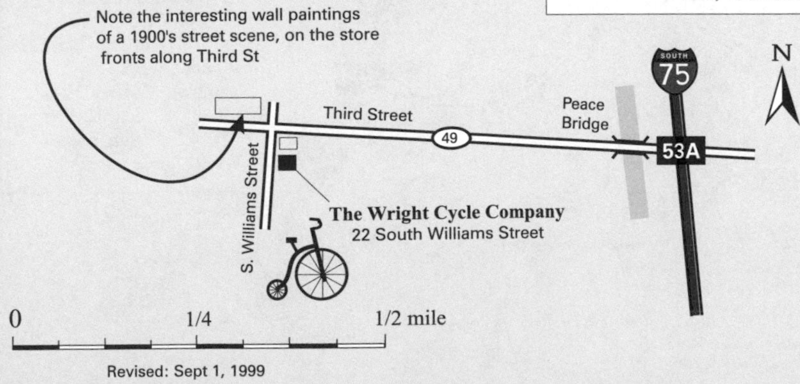

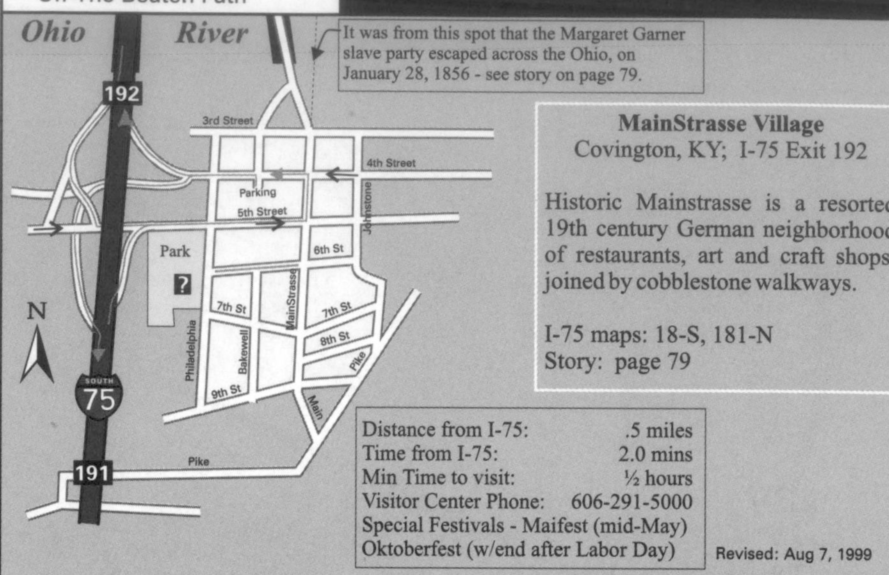

DOWNTOWN LEXINGTON

Lexington, KY; West of I-75 Exit 115 or 104

Most I-75 travelers bypass Lexington, but a short visit will add only ½ hour to your journey. Here's how to navigate through this historic city.

I-75 maps: 21-S, 178-N

Story: page 83

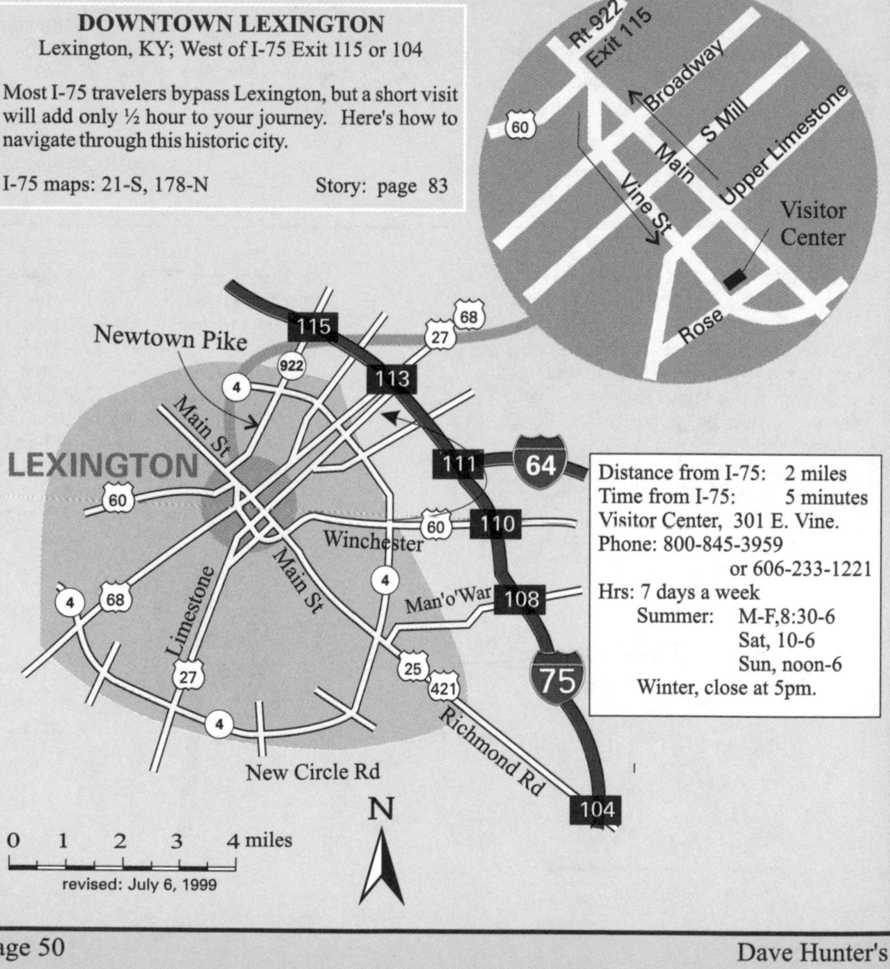

Rt 922 Exit 115
60
Broadway
S Mill
Upper Limestone
Main
Vine St
Visitor Center
Rose

115
68
27
Newtown Pike
922
4
113
Main St
LEXINGTON
111
64
60
110
Winchester
Main St
Limestone
4
Man'o'War
108
4
68
75
25
421
27
Richmond Rd
4
New Circle Rd
104
N
0 1 2 3 4 miles
revised: July 6, 1999

Distance from I-75: 2 miles
Time from I-75: 5 minutes
Visitor Center, 301 E. Vine.
Phone: 800-845-3959
or 606-233-1221
Hrs: 7 days a week
Summer: M-F, 8:30-6
Sat, 10-6
Sun, noon-6
Winter, close at 5pm.

VICTORIAN GEORGETOWN

Georgetown, KY; West of I-75 Exit 126

Georgetown has more than 100 historic buildings on the National Register of Historic Places—many of them on Georgetown's Main Sreet.

I-75 maps: 20-S, 179-N Story: page 82

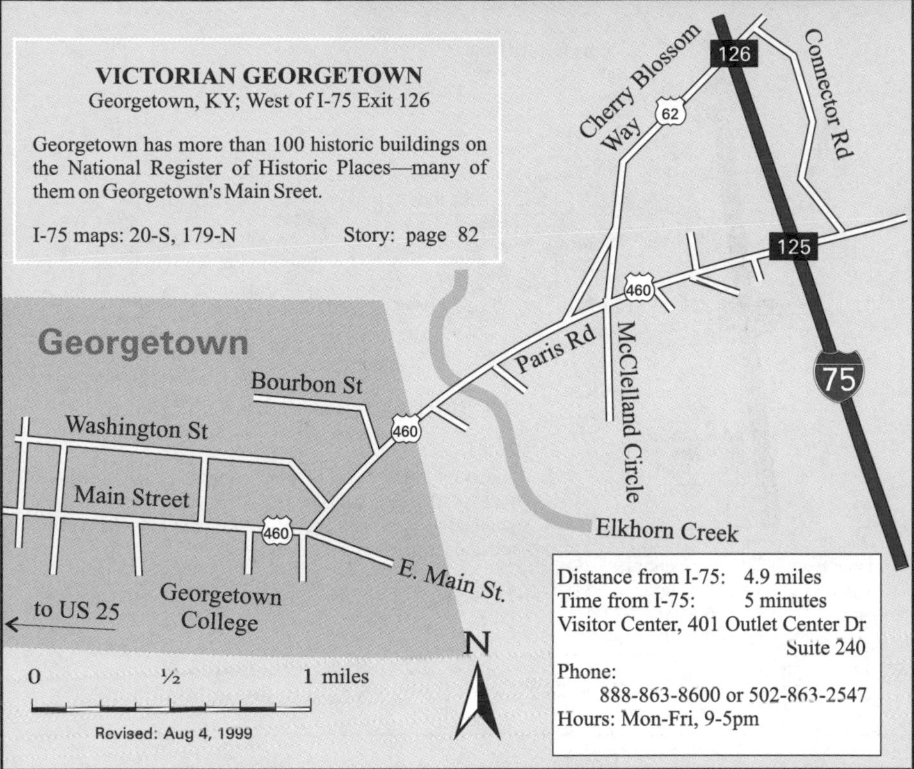

Georgetown
Bourbon St
Washington St
Main Street
460
E. Main St.
Georgetown College
to US 25
Paris Rd
McClelland Circle
Elkhorn Creek
Cherry Blossom Way
62
126
125
Connector Rd
75
N
0
½
1 miles
Revised: Aug 4, 1999

Distance from I-75: 4.9 miles
Time from I-75: 5 minutes
Visitor Center, 401 Outlet Center Dr Suite 240
Phone: 888-863-8600 or 502-863-2547
Hours: Mon-Fri, 9-5pm

WHITE HALL

Richmond, KY; West of I-75 Exit 95

Home of Abraham Lincoln's friend, and Kentucky's most colorful historical figure - Cassius Marcellus Clay. This magnificent Georgian style home dates from 1798 and is open to the public.

I-75 maps: 22-S, 178-N Story: page 84

N
0
1
2
3 miles
Revised: Aug 21, 1999
River
Fort Boonesborough State Park
Coones Ferry Road
Old Boonesborough Rd
McKinney Lane
Rt 627 East to Boonesborough
Rt 3377 Lost Fork Rd
White Hall
Rt 627 West to White Hall
75
95

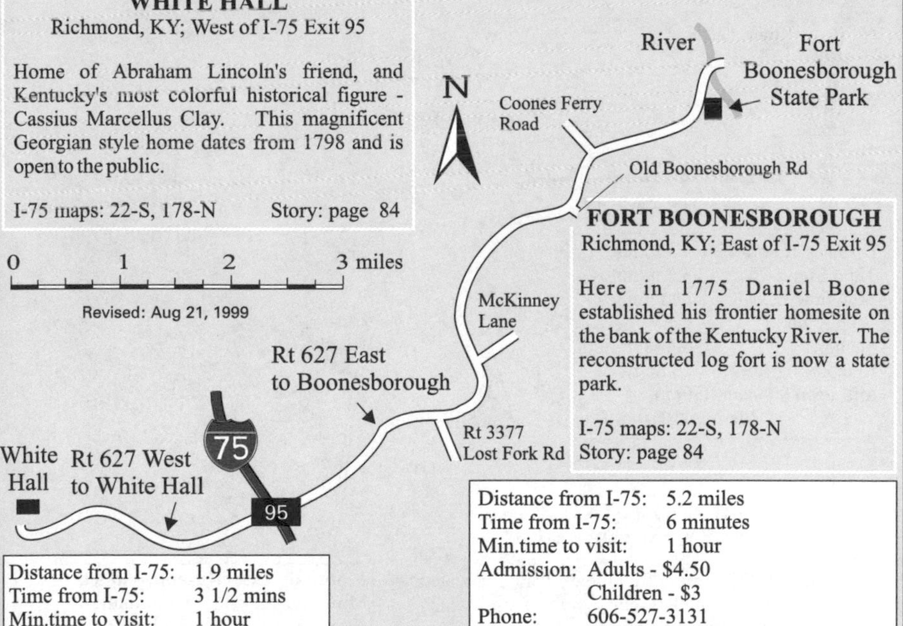

FORT BOONESBOROUGH

Richmond, KY; East of I-75 Exit 95

Here in 1775 Daniel Boone established his frontier homesite on the bank of the Kentucky River. The reconstructed log fort is now a state park.

I-75 maps: 22-S, 178-N
Story: page 84

Distance from I-75: 1.9 miles
Time from I-75: 3 1/2 mins
Min.time to visit: 1 hour
Phone: 606-623-9178
Adult/Child: $4.00/$2.50
Hrs: Apr 1-Labor Day, 9-5:30 daily
Labor Day-Oct 31, phone.

Distance from I-75: 5.2 miles
Time from I-75: 6 minutes
Min.time to visit: 1 hour
Admission: Adults - $4.50
Children - $3
Phone: 606-527-3131
Hours: Apr 1-Labor Day - Daily 9-5:30pm
After Labor Day-Oct 31
-Wed-Sun 9-5:30pm
Closed in winter months

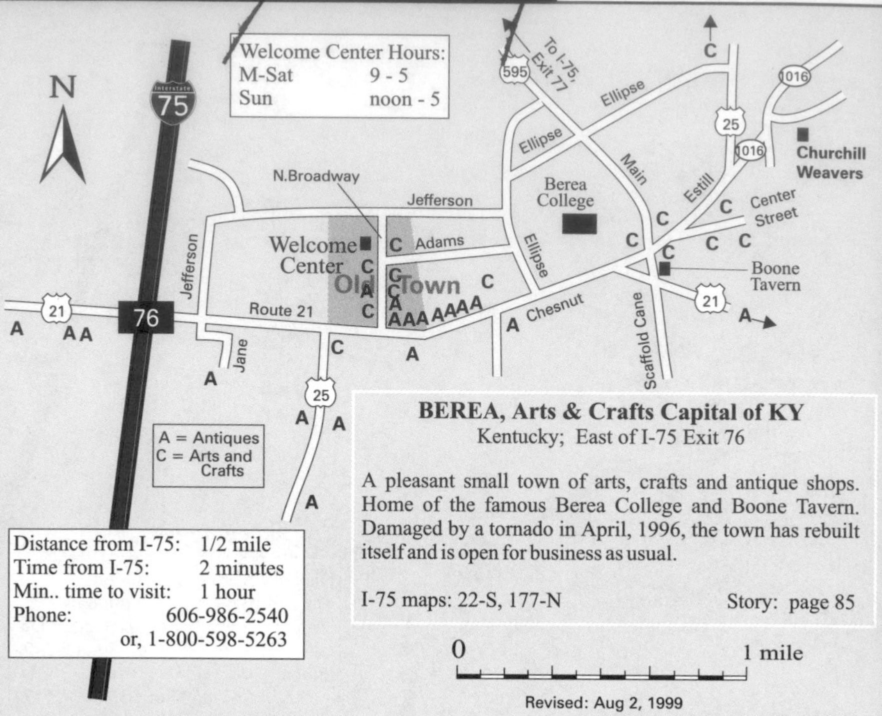

Welcome Center Hours:
M-Sat 9 - 5
Sun noon - 5

A = Antiques
C = Arts and Crafts

BEREA, Arts & Crafts Capital of KY

Kentucky; East of I-75 Exit 76

A pleasant small town of arts, crafts and antique shops. Home of the famous Berea College and Boone Tavern. Damaged by a tornado in April, 1996, the town has rebuilt itself and is open for business as usual.

I-75 maps: 22-S, 177-N Story: page 85

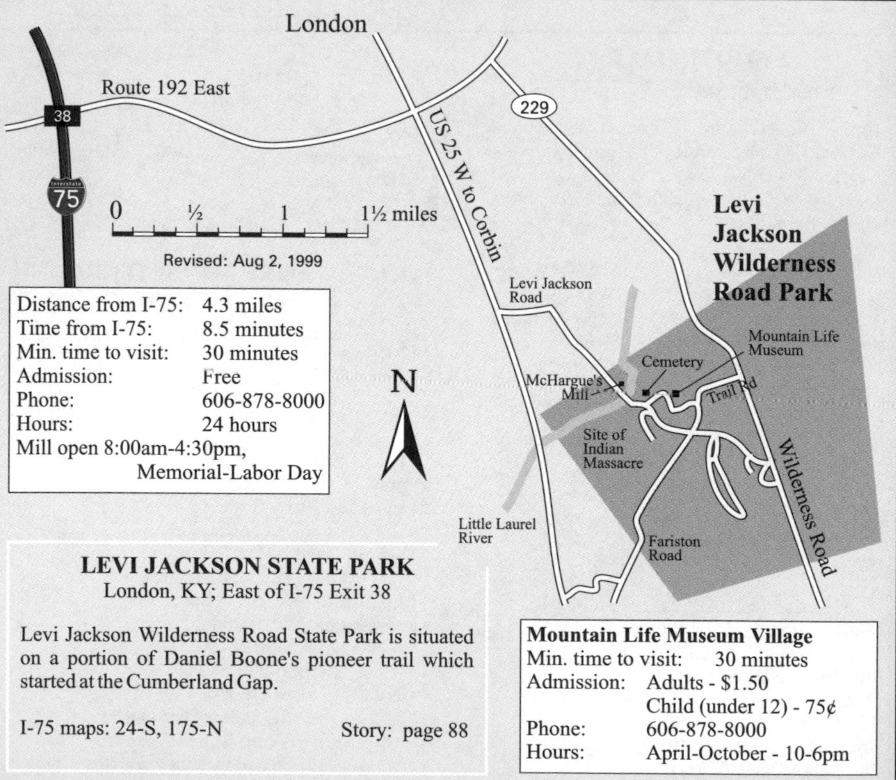

Distance from I-75:	1/2 mile
Time from I-75:	2 minutes
Min.. time to visit:	1 hour
Phone:	606-986-2540 or, 1-800-598-5263

0 — 1 mile

Revised: Aug 2, 1999

0 ½ 1 1½ miles

Revised: Aug 2, 1999

Distance from I-75:	4.3 miles
Time from I-75:	8.5 minutes
Min. time to visit:	30 minutes
Admission:	Free
Phone:	606-878-8000
Hours:	24 hours
Mill open 8:00am-4:30pm, Memorial-Labor Day	

LEVI JACKSON STATE PARK

London, KY; East of I-75 Exit 38

Levi Jackson Wilderness Road State Park is situated on a portion of Daniel Boone's pioneer trail which started at the Cumberland Gap.

I-75 maps: 24-S, 175-N Story: page 88

Mountain Life Museum Village

Min. time to visit:	30 minutes
Admission:	Adults - $1.50 Child (under 12) - 75¢
Phone:	606-878-8000
Hours:	April-October - 10-6pm

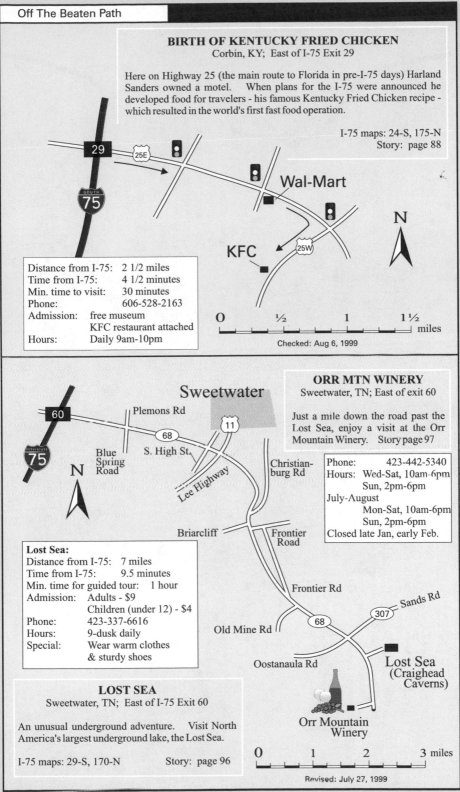

BIRTH OF KENTUCKY FRIED CHICKEN

Corbin, KY; East of I-75 Exit 29

Here on Highway 25 (the main route to Florida in pre-I-75 days) Harland Sanders owned a motel. When plans for the I-75 were announced he developed food for travelers - his famous Kentucky Fried Chicken recipe - which resulted in the world's first fast food operation.

I-75 maps: 24-S, 175-N

Story: page 88

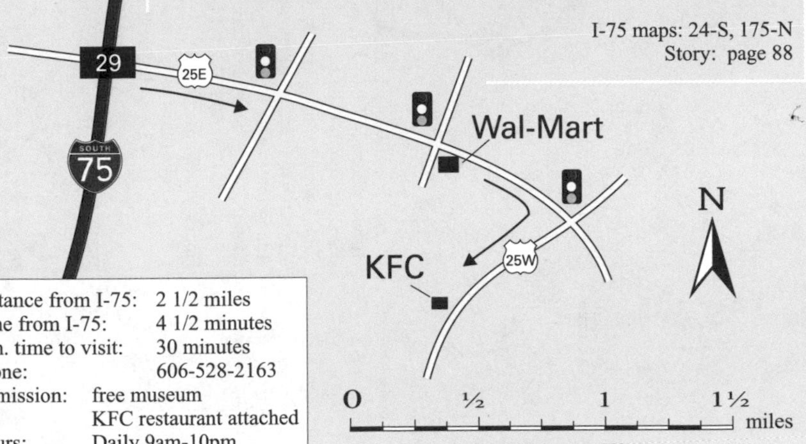

Checked: Aug 6, 1999

Distance from I-75:	2 1/2 miles
Time from I-75:	4 1/2 minutes
Min. time to visit:	30 minutes
Phone:	606-528-2163
Admission:	free museum KFC restaurant attached
Hours:	Daily 9am-10pm

ORR MTN WINERY

Sweetwater, TN; East of exit 60

Just a mile down the road past the Lost Sea, enjoy a visit at the Orr Mountain Winery. Story page 97

Phone:	423-442-5340
Hours:	Wed-Sat, 10am-6pm Sun, 2pm-6pm
July-August	Mon-Sat, 10am-6pm Sun, 2pm-6pm
Closed late Jan, early Feb.	

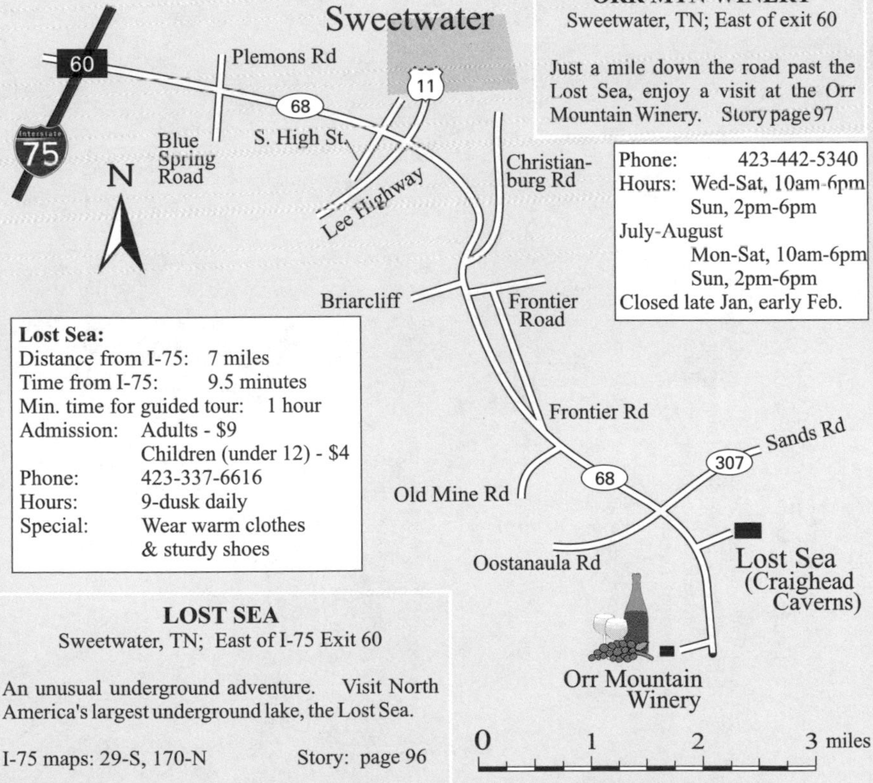

Revised: July 27, 1999

Lost Sea:

Distance from I-75:	7 miles
Time from I-75:	9.5 minutes
Min. time for guided tour:	1 hour
Admission:	Adults - $9 Children (under 12) - $4
Phone:	423-337-6616
Hours:	9-dusk daily
Special:	Wear warm clothes & sturdy shoes

LOST SEA

Sweetwater, TN; East of I-75 Exit 60

An unusual underground adventure. Visit North America's largest underground lake, the Lost Sea.

I-75 maps: 29-S, 170-N

Story: page 96

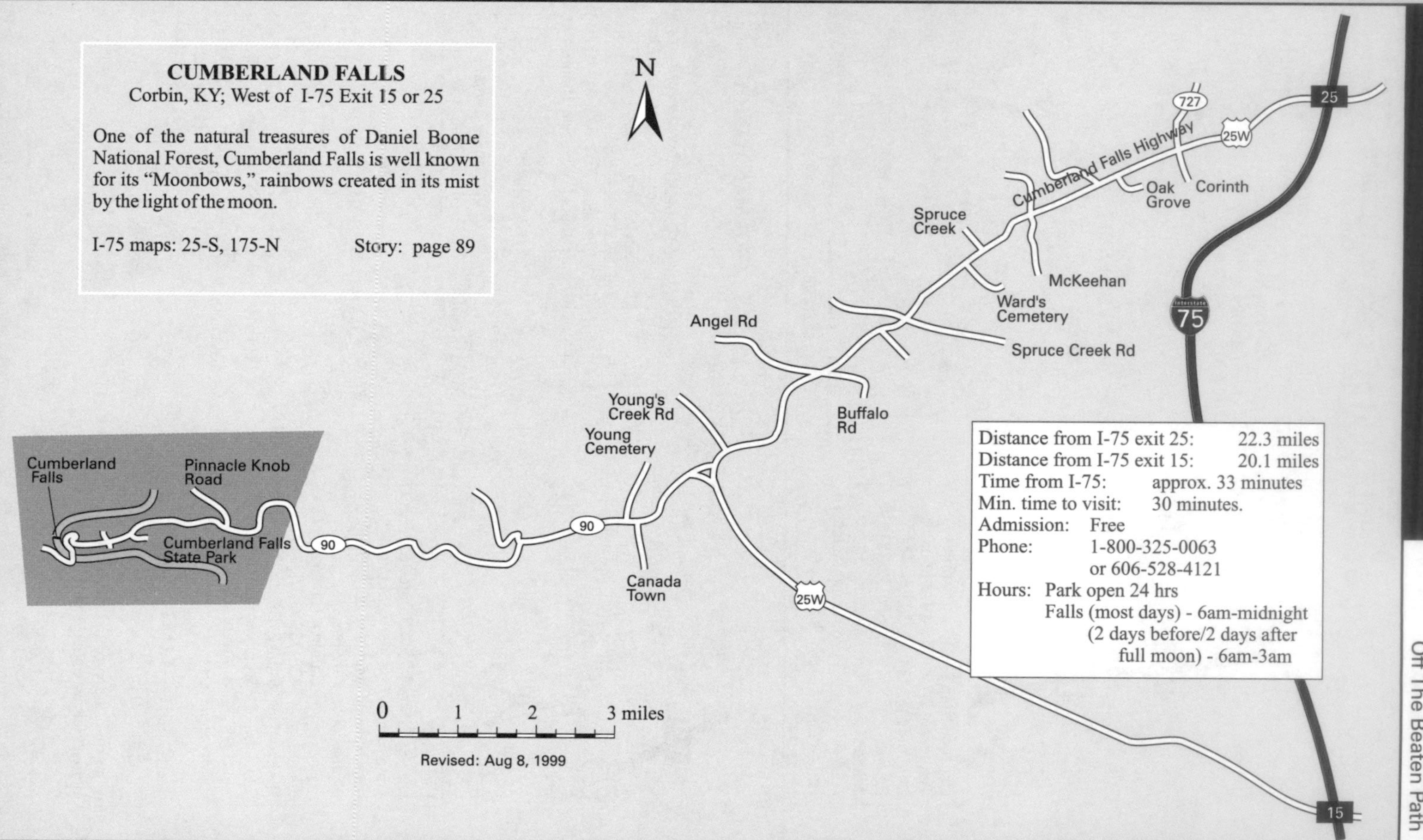

CUMBERLAND FALLS

Corbin, KY; West of I-75 Exit 15 or 25

One of the natural treasures of Daniel Boone National Forest, Cumberland Falls is well known for its "Moonbows," rainbows created in its mist by the light of the moon.

I-75 maps: 25-S, 175-N

Story: page 89

Distance from I-75 exit 25: 22.3 miles
Distance from I-75 exit 15: 20.1 miles
Time from I-75: approx. 33 minutes
Min. time to visit: 30 minutes.
Admission: Free
Phone: 1-800-325-0063
or 606-528-4121
Hours: Park open 24 hrs
Falls (most days) - 6am-midnight
(2 days before/2 days after
full moon) - 6am-3am

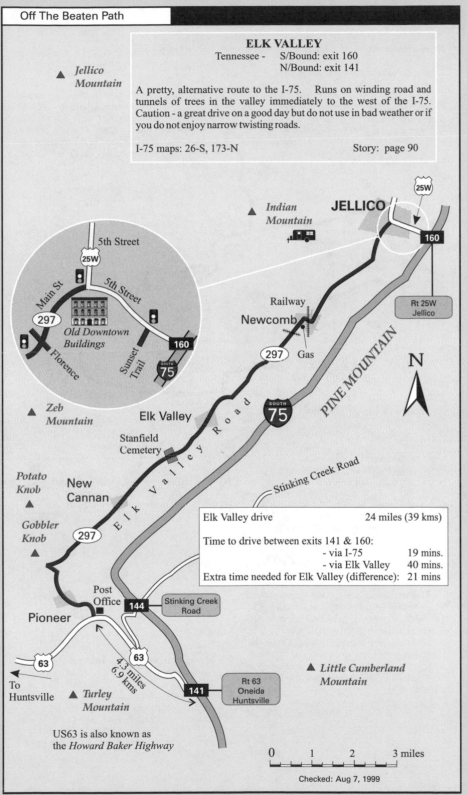

ELK VALLEY

Tennessee - S/Bound: exit 160
N/Bound: exit 141

A pretty, alternative route to the I-75. Runs on winding road and tunnels of trees in the valley immediately to the west of the I-75. Caution - a great drive on a good day but do not use in bad weather or if you do not enjoy narrow twisting roads.

I-75 maps: 26-S, 173-N

Story: page 90

Jellico Mountain

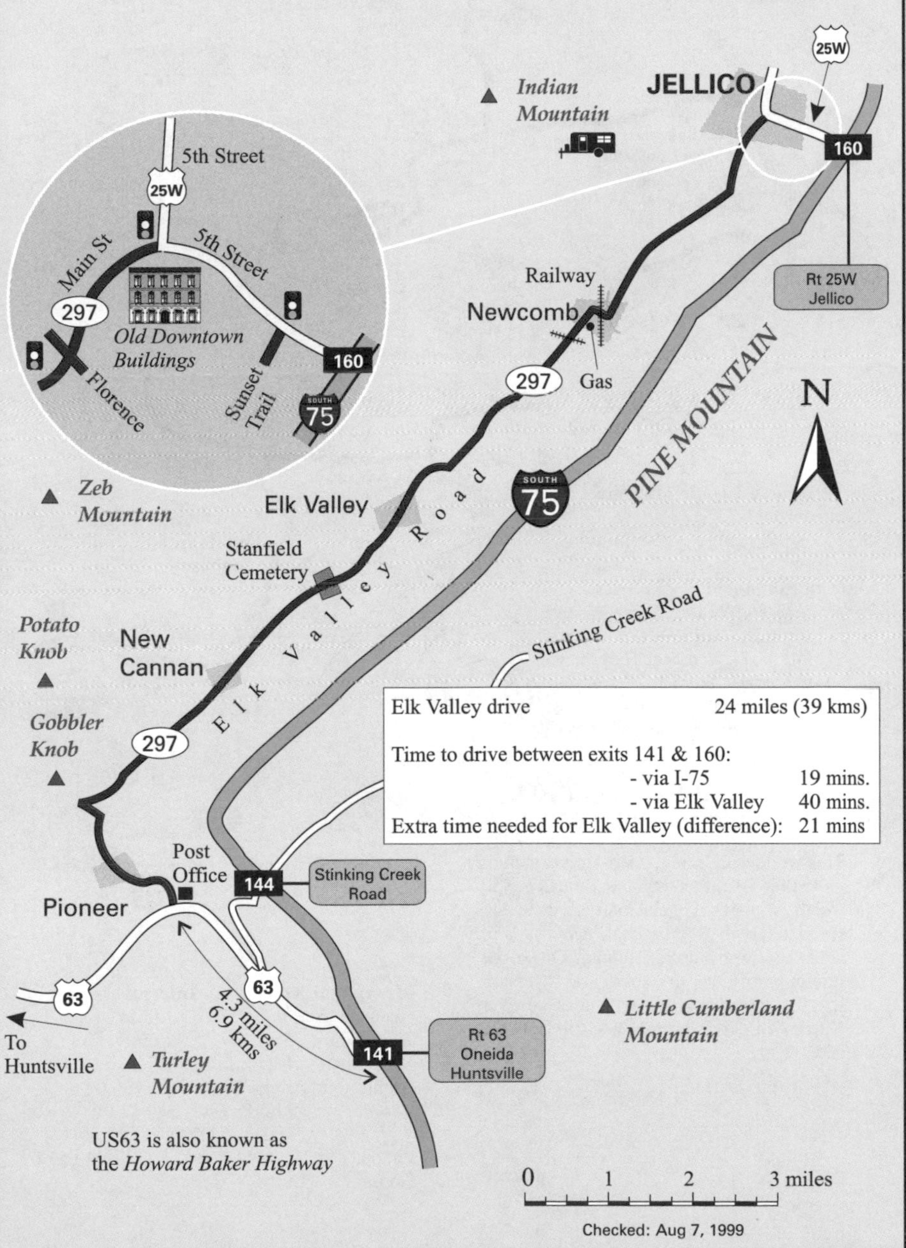

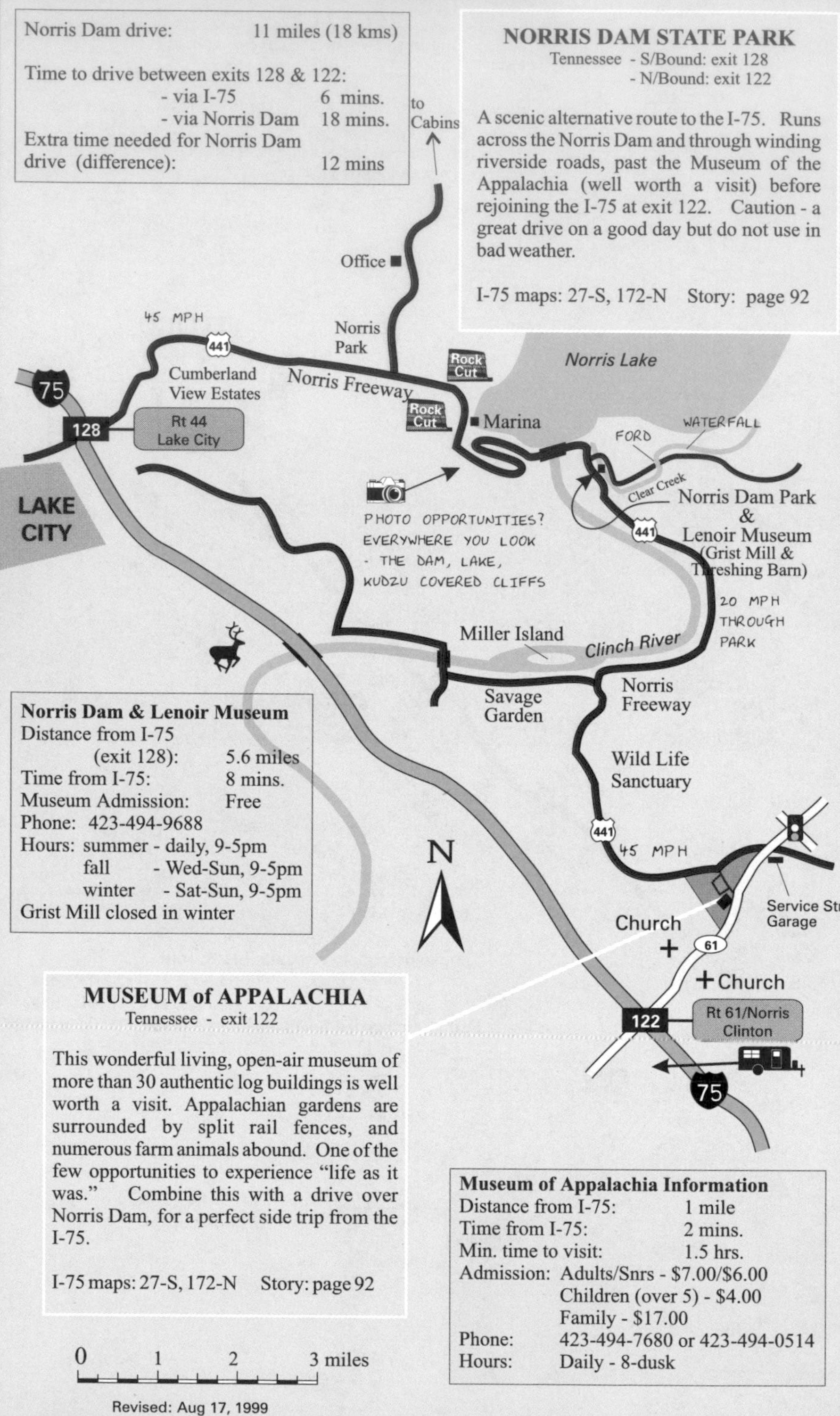
Norris Dam drive: 11 miles (18 kms)
Time to drive between exits 128 & 122:
- via I-75 6 mins.
- via Norris Dam 18 mins.
Extra time needed for Norris Dam drive (difference): 12 mins
NORRIS DAM STATE PARK
Tennessee - S/Bound: exit 128
- N/Bound: exit 122
A scenic alternative route to the I-75. Runs across the Norris Dam and through winding riverside roads, past the Museum of the Appalachia (well worth a visit) before rejoining the I-75 at exit 122. Caution - a great drive on a good day but do not use in bad weather.
I-75 maps: 27-S, 172-N Story: page 92
to Cabins
Office
Norris Park
45 MPH
441
75
128
Cumberland View Estates
Norris Freeway
Rock Cut
Rock Cut
Marina
Norris Lake
Rt 44 Lake City
LAKE CITY
FORD
WATERFALL
Clear Creek
Norris Dam Park & Lenoir Museum (Grist Mill & Threshing Barn)
PHOTO OPPORTUNITIES? EVERYWHERE YOU LOOK - THE DAM, LAKE, KUDZU COVERED CLIFFS
20 MPH THROUGH PARK
Miller Island
Clinch River
Savage Garden
Norris Freeway
Wild Life Sanctuary
Norris Dam & Lenoir Museum
Distance from I-75 (exit 128): 5.6 miles
Time from I-75: 8 mins.
Museum Admission: Free
Phone: 423-494-9688
Hours: summer - daily, 9-5pm
fall - Wed-Sun, 9-5pm
winter - Sat-Sun, 9-5pm
Grist Mill closed in winter
N
45 MPH
Service Stn Garage
Church
61
Church
122
Rt 61/Norris Clinton
MUSEUM of APPALACHIA
Tennessee - exit 122
This wonderful living, open-air museum of more than 30 authentic log buildings is well worth a visit. Appalachian gardens are surrounded by split rail fences, and numerous farm animals abound. One of the few opportunities to experience "life as it was." Combine this with a drive over Norris Dam, for a perfect side trip from the I-75.
I-75 maps: 27-S, 172-N Story: page 92
Museum of Appalachia Information
Distance from I-75: 1 mile
Time from I-75: 2 mins.
Min. time to visit: 1.5 hrs.
Admission: Adults/Snrs - $7.00/$6.00
Children (over 5) - $4.00
Family - $17.00
Phone: 423-494-7680 or 423-494-0514
Hours: Daily - 8-dusk
0 1 2 3 miles
Revised: Aug 17, 1999

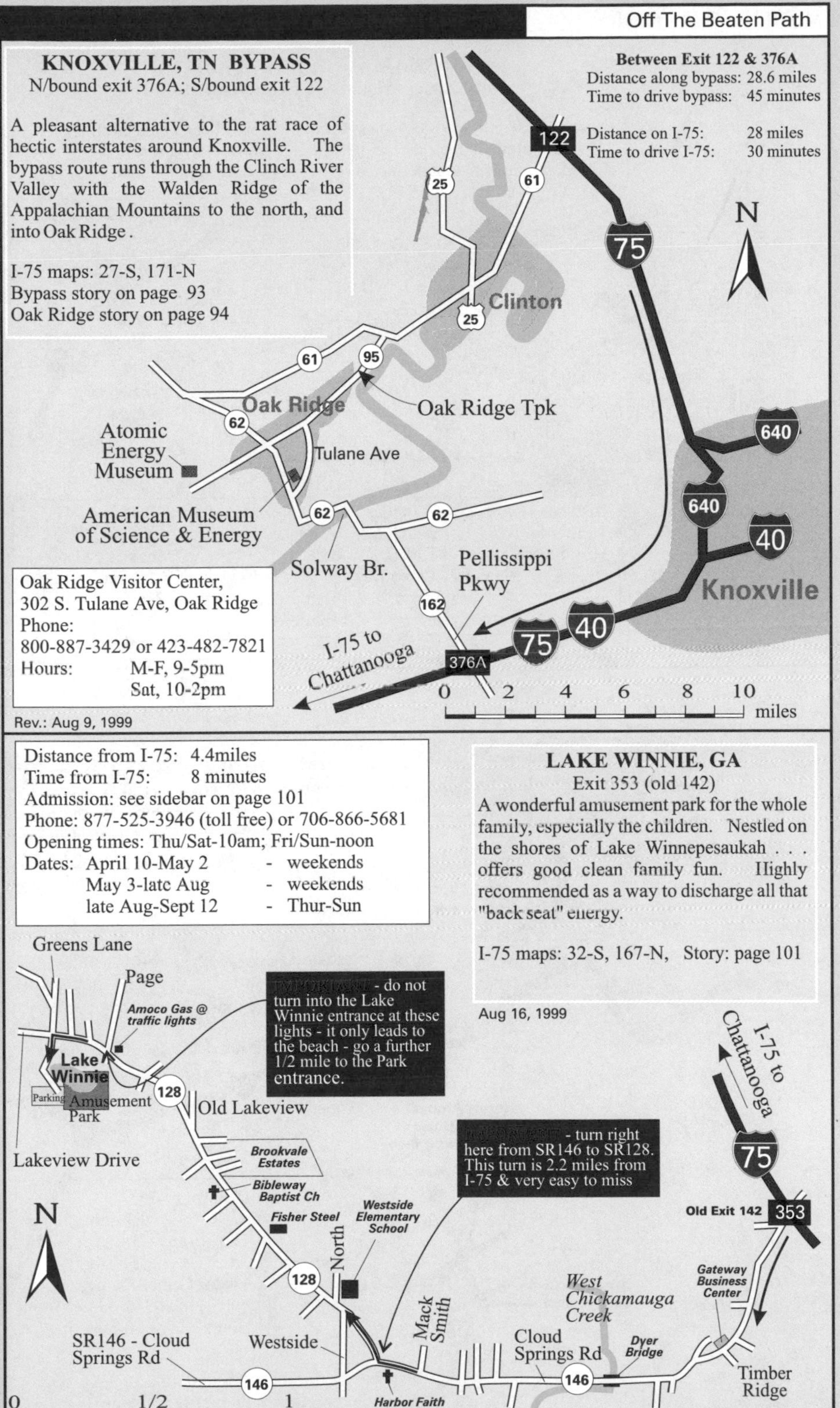
KNOXVILLE, TN BYPASS
N/bound exit 376A; S/bound exit 122
A pleasant alternative to the rat race of hectic interstates around Knoxville. The bypass route runs through the Clinch River Valley with the Walden Ridge of the Appalachian Mountains to the north, and into Oak Ridge.
I-75 maps: 27-S, 171-N
Bypass story on page 93
Oak Ridge story on page 94
Between Exit 122 & 376A
Distance along bypass: 28.6 miles
Time to drive bypass: 45 minutes
Distance on I-75: 28 miles
Time to drive I-75: 30 minutes
122
25
61
75
N
Clinton
25
61
95
Oak Ridge
Oak Ridge Tpk
62
Atomic Energy Museum
Tulane Ave
640
640
American Museum of Science & Energy
62
62
40
Solway Br.
Pellissippi Pkwy
Knoxville
Oak Ridge Visitor Center,
302 S. Tulane Ave, Oak Ridge
Phone:
800-887-3429 or 423-482-7821
Hours: M-F, 9-5pm
Sat, 10-2pm
162
I-75 to Chattanooga
75
40
376A
0 2 4 6 8 10 miles
Rev.: Aug 9, 1999
Distance from I-75: 4.4miles
Time from I-75: 8 minutes
Admission: see sidebar on page 101
Phone: 877-525-3946 (toll free) or 706-866-5681
Opening times: Thu/Sat-10am; Fri/Sun-noon
Dates: April 10-May 2 - weekends
May 3-late Aug - weekends
late Aug-Sept 12 - Thur-Sun
LAKE WINNIE, GA
Exit 353 (old 142)
A wonderful amusement park for the whole family, especially the children. Nestled on the shores of Lake Winnepesaukah . . . offers good clean family fun. Highly recommended as a way to discharge all that "back seat" energy.
I-75 maps: 32-S, 167-N, Story: page 101
Aug 16, 1999
Greens Lane
Page
Amoco Gas @ traffic lights
- do not turn into the Lake Winnie entrance at these lights - it only leads to the beach - go a further 1/2 mile to the Park entrance.
Lake Winnie
Parking
Amusement Park
128
Old Lakeview
I-75 to Chattanooga
Lakeview Drive
Brookvale Estates
- turn right here from SR146 to SR128. This turn is 2.2 miles from I-75 & very easy to miss
75
Bibleway Baptist Ch
N
Fisher Steel
Westside Elementary School
Old Exit 142
353
North
128
Gateway Business Center
West Chickamauga Creek
Mack Smith
SR146 - Cloud Springs Rd
Westside
Cloud Springs Rd
Dyer Bridge
146
146
Timber Ridge
0 1/2 1 miles
Harbor Faith Ch of God
Dietz (traffic lights)

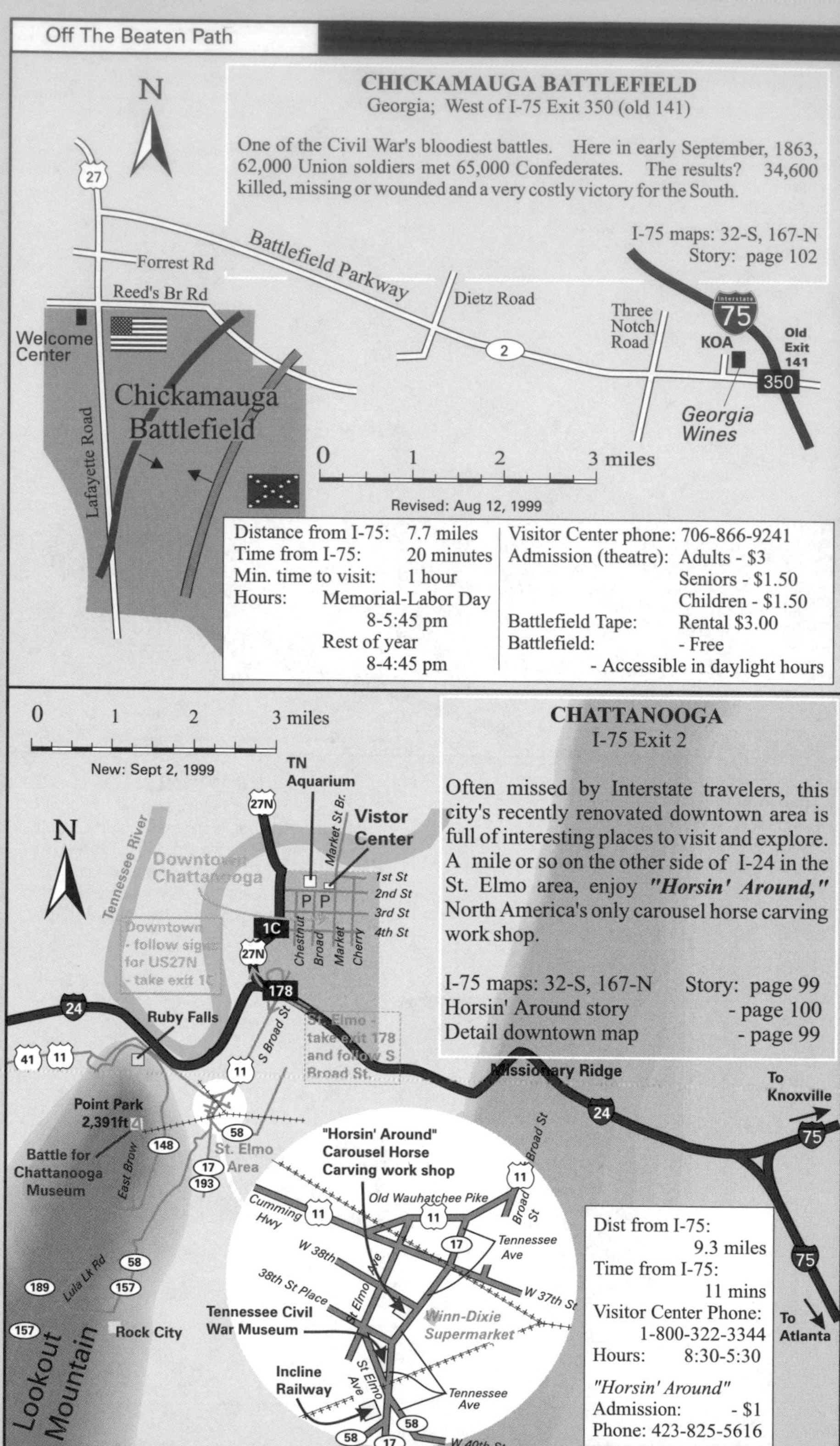
CHICKAMAUGA BATTLEFIELD
Georgia; West of I-75 Exit 350 (old 141)
One of the Civil War's bloodiest battles. Here in early September, 1863, 62,000 Union soldiers met 65,000 Confederates. The results? 34,600 killed, missing or wounded and a very costly victory for the South.
I-75 maps: 32-S, 167-N
Story: page 102
N
27
Forrest Rd
Reed's Br Rd
Battlefield Parkway
Dietz Road
Three Notch Road
75
KOA
Old Exit 141
350
2
Welcome Center
Chickamauga Battlefield
Lafayette Road
Georgia Wines
0 1 2 3 miles
Revised: Aug 12, 1999
Distance from I-75: 7.7 miles
Time from I-75: 20 minutes
Min. time to visit: 1 hour
Hours: Memorial-Labor Day 8-5:45 pm
Rest of year 8-4:45 pm
Visitor Center phone: 706-866-9241
Admission (theatre): Adults - $3
Seniors - $1.50
Children - $1.50
Battlefield Tape: Rental $3.00
Battlefield: - Free
- Accessible in daylight hours
CHATTANOOGA
I-75 Exit 2
Often missed by Interstate travelers, this city's recently renovated downtown area is full of interesting places to visit and explore. A mile or so on the other side of I-24 in the St. Elmo area, enjoy *"Horsin' Around,"* North America's only carousel horse carving work shop.
I-75 maps: 32-S, 167-N
Story: page 99
Horsin' Around story - page 100
Detail downtown map - page 99
0 1 2 3 miles
New: Sept 2, 1999
TN Aquarium
Vistor Center
Market St Br.
27N
N
Tennessee River
Downtown Chattanooga
Downtown - follow signs for US27N - take exit 1C
1C
1st St
2nd St
3rd St
4th St
P P
Chestnut
Broad
Market
Cherry
178
24
Ruby Falls
S Broad St
St. Elmo - take exit 178 and follow S Broad St.
41 11
11
Missionary Ridge
To Knoxville
Point Park 2,391ft
Battle for Chattanooga Museum
148
East Brow
58
St. Elmo Area
17
193
"Horsin' Around" Carousel Horse Carving work shop
Old Wauhatchee Pike
Broad St
Cumming Hwy
W 38th
Tennessee Ave
38th St Place
St Elmo Ave
W 37th St
Winn-Dixie Supermarket
Tennessee Civil War Museum
Incline Railway
Tennessee Ave
W 40th St
Lula Lk Rd
189
157
Rock City
Lookout Mountain
To Atlanta
Dist from I-75: 9.3 miles
Time from I-75: 11 mins
Visitor Center Phone: 1-800-322-3344
Hours: 8:30-5:30
"Horsin' Around"
Admission: - $1
Phone: 423-825-5616

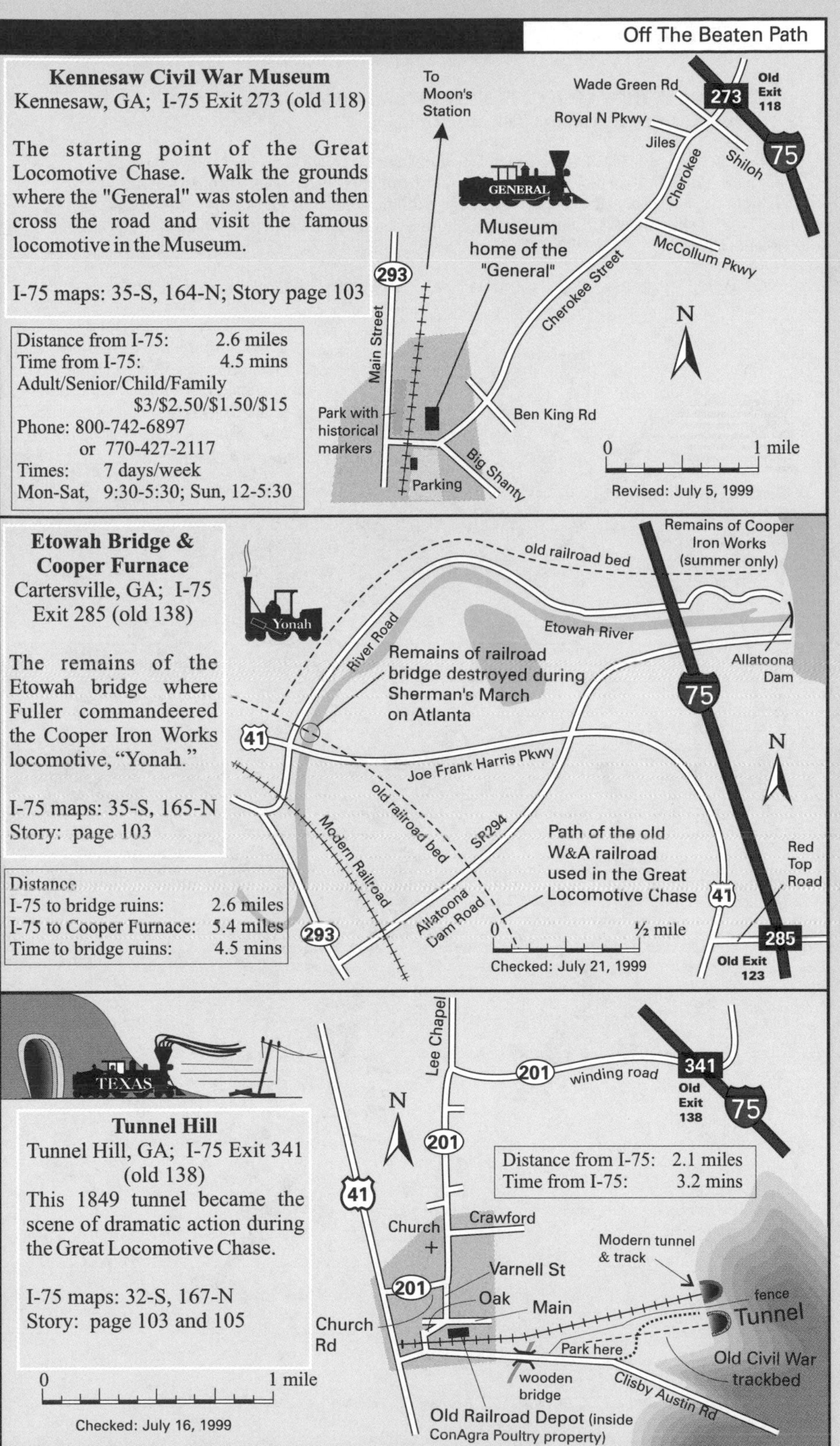

Kennesaw Civil War Museum

Kennesaw, GA; I-75 Exit 273 (old 118)

The starting point of the Great Locomotive Chase. Walk the grounds where the "General" was stolen and then cross the road and visit the famous locomotive in the Museum.

I-75 maps: 35-S, 164-N; Story page 103

Distance from I-75:	2.6 miles
Time from I-75:	4.5 mins
Adult/Senior/Child/Family	$3/$2.50/$1.50/$15
Phone:	800-742-6897 or 770-427-2117
Times:	7 days/week
Mon-Sat,	9:30-5:30; Sun, 12-5:30

Etowah Bridge & Cooper Furnace

Cartersville, GA; I-75 Exit 285 (old 138)

The remains of the Etowah bridge where Fuller commandeered the Cooper Iron Works locomotive, "Yonah."

I-75 maps: 35-S, 165-N
Story: page 103

Distance	
I-75 to bridge ruins:	2.6 miles
I-75 to Cooper Furnace:	5.4 miles
Time to bridge ruins:	4.5 mins

Tunnel Hill

Tunnel Hill, GA; I-75 Exit 341 (old 138)

This 1849 tunnel became the scene of dramatic action during the Great Locomotive Chase.

I-75 maps: 32-S, 167-N
Story: page 103 and 105

Distance from I-75:	2.1 miles
Time from I-75:	3.2 mins

RESACA CIVIL WAR BATTLEFIELD and CEMETERY

Resaca, GA; Cemetery east of I-75 Exit 320 (old 133)

A bloody Civil War battle (5,547 men killed or injured) was fought here, between the 13th and 15th of May, 1864, as the Confederate Army was beaten back towards Atlanta. To help you understand the scope of this large battlefield, the mile markers are shown on the I-75. Directions and distances refer to the Confederate Cemetery which is well worth visiting.

I-75 maps: 33-S, 166 Story: page 107 and Civil War Sidebar, page 108

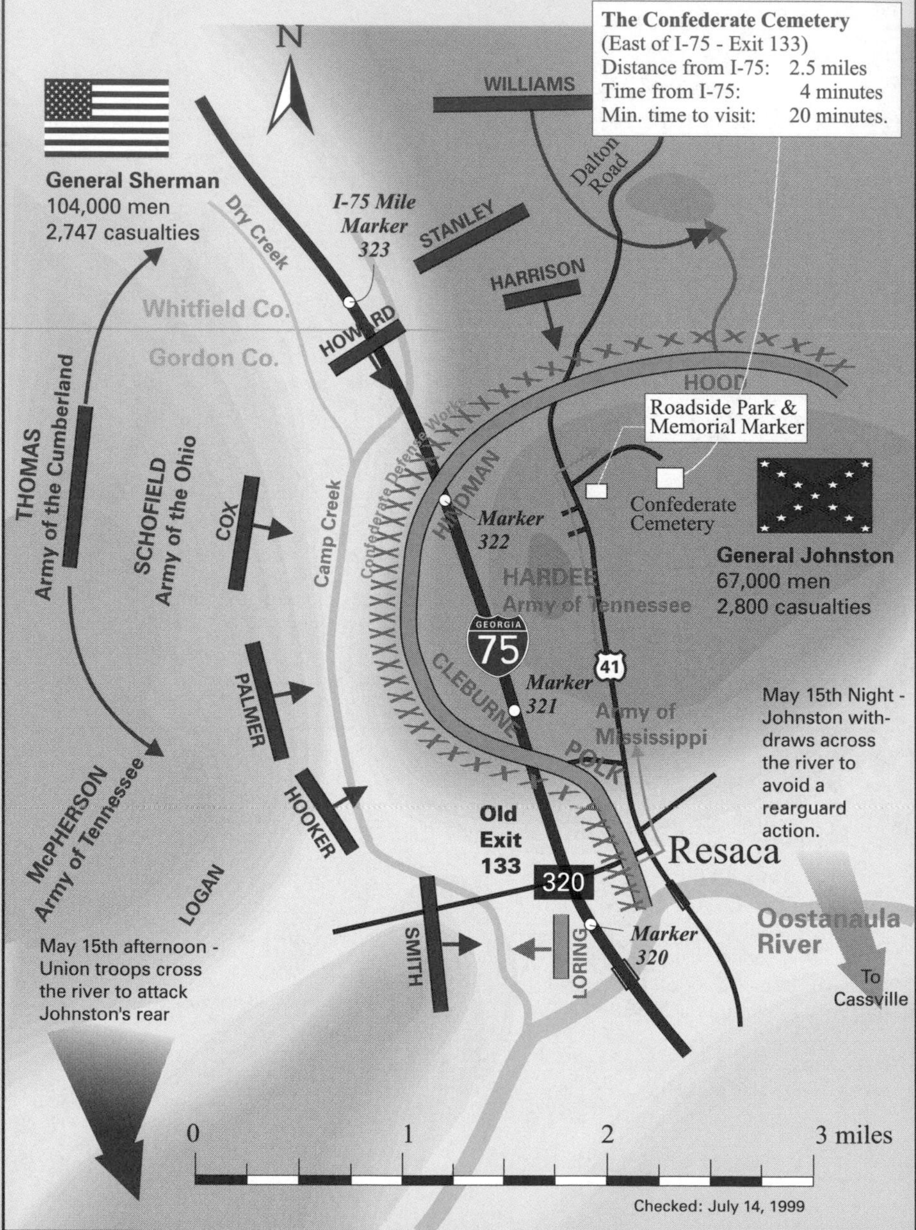

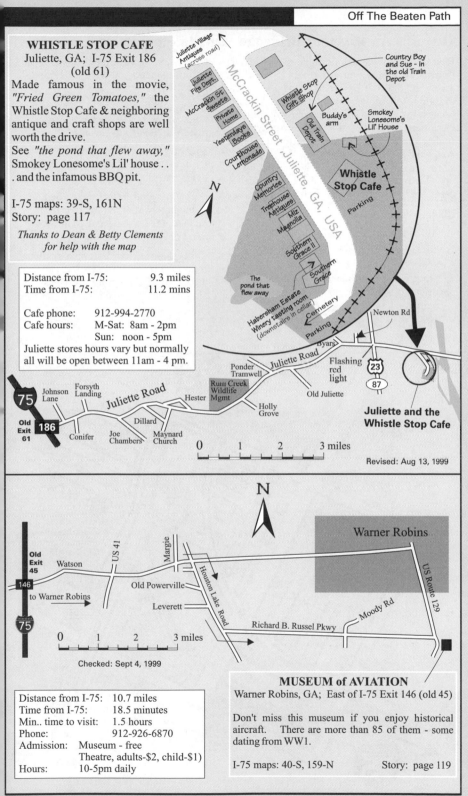

WHISTLE STOP CAFE

Juliette, GA; I-75 Exit 186 (old 61)

Made famous in the movie, *"Fried Green Tomatoes,"* the Whistle Stop Cafe & neighboring antique and craft shops are well worth the drive.

See *"the pond that flew away,"* Smokey Lonesome's Lil' house . . . and the infamous BBQ pit.

I-75 maps: 39-S, 161N

Story: page 117

Thanks to Dean & Betty Clements for help with the map

Distance from I-75:	9.3 miles
Time from I-75:	11.2 mins

Cafe phone: 912-994-2770

Cafe hours: M-Sat: 8am - 2pm; Sun: noon - 5pm

Juliette stores hours vary but normally all will be open between 11am - 4 pm.

Juliette Village Antiques (across road)
Juliette Fire Dept.
McCrackin St Sweets
Private Home
Yesterdays Books
Courthouse Lemonade
Country Memories
Treehouse Antiques
Miz Magnolia
Southern Grace II
Southern Grace
The pond that flew away
Habersham Estate Winery tasting room (downstairs in cellar)
Cemetery
Parking
McCrackin Street, Juliette, GA, USA
Whistle Stop Gift Shop
Old Train Depot
Buddy's arm
Country Boy and Sue - in the old Train Depot
Smokey Lonesome's Lil' House
Whistle Stop Cafe
Parking
N
Newton Rd
Byars
Juliette Road
Flashing red light
23
87
Ponder Tramwell
Rum Creek Wildlife Mgmt
Old Juliette
Hester
Holly Grove
Juliette Road
Johnson Lane
Forsyth Landing
75
Old Exit 61
186
Conifer
Joe Chambers
Dillard
Maynard Church
0 1 2 3 miles
Juliette and the Whistle Stop Cafe
Revised: Aug 13, 1999

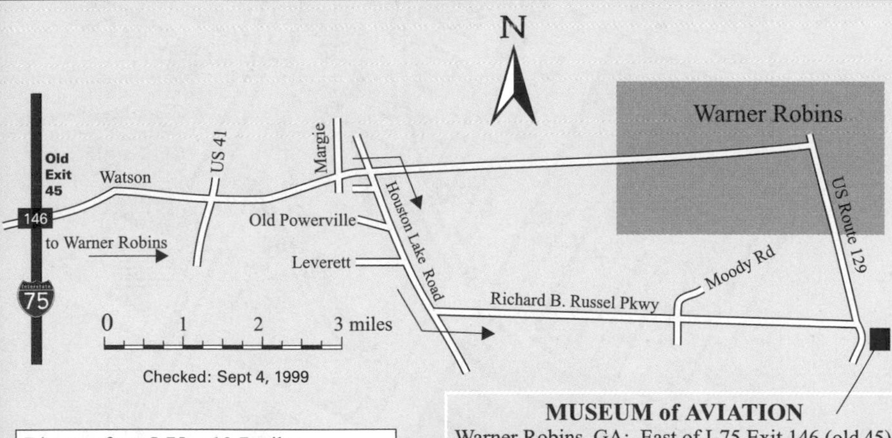

MUSEUM of AVIATION

Warner Robins, GA; East of I-75 Exit 146 (old 45)

Don't miss this museum if you enjoy historical aircraft. There are more than 85 of them - some dating from WW1.

I-75 maps: 40-S, 159-N

Story: page 119

Distance from I-75:	10.7 miles
Time from I-75:	18.5 minutes
Min.. time to visit:	1.5 hours
Phone:	912-926-6870
Admission:	Museum - free; Theatre, adults-$2, child-$1)
Hours:	10-5pm daily

Detroit's Ambassador Bridge to Canada - and Back

Finding the Ambassador Bridge to Canada from the I-75 is easy - just take exit 47B, drive across the lights at Lafayette and you are at the bridge toll booths. Getting back onto I-75 South is not so easy. This is nothing to do with Customs or Immigration, it is more to do with finding the I-75 again. Incidentally, the I-75 is called the "Fisher Freeway" in Detroit. The signs are quite confusing and depending upon the season, covered by foliage in some cases. We have included this map to help you.

Finding the I-75 South

1. After clearing Customs, drive across the lights at Porter. Do not go down the I-75 ramp to your left - it goes north!
2. Move into left turn lane after passing Bristol (a small side street on your right).
3. Turn left at the Vernor intersection lights.
4. On Vernor, move immediately into the left turn lane as you cross the bridge over the I-75.
5. At the next lights, turn left onto Fisher Freeway W. Ignore sign at the corner that says "Bridge to Canada."
6. Stay on "Fisher Freeway West" - past Bagley, Lambie, Howard, 25th St, to the lights at Grand Boulevard.
7. Pass Vinewood, Hubbard and Scotten. Immediately after the lights at Clark, move to the left lane and go down the ramp onto the I-75 South.
8. If this ramp is closed for construction, continue on along the service road - there are at least 3 more I-75 Southbound ramps ahead.

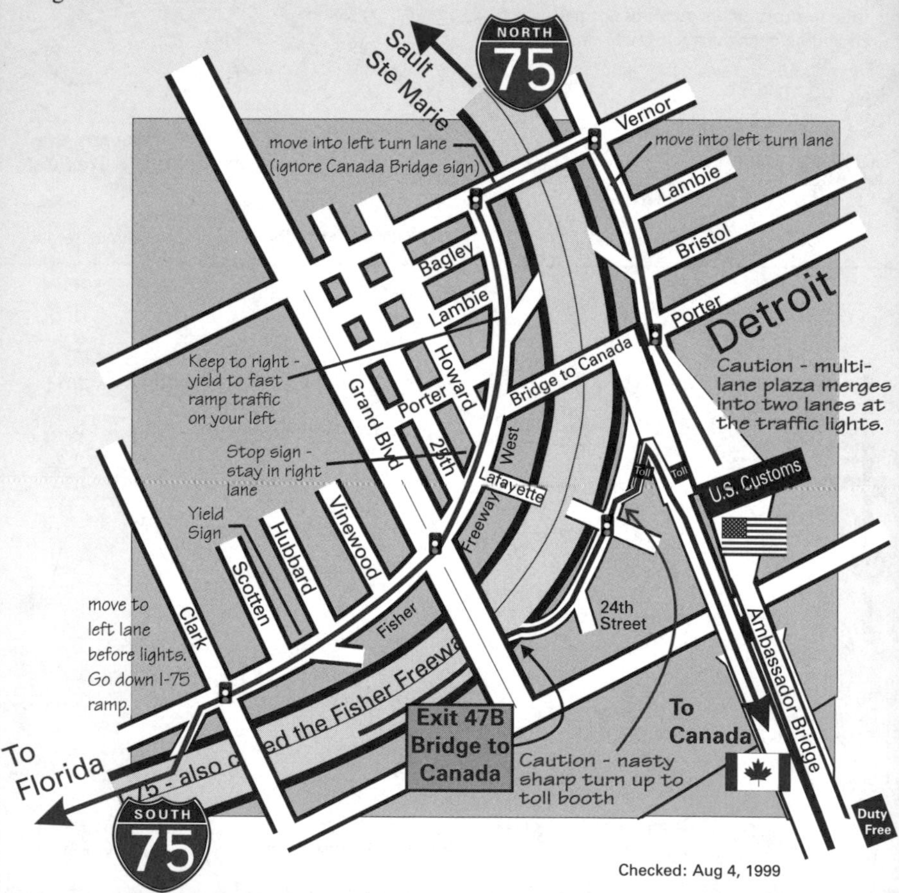

Along the I-75

A journey along the Interstate-75 can either be a boring, fast-paced ride between two points, or an exciting adventure–a chance to learn more about one of the most fascinating and historically rich areas in North America–much of it right alongside the highway.

For instance, did you know that as you drive the freeway you will pass the site of a War of 1812 massacre, drive across two Civil War battlefields, cross a two hundred year old pioneer path, traverse an area which not long ago was a swamp infested with rattlesnakes and panthers and travel across the bed of an ancient tropical sea?

In a more modern vein, you will pass by stealth bombers, moon rocks, an electronic road surface and a plant building the F22 Raptor - the US fighter aircraft for the 21st Century. You will also pass by the "Kryptonite" room—a room so secret that only a few people are authorized to enter.

These are just a few of the wonders described in the following pages. Mile-by-mile, we take you down the I-75 from Detroit to Florida, revealing the secrets, sights and attractions along the way.

Based on an imaginary three day journey from the dead of Michigan's winter to Florida's summery sun, you will also find sprinkled through these pages the history behind the place names you will encounter along the way, our **"Special Reports,"** detailed information about sights of particular interest along the way and great Saving Tips. We know you will find this section one of the most enjoyable in this book.

INSIDER TIPS

Throughout the following sections, you will find our famous "Insider Tips"—hints of special significance to help you save money and have a more enjoyable journey. In some instances, we recommend specific I-75 facilities which, from our personal knowledge (often first brought to our attention by our readers–see page 203) offer exceptional value or an unusual (and worthwhile) experience. None of these establishments have paid for this recommendation–we accept no commercial advertising in this guide. In fact, none of them knew they were being inspected at the time of our visit.

Here is where you get the REAL local knowledge.

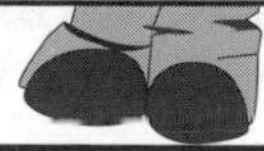

Interstate 75 is dedicated as the
"Blue Star Memorial Highway"

BLUE STAR
MEMORIAL HIGHWAY
A tribute to the Armed Forces
that have defended the
United States of America

Magic of the I-75

People ask us why we enjoy the Interstates so much. To many travelers, they are just a means of getting from here to there and they find them downright boring. To us, though, there is magic in these freeways ... and the I-75 is one of the best.

As we move through the changing scenery, in our mind's eye we are looking through the windows of a time machine–in the winter we move through rapidly changing seasons, and at all times we journey through pages of history. That rolling hill over to the left was probably carved by a massive glacier ... those rock cuts ahead reveal the bed of an ancient tropical sea ... and these strata hide the mysteries of the days when dinosaurs roamed the land. Around this corner lies a Civil War battlefield, and down yonder is a long forgotten war of another time, when Americans attacked Americans. And if you want to stay in the present, there is always the diversity of the scenery, wildlife and plants you find along the way. Let's journey south from Detroit and I'll try to show you what I mean . . .

I-75 Michigan Exit 46 - Winter - Detroit:

It's January 4th and we have started our journey down the Fisher Freeway (Detroit's I-75 expressway) crawling behind the blue flashing light of a slow moving snow plow. Last night's storm has dumped 18 inches of snow across the State. The grating and ringing of the plow's blade as it cuts a swathe with sparks flying into the frosty air, leads our small procession of cars southward. But we don't care for we know that Michigan's and Ohio's winter will rapidly change into Kentucky's and Tennessee's "spring," and then into the warmer temperatures of Georgia, and finally the full blown warmth of Florida's "summer" . . . and all in a few short days. The anticipation is too much to bear.

Before we start though, let's tune into WWJ 950AM to get the latest traffic reports for the road ahead.

MI Exit 15 - Monroe & General Custer: This exit leads to one of the oldest communities in Michigan, the historic town of Monroe (settled by the French in 1780). General George Custer (of Civil War and Little Bighorn massacre fame) lived here for many years before joining the army and making a name for himself in the Cavalry.

There are more than 23 sites and buildings associated with General Custer in Monroe. The Monroe Museum produces a brochure listing all the sites. Unfortunately, many are not open to the public.

One of the most interesting is the privately owned Nevin Custer farm, just west of Monroe on the north bank of the Raisin River. George and his brother, Nevin, purchased the farm in 1871, five years before his death at Little Bighorn. George's favorite horse, Dandy is buried in the orchard near the

WHAT'S IN A NAME?

Indian terms, historical characters, national heroes, town site descriptions–place names weave a colorful tapestry as we journey along Interstate-75. In some cases, early pioneers and settlers from east coast regions transferred the names of their original home towns to their new settlements (e.g.. Milford, Ohio), thereby perpetuating British and European names in the U.S. interior.

Throughout the following pages, we explain the meanings behind some of the more interesting place names encountered as we travel southbound to Florida:

barn. Visitors to the farm have included Buffalo Bill Cody and Annie Oakley.

Today, Custer is remembered by a statue of him riding his rearing horse, sword poised in his arm. The statue, "Sighting the Enemy" was unveiled in 1910 by his widow, Elizabeth (Libbie) Custer and President Taft.

MI Exit 14 - Battle of the Raisin River (map on page 48): Just west of this exit on the north bank of the Raisin River, lays the site of an early settlement called Frenchtown. It was here that one of largest battles between the British and American Armies took place during the War of 1812.

On the evening of January 18, 1813, Frenchtown was occupied by an American force detached from an army recruited in Kentucky during the previous summer. The seven hundred men had faced a small British force earlier that day and, after hours of tree to tree fighting, had driven them back north towards Detroit.

Several days later their leader, General Winchester, arrived with the remainder of the troops, bringing the army to a strength of 934 men.

In the quiet pre-dawn of January 21st, a huge British force of 597 British soldiers supported by 800 Indians, crept towards Frenchtown to take their revenge. The attack lasted less than twenty minutes before the American right (closest to the I-75) was outflanked and the men retreated to the river. Of the 400 men who fled, over 200 were killed and 147 were captured - including General Winchester.

The remaining 500 Kentuckians, fighting from behind picket fences at Frenchtown, were unaware of the collapse on their right, and successfully drove off three fierce British attacks with their rifles. When they saw a British officer come towards them with a white flag, they thought that the British were going to surrender. They were surprised when the officer gave them orders from their own General, now a prisoner of the British, to surrender.

After the surrender, the British withdrew and the Americans gathered their dying and injured to the settlers' homes in Frenchtown. The following morning, the Indian forces attacked, burning and plundering the homes and scalping the American wounded. Over 60 were killed–the action became known as the "Massacre of the Raisin River."

The massacre shocked and enraged settlers throughout the Old Northwest Territory (today's Michigan). Ten months later, American troops chased the British army from Detroit to London, Ontario where a major battle took place on the banks of another river–Ontario's River Thames. During this battle, the famous Indian chief and friend of the British, Tecumseh, was killed. The American battle cry at this engagement? "Remember the Raisin!"

See phone, hours, and details on page 48.

MI Exit 9 - Lake Maumee: We cross through the plains south of Monroe giving little thought to the scene a million years ago when melting glaciers hundreds of feet thick formed an ancient lake which ran right across this section of Michigan and down as far as Exit 159 (Findlay) in Ohio. Geologists named it Lake Maumee and its water surface was about 230 feet above the present position of our car. How can scientists tell? They found the beach ridges of the lake permanently etched into rock at an elevation of 800 feet above sea level (we are driving at 570 feet above sea level). The lake finally broke through the Grand River Valley in Michigan

MICHIGAN - *an old Indian word of unknown origins. It could come from Mishi-mikin-nac or "swimming turtle," a descriptive term used to describe the shape of some of Michigan's land, or from Mitchisawgyegan (michi gama), an Indian term meaning "Great Lake."*

DETROIT - *from the French word "d'etroit" (of the strait). Founded on July 24th, 1701, by French explorer Antoine Cadillac, the early settlement lay on the stretch of land between Lake Erie and Lake St.Clair.*

OHIO -*early French explorers discovered the Ohio River, and used Iroquois words such as Oheo (beautiful) to describe it. The explored territory later acquired the name.*

TOLEDO - *because of its industrial heritage, named after the Spanish town of Toledo famous throughout history for "Toledo Steel."*

and as its water level fell, the current shoreline of Lake Erie appeared.

Ohio Exit 210 - Toledo and the Ohio-Michigan war: It is 1835 and this is where we find our forgotten war. The land between this exit and Ohio Exit 199 is disputed territory and both Ohio and Michigan have laid claim to it. That large crowd of men over there marching down the road with flintlock muskets slung over their shoulders is Michigan's Army led southward by Governor Mason (the stout, black hatted fellow on the roan horse). They are on their way to attack the small settlement of Toledo and settle this question once and for all. They don't know yet but before the week is out, they will capture one of Toledo's founding fathers and hold him as a prisoner of war. Congress will finally have to intervene. The war that has broken out will be resolved by awarding the territory to Ohio, and granting Michigan full statehood in 1837 along with all the copper and iron rights in the peninsula to their north.

The issue of "who owns Toledo" will not go away. As recently as the summer of 1992, an editorial appeared in Toledo's principal newspaper. The Blade, questioning the ownership of Toledo by Ohio. Many still would like to cede the city to Michigan.

OH Exit 199A - US Glass Specialty Outlet: If it's made from glass or ceramic, you will probably find it here in the two large showrooms of this glass and ceramic factory outlet store. Just half-a-mile east of I-75 along Miami Street (Route 65)–see map below–the retail counter is open 6 days a week, M-F 9-5:30, Sat 10-4. You can even visit the glass blowing studio (hrs: 11-4) and even have certain purchases personalized by having your name etched into the glass. ☎ 419-698-8046.

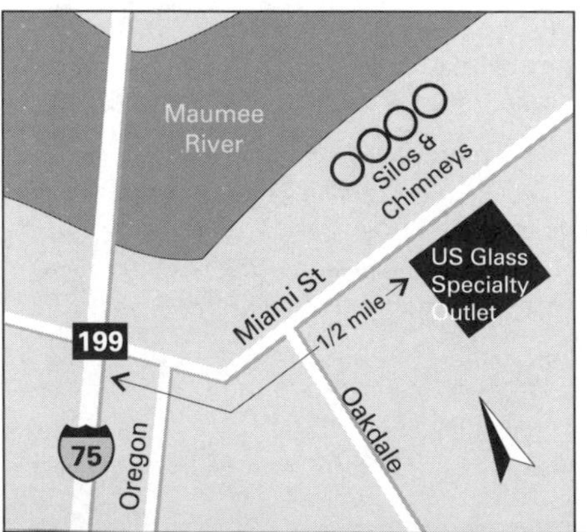

OH between Exits 198 & 163 - The Black Swamp: You wouldn't have wanted to be here 125 years ago, for this entire region (about the size of Connecticut) was the dreaded Black Swamp. A dense, dank, gloomy forest populated mainly by deer, panthers, rattlesnakes, wolves and bear. The ground was an evil boggy quagmire of black muck which sucked pioneers down to their knees and if the animals and insects did not get them, then malaria probably would. In 1850, farmers decided to try to drain the area, and by 1890 more than 22,000 miles of ditches had drained the land and revealed the rich fertile farmland beneath. In 40 years, the stinking swamp had been transformed into the productive farms of today's Ohio.

OH Mile 195 southbound: - Beware of the Ohio "Bear in the Air"–all the way south to Cincinnati. Ohio leads the nation in traffic tickets issued by Highway Patrol aided by aircraft. Every time we drive through here when the weather is clear, our police radio scanner provides us with the most fascinating entertainment.

> *"Unit 37, this is Eagle 2. Red Camaro overtaking the southbound RV at marker (mile marker) 188. Clocked at 82."*
>
> *"Vascar 82 . . . Roger."*

And sure enough, looking up through our sun roof is a speck of a high-winged single engine plane circling the interstate ahead at about 2,000 feet . . . and from the scanner radio speaker, the sound of a siren as a patrol car gets up to speed after the recalcitrant vehicle. Sure enough, a few miles further on, we pass the two sitting on the side of the road "doing business."

See the "Radar" article on page 140 for more information on the different speed control techniques used on the I-75.

OH Exit 192: Fort Meigs (map on page 48): After the massacre of the Kentucky troops at the Raisin River in January, 1813 (see Michigan, Exit 14), fighting between the British and the Americans came to a temporary halt due to severe winter weather. U.S. Major General Harrison decided to build a new fort on the south banks of the Maumee River, named after the Governor of Ohio, Return Jonathan Meigs.

Originally designed as a temporary supply depot, it quickly becomes central to the protection of Ohio from the British Army. Fort Meigs has achieved major strategic status, for if it falls, Michigan and Ohio will become conquered territory of the British.

At its peak it housed more than 2,000 American regulars from Ohio, Kentucky, Pennsylvania and Virginia.

In late April, 1813, however, the fort is badly undermanned with twelve hundred troops of which only 850 are fit for duty–and of these, half are untrained. Will they be able to with stand the coming British attack? To protect his forces, Harrison orders long embankments of earth built across the fort parade grounds so his troops can burrow down into the muddy earth, behind them.

At 11 a.m. on May 1st in chillingly wet weather, a British force of two thousand lays siege to Fort Meigs, pounding its muddy earthworks and wooden blockhouses with 20-30 artillery pieces, for four days. Twenty-four pound cannon balls, red hot 12 pounders, mortar shells and fragmentation bombs rain down on the fort sending deadly iron and wood splinter fragments in all directions. Over the duration of the siege, thousands of such iron missiles will pound the fort and yet cause surprisingly little injury.

Six days later, reinforcements under Brigadier-General Green Clay arrive in the fort and although the buildings and earthworks have been badly mauled, the American flag still flies and the garrison has held tight. So the siege is lifted and the British withdraw and return northward into Ontario to the disappointment of their Indian allies under Chief Tecumseh, who had been waiting to take the fort and enjoy another "Frenchtown" massacre.

Two months later, the British Army makes another attempt to take the fort—which also fails.

Today, you can wander around this historic eight acre stockade overlooking the Maumee River, peer into the gloomy interiors of the log blockhouses and cast your mind back to the heroes who held this fort against a far superior force. Guides in period costume explain the actions which took place, and demonstrate some of the crafts of the time. Exhibits illustrate the 1812 War.

See phone, hours, and details on page 48.

Escape Routes - The Old Road to Florida: By now, you will have noticed that our maps show not only the I-75, but parallel side roads so that should the traffic become heavy ahead, you know how and where to get off the interstate to bypass potential problems.

Most of these "escape" routes follow the traditional north-south route used by Florida snowbirds long before I-75 was built. US 25–the "Old Dixie Highway"–in the North and US41 through the South.

During the interstate's construction, many lands and buildings were expropriated to make way for the "super slab." Some survived physically but died as business disappeared. Later on when we reach exit 29 in Kentucky, I'll explain how a local motel owner took advantage of this situation to start the world's first "fast food" business.

OH Mile 186 - RWIS: I bet you thought that the I-75 road surface beneath your wheels was just that - a road surface. Not any more! In this section of Ohio, in sections north of Cincinnati and on Atlanta's I-75 in Georgia, the road surface acts as part of a giant input device which feeds information to traffic computers. Wire loops in the road record information and devices beside the road (see the microwave tripods at mile marker 105) send other types of data to a central comput-

Money Saving Tip

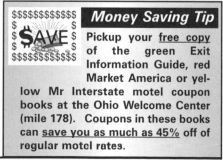

Pickup your free copy of the green Exit Information Guide, red Market America or yellow Mr Interstate motel coupon books at the Ohio Welcome Center (mile 178). Coupons in these books can save you as much as 45% off of regular motel rates.

er. This is all part of Ohio's multi million dollar Traffic Information System (OTIS).

In fact, you are just about to pass one of the input devices at mile marker 186. The pole with the weather vane and wind cups (known as an anemometer) in the median strip and the coils of wire you've just passed over are gathering all sorts of information and sending it electronically to the Ohio Department of Transport's Road and Weather Information System (RWIS).

Now here's the amazing part. If you have a computer which can be hooked up to the internet (many people do today for sending and receiving electronic mail), you can connect your unit to the RWIS computer and get instant information about the road surface (dry, rain, ice, snow, etc), construction and the weather on Ohio's I-75. The World Wide Web address is a bit of a "mouthful" so enter it carefully and then save it (i.e., "bookmark" it) for future use:

http://webapp1.dot.state.oh.us/otis/otis_search.asp

By the way, if you missed the sensor at this mile marker, you have a chance to see another one in the median strip just after exit 168.

Speaking of hi-tech matters, I noticed a piece in the newspaper recently announcing that in the year 2002, automobile manufacturers will move away from the 12 volt car electrical system and start to use 36 volt batteries charged with 42 volt alternators. This change will provide the necessary power to keep up with the much larger demands on "on-board" electricity as we add more electronic devices - cell phone, faxes, navigational computers, etc. It will also have the added advantage of requiring smaller gauge wire to deliver power to individual components thereby greatly reducing the amount of copper (and weight) used in the 2002 vehicle. Further weight will be saved by having the alternator double as the starter motor.

Those of us old enough will remember when we shifted from 6 to 12v batteries, and from positive to negative chassis ground.

OH Exit 181 - BGSU: As we run southward, we pass the stadium and campus of Bowling Green State University. Founded in 1914, BGSU has developed into a major college campus of more than 100 buildings spread over 1,300 acres, and providing a diversity of programs to approximately 18,000 students.

OH Exit 178 - Ohio Welcome Centers: I always make a point of pulling into the Welcome Center at mile 178 to say hello to the knowledgeable counter staff of Marian, Blanca and Quinn. As Marian says, they have excellent information about Ohio's state parks . . . and of course, are fully briefed about any construction ahead.

If you are northbound, then you will have the pleasure of saying "hello" to Rose, Mary and Kate. They are our Bowling Green and Toledo experts.

OH Exits 167, 164 & 157 - Ancient Ridge Highway: As the ancient Lake Maumee slowly receded to existing lake levels, it left beach ridges and sand dunes which can still be seen. Since these were on high ground, the Indians used the ridges for their trails through areas such as the Black Swamp. Pioneers cut their paths on top of Indian tracks, and these eventually evolved into the early roads and then the highways of today. I-75 crosses three

Insider Tip
The Diner

Remember good old fashioned diners? Well we've found a classic for you, complete with neon signs, black & white checker patterns, streamlined chrome and glass brick walls, oval "porthole" windows . . . and of course, 1950's music.

Happy servers in red tops and black skirts move around the glitzy interior taking hamburgers, floats, and other treats to the red and black leatherette booths, while the Big Bopper sings "Chantilly Lace" in the background.

The menu is quite extensive with "light" food for those with special needs- soups, salads, regular entrees - all are very reasonably priced. The diner is open 24 hours and serves breakfast, lunch and dinner; it's a "real cool" find. ☎ 419-424-1661.

Take Findlay exit 159 and turn west and then right as if going to Cracker Barrel. You can't miss the diner.

highways which have been built on the backs of ancient Lake Maumee beach ridges–Route 18 at Exit 167, Route 613 at Exit 164, and Route 12 at Exit 157.

OH Exit 161 - I-75's Antique Roadshow: Those who watch this popular TV program will know that valuable treasures can still be found hiding among the bric-a-brac of antique malls and flea markets - and I-75 is particularly rich with such places.

To the right at this exit is Jeffrey's, Ohio's largest antique mall. Over 700 feet long (2 football fields end to end) and occupying 40,000 square feet. It is home to 300 dealers who are there from 10-6pm daily, year round.

And this year you can probably get that special "find" for an excellent bargain price. Last summer, Jeffrey's was very difficult to reach due to construction at exit 161, and I noticed that the number of cars parked outside the mall was much smaller than usual. This year, I suspect the dealers will be more than willing to bargain with low prices, to make up for a poor year.

OH Exit 157 - Findlay: This is not exactly on the I-75 but since so many people break their journey for an overnight stop at Findlay, I thought I would mention something that has fascinated me since I started writing *"Along the I-75"* in 1992.

At that time, because of an accident I was routed off I-75 and had to drive down County Road 220 which eventually runs into Findlay's Main Street. That's when I saw it! It's has to be the most grotesque and yet beautiful Victorian house in the world . . . best viewed in the evening as the sun is slowly sinking behind it in the west. A perfect Halloween property . . . go and judge for yourself.

The house was built in 1883 on part of a 300 acre farm by the Bigelow family and has only had three owners since. It has seven fireplaces and many of the original gas jets, including one on the staircase newel post shaped like a dragon, which breathes actual fire through its nostrils! The beautiful main staircase of carved butternut wood, curves up to to the second story in front of a magnificent stained glass window.

The *"House on the Hill"* is so impressive that master magician David Copperfield used it as a setting for his spectacular "burning house" illusion, in his 1995 TV special.

To find "my" house, take exit 159 east (Trenton Avenue) for 1 mile until you reach Main Street. Turn left at the lights and go north 1 mile until you reach the point just above the Bigelow Avenue traffic lights where Main Street changes from two lanes to one–the house is immediately to your left. Catch it silhouetted in front of a sinking sun and you'll never forget it.

Some other notes of interest about Findlay. It was originally founded when natural gas was discovered in the area during the 1800's. This period was known as the great Ohio Natural Gas Boom (no pun intended!).

Findlay also bills itself as the "Flag City, USA"—a "tip of the hat" to the patriotism of Findlay's citizens. A drive down Main Street in the summertime will attest to this since virtually every building is dressed with a flag or red, white and blue bunting.

Mile 150 - Foxtrot Delta Yankee: Just to the east of the I-75 at mile 150 is a round squat building with radio antennas on top. This is a signpost of sorts–an electronic signpost for aircraft called a VOR, or VHF Omnidirectional Range. It sits there transmitting its identification code, FDY in morse to anyone tuned into its navigation frequency.

Why does it do this? Just as interstates guide our car from city to city, aircraft are guided from place to place along invisible highways in the sky called, "airways." And just as interstates are given "I" numbers, airways are given "V" numbers, and their intersections are marked with VORs and other radio aids to navigation, to keep the aircraft on course.

For instance, if we were to travel

FINDLAY - *after James Findlay and a fort he built in this area during the 1812 war with Britain. Findlay later became the Mayor of Cincinnati for two terms and a Brigadier-General with the state militia.*

the major air-route from Toledo to Cincinnati, which over-flies the I-75 or just to its east for most of the journey, our flight plan would be as follows:

Take off at Toledo and join the airway **V47** at the **Victor-Whiskey-Victor** VOR - fly 30 miles to the **Foxtrot-Delta-Yankee** VOR (the one beside you at mile marker 150) - continue airway V47 for 42 miles to **Romeo-Oscar-Delta** VOR–and continue V47 for 82 miles to the **Charlie-Victor-Golf** VOR and Cincinnati's air traffic control zone.

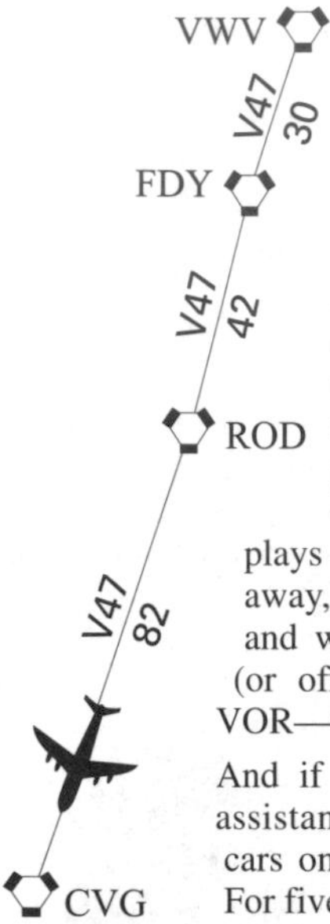

As the journey proceeds, the pilot tunes in the frequency of the next VOR on the plane's navigational equipment, and displays indicate the distance away, the bearing towards, and whether the plane is on (or off) course for the next VOR—"highways in the sky."

And if you wish this sort of assistance was available for cars on the ground, well it is. For five years now, I have been navigating the interstates with a special navigational computer in our car (called a GPS system - available at many marine supply stores for less than $500) which picks up radio signals from satellites in space and tells me exactly where I am, how fast I am going, which direction and how far away is my next destination point and when I will arrive there given the speed I am currently traveling.

I also use the Delorme/AAA Earthmate system described on the next page.

And now let's step back several hundred years in terms of navigation . . .

OH Mile 142 - Yesterday's Virginia: What a difference a few hundred years make. If it had been possible to travel the I-75 route southward in 1784, you would now be leaving Connecticut and entering Virginia ... and after leaving Virginia 300 miles south of here, you would enter the Carolinas before arriving at the Florida border.

According to a map drawn in 1784 by Abel Buell, the four Atlantic states of Connecticut, Virginia, North and South Carolina stretched westward from the sea to the Mississippi River. Territorial disputes led to much of this land being designated as *"Northwest Territory"* (present day Michigan, Indiana, Ohio, Kentucky and Tennessee) in 1787.

Thomas Jefferson, a Virginian Congressman at the time, proposed that the land be sliced

Insider Tip
Bistro on Main, Findlay

Several readers' letters led me to this lovely restaurant housed in an old Victorian building on Main Street in Findlay. From the moment you pass under the green awning and enter the warm interior with its mellow wooden booths, etched glass, old brickwork walls and tin ceiling, you know you are in for a treat. But it doesn't stop with the decor. The staff is friendly and welcoming . . . and the menu of Northern Italian food is out of this world.

Owner Alisa McPharon loves cooking and her passion is to please her patrons. If it's not on the menu, she suggests you ask for it and will even go as far as going out to get the ingredients if it isn't on hand. Alisa's father, Edward, will probably seat you when you arrive. The night we were there, Kathy and I enjoyed sweet bread with creamy honey butter, a salad with raspberry vinegarette dressing, baked penne followed with my favorite of all desserts, a magnificent creme caramel.

All entrees are reasonably priced and the menu is supported with an excellent wine list. The Bistro is open for lunch 11-2:30 and dinner 5-10:30, 6 days a week (closed Sunday) ☎ 419-425-4900.

Bistro on Main is easily reached from I-75 exit 157: travel east along W Main Cross St (Rt12) for 1.2 miles; turn right onto S. Main St and drive south 2 blocks. Bistro on your left at number 407. Say "hi" to Alisa and Edward for me when you arrive . . . and enjoy.

Hi Tech Mapping in your Car

Did you know that you can have mobile colored digital mapping for $150? But you'll need a laptop computer (with a CD-ROM drive) which will run in your car.

Delorme Mapping sells a product called "Earthmate." Its a tiny GPS receiver (about the size of a deck of cards) which plugs into your laptop's serial port. The product also includes a CD-ROM called Map n Go (produced in conjunction with the AAA) and together, this provides the software to display a colored map of your exact location—anywhere in the USA. It also plots your path as you move.

In cities, it even displays side streets — invaluable if you are in a strange area. You can even download up-to-date weather and construction information prepared by the AAA, from a special Delorme site on the Internet.

The tiny Earthmate receiver sits on your dashboard and receives signals from satellites through the windshield, so no special installation is needed beyond plugging it into your cigarette lighter and your laptop.

And here's the incredible part–once you have entered the start, finish and intermediate stopping points of your trip into the computer, it will actually talk to you and tell you when you are approaching a turn, and how many miles it is to the next stage of your journey. So there is no need to look at the colored map on the computer screen as you drive.

Best of all, the Earthmate and accompanying AAA Map'n'Go CD-ROM only costs $149.95 . . . an absolute bargain!!! You of course, provide the laptop. Give Delorme a phone call at 1-800-569-8313 if interested. You can order the device over the phone with VISA or MASTERCARD. It is also available from many AAA clubs.

into fourteen new states, with names such as Cherronesus, Assenesipia, Illinoia, Michigania and Polypotamia. Congress rejected this proposal however and granted statehood to Kentucky and Tennessee in 1792 and 1796, respectively. In 1803, the eastern part of the remaining Territory gained statehood — with the Iroquois Indian name for beauty–"Ohio."

OH Mile 142 - GROB: I bet you are wonder ing what the impressive GROB plant right beside Bluffton Airport, is all about. GROB (pronounce the "O" like in "sew") is a German company that services aircraft and does machine tooling.

OH Mile 141 - Wildflowers: If we were driving through here in the summertime, we could not help notice the masses of wildflowers along the banks and median of the I-75. Blues, mauves, pinks and whites. Like many other states, the Ohio Department of Transportation has an active wildflower planting program which provides motorists with a rainbow of colors at more than 200 sites throughout the State.

Begun in 1984, the Ohio program now annually plants more than 2,000 pounds of wildflower seed along the roadsides. In addition to providing carpets of red, blue and yellow flowers, the program helps preserve native vegetation and reduces costs along the way. But today is January, and the plants lie asleep beneath their blanket of snow, awaiting the warm breath of spring to awaken and bloom once again.

Between mile markers 137 and 138, the Ohio Department of Transport have placed a sign announcing their Tree Source program, which is a similar initiative—planting trees for Ohio.

OH Mile 133 - Lincoln Highway: On an overpass above us is US Highway 30–the Granddaddy of all of our super-roads–the old "Lincoln Highway." It is the route which taught the young 29 year old Dwight Eisenhower that America's roads were inadequate for heavy transportation (see "The National Interstate Defense System"–page 136). The first of the transcontinental roads, it was originally a Dutch settler's trail called the "Old Plank Road" starting near Philadelphia and linking with Indian paths

through Ohio and the mid-west. It connected with the Oregon Trail in the Platte Valley and then ran through the mountains and past Salt Lake for the Overland Stage Route into California.

In 1912, Carl Fisher, a visionary from Indianapolis, tried to raise funds to develop this route into the first proper road across the nation–but little progress was made. Eventually, Fisher's dream came true as the Federal Government began its freeway building program, and the Old Lincoln Highway became the US 30 and I-80, a continuous modern route from Philadelphia to San Francisco.

OH Exit 127 - US Plastics Corp: As you approach exit 127, you cannot miss the huge US Plastics Corporation plant on the right-hand side of the interstate. We decided to go in and have a closer look, and found ourselves in an incredible world of plastic. The US Plastic retail outlet covers 18,000 square feet and according to one of their sales staff, has the largest assortment of plastic goods in the world. If you have a plastic product need . . . no matter how unusual . . . you will probably find it here.

To reach US Plastic, go west at exit 127 and turn right on to Neubrecht Road. Run north parallel to the I-75 for ½ mile and US plastic is on your right. It's well sign-posted. Store hours are M-F, 8-5:00pm. ☎ 800-537-9724 or 419-228-2242.

OH Mile 124 - Lima's Kryptonite Room: A mile or so to the west of the I-75 is a manufacturing factory of General Dynamics Land Systems Division, the Lima Army Tank Plant. Here they build, unarguably the best army tank in the world—the famed M1 Abrams Main Battle Tank. During the Gulf War, this sophisticated machine proved itself with top honors—in fact, it was found to be unstoppable and virtually indestructible.

In one incident, the crew abandoned a tank mired in mud and were ordered to destroy it. A nearby M1 fired two 120mm rounds into it with no effect. Then the abandoned tank's ammunition was detonated. The end result was very little damage—in fact, the tank was

finally recovered and found to be operational with the exception that its gun sights needed to be realigned. The secret of this super strength armor is just beyond the I-75, and this brings us to Lima's "kryptonite" room.

In his excellent book, "Armored Cav," Tom Clancy takes us for a tour of the plant and gives insight into the M1 manufacturing processes. Based on a British innovation called Chobham armor, the M1's outer shell uses interleaved layers of high quality steel alloys and ceramic. But that's not all, using a deep secret "black art" process in the Kryptonite room, a layer of depleted uranium is somehow bound to the armor shell, more than doubling its effectiveness. Superman would be proud!

OH between Miles 116 and 91 - Ohio's Ice Age: A glance out of the side window at the snow laden landscape gives a sense of what it must have been like during the Pleistocene Ice Age. At that time, huge glaciers rumbled southward from Canada dragging boulders, rocks and other debris which slowly ground the Ohio countryside down under their massive weight. As the earth warmed and the glaciers melted and receded, the rubble was left in large ridges known as "end moraines" - gigantic piles of debris which were slowly assimilated into the surrounding landscape. The I-75 between Lima and Piqua is rich with such moraines–a good view of a typical glacial moraine can be seen by looking behind your car and to the right (northward) at Mile 114.

OH Exit 111 - Neil Armstrong Air & Space Museum: If you are older than 35, I am sure you remember the hazy TV pictures on July 20, 1969, of Neil Armstrong climbing down the ladder of the Lunar Exploration Module, "Eagle," and saying–"That's one small step for a man; one giant leap for mankind." Neil Armstrong was the first human to set foot on the moon.

Neil was born and raised in Wapakoneta, just

LIMA - *(pronounced "lime-er") for Lima, Peru.*
WAPAKONETA - *possibly named after a Shawnee Chief.*

to the west of the I-75. Here he used to build model aircraft and work part time at the local pharmacy.

Today, there is a magnificent museum just to the west of I-75, to honor his achievements and showcase exhibits from America's space program. Built by the state of Ohio, the museum is housed in the low gray concrete building that looks like it has a white golf ball on top. Inside, there are seven galleries devoted to the history of space exploration. Exhibits include moon rock and meteorite samples, rocket engines, space suits, actual space rockets and spacecraft.

A special display records the early days of space exploration, including many personal items and Russian space artifacts.

Aspiring astronauts can try their hand at the new space shuttle landing simulator. This unit uses actual computer programs designed to help train the shuttle crew. After a short training session, you take over the controls and have command of the shuttle on its final approach.

The Neil Armstrong Air and Space Museum is very easy to find. Simply take exit 111 west; turn right at the first road and you are in the museum parking area. The museum is open from March to November, Mon-Sat 9:30-5pm; Sun, noon-5pm. Closed major holidays. Admission for adults/seniors/children is $5/$4.50/$1.25. ☎ 800-282-5393 or 419-738-8811.

Before leaving this area, I must share one of my favorite Neil Armstrong stories with you. As he started to climb the ladder of the Lunar Landing Module and leave the surface of the moon, NASA flight controllers noticed that he looked up towards Earth and said, "Good luck, Mr. Gorski."

For years, nobody knew what he meant although he was questioned about it during many of his press interviews. Many thought it might have something to do with the Soviet space program, although nobody knew of an astronaut named "Gorski."

Several years ago, the story was revealed. When Armstrong was a young lad growing up in Wapakoneta, a family called Gorski lived next door.

One day, he accidentally hit a baseball into the Gorski's back garden. As he jumped the fence to retrieve the ball, he heard Mrs. Gorski's voice raised in argument, "Sex . . . sex? I'll give you sex when the kid next door walks on the moon!"

OH between mile 105 & 101 - RTMS: Do you remember the days when traffic on a road was counted by means of a rubber hose clamped across the road surface? The wheels of a car running over the hose caused air compression which operated a mechanical counter in a control box at the roadside. Those days have certainly changed.

Along this section of I-75, you'll see the latest in traffic counting technology - the tripod mounted Remote Traffic Microwave System, or RTMS. Now what is particularly clever about this system is that it sends a microwave beam across all the lanes (northbound and southbound) and it has the ability to determine which of the lanes the vehicle is traveling in and whether it is a large or small vehicle. RTMS can actually slice its measurement beam into 8 zones and count the types of vehicles according to the lane of travel.

Although used for a number of traffic statistic and control purposes, this particular group of sensors has been set up by the Civil Engineering Department of the University of Cincinnati, to test controls for freeway work zones.

PIQUA - *the French explorer derivation of the name of a local Shawnee Indian tribe, from which the famous Indian Chief Tecumseh rose to fame.*

TIPP CITY - *from the Tippecanoe River. Tippecanoe comes from the Potawatami Indian name (Kithtippecanumk) for the "Buffalo Fish" which populated the river.*

DAYTON - *named in 1796 after General Jonathan Dayton, a soldier in the Continental Army of 1776, and later a statesman. In 1795 he served as Speaker in the House of Representatives and between 1799-1805 was a U.S. Senator. During his senatorial term, he was implicated in the conspiracy of Aaron Burr.*

OH between Mile 104 & 99 - Lost River Teays: Ohio is rich in its ancient geological history. Between these mile markers, you are crossing the location of the lost River Teays. It was a major North American river of pre-glacial times and its valley was as much as 400 feet deep below the present position of the I-75. But the glaciers spelled its death. The rubble they dragged along blocked the course of the Teays, burying the valley–erasing it from the landscape forever.

OH Exit 102 - Jackson Center - Airstream Trailer tours: If you are an RVer (Recreational Vehicle owner, to those who aren't), you will probably be interested to note that the famous Airstream Trailer plant is located 7 miles east of I-75 at this exit, in the town of Jackson Center. Each weekday at 2 p.m. (year round except during their July plant closing) they give a free tour of their plant, and an opportunity to see how these beautiful classic aluminum trailers are built. ☎ 937-596-6111.

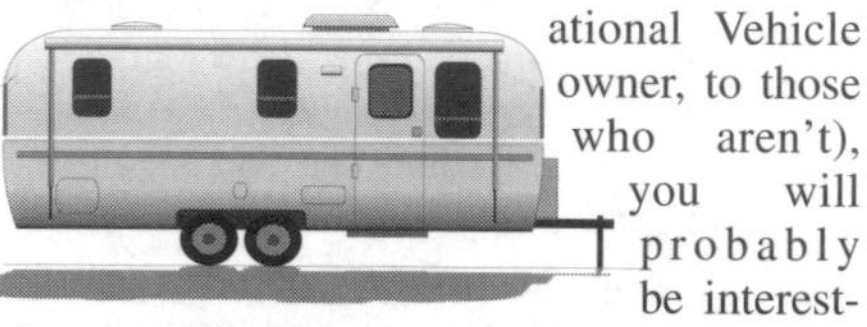

OH Mile 80 - Dayton Traffic: Now is the time to start thinking about the traffic as you approach Dayton, twenty miles ahead. Tune in to WONE-AM 980 "Air Watch" (or WTUE-FM 104.7) for the award winning traffic reports of Major Dick Hale–"The Dixter"–he'll keep you rolling.

OH Exit 73 - Victorian Town of Troy: Tired of the freeway? You might like to take this small detour through the very pretty town of Troy. Built on the banks of the Great Miami River in 1807, Troy has much to offer in the way of interesting architecture. In fact, some of the homes have been lived in for more than 150 years. The focal point is the Troy Public Square where routes 41 and 55 intersect. Here you will find many historical buildings listed on the National Register of Historical Places, such as the lovely red brick Dye building, fronted with the fountain and flower beds.

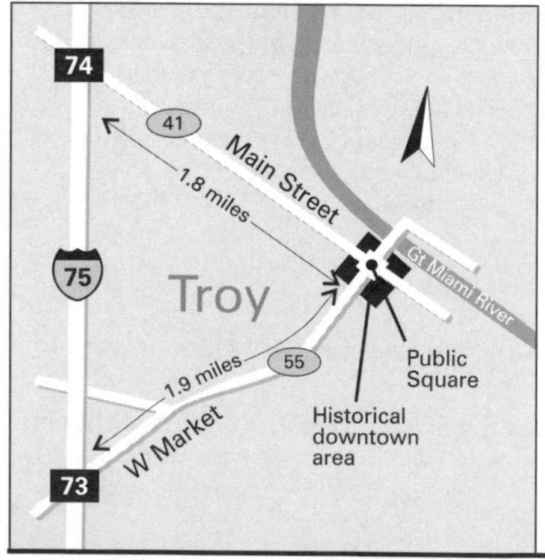

The Miami County Visitors Bureau is located at 405 SW Public Square, Suite 272 ☎ 800-348-8993; pick up their map of the downtown area . . . and stroll around for a while.

Mile 57 - Dayton: As we negotiate the traffic of Dayton's freeway on our journey south, we give little thought to the huge role this Ohio city played in the world of aviation. And yet, it was here just west of the I-75 that the whole concept of powered flight was born—in the printing and bicycle repair shop of Orville and Wilbur Wright. A few miles to the east of the interstate is the USAF Museum which contains the largest collection of military aircraft (ancient and modern) anywhere in the world, and finally, a few miles down the I-75 is an airport from which a replica of the Wright Brothers' original design is still flown. Let's spend a few minutes off the interstate to visit some of these fascinating places.

OH Exit 58 (northbound-54C) - USAF Museum (map on page 49): You must visit this awesome museum if you have any interest in man-made flight. Nearly 300 military aircraft and missiles fill three halls, and range from very early "string and paper" efforts such as the Wright Flyer and Bleriot plane from 1909, to the most modern non-secret and experimental aircraft around. Some exhibits that particularly caught my interest were the original Wright wind tunnel, a space suit made by Litton in 1955 and the F-117 angular *Nighthawk* stealth fighter of Gulf War fame.

Among the technology on display in the Modern Flight Hanger is the awesome XB-70 *Valkyrie* experimental Mach 3 bomber with its long overhanging nose and cockpit. It looks so secret and yet it was rolled out 32 years ago in 1966; it makes you wonder what they are flying now that they **cannot** display?

In the Air Power Gallery you will find several exhibits which will make you stop and think about how fragile life was during the "Cold War" period. Atomic and thermonuclear bomb casings–about the size of a

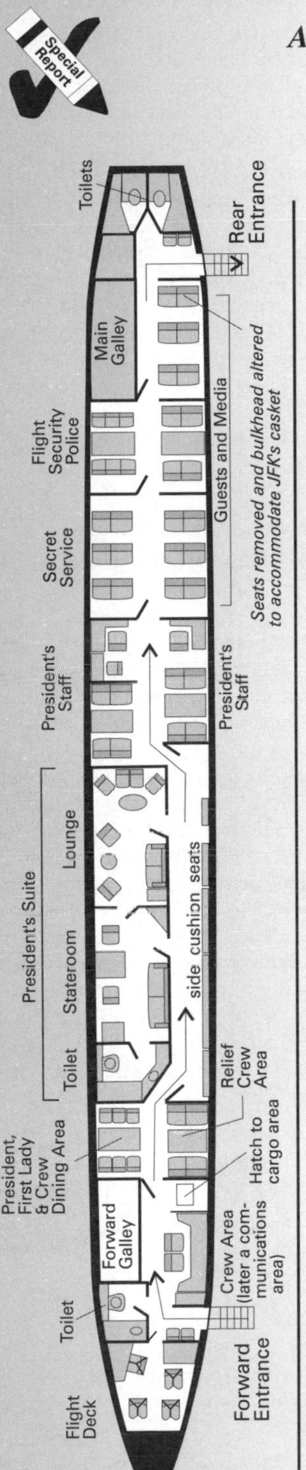

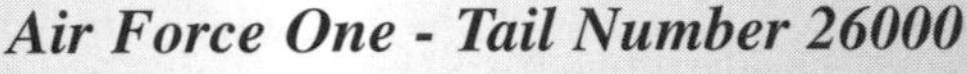

Air Force One - Tail Number 26000

"Wright-Patterson, this is Sam 26000." This is the air traffic message which heralded the arrival of one of the nation's most famous aircraft to the USAF Base at Dayton, in 1998.

Boeing 707(Air Force designation C-137C), number 26000 was *"Air Force One"* for Presidents Kennedy, Johnson, Nixon from 1962 to 1973 . . . and on one occasion when his official airplane was unavailable, President Clinton. This aircraft took Kennedy to Dallas in November, 1963 and returned his body to Washington, DC., following his assassination. Sections of the bulkhead at the rear entrance (opposite the main galley) had to be cut away so that Kennedy's casket could be carried into the plane and set on the floor in the rear seating area. Mrs. Kennedy stayed with her husband for the trip back, sleeping on the floor beside him. On that fateful day, Johnson was sworn in as the 36th President in the main cabin area as 26000 sat on the ground at Love Field, Dallas.

In later service, Number 26000 carried Nixon to meet the Apollo 11 crew after their trip to the moon (1970), took Henry Kissinger to Paris for secret meetings with the North Vietnamese and conveyed Nixon on his historic "journey for peace" to China (1972). In 1981, 26000 transported former Presidents Nixon, Ford and Carter to Cairo for the funeral of Anwar Sadat, and flew Britain's Queen Elizabeth to the West Coast during her 1983 visit to the USA.

Presidential aircraft are proudly flown by the 89th Airlift Wing of the USAF. The aircraft are only designated *"Air Force One"* if the President are actually on board–otherwise, a code name and the tail number is used. While on Presidential service, 26000 carried two complete flight crews and could accommodate a maximum of 60 staff and guests. She can fly at 604 mph and has a cruising range of 6,000 miles.

Some interesting notes about 26000 as *"Air Force One."* Originally the color scheme was silver. Jacqueline Kennedy suggested the distinctive robin egg blue color scheme which is still in use today in modified form.

President Kennedy liked to board by the rear door; Johnson and Nixon boarded via the front door.

Johnson substantially altered the layout. Solid bulkheads were replaced with clear material so Johnson could see and address all who were on board; he also had a desk and chairs which could be raised or lowered electrically so he could sit higher than those he was meeting. The current presidential suite was moved to the center of the airframe in 1983.

large office desk–give a new meaning to "do not touch."

Don't miss the Presidential Aircraft Hanger, and in particular, Boeing 707, tail #26000. This was the jet airliner which served Presidents Kennedy, Johnson and Nixon as Air Force One (see Special Report on page 75).

Number 26000 is open for public display and you may actual walk through the cabins which have been restored to the configuration used during President Kennedy's time. As soon as you arrive at the Museum, pick up your free pass from the information desk so you can drive your car over to the Presidential Aircraft Hangar, where you may also see President Roosevelt's C-54 "Sacred Cow," President Truman's VC-118 "Independence," and President Eisenhower's VC-121 "Columbine III."

New exhibits this year include the Holocaust exhibit, Berlin Airlift and a diorama of WWII Berlin bomb ruins.

Chillingly, you enter the Holocaust exhibit under the stark wrought iron sign - *"Arbeit Macht Frei"* meaning *"Work Brings Freedom."* Nazi Rudolph Hess required that these words be installed over the entrance gates of Auschwitz, and other concentration camps. Beyond is a very rare concentration camp uniform, which was worn by prisoner 114600 Moritz Bomstein.

Nearby, a display case contains an old violin, and with it a rather poignant story. In November, 1938, 15 year old Robert Kahn of Manheim, Germany, was forced to stand on the balcony of his home and play Nazi songs on it while his family was rounded up for shipment to concentration camp. Robert managed to escape, but only after he hid the violin inside the building.

He reached the USA and joined the army where he was able to serve in the forces which helped liberate Europe. After the war, he recovered the violin which had survived the bombings in its hiding place.

In another section of the building, a diorama shows bomb ruins in Berlin. Amidst the rubble lies a golden eagle with its outspread wings - the icon of the Nazi party. This eagle was one of two which stood either side of the entrance to Hitler's office in the Reich Chancellery. Several feet away, is a battered bust of Hitler, with bullet holes through the head.

Elsewhere, you will find one of the Defense Support Program"Star Wars" satellites which help form part of a protective umbrella over North America, and the very latest of fighter technology, the F22 Raptor.

But a visit to the USAF Museum is more than just wandering around and admiring the hardware. I urge you to make time for the emotional experience of the IMAX theater. With its high six-story, wide screen, you feel as if you are actually strapped into the cockpit and it is here that you can come the closest to experiencing flight as you ride with the Blue Angels or glide over the glorious peaks of Hawaii.

See phone, hours, and details on page 49.

OH Mile 52.5 - The Wright Cycle Company (map on page 49): Just a third of a mile to the west is one of the most important historical landmarks in the World–the Wright brothers bicycle and printing shop. It's hard to imagine that this 19th century building on a quiet side street was the birthplace of aviation as we know it today. And yet it was here that Orville and his brother, Wilbur, ran their printing and bicycle repair business, and by the evening's oil-lamp light developed the concepts of powered flight. It was here at 22 South Williams Street - the fourth of five locations for the brother's cycle business - that they read about some flying experiments in Germany. They felt that the concepts were wrong, and built a wind tunnel on the premises to test out a different theory which eventually led to their famous Wright Flying Machine, and the inaugural flight at Kitty Hawk, NC, in 1903.

As we left this "cradle of flight," it was eerie to hear the rumble of a jet far overhead as a modern airliner climbed away from earth and up into the stratosphere.

The Wright Bicycle Shop is only half a mile west (3 minutes) of the southbound I-75 at exit 53A, and the return is easy (see map). See phone, hours, and details on page 49.

OH Exit 52 - Shawnee War Parties: Two hundred years ago you would be in the heart of Indian country, for the main Shawnee camp of Old Chillicothe lay on the banks of the Little Miami River, just thirteen miles to the east. The Shawnee were the most fierce of the Ohio tribes. Their war parties ranged the countryside down to the mountains in South Kentucky (Cherokee lands), often attacking the white settlers who were invading their lands from the east.

In 1778, the famous frontiersman Daniel Boone was captured by the Shawnee Chief Black Fish, and for four months lived as a member of the Shawnee tribe at Little Chillicothe. Learning of an Indian plan to attack his home at Boonesborough (just east of exit 95 in Kentucky) he escaped and made his way through the country alongside today's I-75 route, in time to warn the Boonesborough settlers.

OH Exit 38 - Flier B: A final link with Wilbur and Orville Wright lies several miles off the I-75 to the east—an actual flying reproduction of the Wright Flier B–the military version used by the US Army Signal Corp in 1911. This was the first mass produced powered airplane, and was build by The Wright Company between 1910 and 1911.

The Flyer is housed in a look-alike Wright hangar, where visitors are invited to examine it as closely as they like. It is certainly an unusual experience to approach the "Wright Bros." hanger walking through a group of Cesnas and other modern planes, to see the Wright Bi-plane poking its nose out through the hanger door.

For those who like statistics, Flier "B" has a wingspan of 40'11"; height 10'8"; length 31'11" and weighs 3,400lbs. Her take-off speed is 41mph and she can cruise at a maximum altitude of 2,500 feet above sea level at 60 mph. She has a flight endurance of 2 hours and a range of 100 miles. Her landing speed is 45 mph.

She is driven by a 225hp Lycoming engine (H10-360 F1AD) with belt drives to her two rear-facing wooden propellers

The flyer is based at the Dayton-Wright Bros. Airport, which is reached by taking I-75 exit 38. Go east 2 miles on Rt 73 to Rt 741 (Springboro Pike). Turn left and go north on Rt 741 for 2.8 miles—the airport is on your right. Hours: Tues, Thurs and Sat 9-2:30; admission free. ☎ 937-885-2327.

Incidentally, you can take an actual flight in the flier for $125! For this, you get a pre-flight briefing, a certificate attesting to your "historical" flight, and a special exclusive memento tie–phone for times and details.

OH Exit 38 - Crafter's Heaven: It would probably be easier to list handcrafts that are not carried–leathercraft and woodworking, for instance–but supplies for virtually everything else are carried in this huge warehouse retail outlet just west of the interstate. Pickup a free catalog just inside the door . . . and if you are reading it in your motel room that evening and find something else you need–they have a mail order service.

Factory Direct Craft Supply is at 315 Conover Drive. As you leave I-75, turn west onto State Route 73 and then immediately left onto Conover Drive. The craft supply outlet is halfway down on the right. Hrs: M-F 10-7; Sat 10 6; Sun 11-5. ☎ 1-800-252-5223 or 513-743-5855.

OH Exit 29 - Flea Market Paradise: If you enjoy flea markets, then the north-east and north-west sides of exit 29 must be pure paradise. Trader's World (to the east) and Turtle Creek (to the west) markets are open on weekends from 9-5pm, all year round.

Exit 29 - Tim Horton: Canadian travelers will be delighted to find one of the first I-75 outlets of their favorite Tim Horton coffee and doughnut chain, right here just east of exit 29. Named after Toronto Maple Leaf hockey star, the Tim Horton chain was purchased by Wendy's International in 1995–so of course, the Tim Horton is right alongside the Wendy's!

Mile 28 - Welcome Center: Need a friend miles from home? Then go on in and say "hi" to Joyce, Sheila or Beverly at the southbound welcome center.

On the northbound side of the road, Rene, Serena and Jerome will also help you on your way.

They all know this book and love chatting with my readers.

OH Mile 24 - Voice of America (VOA): To

MIAMISBURG - *after the Miami Indians, a tribe of the Algonquins who lived in this area, until driven by settlers westward to Indiana, Kansas and Oklahoma. The name probably originates from the Objibway word "Oumaumeg" meaning "People of the peninsular."*

the east, the tall towers and curtain antenna arrays of the former VOA transmitter station have now gone. For more than 50 years, this station has been transmitting its signals for the Voice of America and U.S. Armed Forces Radio & Television Service . . but no more. Government budget cuts and the end of the "cold war" have seen the demise of the facility.

During WWII, the station played a major part beaming messages of freedom into the heart of Nazi Europe. As you drive by now, it's strange to think that this tiny parcel of land east of I-75 once incensed Hitler so much that he screamed about *"the propagandists in Cincinnati."*

OH Mile 25 - Cincinnati's Traffic System: If you have a phone in the car, now is the time to dial 211 (Mon-Fri) for Cincinnati's ARTMIS Advanced Regional Traffic Management & Information System, and decide whether to take the bypass (coming up in nine miles) or continue on I-75 through the city.

If you don't have a cell phone, don't despair, an electronic overhead sign just past mile marker 20 will help you with your decision. You can also reach the same service by dialing 211 from a touch tone phone within the area or 513-333-3333.

After dialing 211, follow the prompts. Dial 751* (when prompted) to get information covering the traffic situation from mile 22 down to mile 4. Also dial 275* for the bypass. All traffic information is updated hourly.

OH Exit 21 - Hidden Treasures: There is a neat little antique shop east on Cin-Day Road at this exit. Less than half-a-mile from I-75, you'll find it on your right hand side as you enter the quaint town of West Chester. It's a pleasant change from the sprawling antique malls along the freeway. Hrs: Tu-Sa, 11-7, Sun, 1-6. ☎ 517-779-9908

OH Miles 20 to 14 - Ohio's Tropical Sea: You are now traveling across the ancient bed of a warm, shallow tropical sea (Paleozoic Era–Ordovician Period–400 million years ago). The shale and limestone outcrops along the I-75 are rich in fossils, particularly around Miles 20.5 to 19.5 and 14.8 to 14.3. As the teeming sea-life of small animals (examples, trilobites, primitive fish) and other life forms died, they settled to the bottom and slowly over millions of years, became the familiar layered (geologists call it sedimentary) rock that you see in exposed roadside rock cuts on your journey down the I-75. Often, the ancient animals' hard shells and skeletons remained intact in the rock, creating the fossils of today.

OH Exit 16 (Southbound) - RVs and Cincinnati: This isn't sign posted very well but if you are driving an RV or pulling a trailer, unless you are intending to stop in Cincinnati you must now take the bypass (I-275 East) at exit 16. This is a new rule to minimize the "heavy vehicle" traffic using Covington Hill in Kentucky.

OH Exit 14 - Sneaky Pete: As you approach the concrete pillars of the overpass by exit 14, watch your speed *very* carefully. The pillar near the slow lane soft shoulder is a favorite hiding place for radar equipped patrol cars. The officers park their cars hidden behind the pillar and beam their radar guns at the oncoming southbound traffic as it leaves the 65 mph zone and enters the 55 mph speed reduction.

OH Exit 4 - Doris Mary Ann Von Kappelhoffen: Doris Kappelhoffen was born in 1924, about four miles east of here. She loved to dance and wanted to become a ballerina. In 1936, she and her dance partner Jerry Doherty won a local competition which enabled them to go to Hollywood. When she returned to Cincinnati in 1938, she was seriously injured when a train hit the car she was riding in, severely damaging her right leg. Any thoughts of a dancing career were over so her mother suggested she take singing lessons and this led to a singing engagement on Cincinnati radio station WLW-AM.

Local band leader Barney Rapp "discovered" her and the first song she sang with his band was "Day after day." Rapp suggested that if she was going to have a show career that "Kappelhoffen" would not be a great draw on a marque. So remembering her first "professional" song, she changed her surname to "Day."

CINCINNATI - *settled in 1788 and called Losantiville, the Governor of the then Northwest Territories renamed the village after a Revolutionary War officers' association called the Society of Cincinnatus, which in turn was named after Lucius Quinctius Cincinnatus (519 B.C.), a Roman dictator and soldier who was also a keen farmer.*

The rest is history. Doris Day went on to tour with Les Brown's band for $75 per week, and gained the fame which moved her back to Hollywood and the world of movies. "Que sera, sera - whatever will be will be."

Mile 0 - Oprah's *"Beloved"*: Speaking of movies, have you seen the intensely powerful Oprah Winfrey movie, *"Beloved?"* If you have you will know the non-supernatural part of the story is based on a true incident involving a party of escaped slaves. But did you know that the slaves were owned by a man whose estate was at Richwood in Kentucky (I-75, exit 175) and that the escape took place across the great Ohio river, just to the east of here.

An historical marker on the south bank of the river records the event:

> *"On a snowy night in January, 1856, seventy slaves fled at the foot of Main Street* (in Covington, Kentucky) across the frozen Ohio River. A Margaret Garner was in the group. When arrested in Ohio, she killed her little daughter rather than see her returned to slavery. This much publicized slave capture became the focus of national attention because it involved the issues of Federal and State authority"*

**Editor's note: see map on page 50*

This incident happened 143 years ago, eight years before the start of the Civil War. Here is the story behind the escape.

A 22 year old slave called Margaret or Peggy Garner (Oprah Winfrey's Sethe in the film, "Beloved") worked in the cookhouse of owner Archibald Gaines' estate, Maplewood in Richwood, Kentucky. Rather than remain in bondage, Margaret decided to escape to the "free" state of Ohio.

Accordingly, Margaret and her husband, Robert, gathered their four children and met with twelve others at the Richwood Presbyterian Church, where they used a large sled drawn by two horses to gallop through the snowy night, northward to Covington. Here they abandoned the sled and crossed the frozen Ohio on foot.

The Garners sought the "safe" house of a former slave, Kite. This was their undoing since the slave owners were in hot pursuit and quickly discovered that the Garners were hiding at the Kite home (the other slaves went elsewhere and were able to escape via the "Underground Railroad" to Canada. Surrounded by a posse of men, a battle commenced at the Kite home during which one of the deputies was shot. The door was broken down and seeing there was no escape, Margaret took a knife and killed her youngest daughter, Mary, so she would never have to suffer the horrors of slavery.

The trial that followed raised many legal and moral questions about slave ownership since one of the key arguments was that Margaret and her children were not slaves, but free due to earlier circumstances. Sadly however, the Court's decision was to return her to slavery in Kentucky. She died in 1858, still a slave.

KY Exit 192 - Mainstrasse (map on page 50): Just across the Ohio River in Covington, North Kentucky, lies a rather unusual community—Mainstrasse Village. Covering approximately five blocks, this restored 19th century German neighborhood includes parks, antique, art and craft shops, and of course, restaurants serving fine Bavarian food such as sauerbraten, schnitzel and wurst, washed down with German lager.

The village people are proud of their heritage and offer old world service. Summer or winter, its fun to wander the cobbled walkways and visit establishments such as the Linden Noll Gift Haus or Mainstrasse Arts. Or sit under the trees near the Goose Girl fountain watching others go by while listening to the glockenspiel tower playing its 43 bell carillon in the nearby park.

If you are driving on the I-75 at lunch time, you might consider a quick detour to either the Mainstrasse Pub, the Strasse Haus or Wertheim's as a change from your normal fast food stop. Evening fine dining is provided by Wertheim's Gasthaus Zur Linde, whose menu specializes on German food but also caters to other tastes.

To find Mainstrasse from the southbound I-75, immediately after crossing the Ohio River

KENTUCKY - *a Wyandot Indian name "Kentahteh" meaning "land of tomorrow," or as early settlers used to call it - Caintuck.*

Insider Tip
Best BBQ Ribs on the I-75

We are almost reluctant to share this one since it is so good and we just don't want it spoiled with success. In our opinion the best BBQ ribs on the I-75 between Detroit and Florida are at Burbank's Real Bar-B-Que, Florence, Kentucky (1/2 mile east of I-75 in the Oldenberg Brewery complex, at exit 186, 7 miles south of Cincinnati).

The ribs are *"out of this world"* with your choice of their homemade Texan BBQ sauces...oh yes, and the prices are very reasonable.

Since mentioning this gem in our first I-75 book, many readers have written to me agreeing that this is well worth the stop. After your meal, choose your favorite BBQ sauce and take a bottle along with you. ☎606-341-2806 Hrs: 11-10:30, Fri/Sat, midnight.

(Brent Spence Bridge), take exit 192 and turn left onto Fifth Avenue; follow map on page 50. I suggest you turn right at Philadelphia Street and visit the Visitors' Center which you will find within the park at Philadelphia and Sixth Street.

KY Mile 192 - Covington Hill: If you are prone to a "lead foot" and frustrated after the slow traffic of downtown Cincinnati, take our advice and do not speed up (or down) the Covington Hill—also known locally as, "Death Hill" for very good reasons. It is famous for its aggressive speed control policing.

Incidentally, you'll bc pleased to know that the number of trucks using Covington Hill has been greatly reduced. All "through 18 wheelers" must now use the I-275 bypass.

KY Exit 185 (Northbound) - RVs and Cincinnati: This isn't sign posted very well but if you are driving an RV or pulling a trailer, unless you are intending to stop in Cincinnati you must now take the bypass (I-275 East) at exit 185. This is a new rule to minimize the "heavy vehicle" traffic using Covington Hill in Kentucky.

KY Exit 186 - Oldenberg Brewery: About half a mile to the east on Buttermilk Parkway is a micro brewery and brewing museum you can tour. Oldenberg brews traditional non-pasteurized beers using barley and wheat. After the tour, tastings are conducted in the brewery hall, giving you an opportunity to taste their wares (charge for tastings).

Insider Tip
The Gatehouse

Renowned locally for its prime rib , the Gatehouse Bar & Restaurant is a castle complete with a moat!. Meals are a little more expensive than Burbank's (entrees run from $16.95-$21.95, but they include a salad bar, and the quality is excellent.

To find the Gatehouse, follow the directions in the Burbanks Insider Tip. Where the driveway curves back towards the Oldenburg Brewery and Burbanks, continue straight on into the Drawbridge Estates, as if you are going back to I-75. The Gatehouse will be ahead of you. Hrs: 5:30pm-10:00 ☎ 606-341-3800

To make this a complete dining experience, visit either "Burbanks" or the Gatehouse, two of our favorite restaurants which are on the premises (see Insider Tips above).

Oldenberg Brewery is open all year, 7 days a week, 10-5, tours every hr. ☎ 606-341-2802.

KY Mile 175 - Richwood: It's hard to imagine that this tranquil Kentucky countryside was once a stronghold of slavery. And yet, 143 years ago, this is where the sad story of Margaret Garner's escape started. The Richwood Presbyterian Church where the slaves met on the night of the escape is still here. The Maplewood Plantation where Margaret was kept in bondage was rediscovered by Ohio writer, Joanne Caputo at 1154 Richwood Road. The main plantation house burned to the ground in the 1900's but the

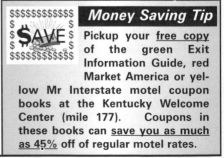

Money Saving Tip

Pickup your <u>free copy</u> of the green Exit Information Guide, red Market America or yellow Mr Interstate motel coupon books at the Kentucky Welcome Center (mile 177). Coupons in these books can <u>save you as much as 45%</u> off of regular motel rates.

Insider Tip
Great Food! - Country Grill

Just a few seconds west of I-75 at exit 159, is a clean, family run restaurant which makes a very pleasant change to the larger chain "food factories." It is easy to spot the Country Grill as you come off the interstate. It sits on the side of a small hill (which gives its dining room a nice panoramic view of the lush Kentucky countryside), on the south (your left) side of the road. Ample parking is provided both in front of the restaurant and in a lower level (inc. RV parking) just below the building.

All meals are prepared on the premises from fresh ingredients by Chef Mark. Table service is wonderful; Barbara and John are the owners and take a close interest in their guests. They will probably seat you at your table.

The Country Grill is a rare find—I know you will enjoy it—we do and heartily recommend it. Hrs: 8-10, ☎ 606-824-6000

cookhouse (where Margaret worked) and the smokehouse still exist.

KY Mile 169 - Advantage-75: Are you curious about the "Advantage-75" signs that you see at truck weigh stations? This is an electronic scanning system which uses computers to automatically identify the equipment rolling through the weigh scales. Introduced in 1994 at a cost of $150,000 per weigh station, it is now speeding trucks through the documentation process at many of the I-75 weigh stations.

This is the beginning of the elimination of interstate weigh stations. Eventually, all trucks will carry mini-transmitters (transponders) similar to those used by aircraft for traffic control purposes. A truck will roll down the I-75 without slowing down, pass a road side scanner which reads the truck's load and destination data, drive over an electronic plate in the right lane road surface to record the load's weight, and get a green signal in their cab which indicates that they may continue—or a red signal to pull over for an inspection. Electronic sensors will monitor the other lanes to ensure that no trucks bypass this invisible data collection system.

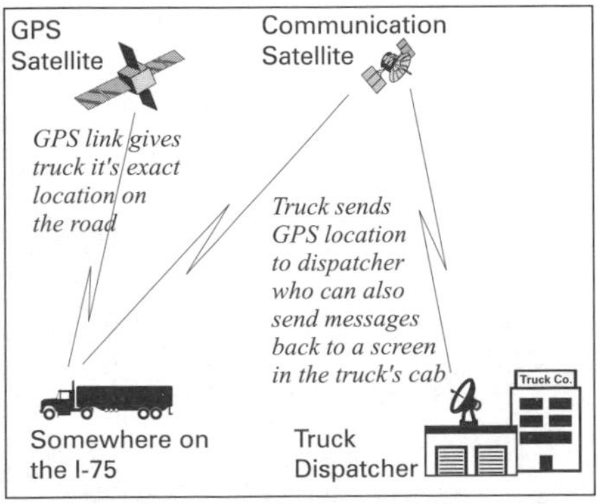

GPS Satellite

Communication Satellite

GPS link gives truck it's exact location on the road

Truck sends GPS location to dispatcher who can also send messages back to a screen in the truck's cab

Truck Co.

Somewhere on the I-75

Truck Dispatcher

Another technology used in many truck fleets today is the global position satellite (GPS) system which constantly records the exact location of a truck anywhere in North America. This information is uploaded from the truck to a satellite in space (look for the flat round antenna usually on the cab roof) and then down to the truck company's central dispatch computer. This means that head office knows exactly where each truck is located at any time, how fast it is going and in which direction. This information coupled with data about the load, enables truck dispatchers to reroute their vehicles to maximize their transportation efficiency. Oh yes, truck drivers are instructed of such changes "on the roll" by a satellite pager system which gives them a visual message from their dispatcher right in their cab. No wonder, some companies are beginning to require a university degree for new truck drivers!

KY Exit 136 - Blue Grass: Sixty miles back we passed over the mighty Ohio River and into Kentucky. Is it possible that the air temperature is a mite warmer? Certainly there is no snow here as we drive through the gently rolling Kentucky countryside. The scenery is very pleasant, but try as we might, we cannot see any famous bluegrass–and yet it is supposed to be all around us–but the grass is distinctly green!

So what is Kentucky Bluegrass? It is a type of grass that grows lushly in the State's rich limestone soil. It is not really blue–it's green, but in the spring, Bluegrass develops bluish-purple buds that when seen from a distance in large fields provide a rich, blue cast blanket.

Nobody knows where it came from but early pioneers found it growing in abundance when they crossed the Appalachian Mountains in their wagons. They shipped it back east and soon traders began asking for the "blue grass seeds from Kentucky" ... and the name stuck.

KY Exit 129 - Toyota: Toyota Motor Manufacturing USA Visitor Center conducts public tours of its facilities where about 400,000 cars and 350,000 engines are made annually. After an introductory video, you are taken on a guided tram ride through the stamping, body welding and assembly shops. Here is your chance to watch robots at work!

Drive east from the I-75 towards the plant chimneys—you can't mistake them.

The plant's tours take place as follows:

June-August; Tues & Thurs; 8:30, 10, noon, 2 & 6 pm. Wed and Fri; noon and 2.

The plant is closed the first week in July.

Sept-May; Tues & Thurs; 8:30, 2 & 6 pm. Wed and Fri; 2pm only.

Reservations are necessary so phone ahead to get your tour times. Children must be at least 8 years old. ☎ 502-868-3027 or 1-800-866-4485.

KY Exit 126 - Georgetown (map on Page 51): Just to the west of I-75 at this exit is the pleasant community of Georgetown. If you have a few minutes to spare, a drive down and back up Main Street is well worthwhile (I-75 is easy to rejoin). Brick sidewalks, old-fashioned lamp posts and more than 100 buildings listed on the National Register of Historic Places make this short sidetrip a visit to a bygone era of America.

Incidentally, a historical marker at the west end of Main Street tells us that the first bourbon whiskey was made here. Named after Bourbon County, Georgetown founder Rev. Elijah Craig set up a still at the Royal Spring in 1789 and brewed the first batch of this potent potion. Ironically, Scott County (in which Georgetown lies) is dry (i.e. doesn't sell or serve spirits)!

KY Exit 120 - Kentucky Horse Park: Kentucky is famous for its horses and horse breeding, and Lexington is at the heart of horse country. If you have equine leanings (translation - horse lover) then you owe it to yourself to stop at the Kentucky Horse Park (exit 120, Iron Works Pike–go east for ¼ mile).

Here you will be welcomed by a statue of that most famous horse of all–Man O'War, who is buried at the park. The Visitor Center has a spectacular film presentation, "Thou Shalt Fly Without Wings." Journey through time and trace the history of horses from prehistoric to modern times, along the spiral ramp of the International Museum of the Horse.

Afterwards, take the park shuttle, horse-drawn carriage or horseback (in snowy winter, horse-drawn sleigh) and enjoy the beautiful Kentucky park with its many horse related activities. The park houses an educational department where students are trained in skills to enter careers in the horse industry, so there is always something going on.

The park is open from 9-5pm. There is a parking charge of $2. Apr to Oct–every day; Nov to Mar–open Wed to Sun. Admission: adult/senior/child (summer) $9.95/$9.45/ $4.95 (winter) $6.50/$6/$4.50. ☎ 800-568-8813 or 606-233-4303.

KY Exit 120 - Ironworks Pike: An interesting note of history here. This road got its name from the early 1800's transport route which ran from the Slate Creek Ironworks about 40 miles east of Lexington, to Frankfort on the Kentucky River. War materials from the Ironworks were carried along this

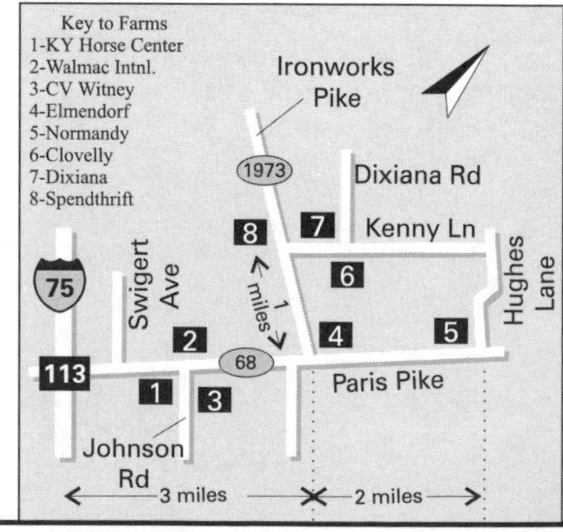

road for shipment by river down the Mississippi to Andrew Jackson in New Orleans during the War of 1812.

KY Exit 113 - A Scenic Diversion: If you have a little time on your hands and would like to see some of the lush Kentucky horse farm land close up, you might enjoy the drive eastward from this exit, along Paris Pike–route 68. Designated a "Scenic Route" you will travel past the brick walls and white fenced meadows of horse farms such as Walmac International, Bittersweet, Clovelly, C.V. Whitney, Elmendorf, Normandy, Spendthrift and Dixiana-Domino. Many of these farms have bred thoroughbred champions running in major events around the world, most notably in the USA and France. Man o' War's sire, Fair Play and dam, Mahubah, are buried on Normandy Farm. CV Whitney's Farm is often host to film stars, international business and political figures.

The drive takes you 3 miles to the junction of Rt 1973 (Ironworks Rd), a further 2 miles takes you to Hughes Lane where you turn left. Turn left again in one and three-quarter miles onto Kenny Lane and left again onto Ironworks Road in 2 miles. One mile down Ironworks Road brings you back to the Paris Pike, where you turn right to drive the 3 miles back to I-75. Total? Thirteen miles of wonderful Kentucky countryside–twenty minutes of pure pleasure.

If short of time, just drive the 3 miles to the junction of Rt 1973, carefully turn around and drive back to the interstate.

KY Exit 110 - Lexington Downtown area (map on page 50): One and a quarter miles south on Newtown Pike (route 922) will bring you to the Lexington downtown area. Lexington was a settlers' campsite in 1775 and yet had become a bustling commercial center within twenty five years. Turn onto West Main Street, bear right onto Vine (one way), cross Broadway, S Mill, Upper, Limestone and stop at the Visitor Center at Vine and Rose (301 E. Vine St; ☎ 800-845-3959 or 606-233-1221.

I suggest you pick up a map and a guide book here for there is lots to see and do in Lexington.

While at the Visitors Center, pick up a copy of "Bluegrass Country Driving Tour," which includes the "Lexington Walk & Bluegrass Country Driving Tour." It has some wonderful short tours in the countryside around you, including some alongside the I-75 in the direction you are traveling.

KY Exit 108 - Man O'War: Man O'War Boulevard is of course, named after the famous Kentucky thoroughbred which put many new records into the book. The horse was said to have had a 25 foot stride and was once clocked at 43 MPH during a workout. Lexington is thoroughbred horse country. The lush grass meadows growing on limestone soil make ideal horse grazing conditions. As you travel the I-75, the neat horse farms to the east with their trim plank fences–Kingston, Shandon, Winter Hill and Meadowcrest–are a delight to the eye. Check our I-75 maps–we have named them for you.

KY Exit 108 - Mega shopping? For many years, the land at this exit has been a horse farm. The farm has now been sold and the area is fast turning into THE mega shopping experience on I-75. Called Hamburg Pavilion, many "big box" stores have already opened here, anchored by a huge Meijer 24 hour superstore and Target. Barnes & Noble super bookstore is here (need another copy of this book? B&N have it in stock!) within just seconds of exit 108 . . . and so are other well known stores such as Office Max, Radio Shack, Old Navy, Garden Ridge, etc. A multi screen movie theatre (Regal Cinema) will open soon and with all sorts of new lodging accommodation opening across the road, this exit will probably become one of the favorite stop-over spots for the Florida bound "snowbird."

KY Mile 98 - Hawks: As we cross the Kentucky River, the road becomes more hilly for we are in the region known as the Kentucky Knobs. Geologists refer to this area as the Jesamine Dome, an area of sedimentary rock that was uplifted millions of years ago. You might see the occasional red fox as you drive through the countryside.

LEXINGTON - *named in 1775 after Lexington, Massachusetts, by a group of colonial hunters who camped close by after the first skirmish with British troops during the War of Independence.*

Two or three hawks glide above us, riding the air currents of the ridges, their sharp eyes focused on the ground looking for the tiny, almost imperceptible movement of a delectable field mouse or baby rabbit. Suddenly, one of them swoops down–sharp talons extended earthward– dropping like a stone. You look away knowing that once again a small animal has given its life to ensure that in death, life goes on. Such is Nature's food chain.

KY Exit 95 - Fort Boonesborough (map on page 51): Just five miles east (about an eight minute drive) along route 627 lies Fort Boonesborough–a reconstruction of the wooden fortified settlement built by Daniel Boone in 1775. As you wander around inside the wooden stockade you may visit the settlers in their period costumes and watch them make soap, spin wool, and practice many other frontier arts and crafts. Most of the products made at the fort can be purchased in the adjacent gift shop. It's a great way to learn more about the hard life of a pioneer.

In 1778, Boone escaped from an Indian village in Ohio (Little Chillicothe–Ohio exit 52) and returned here to warn the settlers of an impending Indian attack. With the help of the British Army, the Indians lay siege to this fort for ten days. Heavy rains and the strong defense by Boone and his men broke the siege. On the tenth day the Indians gave up, disappearing into the trees around the fort.

As you peer through the half opened gateway into the dappled sunlight of the still green forest beyond, its easy to imagine that the cawing sound you just heard was not a bird but one of a Shawnee war party signaling the band to move closer to the stockade walls.

If you are planning to visit White Hall (see next paragraph), you can save money by buying a combination ticket which covers both attractions.

See phone, hours, and details on page 51.

KY Exit 95 - White Hall (map on page 51): In the opposite direction just 1.9 miles (3½ minutes) to the west lies the famous White Hall. This magnificent Georgian and Italianate building was the home of Cassius Clay, one of Kentucky's most colorful and historical figures–a noted abolitionist, politician, publisher, Minister to Russia, and friend of Abraham Lincoln. White Hall is really two houses in one. The original Georgian building–Clermont–was built in 1798, by Clay's father, Green. In the 1860's while Clay was on service in Russia, his wife, Mary Jane supervised the construction of the second house, over the original Clermont building. The transformed building designed by prominent architects Thomas Lewinski and John McMurtry became known as White Hall.

KY Exit 90A - Richmond: Another attractive I-75 community which has managed to protect its 19th century heritage. Its downtown Main Street heritage area lies just over two miles east of the interstate, from this exit.

Route 169 (Tates Creek Road) runs west out of Richmond where in about 12 miles it reaches the Ohio River and the famous Valley View Car Ferry, Kentucky's oldest continuous business.

It's along this road that the famous pioneer and explorer, Christopher "Kit" Carson was born in a small log cabin beside Tates Creek,

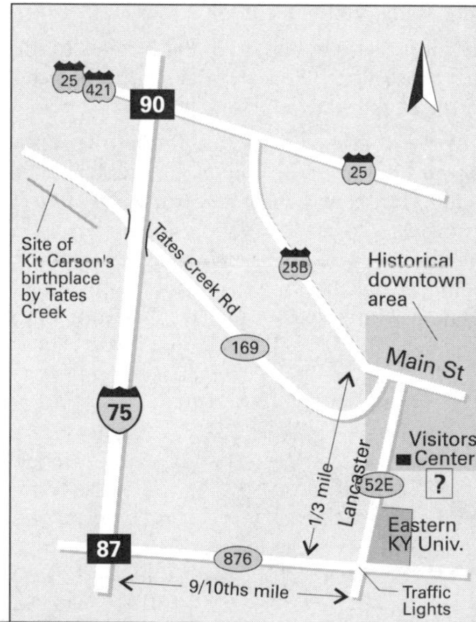

RICHMOND - *named by early settlers after the capital of Virginia, which in turn was named after Richmond, Surrey, England.*

on Christmas Eve, 1809. Kit Carson, went on to become a living legend as a frontiersman. His skill as a hunter and rifleman was thought by many to be second to none. The publication of his adventures during his 1842-1844 exploration of the West were widely read in the eastern cities and spurred many on to life on the new frontier.

Mile 86 - Sedimentary Rock: We pass through an interesting cut of stratified limestone–successive layers of sedimentation from an ancient tropical sea which have been heaved up by the Earth's colossal, mountain folding forces. In summer, this cut is particularly pretty–topped with stands of young lush trees and carpets of wildflowers.

KY Exit 76 - Berea (map on page 52): Literally seconds off the I-75, the small town of Berea just to the east is a hidden jewel that many drive by in their haste to reach Florida. If you enjoy crafts and antiques, make sure you plan an overnight stop here for Berea is exciting and vibrant. In 1988, it was designated the *"Craft Capital"* of Kentucky by State Legislature.

The largest concentration of working studios and craft galleries can be found in "Old Town Berea," located near the Berea Welcome Center on North Broadway (see map).

I suggest you go to the Welcome Center first and get a copy of their excellent Berea guide and fold-out map its a great help in navigating you around the town. You'll find the Center housed in the town's original 1917 L&N Railroad Depot building. See phone, hours, and details on page 52.

Don't miss the historic Boone Tavern located in the heart of College Square along with numerous galleries and shops. At last count, Berea is home to over 40 craft shops and galleries, 18 antique shops or malls, and more than 30 restaurants.

Berea is also home to Berea College, a liberal arts establishment where students receive a free education in return for work in the school's various departments and programs. Interesting student-guided tours of the campus are offered daily, departing from the Boone Tavern.

Historic Berea, where the bluegrass meadows meet the rugged mountains, is truly a living celebration of the Appalachian culture. Stop for a night and enjoy it.

KY Mile 73 - Rock Springlets: We are approaching the Cumberland Mountain region of Kentucky, an area rich with timbered ridge scenery, dense stands of forest, and interesting rock cuts. A favorite of mine is on the west side of the interstate at Mile 63. The face of the cliff is covered with vines and the rock often weeps from hidden springlets of ground water. In the warm sunlight of a spring day, it is magical.

KY Exit 62 - Renfro Valley: Renfro Valley Entertainment Center is one of Kentucky's best kept secrets. Just 15 miles south of Berea, the beautiful Valley is known as "Kentucky's Country Music Capital."

Fiddling, banjo picking, singing, clogging, bluegrass, and vaudeville comedy make up the best country music and entertainment show this side of Nashville. The two barn theatres host eleven live shows weekly, plus a full schedule of Headliner concerts and special events. Many stars have graced the Renfro Valley stages . . from Red Foley to the Osborne Brothers, or Loretta Lynn to John Michael Montgomery. Enjoy the Renfro Valley Barn Dance, Jamboree, Mountain Gospel Jubilee, Festivals and the traditional Renfro Valley Gatherin'.

Take some time to visit the new Historical Cabins & Craft village, tour John Lair's Theater, and enjoy down-home cooking at the log Lodge's famous Boarding House suppers, or snacks at Old Joe Clark's eatery. On the premises you'll discover a new RV Park and miniature Golf.

The Valley's musical venues run from March to December. From May to October, the entertainment of various forms, run from Wednesday to Sunday. The

BEREA - *for the Biblical city in ancient Syria.*

ROCKCASTLE RIVER - *named for the castle-like rock formations along its course.*

Geology and Dinosaurs along the I-75.

The I-75 winds its way across an ancient land with many rock cuts revealing the geology of very early times.To help you understand the age of the land around you and the life forms which were present at that time, here is a simplified chart of the Geological Time Scale.

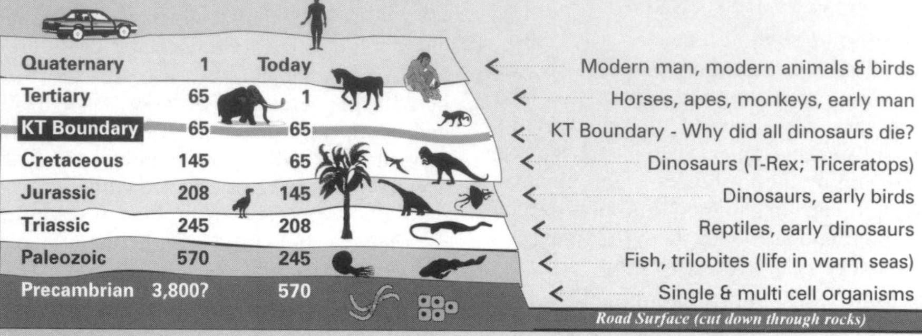

Think of the Time Scale as an eight layer cake; each layer representing a period of time (numbers are in millions of years). The oldest layer is at the bottom and the newest (today) is at the top:

Incidentally did you notice that according to the chart, Tyrannosaurus Rex, the huge flesh eating monster in the movie "Jurassic Park" was not around in the Jurassic period? It did not appear until the Cretaceous Period, 63 million years later–the movie should have been called, "Cretaceous Park."

continued top or next page

programs and stars vary, so its best to call ahead at 1-800-765-7464 for your reservations. At the very least, there is a Barn Dance every Saturday night and a Sunday Gatherin' every Sunday morning at 8:30 am.

KY Mile 61- Interstate Engineering: As we drive through more rock cuts, we cannot help wondering about the massive engineering and construction task presented to the I-75 road builders. The roadbed was built through anything which stood in its path. At times, the I-75 cuts deep into the side of a hill and at others, it traverses a short valley on top of an embankment.

At this mile marker, you notice how the rock face on both sides of the road has been blasted and cut back in steps. If you look carefully, especially when the sun casts shadows across the rock, you will often see evidence of the original explosion shafts running vertically down the rock face. These were drilled down through the earth a few feet apart, along the line of the rock face. Dynamite charges dropped down each hole were set off at the same time, slicing the earth away from the face where it could be gathered and trucked away at the road bed.

The building of America's Interstate system is often quoted as the largest public works project of all human times–larger than the building of the Egyptian Pyramids; broader in scope than the digging of the Suez Canal–this truly must be so. As we whiz by on our way to Florida, we take our hat off to you the builders of the I-75. Thank you all for your Herculean work.

KY Mile 56 - Daniel Boone National Forest: We are about to cross a stretch of the Daniel Boone National Forest. From the I-75, it doesn't look very big but most of it lies to the east and west of us. In fact it covers 21 counties and over 670,000 acres of rugged terrain - steep slopes, narrow valleys, picturesque lakes, rocks and cliffs. It is a primary recreation area with many miles of hiking trails and opportunities for outdoor activities such as picnicking, camping, fishing and water sports.

There is even a hunting area where only pioneer weapons such as muzzle loaded flintlocks or long bows may be used. All modern firearms are banned.

Special Report–continued from top of previous page

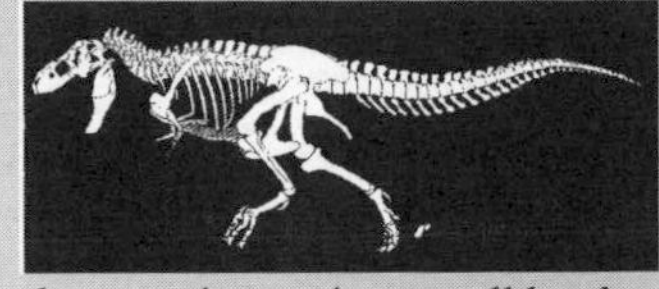

Dinosaurs disappeared 65 million years ago, possibly as the result of a major natural catastrophe. Geologists have identified a dark narrow band of material called the KT Boundary, which appears in rock strata of that time. This layer contains iridium, an element rare on earth but common in asteroids. It also contains tectites, small beads of glass fused under tremendous pressure and heat (most powerful nuclear bomb times 500,000). One theory is that a 6 mile wide asteroid collided with the earth (the Chicxulub Crater) in the ocean off the Yucatan Peninsula, Mexico, causing a massive, earth circling cloud of sulphur fog and debris. This blocked the sun plunging the world into a dark cold ice age, killing all land animals in the process. The KT Boundary may consist of debris from this cloud which settled back onto the earth's surface and was gradually covered by later geological layers.

As we drive along I-75 we travel over an ancient section of landscape, for time has seen many of the more recent geological layers eroded away. Today, the surface geology is often the rocks of the seventh Paleozoic period–a time when warm tropical salt seas covered the land. During that period, sediment suspended in the sea water continually dropped to the bottom accompanied by dead fish, shell invertebrates and vegetation debris. Over time, the ocean bed hardened layer by layer into sedimentary rock such as limestone and shale; the trapped fish and shell remains became the fossils which can be found today in the sedimentary (many-layered) rocks of the cuts along the I-75. All the way from Ohio, through Kentucky and Tennessee and down into Georgia, the surface geology is of this Paleozoic period.

But what about the Dinosaurs? Did they ever stalk the lands through which the I-75 now runs? Not according to the surface geology for this is too old. But marine dinosaur bones of the late Cretaceous period have been found in southwest Georgia.

As we cruise down the freeway on automatic control at 65 MPH, we often think about the hard life of the early pioneers as they pushed their way inland from the settlements of the Atlantic shore. The Appalachian Mountains blocked their path and until the Cumberland Gap was discovered, the journey by ox-drawn wagon laden with all their household possessions was next to impossible. Measuring their forward progress in days–not minutes–they overcame obstacle after obstacle to achieve Utopia ... that wonderful land just beyond the next misty horizon.

And the difficult terrain of their journey was not the only hazard. As the War of Independence raged on the Atlantic Coast the British Army incited the warlike Indians of Ohio and Kentucky to attack the pioneers and turn them eastward again. Soon small bands of Miami, Wynadot, Shawnee and Cherokee braves were treading the paths in the forests beside which we now travel, to ambush the settlers and tomahawk them to death.

In 1775, a man called Henderson formed the Transylvania Company and purchased the lands we now know as Kentucky from the Cherokee Indians–his wish was to sell land grants to white settlers from the east, and he hired Daniel Boone to help with this mission.

The country we are now passing through is named in honor of Boone, for it was he who blazed the Cumberland Gap trail in 1775 and opened the way for pioneers to follow his Wilderness Trace through the Cherokee lands into the Land of the Big Meadow–"Caintuck."

In the next few miles, as the I-75 curves, you will actually cross Daniel Boone's original pioneer's trail twice (see I-75 map pages 24-S and 175/176-N). Half a mile beyond mile marker 47, the "Wilderness Trace" comes from the northeast and runs

Special Report

Birth of the World's Fast Food Business

Hidden in the valley just to the east of the Interstate in south Kentucky is a gem of a discovery–the birth place of America's (and the world's) fast food industry. For this is where Harland Sanders ran his Sanders Court Motel and Restaurant for many years (long famous with travelers for its clean rooms, country hams and pecan pie), right alongside the main route to Florida - Highway 25 (see map on page 53).

Imagine Mr. Sanders' consternation in 1956 when he learned about the Government's plan to build a super highway (the I-75) to Florida just two miles to the west of his property. Sixty-six year old Sanders decided that his reputation for good wholesome food could continue to attract customers so he set about developing a new type of food for the traveler which they could take along on the road with them–deep fried chicken.

The rest, of course, is history. His 11 secret herbs and spices combined with pressure frying techniques, developed into his famous Kentucky Fried Chicken, the first fast food business in the world. Later, the Commonwealth of Kentucky honored him by granting him the title of Colonel, and the name "Colonel Sanders Kentucky Fried Chicken" was born.

How much money did Harland Sanders' Motel and Restaurant make? Here are his financial results for 1945:

RESTAURANT	- Food Sales	$1,847	
	- Cost of Sales	1,081	
	- Net Food Sales	$766	
	- Expenses	777	
	- **LOSS**	$10	$11
MOTEL	- Revenue	$906	
	- Expenses	542	
	- PROFIT	**$364**	364
TOTAL PROFIT FOR 1945			**$353**

Today, you may visit the free museum which includes a typical Sanders Court motel room, the Colonel's office and the kitchen where he developed his special recipe. You can sit in the original restaurant which was restored and re-opened in September 1990, and eat where it all began! Order the Colonel's original recipe from the adjoining modern KFC (Kentucky Fried Chicken) store.

parallel on the east (left) side of the I-75, until it crosses over to the west at Mile 45.5. It runs immediately adjacent to the I-75 on the west (right) side, until it re-crosses just south of Mile 44.

The modern terrain matches the 200 year old frontier trail well. It is still easy to imagine those deerskin clad woodsmen with their wide brimmed beaverskin hats and their flintlock muskets crooked over their arms. We can still hear the rumbling of the wagon wheels and the snorting of the pack horses as the first settlers move northward on their journey to Boonesborough, Kentucky.

KY Exit 38 - Levi Jackson State Park (map on page 52): Nine minutes to the east of this exit lies the Levi Jackson Park. Levi Jackson was born in 1816, the son of an early pioneer. Through the years, the Jackson family acquired many acres of land including a section of Daniel Boone's original trail. In 1931, Jackson's son donated large sections of his holdings to the State, to be protected as park land named in honor of his father.

Within the park lies the site of Kentucky's worst Indian massacre–Defeated Camp. During the night of October 3, 1786, under a hunter's moon, the McNitt party became the victims of a bloody Indian massacre in which at least 24 of the travelers were killed.

The group of approximately 60 pioneers, representing 24 families, had been traveling for over a month and had stopped for the night on the Boone Trace near the Little Laurel River.

Indians, Shawnee and Chickamauga were in the area to observe religious ceremonies. A war band may have become disturbed when it observed the settlers singing and playing cards at their overnight camp–also a sacred Indian place beside the river.

CORBIN - *named after James Corbin Floyd, a circuit judge (traveling magistrate who rode the district by horse, dispensing justice within the various rural communities).*

Insider Tip
Cumberland Inn - "Our Tranquility Base"

Cumberland Inn is such a great find that I am almost reluctant to share it.

Just a few minutes east of the I-75 at exit 11, Cumberland Inn (formerly Cumberland Lodge) was built with—no expenses spared—by Cumberland College to serve as a conference center for its many faculty and alumni programs. This facility is managed by Marriott Conference Centers, who often make extra rooms available to the public starting at $69.00 (10% discounts for seniors and AAA) year around. The inn's phone number is 800-315-0286 (606-539-4100).

And the rooms are exactly what you would expect at an up-scale conference facility. Quiet, wonderfully clean and very well equipped. Hair drier, iron and ironing board, coffee equipment, an electronic calendar on the TV–no detail is missed, even the shower curtain rings have bearings! But would you expect less? In the past, two U.S. Presidents have visited the Cumberland Lodge.

The Athenaeum dining room is superb–friendly service, real table linen, napkin rings and silverware—and great food. Surrounded with library shelves bearing more than 400 books and entertained by an automatic grand piano, I can't think of a better way to spend an evening after a day on the interstate. The price? Our evening meal for two people came to just more than $25, less tip.

Oh yes, if you have time don't forget to visit the fascinating wildlife museum and gift shop on the premises. They are both housed in the building next to the main entrance. The Lodge setting is so peaceful—it really is a wonderful way to break your interstate journey—we call this our "Tranquillity Base" in Kentucky.

The scalped bodies were found later by local settlers, who buried the remains by the camp. During the raid, up to ten pioneers were taken prisoner, including 8 year old Polly Ford who spent nearly 15 years living with the Indians before being rescued.

Phone, hours, and details are on page 52.

KY Exit 29 - KFC (see page 88; map on page 53)

KY Exit 25 - Cumberland Falls (map on page 54): If you have time to explore some of the rugged Kentucky countryside, then I heartily recommend this side trip to the Cumberland Falls. Realize however that it will take just over an hour to drive there and back, and you will need a minimum of 30 minutes to enjoy the scenery when you arrive.

Cumberland Falls State Park is part of the Daniel Boone Forest, and is very typical of the unspoiled countryside of pioneer times. The Falls themselves are quite spectacular–a

Kudzu

Special Report

If it is summer and you look across to the northbound lanes at Tennessee mile 78, you will see an incredible stand of Kudzu (pronounced *cut-zoo*, with the stress on the first syllable). This prolific vine (Pueraria) grows rapidly, covering everything in its path. You often see it in South Tennessee or Georgia covering telephone poles, fences and surrounding trees. Brought to America from Japan in 1876, it was first grown in the Japanese Pavilion at the Philadelphia Centennial Exposition and then became popular as a house plant.

Until 1955, it was used to stop soil erosion in the South, but it escaped and rapidly became a menace to the point where it has been described as a "national disaster." Growing as much as a foot a day in hot weather, the vine develops roots wherever its leaves touch the ground. In one season, it can easily grow 100 feet away from its original stem, enveloping everything in its path. The good news, however, is that cattle like to eat it, and it has been used for its herbal and medicinal properties. Recently, it has been found to be very useful in alcohol addiction therapy.

Kudzu

125 foot curtain of water plunging 60 feet into the boulder strewn gorge below. The mist of Cumberland Falls creates the magic of the "moonbow," a rainbow only visible on a clear night during a full moon. This unique phenomenon appears nowhere else in the Western Hemisphere. Phone the park number provided on the map for moonbow viewing dates and times. See phone, hours, and details on page 54.

KY Mile 8 & 3 - Mountains: Soon we will be crossing the Kentucky–Tennessee border and climbing from Jellico up into the sky. At Kentucky Miles 8 and 3, the freeway ahead gives us a glimpse of what is to come–a panoramic view of the mountain ridges to the south. Taylor, Patterson, Vanderpool, Chestnut Oak, Walnut and Brushy Mountains march across the horizon and recede into the bluish hazy distance.

KY Mile 1 (n/bound) - Welcome Center: Say hello to Irene if she is on the counter.

Tennessee Mile 161 (n/bound) - Graveyard: Many people notice the tiny graveyard beside I-75 just before this mile marker. Here is stark evidence of the way the interstate planners slashed the new freeway across landscape, dividing businesses, farms, homesteads, and in this case - separating the local folk from their departed loved ones. The graveyard is lovingly maintained by the Gibson, Hyslope, Corbin and Parrott families; the cemetery is always well groomed and the flowers fresh and bright.

Tennessee Mile 161 - Welcome Center: It's always a joy to stop at this well maintained Welcome Center. Say hello to Rick, Barbara, Joyce or Debbie, who are usually at the counter helping travelers with their journeys through Tennessee.

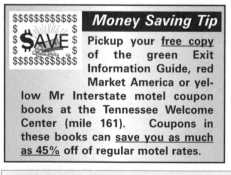

Money Saving Tip

Pickup your free copy of the green Exit Information Guide, red Market America or yellow Mr Interstate motel coupon books at the Tennessee Welcome Center (mile 161). Coupons in these books can save you as much as 45% off of regular motel rates.

TN Exit 160 - Jellico: The small town of Jellico guards the northern gateway to the southernmost range of the massive Appalachian Mountains chain which sweeps across the northeast U.S.A., from New Brunswick, Canada to the Carolinas and Tennessee. Jellico, possibly named after the mountain Angelica plant which was used by settlers to brew an intoxicating drink called "Jelca," was settled in 1795 and incorporated in 1883. Some say the town was incorporated to provide a legal means of selling Tennessee whiskey.

It is remembered for a terrible train crash which occurred here during WWII. A speeding train hauling 15 cars loaded with over 600 soldiers on their way to army camp, derailed and crashed into the deep gorge of the Clear Fork River, about 1½ miles to the east. More than 35 men were killed.

If you have time (this will only take you an extra 21 minutes) and the weather is reasonable, I suggest you turn off the I-75 at exit 160, drive through Jellico and take the Elk Valley road which parallels the interstate. It rejoins the I-75 at exit 141. For those who ply the freeway year after year, this might be a refreshing break. To help you, there is a detailed map of this side trip on page 55.

As you drive through the Jellico main street, note the old storefronts on either side. This is an unusual opportunity to see some really old buildings in their original state. Although they are designated as historical landmarks, they have not been renovated.

Route 297 continues on past the buildings and becomes a very pleasant country byway through leafy tunnels formed by overhanging trees, winding corners and occasional vistas to the east of the I-75 as it climbs over Pine Mountain (not recommended for RVs).

TN Mile 159 - Pine Mountain: The road seems to climb forever as it starts its four mile ascent toward the highest point on our southward journey. We are climbing the Pine Mountain Ridge with Elk Fork Valley and

TENNESSEE - *after the major Cherokee Indian town of Tanasi, located on the river which is now known as the Little Tennessee, in the eastern part of the State.*

JELLICO - *named after the Angelica plant which grew in these mountain areas. Early settlers were said to have made an early moonshine from it— an intoxicating drink called, "Jelca" or "Gelca."*

Insider Tip
Louie's on the Lake

Less than half-a-mile just to the east of Tennessee exit 134 is the Cove Lake State Park which in itself is well worth the short break in my interstate journey. But my mission is to try the offerings of a new family style restaurant crowning a hilltop overlooking the lake–*"Louie's on the Lake."*

Open for lunch and dinner, the menu is interesting and reasonably priced. Kathy and I enjoyed 'Tater Skins and Spinach Artichoke Dip, followed by Delmonico Steaks. A nice change from the fast food "factories" along the interstate.

Kids foods are also provided for the younger travelers and patio service is available during warmer weather.

Louie's is open year-round, from 11am–9pm, 7 days a week. Call 423-566-6676 for further information.

Jellico Mountain to our right; the Cumberland Mountain range to our left. The I-75 tops at Mile 147, and then, as it starts its descent to Caryville, we come across one of the most famous exit signs on our journey - the one that every I-75 traveler remembers:

TN Exit 144 - "Stinking Creek Road": With all the names available to county planners, how did "Stinking Creek" ever get its name? As usual, the answer is rooted in history.

Many years ago, there was a very harsh winter in the Tennessee mountains and wildlife were unable to forage and find food. They gathered at the local creek where water and sustenance had always been plentiful but the creek was frozen; eventually the animals died of starvation and thirst. In the Spring, all the carcasses thawed out and soon a horrible stench pervaded the area. So with great imagination, the creek was named "Stinking Creek."

TN Mile 137 - Devil's Racetrack: About 1/4 mile to the east of the interstate is a cone-

The "New Deal" and Tennessee Valley Authority (TVA)

As you travel through Tennessee, you will encounter the massive works (Norris Dam & Chickamauga Dam, for example) of the Tennessee Valley Authority, the TVA . . . what's it all about?

In the 1930's, the country was hurting from the effects of the Great Depression, and nowhere was this more evident than in the state of Tennessee. Newly elected President Franklin Roosevelt decided that the answer was to put the country back to work, and in 1933 proposed a "New Deal" which created many public works agencies and projects thus producing employment, and jump starting the economy.

In Tennessee and surrounding states, a major need was electrical power so work projects were implemented to build dams and generating plants on the Tennessee River. Whole towns, such as Norris, TN were created to house the workers for these projects. Senator George Norris of Nebraska led a fight to create an agency to keep such projects out of private hands, and the Tennessee Valley Authority (TVA) was born.

During the Second World War, the TVA's ability to produce massive amounts of electrical energy was fundamental to the development of the atomic bomb (see story about Oak Ridge). Today, the TVA is a powerful agency controlling all water issues such as power generation, flood control and navigation on the state's river system.

NORRIS - *named after George William Norris, Senator and a great champion of public electric power. Norris was instrumental in promoting the Tennessee Valley Authority (TVA) as the agency to harnessing the power of water. The town of Norris was built to house the builders of the Norris Dam.*

Insider Tip
Golden Girls Restaurant

No, not the TV *"Golden Girls"* but the four Golden family sisters who really know how to operate a great restaurant.

Owners Ann & Jeanné, and sisters Becky and Kathy run a restaurant that is very popular locally. Excellent food, attentive service and reasonable prices add up to superb value.

You know its good when you see the many police cars parked outside at meal time.

Go west at exit 122. The Golden Girls restaurant is a log building (set back a bit) on your right hand side. Hours are 6am-10pm. ☎ 423-457-3302

shaped hill with vertical runs of sandstone rock up its sides. This is the "Devil's Racetrack," a formation of Pennsylvanian rock (late Paleozoic Age–see the geological strata diagram on page 86), about 340 million years old. People come from miles to explore this unique geological feature, rich with fossils.

TN Exit 128 - Norris Dam; map on page 56): Here is another opportunity to take a short scenic trip off the I-75, for very little extra investment in time. This side trip across the picturesque Norris Dam will only add an extra 12 minutes to your journey, and bring you back to the I-75 at exit 122.

For a really interesting time, you might wish to visit the Lenoir Museum at the Norris Dam State Park or the Museum of Appalachia (see Insider Tip), before rejoining the interstate.

During the summer, Kathy and I stopped at the Grist Mill, just below the Museum on the east side of the dam, and chatted with a Park Ranger. She told us that the road below the

Insider Tip
Museum of Appalachia - A Mountain Man's Gift to the Future

When you arrive at the Museum of Appalachia and enter the main building, you know that you have come to a special place. The smell of warm, freshly baked bread wafts by as you purchase your tickets. You follow the signs to this huge outdoor museum, passing the brick fireplace where a flaming log pops and snaps on ancient andirons. These are all good omens.

As you move out into the bright mountain sunlight, it's as if you have stepped back into time. Nestled close to some rounded stacks of hay are several sheep while a small herd of Scottish Longhorn cattle drink by a small pond. Across the meadow, come the sounds of fiddle and banjo as a group on the verandah of an old mountain house, enjoy a few moments away from field chores.

For this is a living mountain village–the Museum of Appalachia. A wonderful experience of 32 original mountain buildings, displayed in such a way that you would believe the inhabitants have just stepped out back for a few minutes.

A well organized indoor museum displays many artifacts and examples of Appalachian mountain living. Of particular interest are the many different types of musical instruments, including a long horn which was used by Grandma for warning everybody within miles, about "revenue men" in the valley.

To John Rice Irwin, founder of this wonderful museum, it has been an ongoing labor of love. And this dedication shows in the detail around you. John Rice's friend, Alex Haley, paid him the greatest compliment when he said,

> *"This museum is evidence of John's love of the land, his love of his mountain culture, his love of the mountain people who came before him. One cannot walk these grounds and through these cabins without savoring the spirit and strength of a people rich in culture and heritage. You can feel them here, and this is the unique dimension that makes the life work of John Rice Irwin so extraordinary."*

John Rice has created a true gift for future generations–we heartily recommend it.

See map on page 56 for phone number, hours and other details.

Grist Mill led to a ford and waterfall . . . so off we went. We discovered a narrow leafy road which ran alongside Clear Creek. After driving slowly through the shallow ford, we found the waterfall. Below it, the creek meandered across a bed of small rocks and pebbles, in a small valley speckled with yellow winged butterflies–a beautiful sight on a warm, sunny day. The whole adventure only took fifteen minutes; if you would like to repeat our adventure, just follow our "waterfall" road on the Norris Dam map in the "Side Trip" section.

Just to the west of Norris Dam lies the Norris Dam State Park. I was intrigued to find that you can rent cabins within the park–10 of them are labeled deluxe, or "AAA," 19 are rustic, or "AA." More about this in the Lodging–Section 6–of this guidebook.

TN Exit 122 - Museum of Appalachia (see page 92; map on page 56)..

TN Exit 122 - Bypass Knoxville via Oak Ridge (map on page 57): Sometimes it would be great to get off the I-75 for a little while . . . and Exit 122 provides such an opportunity. Rather than continue running south and through the sometimes heavy traffic of Knoxville's I-40, you might want to consider "cutting the corner" and taking the "country route"—Route 61—over to Oak Ridge (see Tennessee exit 376A for the story of Oak Ridge and the Atomic Bomb), and then down Route 62/162 to rejoin the I-75 west of Knoxville at I-40/I-75 Exit 376.

The route crosses the Clinch River 3.6 miles from the I-75 just east of Clinton, and then winds around a bit as it follows the northern bank of the Clinch River with the Walden Ridge of the Appalachian Mountain chain to the north. 5.3 miles from I-75 you will go through local traffic on East Clinch Avenue in downtown Clinton, but this quickly passes. Five miles west of Clinton, join Route 95 (Oak Ridge Parkway) and drive 5.5 miles into the town of Oak Ridge where you join Route 62 (Illinois Avenue). South of Oak Ridge after 5.2 miles, you cross the Clinch River on the Solway Bridge; a mile further take Route 162—Pellissippi Parkway—for 6.2 miles down to rejoin the I-40/I-75 as it runs towards Nashville/Chattanooga. The total distance is 28.6 miles (about 40 minutes). If you stay on I-75, your distance will be about the same but depending upon traffic, should only take you 30 minutes.

If you would like to take this alternative route, follow the sidetrip map on page 57.

TN Mile 107 - <u>Southbound</u> Driving Notes: As the I-75 swings down and around Knoxville, it briefly joins and assumes the mile marker numbers of other interstates.

First we join the westbound branch of the I-640 (the Knoxville northern "ring road") for a few miles. Take care as you approach I-75's exit 3 where it appears the main road (2 lanes) goes off to the east. You don't want that! Instead, stay well over in the right lane (the I-75) which becomes a single lane ramp for ½ mile until you join the high speed traffic of the I-640.

After three miles, you again bear right as the I-640/I-75 combination joins the I-40 west to Nashville/Chattanooga. On the ramp, the two lanes quickly become one, so move left as soon as possible—and move left again once on the I-40 since the single ramp lane also disappears. The mile markers change once again—this time to a 380 series. Watch for police along this stretch since it is actively patrolled for out of state speeders (the "locals" seem to whiz by at excessive speeds

Insider Tip
Great American Buffet

If you love buffets, then this is for you. Three hot tables with over 35 different items, two salad tables with over 28 items - and a huge dessert table. And the prices don't hurt either - $6.49 for lunch and $8.49 for dinner (knock off a $1 if you are a senior). It's no wonder that the Great American Buffet is so popular.

Go west at exit 108 and look for the restaurant on your left.

The hours are M-Th, 11am-10pm; F-Sat, 11am-11pm; Sun brunch, 9am-noon; Sun noon-10pm. ☎ 423-687-8773

KNOXVILLE - *originally called White's Fort, in 1791 it was renamed after General Henry Knox (1750-1806), a soldier during the American Revolution. General Knox was the army Commander in Chief (1783-84) and the Nation's first Secretary of War under President Washington (1785-95). The main depository of the Nation's gold bullion, Fort Knox, is also named after him.*

with complete immunity).

Watch for construction around mile markers 279 and 380 where new overpasses and ramps are being built.

TN Exit 376A - Oak Ridge (map on page 57): 12.3 miles to the north of the I-40/I-75 lies a city built in 1942, for the workers of Clinton Engineering Works. A city so "secret" that it was on no map and anybody asking casual questions about it would be investigated by the FBI as a possible spy.

In 1939, the US Government realized that the Nazis in Germany understood the possibilities of an atomic bomb. Their scientists had recently succeeded in splitting atoms of uranium at Berlin's Kaiser Wilhelm Institute. An atomic bomb in the hands of the Nazis would have guaranteed world dominance by the Germans so it was important that the USA protected its interests by similar development as quickly as possible.

President Roosevelt, through a new organization known as the Manhattan Engineering District (MED) authorized a full-scale bomb development program. The MED identified three secret sites to perform various functions in the research. Site W at Hanford, WA was chosen as the plutonium production location; site X in Tennessee chosen for uranium production, and site Y was a lonely mesa in New Mexico called Los Alamos . . . here the various components from "W" and "X"would be assembled under the direction of Robert Oppenheimer, and the finished bomb tested.

In 1942, the Manhattan Project–the development of the World's first atomic bomb commenced operations under the leadership of MED's Colonel (later Major General) Leslie Groves.

Site X was a series of three valleys northwest of Knoxville, named after one of its ridges– Black Oak Ridge. It was chosen for the manufacturing operations required to extract radioactive uranium (U235), because of the availability of huge amounts of hydro-electricity generated by the TVA dams; the valleys offered shelter to adjacent operations should one of the plants explode, and finally, it was very sparsely populated by farmers who could be easily relocated. It's remoteness also helped with the security issues.

So the secret city of Oak Ridge was born; very few residents were allowed to leave it and until 1949 it could only be visited by special permit. Three plants with code names K25–uranium extraction and enrichment, X10–atomic pile and Y12–uranium atom separation were built in parallel valleys under another secret organization, the Clinton Engineering Works. The entire area, including the town of Oak Ridge with housing and amenities for all the workers, was enclosed by a barbed-wire fence with access controlled by seven gates. Life in the area was very basic and made difficult by the ever present mud.

Today things are much different, an excellent visitors' center and several attractions—the American Museum of Science and Energy, New Bethel Church (where the Project scientists used to meet), the Graphite Reactor and the K-25 visitor overlook — are well worth a visit for those interested in the birth of the Nuclear Age.

The operations at Oak Ridge continue to do the impossible. Whenever an "impossible" but essential project is needed, business and the military turn to the Oak Ridge National Laboratory for answers. While I was last there, the Museum was displaying ORNL's latest success, a completely sterile surgical operating room which could be parachuted to the ground, in a folding package no larger than 10' x 10' x 10'.

The Visitor Center and Museum of Science & Energy phone numbers, hours and other details are on page 57.

TN Exit 373 - Farragut: see page 95 - the Insider Tip for the Apple Cake Tearoom at this exit.

Insider Tip
Calhoun's Ribs

In my never ending search for the "Best BBQ Ribs on the I-75," I have to rate Calhoun's in Knoxville as a close contender to Burbank's in Kentucky. I'll let you be the judge.

Calhoun's is just two minutes off the Interstate and easy to find–take exit 376B (I-140E–Pellissippi Parkway) and leave after 6/10ths mile at exit 1A (Kingston Pike N, US11E, US70), Go through traffic lights at Mabry Hood and Calhoun's - a wooden barn-style building with dark red roof - is immediately on your right. ☎ 423-673-3444

Insider Tip
Apple Cake Tea Room

One of the most pleasant luncheon experiences between Detroit and Florida is to be had at the Apple Cake Tea Room, just to the south/east of I-75/I-40 at exit 373, on Campbell Station Road. Housed in a cozy log cabin, the minute you enter the door you know this is going to be a special dining occasion; pine wood and tasty home cooking aromas greet your senses and prepare you for the meal to follow.

But before you order, take a look around the carefully decorated interior. The Henry family has lived in Farragut for many generations and with great pride, Apple Cake owner Mary Henry furnished the interior with many of her treasured family photos, antiques, quilts and other mementos. If it's not too busy and the room is not in use, ask Mary to show you the private bridal reception room upstairs. On display setting the scene is a wedding gown that was discovered in Mary's grandmother's attic. It's worth the climb up the winding staircase.

The other thing that is evident about the Apple Cake is the wonderful service. Mary's enthusiasm is shared by her staff who all care that you have an enjoyable visit. It couldn't be better.

But now to the menu. First, a very presentable French Onion soup and then on to the main course. There are a number of sandwich choices; I enjoyed the grilled chicken sandwich on a fresh croissant. Side orders of honey butter, cheese toast and banana nut bread help round out the course. And then at the suggestion of several local people who were also enjoying lunch, we bypassed the house speciality dessert–apple cake–and tried the glazed fruit dish. Definitely an excellent choice; the glaze syrup is memorable! But don't ask for the recipe . . . it's a family secret and only available if you buy the business!

And now a word to the guys . . don't be put off by the words, "Tea Room" in the restaurant's name; I'm sure you'll enjoy the experience as much as your wife. The food is excellent, helpings plentiful and prices reasonable. I will certainly be back.

To find the Apple Cake Tea Room, take Exit 373, south/east towards Farragut. The Apple Cake is in Appalachian Log Square plaza on the left side of Campbell Station Road, almost immediately opposite the Pilot gas station. Hours: Mon-Sat. 11am-2:30pm ☎ 423-966-7848

Also at exit 373, is an interesting antique shopping mall–Campbell Station Antiques. Located in the Station West Center next to Cracker Barrel, this 10,000 square foot antique emporium has everything from antique clothing to rare books. Open daily, M-Sat, 10-6; Sun, 1-6. ☎ 423-966-4348.

TN Exit 368 - Driving Notes: Here the I-75 leaves the I-40, and continues south towards Chattanooga. I-75 mile marker numbers resume.

TN Mile 81: Those who drove to Florida in the pre-I-75 days will remember the classics of roadside advertising—*Burma Shave* and *Rock City*. Most of these were discontinued when federal legislation required the removal of all private roadside signs along the interstates, but several have survived.

"Rock City" signs were very prolific and adorned the roofs of barns, outhouses, and farm buildings throughout the South (Rock City is an attraction in Chattanooga), announcing the number of miles you had to travel to "See Rock City." If you look very carefully to the left at mile marker 81, you will see a barn with an original "Rock City" sign painted on its roof.

FARRAGUT - *"Damn the torpedoes - full speed ahead!" was the famous command of Rear Admiral David Farragut, as he led his Union fleet to a Civil War victory through the mines in Mobile Bay on August 5, 1864. The town of Farragut is named in his honor.*

A word about wine tastings—we know that drinking and driving don't mix but on a normal winery tour you will rarely consume more than a glass of wine in total, even though you may try many different varieties.

Your host will recommend you start with dry reds and whites, and proceed through the tasting to sweet and dessert wines. He or she will pour a small amount into a clean wineglass.

Experienced wine tasters hold the glass up to the light while gently rocking it to see wine's color and viscosity ("body"), sniff each wine while rolling it around in its glass to appreciate its smell ("bouquet"), sip it and swill it around their mouth and then spit the sample out into a wine spittoon. In this manner, they can appreciate all the attributes of several wines without absorbing much alcohol.

Tasting can take as long or as little time as you please, but we recommend ½ hour as being reasonable.

Tennessee Wineries: You don't have to go to Sonoma or Napa Valley in California to enjoy free winery tours and wine tastings. Southeast Tennessee is fast becoming known for it fine American wines and there are three wineries where you can enjoy these pleasures within minutes of the I-75.

Recently, Tennessee vineyards have taken bronze, silver and gold medals in national and international competition. The fine wines of this area are slowly becoming "known" through the wine growing world. Today, more than 200 wine growers practice their art throughout the state continuing a long standing Tennessee tradition.

And you don't have to be a "wine snob" to enjoy these tours either. Nobody is going to worry if you can't tell the difference between a Chardonnay and Seyval Blanc—your hosts only wish is that you enjoy yourselves and leave with a better understanding of their excellent products.

Let's stop now, and enjoy a visit with some of these wine growers:

TN Exit 76 - Loudon Valley Winery: Less than 2 miles to the east of I-75's exit 76 (Sugar Limb Road), nestled on a crest overlooking the great Tennessee River is this Gold Medal winery. Owner Stan Dylewksi and his assistant, Brenda, enjoy managing the ten acres of vineyards—containing fifteen varieties of American, French-American hybrid and European (Vinifera) grapes—meeting people and showing them around this impressive estate.

In addition to the tour and tastings, you might enjoy stretching your legs after a long drive by going on a short nature trail hike through the virgin tree stands and down to the river. In the spring and summer, the many wild flowers along the path make this a particular treat. Take along a picnic and delight in the riverside tranquillity.

To find the winery, take exit 76–Sugar Limb Road and on the south side of I-75, immediately turn right onto Hotchkiss Valley Rd, travel west for two miles and turn left onto Huff Ferry Rd, follow this road for one mile to its end where you'll find the Loudon Valley Winery overlooking the Tennessee River.

The winery is open for tours and tastings, from 10-6 p.m., Monday to Saturday, and from 1-5 p.m. on Sunday.

TN Valley Winery: A quarter of a mile to the west of I-75 exit 76 (Sugar Limb Road) lies the entrance to the Tennessee Valley Winery. Here, the Reed family—Jerry, Tom and Chris Reed—continue practicing the Tennessee wine making tradition, producing more than 12,000 gallons of table wines each year from their 32 acres of plantings at the Wildwood Vineyards, located 15 miles south in Roane County. Wine-maker, Tom, is proud of the fact that the family's estate has won medals and awards from all over the United States.

Tours, tastings and picnic facilities are all available here; Tom invites you to stay a while and enjoy a picnic lunch on the sundeck. Enjoy the winery tours and tastings, from 10-6 pm, Mon-Sat, and from 1-5 pm on Sunday.

TN Exit 60 - Lost Sea (see map on page 53): Seven miles to the east of I-75 (9 1/2 minutes along Route 68) lies North America's largest underground lake–the "Lost Sea." Listed in the Guinness Book of Records, the

LOUDON - *after a very unsuccessful Commander in Chief of British forces during the French and Indian wars - John Campbell, 4th Earl of Loudon (1705-1782).*

huge body of water lies within the Craighead Caverns, and covers 4.5 acres. A trip across its surface in a glass bottomed boat allows you to see the many huge speckled trout in the crystal clear water below.

It is an eerie experience as you glide across the mirror lake in the dimly lit limestone cavern; unusual rock formations, mineral deposits and strange cave flowers heighten the mystery.

During the Civil War, the caves were a source of saltpeter for gunpowder. Close your eyes and imagine smoky lanterns casting their flickering shadows on the cavern walls as Confederate soldiers swing their pickaxes. Listen to the ring of metal against stone. These are spooky surroundings.

If you decide to tour the caves, dress warmly because below ground, the air is a constant 58 degrees summer or winter. Also wear solid shoes–the tour includes a walk of about 3/4 mile. See phone, hours and other details on page 53.

TN Exit 60 - Coca Cola shop: Do you collect Coca Cola memorabilia? If you do, then don't miss the Coca Cola shop tucked in behind the huge flea market building, just to the west at exit 60. Apart from all the Coca Cola paraphernalia, there are shelves holding hundreds of bottles of Coke from just about every place or venue where commemorative bottles were produced. Need an unopened bottle of Coke from the Atlanta Summer Olympics or the 1986 World Series - they've got it.

SUPERBOWL
1973

TN Exit 60 - Orr Mountain Winery (map on page 53): Just east of the entrance to the Lost Sea lies Orr Mountain Winery. Lying on a peaceful hillside with a spectacular view of the valley between Mount Le Conte and Starr Mountain, owners Sue and Harry Orr invite you to enjoy the "grape experience from vine to wine." In the spring, "be thrilled at the new shoots bursting forth," and at all times, "see the process of turning great grapes into fine wines as they go from press, to vat, to tank, to bottle."

One mile past the Lost Sea attraction, turn right (at the blue Winery sign) onto CR-117, go one mile and turn right onto CR-121, and follow the signs for 500 yards. See phone, hours, and details are on page 53.

TN Mile 52 - "The World's Best Ice Cream: Once again, I put on my reporter's hat and left I-75 at Tennessee's exit 52 (Mt. Verd Road) and followed route 305 eastwards for 4.3 miles (6.9 kms) through pleasant countryside towards Athens, to visit Mayfield Dairy Farms and sample their "World's Best Ice Cream."

Mayfield Dairy is well marked on the left side of the road, you can't miss the big round brown and yellow billboard at Mayfield Lane that says "Mayfield Dairy Farms–Home of the World's Best Ice Cream."

Full of anticipation I headed right for the Visitor Center's ice cream parlor to interview the staff and sample the wares.

I'm impressed! The "World's Best" accolade was awarded by no less an authority than Time Magazine, in an article published on August 10, 1981. Now I have not tasted all the ice creams in the world so am really in no position to judge, but I've got to tell you that the thick, creamy, smooth, yellow vanilla ice cream I sampled was up to expectations . . . and far beyond.

Just to make absolutely sure (after all, someone has to do it), I also checked the newest flavor, "Banana Split," an interesting blend of banana cream, pecans and cherries, and "Brown Cow," vanilla and fudge.

They mentioned that this year's favorite with the children is "Superman," vanilla with yellow, blue and pink swirls - so I had to try that too. Somebody has to do it!

If you have extra time, you might like to take the very interesting tour of the ice cream and milk processing plant. Ever wonder . . . "How *do* they put the stick inside the ice cream bar?" "How they make the different flavors of ice cream?" After a film presentation, you'll see the bottling of milk and production of ice cream and other food items and all will be explained.

The ice cream parlor at Mayfield Dairy is open May to October: Mon-Sat, 9am-5pm - closed Sundays and major holidays. November to April: Mon-Sat, 9am-2pm. Ice cream prices are very reasonable, starting at 75¢ for a mini-scoop, $1 for a single scoop, $1.50 double and $2.00 for a triple.

Plant tours are held every half-hour–Mon-Fri, 9am-5pm (last tour 4pm); Sat., 9am-2pm (last tour 1pm)–closed Sundays and major holidays. The ice cream plant is not operational on Saturdays; the milk plant is not operational on Wednesdays. Admission is free; comfortable slip-resistant shoes are recommended for the plant tour. Further information? ☎ 423-745-2151 or 1-800-629-3435.

TN Mile 44 - Electronic Fog Advisory System: Born out of tragedy, you are about to enter a very "high-tech" stretch of freeway - the Hiwasee River Valley electronic fog advisory system.

Fog has always been a problem on this section of the I-75, particularly because of paper mills on the River. In December, 1990, there was a terrible traffic accident of massive proportions caused by fog enshrouding the I-75. On the southbound downgrade towards the River, (mile markers 38-36) cars and trucks piled into one another due to the poor visibility. The end result? Thirteen killed, 50 injured and damage to 83 cars and trucks.

Today, there is a very sensitive electronic system in place to advise you of safe speeds. Rather like an optical smoke detector, the system constantly monitors the clarity of the air between its sensors (if you look closely you will see the monitoring devices on some of the poles) and translates the results via a computer into safe driving speeds and advisory warnings, on the electronic gantry and roadside signs.

Incidentally, if you rely on a radar detector, you might as well turn it off through this stretch since the fog system emits signals in the "X" band frequencies and your detector will go off as you pass each sign pole. In fact, the police hope that this will lull you into false security and often set up their radar trap towards the end of this stretch–just when most drivers assume that their detector is emitting another false alarm.

TN Mile 42 - Spanish Explorers: And now for a change of pace. In May, 1539, the Governor of Cuba, Don Hernando de Soto landed in Tampa, Florida, and started an extensive exploration of North America with an army of 600 men.

For more than four years, he traveled over 4,000 miles while searching for gold and silver . . . and a north passage to China. Ranging up the US mainland through Georgia, he led his army into the Carolinas, Tennessee . . . and as far away as modern Chicago, until he turned southward through Missouri and into Arkansas where he died in 1542.

Extensive journals were kept documenting his exploration and since most of the Indian sites mentioned are known today and many modern roads are built over early Indian trails, the track taken by his expedition is well known today. The path of the modern I-75 crosses the path of de Soto and his army in two places–Athens, Tennessee and Perry, Georgia.

From his journals for May, 1540, we know that while in Tennessee he spent a night at Madisonville. The next day an Indian chief visited him and led him to Athens. Here he was joined by a scouting party he had sent up the Tennessee Valley towards Knoxville, where they discovered Indian mines.

He and his army then traveled to, and camped on, Hiwassee Island, at the confluence of the Hiwassee & Tennessee Rivers. Examination of the terrain indicates that he would have crossed the modern path of the I-75 in the vicinity of this mile marker.

TN Mile Marker 18 - Radar Alert: Be careful here just in case the traffic ahead of you suddenly brakes! The I-75 runs downhill and gently curves to the left—thick trees line the median zone.

HIWASSEE RIVER - *Cherokee Indian word meaning "meadow."*

BRAINERD - *named after David Brainerd, a pioneer missionary among the Cherokee Indians.*

CHATTANOOGA - *probably from a Cree Indian word meaning "rock rising to a point" (Lookout Mountain).*

At the bottom of the hill (and curve) an emergency vehicle path cuts through the trees between the south and northbound I-75 lanes, and here the police love to hide with radar beamed up the hill. Cars cannot see them until they are right on top of the radar trap and speeders violently brake to avoid a ticket (it doesn't work).

Watch the traffic ahead of you as you descend this hill. We don't want you to rear-end a speeder.

TN Exit 4 - Chattanooga Choo-Choo: As a kid, I used to love the distinctive smell and noise of steam locomotives as they chugged their way through the countryside. Now you can experience it (again . . . if you are over 40 years old!) with a ride on the Tennessee Valley Railroad.

You board your coach at the Grand Junction Station and travel to downtown Chattanooga behind ex-Southern Railway #4501, ancient Central Georgia #349 or perhaps locomotive #610 or #630. Follow the Civil War track of the Tennessee & Georgia Railroad, which was a vital supply link, first for the Confederacy and then for the Union as the tides of war shifted in 1863. You can almost taste the history as as it winds through the Chattanooga country and into the darkness of the 1858 Missionary Ridge tunnel.

Afterwards, enjoy the audio-visual show and railroad exhibits, visit the repair shop or browse the gift store.

To find Grand Junction Station which is 3.8 miles from the interstate, take I-75 exit 4 (Chickamauga Dam) and follow Route 153 north to the fourth (Jersey Pike) exit. Follow the signs to "TVRM" on Cromwell Road.

The Railway runs on full service (10am-5pm) June to August, and partial service (10am-2pm) April, May, Sept, Oct and November. It's charters and school groups only from December to March, but phone them anyway, there may be an group scheduled with space available when you are in the area.

Fares are adults/children: $8.50/$4.50.
☎ 423-894-8028.

TN Exit 2 - Chattanooga (main map on page 58, downtown map to left): Many people bypass Chattanooga because it seems such a long trek to the west of I-75, but for those that make the effort, the drive to the downtown area is quite scenic and interesting as the road winds down the face of historic Missionary Ridge. Besides, the trip from I-75 exit 2 is not that long–9.3 miles; about 11 minutes–and over the last few years

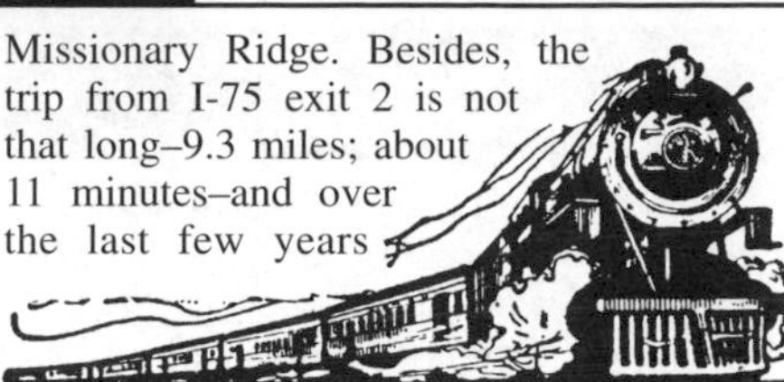

downtown Chattanooga has experienced a renaissance and grown into a wonderfully interesting place for visitors.

To reach downtown, take I-75 exit 2 (I-24 West). At exit 178 (Downtown) take US27 North to exit 1-C (4th Street), turn left at the second traffic light (Broad Street)–ahead of you is the Tennessee Aquarium with the Visitors Center to its right. You'll find parking lots on either side of the street just before these buildings as well as in front of the Visitors Center.

Tennessee Aquarium: Gone are the days of dark, dank rooms with small thick glass apertures separating fish and viewer. The Tennessee Aquarium is a "4th generation facility, an aquarium which tells a story as you wander down through its thematic galleries.

You start your self-guided tour by following the flow of the Tennessee River, from its

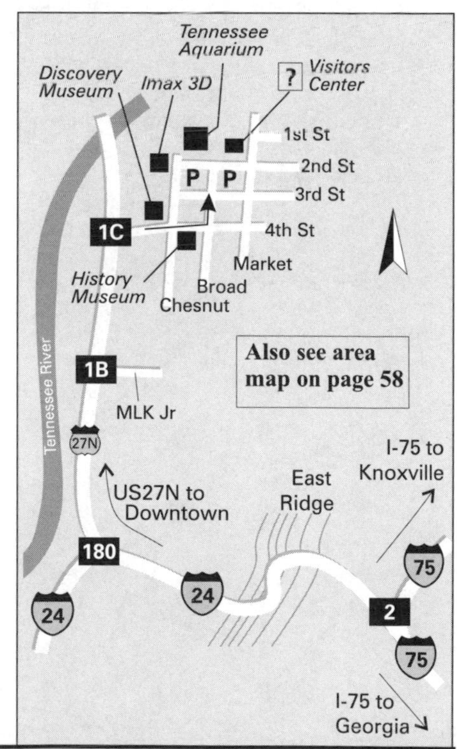

Insider Tip
Horsin' Around

"Horsin' Around" is a magical experience. It's a wood carving workshop where horses, frogs wearing pants, unicorns, cats and other wonderful creatures, mythical and otherwise, are carved and painted to a glossy finish - in preparation for old fashioned carousel rides. In fact, it's the only carousel horse carving place in North America, if not the World.

The carvers are all volunteers and are passionate about their work. They have come from across the USA to work with master carver Bud Ellis . . . and they love to talk to the visitors about the different projects that are underway.

Now "Horsin' Around" is not one of your normal tourist attractions. It is housed in an old grey factory building across from the Winn-Dixie Supermarket on Tennessee Street. You climb the old wooden stairs and at the top, a $1 donation is requested from each visitor - young or old. But you are free to wander around and talk to the carvers, smell the fresh bass wood and paint, and enjoy the experience. Watch the childrens' eyes and you'll understand what I mean when I say that this is a very rare and magical experience - nothing in Disney World will match it!

See the Chattanooga map on page 58 for directions. Working (visiting) hours are M-Th, 9am-8pm; F 9am-5pm; Sat 9am-6pm. ☎ 423-825-5616.

beginnings in the Appalachians, into the great Mississippi and onward towards the salt waters of the Gulf of Mexico. Fabulous vistas of birds, animal and marine life accompany your journey as you descend through the aquarium building. First, the Appalachian Cove Forest with its dripping rocks, ferns, moss covered trees, mountain streams and otter pool. Then to the Tennessee River Gallery where you examine (above and below water) the huge "Nickajack" and "Reelfoot" lakes. "Discovery Falls" takes you through an interactive educational gallery where children (and adults) may examine various specimens at close range. And finally, on to the Mississippi Delta—a recreated cypress swamp where snakes, alligators and other fearsome reptiles live—and the Gulf of Mexico, the aquarium's only salt water tank.

The Aquarium hours are: May 1-Labor Day: M-Th, 10-6; F-Sun, 10-8 Rest of year: 10-6 daily. Admission is adults/children $10.25/$5.50 – children under 3yrs are free.

The Aquarium also has an Imax 3D theater showing nature oriented films with images that leap off the screen. Tickets are $6.75/$4.75. Combination aquarium & theater are also available at $14/$8.50. ☎ 800-262-0695 or 423-265-0695.

Other downtown attractions: Here are some other downtown attractions you might enjoy; pick up information from the Visitors Center (see map):

- Creative Discovery Museum
- Hunter Museum of Art
- Medal of Honor Museum
- Regional History Museum
- Tow & Recovery Hall of Fame
- An interesting place to eat
  – Sticky Fingers, (cor. Broad & 5th).

St. Elmo and Lookout Mountain (see map on page 58): On the other side of I-24 rises Lookout Mountain, peaking at 2,391 feet. On the mountain you'll find other Chattanooga attractions - Battle of Chattanooga Museum, Incline Railway, Ruby Falls and Rock City. The drive up the mountain (see map) to the Point Park at the top is well worth the effort.

Insider Tip
Lake Winnie - Family Fun

This is a very well kept secret; a "family fun" place locals rave about. An old fashioned style amusement park but with one key difference–no alcohol, no bad language, ultra clean grounds, neatly dressed and very polite employees . . . and good "ride" value for your money. In fact, a place where you will have absolutely no concerns about taking your children, no matter whatever age.

The Lake Winnie (short for Lake Winnepesaukah) Amusement Park has has been in the business of entertaining north Georgian and southern Tennessee families for more than seventy years. *Travel & Leisure* magazine rated it as one of America's top 10 family amusement parks.

A good variety of 33 rides will keep the young ones entertained–water splash rides (I'm assured that bathing suits aren't necessary on any of the water rides–you don't get wet!), paddleboats, pirate ride, Cannonball Roller Coaster, Alpine chairlift, antique carousel, ferris wheel, train ride, Pipeline Plunge water ride–and much, much more. There are also clean food stands throughout the grounds, or you can take a picnic.

General Manager George Bergethon is out in the park all the time, making sure that there are no problems and everybody is just having a good time. This is a highly recommended family fun place.

Open late-April to mid-May and late-August to mid-September, weekends only ; Mid-May to late-August, Thurs to Sunday. Phone for hours. ☎ 706-866-5681 or 877-525-3946

Park admission, adults/children–$3/$2, children under 3 yrs free.

Ride tickets (rides require from 2-6 tickets) single - .60, 14 - $8, 28 - $16, unlimited rides $15.

To find Lake Winnie, see the map on page 57.

But for me, two of the best area attractions are near the foot of the Incline Railway, on St.Elmo Street.

The new Tennessee Civil War Museum houses an excellent collection of exhibits and information about the "War Between the States." The museum is open daily from 10am-6pm. ☎ 423-821-4954

The other attraction is "Horsin' Around" (see Insider Tip), and is an absolute MUST if you are traveling with children.

Georgia Mile 353 - Georgia Exit Numbers: Finally, Georgia has decided to adopt the "mile marker" exit numbering system recommended by the Federal Department of Transport and adopted by most other states (Florida will now be the only I-75 exception).

For instance, the first Georgia exit you encounter as you drive south was exit 142 (Route 146/Fort Oglethorpe) at mile marker 353. The new signage will show it as exit 353.

Starting January, 2000 and ending in June, the exit number signage on all Georgia interstates will be changed to reflect the new numbers. For a few years, the old exit number will also be shown.

Throughout this book, we decided to change to the new exit numbers immediately but include the old exit number alongside. This will help those who drive to Florida in late 1999 (under the old numbers) and return next Spring when the exit numbers will probably have changed on I-75.

So here we go with the new (and old) exit numbers.

GA Exit 353 (Old 142) - Lake Winnie (map on page 57): A wonderful family fun place–see insider tip, above.

GEORGIA - *in honor of King George II of England, by early explorer James Oglethorpe who received a Royal Charter in 1733, to settle the area.*

CHICKAMAUGA - *a Cherokee Indian name whose meaning is either "sluggish or dead waters," or "boiling waters."*

A Short Latin Lesson for the South

Special Report

As you visit museums and historic locations in the South, you will often encounter the terms *antebellum* and *postbellum*. These refer to the periods before the Civil War (also known as *The War between the States*, in the South) and after the Civil War, respectively. For instance, a plantation house might be described as Antebellum, meaning that it was built before 1861.

The terms come from the Latin, Ante meaning Before, Post meaning After, and Bellum meaning War. An easy way to remember these is to think of two other Latin terms familiar to everyone–a.m. meaning Ante Meridiem, or Before Noon (morning), and p.m. meaning Post Meridiem, or After Noon (afternoon).

Incidentally, Confederate President Jeff Davis and General Bragg met beside the Lake on the eve of the Battle of Missionary Ridge, in nearby Chattanooga.

GA Mile 352 - Welcome Center: One of my favorite stops on our I-75 trips is to pull in here, chat with the excellent staff and find out what is new within the State of Georgia. Say hello to my friends, Janice, Teresa, Carole and Manager Jo Anne, if they are on the counter that day. They all know and love Georgia.

GA Exit 350 (Old 141) - Georgia Winery (see Chickamauga map on page 58): The warm sunshine and distinctive soil of Georgia assures a strong wine industry which, in fact, has been around since 1730. Wineries such as Cavender Castle, Chateau Elan, Chestnut Mountain, Fox Wineries, Habersham Vineyards guarantee a good choice of varietal grape products . . . and the tasting room for one of the wineries, Georgia Wines, is just around the corner. Take exit 350 (old 141 - Battlefield Parkway) and travel 300 yards west until you see the KOA sign on your right. Turn right . . . and the tasting room is immediately on your right. Vineyard Master, Maurice, or Wine-maker, Patty, will help you with your choices. Georgia Wines is open Mon-Sat: 11-6pm. ☎ 706-937-2177

Money Saving Tip

Fill up with gas as soon as you can–even if you only need a 1/4 of a tank. Georgia has the cheapest gasoline in the USA.

Money Saving Tip

Pickup your <u>free copy</u> of the green Exit Information Guide, red Market America or yellow Mr Interstate motel coupon books at the Georgia Welcome Center (mile 352). Coupons in these books can <u>save you as much as 45%</u> off of regular motel rates.

GA Mile 350-Exit 141 - Chickamauga (map on page 58): After visiting Georgia Wines, you can continue westward along Battlefield Parkway to visit the well preserved battlefield of Chickamauga (about 20 minutes to the west). Phone, hours and other details on page 58. For many miles south of Chattanooga, the I-75 follows General Sherman's Union Army campaign to burn and destroy Atlanta–at Miles 338 and 323, the freeway runs right through the battlefields of Rocky Face Ridge and Resaca, respectively. And at Georgia Exit 149 (old 46 - Unadilla), you can follow the Andersonville Trail to visit the Confederate's dreaded Andersonville Prisoner of War Camp. It lies about 42 miles southwest of I-75.

GA Exit 348 (Old 140) - Ringgold & the Great Locomotive Chase (see special report on next 3 pages, side-trip maps on page 59, and detail I-75 maps between GA exit 348 (old 140) and exit 273 (old 118): One of the best known adventures of the Civil War– made even more famous by a Walt Disney movie, "The Great Locomotive Chase," starring Fess Parker - was exactly that . . . an epic chase where a steam locomotive stolen by Union soldiers, was chased through the

RINGGOLD - *in memory of Samuel Ringgold, professional soldier and Indian fighter who died of wounds received in action during the Mexican War, 1846.*

OOSTANAULA RIVER - *Cherokee name, "place of the rocks across the stream," for a shallow place to ford.*

The Great Locomotive Chase

During the Civil War, the Western & Atlantic railway line between Chattanooga and Atlanta was of great importance to the Confederacy, moving freight and soldiers between these two important railway centers. This vital link was a single track railway with passing tracks at various stations along the route. Kentuckian James Andrews, a Federal spy, devised a plan to steal a train near Atlanta and destroy the track and bridges along this line as he traveled northward. Andrews' tiny band of Union soldiers became known as Andrews' Raiders, and the subsequent actions of Saturday, April 12, 1862—the Great Locomotive Chase.

Note: This Special Report tells the story of the chase from the theft of the "General" at Big Shanty (Kennesaw–exit 273 - old 118) to its conclusion at Ringgold (exit 348 - old 140). If southbound on I-75, I suggest you read this report first so you understand the significance of the various locations as you run south towards Kennesaw. The entire adventure is shown on the detail map pages, supported with three special sidetrip maps on page 59. Numbers in the report refer to the locations marked on the detail maps—numbers in circles represent Andrews Raiders' (Union) actions; numbers in squares represent Fuller's (Confederate) actions.

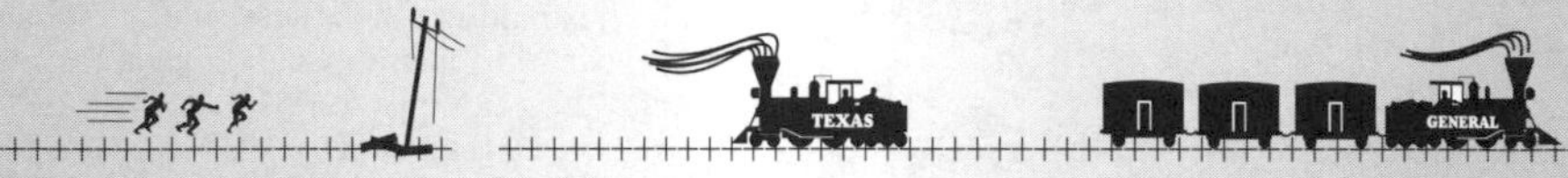

1. 5:30 a.m.—on a wet, rainy day, James Andrews and 23 Union soldiers from Ohio ride from Marietta to Big Shanty (Kennesaw) as passengers on a northbound train pulled by the locomotive, General. William Fuller is the train's conductor
2. 6:00 a.m.—while the train stops for breakfast at Big Shanty, Andrews' Raiders capture the General and with three box-cars, head north towards Chattanooga. Andrews and two men ride the locomotive while the rest of the armed band are hidden inside the box-cars.
3. 6:10 a.m.—Fuller, disturbed at breakfast and believing that Confederate conscripts had stolen his train to get clear of Big Shanty's army camp and would shortly abandon it, decides to give chase on foot. The General's engineer, Jeff Cain and a railroad engineering foreman, Anthony Murphy run with him.
4. The General runs out of steam a few miles up the track from Big Shanty. Andrews did not realize that the boiler dampers had been closed while the crew were at breakfast. The dampers were quickly opened and fires re-stoked with oil-soaked wood while the Raiders cut trackside telegraph wires to prevent "intercept" messages going north.

   After a quick run north, the General arrives at Moon's Station, and the Raiders "borrow" an iron bar from a track repair crew. The Raiders intend to remove rail sections behind them to halt pursuit, but later find the bar is inadequate for the task.
5. A breathless Fuller and companions arrive at Moon's Station, and take a pole-car. The three continue their pursuit by poling the car northward at 7-8 mph.
6. After passing through Acworth Station, the Raiders stop and cut more telegraph wires and damage a rail section.

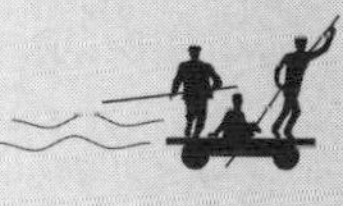

7. The General halts just below Allatoona to cut telegraph wires.
8. Andrews sees the Yonah, a work locomotive belonging to the Cooper Iron Works on the north banks of the Etowah River, with steam up. He is concerned since he knows that if a pursuit message gets this far north, there is now an operational locomotive and armed crew, to give chase. He does not stop since destroying the Etowah Bridge would not fill a purpose now.
9. The General pulls up at Cass Station (near Cartersville). Andrews convinces a suspicious railway worker that he is carrying much needed gunpowder north to the Confederate Army. The patriotic worker gives Andrews his only railway schedule so that Andrews can plan his northbound run to meet and pass southbound trains at appropriate stations.
10. The Raiders pull into Kingston Station, a major passing point on the railroad. Here they wait for a southbound train but when it finally arrives, they find that there are two

unscheduled southbounds on the same track section. The Raiders are forced to wait until the next section of track is clear. In the meantime, the station personnel are getting very suspicious of the northbound "gunpowder" train.

11. Fuller cannot stop the pole-car in time and it runs off the track at the broken rail section, dumping the crew and car down an embankment. Uninjured, they carry the car back up and resume the chase. After an epic pole-car journey of 20 miles, Fuller and crew arrive at the Etowah River and commandeer the Yonah.

12. After a wait of more than an hour, the General pulls out of Kingston to continue its northbound journey, just eight minutes before the arrival of Fuller aboard the Yonah. Andrews is now aware that pursuit is close since he has heard the frantic whistle of the Yonah as it approaches Kingston.

13. Fuller cannot get past the southbound trains so once again, he and his companions take to foot, running across the Kingston railroad yards to commandeer another locomotive, the William R. Smith. They give chase northwards towards Adairsville Station. To warn of obstructions, Fuller hangs onto the locomotive's cowcatcher while scanning the track ahead.

14. Aware that a chase is now on hand, the Raiders stop to cut wires and pile railroad ties across the track as a delaying tactic.

15. Several miles further, the Raiders stop to remove a rail section but find that their crowbar is too small to easily pull the spikes. By brute strength, the men manage to bend and snap a rail and throw it in the bushes.

16. Feeling safe once more, the Raiders pull into Adairsville Station where they find a long southbound train pulled by the locomotive, Texas. The suspicious engineer refuses to pull his train forward to clear the north switch of the passing track. After another delay, Andrews manages to convince the driver, and tries to send him southbound to either collide with their pursuers or derail on the broken section.

17. The William R. Smith is stopped in time to avoid being derailed by the missing section of rail. Fuller and company take off on foot for the third time, running up the track where they manage to flag down the southbound train pulled by the Texas.

18. They hear the engineer's story and commandeer the Texas for their chase—running in reverse. As they pass through Adairsville, Fuller, without stopping the train, uncouples the cars, runs ahead, turns the switch to a side track diverting the cars into it, returns the switch for the mainline movement, jumps back on board the Texas and the pursuit continues unencumbered by the weight of the cars.

19. The Raiders hear the whistle of the Texas to the south. They create as high a head of steam as possible by burning wood soaked in oil. The General careens up the railroad, leaning out and almost toppling on the curves.

20. The General and the last train southbound from Chattanooga pass at Calhoun Station without incident.

21. As the Texas steams through Calhoun a few minutes behind the General, Fuller spots a 13 year old telegraph boy, and grabs him onto the moving train. He writes a telegram to the Confederate commander in Chattanooga.

22. Desperately, the Raiders stop and attempt to remove a rail section but are only able to bend it slightly out of shape. They also cut the telegraph wire. They quickly scramble back on board when they see their pursuer for the first time–the reversed Texas with a full head of steam charging in their direction.

23. The Texas miraculously rides right over the damaged rail section.

24. Around a curve and out of sight, the Raiders uncouple a box car and let it run down a grade onto Fuller, who reverses his direction of travel to "catch" the box-car. He couples it to the Texas' tender and resumes the chase with the box car leading.

25. The Raiders do not have time to burn and destroy the covered Oostanaula River Bridge (a major target) so drop the second box-car in its center span hoping to slow down the pursuers. As before, the Fuller "catches" the box-car, couples it and later drops them both at a siding near Resaca Station.

26. A mile north of Resaca Station, Andrews cuts the Calhoun-Dalton telegraph wire and piles ties across the track.

27. The tactic of dropping railroad ties onto the track works to delay the Texas. Each time, the engineer must throw the locomotive into full reverse, skid to a halt while Fuller and his men jump down, clear the track and start on their way again. Seeing this, Andrews decided to punch a hole through the rear wall of the remaining box-car, and drop a succession of ties on the track

behind him.

28. Aware their pursuers are close again, the Raiders stop to cut wires and pile railroad ties across the track as a delaying tactic. Just south of Green's Station (Tilton), the Raiders stop again and attempt to remove a rail. They can only pry it out of shape, however. Andrews puts another rail underneath the bent rail, to try and derail the fast approaching Texas.

29. Thinking the damaged rail will have stopped the pursuit, a mile north of Tilton, Andrews' Raiders stop to take on much needed wood and water, but have to cut this short when they hear the whistle from the fast approaching Texas again. For the second time that day, the Texas has managed to run over damaged railway track without derailing.

30. After two more miles, the General stops again. Telegraph wires are cut and the track obstructed.

31. The Raiders decide to speed through Dalton, a major Confederate camp. A mile north of Dalton, they stop to cut the telegraph wire to stop messages getting through but they are unaware that minutes behind them, Fuller has dropped off the boy telegraph operator, who manages to get a portion of the message through to Chattanooga.

32. A few miles ahead is the Tunnel Hill railroad tunnel, and the Raiders discuss whether to ambush the Texas or perhaps travel through the tunnel and then reverse the General locomotive back towards the pursuing Texas for a collision. They decide to speed on northwards.

33. The Texas approaches the smoke filled tunnel. They cannot see ahead and are aware of what the Raiders might plan. Fuller decides to plunge into the tunnel's darkness at full speed, regardless of safety.

34. To their horror, Andrews looks back and sees the Texas emerge from the tunnel hard on their heels. They are approaching a covered wooden bridge across the Chickamauga River so he orders the last box car set on fire and then uncoupled in the middle of the bridge. Wet wood and the driving rain of the hour prevents this last attempt to escape, from working.

35. After a frantic dash through Ringgold, the Raiders are out of wood and oil and the General is slowing down. Andrews orders his men to jump from the train and find their own ways back to Union lines.

The mission failed because of the dogged pursuit by the General's conductor, William Fuller. Of the Raiders, sixteen were captured and eight were able to escape back to the safety of the Union. Of the captured men, eight were taken to Atlanta (including James Andrew) where they were hanged. Six were exchanged and two were "enlisted" in the Confederate Army. After the war, most of the surviving Raiders were awarded the Medal of Honor.

Continued from page 102

Georgia countryside by its Southern crew, who used their feet, a push car, and three other locomotives before they successfully recaptured their errant ward.

But best of all, the route of this chase from Kennesaw in the south, to Ringgold in the north, criss-crossed the path of the modern I-75 as it winds its way from the Tennessee-Georgia border towards Atlanta. We have mapped this chase alongside the modern interstate for you on southbound map pages 32 to 35 & northbound map pages 164 to 167.

GA Exit 341 (Old 138) - Tunnel Hill (map on page 59): Interesting things are happening at the famous 1850 railroad tunnel at Tunnel Hill, which played such a significant role in the Civil War's Great Locomotive Chase (see page 103) and in General Sherman's 1864 Atlanta Campaign.

$875,000 has been allocated by Georgia DOT and Whitfield County to preserve the 1,477 foot tunnel and its imposing arches. By March, 2000, tunnel owner Ken Holcomb (who also owns and has restored nearby Clisby-Austin House) plans to have opened a historical park at its mouth so all may enjoy it.

Clisby-Austin House is also a special Civil War site. It was used as a hospital during the war and later, as General Sherman's HQ during his campaign against Atlanta. After General John Hood lost his leg at the battle of Chickamauga, he and the limb were transferred to the House; the leg was buried in a nearby cemetery.

To find the tunnel, follow the map on page 59 to Tunnel Hill. Once you have driven across the bridge, park your car on the left of the

Insider Tip
Flammini's - An Italian Family Dining Experience

Have you ever been to an Italian family feast . . . one where everybody knows everybody, people wander around and talk to people at other tables, everybody is happy and smiling and laughter fills the air. Well, *Flammini's Cafe Italia* in Dalton is just like that. Even if you are far from home, the minute you poke your head through the door and past all the family photos, you are made warmly welcome by owner Pete, or perhaps his parents, Jack and Pat. You *know* you are going to have a wonderfully, enjoyable evening among new friends. Tiny lights twinkle throughout the dining area, and everybody–from the staff to the patrons is obviously having a good time.

The Flammini's are from the Marche region of Italy near the Adriatic Sea, and serve traditional foods from the small towns in the region . . . recipes which have been handed down through the generations of the Flammini family. Beef, seafood, veal or chicken in various preparations can be served with your choice of nine different pastas. And of course, they serve dining room pizzas. After our tasty main course of Veal Marsala (veal sauteed in marsala wine with mushrooms) and capellini (angel hair) pasta, Pat Flammini insisted that I sample a taste of traditional Tirami Su dessert (ladyfingers, soaked in rum, layered with mascarpone cheese and coffee whipped cream) . . . it's to die for! Incidentally, the Flammini's haven't forgotten those with dietary concerns, and offer a number of light and child meals.

The entire dining experience at Flammini's is best summed up by their own menu notes . . . "in our family, there is always plenty of food and room for one more at the table. At Flammini's there will be food in generous portions and we'll consider you as part of our family." Believe me, they mean it!

Buon Appetito

Flammini's Cafe Italia is at 1205 W. Walnut Avenue, Dalton. To find it, take exit 333 (old 136) and drive east along Walnut Avenue, through the lights at Tibbs Road–look for the yellow sign with black writing on your right–7/10ths of a mile from I-75. Open for lunch on Thurs and Fri only. Hours: Mon-Wed, 5pm-9:30pm; Thur-Fri, 11am-10pm; Sat, 5pm-10pm. Closed Sunday. ☎ 706-226-0667

road before the hill and you can walk right up the strip of land between the modern railroad track and the old rail bed, right up to the mouth of the old tunnel.

GA Mile 339 - Battle of Rocky Face Ridge: Ahead of you looms the craggy heights of Rocky Face Ridge, shielding the strategic town of Dalton behind. Here, for eight days starting on May 7th, 1864, Confederate General Joseph Johnston held off General Sherman's Army of the Ohio, under the command of Major General Schofield. The Rebs were well entrenched along the ridge (known locally as "Buzzards Roost") and as you can see, the terrain was very difficult for the attacking forces. In places, the men could only advance along its precipitous paths in single file; General Sherman described this gap as "the door of death."

While the General Schofield pursued his attack, Sherman decided to outflank the Confederates and sever the railroad further south. On May 9th, he sent his Army of the Tennessee to the west through Snake Creek Gap and down towards the sleepy, Georgian town of Resaca (mile marker 320). On May 11th, realizing the assault on the Ridge was impossible, Sherman left a token attacking force and followed his main army down towards Resaca. Johnston found out about this flanking movement from prisoners a day later, and rapidly pulled his troops from the "Door of Death" and retreated to defend the railroad at Resaca.

GA Exit 333 (Old 136) - Dalton: You have passed the signboards advertising carpet sales at Dalton on your journey south, but have you ever wondered ... why Dalton? Well Dalton bills itself as the Carpet Capital of North America, and it all started with one young farm girl, Catherine Whitener, supporting her family in the early 1900s by making tufted bedspreads and scatter rugs at home. Other women joined her and soon Dalton had a booming cottage industry, saving the area from the pangs of the Depression. By the 1950s advances in machinery and dyeing opened the door to the modern carpet industry. The entrepreneurial spirit of the local residents turned the cottage bedspread industry into multi-billion dollar carpet manufacturing. Today, more than 65% of the world's carpets are made in Dalton!

Incidentally, did you know that the nation's first gold rush did not occur in California, but in Dahlonga, Georgia, 93 miles east along Route 52 from I-75 exit 333 (old 136). In 1828, the area boomed and more than $6 million in gold coin was minted at the Dahlonga Mint before the Civil War closed it down.

Today, you can pan for gold in several locations as well as visit some of the 19th century mines and an interesting Georgia State Park museum. Mon-Sat, 9-5; Sun 10-5. Admission, adult/child–$3/$2.
☎ 706-864-2257.

GA Exit 320 (Old 133) - Battle of Resaca (see map on page 60 and Sidebar on page 108): At mile marker 323, you are just about to drive right across the Civil War battlefield of Resaca. See the Special Report above for a description of the battle.

Nowhere can the atmosphere of that day in 1864 be better felt, than at the Confederate Cemetery just a few minutes east of the I-75. The map on page 60 will help you find it.

The first time I visited this site, it was dusk and I was by myself. It was lonely and yet somehow peaceful–just row upon row of old but tidy graves–in the soft fading light filtered through the leafy boughs of the trees above.

The United Daughters of the Confederacy had recently put tiny flags by many of the tombstones, so even 130 years later, the men are still cared for. Imagine the anguish of wives and daughters, of families left behind who didn't know where their men had gone. But we know where they went–their journey ended here.

GA Exit 317 (Old 131) - New Echota and the Cherokee Nation: During the early 1800's, north Georgia was the heart of the sovereign Cherokee Indian Nation. By this time, the Cherokee were the most progressive Indian tribe in North America.

In 1821, they became the first American Indians with a written language, invented by Sequoyah. New Echota, the Cherokee national capital, was located just half a mile from here (take exit 317 - old 131 - and follow Rt 225 east for 1 minute). There, a constitutional government with executive, legislative and judicial branches ruled the nation. Once the largest town in this area, New Echota consisted of houses, stores, taverns, a Council house, Supreme Courthouse, and a printing office which published a national bilingual newspaper, the Cherokee Phoenix.

In 1838, the Cherokee were rounded up at gun point and imprisoned by state and federal armies. Later that year, these peaceful people were forced to what is now Oklahoma. Four thousand Cherokee died on the terrible march west known as the "Trail of Tears."

Today, you may visit New Echota where the State of Georgia maintains an excellent museum and seven of the original houses.

The historic site is open Tues.-Sat, 9-5, Sunday 2-5:30pm. Admission adults/children–$2.50/$1.50. ☎ 706-624-1321.

GA Mile 310 - Mercer Air Field: Across the freeway beside the northbound lanes is a field containing vintage aircraft - the collection of local businessman, E L Mercer. Representing aircraft from WWII, the Korean War and Vietnam eras, sadly, they have deteriorated

Insider Tip
Born to Shop, Dalton Style

In case you didn't already know, there's excellent factory outlet shopping–the West Point Pepperill Mall - on the east side of Exit 333 (old 136). And with great forethought Hampton built an excellent inn within easy walking distance right alongside the mall. So, you can park your car at the inn - shop–go back to your room–shop–go back to your room–shop, etc. Note: a ground floor room might be your best bet. The inn also provides an excellent free breakfast.

An outlet shopper's dream come true!

I-75 and the Civil War

As you drive through north Georgia, you will pass a number of nearby Civil War battlefields–Chickamauga and Chattanooga's Lookout Mountain. The I-75 follows the route of Sherman's march toward Atlanta with its resulting destruction by flame - and you will actually drive through two of the battlefields (see Resaca map on page 60).

Imagine the scene–it is May 13,1864. Strung out across the path of the southbound I-75 a few yards south of mile marker 323 is a thin line of young men crouched in hurriedly constructed trenches cut deep into the red Georgian earth. Banks of rubble have been thrown forward to give added protection from the whining Minie balls which zip overhead like angry hornets waiting to administer the sting of death. A fountain of red soil suddenly shoots skyward in front of them, followed by the vibration of the ground shock wave and deep crumping sound of a distant explosion. A Confederate field gun is ranging in on their position.

Sweltering under the hot Georgian sun in their heavy flannel uniforms of dark blue, they wait their officer's command to rise up and charge over the rough ground toward the wooded rise where they can see the gray hunched shapes of the Confederates behind log spiked palisades. Behind the wooden barriers, the distinctive saltire cross of the red and blue Battle Flag floats lazily overhead.

On closer look, the mud and sweat streaked faces are of very young men–frightened, quietly exchanging comments of bravado in nervous, throat-tightened voices. Many, only in their sixteenth or seventeenth year, will not see nightfall.

They are showing the strain of the Atlanta campaign–many escaped death only a few days earlier facing the same enemy in the battle of Rocky Face Ridge, 14 miles north of here. They were lucky, for they survived and flanked General Johnston's Gray forces who have now retreated southward to make yet another stand here–at Resaca–as the Rebels fall back toward Atlanta's

Continued top of next page

over the years and are probably not flyable now.

GA Exit 293 (Old 126) - Weinman Mineral Museum: If you enjoy rocks and precious stones, there is a treat in store for you just minutes off the I-75 at this exit–the William Weinman Mineral Museum. More than 2,000 exhibits are displayed in three halls. The Georgia room contains many specimens native to the State, as well as a simulated cave and waterfall. Indian artifacts dated back to 8,000 BC and fossils as early as the Paleozoic Era (see chart on page 86) are displayed in a second room, while a third contains the international Mayo collections.

Children can touch the skull (replica) of a 30 foot Triceratops Horridus dinosaur or try their hands at gold panning and mineral classification while parents peruse the Gift Shop. The Museum is closed on Mon. Hours for Tues-Sat are 10-4:30pm; Sun, 1-4:30pm. Admission is Adult/Senior/ Children (6-11); $3.50/$3/$2.50.

To find the museum, take exit 293 (old 126) and go west for a few yards on route 411. Turn left onto Mineral Museum Drive which is just past the Holiday Inn. ☎ 770-386-0576.

GA Exit 288 (Old 124) - Original Coca-Cola sign: Take Rt113 2.7 miles west to Cartersville, and you will run right into the Cartersville Main Street and historical downtown area. Just over the railroad tracks on West Main Street is the Young Brothers Pharmacy, and it was on the outside wall in 1894 that a Coca-Cola syrup salesman painted the first outside painted-wall Coke advertisement in the World. Visit the historic pharmacy and

CARTERSVILLE - *for Colonel Farish Carter (1780-1861), an early landowner.*

MARIETTA - *for Marietta Cobb, believed to have been the wife of Thomas Cobb, after whom Cobb County is named.*

main defense line in a losing war.

These are the men and boys of the General Sherman's 35th Indiana, under the command of Brigadier General Stanley. Little do they know that the Confederates have already spotted a weakness to the left of their line and at 4 o'clock that afternoon, six divisions of General Hood's best Rebs will charge down the slope and drive them from their position. The situation will be saved by the 5th Indiana gunners firing double-shotted canister into the Grays, and the timely arrival of General William's Union Army of the Cumberland, currently positioned a mile to their right.

Before the end of this battle three days later, 5,547 men and boys will have been killed or injured, and the Confederates will be forced to pull back to make yet another retreating stand at Cassville, opening the door to Sherman's Union victories at New Hope Church, Kennesaw Mountain ... and ultimately, Atlanta.

All this action, which involved over 171,000 men, took place right across the ground you are traveling as you approach Exit 320 (old 133). The map on page 60 relates the I-75 mile markers to the battlefield.

After driving through the 35th Indiana's Union line positions (just south of Mile 323), you pass through the Confederate defenses (just north of mile marker 322) of General Hood and then cross the Confederate encampment and back through the Rebel army's southernmost defense lines (just south of mile marker 321) manned by the troops of Generals Cleburne and Polk. At Exit 320 (old 133), you are in no man's land between the forces of Cleburne and the Union attackers of Major Generals Loring and Smith. The Oostanaula River forms the southern boundary of the battlefield.

see how the sign was discovered and restored . . . and of course, enjoy a Coke while you are there.

GA Exit 288 (Old 124) - Etowah Indian Mounds: Five miles (15 minutes) to the west along route 113 (2.3 miles past the Coke sign) is an early Indian townsite on the banks of the Etowah River. Dated from 1000–1500 AD, the remains of three flat topped ceremonial mounds and a moat which encircled the town remain. Archeological digs have yielded many finds which are on display at the park's Visitor Center.

To find the Etowah Mounds State Park, drive west on route 113 towards Cartersville, left on Etowah Drive, continue on Indian Mounds Road. The park is open Tues-Sat, 9-5; Sun 2-5:30pm. Admission is Adult/Children; $3/$2. ☎ 770-387-3747.

GA Exit 285 (Old 123) - Etowah Bridge and Cooper Iron Works (map on page 59): Follow the map and visit remains of the Etowah Bridge where the locomotive, Yonah was commandeered during the Great Locomotive Chase.

GA Mile 281 - Allatoona Lake: In 1965, another civil war of sorts took place here. At issue was the building of the I-75 in a straight line from Chattanooga to Atlanta, for it was designed to go right through the center of Lake Allatoona and surrounding woodlands,

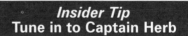

Insider Tip
Tune in to Captain Herb

Mile 285–Just a reminder, you are twenty six miles north of the point where the Atlanta bypass leaves I-75 to circle around the city to the west. Now is the time to start thinking about whether you are going to bypass Atlanta or stay on I-75 and go right through.

Why not tune in Captain Herb on 750 AM and get a traffic report? See page 193 for Atlanta rush hour times and page 195 for the bypass map.

Insider Tip
Red Top Mountain

Just to the east of I-75 is one of Atlanta's favorite week-end retreats, *Red Top Mountain State Park*. It is so close to the interstate, that it is an interesting diversion just to drive in and spend ten or fifteen minutes touring its treed winding roads, just to throw off the cloak of stress gathered while driving the freeway. Drive slowly though since the park abounds with wildlife. We have seen deer grazing beside the road and red foxes can often be seen.

Red Top is named after the rich red color of the area's soil, caused by the very high iron-ore content. You might wish to visit the park lodge which is 2.1 miles from the park entrance–just follow the excellent park signage. The Lodge is extremely clean and maintained to very high standards; it also has a restaurant which is open for all meals which are served buffet style. More on staying at Red Top Lodge in Section Six – *"Interstate-75 Lodging"* – of this guide.

If in the mood, you may enjoy stretching your legs along one of the many hiking trails. The 3/4 mile long *Lakeside Trail* starts at the Lodge parking lot and makes a loop bordering the Lake. It is paved and quite suitable for wheelchair access. Be sure to stop and see the 1860's log cabin along the way.

The park entrance is 1.2 miles from I-75, exit 285 (old 123). Drive east along Glade Road and across the Bethany girder bridge which crosses a section of Allatoona Lake, and into the park entrance. There is no entry fee although if you decide to park, there is a $2 parking fee. The park is open year round.

on a causeway–and that's where the battle lines were drawn. The resulting fight ground to a halt the completion of the first continuous Interstate to Florida's border. Twelve years later, with the last lawsuit dismissed and the road's path relocated somewhat to the west of its original plan, Georgia's Governor Busbee and U.S. Transportation Secretary Adams cut a red, white and blue ribbon and the traffic began to flow over the I-75's last (and most controversial) link. The date was Wednesday, December 22, 1977; 21 years after construction of the I-75 had officially begun.

As Governor Busbee said, "it is now possible to drive from Canada to the Gulf of Mexico without stopping for a single traffic light or stop sign." In a message to those present at the ceremony, President Carter called it "the most important interstate route in the nation."

GA Exit 273 (Old 118) - Kennesaw Civil War Museum (map on page 59): After following the route of the Great Locomotive Chase backwards all the way down from Ringgold, you can now visit the actual restored locomotive, "General" and the place where she was seized on April 12, 1862. In fact, the parking area opposite the Museum is right at Big Shanty where the crew stopped the train for breakfast that fateful morning.

It is also worth noting that the other major locomotive involved in the Chase, the "Texas," is on display in Atlanta at the Cyclorama. ☎ phone 404-658-7625 for directions and information.

GA - somewhere north of Atlanta: speaking of trains, someday you might see electric passenger coaches whizzing along beside the interstate - at 310 miles per hour. In 1998, President Clinton signed a bill allocating substantial funds to build an experimental 40 mile track along the interstate corridor, to test

ATLANTA - *formerly named "Terminus" (in 1837 for the southern end of the Western & Atlantic Railroad), and changed to "Marthasville" in 1843 to honor Gov.. Wilson Lumpkin's daughter. Finally to "Atlanta" in 1845, suggested by the word "Atlantic" in the name of its most important industry, the W&A Railroad.*

CHATTAHOOCHEE RIVER - *Cherokee name probably, "marked rocks," for painted stones found in the river.*

high speed trains operating using the magnetic levitation (maglev) technology already in final test in Germany and Japan. Similar U.S. tests will be conducted on the Baltimore-Washington, DC, Pittsburgh-Corapolis corridors, and at a site to still be announced in southern California.

GA Exit 271 (Old 117) - Speed Zone: Have you ever wanted to drive a race car, or pilot one of those drag strip monsters down the track? If so, Speed Zone is for you. As its brochure states, "you are about to enter a 12 acre park completely dedicated to speed, racing and competition. It is the closest thing to professional racing ever offered to the public."

The attraction offers a number of challenges - you can ride the powerful Eliminator dragsters (3 races for $15), drive the Turbo Track ($5 for 5 minutes), handle the Slick Trax ($5 for 5 minutes) or master the Grand Prix circuit ($2.50 per lap). A special ticket deal is also available which gives $30 of racing for $25.

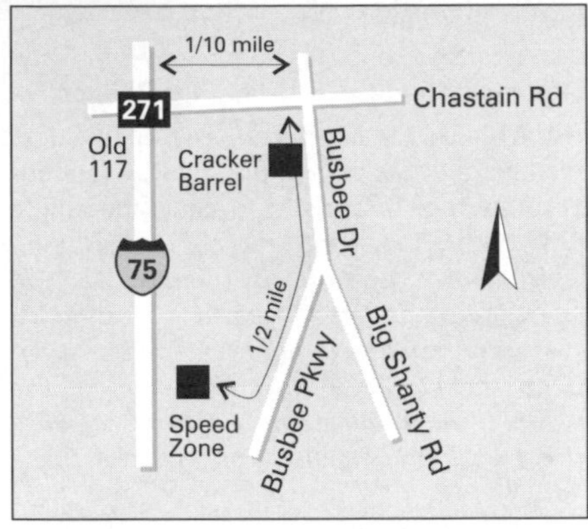

Speed Zone is geared primarily to 18 to 35 year olds, but younger family members (42" or taller) may ride as passengers on the Turbo or Grand Prix tracks during daylight hours. Youngsters over 5' tall, may also drive a special car on the Turbo Track during daylight hours.

It seems to me that Speed Zone might be an excellent way to discharge all that youthful

Insider Tip
Harry's Farmers Market

If you have ever visited Atlanta for any length of time, you will have certainly heard about Harry's Farmers Market. Harry's is sort of difficult to describe . . . think of it as a "super box" department store for fruit, vegetables, fish, meat, deli, cheese and bakery items, with aisles three times as wide as the average supermarket. All I know is that when you walk into Harry's your senses are immediately affected; the sights, aromas, freshness, tastes and sounds are unique and unforgettable. The store is fast becoming a tourist attraction (the salad and soup bar is perfect for travelers passing through) as well as a fabulous shopping experience for locals. If it grows or swims, the store probably stocks it.

With more than 1,200 fresh produce alone, Harry's covers the full range including organically grown and exotic ethnic vegetables. Ever try Coco Malagna? . . . they have it. Seafood-wise, they stock up to 300 items daily (try Harry's famous *smoked salmon Californian roll*). The Deli has 85 types of deli meat, 400 different cheeses and the bakery offers 200 different items baked daily. Wash all of this down with one of the 75 different coffee blends.

Two cautions: Unlike a regular supermarket, the aisle in Harry's winds around continuously with no escape routes. Once committed to the store you have to keep going, although I suppose you can always retrace your path and go out the "in" door. Secondly, if buying lunch here, there is nowhere to sit–other than your car!

To reach Harry's, take exit 263 (old 112 - Marietta Parkway–State Route 120E) east towards Roswell, at the first light turn left onto Powers Ferry Road. The store is approximately 1 mile up on the left hand side in the Harry's Crossing Plaza.

What more can I say except *"I'm just wild about Harry's"* and wouldn't dream of passing exit 263 without stopping for a gastronomical visit.

energy that can build up during a long car journey. Speed Zone hours are Sun-Thur, 11:30am-11pm; Fri-Sat, 11:30am-1:00am.

GA Mile 262 - Marietta: The huge Lockheed plant to the east of the freeway reminds us of another I-75 claim to fame. Quoting a 1987 Forbes magazine article, *"the I-75 symbolizes America's industrial renaissance. In recent years it has attracted an estimated 15% of America's capital spending on manufacturing, and the dollars keep coming. The Japanese have put about a quarter of their direct U.S. investments alongside the Interstate."*

It is true–think about the massive manufacturing plants you have passed along the way - Mazda's U.S. car plant in Flat Rock, Michigan; Honda's Anna, Ohio, engine plant; General Electric's Cincinnati un-ducted jet aircraft engine center; Toyota in Georgetown, Kentucky; Martin Marietta around Knoxville; Komatsu Ltd. in Chattanooga; Lockheed and Northrop in North Georgia; Ford's Sable and Taurus automobile plant in South Atlanta; McDonnell Douglas in Macon - and these are just a few.

One of the most impressive hi-tech projects currently underway by I-75 is the production of the USA's new fighter aircraft, the F-22 Raptor, at Lockheed in Marietta. This very advanced fighter is designed to replace the aging F15 as America's front-line air superiority fighter; deliveries will start in 2002.

Designed to continue the USA's combat dominance in the air for the first quarter of the 21st Century, the Raptor combines stealth, maneuverability (hovering, flying backwards, etc.), supersonic cruise speed without an afterburner and very advanced integrated avionics (aviation electronics).

The latter is very impressive indeed. Each F22 will have computing power equal to two Cray Supercomputers, and will have the ability to automatically link up with other aircraft in its flight and exchange data without pilot intervention. For instance, each fighter can quickly determine on its display unit, all characteristics of the other F22's in its flight - fuel loads, weapons available, target locks, etc. - all without voice communication.

The first F22 Raptor took off from Dobbins AFB on September 7, 1997, and climbed to 15,000 feet in the skies over Marietta and I-75, in seconds.

As Forbes went on to say, *"I-75 slices right through the middle of the country where the supply of workers is ample and eager, the taxes and the cost of living remain low, and land can still be had for as little as $1,000 an acre."*

GA Mile 260 - Atlanta's Advanced Traffic Management System: You have just passed under one of the electronic gantry signs of Atlanta's Advanced Traffic Management System, or ATMS, billed as the most sophisticated traffic management system in the World.

Many technologies such as video camera and road sensors feed information into a control center where the information is analyzed and up-to-date traffic information messages relayed back to travelers via the overhead signs (there are five over the I-75 in the Atlanta area)—and eventually to in-car navigational displays, hand-held Personal Communication Devices (for people walking), on-line computer services and cable TV. The overhead signs should be a great help in driving through or around Atlanta. They will also give you a final check on whether to take the bypass (coming up in another mile) or not.

GA Mile 258 - Atlanta Express Lanes: Another much needed innovation to help traffic move on the I-75 through Atlanta is the introduction of restricted High Occupancy Vehicle (HOV), or express lanes.

From mile marker 258 to 237, the left hand lane is dedicated to public and emergency vehicles, and cars with two or more people on board. Unlike many other cities though, the Atlanta Express Lanes are ***restricted to this traffic 24 hours a day, 7 days a week.*** Watch for the black diamond sign and double dashed lines marked on the road, which identifies the restricted traffic lanes.

Incidentally, the signage reads "two person car pools" but we have checked with the Atlanta authorities and any private car (even with out-of-state license plates) with two or more people in it may use the express lanes. A special "car pooling" permit, as some readers thought, is not necessary.

A small word of caution. Since the express lanes occupy the freeway's left hand lane and the I-75 running through Atlanta has some exits which also exit to the left, be very careful that you don't accidentally leave the I-75 at those exits. There are however, several points where due to the "basket weave" of other interstates joining and leaving I-75, the express lanes appear to leave the normal flow of I-75 traffic. The express ;lanes are clearly marked "I-75" with an arrow. Follow these with confidence since they rejoin I-75 a little further on. Just feel good about the fact that you are in the express lane and moving . . . whereas the rest of the I-75 traffic is probably standing still!

GA Exit 250 (Old 102) - Atlanta 1996 Olympic Games: It would be hard to ignore the passing of the 1996 Centennial Olympic Games which were held in Atlanta that year. Some of the landmarks that became familiar to us during the Games are still visible from the I-75. Here's a quick run-down.

Olympic Village - At mile 251, the I-75 runs alongside the site of the Olympic Village (on the right side of the freeway). The buildings are easily recognized by their red brick and tall peak roofs.

Just south of mile 251, are more buildings—in this case high rises—of the large Olympic housing complex.

Centennial Olympic Park - About 3/4 mile behind these is the Centennial Olympic Park area, gathering place for the many Olympic fans and site of the fateful bombing of July 27, 1996.

The Varsity - at exit 249D (old 100) lies one of Atlanta's famous landmarks which I'm sure played a major role during the Olympics, The Varsity drive-in restaurant.

Now there are several things you need to know about The Varsity before you decide to eat there. It can be crowded, noisy . . . in fact, sometimes raucous . . . but it's an Atlanta institution. Anybody who is anybody in Atlanta has eaten there. Presidents Carter, Bush, and most recently, Clinton have graced The Varsity dining rooms where you can choose the room according to the TV channel you would like to watch; they probably decided upon the CNN room.

No matter how crowded it is (they serve over 10,000 customers a day), the orders move quickly over the many sales positions along the 150' stainless steel counter.

"Whad'll ya have?? whad'll you have??" is the constant cry. As owner Frank Gordy says, "Have your money in your hand and your order in your mind and we will get you to the game on time."

Alternatively, you can sit in your car and one of the car-hops will come and take your order. If you get Flossie Mae, the menu will be sung to you!

You will either love or hate The Varsity, but it will be an unforgettable experience. If you see Frank say "hello" to him from me; his wife Evelyn is usually there as well - if you see her, ask her about the old days of Atlanta - she'd love to chat with you.

If driving south on I-75, take exit 249D (old 100), turn left and The Varsity is immediately on your left just across the bridge. Pull into the first driveway (before the building) for car-hop service or regular parking.

When you leave, drive around the back out onto Spring St, cross the traffic lights at Ponce De Leon and across North Ave., stay left past the I-75 North ramp until you see the I-75 South sign - follow the I-75S ramp back down onto the freeway (also known as the Atlanta Downtown Connector).

If driving north, take exit 249D (old 100), cross Spring St and turn left when you reach West Peachtree, turn left again at North Avenue and you will see The Varsity across the road from you.

When you leave, follow the directions above for southbound travelers but take the I-75 North ramp instead.

Turner Field (Olympic Stadium) - At mile 246, on your left is the newly named Turner Field (named after cable TV and CNN mogul Ted Turner), site of the Olympic Opening and Closing ceremonies. The stadium is now home of the Atlanta Braves baseball team.

Olympic Torch - Just to the north of the Stadium is the distinctive open girder statue of the Olympic Torch, honoring the Games.

Mile 239 - World's Busiest Airport: At mile 239, you might notice lights on top of stalks in I-75's median. These are the final approach lights of runway 27R, of the world's busiest airport, William B Hartsfield International.

Insider Tip
Tokyo Japanese Steak House

For a change of pace, you might enjoy dining Teppanyachi style at this restaurant where the chef prepares your steak, chicken or shrimps (and performs) right at your table. The special teppa tables with their hot cooking surfaces seat 8 people. With a friendly group, the show can be spectacular - so introduce yourselves to others when you arrive - you'll soon be having a great time! Meals are all inclusive and include soup or salad, entree, dessert and beverage.

The Tokyo Japanese Steak House is located at 3688 HIghway 138. Go east at exit 228 (old 75); the restaurant is located in the last shopping plaza on your right just before you reach the I-675 ramp.

Hours: Mon-Thur 4:30-10pm; Fri-Sat 4:30-11pm; closed on Sunday
☎ 770-506-8866

Built on land originally owned by Asa Chandler, the founder of The Coca Cola Company, as the site of his auto race track, Hartsfield was recently named the world's busiest airport by the Geneva based International Airport Council. Currently, Atlanta handles 73.5 million passengers a year, compared to Chicago O'Hare's 72.4 million.

GA Exit 237 (Old 78) - Georgia Farmers Market: Just to the east of I-75 lies the huge Georgia Farmers' Market. To reach it, turn off at Exit 237 (old 78) and go east to the second traffic light. Turn left into the double gates and follow the left hand lanes marked Shed Area–"Georgia Farmers" (don't worry–it's open to the public even though it looks commercial)–follow the lanes around the building and there you will find sheds with stands selling–pecans, onions, tomatoes, peanuts–every type of fruit and vegetable you ever wanted.

GA Exit 233 (Old 76) - Road to Tara Museum: We are in the Deep South and the names "Jonesboro" and "Clayton County" on the road signs strike a chord–for we are in "Gone With The Wind" country.

Yes, I know that Margaret Mitchell's great book was a work of fiction ... but wasn't Jonesboro where Scarlett O'Hara used to drive her buggy five miles to catch the train to Atlanta? And, my map shows me that the Flint River which flowed through Tara's grounds, is just to the west. So while in the mood, let's go and visit the "Road To Tara" Museum which is housed very appropriately in the Jonesboro Railroad Depot building.

The first thing that strikes me as I enter the door is the green drapery dress worn by Scarlett when she went to visit Rhett in jail to try and borrow money from him to pay the taxes on Tara. The museum is filled with such mementos - from the movie, "Gone With The Wind" and from Margaret Mitchell's personal life. For any "GWTW" fan, it's an absolute must.

And if you're really lucky, Scarlett might sweep into the room in the form of Miss Melly Meadows, who is the official "Scarlett" of Clayton County. You cannot tell the difference between Vivien Leigh and Melly - they are exact look-alikes.

The "Road To Tara" Museum is open Mon-Sat, 10am-4pm. ☎ 770-210-1017

Well, perhaps we had better move on before I start to imagine Rhett Butler and Ashley Wilkes riding out of the mist on their way to

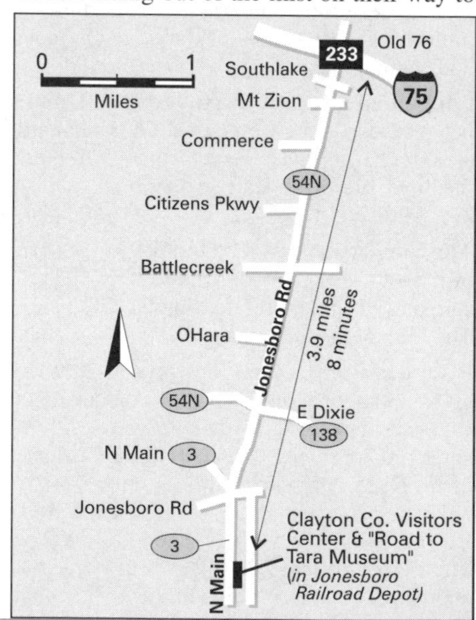

JONESBORO - *originally called "Leakesville," it was renamed after Samuel Jones, an engineer who revived the Macon & Western, a bankrupt railroad.*

Insider Tip
Golf Heaven - The Inn at Eagle's Landing

We have a real treat for those of you who love to occasionally pamper yourselves with luxury, and it includes if you wish, a round of golf on one of the finest private courses in Georgia.

The management of the lovely gated Inn at Eagle's Landing (just south of Atlanta) has offered readers of *Along Interstate-75* a special weekend price which includes a large deluxe room with executive amenities, afternoon wine & hors d'oeuvres reception in the Tee Lounge, late night cookies & a hot beverage beside the brick fireplace in the sumptuous mahogany and leather living room and an excellent continental breakfast overlooking a world class golfcourse. Of course, you also have the use of their fully equipped fitness room and two swimming pools. An in-house spa and the private dining room in the golf Clubhouse are also available to you.

Now, the golf course is a world-class championship course designed by the acclaimed Tom Fazio and home to one of the LPGA championships. Here's a sample - hole 8, 207 yard, par 3 - "beautiful and treacherous, considered one of the most difficult par 3's in Georgia. Elevated tee to a long, narrow and rolling green menaced by a creek on the left."

Non-golfers might enjoy the clay and hard tennis courts, or simply sitting out on one of the Inn's balconies or perhaps the patio beside the goldfish pool, enjoying magazines or a novel and delighting in the fresh air of the surrounding woods.

If you would like to take advantage of this offer which is $100 per evening (a 40% discount from the regular rates), please give Director of Sales John Couey a call at 770-389-3118; make sure you mention *Along Interstate-75*. Should you wish to arrange a round of golf, mention this to John and he will explain the various green fee options open to you. This very generous offer expires on October 31, 2000.

Although, reservations are preferred to avoid disappointment, the staff will do their best to accommodate you if you arrive without previous arrangements. Just press the bell at the gate and again, make sure you mention you are a reader of this book.

To reach the Inn, take exit 224 (old 73 - Eagle Landing Parkway) and drive east for 1 mile, turn right just after the Publix plaza onto Country Club Drive. The gates to the Inn at Eagle's Landing are a short distance down the road on the left.

Twelve Oaks.

GA Exit 224 (old 73): see the Golf Heaven Insider Tip above.

GA Exit 221 (Old 71) - McDonough Square (see map next page): There's a lovely town square of a bygone era a few miles off I-75 at McDonough. In it's center sits a white stone memorial to the "War between the States," shaded on all sides by old leafy trees. Sitting in the sun on one of the wrought iron benches at the side of the square, it is easy to close one's eyes and imagine that you hear the excited voices of an early Confederate muster at the beginning of the war when McDonough's youth were going to go up north to "whop them boys in blue" . . . or perhaps the concerned shouts of the city's merchants on the evening of November 15, 1864, when they heard that the 17th Corps of Sherman's Army was camped nine miles north of McDonough at Stockbridge, and intending to head in their direction the following morning.

MCDONOUGH - *in honor of War of 1812 naval hero, Commodore Thomas McDonough (1783-1825). During the 1812 naval campaigns on Lake Champlain, he fought and won the battle of Plattsburgh which caused the British forces to retreat back to Canada.*

FORSYTH - *for John Forsyth (1780-1841) who was Governor of Georgia in 1827 and Secretary of State between 1834-41, under Presidents Jackson and Van Buren.*

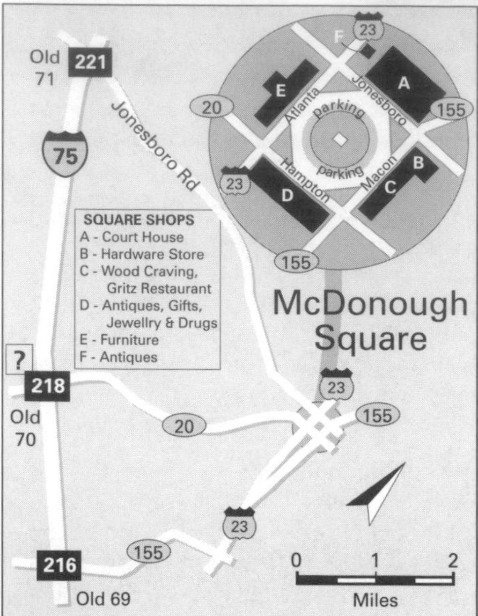

Thanks to the skirmishing actions of the Kentucky 4th Mounted Infantry ("The Orphan Brigade"), the Feds decided to move off in another direction as part of Sherman's right wing of his devastating "March to the Sea" - saving McDonough from possible pillage and burning.

Today, the square is surrounded on three sides by interesting stores to poke around in. From the old general store - McDonough Hardware to various antique and gift shops. Southern food is served at the Gritz Family Restaurant. On the north lies the imposing Henry County Courthouse.

The McDonough Square is one of those small treasures which never gets adequate mention in the glossy travelbooks - enjoy a bygone era.

Insider Tip
Falls View Restaurant

Visitors from the Magnolia State and local folk agree, *"this is the best catfish restaurant this side of the Mississippi."* Located across the road from High Falls State Park, it's tucked back in a wooded setting, with a real fireplace to provide comfort on the cooler days.

The menu offers many seafood items as well as steaks, chicken and hamburgers . . . the prices are very reasonable. Service is provided by owner Tommy Wilson, the Wilson family and their staff. Say "hello" to Tommy for me and tell him I sent you.

To find the Falls View Restaurant, take exit 198 (old 65) and drive 1.4 miles east towards High Falls Park. Watch for the restaurant parking area on your right, after passing Exxon.

Hours: Tue-Thurs, 4pm-9pm; Fri-Sat, 4pm-10pm. ☎ 912-994-6050

GA Exit 218 (old 70) - McDonough Visitors' Information: Need area tourist information? The McDonough Chamber of Commerce is at this exit immediately to the west of I-75 on the north side (your right) of the road.

GA Exit 201 (Old 66) - Buckners, A Different Dining Experience: Buckners Family Restaurant and Music Hall is certainly an unusual dining experience, for they combine great southern cooking with gospel singing (Thursday, Friday and Saturday evenings).

The buffet meal (served at round communal tables with lazy susan food trays in the center) gives a choice of two entrees each day and is all inclusive. A typical day might include southern fried chicken, BBQ pork or beef, mashed potatoes, stewed tomatoes, cream corn, black-eyed peas —followed with peach cobbler for dessert.

After your meal, wander around the tables and make new friends, for owners Glen and David Buckner encourage that type of informal, down-south atmosphere.

Buckners are closed on Monday and Tuesday. On other days they open from 11:30-8:00 pm. Please note that there can be line-ups on Saturday evening.

GA Exit 198 (Old 65) - High Falls State Park: Less than two miles east of the I-75 is a pretty place to pause—perhaps for a picnic beside the 100 foot waterfall—the High Falls State Park. Incidentally, an excellent overnight stop for RVers.

GA Exit 186 (Old 61) - Juliette - Whistle Stop Cafe (see page 117; map on page 61).

Southern Grace, Juliette - I must mention my very special place here . . . the two rocking chairs on Betty's front porch or the two rockers down in the wine cellar where it is cooler. It's wonderful to sit here and chat with Betty and her son, Dean. Ask Dean about

Whistle Stop Cafe & Fried Green Tomatoes

Special Report

Did you enjoy *"Fried Green Tomatoes?"* No, not the Southern dish—the movie. That wonderful warm story about how Evelyn Couch rediscovers herself while listening to 83 year old Ninny Threadgoode (Jessica Tandy) tell about life in Whistle Stop, Alabama, with Ruth, and her best friend, the rebellious Idgie. Well, Whistle Stop is not in Alabama, but a few miles east of the I-75 at exit 186 (old 61) in Georgia. The film company took over the town and people of Juliette, Georgia . . . and turned it into Whistle Stop.

I decided to visit the movie set (it's still there and now houses various antique and craft shops) and see if the *Whistle Stop Cafe* really exists. Well it does . . . the movie company left long ago but the spirit of Whistle Stop lives on in the warmth and charm of Juliette's people.

Whistle Stop Cafe owners Jerie Williams & Robert Williams, Betty Clements and her son, Dean, of the *Southern Grace* country collectibles shop & Habersham Wines, Donna & Larry Pierce of McCrackin St. Sweets, and the many other fine people of Juliette are just as friendly and heart-warming as the folk in the movie. I arrived expecting to spend half an hour chatting with various residents gathering information to write a story, and left three hours later as "family." Juliette and its people have this effect on you.

The center of activity is the *Whistle Stop Cafe* (yes–they do serve Fried Green Tomatoes as well as other Southern delicacies) where Jerie maintains her business office in one of its old wooden booths. As you sit and chat, people come and go and, of course, you are introduced and meet them all. Despite the success of the film which has brought worldwide fame to the cafe and Juliette, Jerie is determined to maintain this spirit and not let it become another "plastic" commercial tourist attraction. In fact, I went back the following morning (the Cafe is open from 8am–2 pm, Mon-Sat; noon–5 pm, Sunday; phone 912-994-3670) and Jerie cooked me a breakfast of . . . yes, you guessed it . . . FGTs!

Across the street, Betty not only runs the *Southern Grace* and two other stores next door, but also a wine and tasting room down the cellar steps. Here you can sample Georgia's *Habersham Estate* wines such as , Cherokee Rose, Belle Blush, Granny's Arbor, Scarlett, Peach Treat . . . then there is *Miz Magnolia* and *Treehouse Antiques* (Ruth and Idgie's house in the movie), and so on up Juliette's main McCrackin Street until you reach the Firehall (see map of the street on page 61). The twelve or so shops have varying hours but you should find them all open between 11-4 p.m.

Fried Green Tomatoes Recipe

reprinted with kind permission of
Jerie Williams, Whistle Stop Cafe

2 firm medium-sized green tomatoes

¼ teaspoon of salt

¼ teaspoon of pepper

½ cup of white cornmeal

¼ cup of bacon dripping

Cut tomatoes into ¼ inch slices. Sprinkle with salt and pepper; dredge in cornmeal. Heat bacon drippings in a heavy skillet; add tomatoes and cook over medium heat until browned, turning once.

Yield: 2-3 servings.

Thirsty? Try Grandma Huber's wonderfully sweet and thirst quenching - "lemonade made right!" at McCrackin Street Sweets, just beside the Fire Hall. A photograph of Grandma (just inside the door as you enter) ensures that "all the makins' are right." Try the cream fudge as well.

In today's hectic pace, a sidetrip to Juliette is a much needed break to recharge the soul—it's a short trip to another time and age and I heartily recommend it. Jessica Tandy's parting line in the movie mentions the Whistle Stop Cafe . . . *"It was never more than a little knockabout place but when I look back on it . . . it's funny how a tiny place like this brought so many people together."* Jerie, thanks to you and the wonderful folk of Juliette, it still does.

Juliette, Georgia is 9 miles (11 minutes) east of I-75 at exit 186 - old 61 (see map on page 61). Oh, and when you get there, please say "hi" to Jerie, Betty, Dean, Larry, Donna and all the Juliette folk for me.

Insider Tip
Sweet Sue's . . . a Soda Fountain Experience

Driving south of McDonough, I tuned my radio to my favorite Macon "oldies" radio station, WAYS 99.1FM, and settled back to the slow swinging cadence of that old Dinah Shore standard, *"gonna take a sentimental journey."* Little did I know that in a few minutes I would be taking my own sentimental journey by stepping back in time, into the "Norman Rockwell" interior of Sweet Sue's Tea Room, at Bolingbroke, Exit 15 (old 4) on the I-475 Macon Bypass.

This is the perfect lunch stop. Not only is the food fresh and tasty but owners Beverly and Jim Mickle have made the soda fountain of old, a "house speciality." Jim is the resident *"fizzician"* and can whip up old fashioned delicacies such as lemon-lime, strawberry or cherry phosphates, fountain specialities such as coke and root beer floats, banana splits and traditional sundaes in a minute. But I've got ahead of myself—back to lunch!

You must try the home-made daily soup. You don't have to ask what it is (unless there are some things you just cannot eat), I know you'll enjoy it; subtle tastes of herbs and spices make this a wonderful taste experience. I followed this with a fresh garden salad and a bacon, lettuce and tomato sandwich on a croissant. I won't tell you how many "fountain items" I had for dessert.

For the mid-afternoon crowd, Sweet Sue's serves either a Southern Afternoon (finger sandwiches, cheese wafers, nut bread & lemon curd tarts) or Lord Bolingbroke (cucumber sandwiches, scones, clotted cream, jam, lemon curd, shortbread) Tea Tray. These can be had for one or two people at reasonable prices. Sweet Sue's is open Mon-Sat 11-4, with tea trays served between 2 - 4pm. If you decide to visit, say "hi" to Bev and Jim for me. They're a delightful couple.

Soda Fountain Culture, by Beverly Mickle

The soda fountain saga started in 1767 in England where Joseph Priestly pioneered carbonated water. It was sold in a Philadelphia drugstore in 1825 as a cure for indigestion. That idea reinforced in the late 19th century when, for similar reasons, Dr. John Pemberton concocted a mixture of lime juice, sugar, extracts of vanilla and coca, 7 flavoring oils, citric acid, water, caramel and alcohol—which he called Coca-Cola—and peddled it at an Atlanta pharmacy. At about the same time, ice cream—which had been around for years—was introduced to carbonated water, and the ice cream soda was born. By 1893, it was being hailed as the national beverage; legend has it that to circumvent blue laws banning sinful Sabbath soda sipping, fountain keepers skipped the soda and dumped syrup on the dish to create the "Sunday," later renamed sundae. Shakes, malts, sundaes, parfaits and banana splits soon appeared and thanks to the 1904 St. Louis World's Fair, ice cream cones, too. By 1910 there were more than 100,000 soda fountains in the USA. Many were stand alone businesses, some seating up to 400 customers; others were found in drugstores. They all had similar features, long, marble counter, tile floor, elaborately tooled back-bars, metal chairs and tables, and an open, airy atmosphere. The heyday of the soda fountains was in the 1920's. They were an important cultural contribution to the American scene, providing a sociable place where patrons could linger, gossip and swap stories. The soda fountain was also a place where a lady could go unescorted.

Growing up, one of my first jobs was being a "soda jerk" in Vineland, where my father, Dr. "Doc" John Wadley was pharmacist.

MACON - *after Nathaniel Macon (1757-1837), an American Revolutionary patriot and politician.*

ECHECONNEE CREEK - *from Creek Indian, "place where deer are trapped."*

Insider Tip
Macon - the Jewel of the South

Without a doubt, Macon is the *"Jewel of the South"* and yet so many travelers intent on getting to Florida, pass it by. Why not arrange to spend a night here (see Saving Tip below)–located on the banks of the Ocmulgee (oak-mul-gee), it is full of history (General Sherman spared the town on his march to Savannah) and things to do.

Here's are several suggestion for an interesting visit. Try and take the excellent Sidney's Tour of historic Macon ☎ 912-743-3401. You'll see major sites such as Sidney Lanier's (Georgia's foremost poet) cottage, Hay House, Cannonball House, Tubman African American Museum . . . all in an air-conditioned bus.

If you enjoy ancient history, don't miss the Ocmulgee National Monument Indian village park (dated back to 9,000BC), visited by Hernando de Soto in 1540.

Modern attractions? Georgia Music Hall of Fame, The Museum of Arts & Sciences, Planetarium, and of course, Macon Mall (see Macon area map on page 196).

For a splurge, try and spend a night at Macon's 1842 Inn. It's not cheap but well worth it. It's also the home of the best Mint Juleps in the South!

Money Saving Tip

If planning to spend the night in Macon, tell BJ (or other staff at the Macon Welcome Center), and let them make arrangements for you. Tell them what your budget is–they can often arrange much better rates (assuming availability) than you could by yourself.

local history–he's very knowledgeable. Notice the clock behind the counter. Betty keeps "River Time" because she doesn't like to change it in the spring or fall . . . *"and the nearby Ocmulgee River keeps the same time year round."*

Mile 180 - Macon Welcome Center (see map on page 196) - "BJ" : I cannot go by here without stopping to say "hello" to that wonderful Southern lady, BJ, and her warm associates on the staff of the Macon Welcome Center. Right now they are tucked away in a trailer (down the path behind the restroom building), but one day–perhaps early this year - they will occupy the new Center building.

BJ and I go back a few years. She has tried to teach me to pronounce "kudzu" in the Southern manner . . . but with my English accent getting in the way, I think she has given up!

GA I-475 Exit 15 (Old 4) - Bolingbroke: Virtually everybody heading south on the I-475 Macon Bypass misses Bolingbroke. This tiny village of antique, craft shops and a tea room lies just seconds off the I-475 east of exit 15 (old 4). See Insider Tip —"Sweet Suc's Tea Room"—on page 118.

GA I-475 Exit 9 (Old 3) - Pollys: If you like fried shrimp, then don't miss Polly's Restaurant. It's located just to the west of this exit in a small plaza on your right - alongside the Young America Music School. When you first enter, it appears to be a small lounge/bar. But there is a lot more seating the other side of the bar area in the well lit enclosed patio (a non smoking area). Owners Polly and Junior Mills will look after you.

Hrs: Mon, 11am-2pm, 5-9pm; Tue-Sat, 11am-2pm, 5-10pm. ☎ 912-757-9926.

GA Exit 146 (Old 45) - Museum of Aviation (map on page 61): A CGM-13 Martin Mace guided missile on the south eastern corner of this exit highlights the fact that nearby Warner Robins is a USAF town. It is also home to the Museum of Aviation. With over 85 aircraft on display (and growing), it is the second largest Air Force museums in the USA.

The best part is that you can get close. In fact a number of the larger aircraft are parked outside and you can

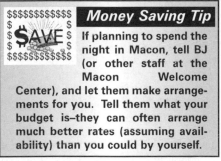

SR-71
"Blackbird"

walk right up and around them. The collection covers all the years from the 40's, but is not dated. For instance, you can get close to an SR-71 Lockheed "Blackbird" and F-15A McDonnell-Douglas "Eagle." Although 34 years old, the SR-71 remains one of the fastest and highest flying aircraft (that we are told about!). It can fly 15 miles above the earth's surface at 2200mph, enough speed to cross the USA from coast to coast in one hour – awesome!

Phone, hours and other details on page 61.

GA Exit 135 (Old 42) - Visitor Center: To the east of the I-75 at this exit is an excellent Visitor Center for anybody spending time in this "Peach Festival" area. It is well stocked with maps and brochures, and friendly advice. M-Sat, 8:30-5. ☎ 912-988-8000.

You will also find the Georgia National Fairgrounds at this exit.

GA Mile 130 Hernando de Soto: At Tennessee mile 42, I explained how in 1539, Don Hernando de Soto, the Spanish explorer led his army of 600 men on a journey of exploration of the North American continent. As he moved northward through Georgia, his journal for March, 1540, records how he marched from Montezuma (about 15 miles west of I-75 mile marker 125), crossed Beaver Creek and arrived at an Indian village at Perry where he observed the women spinning silk from the fibers of mulberry trees. His army would have crossed the terrain of the modern I-75 around mile marker 130. Several days later, the army moved on towards modern Macon and crossed the "Great River"–the Ocmulgee.

GA Mile 133 - an Epiphyte: Now we are south of Macon, the large sprawling industrial concerns of northern Georgia have disappeared. The stands of conifers in the sawmill pinelands and trees draped with Hanging Moss give a much more relaxed, laid back appearance to the roadside. To me, Hanging (or Spanish) Moss (Tillandsia Usneoides) is always the guarantee that you are beyond the most southern snowline. It is a peculiar plant, not a moss and not a parasite as many people believe. It is in fact an Epiphyte–a plant that does not grow in soil but clings to another plant or tree for support and lives on the air surrounding it.

GA Exit 127 (Old Exit 41) - Henderson Village: Barely one mile west of this exit is a fascinating alternative to the interstate motel - an 18 acre village of deluxe overnight lodging and fine dining complemented with formal gardens, fountains and a 3,500 acre hunting preserve (game shooting and wild boar hunting). Definitely not for the budget minded traveler, but perhaps the ultimate stopover for that special occasion. A fine way to celebrate a birthday or anniversary while on the road to or from Florida.

But let's talk about the restaurant . . . it's housed in the beautifully renovated Langston House (1838), decorated throughout with original antiques and divided into small intimate dining rooms. Renowned chef, Garry Kensley has been attracted from Europe where he earned the "Restaurant of the Year" award for two years in a row, as well as many other European accolades, including a gold medal for his bread.

The menu items change from day to day and might include such delicacies as honey and lime barbequed salmon filet or southern fried crabcakes; grilled swordfish with a creamy crab sauce or chicken with a lemon thyme

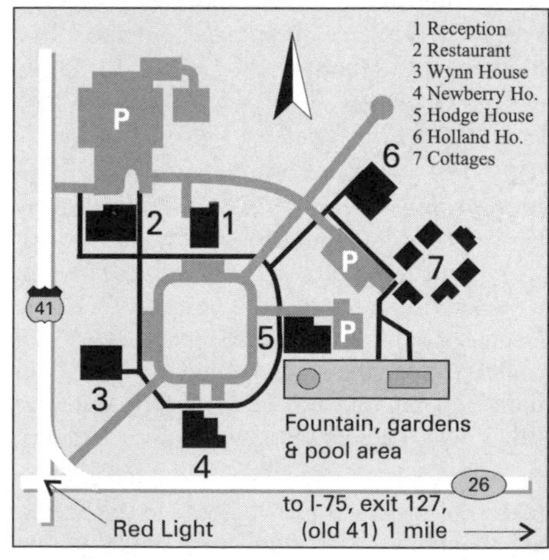

PERRY - *"We have met the enemy and they are ours" was the naval signal sent by Oliver Hazard Perry (1785-1819) after he beat the British fleet on Lake Erie during the War of 1812. Perry is named in honor of the war hero.*

and ginger mousse – the menu for the day is bound to be mouth-watering!

Incidentally, prices are quite reasonable with a two course lunch for under $12 or a three course dinner for under $28.

And now to the lodgings. Henderson Village is an assembly of old historical buildings from the area–local homes and tenant farmer cottages, all completely renovated and decorated in the finest fashion for a deluxe stay. Winding brick paths meander through the Village, moon lights in the trees and old fashioned gaslamps light the way during the evening.

I was really taken by the tiny square of six inward facing cottages. As you cross the verandah and enter the door of each, you immediately notice the wonderful aromas of cedar and bayberry.

All the old architectural features that make these buildings so endearing, have been kept. Some have wooden shingle roofs while others have tin, but all are completely modernized and weather-tight. Modern heating and air-conditioning is hidden away where you cannot see it. Beautiful old brick hearths (retrofitted with safe but very authentic looking gas fireplaces with glowing embers) along with functional antique furnishing ensure warm and comfortable interiors.

All buildings have at least one porch; some with porch swings, others with rocking chairs or wicker furniture. There is something special about sitting out and quietly rocking the time away, on a warm southern night.

Mornings are special too. I can just imagine staying at the Holland House (early 1900's) having breakfast on the porch served by the Langston House restaurant's silver tray room service. No expense has been spared in Henderson Village to evoke the atmosphere of a peaceful but bygone era.

General Manager Stuart Macpherson has kindly invited readers of *"Along Interstate-75"* to take a break from the highway, to come and enjoy the grounds, relax and wander around this unusual community and perhaps, sample some of the delicacies at the Langston House. For a fully pampered and relaxing stay–away from the pressures of the I-75 drive, Henderson Village has much to offer .

Restaurant hours are 7:00-9:30am for breakfast, 11:30-2:30pm for lunch and 6:00-9:00pm for dinner–Tues to Sat. Sunday brunch is from 11:30-2:30pm. For further information and reservations, phone toll free 888-615-9722, or 912-988-8696.

GA Mile 115 - Peanuts and Irrigation: The fields just to the west (right) of you here are peanuts. The large wheeled girder units are used for irrigation.

GA Mile 111 - The Tax Day Tornado: April 15, 1999, presented a big shock to the people of Vienna, Georgia . . . for not only was it income tax filing day but at 10:20 in the morning, a severe tornado (rated F3 - 158-206 mph winds) touched down in nearby Vienna. Along its 16 mile (½ mile wide) path, it destroyed 105 buildings and seriously damaged 65 others before tearing across I-75 at this point. Luckily, the most serious injury to the 25 people who were hurt during the storm, was a broken leg.

GA Exit 109 (Old 36) - Georgia Cotton Museum: The history of Georgia and the history of cotton have long been closely associated, and now a new museum ½ mile west of I-75 tells all with some very attractive exhibits. Did you know for instance, that the first Georgia cotton was brought from England in 1733 and planted in the Trustees Garden in Savannah; or that Georgia was the first state to produce cotton commercially?

For more than 250 years, "King Cotton" as it was known played a major role in building the economy of Georgia—until it was almost wiped out by the Boll Weevil. But it has come back and today is a major Southern crop again.

The museum is more than just a collection of artifacts. It includes information about the slave issues. It demonstrates the tools used, including Eli Whitney's Cotton Gin (for removing seeds from the white cotton lint) and a weighing beam used to weigh cotton bales. Samples of cotton in various stages of growth are available so you can actually touch and feel Georgia's number one cash crop.

If you've ever wondered about cotton then you're in the right place. Museum custodian Margaret Hegidio knows cotton and loves to chat with her

Insider Tip
A Visit to Ellis Bros.—a family Pecan Farm

"We're Nuts . . . " is the slogan of Ellis Bros. Pecans, and if there's anything you want to know about this local nut, Elliott Ellis is your man. Just east of I-75 the Ellis family has been farming pecans for three generations. In fact, the pecan trees in the grove just to the north of their retail store were planted in 1918, just after the end of WWI. Pecans are harvested by air blasting them onto strips of ground kept clear of cover between the trees. Elliott took me for a tour of his shelling plant behind the store and I was surprised at the control he must maintain over the humidity. Quality control is very high in their process and he is very proud of the fact that in 1992 they won the Georgia Family Business of the Year Award.

In the store, you will find just about every type of coated pecan—coffee, honey, ginger and chocolate, to name a few. Irene Ellis has an in-house candy kitchen with four marble topped tables to supply this need. The Ellis' also grow and make the wonderful Mayhaw Jelly (see below) as well as sell almonds, cashews, peanuts—and five varieties of pecan incl. Stuart, Desirables, Papershells (Schley/Sumner).

To reach Ellis Brothers, take exit 109 east (old 36 - route 215) and take first left (Tippetville Rd) at the Ellis Bros. sign. Ellis Bros. is well marked, about ¾ mile on left. The store is open 7 days a week, 8am-7 pm; phone: 1-800-635-0616 or 912-268-9041.

As you travel through this section of Georgia, you are traveling through an area that offers a rare gastronomical delicacy—Mayhaw Jelly.

Mayhaw jelly is made from the tart red berry that grows in the swamps and bogs of Southwest Georgia. The Mayhaw trees grow wild in such a small geographic area that the berries are highly prized and the tart sweet jelly hoarded for special occasions. I enjoy mine (whenever I can find it) on hot, buttered toast.

Mayhaws are called berries, but technically they are a member of the haw or apple family. In May, the red berries fall to the ground or in the water and are gathered by hand or scooped out of the water by fishnets. The berries are boiled and squeezed to get the clear coral colored juice that is made into the "best jelly in the world." If you find a jar of wild Mayhaw Jelly, buy it! It's a rare delicacy.

visitors–and Dooly County, Georgia is one of America's major cotton crop areas. As one early traveler to the area wrote, *"when you visit Dooly County in the Fall, you can enjoy the "snow of the South. The cotton is so thick and so white that it appears to be snow on the ground with bright green trees framing the view."*

Museum hours are: Mon-Sat, 9:15-4pm, closed Sunday. ☎ 912-268-2045

GA Mile 103 - Pecan Orchard: If you didn't have time to stop and visit the Ellis Bros. at exit 109 (old 36), here's your chance to see a grove of pecan trees beside the interstate. Look for an orchard of trees on the right (west) side as you travel south, between exits 104 (old 35) and 102 (old 34).

GA Exit 101 (Old 33) - Cordele: Worthy of note–we are just passing the first palm tree north of Florida. It's to the right (west) of the freeway, halfway between the I-75 and the Holiday Inn property.

If you take this exit to buy gas, you might be surprised to see a Titan Rocket. The Titan

CORDELE - *after Cordelia Hawkins, daughter of Colonel Samuel Hawkins, president of the Savannah, Americus and Montgomery railroad.*

TIFTON - *for Nelson Tift (1810-91), an officer in the Confederate Army and U.S. representative from 1868-69.*

was an early rocket and contained many unusual and exotic materials–these have led to corrosion. In the late 1980's, engineers came from the air force desert "bone yard" at Davis- Monthan AFB, Arizona, to renovate this particular Titan.

GA Exit 101 (Old 33) - Cotton: Just south of this exit on your right is a cotton field which may or may not be of interest depending upon whether you are a Northerner or Southerner. If you missed the Cotton Museum at exit 109 (old 36), here's your chance to see a cotton field from your car.

Keep an eye on this field—green for most of the summer, it bursts into a field of thigh high cotton balls in mid-August.

GA Exit 101 (Old 33) - Vidalia Onions: Vidalia onions are well known all over the world for their unusual sweetness and flavor. In fact they are so sweet they have a higher sugar (fructose) content than Coca-Cola. They are also tearless!

Why do they taste so different, after all they are an ordinary variety of onion? It's due to the local sandy, low-sulphur soil in the Vidalia area (85 miles to the east along Rt280 of this exit). This was discovered by accident in 1931 when local resident Mose Coleman planted some onion seeds from Texas, and could not believe the sweet, juicy results. They were so good that they could be eaten raw.

Today, Vidalia onions have grown into a multi-million dollar business. Just like fine wines, only onions grown in certain areas are allowed to bear the Vidalia logo. The best time to buy is in the spring. After shopping around, we have found the Vidalia onions products–relish, etc.–carried by Cracker Barrel's Country Stores to be the best consistent value. Genuine Vidalia onions may be found at many local supermarkets, but you might wish to shop at the Georgia State Farmers Market (exit 237 - old 78) if driving north.

GA Exit 78 (Old 26) - Jefferson Davis Park: May 10, 1865–pity poor Jefferson Davis, ex-President of the Southern Confederacy. He had been on the run from his Capital, Richmond in Virginia, since early April and had a $100,000 reward of gold on his head. With his wife, an escort of 20 men and $300,000 in gold and silver from the Confederate Treasury, the party decided to camp in a pine grove beside a stream.

Imagine their feelings when they were woken up in the early morning by two Federal cavalries shooting at each other and everything else in sight. A soldier aimed at Jefferson but his wife offered herself as a target instead. Jefferson surrendered quickly to save her life.

A colonel rode up and said, *"Well, old Jeff, we've got you at last."*

This action took place at the Jefferson Davis Park—15.6 miles (18.5 mins.) east of the I-75 at this exit.

By the way, the Confederate Treasury disappeared and has never been found—but no digging is allowed in the park!

Sixteen miles may seem like a long way to drive for such a destination, but if you are a true Civil War buff, you will not regret it. For me, as I stand looking down the grass slope across the location of the Davis' encampment, and along the track of the old 1800's road with its log bridge across the creek, it is still possible to imagine the poignancy of the event 135 years ago as two groups of Union soldiers fought each other for the honor of capturing the scared group.

Incidentally, the State of Georgia has recently taken over the property and is bringing the park and museum up to State Park standards.

GA Exit 63B (Old 20) - Georgia Agrirama: Two minutes west on Eighth Street, country life in the late 19th century is the focus of this living outdoor museum. The town's guides wear costumes from the period and practice the trades and skills which would have been required to live in this rural community.

Insider Tip
Pit Stop Bar-B-Que

By now, you probably know that my two loves when I travel are history and eating. In fact, some people have even subtitled this book, *"Dave eats his way to Florida!"* But I don't want you to miss this excellent Pit BBQ restaurant just to west of I-75 at exit 55B (old 20). After your meal, go and visit the smoke house at the back.

Hours: Tue-Thur, 11am-9pm; Fri-Sat, 11am-10pm; Sun, 11am-9pm; closed Mondays ☎ 912-387-0888

As you wander around the town, visit the steam-powered sawmill, water wheel grist mill, smokehouse, sugar cane mill and turpentine still, among other rural industries. All in all, a pleasant way to spend an hour or so, off the road.

Agrirama is open: Jun-Aug, Tues-Sat, 9-5, Sun 12:30-5; Rest of year, Mon-Sat, 9-5. Admission: Adult/Senior/Child (4-16) $8/$6/$4 ☎ 912-386-3344.

GA Exit 62 (Old 18) - Tifton's Historical Buildings: Follow route 82 for 1 ½ miles east to Tifton's downtown area, where you will find twelve city blocks featuring old homes from the late 1800's to 1930's nestled among shade tree streets. See the neon lighted theater and historic churches and over 30 shops in restored buildings. Seventy percent of these buildings are on the National Register of Historic Buildings. This is ideal for a walking tour—an opportunity to get out of your car and stretch.

GA Exit 62 (Old 18) - Adcock Pecans: Just to the east of this exit is Adcock Pecans, the huge retail outlet of the Sunbelt Plantation company. I'm always impressed with the huge array of jellies, jams, relish, salsa, sauces and spreads on display. At the last count, there were 88 different varieties in stock, from pumpkin butter to guava jelly to chow chow-you never know what you'll find.

Money Saving Tip

Before you leave Georgia, fill up with gas - even if you only need a 1/4 of a tank. Georgia has the cheapest gasoline in the USA.

GA Exit 55 (Old 14) - Magnolia Plantation: I can never seem to get my car (or my wife, Kathy) past the Magnolia Plantation without a mandatory stop to check out their large stock of local relishes, honey, jellies, jams or marmalades. We always come away with at least a few jars of Vidalia Onion relish.

GA Mile 43 - Florida Welcome Centers?: By now you will have noticed roadside signs

Insider Tip

Your Private Club beside the Interstate

One day, a group of ardent golfers got together and discussed what they would like in a clubhouse if they were to design it. Of course, one of the priorities was to have sleep-over facilities so they could be close to the golf course early in the morning. Thus was born the Clubhouse Inn concept. Today, eighteen of these special "clubhouses" exist and as luck would have it, one is just beside the I-75, east at exit 18 (old 5), in Valdosta, Georgia (another is in Knoxville).

We decided to try it. The intriguing thing is that when you register, you don't check in as a guest but as a member. And with membership comes privileges . . . a cocktail reception (with 4 free drink coupons), bar snacks, free movie channel, free coffee or tea all day or night and a hot breakfast buffet in the morning. The facilities are excellent as well–nicely appointed room, outside patio area for sitting and a warm pool. Every so often, they hold a BBQ for members outside beside the swimming pool. If you're not there when this happens though, there's a good choice of restaurants at this exit, including an Outback Steakhouse right next door.

Try and say 'hello" to the Clubhouse's General Manager Felecia Barnes; she loves the hospitality business and it really shows. I was impressed to see her in the front office at nighttime and yet helping clear breakfast dishes away early the next morning. Jeff Stubbs, the director of sales is another friendly "Clubhouse" face. They, and the rest of their staff, always enjoy their guests and make you feel very welcome indeed.

Although a little more expensive than other motels at the Valdosta exit, the added benefits more than offset the added costs. I know that the next time we are stopping in Valdosta, we'll definitely head to our *"private club beside the interstate."*

advertising Florida Welcome Centers at exits ahead. Some even advertise free or discounted Disney tickets. But common sense indicates that of course, an official Florida Welcome Center would be located in Florida, not Georgia - and it certainly would be on the southbound side of the road!

There is only one I-75 official Florida Welcome Center and that is at Florida mile-marker 471, or 44 miles ahead (see next page).

Most of these other places are Orlando area condominium sales outlets. They want you to commit to spending several hours visiting their condo site in Florida after which, you are taken into a "gift" room where you can choose from items which often include discounted WDW tickets.

They will actually book a time and date at the "Welcome Center" and some even require a small deposit to ensure you turn up.

GA Mile 32: Another stand of Hanging (Spanish) Moss to the right of the I-75 reminds me of the *"Legend of the Spanish Moss"* -

There's an old, old legend that's whispered by Southern folk,
About the lacy moss that garlands the great oak;
A lovely princess and her love, upon their wedding day,
Were struck-down by a savage foe amidst a bitter fray;
United in death they're buried, so the legends go
'Neath an oak's strong, friendly arms, protected from their foe;
There as was the custom, they cut the bride's hair with love
And hung its shining blackness on the spreading oak above;
Untouched, undisturbed it hung there, for all the world to see
And with the years, the locks turned gray, and spread from tree to tree.

Georgia Mile 27 - Disney Radio: Turn on your car radio to 910 AM. You will know that you're close to the Florida Border because Disney is in the air.

GA Exit 16 (Old 4) - Valdosta's Barber-House: Four miles and 10 minutes east of the I-75 (turn left onto Ashley St.), you will find an old Southern home of the neo-classical style. Built in 1915 for one of the early bottlers and promoters of Coca-Cola, its marble steps, six Ionic columns and wide portico symbolizes the Georgian Mansion of the deep south.

Today, it houses the County's Chamber of Commerce, and is open Mon-Fri, 9-5 pm. ☎ 912-247-8100.

GA Exit 13 (Old 3a) - Wild Adventures: West of I-75, 4.4 miles along the Old Clyattville Road, wild and exotic animals rule the Georgia landscape in a new attraction—Wild Adventures. Part zoo, part amusement park and part stage show entertainment, Wild Adventures is quickly becoming a "must-see" stop for I-75 travelers heading towards Florida or on the way back up north.

Owner Kent Buescher is fulfilling a dream by adding many other animals to his 170 acre property, originally a horse farm. Lions, tigers, a black bear, giraffes, alligators, zebras, 70 monkeys and more provide a realism to Wild Adventures safari rides.

But that's not all. For the young in heart, 20 amusement rides such as Pharaoh's Fury, Chaos, Tiger Terror and the Giant Wheel are guaranteed to provide an adrenaline rush. Slower rides such as bumper boats, swings and the Carousel keep the younger (and perhaps, senior) family members happy.

Finally, Wild Adventures is proud of its "Big Name" shows and concerts. Stars such as Chubby Checker and Waylon Jennings provide outstanding entertainment for the enjoyment of the lawn chair and "blanket-on-the-grass" audience. I suggest you phone ahead to find out who is "on stage" the day you plan to visit.

Owner Kent has injected more than

ADEL - *by homesick eastern settlers, second and third syllables from their home town name, "Philadelphia."*

VALDOSTA - *From "Val d'Aosta" meaning "vale of beauty." This was the name of the northern Italian estate of Governor George Troup.*

$10 million into Wild Adventures to ensure a fun experience for the entire family. Recently, he announced that $50 million more would be spent as part of a 5 year expansion which will include many new rides and a water park. The first phase of this program recently added 16 new rides to the park.

All of this comes with a one price admission for everything–animals, safari, amusements and shows. The all inclusive admission is: adults/snrs/children: $14.95/$12.95/$10.95;

Hours vary greatly according to season and day of the week. Phone for information. ☎ 912-559-1330.

Georgia Mile 2 - Northbound Welcome Center: If you are traveling north from Florida don't forget to stop and say hello to the friendly staff at the Georgia Welcome Center. Manager Beth Cody and her staff of Barbara, Cathy, Leigh and Missy are all very knowledgeable and will help make your journey north through Georgia, as interesting as possible.

Incidentally, please note that the restrooms close at 11:30 at night, and re-open at 7:30a.m.

Florida Mile 471 - Florida Welcome Center: Don't forget to stop here for your free orange or grapefruit juice. The information section is well stocked, and open from 8–5pm daily.

Incidentally, if you arrive here after hours go over to the paper boxes outside the vending machine area—you will find a good supply of the free Florida motel and restaurant guides, and coupon books here.

Recently, "Visit Florida," the State's tourism marketing agency added a toll free number, 1-800-656-8777, to help tourists with emergency and non-emergency situations. So if you have lost travel documents, need directions or have a medical or non-medical emergency, give one of their operators a call.

It seems like years since we left the snow and ice of Detroit, and yet it has only been a few short days. We have discovered Summer in January, visited some interesting places and had a lot of enjoyment along the way. I must leave you now, and head back north. Enjoy your time in the sun.

Money Saving Tip

Pickup your free copy of the green Exit Information Guide, red Market America or yellow Mr Interstate motel coupon books at the Florida Welcome Center (mile 471). Coupons in these books can save you as much as 45% off of regular motel rates.

Don't forget the special free Florida restaurant coupon books either.

Insider Tip
Country Kitchen Quail

By now if you've been following my *Insider Tips*, you probably think that I have eaten my way to Florida! I admit, I do enjoy food so . . . when somebody mentions a restaurant in South Georgia that serves BBQ quail, I just have to go to check it out.

Now, a word of explanation . . . Quail is a wild game bird common in this area. In the Fall, hunting groups will often gather for organized shooting parties.

The Farmhouse Restaurant at Lake Park (Exit 5 - old 2) specializes in quail, although they buy their birds from a game farm, so they are not wild. They are always on the menu either grilled or deep fried, but from time to time, the Farmhouse also has an outdoor BBQ special.

If you are passing through this area, you might want to try this local delicacy.

FLORIDA - *named by explorer Ponce de Leon, who discovered the land on Easter Sunday (Pascua Florida), in 1512. Florida means "flowering" in Spanish. Ponce de Leon's original Florida claim encompassed all the land up to and including Newfoundland in Canada.*

Useful Information

Local Knowledge - if you have it you will always feel comfortable as you travel. Here is the "local knowledge" section:

"Where can I get local traffic information on my car radio?"

"Is it OK to use my radar detector in Georgia?"

"Should I gas up in Kentucky or Tennessee?

"There's a tornado alert for Preble County - is that close?"

These are the sort of questions answered in this section. In fact, if you can think of other questions which need answers, let me know (see page 203), and I will try and oblige in a future edition:

INTERSTATE-75 RADIO GUIDE

Area (Southbound Sequence)	Best Traffic	Misc Music	Soft Pop	Oldies	Top Pops	Special Programming Public	Classical	All Talk	News	Sports	Rock	Jazz	C&W	Religion
Detroit, MI	950AM	100.3	95.1	1450AM	95.5	91.7	89.9	760AM	950AM	1130AM	101.1	105.9	99.5	103.5
Toledo, OH	1370AM	105.5	101.5	93.5	92.5	91.3	91.3	1230AM	1430AM	1220AM	104.7	97.3	99.9	90.3
Lima, OH	1150AM	103.7	98.1	95.7	92.1	90.7	90.7	1200AM	1150AM	1220AM	93.1	90.7	107.7	97.7
Dayton, OH	980AM	107.7	99.9	95.3	92.9	90.9	94.1	1290AM	1410AM	1220AM	104.7	94.9	99.1	93.3
Cincinnati, OH	700AM	94.1	98.5	103.5	101.9	91.7	90.9	550AM	700AM	1220AM	102.7	94.9	105.1	93.3
Lexington, KY	590AM	104.9	102.1	1380AM	94.5	88.9	88.9	590AM	590AM	1300AM	100.1	91.3	92.9	95.3
London, KY	1400AM	107.3	102.7	740AM	107.3	90.9	--	1070AM	1240AM	--	103.5	--	99.5	950AM
Jellico, TN	810AM	102.7	--	102.1	102.7	91.9	--	640AM	910AM	1240AM	103.5	--	99.5	92.7
Knoxville, TN	990AM	97.5	--	105.3	104.5	91.9	91.9	670AM	850AM	990AM	103.5	--	107.7	96.3
Athens	--	97.5	92.3	102.1	93.9	91.9	90.5	580AM	850AM	--	106.5	--	101.7	98.3
Chattanooga, TN	107.9	101.7	92.3	107.9	105.5	88.1	90.5	102.3	1150AM	102.3	106.5	93.7	100.7	98.3
Dalton, GA	850AM	104.5	92.3	107.9	105.5	88.1	90.5	1430AM	850AM	--	106.5	93.7	98.9	1530AM
Atlanta, GA	750AM	98.5	94.9	97.1	94.1	90.1	1190AM	750AM	640AM	790AM	96.1	104.1	106.7	1490AM
High Falls, GA	--	92.1	94.9	97.1	94.1	90.1	--	640AM	850AM	680AM	92.9	104.1	106.7	90.7
Macon, GA	99.1	107.9	107.9	99.1	93.7	89.7	89.7	810AM	940AM	96.5	106.3	97.9	92.3	900AM
Cordele, GA	--	104.5	103.9	99.1	94.7	91.1	91.7	680AM	850AM	--	102.9	--	98.3	99.9
Tifton, GA	1340AM	96.9	104.5	97.7	--	91.1	91.7	--	1340AM	--	105.7	840AM	100.3	101.1
Valdosta, GA	1340AM	95.7	105.3	1450AM	95.7	91.7	91.7	910AM	680AM	820AM	107.7	102.7	92.9	101.1

Revised: 8/19/99 Note: all radio station frequencies are FM, unless otherwise noted. ©2000, Mile Oak Publishing Inc.

Radio Along I-75

To the left is a selection of major radio stations which can be received at various locations on the interstate.

There are many other excellent stations which can also be received in each location, but this chart represents a good cross section of the more powerful ones, subdivided by the type of music or programs provided (known as the stations "format" in the radio business).

Where a station's format falls under several categories, we have listed it under the best "fit" for its main programming, or in those areas with only a few stations, under each of the appropriate categories.

Several comments follow:

Best Traffic - covers at least the morning & afternoon rush hours, with unscheduled traffic reports when trouble conditions occur. See also page 193 for the traffic "personalities" of the major urban areas.

Public - stations which are members of either the American Public Radio (APR) or National Public Radio (NPR) systems. Their programming tends to be classical or jazz.

All Talk - we've attempted to provide those stations which offer the popular nationally syndicated shows, such as Doctor Laura Schlessinger or Rush Limbaugh.

Clear Channel AM Radio Stations

Radio signals travel much farther in the dark. To avoid interference, the FCC requires that many stations reduce their night "distance" coverage by performing an antenna "pattern" change at dusk. By agreement, some powerful (50,000 watt) AM radio stations provide nightime extended coverage and their signals can cover as much as 750 miles after dark. This is useful to know if you are on a night drive since you can stay with the same station for many miles. Here are the powerful I-75 "Clear Channel" AM stations:

MI-WJR-760, **OH**-WLW-700, **KY**-WHAS-840, **TN**-WSM-650, **GA**-WSB-750

Police & Weather Phone Numbers; State Gas Taxes

Need to phone the State Police for advice, or do you want to check road conditions to your destination? Listed below are the phone numbers you will need. Use the police number if there is no phone service for road conditions. Please note that the state police numbers shown in the third column are for information only - ***use 911 in an emergency.***

State	Emergency No. Cellular/Reg.Phone	State Police Information	Weather & Road Conditions	Construction Web Sites	Gas Taxes
Michigan	911	517-332-2521	Detroit: 313-961-8686	www.mdot.state.mi.us	25.1
Ohio	911/614-466-2660	614-466-2660	(M-F) 513-241-1010	www.dot.state.oh.us	22.0
Kentucky	911/800-222-5555	502-277-2221	606-666-8000	www.kytc.state.ky.us	16.4
Tennessee	*THP/615-741-2060	615-741-3181	423-521-6300	www.state.tn.us/transport/	21.4
Georgia	*GSP/404 624-6077	404-624-6077	770-455-7141	www.dot.state.ga.us	10.9
Florida	*FHP or 911	850-488-8676	Miami: 305-229-4522 Tampa: 813-645-2606	www.dot.state.fl.us	28.1

Cell Phone Users - *1-800-525-5555 will connected you immediately to the nearest state police dept.*
Note 1 - there are no state phone numbers for construction. All now report this on their Internet sites.
Note 2 - "Gas Taxes" are the cents each state collects from each gallon of gas pumped into your car.

I-75 Traffic Laws

Traffic laws change from state to state. Here is a useful chart which summarizes some of the laws in the six states crossed by the I-75.

STATE	* Minimum Driver Age	Right Turn on Red	Child Restraints	** Mandatory Seat Belt Usage	Radar Detectors
Michigan	18 (16)	Yes	under 4 years old	DR, FP + RP under 16	OK to use
Ohio	18 (16)	Yes	under 4 yrs or 40 lbs.	DR + FP	OK (exc. commercial)
Kentucky	16 (16)	Yes	under 41" tall	DR + all passengers	OK to use
Tennessee	16 (15)	Yes	under 4 years old	DR, FP + RP 4-12	OK (exc. commercial)
Georgia	16 (15)	Yes	under 4 years old	DR + FP	OK to use
Florida	16 (15)	Yes	under 5 years old	DR + FP	OK to use

Notes * Figure in ( ) is minimum age for driver with conditional of probationary license
** DR = driver, FP = front seat passenger, RP = rear seat passenger

The Triple "A" for Help

One of the best investments you can make for a long distance drive is to join the AAA (or CAA in Canada). It doesn't cost a lot of money (annual membership fees vary from area to area but it is usually in the $50-70 range) and yet the peace of mind provided when traveling long distances is well worth the money. Should you experience a breakdown or other car emergency, they are only a national toll free 1-800 phone call away:

USA - 1-800-AAA-HELP Canada - 1-800-CAA-HELP

TORNADO WATCH

Special note: this section is not intended to alarm you - but to make sure that you are well informed and prepared should a Tornado emergency occur in your area, while traveling the I-75.

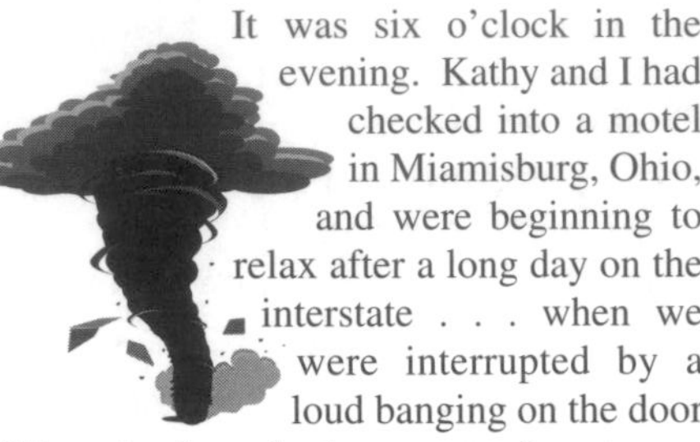

It was six o'clock in the evening. Kathy and I had checked into a motel in Miamisburg, Ohio, and were beginning to relax after a long day on the interstate . . . when we were interrupted by a loud banging on the door - *"Everybody to the basement - three tornados have been spotted in Preble County!"*

Where was Preble County? We had no idea. What should we do to minimize our risk? We did not know. After the emergency was over, I decided to find the answers to these very important questions & share them with you.

Over the last few year's we have certainly gained a heightened awareness of tornados (or twisters, as they are often known), as we

Tornado Safety Tips

If in a sturdy building:

- go to the lowest level, interior room in the building.
- take a flashlight and battery radio.
- stay away from large rooms, such as auditoriums, ballrooms,etc.
- avoid rooms with windows & outside walls.
- hide under something that is sturdy.
- cover yourself with blankets, pillows, coats (to protect from flying debris).
- protect your neck and head areas. Put on a crash or safety helmet, if you have one.

If in a weak structure or RV home:

- get out and seek a sturdy shelter.

If caught in the open:

- lay flat in a ditch face down (1st choice) or behind a sturdy hedge. Cover head with arms.

If in a car:

- get out, and if close to an overpass, crawl up into the "V" created by the concrete banks and the road above.
- If no overpass, find a ditch, hedge or sturdy structure.

Insider Tip
Your Personal Alert System

After this summer's experience, we do not travel the interstate without a Weather Radio with a weather alert feature - in the car or in our motel room. The best type to buy is a unit which receives all 7 of the National Weather Service (NWS) frequencies. It must be capable of receiving the NWS "Alert" signal - this will ensure that your unit will sound an alarm when a NWS alert signal is received. It should also have a built-in backup battery, for emergency use.

Your home unit should be capable of receiving the special Specific Area Message Encoding (SAME) signal - this signal (also known as the FIPS code) enables your unit to give you alerts for your specific area, rather than on a broad county basis. The 6 digit FIPS code for your area is obtained by phoning the toll-free NWS number 1-888-697-7263, and following the automated instructions. The resulting code is punched into your radio unit.

I have tested two Radio Shack units on the road, they meet all the requirements and work very well. During our test run, we actually experienced one Tornado alert, 2 flood warnings and 2 severe thunderstorm alerts. The portable unit we use in our car as we travel is Radio Shack model 12-246 (cost $29.99); it runs on 3 AAA batteries. The second unit has the SAME feature. It is Radio Shack 12-249 and costs $69.99. We use this as our "plug in" unit in our motel at night. If staying for any time in one location,I obtain the FIPS code for the area. The unit has a 9v backup battery and displays alert messages on a screen as well as indicating the alert severity. *(Canadians, please note: the SAME unit uses codes which only apply to land areas in the USA; it is only available in Radio Shack stores in the U.S.).*

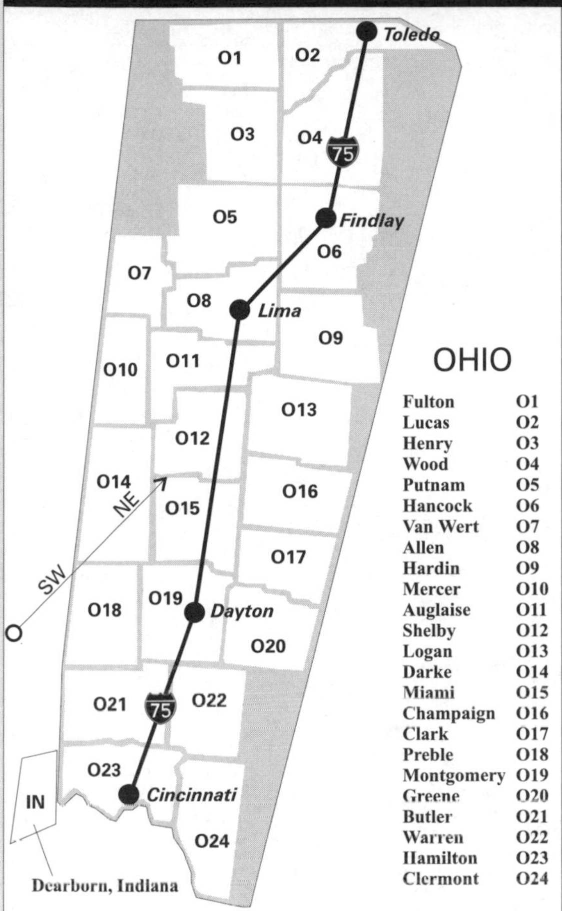

travel. In April, 1996, a section of the small town of Berea was devastated by a tornado which swept across the I-75 and slammed into the "old town" area. And of course, we are all aware of the terrible damage done by a tornado which touched down just east of Kissimmee, Florida during the 1997/8 winter. Here are some tornado facts:

Tornados tend to travel from the south-west quadrant of a storm system to the north east. Never try to outrun a tornado in your car, but if there is clear sky to

A Word About the County Charts

Tornado warnings are usually issued by county. I have shown all the I-75 counties through which you may travel, together with at least one other county either side. The southwest-northeast axis is also shown in each case, since this tends to be the general path of tornado spawning storms.

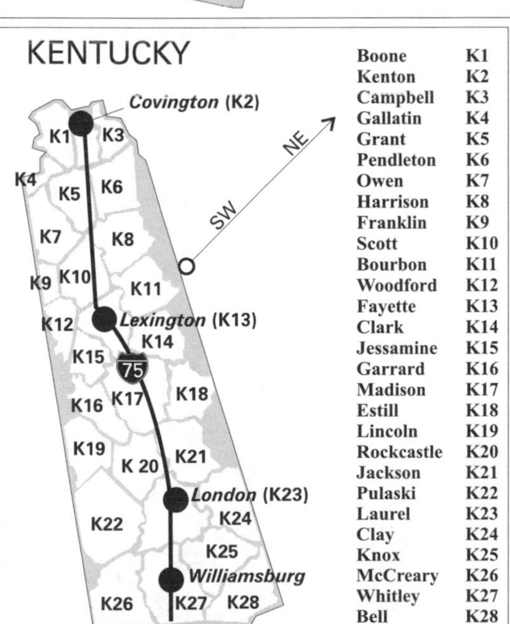

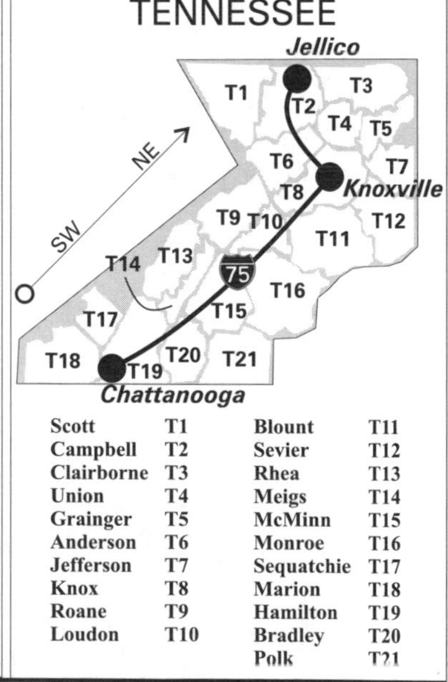

your south-east, that is the direction to go.

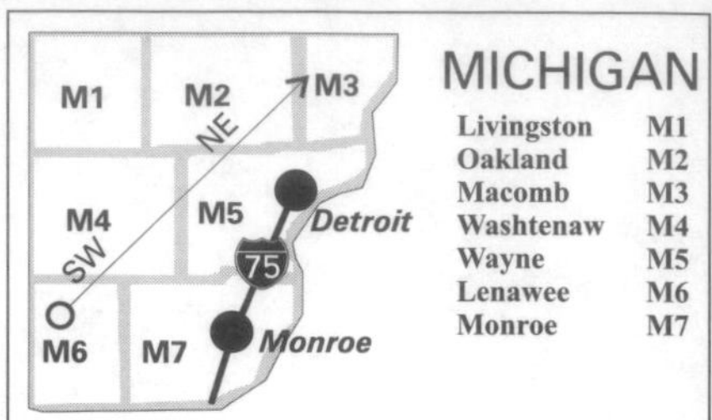

A storm that can spawn tornados is often preceded with lightning, hail and heavy rain. They tend to happen in late afternoon, early evenings during the late-spring/early summer.

Most injuries are caused by flying debris. A tornado can come in many strengths, from one which damages light trees, branches or billboards (known as an F0) to a very rare F5 which can hurtle a wooden plank projectile at speeds up to 200 mph. Pressure differential in tornados does not play a big role in terms of damage. Forget the old wives tale about opening a window on the opposite side to the storm; experts say it makes no difference.

In terms of risk, here are typical tornado frequencies by state, compiled by the National Severe Storm Center in Kansas City -- Texas-189 Kansas-92 Oklahoma-64 Michigan-21 Ohio-61 Kentucky-11 Tennessee-8 Georgia-19 Florida-60.

The I-75 is no more vulnerable to tornados than any of the other major corridor routes between the northern states and Florida. In fact, the tips in this story can be equally as well applied to your home area. I consider my home weather alert system as important as my smoke detectors or security system, and keep it running at all times.

I certainly hope you never encounter a tornado, but if you do at least you are well prepared.

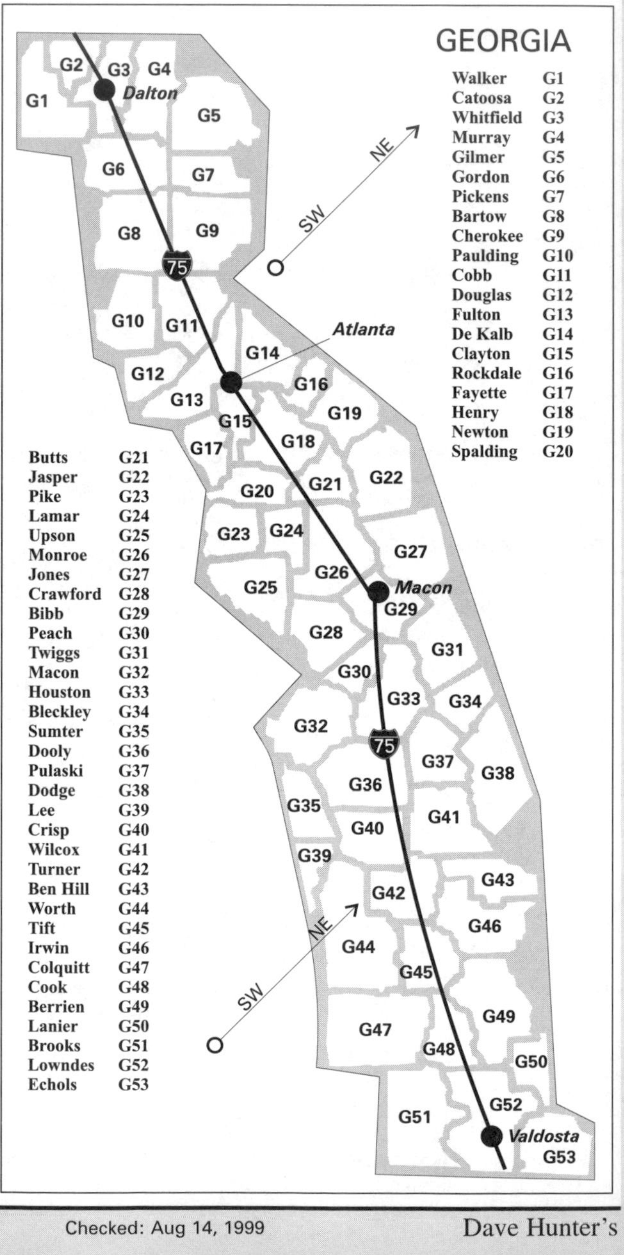

MICHIGAN
M1 M2 M3 M4 M5 M6 M7
NE
SW
75
Detroit
Monroe
Livingston M1
Oakland M2
Macomb M3
Washtenaw M4
Wayne M5
Lenawee M6
Monroe M7

GEORGIA
Dalton
Atlanta
Macon
Valdosta
75
NE
SW
Walker G1
Catoosa G2
Whitfield G3
Murray G4
Gilmer G5
Gordon G6
Pickens G7
Bartow G8
Cherokee G9
Paulding G10
Cobb G11
Douglas G12
Fulton G13
De Kalb G14
Clayton G15
Rockdale G16
Fayette G17
Henry G18
Newton G19
Spalding G20
Butts G21
Jasper G22
Pike G23
Lamar G24
Upson G25
Monroe G26
Jones G27
Crawford G28
Bibb G29
Peach G30
Twiggs G31
Macon G32
Houston G33
Bleckley G34
Sumter G35
Dooly G36
Pulaski G37
Dodge G38
Lee G39
Crisp G40
Wilcox G41
Turner G42
Ben Hill G43
Worth G44
Tift G45
Irwin G46
Colquitt G47
Cook G48
Berrien G49
Lanier G50
Brooks G51
Lowndes G52
Echols G53

INTERSTATE-75 RV PARK & CAMPGROUND SITES

State	I-75 Exit	Direction	Campground	Phone	# of Sites	Open	Rates	Distance in Miles	Driving Directions
MI	18	W	Camp Lord Willing	313-243-2052	288	all year	$16-20/family	1	1 miles West on Nadeau Rd; follow signs to campground
OH	179	W	Fire Lake	888-879-2267	100	4/15-10/15	$17/2people	2½	1½ miles W on 6; ½ m S on 25; ½ m W on Kramer Road
OH	164	E	Pleasant View	419-299-3897	300	all year	$16-18/fam.	1	¾ m E on 613; ¼ m SE on 218
OH	161	E	Shady Lake	419-423-3490	139	all year	$16/fam.	2½	½ m E on 99; 1½ m N on CR 220; ½ m W on 101
OH	145	E	Twin Lake Park	419-477-5255	100	4/15-10/15	$17-25/fam.	3/4	¼ m S on 235; ½ m E on 34
OH	110	E	KOA Wapakonata	800-562-9872	76	all year	$23-24/2p	1½	¾ m E to first intersection; ¾ m N on Cemetery Rd.
OH	82	E	Poor Farmer's	937-368-2449	540	all year	$12.50/fam.	6¾	6 m E on 36; ¾ m S on Lost Creek Shelley Rd.
OH	14	W	Quality Inn RV Park	513-771-5252	11	all year	$25/vehicle	¼	¼ mile west on Glendale-Milford Rd
OH	10	W	Woodland Trailer	513-931-8845	20	all year	$18/2p	4¼	4 m W on Galbraith; ¼ m S on Daly
KY	166	E	KOA Cincinnati - South	800-562-9151	108	all year	$20-23/2p	2¼	¼ m E on 491; 2 m S on 25
KY	159	W	Dry Ridge Camper's Village	606-824-5836	70	all year	$20/vehicle	1.2	50 yds W on 22; 1 m N on Service Rd.
KY	120	E	Kentucky Horse Park S/P	800-370-6416	260	all year	unknown	1	1 m E on 1973
KY	97	W	Clay Ferry Campground	606-626-1330	112	all year	$12-16/2p	2	1000ft W on US 25, 2 miles North on 2338
KY	95	E	Fort Boonesborough S/P	606-527-3131	167	all year	unknown	5.9	4 9/10m E on 627; 1m S on 338
KY	76	W	Oh Kentucky Campground	606-986-1150	120	all year	$10-12/vehicle	1/4	¼ m W on Hwy 21
KY	76	W	Walnut Meadow Campground	606-986-6180	123	all year	$13-14/2p	1/2	½m W on Hwy 21
KY	62	E	KOA Renfro Valley	800-562-2475	110	all year	$15.50-$19.50/2	1½	1½ m N on Hwy 25
KY	62	E	Renfro Valley RV Park	800-765-7464	199	3/1-12/15	$19-21/vehicle	¼	¼ mile east on Highway 25
KY	38	E	Levi Jackson Wilderness Rd S/P	606-878-8000	188	all year	unknown	4.3	2 m E on 192; 2 3/10 m S on 25
KY	29	W	KOA Corbin	800-562-8132	90	all year	$15.50-22/2p	1/2	¼ m W on 770; ¼ m S (follow signs)
KY	11	W	Williamsburg Travel Trailer Park	800-426-3267	56	all year	$10/4p	1/4	¼ m W on Hwy 92
TN	134	W	Cove Lake S/P	615-562-8355	97	all year	unknown	1	east of I-75 on Hwy 25; park entrance on left
TN	122	E	Big Ridge S/P	615-992-5523	52	all year	unknown	12	12 E on Hwy 61
TN	122	E	Fox Inn Campground	423-494-9386	98	all year	$15-20/2p	3/5	3/5 m E on Hwy 61
TN	62	W	KOA Sweetwater Valley	800-562-9224	63	all year	$19-20.50/fam.	1	¾ m W on Oakland; follow signs S
TN	49	E	Athens I-75 Campground	423-745-9199	60	all year	$17-18/2p	3/4	¾ m E on Hwy 30
TN	20	W	KOA North Cleveland	800-562-9039	87	all year	$18-20/2p	1	½ m W on County Rd; follow signs ½ m
TN	1	W	Holiday Trav-L-Park	800-693-2877	171	all year	$19.50-21.50/2p	3/4	¼ m W on Hwy 41; ½ m S on Mack Smith Rd.

INTERSTATE-75 RV PARK & CAMPGROUND SITES

State I-75 Exit Direction	Campground	Phone	# of Sites	Open	Rates	Distance in Miles	Driving Directions
GA 141 W	KOA Chattanooga S KOA	800-562-4167	145	all year	$20.50-23.50/2p	1/4	¼m W on Hwy 2, entrance on right
GA 130 E	KOA Calhoun	800-562-7512	87	all year	$16.95-22.95/2p	1½	1½ m E on Hwy 156
GA 127 W	KOA Cartersville	800-562-2841	117	all year	$15-19/2p	1/4	¼ m W on Cassville Rd.
GA 121 E	Holiday Marina Harbour & CG	707-974-2575	44	all year	$15-18/2p	2¼	¾m E on Glade Rd; 1m N on Tanyard Ck.; ½ m E on Groover's
GA 116 W	KOA Atlanta N (Kennesaw)	800-562-4194	230	all year	$20-26/2p	2 1/10	1½ m W on Barrett; ½ m N on Hwy 41; 1/10 m Battlefield Pkwy
GA 72 W	KOA Atlanta S (McDonough)	800-562-6073	145	all year	$24-26/2p	1/4	¼ m W on Frontage Rd.
GA 65 W	High Falls Campground	800-428-0132	124	all year	$14/family	1/10	1/10 m W on High Falls Rd; entrance on right
GA 61 E	KOA Forsyth	800-562-8614	110	all year	$19-21/2p	3/5	1/10 m E on Juliette Rd; ½ m N on County Rd.
GA 45 W	Candlelight RV	912-956-1880	64	all year	$15/vehicle	1/2	½m W on Hwy 247; entrance on right
GA 43 E	Boland's RV Park	912-987-3371	65	all year	$16.50/2p	1/3	¼ m E on Hwy 341; 1/10 m N on Perimeter Rd.
GA 43 W	Crossroads Travel Park	912-987-3141	64	all year	$17/2p	1/10	1/10 m W on Hwy 341; entrance on left
GA 42 W	Fair Harbor RV Park	912-988-8844	150	all year	$17/2p	1/4	¼ m W of exit 42; entrance on right
GA 31 W	KOA Cordele	800-562-0275	73	all year	$19-22.50/2p	1/4	¼ m W on Rockhouse Rd.
GA 30 W	Southern Gates RV	912-273-6464	46	all year	$17/4people	1/4	¼m W on Deep Creek Rd; entrance on right
GA 29 W	Knight's RV Park	912-567-3334	81	all year	$8.95/2people	1/10	1/10m W on Amboy Rd; entrance on right
GA 16 W	Amy's South GA RV Park	912-386-8441	86	all year	$15/2p	1	1m W on South Central Ave.
GA 10 W	Reed Bingham S/P	912-896-3551	46	all year	unknown	6	6m W on Hwy 37
GA 5 W	River Park	912-244-8397	62	all year	$14/2p	1/10	1/10 m W on Hwy 133
GA 2 E	Eagles Roost Campground	912-559-5192	140	all year	$17/2p	3/5	100 ft E; ½ m S on Frontage Rd

We hope that these I-75 RV Park and Campground tables help you in your travels. We recommend that you purchase a current copy of ***Woodall's Campground Directory*** (from your RV dealer, bookstore or phone, 1-800-323-9076). This comprehensive directory covers all the key parks and campgrounds state by state, across North America.

In addition, if you are not already a member, consider joining the ***Good Sam Club.*** The benefits are numerous, and include discounts at various campgrounds and on propane purchases, special RV insurance, etc. Good Sam publishes the ***Trailer Life Campground and RV Park & Services Directory,*** another excellent source of parks and campgrounds. Phone 1-800-234-3450 for membership information and services.

Both of these directories include information about RV services and suppliers (parts) -- and tourist attractions along the way.

Miscellaneous

A ***"Compendium of Miscellany"*** . . .

. . . interstate facts, figures and nonsensical information you probably don't want to know — like ***what is TEA-21*** or ***how much a highway sign costs?***

. . . or information you definitely ***do*** want to know like, ***where are the most notorious radar traps on I-75?***

It is all here for your delectation!

Plus tips . . .

tips . . .

and more tips . . .

spread throughout the section

The National Interstate Defense System

Just after World War I, the War Department in Washington decided to "wave the flag" and thank the people of America who had generously supported the war effort in many ways. The Department felt that a convoy of America's military Might - tanks, trucks, field guns - driven across the continent from Washington to San Francisco would be a suitable event. The convoy would visit various towns and villages on the way and give the public a closer view of the equipment which had help win the European war.

They turned to a young lieutenant colonel to organize and lead this mission which he did with much enthusiasm. The convoy set off in the summer of 1919. From the first day it was a disaster. The heavy tanks often collapsed the wooden rural bridges and trucks frequently mired to the axles in mud. Two months after the journey started, at an average speed of 6 mph the convoy limped into Oakland, California.

The officer recorded in his memoirs,

"efforts should be made to get our people interested in producing better roads."

Others were also concerned about the state of the nation's roads and in the late 1930's during Roosevelt's administration, plans were finally being laid for a national grid of high speed freeways.

And then came the second war in Europe - World War II. The young Lt. Colonel who led the 1919 convoy had risen in rank and become the Supreme Allied Commander with responsibility for coordinating the invasion of "Fortress Europe." He and his generals watched in horror as Hitler was able to rapidly deploy his troops via the German super-freeway Autobahn system.

The commander of course, was Dwight Eisenhower who in 1953 became President of the United States. On June 29, 1956 - the "official birth date" of the Interstate system - he signed legislation which created a ***"National System of Interstate and Defense Highways"*** – an extensive multi lane limited-access freeway system designed not only to move people quickly from one place to another, but serve as a vital element of defense during a national emergency, so armies can swiftly move along its arteries.

Today however, national defense is less of a concern and the public at large is the beneficiary of what became a miracle of modern engineering . . . the largest coordinated public works program in the entire history of mankind (estimated to be much bigger than the building of the pyramids in Egypt, the construction of the extensive Roman road system in ancient Europe and Asia, or the excavation of the Suez Canal).

Defense isn't entirely forgotten though; sections of interstates have been designed to serve as tactical airstrips during times of crisis. During the 1960's, there was a concern that Soviet forces might attempt an invasion of the US mainland via Cuba. Sections of the I-75 in lower Georgia would have been converted to airstrips to help meet this threat.

Prior to the Interstate System, traveling long distances could be painful; a trip from Detroit to Florida would take 5 to 6 days. Primary roads did not always go in straight lines - they often meandered around the countryside. Frequently they were single lane and at every community along the way, traffic lights, stop signs and local cross traffic slowed the journey. Today, however, I-75 makes the drive to Florida a comfortable and pleasant experience.

TEA-21, and all that . . .

Here are some interesting facts about the Interstate Highway system.

Usage—there are 4 million miles of roads in the USA. The interstates account for 45,744 miles or about 1.1%, and yet interstates carry 23% of the total traffic. The standard interstate should have four 12' wide lanes and 10' wide shoulders, although due to heavier traffic patterns, many states are now expanding old four lane sections to six.

Administration—The highways are administered by the U.S. Department of Transportation, Federal Highway Administration, Washington, DC, in coordination with each State's Department of Highways (DOT). As the owner, each state is responsible for the construction and maintenance of sections of the Interstate system; the Federal Government reimburses the state 90% of its costs.

TEA-21—In June, 1998, recognizing that maintenance and expansion of the interstate system was not keeping up with current and future needs, President Clinton signed new legislation—the *Transportation Equity Act,* known as TEA-21—which will release billions of dollars to the states between now and 2003, to provide funding to improve all transportation systems. Much of this extra funding will be spent on the nation's interstates, it's estimated that Federal spending on highways will increase by about 10 billion dollars during this period.

Numbering—Interstate highways are numbered with two digits according to their route direction. North-South routes are odd numbered, starting in California with I-5 and moving eastward toward the Atlantic coast where we find the I-95. East-West routes are designated with even numbers and start in the south with I-4 in Florida and finish in the North with I-96 in Michigan. This system was chosen to avoid confusion with the older highway numbering system which started with US1 in the East and finished with U.S. 101 in the West.

Even the three digit Interstate extensions and beltways numbers have significance. If the ***first digit is even***, the route is a ***beltway***, bypass or loop around a city (e.g. I-275 around Cincinnati or I-475 around Macon). Incidentally, these beltways were not always designed as bypasses for the convenience of travelers. Planned during the Cold War period, some were designed as a means of allowing the military to bypass the rubble of a nuclear devastated city!

If the ***first digit is odd***, the route is a ***spur*** from the main route into a nearby area (example: I-575 at I-75 exit 268 [old 115] above Marietta, GA).

Signage — Interstate signs are not cheap. The entire system has signage worth over $200 million. An average interchange sign (about 150 sq. feet) costs around $5,000, and overhead suspended truss signs such as those used to signify major divides in an interstate highway can run as much as $35,000. Interstate signs are color coded. Green & white give directions; blue & white signs inform about roadside services (e.g. rest area). The signs are designed to be read 1,000 feet away. At 70 MPH, a vehicle takes 9.7 seconds to cover this distance. Some signs need fast readers!!!

Incidentally, those Lodging-Food-Gas service signs you see as you approach an exit do not necessarily list ALL the services available at the exit. Companies must pay the state to be listed - some decide not to.

Safety — Interstate highways are generally 2½ times safer than other roads. Why? A number of reasons including - multiple lanes smoothing the flow of traffic, divided roads with median barriers reducing or eliminating headlight glare and head-on crash situations, fenced right-of-ways controlling access by animals and pedestrians, no stop signs or traffic lights causing sudden stopping situations, and finally, controlled access of all intersections so that the cross route goes over or under (rather than through) the Interstate — eliminating dangerous cross traffic hazards.

The 500 Mile Day - Breaking it Up

What is the best way of breaking up your driving day so that you don't become overly tired and yet travel a reasonable distance? After many trips along the I-75, we have adopted the following 500 mile/day approach which might also work for others, especially if like us they are "morning" people. It takes advantage of low traffic periods and the time-shifting of meals (it might not work well for families traveling with children) to avoid long delays at restaurants. Here's how the day goes:

Wake up at 6:30 a.m. and plan to depart at 7:30 (get a cup of coffee at the motel if possible, or make it on your portable coffee maker).

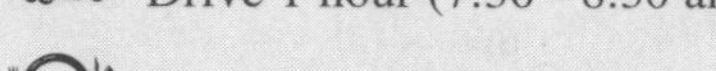

Drive 1 hour (7:30 - 8:30 am) advantage - traffic is very light.

Breakfast (8:30 - 9:15 am).

Drive 2 hours (9:15 - 11:15 am).

Coffee break (11:15 - 11:30 am).

Drive 2 hours (11:30 am - 1:30 p.m.) advantage - lighter traffic.

Lunch (1:30 - 2:15 p.m.) advantage - faster service, main lunch rush is over.

Drive 1¾ hours (2:15 - 4:00 p.m.).

Coffee break (4:00-4:30 p.m.) start planning night stop (about 90 miles ahead).

Drive 1½ hours (4:30 - 6:00 p.m.) - Stop for the night around 6:00 p.m.

Money Saving Tip

After entering a new state, stop at the Welcome Center and get a copy of the free Market America (MA) or Exit Information Guide (EIG). The green, yellow or red covered coupon books can usually be found lying in a pile on the counter or nearby rack. If you don't see them . . . ask for them . . . they will be well known by the Welcome Center staff, but might be under the counter since they are very popular and supplies don't last long.

These publications will save you many $$$$ on your overnight accommodation. They are chock full of discount coupons for motels (independents as well as major chains) along the way. Typically, you will find discounts in the 20-45% range. Bargains we have seen recently were $65 rooms discounted to $36, and $42 rooms to $28. We use the books all the time on each trip (including our vacation stays in Florida) and save literally hundreds of dollars.

Here's how they work - every day each motel listed in the coupon books sets aside a certain number of discount rate rooms based on their occupancy experience from the previous night, and the discounts are provided on a first-come first-served basis to travelers with the discount book coupons. What are your chances of getting a discount room? We normally pull off the road around 6 p.m. and in all our years of traveling have only been turned down three times at a motel of our choice. We quickly found another one nearby which accepted their coupon from the book.

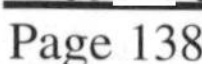

Insider Tip
Crackêr Barrel's Talking Books

Tired of the radio and need something different to pass the time as you drive? Then stop at the nearest Cracker Barrel Store (see the maps for the closest "Cracker Barrel" exit to you) and rent a selection from their "Book on Audio" program. After you've finished listening to it, drop it off at your next Cracker Barrel stop and pick up another. Your total cost if you return it within a week? Three dollars!

These "tape books" cover the full gamut of interests. On a recent trip to Florida, we rented a current John Grisham novel *"The Testament,"* Robert Waller's *"Bridges of Madison County,"* a Daphne DuMaurier classic and *"The Eleventh Commandment,"* by Geoffrey Archer (total cost for all this entertainment – $12). There were even tapes of the latest selections from Oprah Winfrey's popular TV book club.

Dozens of other "books" are available, from Zane Grey to Agatha Christie . . . from P.G. Wodehouse's *"Jeeves"* series to many current non-fiction best sellers, such as Phil McGraw's *"Life Strategies."* There is also an excellent selection of children's stories — including current offering such as, *"Indian in the Cupboard"* — what better way to keep the younger travelers quiet and occupied? The Cracker Barrel staff told us that they often add new titles to keep the selection current.

Here's how the Cracker Barrel tape-book program works. Go to the revolving tape-book stand in any Cracker Barrel store and choose the tapes you want. The price of the tape-book is on the back ($12.99 for a single cassette book and $18.99 for a double, $23.99 — three cassettes and $27.99 for four). You pay the Cracker Barrel staff the full price, and they give you a special receipt for this amount. After enjoying the book on your journey you stop at another Cracker Barrel, turn the tape-book in and receive your money back less three dollars (per week) to cover the rental.

Oh, by the way – while you are there enjoy one of their marvelous country style meals. Their baked potatoes and fresh vegetables are scrumptious. We also enjoy browsing the well stocked country store before or after meals. The merchandise is always unique and reflects the home style atmosphere of this excellent restaurant chain.

The 500 Mile Day - Drive by the Page

"Honey, let's drive three more pages and then stop at that Cracker Barrel shown in Dave's book at exit 373. It's on the left side of the road."

This is one of the most interesting things about *"Along the I-75"* — we have found that you start thinking of your day's drive in terms of the pages you're going to drive . . . rather than miles. Unlike other maps which vary in scale, our maps are designed to the same scale of 25 miles (40 kms) per page. This allows you to relate distance to pages very specifically.

For instance, if you are planning to follow the 500 miles per day plan described on the previous page, this becomes a 20 page day as follows:

Two pages before breakfast—five before morning coffee break—five pages before lunch—four before afternoon coffee—four pages before stopping for the night.

Somehow, this approach seems to make the large distances along the interstate easier to manage . . . and the day go much faster, too. One of our readers, an experienced I-75 driver of many years said, *"the miles seem to whiz by as we turn the pages."*

Traveling with children? See the special "500 Mile Day" on page 145.

Radar

When compared to national highway safety statistics, the I-75 is a very safe freeway. State police mean to keep it that way by actively monitoring speed and issuing tickets for infractions as little as 5 mph over the limit.

Now, I *know* you have absolutely no intention of speeding as you head along the interstates, but solely for academic purposes I thought you might like to update yourself with the new technology waiting to trap the unwary. In the next few pages, I will give you a look at the various devices used by the police to measure car speed and the counter measures available to the public. Radar detectors are legal (for passenger vehicle use) in all the I-75 states but we will also have a quick look at the VG-2, the device used by Highway Patrol to detect the illegal use of detectors in those states where they are banned — the so called, "detector detector."

Radar Guns, Detectors and other High-Tech Toys

When you see radar detectors for sale (truck stops have the best selection - I wonder why?), you will see features with cryptic words such as X, K and Ka bands, VG-2 proof, Lidar and anti-falsing. What do they mean? Here is a short primer:

The early methods of speed measurement - an officer with a stop watch behind a rock, or two pneumatic tubes laid across the road measuring the time difference of the front wheels hitting them - have long disappeared from the enforcement scene, although but surprisingly the stop watch method has been updated as follows:

VASCAR, or **V**isual **A**verage **S**peed **C**omputer **A**nd **R**ecorder is a non-radar method of speed measurement; it makes use of the "distance/time" equation. If you know the distance between two points and can measure the time taken to travel between them, you have the speed of the object making the passage.

In practical applications, VASCAR is used frequently in all I-75 states, but in particular by air patrols (Ohio writes the most VASCAR measured tickets). An officer flying at 2,000 feet will see a car traveling at excessive speed. As the car passes a known point on the road, the officer flips a switch on his VASCAR unit. As the car passes the second measurement point, the officer flips another switch and the unit calculates the speed and displays it on the VASCAR screen. It should be noted that the distance between the two points is always pre-measured and entered into the unit - they are not necessarily the white "T" symbols you see painted on the road surface, but may be natural landmarks unknown to you.

Details of the measurement are quickly relayed by radio to a ground patrol car, to make the arrest (see page 66).

You should note that its most common application is in a moving patrol car with "distance" information being inputted to the unit with a hookup to the car's odometer. The measurement can be made from a patrol car following you or even ahead of you.

X, K & Ka bands refer to the different types of police radar signals detected by the unit. The more expensive detectors ($250 - $400) will respond to all three types of radar signal, with top of the line models also detecting laser guns.

The oldest is the X band, but it is still very active in all the states you will drive through on I-75. Cheap X band detectors are very sensitive to non-speed trap radar

Rear panel of a hand held instant-on Ka band radar gun

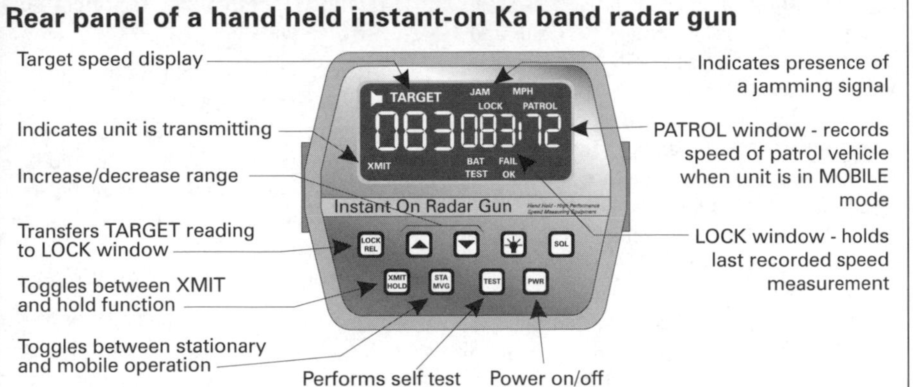

signal sources such as automatic supermarket doors, and often sound their alarm (falsely) even when there is no police unit nearby. Furthermore, the alarm can be inadvertently activated by overtaking vehicles equipped with similar radar detectors. The X band units often have highway (sensitive) or city (less sensitive) switch settings, or automatic "anti-falsing" circuitry to try and overcome these false alarms.

The **K band** detector is less likely to be vulnerable to false alarms since there are very few non-police devices licensed by the FCC to operate within the K band frequencies. This means that when a K band radar detector sounds a warning, you can almost be sure there is a radar trap ahead (or creeping up on you from behind!). From the "Smokey" point of view, the K band gun is more accurate than the X band gun and is therefore the police radar "weapon of choice." The newer "instant-on" K band radar guns (see diagram below) are deadly, since once the alarm sounds, the police have recorded the speed. The guns have ominous names such as the "Stalker," "Bee 36" and the "Shooter" and are very accurate as well as difficult to detect. They can be used from a stationary patrol car or while "pacing" (ie. driving in a traffic flow).

In the diagram above, a car has been registered speeding at 83 mph. The officer locked this speed into the LOCK display so that it can be shown to the driver and used as evidence (some units will retain the display in "memory" or download it to a portable printer). At the time of the reading, the officer was driving at 72 mph in the same direction as the target.

To give you an idea of how likely you are to encounter an X or K band radar gun, there are more than 140,000 X band and 60,000 K band guns licensed to police departments. Many of these K band units are being retro-fitted to Ka band which, along with **LIDAR** (laser) are the new glamour weapons of the Highway Patrol.

The **Ka** units come in two forms — upgraded models of the instant-on K band guns described above, and photo radar. Ka radar guns are now growing in popularity. On a recent I-75 drive to Florida, 60% of our radar "hits" were Ka units.

"Small" and "portable" are the new buzzwords. Recent Ka models introduced to the market include the Genesis II - a portable unit which actually uses the Black & Decker's VersaPak rechargeable battery - just like your portable drill. Kustom Signal's Golden Eagle can differentiate between two speeding cars and Stalker DSR has the ability to lock onto its target just like a fighter aircraft. A synthesized voice advises the officer that he or she has a "lock."

LIDAR (**Li**ght **D**etection **a**nd **R**anging) or

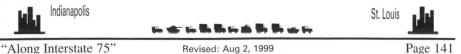

laser technology has been in use for some time now. This is extremely accurate and is in the form of a hand held gun. Laser is detectable by the newer detectors, but, this will probably not help the speeder since laser guns read a vehicle's speed instantly. In other words, if your detector warns you of a laser beam, unless it has reacted to "splash" from a nearby vehicle, the police already have your speed recorded on their screen. Typically, a laser unit has a range of about 1,200 feet - the beam at that point is about 3 feet wide so it takes an officer with a very steady hand to pick off targets with accuracy.

Another "buzz word" you should know about is **VG-2**. As you know, a number of states ban the use of radar detectors (see chart). In these jurisdictions, police cars are equipped with special instruments known as VG-2 units which detect electronic signals emitted through the antenna of illegally installed detectors. To counteract this, some radar/lidar detectors are sold as "VG-2 proof," or "stealth" units — meaning that they cannot be detected by the police VG-2 systems. Tests however, indicate that there is always some leakage, no matter how small.

Finally, an interesting type of counter measure was introduced a few years ago by detector manufacturer, Uniden. Called the **BearTracker** this might just be the answer to all those sophisticated police guns described above.

The BearTracker scanner is installed in your car and detects the stray electrical signals given off by all highway patrol vehicle radio transmitters, whether the radio is being used or not. As you enter a new state, you tap its name into the unit and the scanner will detect that state's Highway Patrol vehicles from up to 3 miles away.

It really works! It is uncanny to have the Bear Tracker signal the proximity of a patrol car, and then see it half a mile further down the road hidden in the trees.

What is the bottom line? Don't speed—apart from the obvious danger to yourself and others (have you ever tried to control a blown front tire at 75 mph?) it can be very costly. The citation is only a small part of this cost; many states now exchange computer information about traffic violations and this can almost certainly ensure that the violator's insurance rates will increase substantially for the next few years.

Do as we do, set the cruise control at 65 mph and drive the right hand lane; let all those others go around you. Did you know that if you drive a consistent 10 mph over the various I-75 speed limits from Detroit to the Florida Border, you will only save 2 hours and 20 minutes on the entire five state journey?

Speed Enforcement on I-75

You will notice the patrol car symbols on the 25 mile-per-page maps — these represent places where we have observed speed traps or stationary patrol cars with some frequency over the past few years. Following is a state by state report on I-75 speed enforcement.

Michigan — Patrol cars: 770+ patrol cars (none unmarked by State law, although some have bumper strobes and rear deck lights) - all are painted a special "state police blue" which is a registered color that no other car owner can use. models: Chev Caprice and Ford Crown Victorias. 20 Mustangs assigned to freeway work, equipped with bumper strobes and rear deck lights. **Methods Used:** extensive stationary and moving radar/laser, Vascar, limited aircraft use. **Known Traps:** nothing significant on the I-75.

Ohio — Patrol cars: 972 patrol cars (none unmarked by State law) - all painted "smoke" gray. models: a few Chevy Corsica and 4X4's, most OHP use Ford Crown Victorias. **Air Patrols:** 11 aircraft

+ 2 helicopters, flown 8,200 hours and average 48,000 speeding tickets annually. Look for high wing, single engine aircraft with red, white and black paint and highway patrol insignia. Special note - Ohio makes the heaviest use of aircraft enforcement in the USA. Some of these aircraft are based at Wapakoneta Airport, several miles west of the I-75 at milepost 107. **Methods Used:** extensive VASCAR air surveillance (as weather permits), stationary and rolling radar (have observed patrol cars using radar guns from exit ramps of rest areas — ready to chase), laser. **Known Traps:** watch for median strip radar traps in the Lima area (between mileposts 133 to 118), and between Dayton and Cincinnati.

Kentucky — Patrol cars: 592 patrol cars (12 unmarked) - most painted gray, with blue light bar on roof - models: some Ford Probes (various colors, tinted windows), mostly Crown Victorias. **Air Patrols:** not used for speed control. **Methods Used:** stationary and rolling radar, "Wolf packs" (where 5-10 police cars will hide around a bend and pull a group of speeding traffic over), and Vascar. **Known Traps:** KSP has been running a Select Traffic Enforcement Program in the Covington, Florence, Walton area for some time now. According to the RADAR organization, two troopers in Boone County were able to raise $47,000 through 400 citations in 10 days work. They have been designated, "I-75's Hardest Working Troopers."

Tennessee — Patrol cars: 870 patrol cars (153 unmarked usually older mid-80 models) - painted 2 tone tan & brown - model: Chevy Caprice, Ford Crown Victorias, a few Chevy Tahoe's with modified engines. **Air Patrols:** not used for speed control. **Methods Used:** stationary and rolling radar, laser, "shoot in the back" radar/laser from overpasses. **Known Traps:** see 25 mile-per-page maps - several specific radar speed traps south of Knoxville are marked — watch for radar cars hiding in the gaps between trees (emergency turn cuts) in the wide median strip.

Georgia — Patrol cars: 768 patrol cars (79 unmarked - usually Ford Mustangs) models: Chevy Caprice, Ford Crown Victoria and Ford Mustangs (brown, or blue/gray with blue light bars). **Air Patrols:** unknown, but used for speed control. **Methods Used:** stationary and rolling radar, laser, "Wolf packs" (see Kentucky), "shoot in the back" radar from overpasses, Vascar. **Known Traps:** see maps.

All States — Drafting: Watch for a patrol car which comes down an I-75 entrance ramp, and joins the traffic. All traffic normally matches its speed. The patrol car will slowly speed up over the next few miles and lead the traffic (which is keeping up. After all, its OK to go at the same speed isn't it?) - right into the arms of a "Wolf Pack."

"I apologize officer, if I was doing anything wrong . . ."

What to do if you get stopped for speeding? Remain calm, remove dark sunglasses if wearing them, roll down your window and keep both hands on your steering wheel. When he or she ask for your license, take it out of your purse, wallet or holder before handing it over.

Never offer excuses, admit to speeding or protest ignorance-instead, apologize to the officer and ask if he/she would issue a warning instead of a ticket. If you know you were going fast, accept the officer's decision gracefully-it's probably overdue.

If you feel you were not speeding, don't protest but do ask what method was used to measure your speed. Try and establish the make and model of equipment used. If the officer is not cooperative, do not pursue it. As soon as possible, join the National Motorists Association (see page 198); they have lots of helpful information about fighting unfair tickets.

St. Louis

Kansas City

Construction Doesn't Always Mean a Slow Trip

When you see those maps with "construction" stamped all over them, the heart tends to sink. But it may not necessarily mean slow travel with long lines of backed up traffic. Let me explain:

Last year, I received my normal information packages from the I-75 state transportation departments detailing scheduled I-75 construction projects for the coming year. From the number of projects described, I expected that 1999 would be the year of the "slow drive to Florida" - and yet after driving the route three times, my impression was that these had been the best drives I had experienced since starting to write *"Along Interstate-75"* eight years ago. Why was that? It set me thinking.

The construction projects we meet on a long distance drive normally falls into one of three categories - emergency repairs, scheduled maintenance (e.g., resurfacing) or new project work (e.g., lane expansion).

Emergency repairs of course, cannot be predicted although as maintenance work increases over the next few years funded through TEA-21, the improved fabric of our interstate system should result in fewer emergencies repairs in the long term.

Now the primary reason people do not like construction is that it affects traffic flow and causes traffic backups. In other words, it slows down their journey.

So how do scheduled maintenance and new projects affect traffic flow?

Reduced speed limits in construction zones do not appear to upset drivers and most are quite happy to continue moving - even at 45 mph - without feeling frustrated. After all, there is a real human element here - the safety of the construction workers on the side of the road is really at risk from high speed traffic.

The merging of traffic lanes in a construction project however is another matter entirely. This situation can bring out the worst in some drivers. Backed up lanes, the "unfairness" of somebody trying to "sneak" ahead on the merging lane - all seem to create impatience and frustration - causes of "driver stress."

So here is the crux of the construction story. We shouldn't be counting construction zones as a measure of how fast or slow our I-75 journey will be, but the number of lane merges along the way. This is why we specifically mark them on our maps.

The good news this year is that although there may seem to be the normal number of construction projects scheduled, there are only two lane merges on the entire distance between Detroit and the Florida Border - and by using our map's brown "escape routes" as we did on a recent I-75 drive, you can easily avoid them!

Radio Grapevine

There's an information grapevine along the I-75 which runs 24 hours a day - 7 days a week, and relays information faster than jungle drums. Better than continuous traffic reports on commercial radio, it reports with unerring accuracy abnormal (fog, snow, accident) road conditions ahead, the best lane to use, where the Highway Patrol are hidden and even inside information about restaurants. It's the soap opera of the radio waves and I guarantee that once you get hooked you will never have a dull or boring Interstate drive again.

Oh yes . . one other thing . . you also have to be able to understand the language. For instance, do you know what the following means? *"Hey 4 wheeler on my backdoor, hope y'all got your ears on 'cause I'm backin' it down"* or, *"South bounders, Smokey taking pictures at marker 114."*

Yep, it's good ole CB radio (Citizen's Band to the uninitiated) that indispensable communication medium of the long-distance trucker's world . . . and we wouldn't drive the I-75 without it.

The 500 Mile Day
- Traveling With Children

"Children, we are going to drive three more pages and then stop at the McDonalds on page 27 with the playground . . . why don't you read me the stories about the next stretch of the interstate as I drive?"

Traveling with children has its own special challenges, and over the years I have received many letter from young parents who have given all sorts of great advise. On page 139, I described the method of "driving by the page" to make the distance go by quickly. Here's a special adaptation of that technique for the younger set:

- Pack the car the night before and let the kids sleep in the clothes they will be traveling in.
- Up at 5:30am - get yourself ready - wake up children and put them in the car. They'll go off to sleep again.
- Drive 4 pages (target 8:30), stop for breakfast - change clothes, brush teeth, etc.
- Drive 4 pages (target 10:30), stop for a rest room break and a run around or outside play time.
- Drive 4 pages (target 12:30), stop for lunch. Fast food facilities with playground areas are shown in red on our maps.
- Drive 4 pages (target 2:30), stop for a rest room break and a run around or outside play time.
- Drive 4 pages (target 4:30), stop for the night. Choose a motel with a pool so they can burn off some energy. Dinner 5:30-6pm. Off to bed early ready for the next day.

Another idea - rotate the car seating arrangement so that mom or dad spend some time in the back seat, and the children get an equal share of the front passenger seat. One safety item to consider though, don't place young children in a car seat where they could be injured should an air bag activate.

CB not only provides scads of information as you travel the Interstate but also peace of mind. You will never be alone at the side of the freeway should you experience a breakdown. With CB on board, you can summons help from your fellow travelers, and in a number of areas, state police and emergency organizations (such as REACT, or **R**adio **E**mergency **A**ssociated **C**itizens **T**eams) monitor the designated highway emergency and general calling channel – channel 9, and will get help to vehicles requesting assistance.

Finally, if this is your first venture into CB, we suggest a passive approach. Tune in to the trucks (channel 19 on I-75) and enjoy the ride. When you are ready to get your feet wet "on the air" try and call a fellow I-75 traveler heading in the same direction — *"Break, for a southbounder."*

Try channel 9 first—if you make contact, switch to another channel that you both agree upon since channel 9 should not be used for general conversation. If you have no luck on channel 9 then try the trucker's channel because this is probably where all the *"4 wheelers"* (private car) are listening— but again, switch to another channel right away after making contact since the truckers like to keep this channel for themselves.

I-75 Exit Numbers

All states number I-75 exits starting with the first exit at the southern end of the state, and numbering northward – but there are two different approaches to the way that the exit numbers are assigned.

Florida uses an old system – it numbers its exits sequentially – that is, the first northbound exit is number 1, followed by exit 2 and so on, until the northern border is reached.

The other five I-75 states use the federally approved "milepost" or "mile-log" approach – a system which is much better for travelers. In this system, the exits are numbered according to the closest roadside mile marker. Since the markers measure distance from the state's southern border, each exit number is also a record of its distance from the border. For example, the first northbound exit in Kentucky is exit 11–because it is 11 miles north of the Kentucky–Tennessee (Kentucky's southern) border.

Why don't we like the Florida approach? You cannot gage your journey's progress using the exit numbers. In Florida, you may know the next exit number but have no idea whether it is one mile away, or ten. In the other I-75 states, you can easily calculate the distances between exits – by deducting the lower exit number from the higher – a real traveler's convenience

Georgia is converting its exit numbering system starting on January 1, 2000, and plans to finish within seven months. Since this edition of *"Along Interstate-75"* will span this period, we decided to convert to the new Georgia numbers immediately throughout the book, but keep the old numbers alongside for reference.

Although Georgia has resisted this change for years, it is interesting to note some of the advantages of the mile-log system GDOT stated in a recent media release:

- *will allow emergency vehicles to get to incidents quicker.*
- *more exact times of arrival to an incident to be estimated.*
- *better travel planning due to more useable distance information.*
- *police and EMS can locate stranded vehicles faster.*

I suspect it has more to do with the fact that this system is the method recommended by the Federal Government . . . and after the new TEA-21 (see page 137) Act went into effect last year releasing billions of dollars to the states for transportation projects, Georgia felt that it should fall in line.

Florida, the ball is now in your court!

Motel 6pm Saving

No reservation? If you are planning to stay at a national chain with a central reservation system, try and arrive at your chosen motel (with MA or EIG discount coupon in hand), a few minutes after 6 p.m.

At 6 o'clock, the central reservation computer system often "dumps" non-guaranteed reservations (ie. those not guaranteed with a credit card and held only to 6 pm).

At smaller properties, the front desk staff often check their reservation file and free up any that are not guaranteed, although this is not as consistent as the large chains.

You should have no difficulty getting your discounted room for the night – at the average motel at least several rooms become available - and you are first-in-line as a paying customer.

$$$ Savings at Disney

A great tip for I-75 users heading for Walt Disney World (WDW) in Orlando. This will save you so much time - almost a day if you had planned to stay for four — that you will most certainly want to pass this one on to your Disney bound friends.

Buy a copy of the *"Unofficial Guide to Walt Disney World,"* by Bob Sehlinger (Publisher: Prentice Hall). This book is jammed full of so many good "behind the scene" time and money saving tips for your Magic Kingdom, EPCOT and MGM Studio visits, that it has quickly become an insider's "must have" for a Disney visit. It tells you where the best and worst food bargains are — which rides to go on first to maximize your attendance time — how to plan your day against the normal crowd patterns and avoid excessive line-ups . . . where and when to make special feature reservations . . . and much more. We have used it and fully endorse the author's statement that it provides the "information necessary to tour WDW with the greatest efficiency and economy, and with the least hassle and standing in line."

Most book stores have it in stock; it can also be easily ordered through book stores elsewhere in the nation (ISBN: 0-02-862616-8). However, be warned that because it is not officially sanctioned by the Walt Disney organization (the reason given is that they already have an "official" guidebook), it is not available at any of the concessions inside Walt Disney World.

To make the best use of this book, buy it before you leave home. Study it—learn the best and the worst—plan your strategy—choose your tactics—and then comfortably "do" four days of Disney World in three . . . comfortable $$$ savings too!

$$$ Savings on Disney Merchandise

Are you and the children heading for Walt Disney World (WDW) in Orlando? If so, you will probably want to buy Disney souvenirs and will find out how expensive the WDW "designer label" can be. The Disney licensed items sold in WDW shops inside the various theme parks are excellent quality, but at regular prices (i.e.. no discounts). Merchandise sold outside the parks may not be so good in quality, and selection is often limited.

There is one place outside WDW however, where you can buy much of the same merchandise that is sold inside the parks — but at a discount. You will get the same quality and selection at a lower price. This is the Character Warehouse in Mall number 2 of the Belz Factory Outlet World, on International Drive, Orlando.

How good are the discounts? For instance, regular "Mickey" ears cost $4.99 at WDW; Character Warehouse sell them for 99 cents. A large stuffed Mickey Mouse (regular $60), sells for $34.99. All of their casual wear bears the original Walt Disney Company labels, such as "Disney Wear" or "Disney Products."

We suggest that you plan to go to the Character Warehouse before you visit WDW. That way you won't be disappointed if there is something you want, but the Character Warehouse does not have it in stock - you can always get it later at the Park. To find the Belz Mall 2, take I-4 exit 29 (Sand Lake Rd. East). Turn left at the lights onto International Drive and continue to the end where it joins Oakridge Road—you can't miss the Belz Mall.

Interstate-75 Lodging

Long distance interstate travelers have differing accommodation needs. Many are "seniors" or retired people who might want to know if the "property" (this is what a lodging facility is called in the hospitality industry) has an attached restaurant (to save walking) or has facilities for the disabled. Some like to drive their car right to the unit door, others prefer the security of limited access properties where a door card is needed to open external doors. Young families on a budget vacation will try and save as much money as possible and will probably look at the "budget" chains such as Motel6, Red Roof or Super8. Still others might wish to relax in a swimming pool after a long day's drive, or just flop down and watch a movie on TV.

Whatever your needs, I-75 lodgings can cater to all tastes. Once you've determined your "style," the next thing is to locate a suitable property at your planned night's destination—and then get down to the fun task of obtaining the best rate for your stay.

Getting the Best Rates: I-75 has been around a long time and it has a lodging surplus along its length - except in March. Because of this, rates can be very competitive and some times, price wars will be apparent in their discounts. ***Hint:*** *use those free motel coupon books which are issued every 3 months (see page 138), to get the very best "price war" rates.*

When you go into a motel, do you ask them if they have a room for a night, and just leave it at that? If you do, you may not be getting the best rates available. After all, purchasing a motel room is no different to purchasing any other consumer product or service. It pays to shop around a bit, even if you do your shopping in the same motel—here's what I mean.

Rates within a property vary depending upon where a room is located (lower vs. upper floor; poolside or facing a highway, etc.) and how it is equipped. Generally, lower priced rooms are on upper levels, face the freeway and have one bed.

Once you've established room location, be aware that most properties usually have different rates for the same room; here's the structure: **a) the "rack" rate**—the standard rate which you get if you just ask for a room for the night, **b) the "senior" or "affiliation" rate** (at many motels the staff are not allowed to ask if you are a member of the AARP or AAA, you must volunteer this information), **c) the "discount coupon" rate**—this is often the easiest to get since discount coupon books are available everywhere (see page 138). But a motel might designate only a few rooms as "coupon" rooms, so it's on a "first come-first served" basis, **d) the "commercial" or "corporate" rate**—everybody, retired or not, can probably produce a business card or has worked for a corporation, use it, and **e) the "preferred" rate**—often the best, not always available.

When I approach the front desk of my selected motel, I first establish what the rack rate is for a standard 2P/1B (2 people/1 bed) room—this becomes my "yardstick"—and then ask for their best discounted, preferred rate. If not available, we then compare "corporate rates" to "discount coupon" and "affiliation" rates. We <u>never</u> pay the "rack rate."

Traveling with Pets: Traveling with pets can be difficult due to rules imposed by some motels - these run from "no pet" facilities to "pets welcome" on a no-charge or a pet deposit/surcharge (usually \$2-\$5) basis.

When questioned, we found that motel operators are not necessarily biased against pets; damage in not an issue (after all they do not surcharge for children who can cause more wear and tear on facilities than pets). They do have problems however with allergic reactions caused to guests staying in rooms previously occupied by pets, and must perform special cleaning to minimize this (it has been found that proteins in pet saliva can be a particular allergy problem).

As pet owners ourselves, we understand that pets are very much part of the family. We recommend the AAA book "Traveling with Your Pet" (see page 198).

To help pet owners, on our maps we have marked **in blue any motel which accepts pets** (they may require deposit or surcharge); exits with veterinarians & animal clinics are identified by this green "V" symbol.

Insider Tip
A Friendly Inn in a Storm

Imagine the scene. Outside your car its a howling blizzard and you've got to find a place for yourself and your family, for the night. You're becoming desperate. The first motel you tried was full up since many interstate travelers had been driven off the road early because of appalling conditions. The last place had doubled their room rates - taking advantage of the conditions.

Ahead, you see the glow of the red and green inn sign through the veil of white across yet another motel parking lot. You pull up under the relative shelter of the front canopy, give your wife the "here we go again" look and head out of the car into the lobby of the Holiday Inn in Monroe, Michigan (exit 15).

A few minutes later, you are out with a room key and a smile on your face. You and your family have a warm safe place to stay for the night. Not only did the Holiday Inn have a room but they offered you their discount rate!

This is a true story from last winter and several *"Along Interstate-75"* readers wrote or phoned me about it.

Last month, I went and visited with Monroe Holiday Inn manager Tarek Merhebi - to thank him on behalf of my readers. I took copies of your letters along with me and left them with Tarek. so he could share them with his staff.

Immediately you meet Tarek, you will like him. When I asked him about the storm and why he didn't take advantage of stranded travelers, he replied with an honesty that is so refreshing these days . . . that his job as an inn keeper is to provide safe, warm and comfortable lodgings for travelers at reasonable cost . . . not to gouge them. After a phone poll of other area motels that stormy night, he decided to maintain his normal rate policy. I am sure that many of his "storm" guests will be back and take their friends with them.

Tarek's Holiday Inn can be reached at 734-242-6000.

Insider Tip
An All-In-One Overnight Stop

Many of my "snowbird" readers are "mall walkers" - so when a reader recommends a comfortable inn with a mall attached to it through an inside door, I know that this is something to share.

The inn in question is the Comfort Inn connected to the Piqua Mall, at exit 82 in Ohio. Not only does the mall provide an excellent exercise opportunity but its access door is open all the time. During mall hours, you might want to take advantage of the food court or restaurants, or just wander around and window shop after a long days drive on I-75.

There is also a multi-screen theater in the mall, so here is your opportunity to catch up on that movie you wanted to see but didn't have time to see back home. A great alternative for the evening, than CNN in your room!

The Comfort Inn is just that . . . a well furnished comfortable inn with excellent rates and a welcoming staff. If you would like to give this inn, mall, movie combination a try, give them a phone call at 937-778-8100; I know general manager Dan Peterson will make you welcome.

This Comfort Inn is a perfect overnight stop in any sort of inclement weather.

Insider Tip
We find the Perfect Motel

It's the little things which turn a good motel room into a great one, and I may have found the perfect match to my expectations . . . at the Baymont (formerly, the chain was called Budgetel), west of the I-75 at Kentucky exit 29.

Here are my first impressions on opening the door with the plastic security card: —a fresh, clean smell in the air—larger than normal, well decorated room with high ceilings—separate vanity-bathroom areas (very important for traveling couples and fast morning getaways)—modular shower with excellent shower head and a GREAT steam extractor fan—lots of lights (5 x 100w + vanity area fluorescent)—large 25" screen TV with moveable (non-tethered) remote control unit—very, very quiet even although next to the interstate—soft, full reclining chair—heavy noise-killing drapes—coffee maker with full supplies.

But I've saved the best until last. I had been driving northbound in a freak winter storm which caused snowy and icy conditions all the way from Atlanta. Coming over Tennessee's Pine Mountain in next to impossible winter conditions was another story and all I wanted to do was get off the road with minimum fuss and into a swimming pool . . . and forget the drive. Imagine my delight when I found that the Baymont maintains its pool at a tepid 97°F (36°C), and that an even warmer bubble-spa is right alongside. Incidentally, the pool is housed inside a large glass enclosure which allowed me to swim in the tension-relaxing warm water while watching the traffic fight the snowy interstate outside.

We ate dinner at the Cracker Barrel restaurant next door. The following morning, we enjoyed a free breakfast and paper in the special "breakfast room," enabling us to make an early start (on a cleared road). This motel is highly recommended.

Insider Tip
Signature Inns - Friendly and Clean

It is small wonder that Signature Inns is the preferred choice of many corporations and travel agents. Started in 1981, this chain focuses on safe, quality accommodations at a reasonable price—all corridors are internal and access is past the front desk only. This safety theme is carried to the rooms which have electronic door locks. The rooms are large, exceptionally clean and well appointed.

Front desk service is always excellent, friendly and helpful. A free Breakfast Express, an all-you-can-eat buffet of fresh fruit, baked pastries, cereal, juices, coffee, etc., is included with your overnight stay, as is a free "USA Today" or "Wall Street Journal." Incidentally if you travel on business, they provide fax service and modem ports for in-room computer use - most also have a microwave and fridge.

When comparing motel rates, don't overlook these extras. For instance, if you buy a morning paper and have breakfast "on the road," you are probably spending another $10 per couple - a stay at Signature Inns saves you these added costs.

And a final point, many organizations claim to excel in "customer service" and many of them do until a problem arises . . . then watch out. Last summer, we watched Signature Inn staff deal with a customer problem. We were very impressed by the manner in which they resolved the situation to *everybody's* satisfaction, turning a disgruntled person into a happy guest. This is REAL customer service. We heartily recommend Signature Inns, for this and all the other reasons.

I-75 Lodging Alternatives

The following sections describe some alternatives to motel lodging. Bed & Breakfasting is an adult alternative, but if you are traveling with children, "lodging in the rough" may be a fun family experience.

Bed and Breakfast: For many years, Kathy and I have enjoyed Bed & Breakfast (B&B) lodgings on our travels through North America. Some of the wonderful places we have stayed include an herb farm in Pennsylvania, with a lobster fisherman in Massachusetts, a haunted house in Salem with a secret door in the wall of our room, with a High Court Judge in Connecticut and in a beautiful "ginger-bread" Victorian home in Cape May, NJ. Each stay has been valuable and unforgettably pleasant experience.

B&B may not be for everybody th. They may be a few extra miles off the freeway, but the drive is usually worth it. You must usually reserve ahead and provide a deposit (charge card number) when you phone. Prices tend to be higher than motel lodging. Often bathrooms are shared between guests and since you are staying in someone's home, the restrictions you would experience staying with friends, normal apply.

Also, you must enjoy people - after all, the best part of the B&B experience is the interesting people (hosts or other guests) you meet. Spending time with them, chatting about common interests, learning about the local countryside or other parts of the country - is one of the most enjoyable things about B&B. If this is not for you, then stick to hotel or motel lodging.

Hidden in the countryside bordering the Interstate-75, are some unique B&B opportunities. Here are some recommended by our readers:

OHIO

Toledo - Cummings House B&B
Restored 1857 manse in historic area; Dbl: $60-90, ☎ 419-224-3219

Findlay - Rose Gate Cottage,
Victorian decor in historic Findlay; Dbl: $50-70, ☎ 419-424-1940

KENTUCKY

Covington - Sandford House,
Historic building, AAA rated 3 diamond, Dbl: $65-100, ☎ 606-291-9133

Georgetown - Log Cabin,
1809 log cabin with period furniture, ☎ 502-863-3514

Lexington - Blackridge Hall,
Georgian mansion on 5 acres, ☎ 502-863-2069 (800-768-9308)

Richmond - Bennett House
Restored 1880's Victorian home, ☎ 606-625-0097

TENNESSEE

Knoxville - Magnolia Manor B&B,
AAA rated 3 diamond, ☎ 423-688-8999

GEORGIA

Ft. Oglethorpe - Capt. Quarters B&B Inn,
Former Cavalry officer's quarters, AAA rated 3 diamond, Dbl: $88-135 ☎ 706-375-4728 (800-487-4728)

Marietta - Stanley House B&B,
Historic, early Victorian, AAA rated 3 diamond, Dbl: $85 ☎ 770-426-1881

Lodgings "In the Wilderness": Want to try something different while you travel? Then consider a cabin in the woods. These are available at some state parks, or at private facilities such as KOA Kampgrounds. Here's the information:

KOA Kamping Kabins - KOA facilities are primarily for RVer's, but many of them have log cabins for rent as well. Some are available year round, others are closed in the winter; many have heaters and/or air conditioning. All have lockable doors, electricity and can sleep 4-6 people in 1 or 2 room layouts. But it is really upscale camping - there are no cooking facilities except for a BBQ or fireplace pit outside - and washing/shower facilities are in a communal building. KOA supply the beds and mattresses; you supply bed linen (or sleeping bags) and towels. To learn more, pickup a Directory at any KOA campground.

State Park Lodging: Many state parks have lodging facilities. Here are two to try:

Norris State Park, TN (see page 92) - this lovely Tennessee park nestled in the woods above Norris Lake has 10 deluxe and 19 "rustic" cabins for rent. The deluxe have 3 bedrooms, full furnished kitchens, TV, wood fireplaces, bath w/shower, heating & a/c - all linens are supplied. The rustics are similar, but smaller. The units normally rent by the week, but give the Park a call, they may have one or two available for one night stays. Reservations: 423-426-7461; toll free 800-543-9335.

Red Top State Park Lodge, GA (see page 110) - just 2 miles east of the Interstate lies Red Top Park with its famous lodge and restaurant. Surrounded with hiking trails winding through the pine trees, with glimpses of Allatoona Lake in the distance, the Lodge is a wonderful place to refresh the spirit.

The lodge's 33 rooms cost (Dbl) $69-79 depending upon day-of-the-week and season. They are often booked but with a little advance planning you could enjoy a peaceful night in the woods on the way to Florida. Reservations: 770-975-0055.

Symbol	Motel	1-800-Phone
BHost	Budget Host	800-283-4678
Baymnt	Baymont Inns	800-301-0200
BestW	Best Western	800-528-1234
C/Ctry	Cross Country Inn	800-621-1429
ClbHse	Clubhouse	800-258-2466
Comfrt	Comfort Inn	800-228-5150
CtySte	Country Inns/Suites	800-456-4000
CrtYrd	Courtyard-Marriot	800-321-2211
CtHrth	Country Hearth	800-848-5767
Days	Days Inn	800-329-7466
Econo	Econo Lodge	800-553-2666
Evoy	Envoy Inn	800-227-7378
ExtStAm	Ext. Stay America	800-646-8000
Fairfld	Fairfield Inn	800-228-2800
H/Inn	Holiday Inn	800-465-4329
Hmptn	Hampton Inn	800-426-7866
HoJo	Howard Johnston	800-446-4656
Jamsn	Jameson Inns	800-526-3766
Knght	Knights Inn	800-843-5644
LaQnt	La Quinta	800-531-5900
MHost	Master Host Inn	800-251-1962
MicroT	Microtel	888-771-7171
Motel6	Motel6	800-466-8356
Mstrs	Masters Inn	800-633-3434
Pssprt	Passport Inn	800-251-1962
QltyInn	Quality Inn	800-228-5151
Ramda	Ramada Inn	800-272-6232
RedC	Red Carpet Inn	800-251-1962
RedRf	Red Roof Inns	800-843-7663
Rodwy	Rodeway Inn	800-228-2000
Rsdnts	Residence Inn	800-331-3131
Scot	Scottish Inn	800-251-1962
Shony	Shoney's Inn	800-222-2222
Signtr	Signature Inn	800-822-5252
Sleep	Sleep Inn	800-753-3746
Supr8	Super 8 Motels	800-800-8000
TravL	Travelodge	800-578-7878
Wingate	Wingate Inns	800-228-1000

More Lodging Information? - see the following ***Insider*** or ***Saving Tips:***

Cumberland Inn, Kentucky (page 89), Hampton Inn, Dalton (page 107), Golf Heaven, Stockbridge, GA (page 115), Macon Reservations (page 119), Private Club motel (page 124), How coupon books work (page 138) and, 6pm Motel Savings (page 146)

Toll Free Reservation Phone Numbers

The chart to the left provides the 800 or 888 (no charge) reservation phone numbers for all of the popular motel chains along the Interstate. The advantage of the 800/888 number system is its convenience, but be aware of two drawbacks.

First, you cannot always use a discount coupon from a free coupon books (Exit Information Guide or Market America) when making an 800 number reservation - some will accept them but most don't. Most motels will however honor a senior (AARP) or AAA discount if you mention it to them over the phone. Make sure you mention it again when you check in.

Secondly, you may be told that the motel of your choice is full. If so, a phone call to the specific motel (get the number from the 800/888 operator) can often find you a room since most motels do not allocate all their rooms to their 800 number reservation system. They usually keep rooms available for last minute local needs.

Northbound Route

From the Florida Border to Detroit

Insider Tip for Northbound Travelers
Northbound Photographs

Driving north with the sun over your shoulder makes the roadside scenery much more interesting and acceptable for mobile in-car photography. In particular, look closely at the rock cuts in north Tennessee and south Kentucky. Early morning sun angled across cuts on the west side of the interstate and late afternoon sun lighting rock cuts on the east will reveal all sorts of interesting things such as the vertical drill holes used for the dynamite charges when the road was being built.

If using an automatic camera from inside the car, don't forget to turn off the auto focusing feature (otherwise it will tend to focus on your car window glass) and set for as high a shutter speed as possible. If you don't have a high shutter speed, then try and "lock" your camera on the subject by panning as the car moves forward.

Never pull on to the soft shoulder for your photograph - an interstate shoulder is a very dangerous place to be and should only be used for emergency stops.

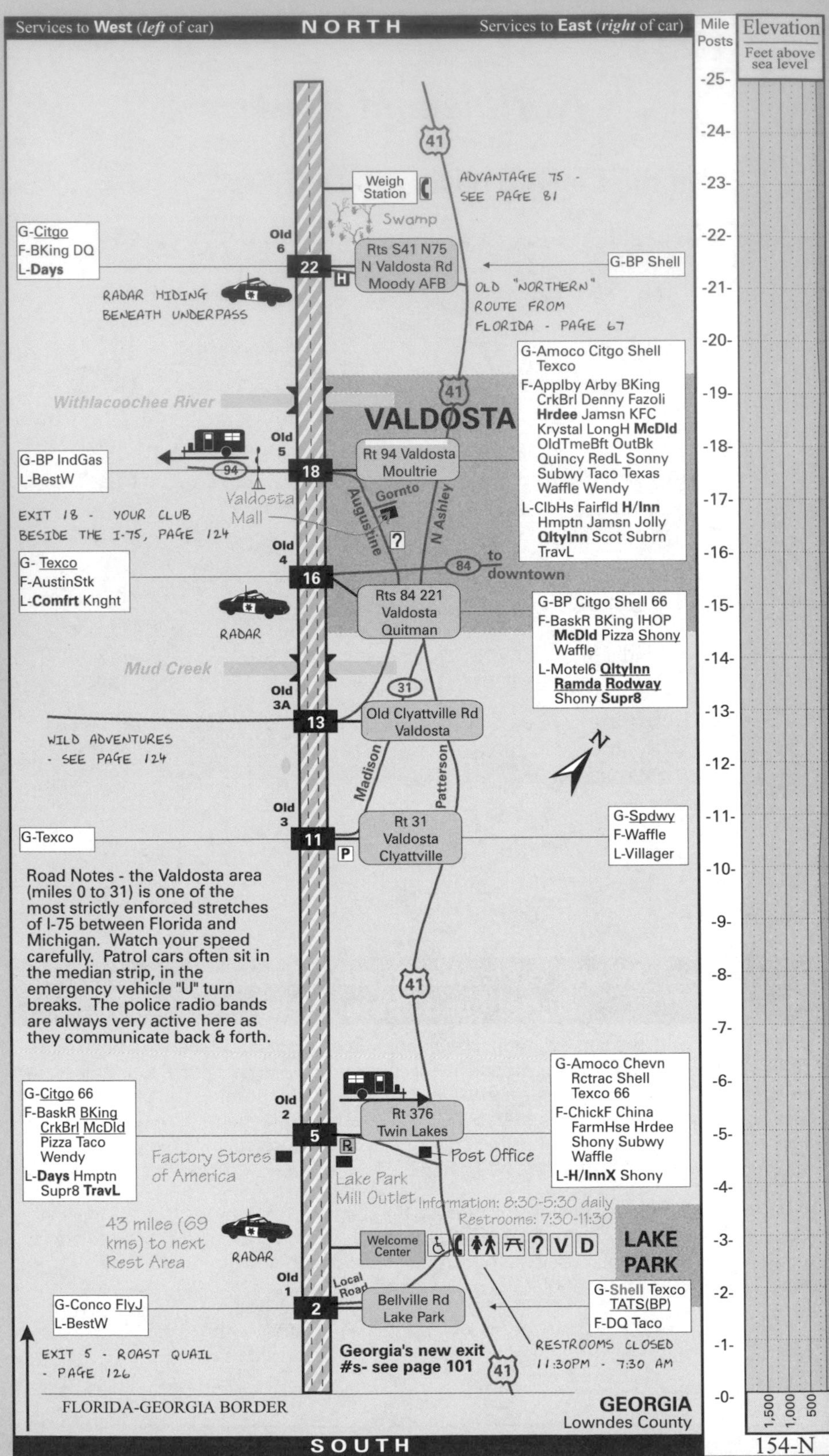
Services to West (left of car)
NORTH
Services to East (right of car)
Mile Posts
Elevation
Feet above sea level
41
Weigh Station
ADVANTAGE 75 - SEE PAGE 81
Swamp
G-Citgo
F-BKing DQ
L-Days
Old 6
22
Rts S41 N75
N Valdosta Rd
Moody AFB
H
G-BP Shell
RADAR HIDING BENEATH UNDERPASS
OLD "NORTHERN" ROUTE FROM FLORIDA - PAGE 67
G-Amoco Citgo Shell Texco
F-Applby Arby BKing CrkBrl Denny Fazoli Hrdee Jamsn KFC Krystal LongH McDld OldTmeBft OutBk Quincy RedL Sonny Subwy Taco Texas Waffle Wendy
L-ClbHs Fairfld H/Inn Hmptn Jamsn Jolly QltyInn Scot Subrn TravL
Withlacoochee River
VALDOSTA
Old 5
18
94
G-BP IndGas
L-BestW
Rt 94 Valdosta
Moultrie
Valdosta Mall
Augustine
Gornto
N Ashley
?
EXIT 18 - YOUR CLUB BESIDE THE I-75, PAGE 124
Old 4
16
84
to downtown
G- Texco
F-AustinStk
L-Comfrt Knght
Rts 84 221
Valdosta
Quitman
RADAR
G-BP Citgo Shell 66
F-BaskR BKing IHOP McDld Pizza Shony Waffle
L-Motel6 QltyInn Ramda Rodway Shony Supr8
Mud Creek
31
Old 3A
13
Old Clyattville Rd
Valdosta
WILD ADVENTURES - SEE PAGE 124
N
Madison
Patterson
Old 3
11
P
G-Texco
Rt 31
Valdosta
Clyattville
G-Spdwy
F-Waffle
L-Villager
Road Notes - the Valdosta area (miles 0 to 31) is one of the most strictly enforced stretches of I-75 between Florida and Michigan. Watch your speed carefully. Patrol cars often sit in the median strip, in the emergency vehicle "U" turn breaks. The police radio bands are always very active here as they communicate back & forth.
41
G-Citgo 66
F-BaskR BKing CrkBrl McDld Pizza Taco Wendy
L-Days Hmptn Supr8 TravL
Old 2
5
Rt 376
Twin Lakes
R
G-Amoco Chevn Rctrac Shell Texco 66
F-ChickF China FarmHse Hrdee Shony Subwy Waffle
L-H/InnX Shony
Factory Stores of America
Lake Park Mill Outlet
Post Office
Information: 8:30-5:30 daily
Restrooms: 7:30-11:30
43 miles (69 kms) to next Rest Area
RADAR
Welcome Center
? V D
LAKE PARK
Old 1
Local Road
2
Bellville Rd
Lake Park
G-Conco FlyJ
L-BestW
G-Shell Texco TATS(BP)
F-DQ Taco
RESTROOMS CLOSED 11:30PM - 7:30 AM
EXIT 5 - ROAST QUAIL - PAGE 126
Georgia's new exit #s- see page 101
41
FLORIDA-GEORGIA BORDER
GEORGIA
Lowndes County
SOUTH
-25- -24- -23- -22- -21- -20- -19- -18- -17- -16- -15- -14- -13- -12- -11- -10- -9- -8- -7- -6- -5- -4- -3- -2- -1- -0-
1,500 1,000 500

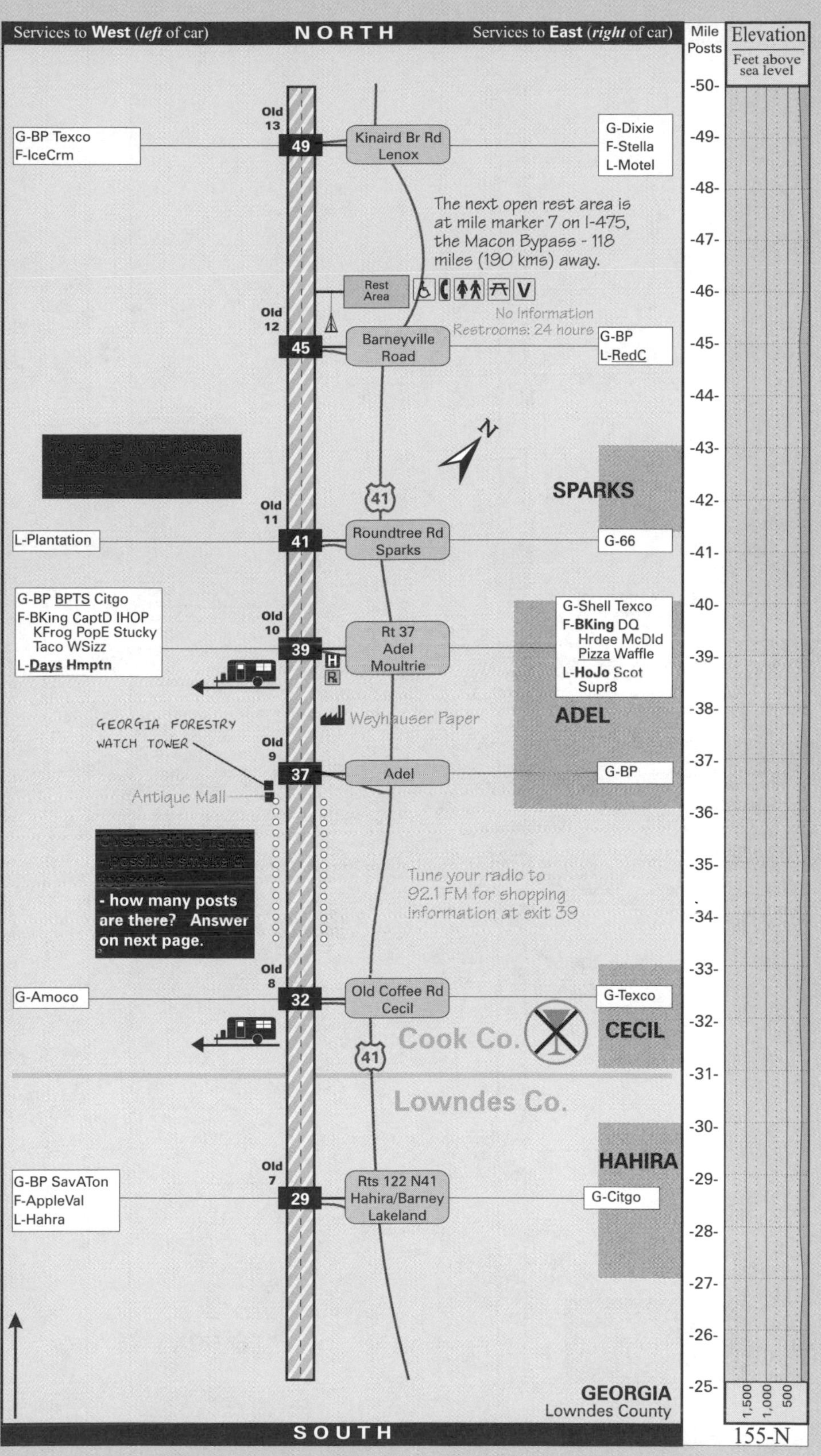

Services to West (left of car)
NORTH
Services to East (right of car)
Mile Posts
Elevation
Feet above sea level
-50-
Old 13
49
G-BP Texco
F-IceCrm
Kinaird Br Rd
Lenox
G-Dixie
F-Stella
L-Motel
-49-
-48-
The next open rest area is at mile marker 7 on I-475, the Macon Bypass - 118 miles (190 kms) away.
-47-
Rest Area
-46-
No Information
Restrooms: 24 hours
Old 12
45
Barneyville Road
G-BP
L-RedC
-45-
-44-
N
-43-
SPARKS
41
-42-
Old 11
41
L-Plantation
Roundtree Rd
Sparks
G-66
-41-
G-BP BPTS Citgo
F-BKing CaptD IHOP
KFrog PopE Stucky
Taco WSizz
L-Days Hmptn
Old 10
39
Rt 37
Adel
Moultrie
G-Shell Texco
F-BKing DQ
Hrdee McDld
Pizza Waffle
L-HoJo Scot
Supr8
-40-
-39-
GEORGIA FORESTRY WATCH TOWER
Weyhauser Paper
ADEL
-38-
Old 9
37
Adel
G-BP
-37-
Antique Mall
-36-
- how many posts are there? Answer on next page.
Tune your radio to 92.1 FM for shopping information at exit 39
-35-
-34-
Old 8
32
G-Amoco
Old Coffee Rd
Cecil
G-Texco
-33-
Cook Co.
CECIL
41
-32-
-31-
Lowndes Co.
-30-
HAHIRA
Old 7
29
G-BP SavATon
F-AppleVal
L-Hahra
Rts 122 N41
Hahira/Barney
Lakeland
G-Citgo
-29-
-28-
-27-
-26-
GEORGIA
Lowndes County
-25-
1,500
1,000
500
SOUTH

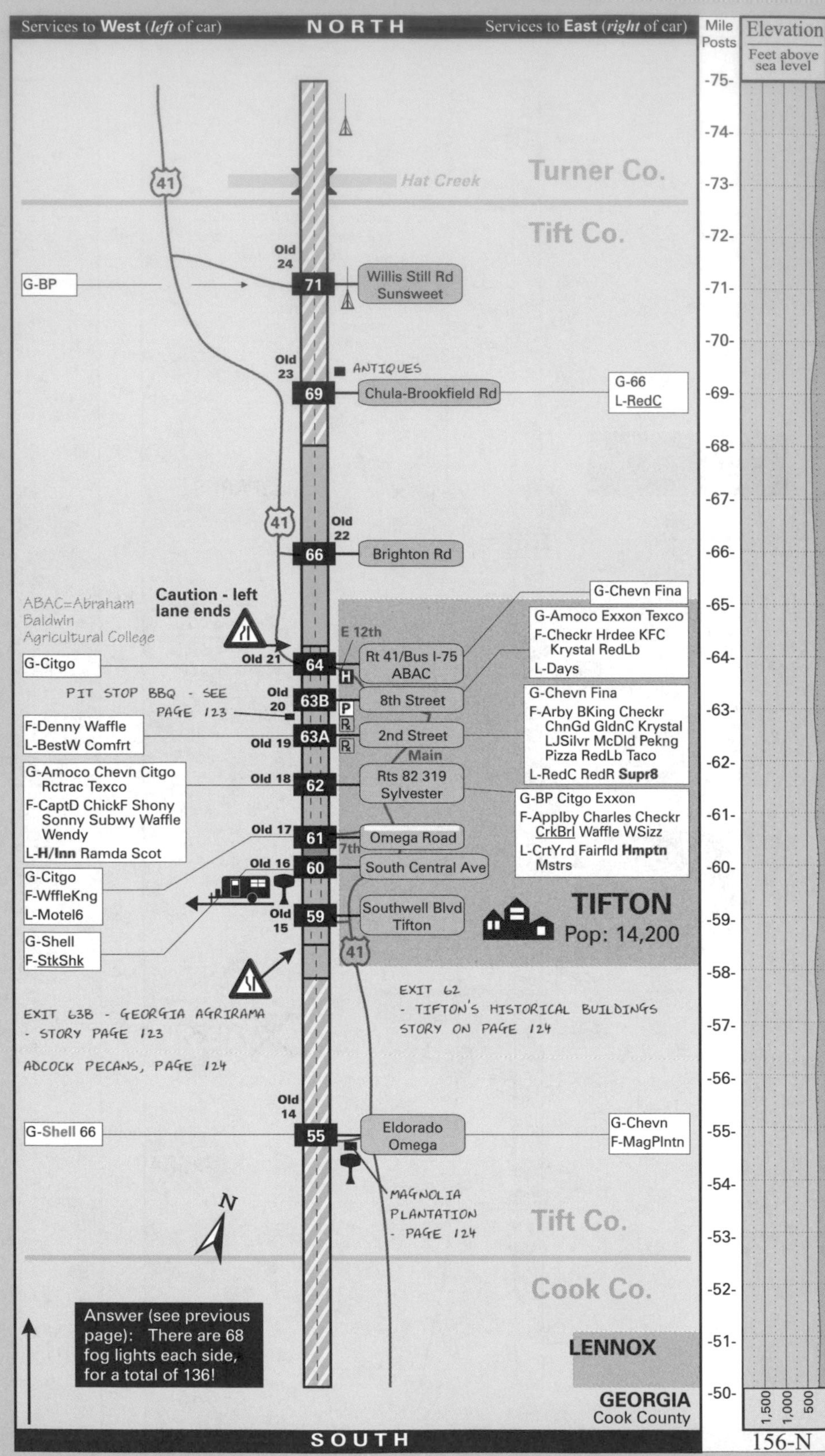

Services to West (left of car)
NORTH
Services to East (right of car)
Mile Posts
Elevation
Feet above sea level
Hat Creek
Turner Co.
Tift Co.
41
Old 24
71
Willis Still Rd Sunsweet
G-BP
Old 23
ANTIQUES
69
Chula-Brookfield Rd
G-66
L-RedC
41
Old 22
66
Brighton Rd
ABAC=Abraham Baldwin Agricultural College
Caution - left lane ends
G-Chevn Fina
G-Amoco Exxon Texco
F-Checkr Hrdee KFC Krystal RedLb
L-Days
E 12th
Old 21
64
Rt 41/Bus I-75 ABAC
G-Citgo
PIT STOP BBQ - SEE PAGE 123
Old 20
63B
8th Street
G-Chevn Fina
F-Arby BKing Checkr ChnGd GldnC Krystal LJSilvr McDld Pekng Pizza RedLb Taco
L-RedC RedR Supr8
F-Denny Waffle
L-BestW Comfrt
Old 19
63A
2nd Street
Main
G-Amoco Chevn Citgo Rctrac Texco
F-CaptD ChickF Shony Sonny Subwy Waffle Wendy
L-H/Inn Ramda Scot
Old 18
62
Rts 82 319 Sylvester
G-BP Citgo Exxon
F-Applby Charles Checkr CrkBrl Waffle WSizz
L-CrtYrd Fairfld Hmptn Mstrs
Old 17
61
Omega Road
7th
Old 16
60
South Central Ave
G-Citgo
F-WffleKng
L-Motel6
Old 15
59
Southwell Blvd Tifton
TIFTON
Pop: 14,200
G-Shell
F-StkShk
41
EXIT 63B - GEORGIA AGRIRAMA - STORY PAGE 123
ADCOCK PECANS, PAGE 124
EXIT 62 - TIFTON'S HISTORICAL BUILDINGS STORY ON PAGE 124
Old 14
55
Eldorado Omega
G-Shell 66
G-Chevn
F-MagPlntn
MAGNOLIA PLANTATION - PAGE 124
N
Tift Co.
Cook Co.
Answer (see previous page): There are 68 fog lights each side, for a total of 136!
LENNOX
GEORGIA
Cook County
SOUTH
-75- -74- -73- -72- -71- -70- -69- -68- -67- -66- -65- -64- -63- -62- -61- -60- -59- -58- -57- -56- -55- -54- -53- -52- -51- -50-
1,500 1,000 500
156-N

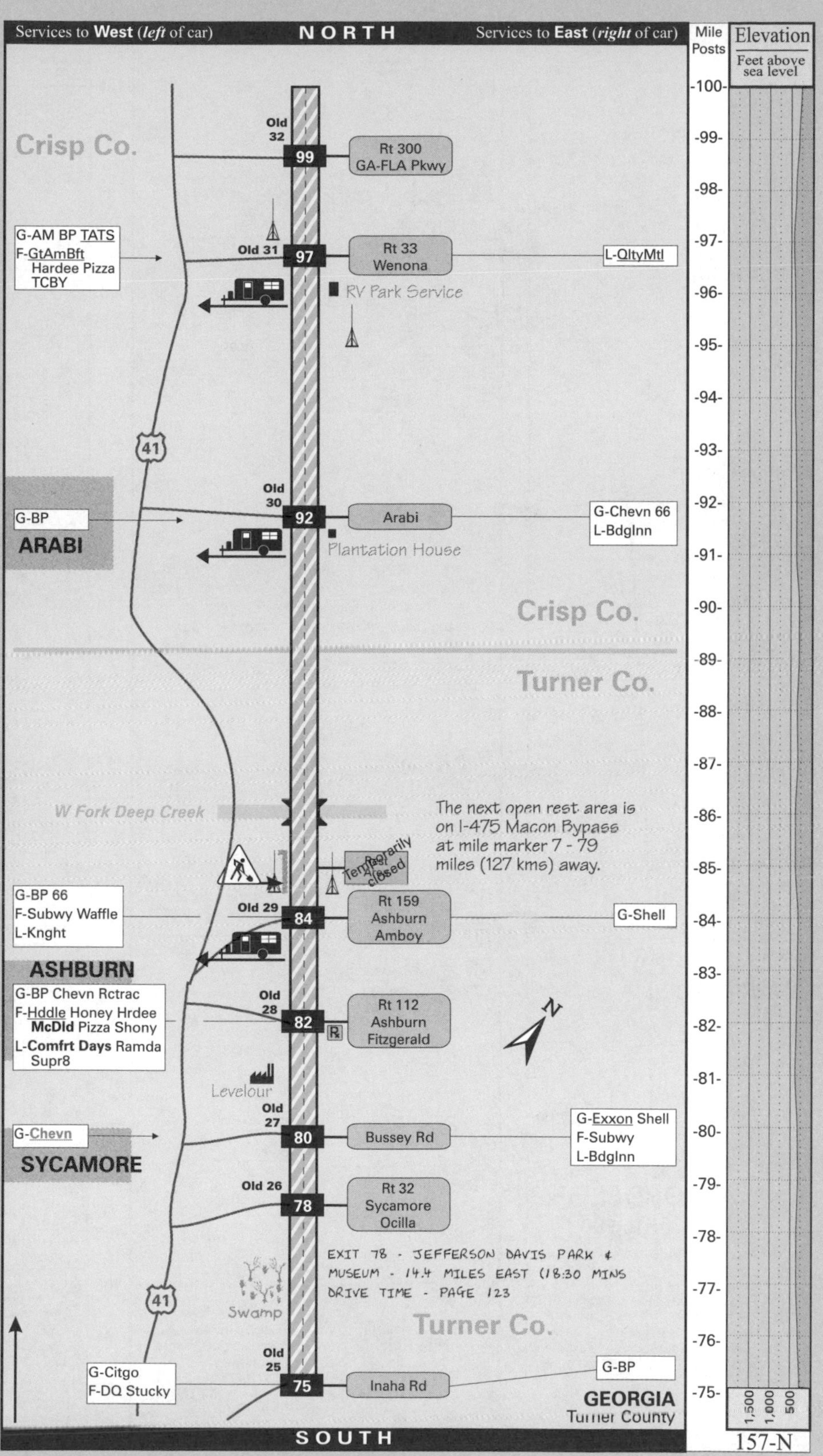

Services to West (left of car)
NORTH
Services to East (right of car)
Mile Posts
Elevation
Feet above sea level
Crisp Co.
Old 32
99
Rt 300 GA-FLA Pkwy
G-AM BP TATS
F-GtAmBft Hardee Pizza TCBY
Old 31
97
Rt 33 Wenona
L-QltyMtl
RV Park Service
41
Old 30
92
Arabi
G-BP
ARABI
G-Chevn 66
L-BdgInn
Plantation House
Crisp Co.
Turner Co.
W Fork Deep Creek
The next open rest area is on I-475 Macon Bypass at mile marker 7 - 79 miles (127 kms) away.
Temporarily closed
G-BP 66
F-Subwy Waffle
L-Knght
Old 29
84
Rt 159 Ashburn Amboy
G-Shell
ASHBURN
G-BP Chevn Rctrac
F-Hddle Honey Hrdee McDld Pizza Shony
L-Comfrt Days Ramda Supr8
Old 28
82
Rt 112 Ashburn Fitzgerald
N
Levelour
Old 27
80
Bussey Rd
G-Chevn
SYCAMORE
G-Exxon Shell
F-Subwy
L-BdgInn
Old 26
78
Rt 32 Sycamore Ocilla
EXIT 78 - JEFFERSON DAVIS PARK & MUSEUM - 14.4 MILES EAST (18:30 MINS DRIVE TIME - PAGE 123
41
Swamp
Turner Co.
Old 25
75
Inaha Rd
G-Citgo
F-DQ Stucky
G-BP
GEORGIA
Turner County
SOUTH
-100- -99- -98- -97- -96- -95- -94- -93- -92- -91- -90- -89- -88- -87- -86- -85- -84- -83- -82- -81- -80- -79- -78- -77- -76- -75-
1,500 1,000 500

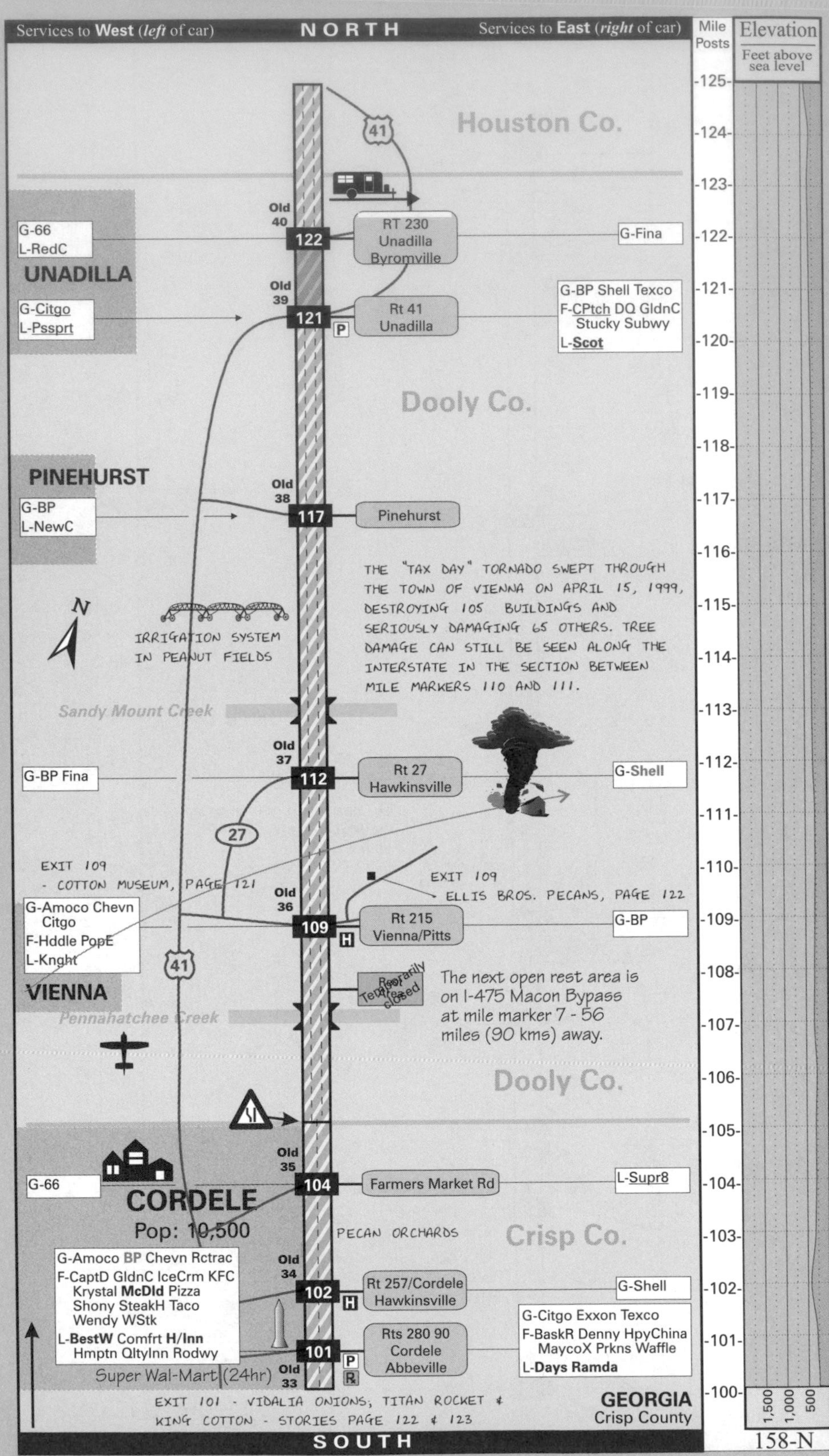
Services to West (left of car)
NORTH
Services to East (right of car)
Mile Posts
Elevation
Feet above sea level
41
Houston Co.
Old 40
122
RT 230 Unadilla Byromville
G-66
L-RedC
UNADILLA
G-Fina
Old 39
121
Rt 41 Unadilla
G-Citgo
L-Pssprt
G-BP Shell Texco
F-CPtch DQ GldnC
Stucky Subwy
L-Scot
Dooly Co.
PINEHURST
G-BP
L-NewC
Old 38
117
Pinehurst
THE "TAX DAY" TORNADO SWEPT THROUGH THE TOWN OF VIENNA ON APRIL 15, 1999, DESTROYING 105 BUILDINGS AND SERIOUSLY DAMAGING 65 OTHERS. TREE DAMAGE CAN STILL BE SEEN ALONG THE INTERSTATE IN THE SECTION BETWEEN MILE MARKERS 110 AND 111.
N
IRRIGATION SYSTEM IN PEANUT FIELDS
Sandy Mount Creek
Old 37
112
Rt 27 Hawkinsville
G-BP Fina
G-Shell
27
EXIT 109 - COTTON MUSEUM, PAGE 121
EXIT 109 - ELLIS BROS. PECANS, PAGE 122
Old 36
109
Rt 215 Vienna/Pitts
G-Amoco Chevn Citgo
F-Hddle PopE
L-Knght
G-BP
41
VIENNA
Rest Area Temporarily closed
The next open rest area is on I-475 Macon Bypass at mile marker 7 - 56 miles (90 kms) away.
Pennahatchee Creek
Dooly Co.
Old 35
104
Farmers Market Rd
G-66
L-Supr8
CORDELE
Pop: 10,500
PECAN ORCHARDS
Crisp Co.
Old 34
102
Rt 257/Cordele Hawkinsville
G-Amoco BP Chevn Rctrac
F-CaptD GldnC IceCrm KFC
Krystal McDld Pizza
Shony SteakH Taco
Wendy WStk
L-BestW Comfrt H/Inn
Hmptn QltyInn Rodwy
G-Shell
101
Rts 280 90 Cordele Abbeville
G-Citgo Exxon Texco
F-BaskR Denny HpyChina
MaycoX Prkns Waffle
L-Days Ramda
Super Wal-Mart (24hr)
Old 33
EXIT 101 - VIDALIA ONIONS, TITAN ROCKET & KING COTTON - STORIES PAGE 122 & 123
GEORGIA
Crisp County
SOUTH
-125- -124- -123- -122- -121- -120- -119- -118- -117- -116- -115- -114- -113- -112- -111- -110- -109- -108- -107- -106- -105- -104- -103- -102- -101- -100-
1,500 1,000 500

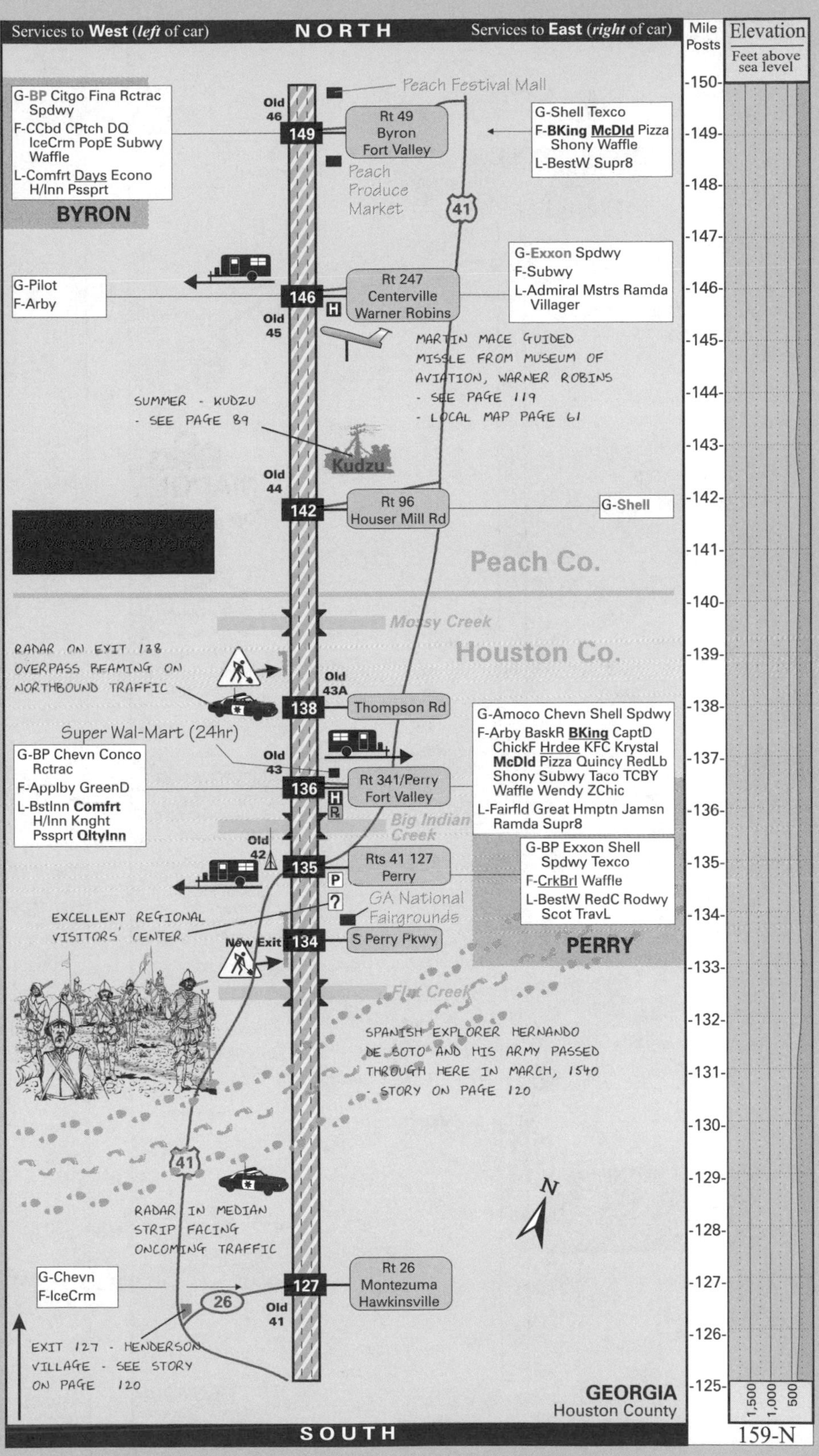

Services to West (left of car)
NORTH
Services to East (right of car)
Mile Posts
Elevation
Feet above sea level
Peach Festival Mall
G-BP Citgo Fina Rctrac Spdwy
F-CCbd CPtch DQ IceCrm PopE Subwy Waffle
L-Comfrt Days Econo H/Inn Pssprt
BYRON
Old 46
149
Rt 49
Byron
Fort Valley
G-Shell Texco
F-BKing McDld Pizza Shony Waffle
L-BestW Supr8
Peach Produce Market
41
G-Exxon Spdwy
F-Subwy
L-Admiral Mstrs Ramda Villager
G-Pilot
F-Arby
146
Rt 247
Centerville
Warner Robins
Old 45
MARTIN MACE GUIDED MISSLE FROM MUSEUM OF AVIATION, WARNER ROBINS
- SEE PAGE 119
- LOCAL MAP PAGE 61
SUMMER - KUDZU
- SEE PAGE 89
Kudzu
Old 44
142
Rt 96
Houser Mill Rd
G-Shell
Peach Co.
Mossy Creek
Houston Co.
RADAR ON EXIT 138 OVERPASS BEAMING ON NORTHBOUND TRAFFIC
Old 43A
138
Thompson Rd
G-Amoco Chevn Shell Spdwy
F-Arby BaskR BKing CaptD ChickF Hrdee KFC Krystal McDld Pizza Quincy RedLb Shony Subwy Taco TCBY Waffle Wendy ZChic
L-Fairfld Great Hmptn Jamsn Ramda Supr8
Super Wal-Mart (24hr)
G-BP Chevn Conco Rctrac
F-Applby GreenD
L-BstInn Comfrt H/Inn Knght Pssprt QltyInn
Old 43
136
Rt 341/Perry
Fort Valley
Big Indian Creek
Old 42
135
Rts 41 127
Perry
G-BP Exxon Shell Spdwy Texco
F-CrkBrl Waffle
L-BestW RedC Rodwy Scot TravL
GA National Fairgrounds
EXCELLENT REGIONAL VISITORS' CENTER
New Exit
134
S Perry Pkwy
PERRY
Flat Creek
SPANISH EXPLORER HERNANDO DE SOTO AND HIS ARMY PASSED THROUGH HERE IN MARCH, 1540
- STORY ON PAGE 120
41
RADAR IN MEDIAN STRIP FACING ONCOMING TRAFFIC
N
G-Chevn
F-IceCrm
127
Rt 26
Montezuma
Hawkinsville
26
Old 41
EXIT 127 - HENDERSON VILLAGE - SEE STORY ON PAGE 120
GEORGIA
Houston County
SOUTH
-150- -149- -148- -147- -146- -145- -144- -143- -142- -141- -140- -139- -138- -137- -136- -135- -134- -133- -132- -131- -130- -129- -128- -127- -126- -125-
1,500 1,000 500

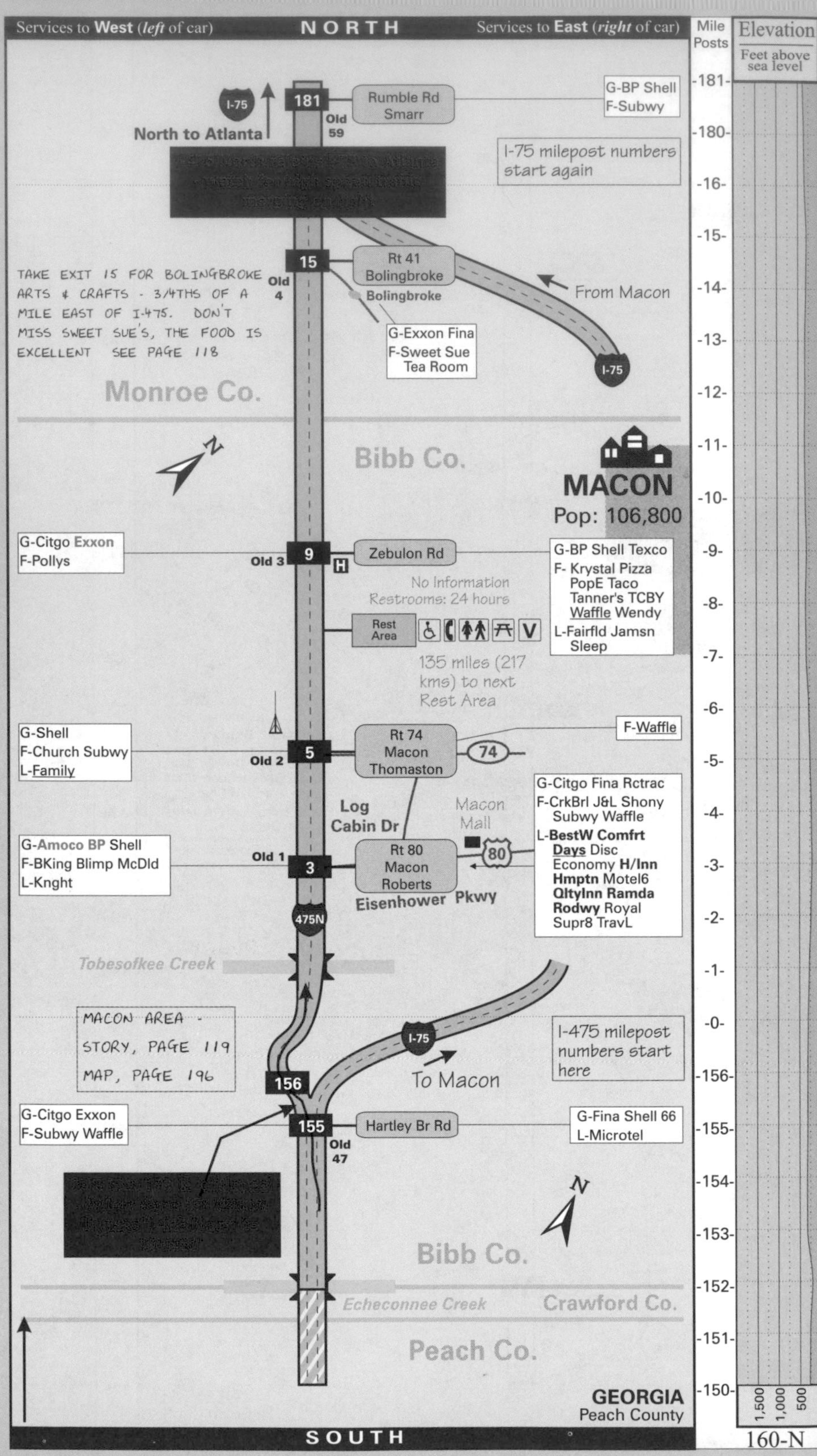

Services to West (left of car)
NORTH
Services to East (right of car)
Mile Posts
Elevation
Feet above sea level
I-75
North to Atlanta
181
Old 59
Rumble Rd
Smarr
G-BP Shell
F-Subwy
I-75 milepost numbers start again
15
Old 4
Rt 41
Bolingbroke
Bolingbroke
From Macon
TAKE EXIT 15 FOR BOLINGBROKE ARTS & CRAFTS - 3/4THS OF A MILE EAST OF I-475. DON'T MISS SWEET SUE'S, THE FOOD IS EXCELLENT SEE PAGE 118
G-Exxon Fina
F-Sweet Sue Tea Room
I-75
Monroe Co.
Bibb Co.
MACON
Pop: 106,800
G-Citgo Exxon
F-Pollys
Old 3
9
Zebulon Rd
G-BP Shell Texco
F- Krystal Pizza PopE Taco Tanner's TCBY Waffle Wendy
L-Fairfld Jamsn Sleep
No Information
Restrooms: 24 hours
Rest Area
135 miles (217 kms) to next Rest Area
G-Shell
F-Church Subwy
L-Family
Old 2
5
Rt 74
Macon
Thomaston
74
F-Waffle
Log Cabin Dr
Macon Mall
G-Citgo Fina Rctrac
F-CrkBrl J&L Shony Subwy Waffle
L-BestW Comfrt Days Disc Economy H/Inn Hmptn Motel6 QltyInn Ramda Rodwy Royal Supr8 TravL
G-Amoco BP Shell
F-BKing Blimp McDld
L-Knght
Old 1
3
Rt 80
Macon
Roberts
80
Eisenhower Pkwy
475N
Tobesofkee Creek
MACON AREA - STORY, PAGE 119 MAP, PAGE 196
I-75
To Macon
I-475 milepost numbers start here
156
G-Citgo Exxon
F-Subwy Waffle
155
Old 47
Hartley Br Rd
G-Fina Shell 66
L-Microtel
Bibb Co.
Echeconnee Creek
Crawford Co.
Peach Co.
GEORGIA
Peach County
SOUTH
-181- -180- -16- -15- -14- -13- -12- -11- -10- -9- -8- -7- -6- -5- -4- -3- -2- -1- -0- -156- -155- -154- -153- -152- -151- -150-
1,500
1,000
500

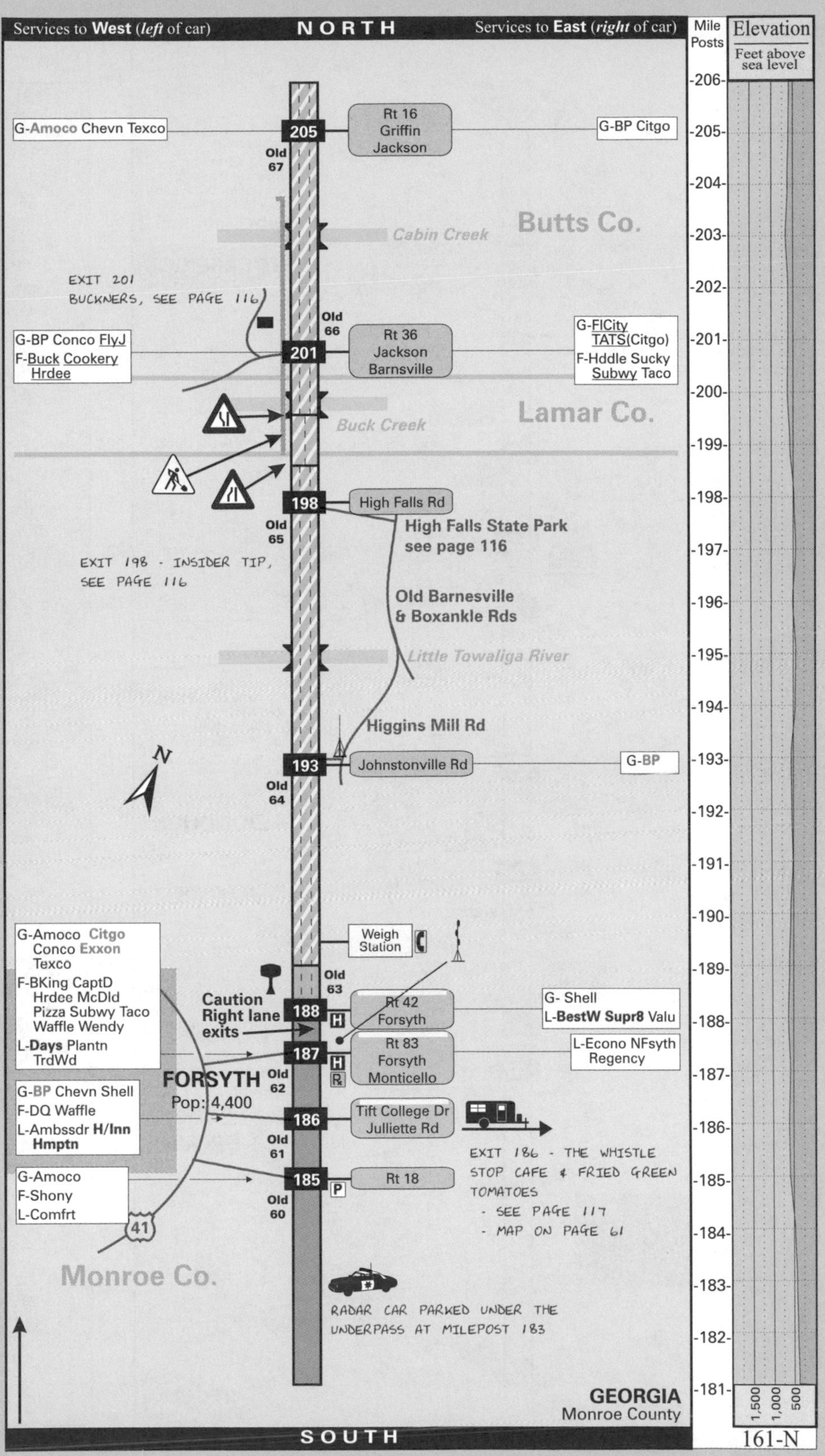

Services to West (left of car)
NORTH
Services to East (right of car)
Mile Posts
Elevation
Feet above sea level
G-Amoco Chevn Texco
205
Old 67
Rt 16 Griffin Jackson
G-BP Citgo
Cabin Creek
Butts Co.
EXIT 201 BUCKNERS, SEE PAGE 116
Old 66
G-BP Conco FlyJ
F-Buck Cookery Hrdee
201
Rt 36 Jackson Barnsville
G-FlCity TATS(Citgo)
F-Hddle Sucky Subwy Taco
Buck Creek
Lamar Co.
198
High Falls Rd
Old 65
High Falls State Park see page 116
EXIT 198 - INSIDER TIP, SEE PAGE 116
Old Barnesville & Boxankle Rds
Little Towaliga River
Higgins Mill Rd
N
193
Johnstonville Rd
G-BP
Old 64
Weigh Station
G-Amoco Citgo Conco Exxon Texco
F-BKing CaptD Hrdee McDld Pizza Subwy Taco Waffle Wendy
L-Days Plantn TrdWd
Old 63
Caution Right lane exits
188
Rt 42 Forsyth
G- Shell
L-BestW Supr8 Valu
187
Rt 83 Forsyth Monticello
L-Econo NFsyth Regency
FORSYTH
Pop: 4,400
Old 62
G-BP Chevn Shell
F-DQ Waffle
L-Ambssdr H/Inn Hmptn
186
Tift College Dr Julliette Rd
Old 61
EXIT 186 - THE WHISTLE STOP CAFE & FRIED GREEN TOMATOES
- SEE PAGE 117
- MAP ON PAGE 61
G-Amoco
F-Shony
L-Comfrt
185
Rt 18
Old 60
41
Monroe Co.
RADAR CAR PARKED UNDER THE UNDERPASS AT MILEPOST 183
GEORGIA
Monroe County
SOUTH
-206- -205- -204- -203- -202- -201- -200- -199- -198- -197- -196- -195- -194- -193- -192- -191- -190- -189- -188- -187- -186- -185- -184- -183- -182- -181-
1,500 1,000 500

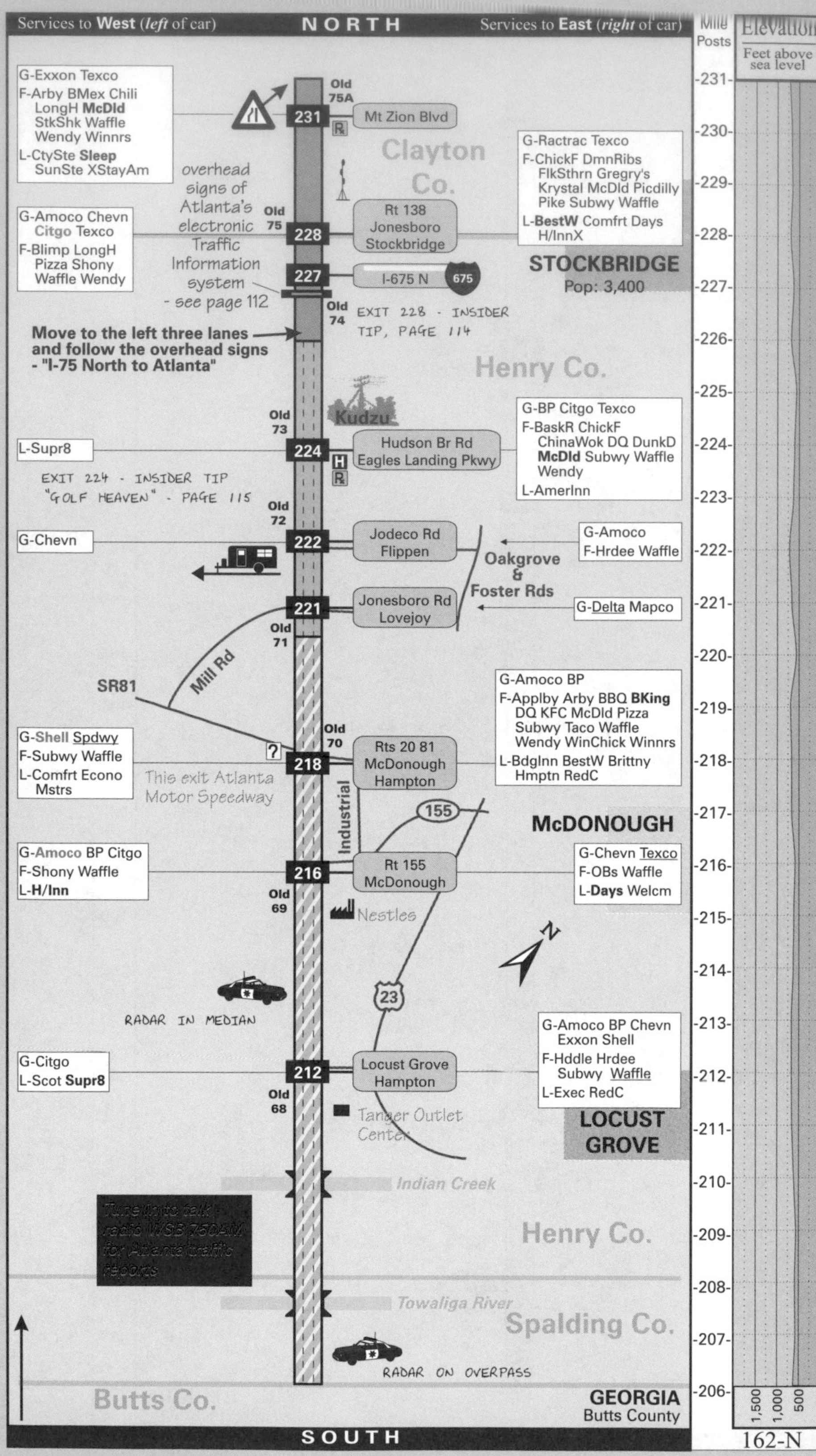
Services to West (left of car)
NORTH
Services to East (right of car)
Mile Posts
Elevation
Feet above sea level
G-Exxon Texco
F-Arby BMex Chili LongH McDld StkShk Waffle Wendy Winnrs
L-CtySte Sleep SunSte XStayAm
Old 75A
231
Mt Zion Blvd
Clayton Co.
G-Ractrac Texco
F-ChickF DmnRibs FlkSthrn Gregry's Krystal McDld Picdilly Pike Subwy Waffle
L-BestW Comfrt Days H/InnX
overhead signs of Atlanta's electronic Traffic Information system - see page 112
G-Amoco Chevn Citgo Texco
F-Blimp LongH Pizza Shony Waffle Wendy
Old 75
228
Rt 138 Jonesboro Stockbridge
STOCKBRIDGE
Pop: 3,400
227
I-675 N
675
Old 74
EXIT 228 - INSIDER TIP, PAGE 114
Move to the left three lanes and follow the overhead signs - "I-75 North to Atlanta"
Henry Co.
Kudzu
Old 73
G-BP Citgo Texco
F-BaskR ChickF ChinaWok DQ DunkD McDld Subwy Waffle Wendy
L-AmerInn
L-Supr8
224
Hudson Br Rd Eagles Landing Pkwy
EXIT 224 - INSIDER TIP "GOLF HEAVEN" - PAGE 115
Old 72
G-Chevn
222
Jodeco Rd Flippen
G-Amoco
F-Hrdee Waffle
Oakgrove & Foster Rds
221
Jonesboro Rd Lovejoy
G-Delta Mapco
Old 71
Mill Rd
SR81
G-Amoco BP
F-Applby Arby BBQ BKing DQ KFC McDld Pizza Subwy Taco Waffle Wendy WinChick Winnrs
L-BdgInn BestW Brittny Hmptn RedC
G-Shell Spdwy
F-Subwy Waffle
L-Comfrt Econo Mstrs
Old 70
218
Rts 20 81 McDonough Hampton
This exit Atlanta Motor Speedway
Industrial
155
McDONOUGH
G-Amoco BP Citgo
F-Shony Waffle
L-H/Inn
216
Rt 155 McDonough
G-Chevn Texco
F-OBs Waffle
L-Days Welcm
Old 69
Nestles
N
23
RADAR IN MEDIAN
G-Amoco BP Chevn Exxon Shell
F-Hddle Hrdee Subwy Waffle
L-Exec RedC
G-Citgo
L-Scot Supr8
212
Locust Grove Hampton
Old 68
Tanger Outlet Center
LOCUST GROVE
Indian Creek
Tune into talk radio WSB 750AM for Atlanta traffic reports
Henry Co.
Towaliga River
Spalding Co.
RADAR ON OVERPASS
Butts Co.
GEORGIA
Butts County
SOUTH
-231- -230- -229- -228- -227- -226- -225- -224- -223- -222- -221- -220- -219- -218- -217- -216- -215- -214- -213- -212- -211- -210- -209- -208- -207- -206-
1,500 1,000 500
162-N

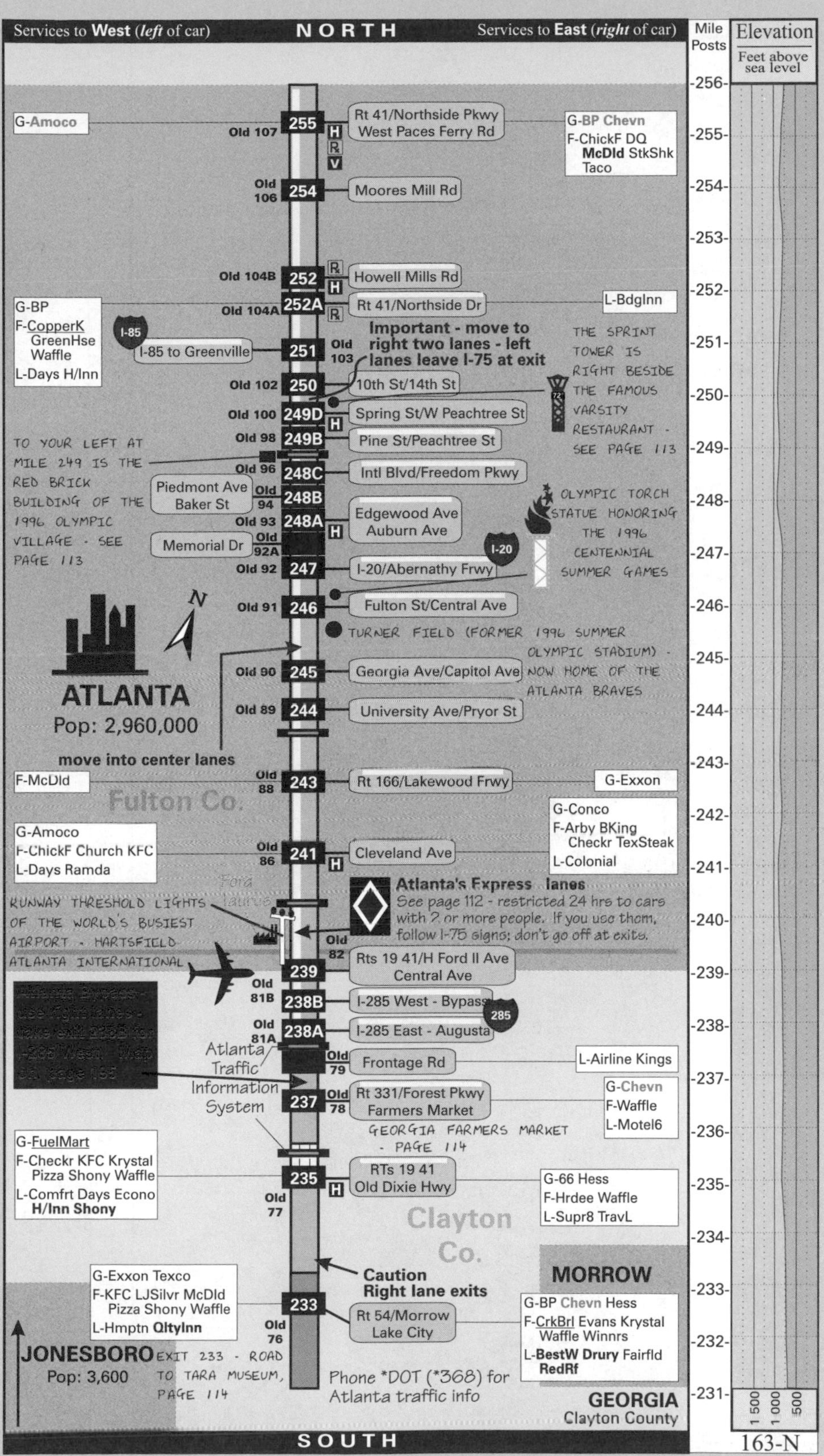

Services to West (left of car)
NORTH
Services to East (right of car)
Mile Posts
Elevation
Feet above sea level
G-Amoco
Old 107
255
Rt 41/Northside Pkwy
West Paces Ferry Rd
G-BP Chevn
F-ChickF DQ
McDld StkShk
Taco
Old 106
254
Moores Mill Rd
Old 104B
252
Howell Mills Rd
G-BP
F-CopperK
GreenHse
Waffle
L-Days H/Inn
Old 104A
252A
Rt 41/Northside Dr
L-BdgInn
I-85
I-85 to Greenville
251
Old 103
Important - move to right two lanes - left lanes leave I-75 at exit
THE SPRINT TOWER IS RIGHT BESIDE THE FAMOUS VARSITY RESTAURANT - SEE PAGE 113
Old 102
250
10th St/14th St
Old 100
249D
Spring St/W Peachtree St
Old 98
249B
Pine St/Peachtree St
TO YOUR LEFT AT MILE 249 IS THE RED BRICK BUILDING OF THE 1996 OLYMPIC VILLAGE - SEE PAGE 113
Old 96
248C
Intl Blvd/Freedom Pkwy
Piedmont Ave
Baker St
Old 94
248B
Old 93
248A
Edgewood Ave
Auburn Ave
OLYMPIC TORCH STATUE HONORING THE 1996 CENTENNIAL SUMMER GAMES
Memorial Dr
Old 92A
I-20
Old 92
247
I-20/Abernathy Frwy
Old 91
246
Fulton St/Central Ave
N
TURNER FIELD (FORMER 1996 SUMMER OLYMPIC STADIUM) - NOW HOME OF THE ATLANTA BRAVES
Old 90
245
Georgia Ave/Capitol Ave
ATLANTA
Pop: 2,960,000
Old 89
244
University Ave/Pryor St
move into center lanes
F-McDld
Old 88
243
Rt 166/Lakewood Frwy
G-Exxon
Fulton Co.
G-Conco
F-Arby BKing
Checkr TexSteak
L-Colonial
G-Amoco
F-ChickF Church KFC
L-Days Ramda
Old 86
241
Cleveland Ave
Atlanta's Express lanes
See page 112 - restricted 24 hrs to cars with 2 or more people. If you use them, follow I-75 signs; don't go off at exits.
RUNWAY THRESHOLD LIGHTS OF THE WORLD'S BUSIEST AIRPORT - HARTSFIELD ATLANTA INTERNATIONAL
Old 82
239
Rts 19 41/H Ford II Ave
Central Ave
Old 81B
238B
I-285 West - Bypass
285
Old 81A
238A
I-285 East - Augusta
Atlanta Traffic Information System
Old 79
Frontage Rd
L-Airline Kings
237
Old 78
Rt 331/Forest Pkwy
Farmers Market
G-Chevn
F-Waffle
L-Motel6
GEORGIA FARMERS MARKET - PAGE 114
G-FuelMart
F-Checkr KFC Krystal
Pizza Shony Waffle
L-Comfrt Days Econo
H/Inn Shony
235
Old 77
RTs 19 41
Old Dixie Hwy
G-66 Hess
F-Hrdee Waffle
L-Supr8 TravL
Clayton Co.
MORROW
Caution
Right lane exits
G-Exxon Texco
F-KFC LJSilvr McDld
Pizza Shony Waffle
L-Hmptn QltyInn
233
Old 76
Rt 54/Morrow
Lake City
G-BP Chevn Hess
F-CrkBrl Evans Krystal
Waffle Winnrs
L-BestW Drury Fairfld
RedRf
JONESBORO
Pop: 3,600
EXIT 233 - ROAD TO TARA MUSEUM, PAGE 114
Phone *DOT (*368) for Atlanta traffic info
GEORGIA
Clayton County
SOUTH
-256- -255- -254- -253- -252- -251- -250- -249- -248- -247- -246- -245- -244- -243- -242- -241- -240- -239- -238- -237- -236- -235- -234- -233- -232- -231-
1 500
1 000
500

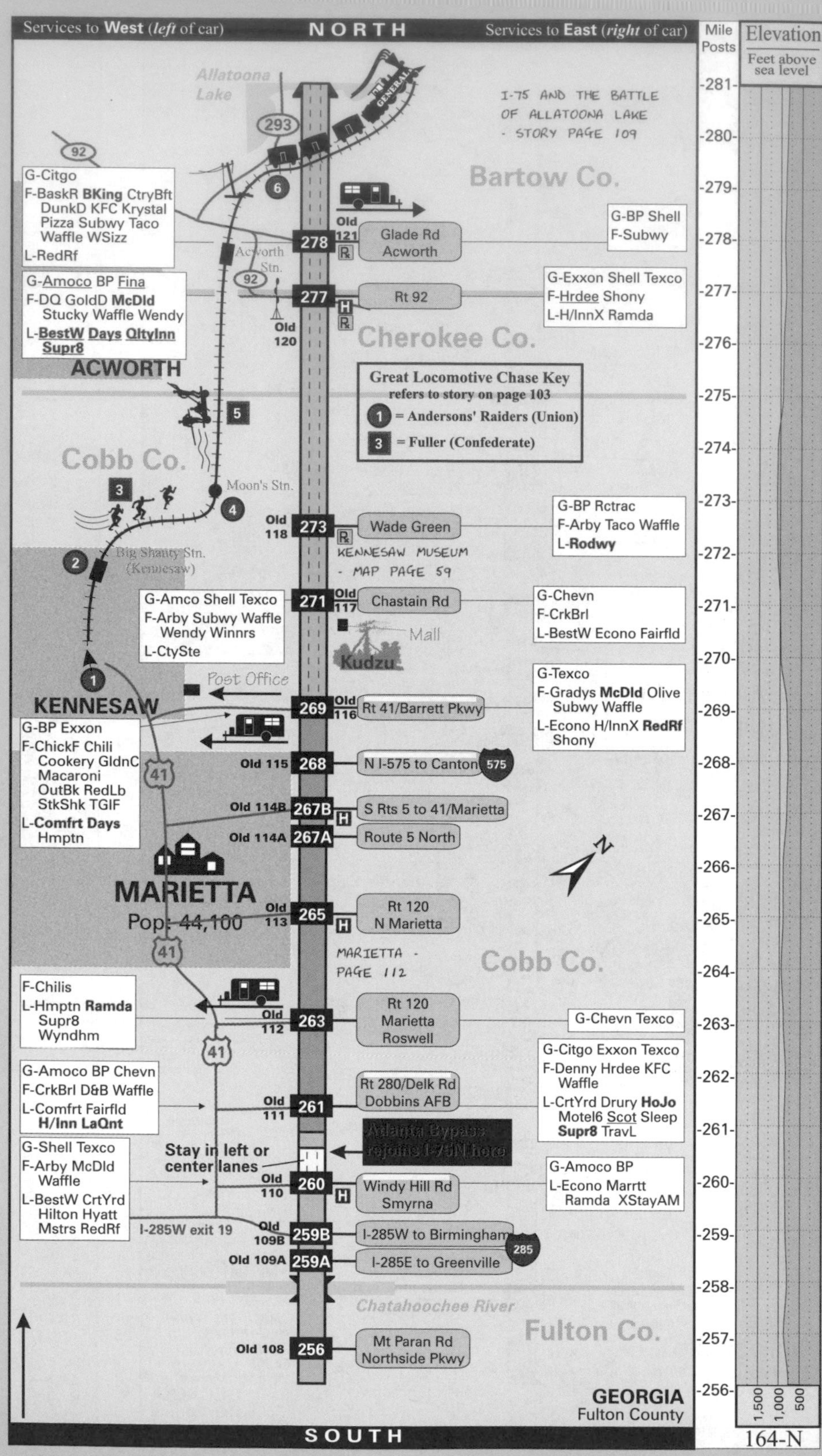

Services to West (left of car)
NORTH
Services to East (right of car)
Mile Posts
Elevation
Feet above sea level
Allatoona Lake
293
GENERAL
I-75 AND THE BATTLE OF ALLATOONA LAKE - STORY PAGE 109
92
G-Citgo
F-BaskR BKing CtryBft DunkD KFC Krystal Pizza Subwy Taco Waffle WSizz
L-RedRf
6
Bartow Co.
Old 121
278
Glade Rd Acworth
G-BP Shell
F-Subwy
Acworth Stn.
92
G-Amoco BP Fina
F-DQ GoldD McDld Stucky Waffle Wendy
L-BestW Days QltyInn Supr8
277
Rt 92
G-Exxon Shell Texco
F-Hrdee Shony
L-H/InnX Ramda
Old 120
Cherokee Co.
ACWORTH
Great Locomotive Chase Key
refers to story on page 103
1 = Andersons' Raiders (Union)
3 = Fuller (Confederate)
5
Cobb Co.
Moon's Stn.
3
4
Old 118
273
Wade Green
G-BP Rctrac
F-Arby Taco Waffle
L-Rodwy
KENNESAW MUSEUM - MAP PAGE 59
2
Big Shanty Stn. (Kennesaw)
G-Amco Shell Texco
F-Arby Subwy Waffle Wendy Winnrs
L-CtySte
271
Old 117
Chastain Rd
G-Chevn
F-CrkBrl
L-BestW Econo Fairfld
Mall
Kudzu
1
Post Office
KENNESAW
269
Old 116
Rt 41/Barrett Pkwy
G-Texco
F-Gradys McDld Olive Subwy Waffle
L-Econo H/InnX RedRf Shony
G-BP Exxon
F-ChickF Chili Cookery GldnC Macaroni OutBk RedLb StkShk TGIF
L-Comfrt Days Hmptn
41
Old 115
268
N I-575 to Canton
575
Old 114B
267B
S Rts 5 to 41/Marietta
Old 114A
267A
Route 5 North
N
MARIETTA
Pop: 44,100
Old 113
265
Rt 120 N Marietta
41
MARIETTA - PAGE 112
Cobb Co.
F-Chilis
L-Hmptn Ramda Supr8 Wyndhm
Old 112
263
Rt 120 Marietta Roswell
G-Chevn Texco
41
G-Citgo Exxon Texco
F-Denny Hrdee KFC Waffle
L-CrtYrd Drury HoJo Motel6 Scot Sleep Supr8 TravL
G-Amoco BP Chevn
F-CrkBrl D&B Waffle
L-Comfrt Fairfld H/Inn LaQnt
Old 111
261
Rt 280/Delk Rd Dobbins AFB
Atlanta Bypass rejoins I-75N here
G-Shell Texco
F-Arby McDld Waffle
L-BestW CrtYrd Hilton Hyatt Mstrs RedRf
Stay in left or center lanes
Old 110
260
Windy Hill Rd Smyrna
G-Amoco BP
L-Econo Marrt Ramda XStayAM
I-285W exit 19
Old 109B
259B
I-285W to Birmingham
285
Old 109A
259A
I-285E to Greenville
Chatahoochee River
Fulton Co.
Old 108
256
Mt Paran Rd Northside Pkwy
GEORGIA
Fulton County
SOUTH
-281- -280- -279- -278- -277- -276- -275- -274- -273- -272- -271- -270- -269- -268- -267- -266- -265- -264- -263- -262- -261- -260- -259- -258- -257- -256-
1,500 1,000 500

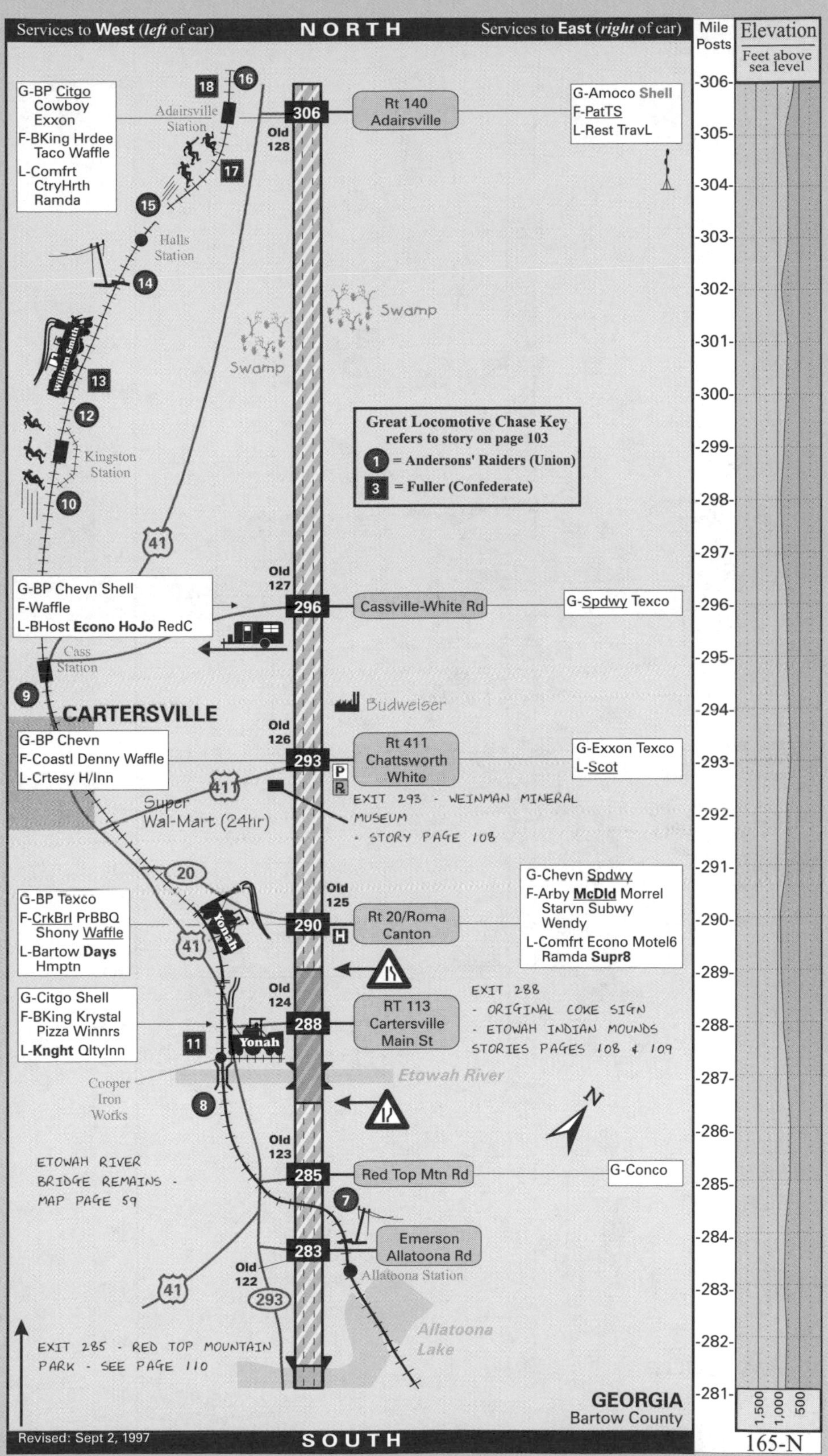
Services to West (left of car)
NORTH
Services to East (right of car)
Mile Posts
Elevation
Feet above sea level
G-BP Citgo Cowboy Exxon
F-BKing Hrdee Taco Waffle
L-Comfrt CtryHrth Ramda
Adairsville Station
306
Old 128
Rt 140 Adairsville
G-Amoco Shell
F-PatTS
L-Rest TravL
Halls Station
Swamp
Swamp
William Smith
Kingston Station
Great Locomotive Chase Key
refers to story on page 103
1 = Andersons' Raiders (Union)
3 = Fuller (Confederate)
41
Old 127
G-BP Chevn Shell
F-Waffle
L-BHost Econo HoJo RedC
296
Cassville-White Rd
G-Spdwy Texco
Cass Station
CARTERSVILLE
Budweiser
Old 126
G-BP Chevn
F-Coastl Denny Waffle
L-Crtesy H/Inn
293
Rt 411 Chattsworth White
G-Exxon Texco
L-Scot
411
Super Wal-Mart (24hr)
EXIT 293 - WEINMAN MINERAL MUSEUM
- STORY PAGE 108
20
G-BP Texco
F-CrkBrl PrBBQ Shony Waffle
L-Bartow Days Hmptn
Yonah
Old 125
290
Rt 20/Roma Canton
G-Chevn Spdwy
F-Arby McDld Morrel Starvn Subwy Wendy
L-Comfrt Econo Motel6 Ramda Supr8
G-Citgo Shell
F-BKing Krystal Pizza Winnrs
L-Knght QltyInn
Old 124
288
RT 113 Cartersville Main St
EXIT 288
- ORIGINAL COKE SIGN
- ETOWAH INDIAN MOUNDS
STORIES PAGES 108 & 109
Yonah
Etowah River
Cooper Iron Works
ETOWAH RIVER BRIDGE REMAINS - MAP PAGE 59
Old 123
285
Red Top Mtn Rd
G-Conco
283
Old 122
Emerson Allatoona Rd
Allatoona Station
293
Allatoona Lake
EXIT 285 - RED TOP MOUNTAIN PARK - SEE PAGE 110
GEORGIA
Bartow County
-306- -305- -304- -303- -302- -301- -300- -299- -298- -297- -296- -295- -294- -293- -292- -291- -290- -289- -288- -287- -286- -285- -284- -283- -282- -281-
1,500 1,000 500
Revised: Sept 2, 1997
SOUTH

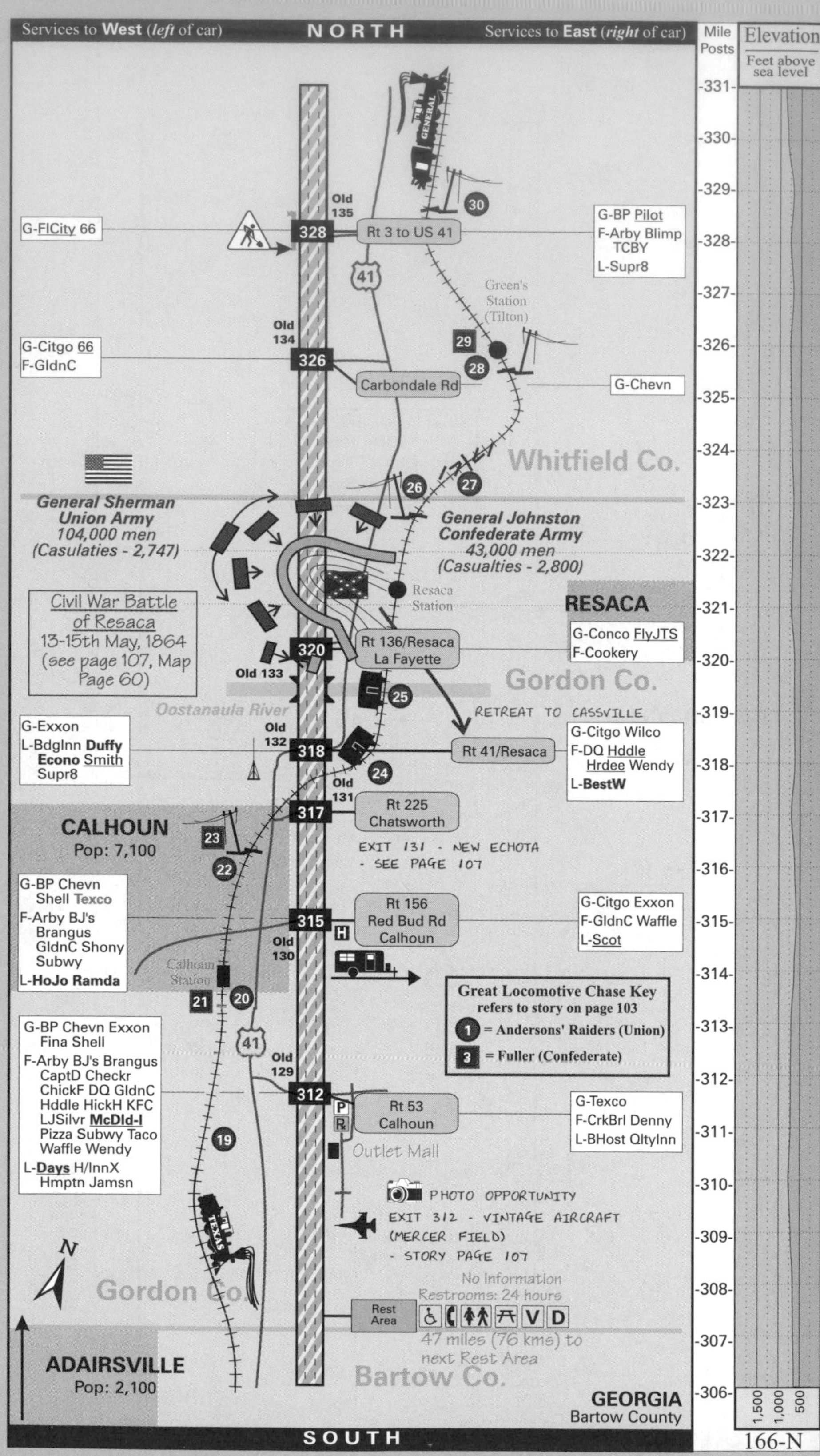

Services to West (left of car)
NORTH
Services to East (right of car)
Mile Posts
Elevation
Feet above sea level
Old 135
328
Rt 3 to US 41
G-FlCity 66
G-BP Pilot
F-Arby Blimp TCBY
L-Supr8
41
Green's Station (Tilton)
Old 134
326
G-Citgo 66
F-GldnC
Carbondale Rd
G-Chevn
Whitfield Co.
General Sherman
Union Army
104,000 men
(Casulaties - 2,747)
General Johnston
Confederate Army
43,000 men
(Casualties - 2,800)
Civil War Battle of Resaca
13-15th May, 1864
(see page 107, Map Page 60)
Resaca Station
RESACA
320
Rt 136/Resaca La Fayette
G-Conco FlyJTS
F-Cookery
Old 133
Gordon Co.
Oostanaula River
RETREAT TO CASSVILLE
Old 132
318
G-Exxon
L-BdgInn Duffy Econo Smith Supr8
Rt 41/Resaca
G-Citgo Wilco
F-DQ Hddle Hrdee Wendy
L-BestW
Old 131
317
Rt 225 Chatsworth
CALHOUN
Pop: 7,100
EXIT 131 - NEW ECHOTA - SEE PAGE 107
315
Rt 156 Red Bud Rd Calhoun
G-BP Chevn Shell Texco
F-Arby BJ's Brangus GldnC Shony Subwy
L-HoJo Ramda
G-Citgo Exxon
F-GldnC Waffle
L-Scot
Old 130
Calhoun Station
Great Locomotive Chase Key
refers to story on page 103
1 = Andersons' Raiders (Union)
3 = Fuller (Confederate)
41
Old 129
312
Rt 53 Calhoun
G-BP Chevn Exxon Fina Shell
F-Arby BJ's Brangus CaptD Checkr ChickF DQ GldnC Hddle HickH KFC LJSilvr McDld-I Pizza Subwy Taco Waffle Wendy
L-Days H/InnX Hmptn Jamsn
G-Texco
F-CrkBrl Denny
L-BHost QltyInn
Outlet Mall
PHOTO OPPORTUNITY
EXIT 312 - VINTAGE AIRCRAFT (MERCER FIELD) - STORY PAGE 107
No Information
Restrooms: 24 hours
Rest Area
47 miles (76 kms) to next Rest Area
N
Gordon Co.
Bartow Co.
ADAIRSVILLE
Pop: 2,100
GEORGIA
Bartow County
SOUTH
-331- -330- -329- -328- -327- -326- -325- -324- -323- -322- -321- -320- -319- -318- -317- -316- -315- -314- -313- -312- -311- -310- -309- -308- -307- -306-
1,500 1,000 500

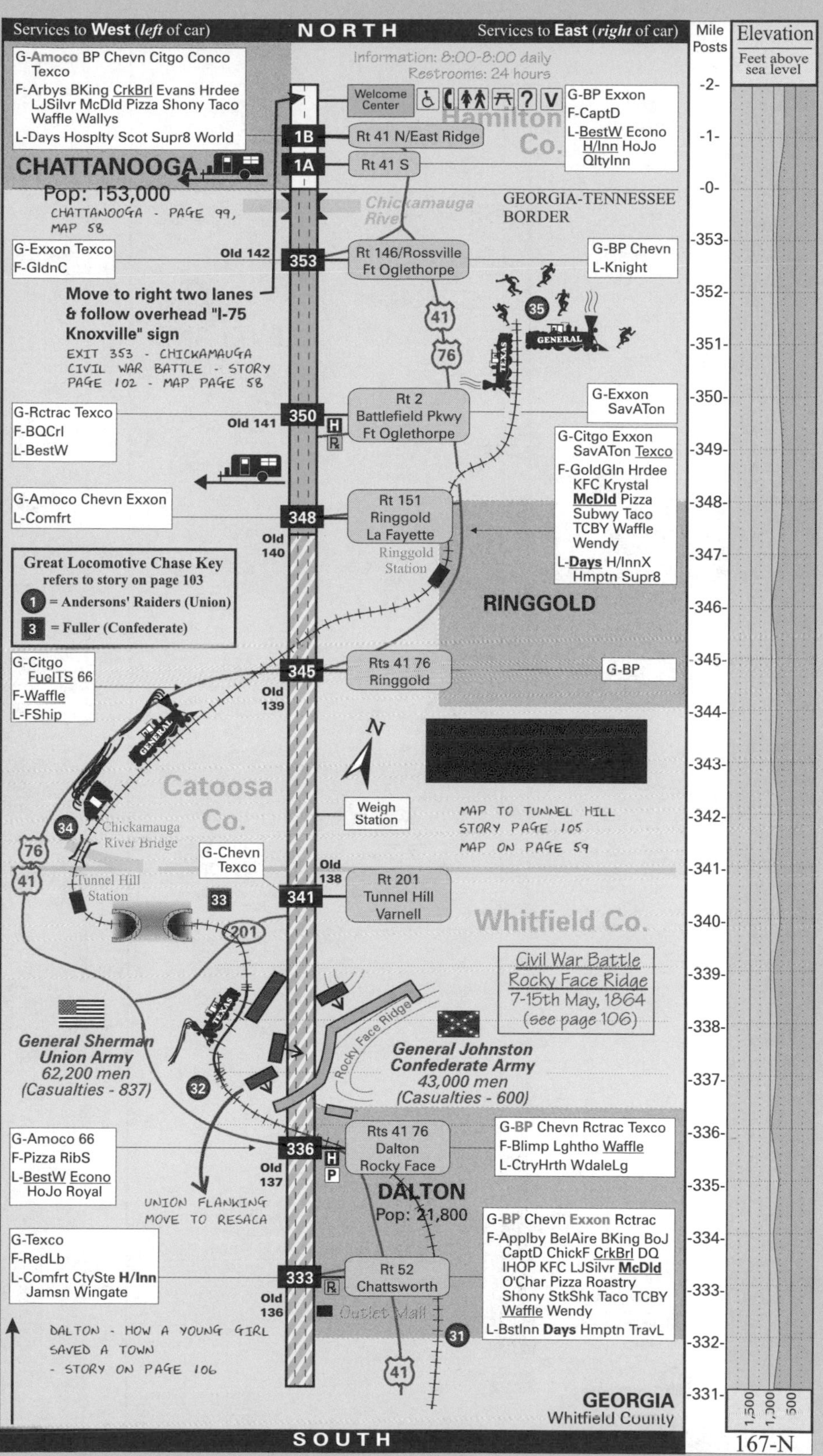

Services to West (left of car)
NORTH
Services to East (right of car)
Mile Posts
Elevation
Feet above sea level
G-Amoco BP Chevn Citgo Conco Texco
F-Arbys BKing CrkBrl Evans Hrdee LJSilvr McDld Pizza Shony Taco Waffle Wallys
L-Days Hosplty Scot Supr8 World
Information: 8:00-8:00 daily
Restrooms: 24 hours
Welcome Center
G-BP Exxon
F-CaptD
L-BestW Econo H/Inn HoJo QltyInn
Hamilton Co.
1B
Rt 41 N/East Ridge
1A
Rt 41 S
CHATTANOOGA
Pop: 153,000
CHATTANOOGA - PAGE 99, MAP 58
Chickamauga River
GEORGIA-TENNESSEE BORDER
G-Exxon Texco
F-GldnC
Old 142
353
Rt 146/Rossville Ft Oglethorpe
G-BP Chevn
L-Knight
Move to right two lanes & follow overhead "I-75 Knoxville" sign
EXIT 353 - CHICKAMAUGA CIVIL WAR BATTLE - STORY PAGE 102 - MAP PAGE 58
41
76
35
GENERAL
TEXAS
G-Rctrac Texco
F-BQCrl
L-BestW
Old 141
350
Rt 2 Battlefield Pkwy Ft Oglethorpe
G-Exxon SavATon
G-Citgo Exxon SavATon Texco
F-GoldGln Hrdee KFC Krystal McDld Pizza Subwy Taco TCBY Waffle Wendy
L-Days H/InnX Hmptn Supr8
G-Amoco Chevn Exxon
L-Comfrt
348
Old 140
Rt 151 Ringgold La Fayette
Ringgold Station
Great Locomotive Chase Key
refers to story on page 103
1 = Andersons' Raiders (Union)
3 = Fuller (Confederate)
RINGGOLD
G-Citgo FuelTS 66
F-Waffle
L-FShip
345
Old 139
Rts 41 76 Ringgold
G-BP
N
GENERAL
Catoosa Co.
Weigh Station
MAP TO TUNNEL HILL STORY PAGE 105 MAP ON PAGE 59
34
Chickamauga River Bridge
76
41
Tunnel Hill Station
G-Chevn Texco
Old 138
341
Rt 201 Tunnel Hill Varnell
33
201
Whitfield Co.
Civil War Battle Rocky Face Ridge 7-15th May, 1864 (see page 106)
Rocky Face Ridge
TEXAS
General Sherman Union Army 62,200 men (Casualties - 837)
General Johnston Confederate Army 43,000 men (Casualties - 600)
32
G-Amoco 66
F-Pizza RibS
L-BestW Econo HoJo Royal
336
Old 137
Rts 41 76 Dalton Rocky Face
G-BP Chevn Rctrac Texco
F-Blimp Lghtho Waffle
L-CtryHrth WdaleLg
UNION FLANKING MOVE TO RESACA
DALTON
Pop: 21,800
G-Texco
F-RedLb
L-Comfrt CtySte H/Inn Jamsn Wingate
333
Old 136
Rt 52 Chattsworth
Outlet Mall
G-BP Chevn Exxon Rctrac
F-Applby BelAire BKing BoJ CaptD ChickF CrkBrl DQ IHOP KFC LJSilvr McDld O'Char Pizza Roastry Shony StkShk Taco TCBY Waffle Wendy
L-BstInn Days Hmptn TravL
31
41
DALTON - HOW A YOUNG GIRL SAVED A TOWN - STORY ON PAGE 106
GEORGIA
Whitfield County
SOUTH
-2- -1- -0- -353- -352- -351- -350- -349- -348- -347- -346- -345- -344- -343- -342- -341- -340- -339- -338- -337- -336- -335- -334- -333- -332- -331-
1,500 1,000 500

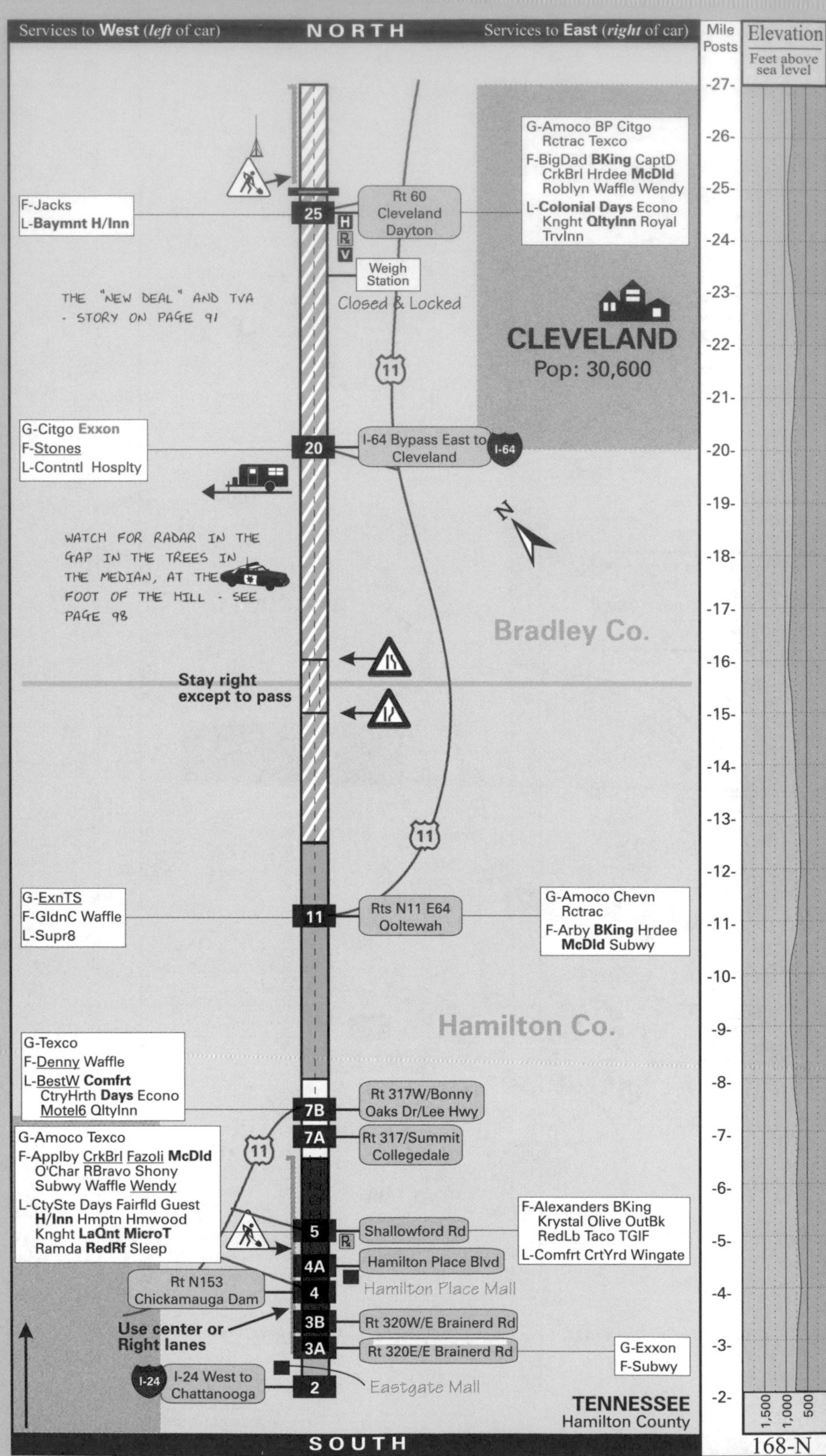

Services to West (left of car)
NORTH
Services to East (right of car)
Mile Posts
Elevation
Feet above sea level
G-Amoco BP Citgo Rctrac Texco
F-BigDad BKing CaptD CrkBrl Hrdee McDld Roblyn Waffle Wendy
L-Colonial Days Econo Knght QltyInn Royal TrvInn
F-Jacks
L-Baymnt H/Inn
25
Rt 60 Cleveland Dayton
Weigh Station
Closed & Locked
THE "NEW DEAL" AND TVA - STORY ON PAGE 91
CLEVELAND
Pop: 30,600
11
G-Citgo Exxon
F-Stones
L-Contntl Hosplty
20
I-64 Bypass East to Cleveland
I-64
WATCH FOR RADAR IN THE GAP IN THE TREES IN THE MEDIAN, AT THE FOOT OF THE HILL - SEE PAGE 98
Bradley Co.
Stay right except to pass
G-ExnTS
F-GldnC Waffle
L-Supr8
11
Rts N11 E64 Ooltewah
G-Amoco Chevn Rctrac
F-Arby BKing Hrdee McDld Subwy
Hamilton Co.
G-Texco
F-Denny Waffle
L-BestW Comfrt CtryHrth Days Econo Motel6 QltyInn
7B
Rt 317W/Bonny Oaks Dr/Lee Hwy
7A
Rt 317/Summit Collegedale
G-Amoco Texco
F-Applby CrkBrl Fazoli McDld O'Char RBravo Shony Subwy Waffle Wendy
L-CtySte Days Fairfld Guest H/Inn Hmptn Hmwood Knght LaQnt MicroT Ramda RedRf Sleep
5
Shallowford Rd
F-Alexanders BKing Krystal Olive OutBk RedLb Taco TGIF
L-Comfrt CrtYrd Wingate
4A
Hamilton Place Blvd
Hamilton Place Mall
Rt N153 Chickamauga Dam
4
3B
Rt 320W/E Brainerd Rd
Use center or Right lanes
3A
Rt 320E/E Brainerd Rd
G-Exxon
F-Subwy
I-24
I-24 West to Chattanooga
2
Eastgate Mall
TENNESSEE
Hamilton County
SOUTH
-27- -26- -25- -24- -23- -22- -21- -20- -19- -18- -17- -16- -15- -14- -13- -12- -11- -10- -9- -8- -7- -6- -5- -4- -3- -2-
1,500 1,000 500

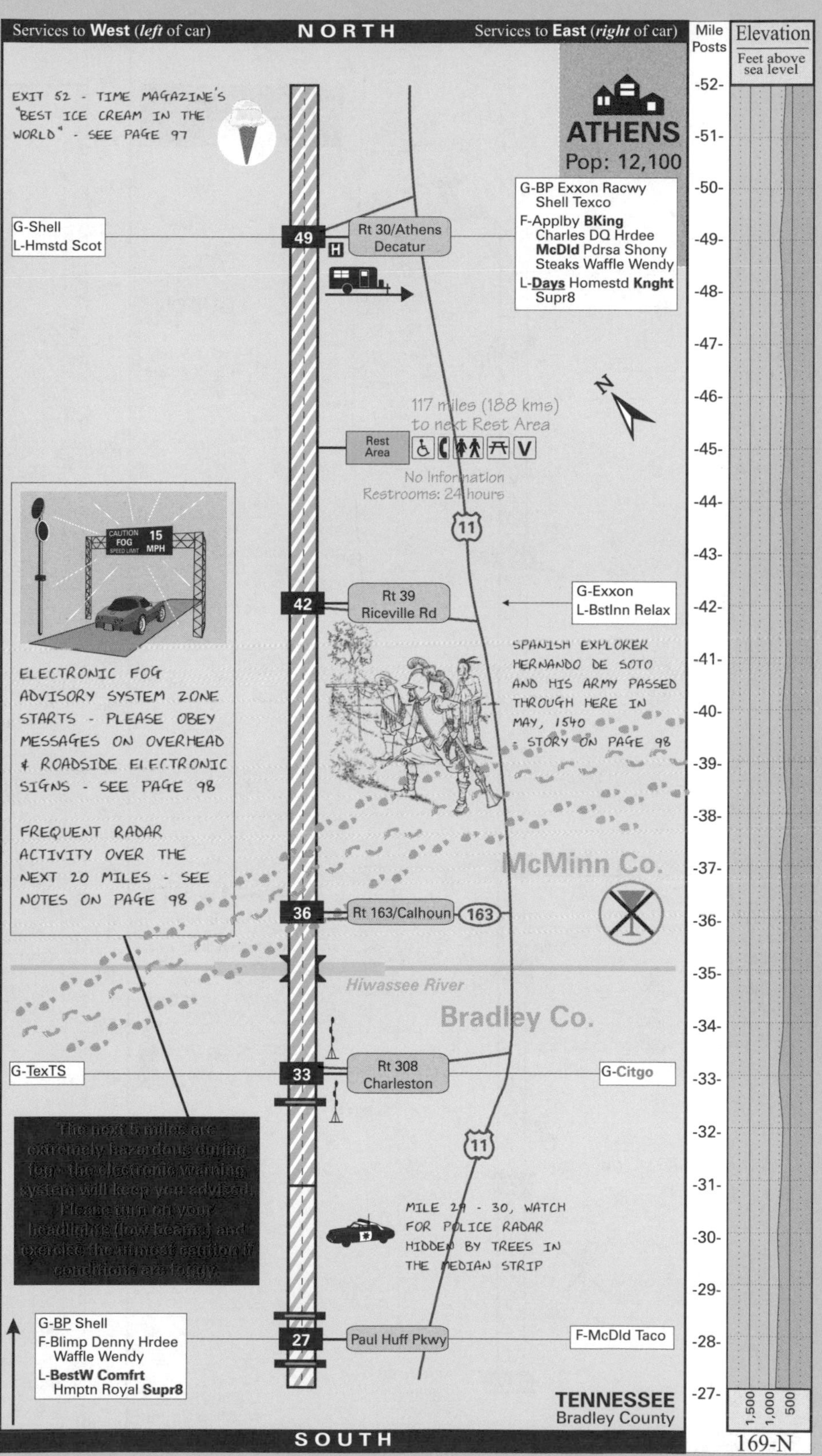

Services to West (left of car)
NORTH
Services to East (right of car)
Mile Posts
Elevation
Feet above sea level
EXIT 52 - TIME MAGAZINE'S "BEST ICE CREAM IN THE WORLD" - SEE PAGE 97
ATHENS
Pop: 12,100
G-BP Exxon Racwy Shell Texco
F-Applby BKing Charles DQ Hrdee McDld Pdrsa Shony Steaks Waffle Wendy
L-Days Homestd Knght Supr8
G-Shell
L-Hmstd Scot
49
Rt 30/Athens Decatur
H
117 miles (188 kms) to next Rest Area
Rest Area
V
No Information
Restrooms: 24 hours
N
11
CAUTION FOG SPEED LIMIT 15 MPH
ELECTRONIC FOG ADVISORY SYSTEM ZONE STARTS - PLEASE OBEY MESSAGES ON OVERHEAD & ROADSIDE ELECTRONIC SIGNS - SEE PAGE 98
FREQUENT RADAR ACTIVITY OVER THE NEXT 20 MILES - SEE NOTES ON PAGE 98
42
Rt 39 Riceville Rd
G-Exxon
L-BstInn Relax
SPANISH EXPLORER HERNANDO DE SOTO AND HIS ARMY PASSED THROUGH HERE IN MAY, 1540 - STORY ON PAGE 98
McMinn Co.
36
Rt 163/Calhoun
163
Hiwassee River
Bradley Co.
G-TexTS
33
Rt 308 Charleston
G-Citgo
11
The next 5 miles are extremely hazardous during fog - the electronic warning system will keep you advised. Please turn on your headlights (low beams) and exercise the utmost caution if conditions are foggy.
MILE 29 - 30, WATCH FOR POLICE RADAR HIDDEN BY TREES IN THE MEDIAN STRIP
G-BP Shell
F-Blimp Denny Hrdee Waffle Wendy
L-BestW Comfrt Hmptn Royal Supr8
27
Paul Huff Pkwy
F-McDld Taco
TENNESSEE
Bradley County
SOUTH
-52-
-51-
-50-
-49-
-48-
-47-
-46-
-45-
-44-
-43-
-42-
-41-
-40-
-39-
-38-
-37-
-36-
-35-
-34-
-33-
-32-
-31-
-30-
-29-
-28-
-27-
1,500
1,000
500
169-N

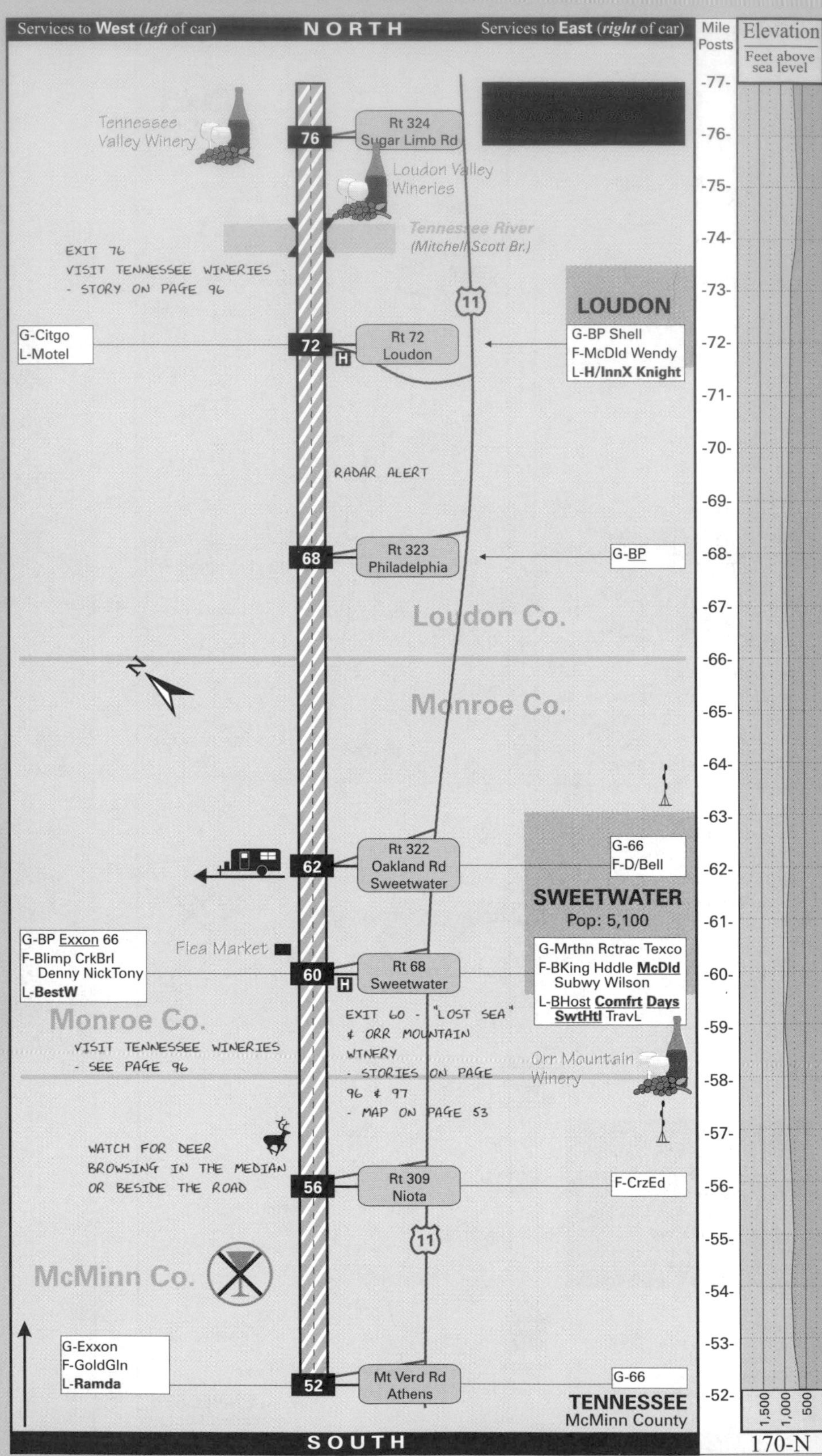

Services to West (left of car)
NORTH
Services to East (right of car)
Mile Posts
Elevation
Feet above sea level
Tennessee Valley Winery
76
Rt 324 Sugar Limb Rd
Loudon Valley Wineries
Tennessee River (Mitchell Scott Br.)
EXIT 76
VISIT TENNESSEE WINERIES
- STORY ON PAGE 96
11
LOUDON
G-Citgo
L-Motel
72
Rt 72 Loudon
G-BP Shell
F-McDld Wendy
L-H/InnX Knight
RADAR ALERT
68
Rt 323 Philadelphia
G-BP
Loudon Co.
Monroe Co.
62
Rt 322 Oakland Rd Sweetwater
G-66
F-D/Bell
SWEETWATER
Pop: 5,100
G-BP Exxon 66
F-Blimp CrkBrl Denny NickTony
L-BestW
Flea Market
60
Rt 68 Sweetwater
G-Mrthn Rctrac Texco
F-BKing Hddle McDld Subwy Wilson
L-BHost Comfrt Days SwtHtl TravL
Monroe Co.
VISIT TENNESSEE WINERIES
- SEE PAGE 96
EXIT 60 - "LOST SEA" & ORR MOUNTAIN WINERY
- STORIES ON PAGE 96 & 97
- MAP ON PAGE 53
Orr Mountain Winery
WATCH FOR DEER BROWSING IN THE MEDIAN OR BESIDE THE ROAD
56
Rt 309 Niota
F-CrzEd
11
McMinn Co.
G-Exxon
F-GoldGln
L-Ramda
52
Mt Verd Rd Athens
G-66
TENNESSEE
McMinn County
SOUTH
-77- -76- -75- -74- -73- -72- -71- -70- -69- -68- -67- -66- -65- -64- -63- -62- -61- -60- -59- -58- -57- -56- -55- -54- -53- -52-
1,500 1,000 500

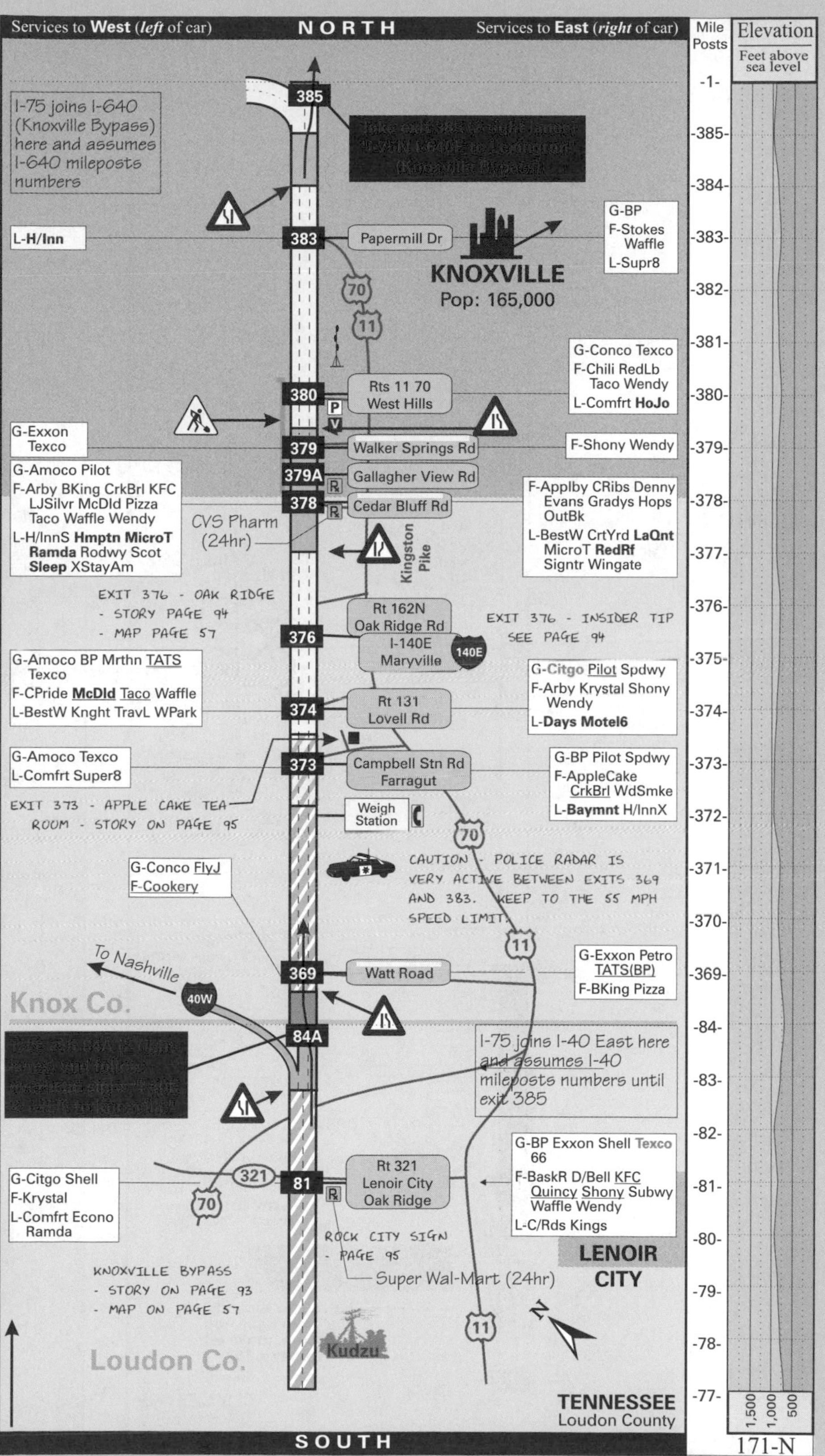

Services to West (left of car)
NORTH
Services to East (right of car)
Mile Posts
Elevation
Feet above sea level
-1-
385
I-75 joins I-640 (Knoxville Bypass) here and assumes I-640 mileposts numbers
-385-
-384-
L-H/Inn
383
Papermill Dr
KNOXVILLE
Pop: 165,000
G-BP
F-Stokes Waffle
L-Supr8
-383-
70
11
-382-
-381-
G-Conco Texco
F-Chili RedLb Taco Wendy
L-Comfrt HoJo
380
Rts 11 70 West Hills
-380-
P
V
G-Exxon Texco
379
Walker Springs Rd
F-Shony Wendy
-379-
G-Amoco Pilot
F-Arby BKing CrkBrl KFC LJSilvr McDld Pizza Taco Waffle Wendy
L-H/InnS Hmptn MicroT Ramda Rodwy Scot Sleep XStayAm
379A
Gallagher View Rd
R
378
Cedar Bluff Rd
R
F-Applby CRibs Denny Evans Gradys Hops OutBk
L-BestW CrtYrd LaQnt MicroT RedRf Signtr Wingate
-378-
CVS Pharm (24hr)
Kingston Pike
-377-
EXIT 376 - OAK RIDGE
- STORY PAGE 94
- MAP PAGE 57
Rt 162N Oak Ridge Rd
EXIT 376 - INSIDER TIP
SEE PAGE 94
-376-
376
I-140E Maryville
140E
-375-
G-Amoco BP Mrthn TATS Texco
F-CPride McDld Taco Waffle
L-BestW Knght TravL WPark
G-Citgo Pilot Spdwy
F-Arby Krystal Shony Wendy
L-Days Motel6
374
Rt 131 Lovell Rd
-374-
G-Amoco Texco
L-Comfrt Super8
373
Campbell Stn Rd Farragut
G-BP Pilot Spdwy
F-AppleCake CrkBrl WdSmke
L-Baymnt H/InnX
-373-
EXIT 373 - APPLE CAKE TEA ROOM - STORY ON PAGE 95
Weigh Station
-372-
70
CAUTION - POLICE RADAR IS VERY ACTIVE BETWEEN EXITS 369 AND 383. KEEP TO THE 55 MPH SPEED LIMIT.
-371-
G-Conco FlyJ
F-Cookery
-370-
11
To Nashville
369
Watt Road
G-Exxon Petro TATS(BP)
F-BKing Pizza
-369-
40W
Knox Co.
84A
-84-
I-75 joins I-40 East here and assumes I-40 mileposts numbers until exit 385
-83-
-82-
G-Citgo Shell
F-Krystal
L-Comfrt Econo Ramda
321
81
Rt 321 Lenoir City Oak Ridge
R
G-BP Exxon Shell Texco 66
F-BaskR D/Bell KFC Quincy Shony Subwy Waffle Wendy
L-C/Rds Kings
-81-
70
-80-
ROCK CITY SIGN - PAGE 95
LENOIR CITY
Super Wal-Mart (24hr)
-79-
KNOXVILLE BYPASS
- STORY ON PAGE 93
- MAP ON PAGE 57
11
N
-78-
Kudzu
Loudon Co.
TENNESSEE
Loudon County
-77-
1,500
1,000
500
SOUTH
171-N

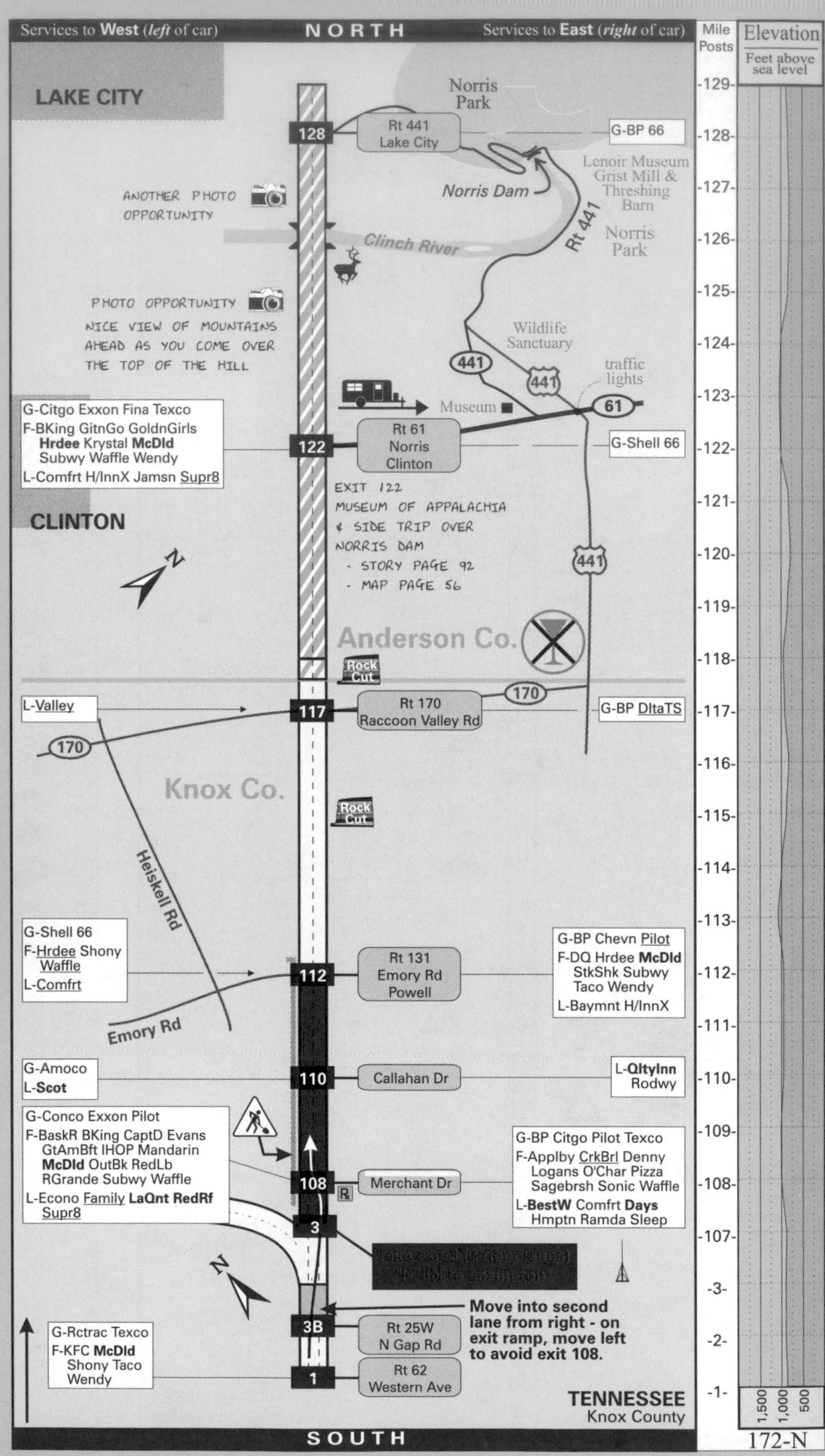
Services to West (left of car)
NORTH
Services to East (right of car)
Mile Posts
Elevation
Feet above sea level
LAKE CITY
Norris Park
128
Rt 441 Lake City
G-BP 66
Lenoir Museum Grist Mill & Threshing Barn
ANOTHER PHOTO OPPORTUNITY
Norris Dam
Rt 441
Clinch River
Norris Park
PHOTO OPPORTUNITY
NICE VIEW OF MOUNTAINS AHEAD AS YOU COME OVER THE TOP OF THE HILL
Wildlife Sanctuary
441
traffic lights
Museum
61
G-Citgo Exxon Fina Texco
F-BKing GitnGo GoldnGirls Hrdee Krystal McDld Subwy Waffle Wendy
L-Comfrt H/InnX Jamsn Supr8
122
Rt 61 Norris Clinton
G-Shell 66
EXIT 122
MUSEUM OF APPALACHIA
& SIDE TRIP OVER NORRIS DAM
- STORY PAGE 92
- MAP PAGE 56
CLINTON
N
Anderson Co.
Rock Cut
L-Valley
117
Rt 170 Raccoon Valley Rd
170
G-BP DltaTS
Knox Co.
Rock Cut
Heiskell Rd
G-Shell 66
F-Hrdee Shony Waffle
L-Comfrt
112
Rt 131 Emory Rd Powell
G-BP Chevn Pilot
F-DQ Hrdee McDld StkShk Subwy Taco Wendy
L-Baymnt H/InnX
Emory Rd
G-Amoco
L-Scot
110
Callahan Dr
L-QltyInn Rodwy
G-Conco Exxon Pilot
F-BaskR BKing CaptD Evans GtAmBft IHOP Mandarin McDld OutBk RedLb RGrande Subwy Waffle
L-Econo Family LaQnt RedRf Supr8
108
Merchant Dr
G-BP Citgo Pilot Texco
F-Applby CrkBrl Denny Logans O'Char Pizza Sagebrsh Sonic Waffle
L-BestW Comfrt Days Hmptn Ramda Sleep
3
3B
Rt 25W N Gap Rd
Move into second lane from right - on exit ramp, move left to avoid exit 108.
G-Rctrac Texco
F-KFC McDld Shony Taco Wendy
1
Rt 62 Western Ave
TENNESSEE
Knox County
SOUTH
-129-
-128-
-127-
-126-
-125-
-124-
-123-
-122-
-121-
-120-
-119-
-118-
-117-
-116-
-115-
-114-
-113-
-112-
-111-
-110-
-109-
-108-
-107-
-3-
-2-
-1-
1,500
1,000
500
172-N

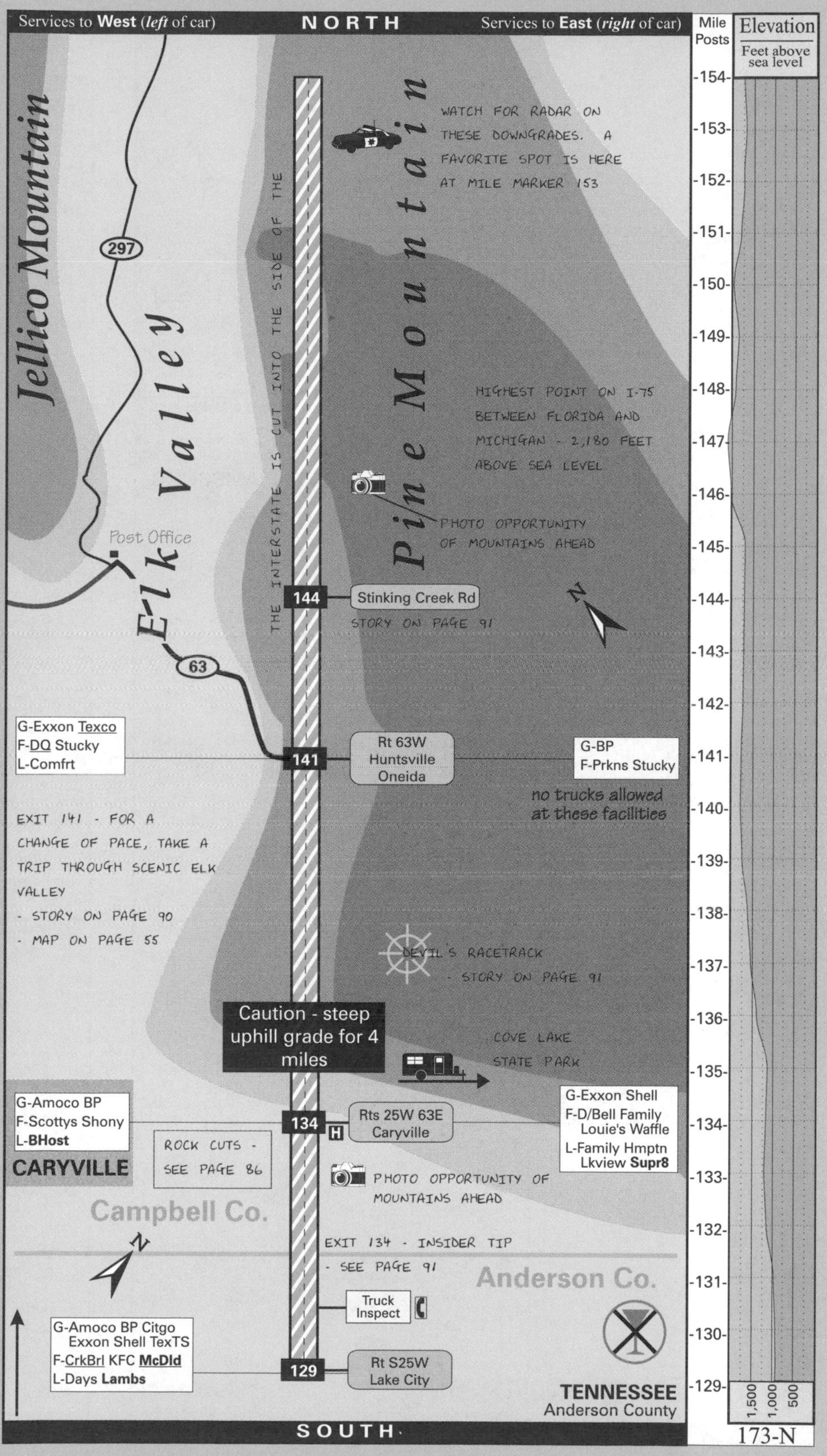

Services to West (left of car)
NORTH
Services to East (right of car)
Mile Posts
Elevation
Feet above sea level
-154-
-153-
-152-
-151-
-150-
-149-
-148-
-147-
-146-
-145-
-144-
-143-
-142-
-141-
-140-
-139-
-138-
-137-
-136-
-135-
-134-
-133-
-132-
-131-
-130-
-129-
1,500
1,000
500
Jellico Mountain
297
Elk Valley
Post Office
63
THE INTERSTATE IS CUT INTO THE SIDE OF THE
Pine Mountain
WATCH FOR RADAR ON THESE DOWNGRADES. A FAVORITE SPOT IS HERE AT MILE MARKER 153
HIGHEST POINT ON I-75 BETWEEN FLORIDA AND MICHIGAN - 2,180 FEET ABOVE SEA LEVEL
PHOTO OPPORTUNITY OF MOUNTAINS AHEAD
144
Stinking Creek Rd
STORY ON PAGE 91
N
G-Exxon Texco
F-DQ Stucky
L-Comfrt
141
Rt 63W Huntsville Oneida
G-BP
F-Prkns Stucky
no trucks allowed at these facilities
EXIT 141 - FOR A CHANGE OF PACE, TAKE A TRIP THROUGH SCENIC ELK VALLEY
- STORY ON PAGE 90
- MAP ON PAGE 55
DEVIL'S RACETRACK
- STORY ON PAGE 91
Caution - steep uphill grade for 4 miles
COVE LAKE STATE PARK
G-Amoco BP
F-Scottys Shony
L-BHost
CARYVILLE
134
H
Rts 25W 63E Caryville
G-Exxon Shell
F-D/Bell Family Louie's Waffle
L-Family Hmptn Lkview Supr8
ROCK CUTS - SEE PAGE 86
PHOTO OPPORTUNITY OF MOUNTAINS AHEAD
Campbell Co.
EXIT 134 - INSIDER TIP
- SEE PAGE 91
N
Anderson Co.
Truck Inspect
G-Amoco BP Citgo Exxon Shell TexTS
F-CrkBrl KFC McDld
L-Days Lambs
129
Rt S25W Lake City
TENNESSEE
Anderson County
SOUTH

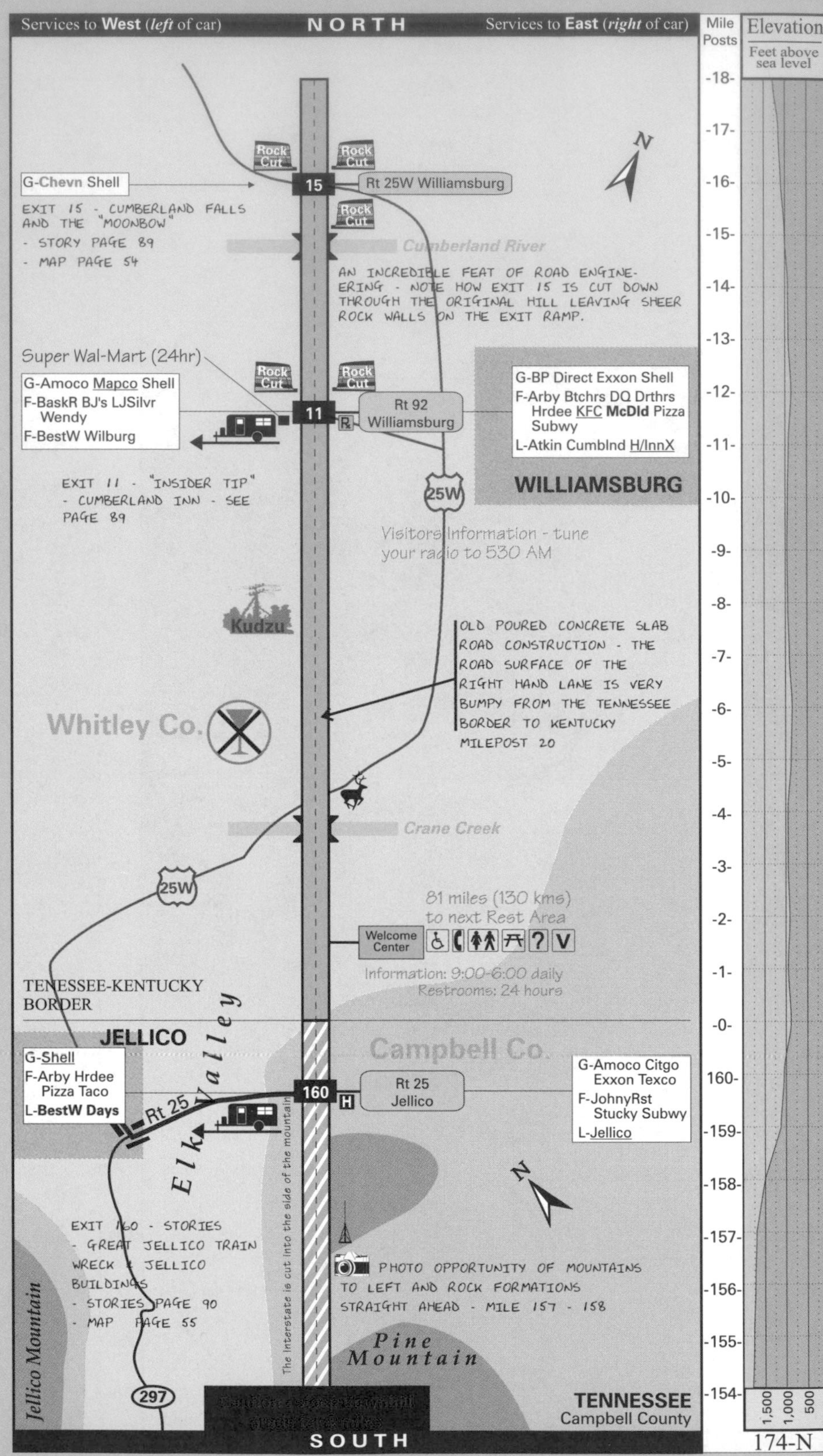

Services to West (left of car)
NORTH
Services to East (right of car)
Mile Posts
Elevation
Feet above sea level
Rock Cut
G-Chevn Shell
15
Rt 25W Williamsburg
EXIT 15 - CUMBERLAND FALLS AND THE "MOONBOW"
- STORY PAGE 89
- MAP PAGE 54
Cumberland River
AN INCREDIBLE FEAT OF ROAD ENGINEERING - NOTE HOW EXIT 15 IS CUT DOWN THROUGH THE ORIGINAL HILL LEAVING SHEER ROCK WALLS ON THE EXIT RAMP.
Super Wal-Mart (24hr)
G-Amoco Mapco Shell
F-BaskR BJ's LJSilvr Wendy
F-BestW Wilburg
11
Rt 92 Williamsburg
G-BP Direct Exxon Shell
F-Arby Btchrs DQ Drthrs Hrdee KFC McDld Pizza Subwy
L-Atkin Cumblnd H/InnX
WILLIAMSBURG
25W
EXIT 11 - "INSIDER TIP" - CUMBERLAND INN - SEE PAGE 89
Visitors Information - tune your radio to 530 AM
Kudzu
OLD POURED CONCRETE SLAB ROAD CONSTRUCTION - THE ROAD SURFACE OF THE RIGHT HAND LANE IS VERY BUMPY FROM THE TENNESSEE BORDER TO KENTUCKY MILEPOST 20
Whitley Co.
Crane Creek
25W
81 miles (130 kms) to next Rest Area
Welcome Center
Information: 9:00-6:00 daily
Restrooms: 24 hours
TENESSEE-KENTUCKY BORDER
JELLICO
Campbell Co.
G-Shell
F-Arby Hrdee Pizza Taco
L-BestW Days
Rt 25
Elk Valley
160
Rt 25 Jellico
G-Amoco Citgo Exxon Texco
F-JohnyRst Stucky Subwy
L-Jellico
The Interstate is cut into the side of the mountain
EXIT 160 - STORIES
- GREAT JELLICO TRAIN WRECK & JELLICO BUILDINGS
- STORIES PAGE 90
- MAP PAGE 55
PHOTO OPPORTUNITY OF MOUNTAINS TO LEFT AND ROCK FORMATIONS STRAIGHT AHEAD - MILE 157 - 158
Pine Mountain
Jellico Mountain
297
TENNESSEE
Campbell County
SOUTH
-18-
-17-
-16-
-15-
-14-
-13-
-12-
-11-
-10-
-9-
-8-
-7-
-6-
-5-
-4-
-3-
-2-
-1-
-0-
160-
-159-
-158-
-157-
-156-
-155-
-154-
1,500
1,000
500

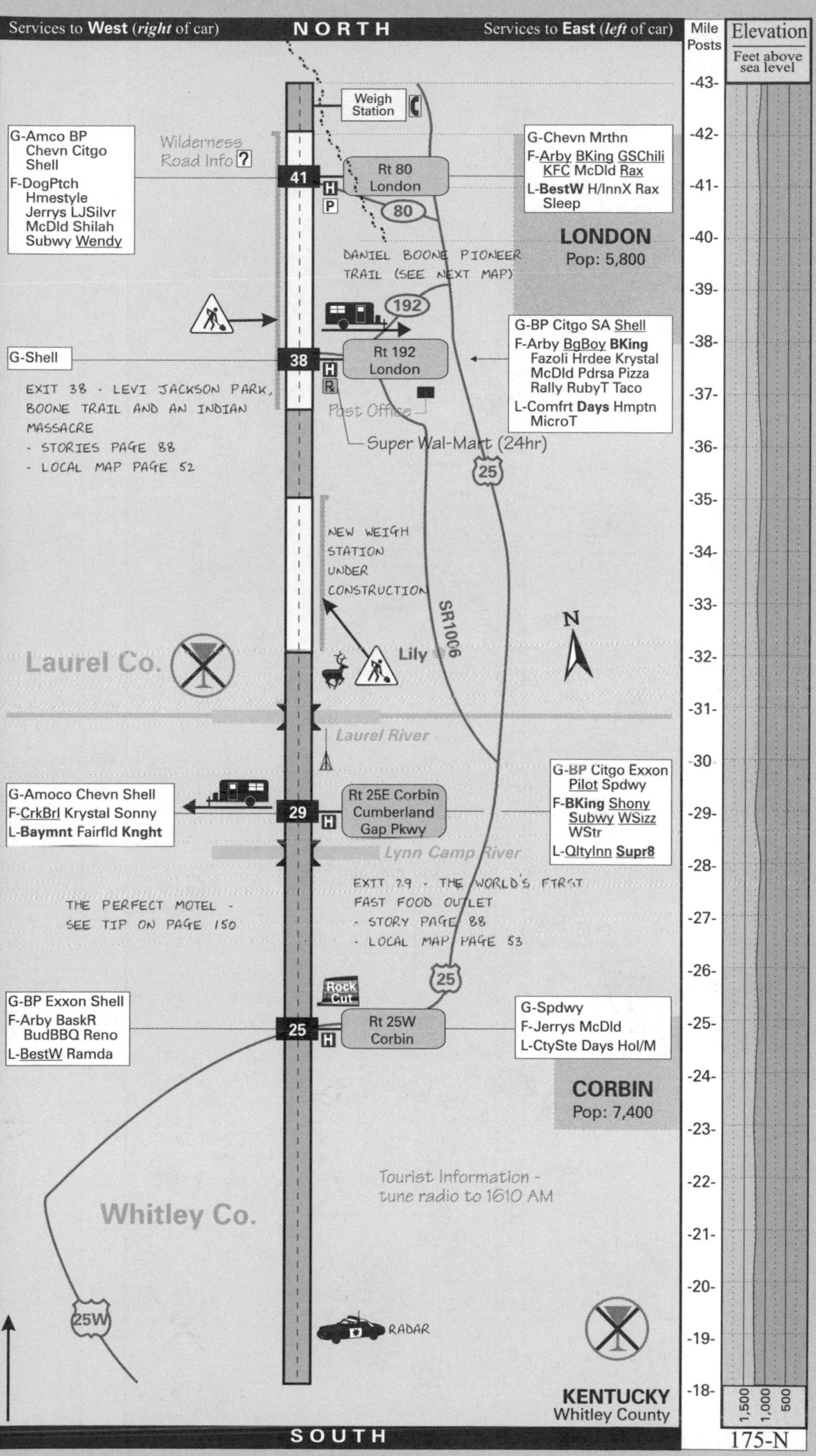

Services to West (right of car)
NORTH
Services to East (left of car)
Mile Posts
Elevation
Feet above sea level
Weigh Station
G-Amco BP Chevn Citgo Shell
F-DogPtch Hmestyle Jerrys LJSilvr McDld Shilah Subwy Wendy
Wilderness Road Info
41
Rt 80 London
80
G-Chevn Mrthn
F-Arby BKing GSChili KFC McDld Rax
L-BestW H/InnX Rax Sleep
LONDON
Pop: 5,800
DANIEL BOONE PIONEER TRAIL (SEE NEXT MAP)
192
G-Shell
38
Rt 192 London
G-BP Citgo SA Shell
F-Arby BgBoy BKing Fazoli Hrdee Krystal McDld Pdrsa Pizza Rally RubyT Taco
L-Comfrt Days Hmptn MicroT
EXIT 38 - LEVI JACKSON PARK, BOONE TRAIL AND AN INDIAN MASSACRE
- STORIES PAGE 88
- LOCAL MAP PAGE 52
Post Office
Super Wal-Mart (24hr)
25
NEW WEIGH STATION UNDER CONSTRUCTION
SR1006
N
Laurel Co.
Lily
Laurel River
G-Amoco Chevn Shell
F-CrkBrl Krystal Sonny
L-Baymnt Fairfld Knght
29
Rt 25E Corbin Cumberland Gap Pkwy
G-BP Citgo Exxon Pilot Spdwy
F-BKing Shony Subwy WSizz WStr
L-QltyInn Supr8
Lynn Camp River
EXIT 29 - THE WORLD'S FIRST FAST FOOD OUTLET
- STORY PAGE 88
- LOCAL MAP PAGE 53
THE PERFECT MOTEL - SEE TIP ON PAGE 150
Rock Cut
G-BP Exxon Shell
F-Arby BaskR BudBBQ Reno
L-BestW Ramda
25
Rt 25W Corbin
G-Spdwy
F-Jerrys McDld
L-CtySte Days Hol/M
CORBIN
Pop: 7,400
Tourist Information - tune radio to 1610 AM
Whitley Co.
25W
RADAR
KENTUCKY
Whitley County
SOUTH
-43- -42- -41- -40- -39- -38- -37- -36- -35- -34- -33- -32- -31- -30- -29- -28- -27- -26- -25- -24- -23- -22- -21- -20- -19- -18-
1,500 1,000 500
175-N

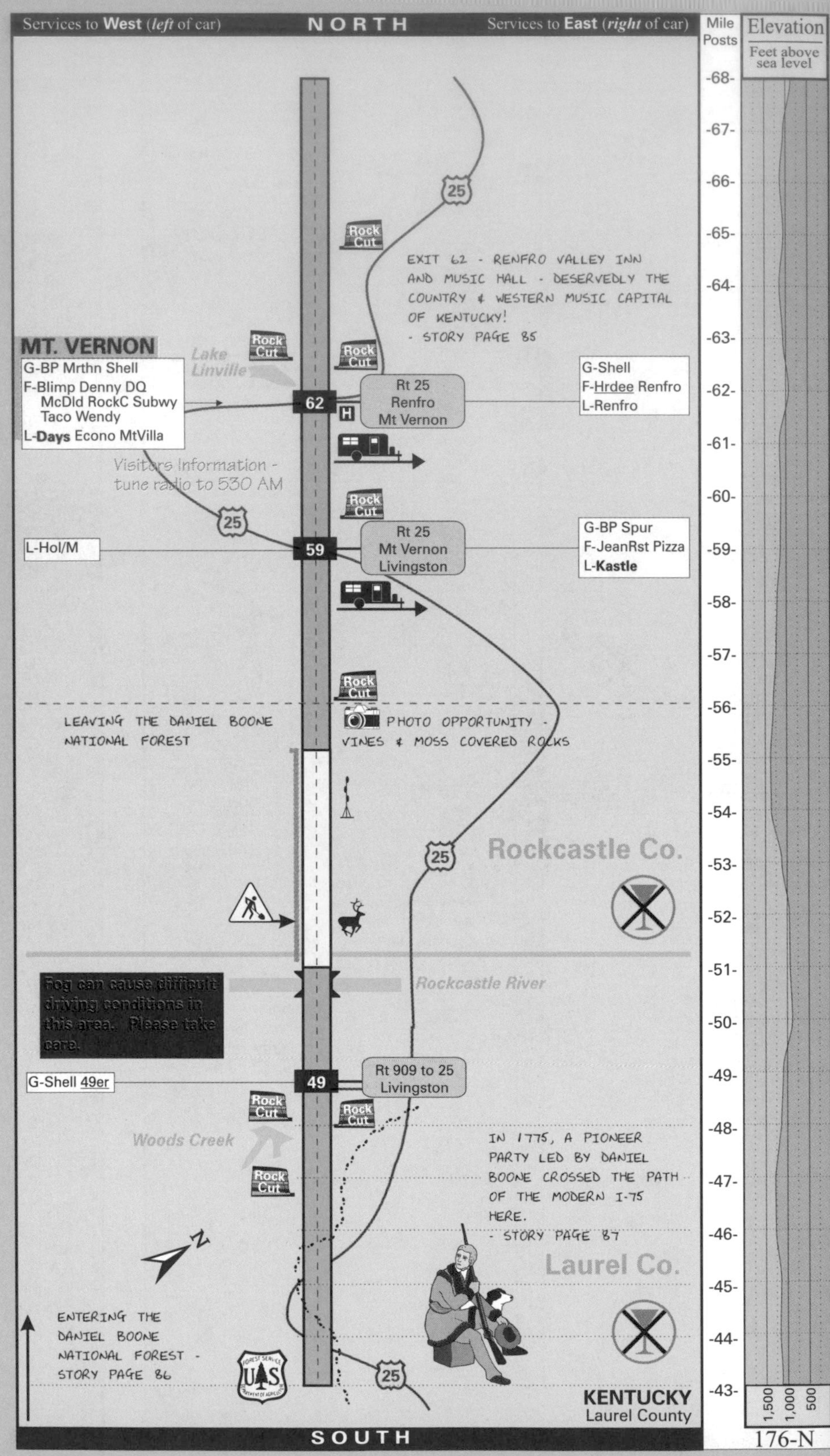

Services to West (left of car)
NORTH
Services to East (right of car)
Mile Posts
Elevation
Feet above sea level
EXIT 62 - RENFRO VALLEY INN AND MUSIC HALL - DESERVEDLY THE COUNTRY & WESTERN MUSIC CAPITAL OF KENTUCKY!
- STORY PAGE 85
MT. VERNON
G-BP Mrthn Shell
F-Blimp Denny DQ McDld RockC Subwy Taco Wendy
L-Days Econo MtVilla
Lake Linville
Rock Cut
62
Rt 25 Renfro Mt Vernon
G-Shell
F-Hrdee Renfro
L-Renfro
Visitors Information - tune radio to 530 AM
25
L-Hol/M
59
Rt 25 Mt Vernon Livingston
G-BP Spur
F-JeanRst Pizza
L-Kastle
LEAVING THE DANIEL BOONE NATIONAL FOREST
PHOTO OPPORTUNITY - VINES & MOSS COVERED ROCKS
Rockcastle Co.
Fog can cause difficult driving conditions in this area. Please take care.
Rockcastle River
G-Shell 49er
49
Rt 909 to 25 Livingston
Woods Creek
IN 1775, A PIONEER PARTY LED BY DANIEL BOONE CROSSED THE PATH OF THE MODERN I-75 HERE.
- STORY PAGE 87
Laurel Co.
ENTERING THE DANIEL BOONE NATIONAL FOREST - STORY PAGE 86
KENTUCKY
Laurel County
SOUTH
-68- -67- -66- -65- -64- -63- -62- -61- -60- -59- -58- -57- -56- -55- -54- -53- -52- -51- -50- -49- -48- -47- -46- -45- -44- -43-
1,500 1,000 500

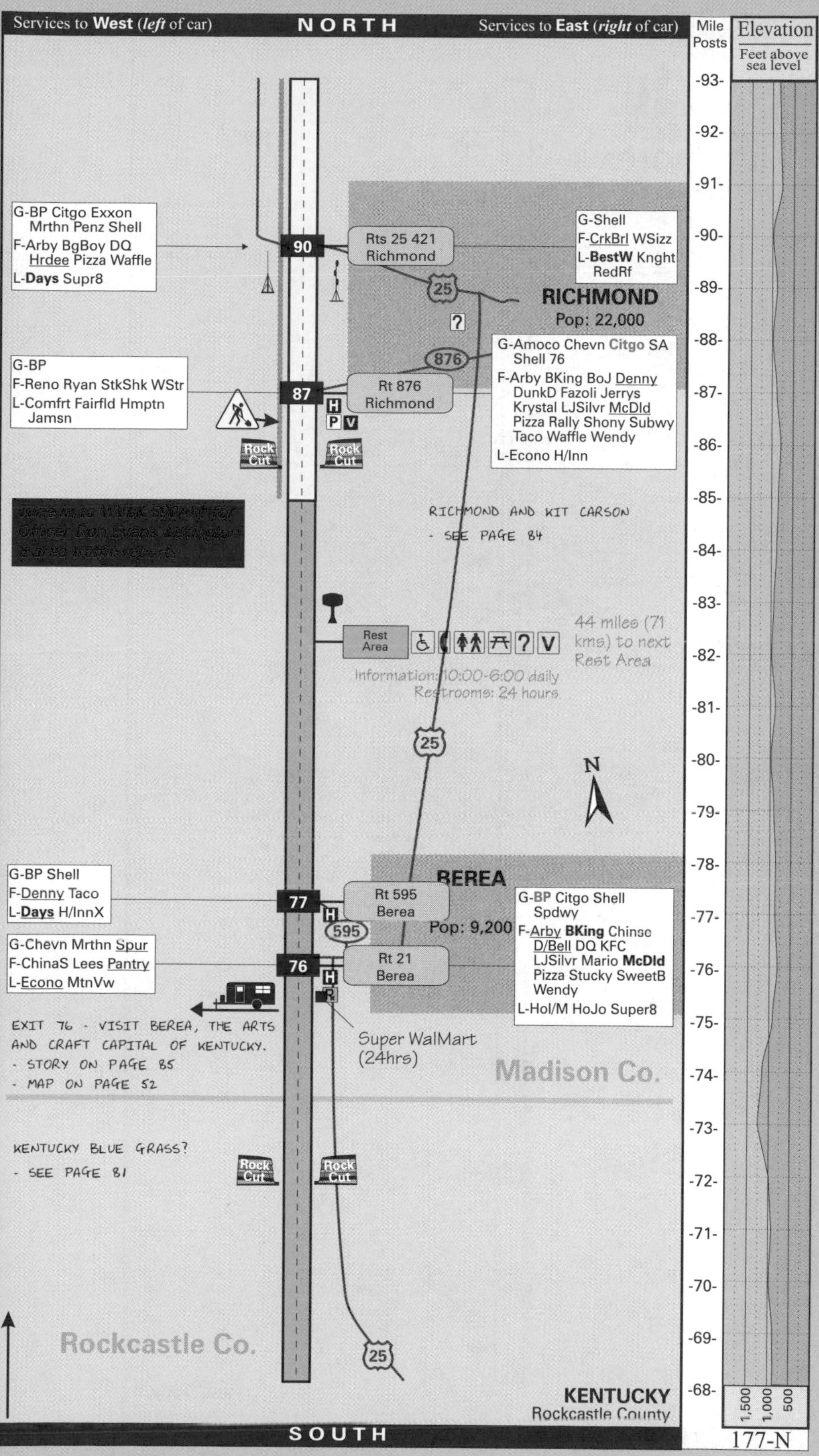

Services to West (left of car)
NORTH
Services to East (right of car)
Mile Posts
Elevation
Feet above sea level
-93-
-92-
-91-
-90-
-89-
-88-
-87-
-86-
-85-
-84-
-83-
-82-
-81-
-80-
-79-
-78-
-77-
-76-
-75-
-74-
-73-
-72-
-71-
-70-
-69-
-68-
G-BP Citgo Exxon Mrthn Penz Shell
F-Arby BgBoy DQ Hrdee Pizza Waffle
L-Days Supr8
90
Rts 25 421 Richmond
25
G-Shell
F-CrkBrl WSizz
L-BestW Knght RedRf
RICHMOND
Pop: 22,000
G-BP
F-Reno Ryan StkShk WStr
L-Comfrt Fairfld Hmptn Jamsn
87
876
Rt 876 Richmond
G-Amoco Chevn Citgo SA Shell 76
F-Arby BKing BoJ Denny DunkD Fazoli Jerrys Krystal LJSilvr McDld Pizza Rally Shony Subwy Taco Waffle Wendy
L-Econo H/Inn
Rock Cut
Rock Cut
RICHMOND AND KIT CARSON
- SEE PAGE 84
Rest Area
44 miles (71 kms) to next Rest Area
Information: 10:00-6:00 daily
Restrooms: 24 hours
25
N
G-BP Shell
F-Denny Taco
L-Days H/InnX
77
Rt 595 Berea
595
BEREA
Pop: 9,200
G-BP Citgo Shell Spdwy
F-Arby BKing Chinse D/Bell DQ KFC LJSilvr Mario McDld Pizza Stucky SweetB Wendy
L-Hol/M HoJo Super8
G-Chevn Mrthn Spur
F-ChinaS Lees Pantry
L-Econo MtnVw
76
Rt 21 Berea
EXIT 76 - VISIT BEREA, THE ARTS AND CRAFT CAPITAL OF KENTUCKY.
- STORY ON PAGE 85
- MAP ON PAGE 52
Super WalMart (24hrs)
Madison Co.
KENTUCKY BLUE GRASS?
- SEE PAGE 81
Rock Cut
Rock Cut
Rockcastle Co.
25
KENTUCKY
Rockcastle County
1,500
1,000
500
SOUTH

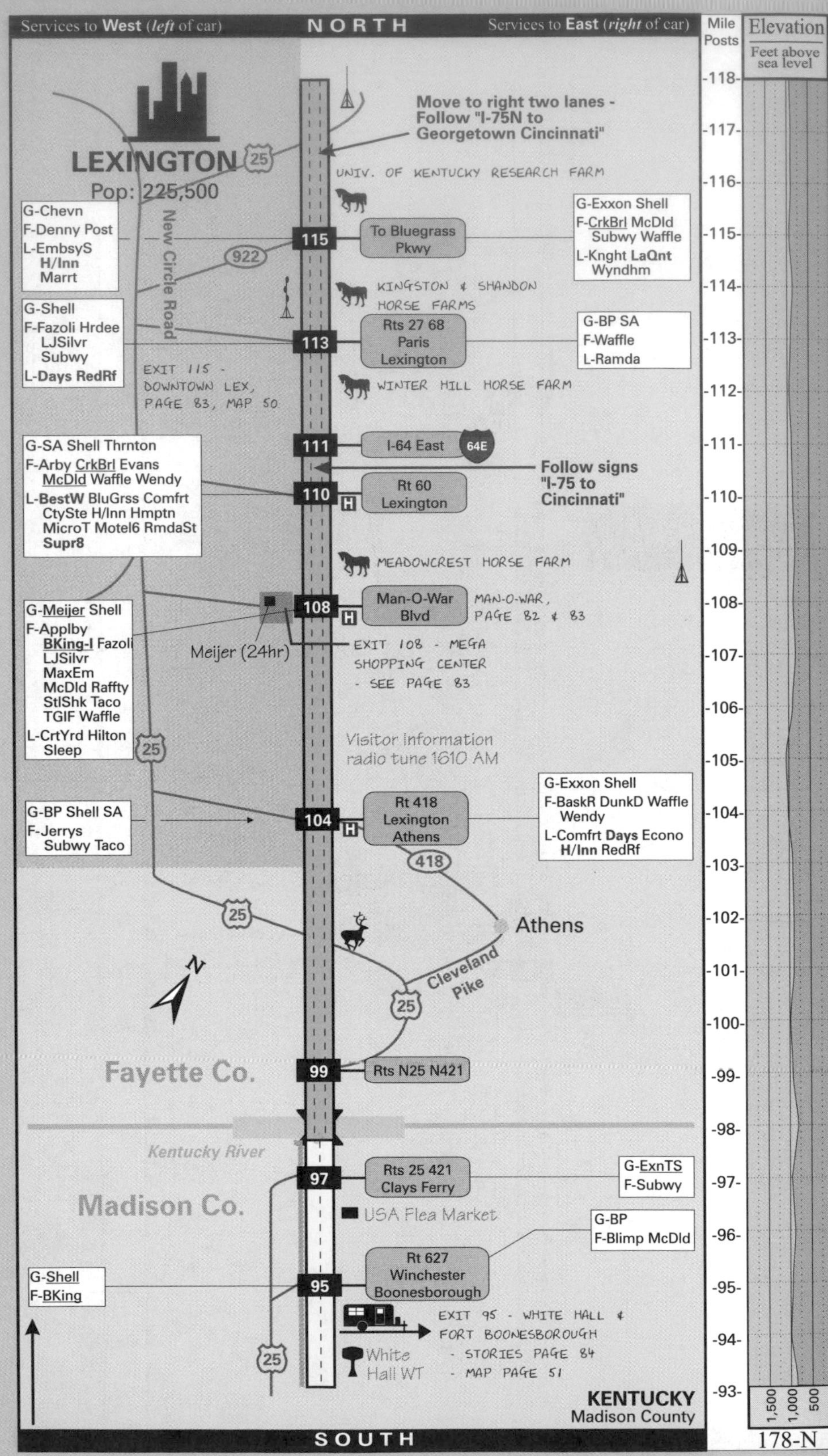
Services to West (left of car)
NORTH
Services to East (right of car)
Mile Posts
Elevation
Feet above sea level
LEXINGTON
Pop: 225,500
Move to right two lanes - Follow "I-75N to Georgetown Cincinnati"
UNIV. OF KENTUCKY RESEARCH FARM
G-Chevn
F-Denny Post
L-EmbsyS H/Inn Marrt
115
To Bluegrass Pkwy
G-Exxon Shell
F-CrkBrl McDld Subwy Waffle
L-Knght LaQnt Wyndhm
922
New Circle Road
KINGSTON & SHANDON HORSE FARMS
G-Shell
F-Fazoli Hrdee LJSilvr Subwy
L-Days RedRf
113
Rts 27 68 Paris Lexington
G-BP SA
F-Waffle
L-Ramda
EXIT 115 - DOWNTOWN LEX, PAGE 83, MAP 50
WINTER HILL HORSE FARM
G-SA Shell Thrnton
F-Arby CrkBrl Evans McDld Waffle Wendy
L-BestW BluGrss Comfrt CtySte H/Inn Hmptn MicroT Motel6 RmdaSt Supr8
111
I-64 East
64E
Follow signs "I-75 to Cincinnati"
110
Rt 60 Lexington
MEADOWCREST HORSE FARM
G-Meijer Shell
F-Applby BKing-I Fazoli LJSilvr MaxEm McDld Raffty StlShk Taco TGIF Waffle
L-CrtYrd Hilton Sleep
108
Man-O-War Blvd
MAN-O-WAR, PAGE 82 & 83
Meijer (24hr)
EXIT 108 - MEGA SHOPPING CENTER - SEE PAGE 83
Visitor Information radio tune 1610 AM
25
G-BP Shell SA
F-Jerrys Subwy Taco
104
Rt 418 Lexington Athens
G-Exxon Shell
F-BaskR DunkD Waffle Wendy
L-Comfrt Days Econo H/Inn RedRf
418
Athens
Cleveland Pike
N
Fayette Co.
99
Rts N25 N421
Kentucky River
Madison Co.
97
Rts 25 421 Clays Ferry
G-ExnTS
F-Subwy
USA Flea Market
G-BP
F-Blimp McDld
Rt 627 Winchester Boonesborough
G-Shell
F-BKing
95
EXIT 95 - WHITE HALL & FORT BOONESBOROUGH - STORIES PAGE 84 - MAP PAGE 51
White Hall WT
KENTUCKY
Madison County
SOUTH
1,500
1,000
500
-118- -117- -116- -115- -114- -113- -112- -111- -110- -109- -108- -107- -106- -105- -104- -103- -102- -101- -100- -99- -98- -97- -96- -95- -94- -93-

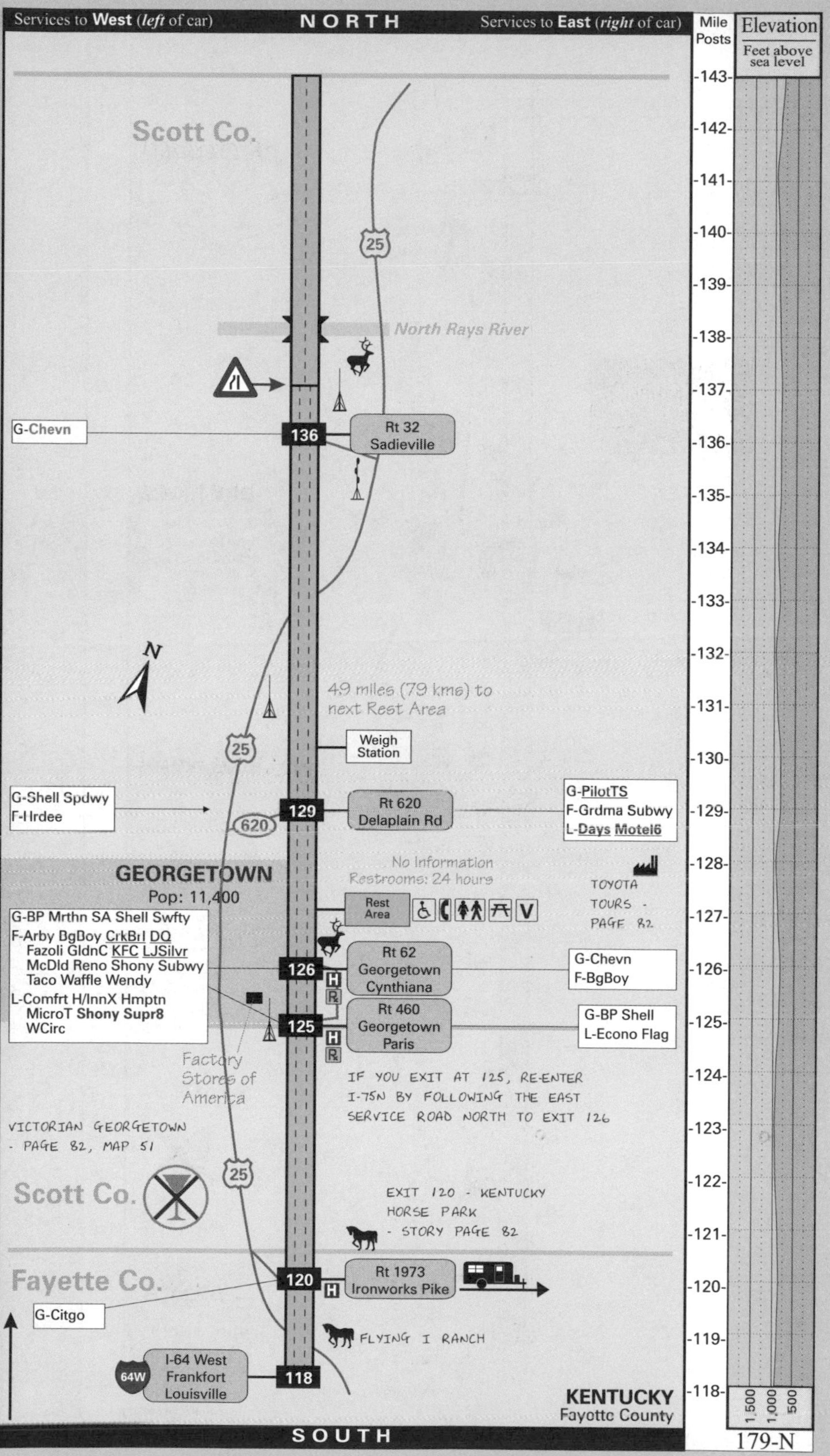

Services to West (left of car)
NORTH
Services to East (right of car)
Mile Posts
Elevation
Feet above sea level
Scott Co.
25
North Rays River
G-Chevn
136
Rt 32
Sadieville
N
49 miles (79 kms) to next Rest Area
Weigh Station
G-Shell Spdwy
F-Hrdee
129
620
Rt 620
Delaplain Rd
G-PilotTS
F-Grdma Subwy
L-Days Motel6
GEORGETOWN
Pop: 11,400
No Information
Restrooms: 24 hours
TOYOTA TOURS - PAGE 82
Rest Area
V
G-BP Mrthn SA Shell Swfty
F-Arby BgBoy CrkBrl DQ
Fazoli GldnC KFC LJSilvr
McDld Reno Shony Subwy
Taco Waffle Wendy
L-Comfrt H/InnX Hmptn
MicroT Shony Supr8
WCirc
126
Rt 62
Georgetown
Cynthiana
G-Chevn
F-BgBoy
125
Rt 460
Georgetown
Paris
G-BP Shell
L-Econo Flag
Factory Stores of America
IF YOU EXIT AT 125, RE-ENTER I-75N BY FOLLOWING THE EAST SERVICE ROAD NORTH TO EXIT 126
VICTORIAN GEORGETOWN - PAGE 82, MAP 51
Scott Co.
EXIT 120 - KENTUCKY HORSE PARK - STORY PAGE 82
Fayette Co.
120
Rt 1973
Ironworks Pike
G-Citgo
FLYING I RANCH
64W
I-64 West
Frankfort
Louisville
118
KENTUCKY
Fayette County
SOUTH
-143-
-142-
-141-
-140-
-139-
-138-
-137-
-136-
-135-
-134-
-133-
-132-
-131-
-130-
-129-
-128-
-127-
-126-
-125-
-124-
-123-
-122-
-121-
-120-
-119-
-118-
1,500
1,000
500

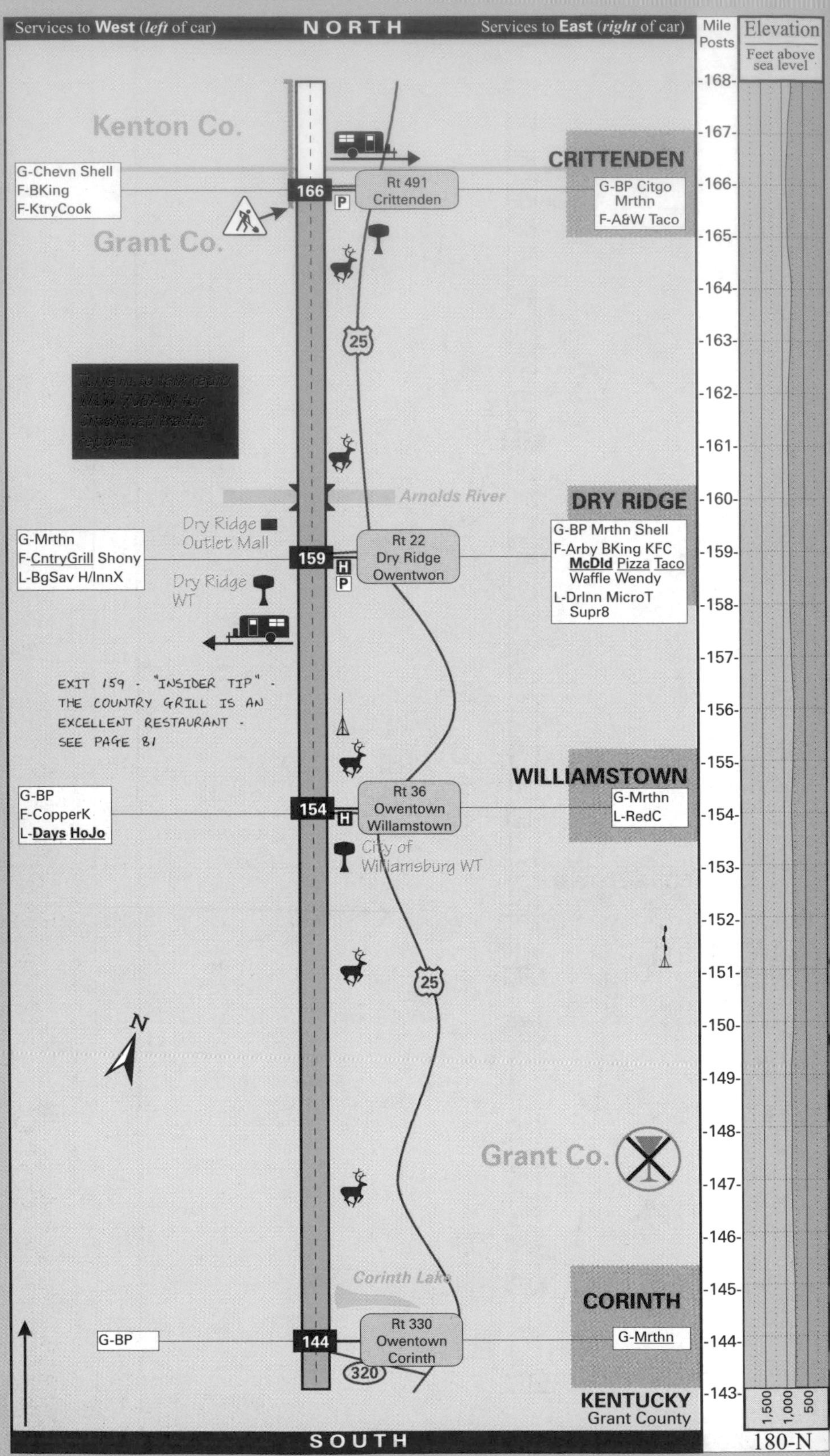

Services to West (left of car)
NORTH
Services to East (right of car)
Mile Posts
Elevation
Feet above sea level
-168-
-167-
-166-
-165-
-164-
-163-
-162-
-161-
-160-
-159-
-158-
-157-
-156-
-155-
-154-
-153-
-152-
-151-
-150-
-149-
-148-
-147-
-146-
-145-
-144-
-143-
Kenton Co.
Grant Co.
CRITTENDEN
G-Chevn Shell
F-BKing
F-KtryCook
166
P
Rt 491
Crittenden
G-BP Citgo
Mrthn
F-A&W Taco
25
Arnolds River
DRY RIDGE
Dry Ridge
Outlet Mall
G-Mrthn
F-CntryGrill Shony
L-BgSav H/InnX
159
H
P
Rt 22
Dry Ridge
Owentwon
G-BP Mrthn Shell
F-Arby BKing KFC
McDld Pizza Taco
Waffle Wendy
L-DrInn MicroT
Supr8
Dry Ridge
WT
EXIT 159 - "INSIDER TIP" -
THE COUNTRY GRILL IS AN
EXCELLENT RESTAURANT -
SEE PAGE 81
WILLIAMSTOWN
G-BP
F-CopperK
L-Days HoJo
154
H
Rt 36
Owentown
Willamstown
G-Mrthn
L-RedC
City of
Williamsburg WT
25
N
Grant Co.
Corinth Lake
CORINTH
G-BP
144
Rt 330
Owentown
Corinth
320
G-Mrthn
KENTUCKY
Grant County
1,500
1,000
500
SOUTH
180-N

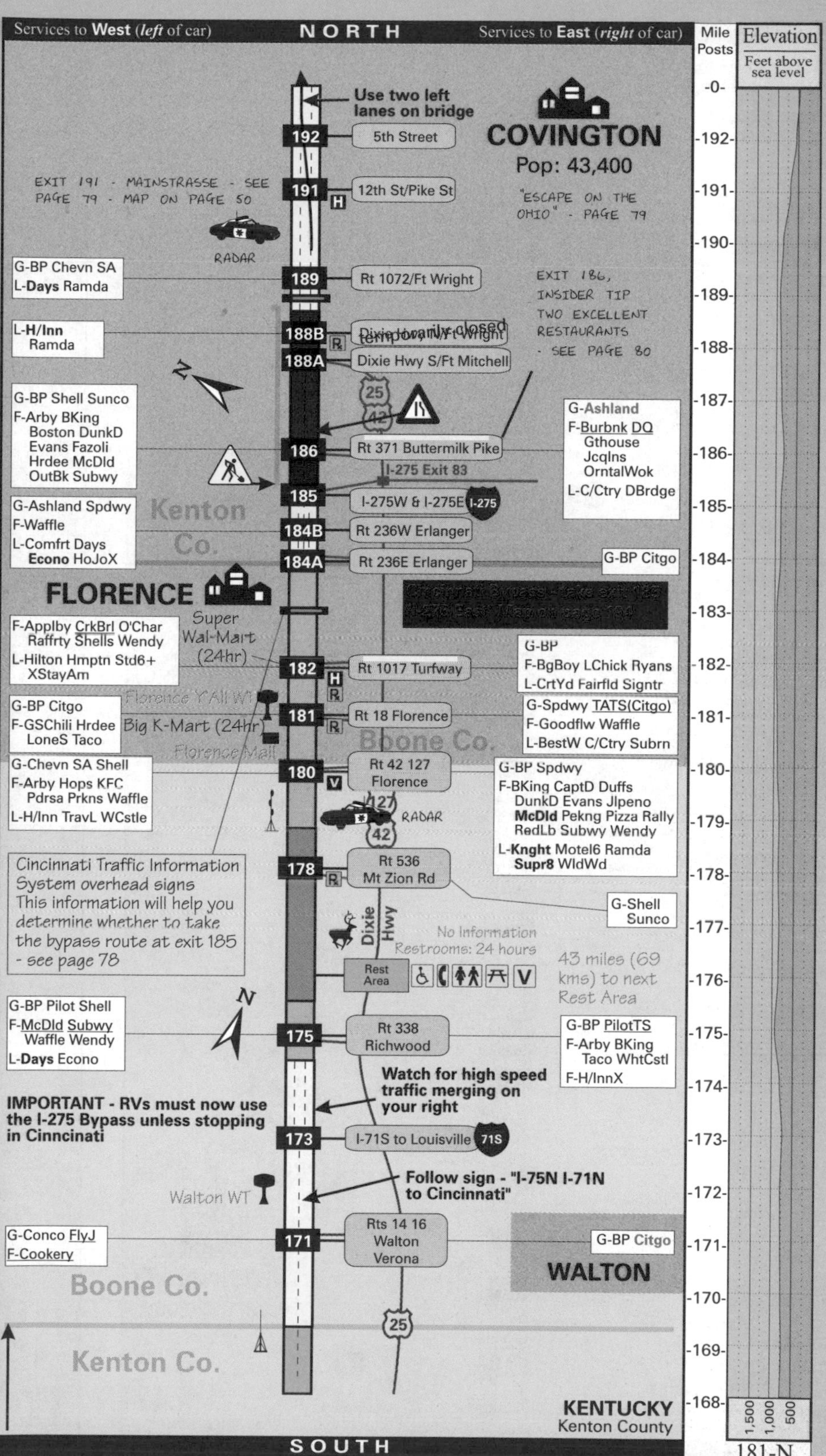

Services to West (left of car)
NORTH
Services to East (right of car)
Mile Posts
Elevation
Feet above sea level
Use two left lanes on bridge
192
5th Street
COVINGTON
Pop: 43,400
EXIT 191 - MAINSTRASSE - SEE PAGE 79 - MAP ON PAGE 50
191
12th St/Pike St
"ESCAPE ON THE OHIO" - PAGE 79
RADAR
G-BP Chevn SA
L-Days Ramda
189
Rt 1072/Ft Wright
EXIT 186, INSIDER TIP TWO EXCELLENT RESTAURANTS - SEE PAGE 80
L-H/Inn
Ramda
188B
Dixie Hwy N/Ft Wright
temporarily closed
188A
Dixie Hwy S/Ft Mitchell
25
42
G-BP Shell Sunco
F-Arby BKing
Boston DunkD
Evans Fazoli
Hrdee McDld
OutBk Subwy
186
Rt 371 Buttermilk Pike
I-275 Exit 83
G-Ashland
F-Burbnk DQ
Gthouse
Jcqlns
OrntalWok
L-C/Ctry DBrdge
G-Ashland Spdwy
F-Waffle
L-Comfrt Days
Econo HoJoX
Kenton Co.
185
I-275W & I-275E
I-275
184B
Rt 236W Erlanger
184A
Rt 236E Erlanger
G-BP Citgo
FLORENCE
F-Applby CrkBrl O'Char
Raffrty Shells Wendy
L-Hilton Hmptn Std6+
XStayAm
Super Wal-Mart (24hr)
182
Rt 1017 Turfway
G-BP
F-BgBoy LChick Ryans
L-CrtYd Fairfld Signtr
Florence Y'All WT
G-BP Citgo
F-GSChili Hrdee
LoneS Taco
181
Big K-Mart (24hr)
Rt 18 Florence
G-Spdwy TATS(Citgo)
F-Goodflw Waffle
L-BestW C/Ctry Subrn
Boone Co.
Florence Mall
G-Chevn SA Shell
F-Arby Hops KFC
Pdrsa Prkns Waffle
L-H/Inn TravL WCstle
180
Rt 42 127
Florence
G-BP Spdwy
F-BKing CaptD Duffs
DunkD Evans Jlpeno
McDld Pekng Pizza Rally
RedLb Subwy Wendy
L-Knght Motel6 Ramda
Supr8 WldWd
127
RADAR
42
Cincinnati Traffic Information System overhead signs
This information will help you determine whether to take the bypass route at exit 185 - see page 78
178
Rt 536
Mt Zion Rd
G-Shell
Sunco
Dixie Hwy
No Information
Restrooms: 24 hours
Rest Area
V
43 miles (69 kms) to next Rest Area
N
G-BP Pilot Shell
F-McDld Subwy
Waffle Wendy
L-Days Econo
175
Rt 338
Richwood
G-BP PilotTS
F-Arby BKing
Taco WhtCstl
F-H/InnX
Watch for high speed traffic merging on your right
IMPORTANT - RVs must now use the I-275 Bypass unless stopping in Cinncinati
173
I-71S to Louisville
71S
Follow sign - "I-75N I-71N to Cincinnati"
Walton WT
G-Conco FlyJ
F-Cookery
171
Rts 14 16
Walton
Verona
G-BP Citgo
WALTON
Boone Co.
25
Kenton Co.
KENTUCKY
Kenton County
SOUTH
-0-
-192-
-191-
-190-
-189-
-188-
-187-
-186-
-185-
-184-
-183-
-182-
-181-
-180-
-179-
-178-
-177-
-176-
-175-
-174-
-173-
-172-
-171-
-170-
-169-
-168-
1,500
1,000
500
181-N

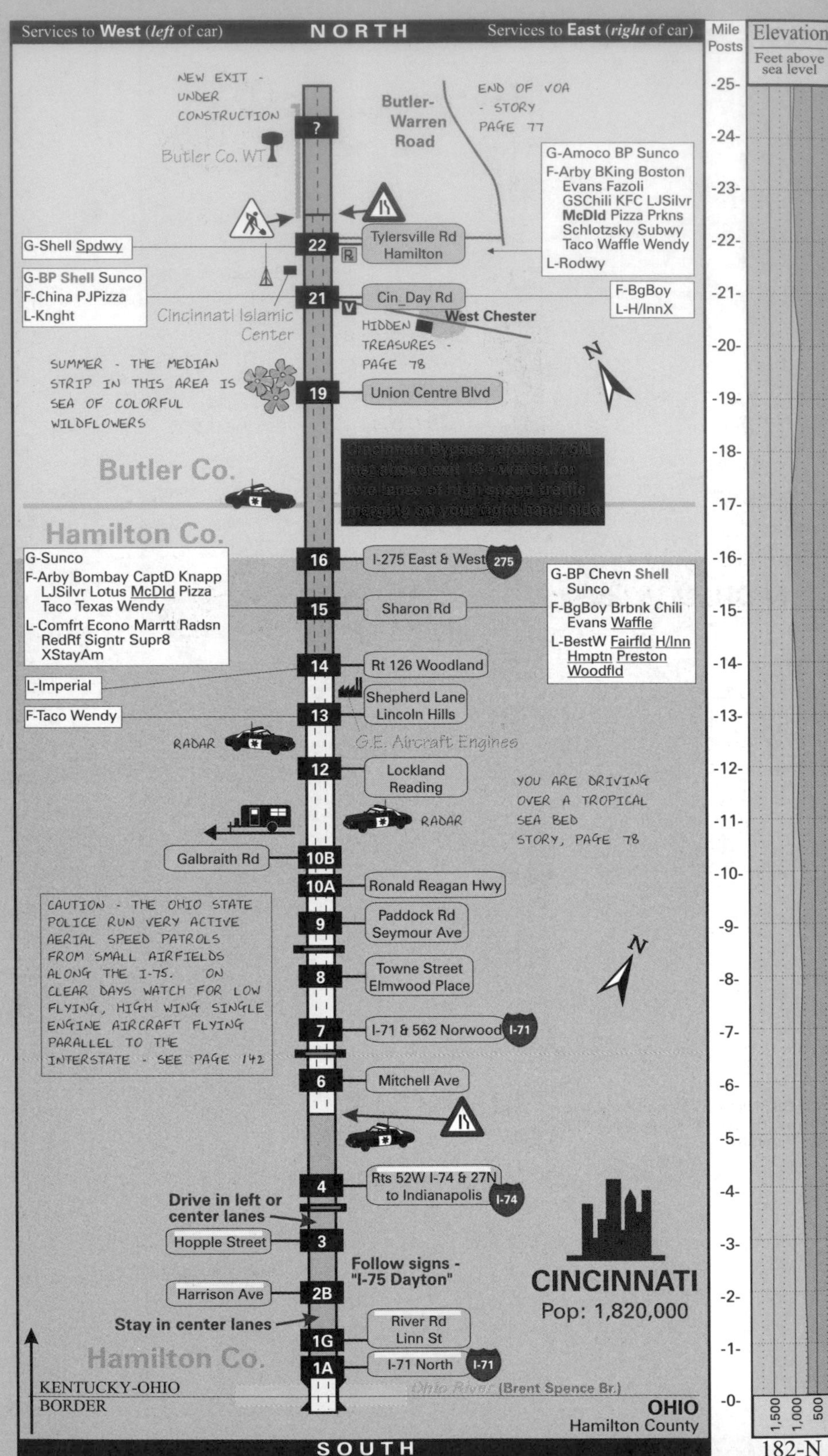

Services to West (left of car)
NORTH
Services to East (right of car)
Mile Posts
Elevation
Feet above sea level
NEW EXIT - UNDER CONSTRUCTION
?
Butler Co. WT
Butler-Warren Road
END OF VOA - STORY PAGE 77
G-Amoco BP Sunco
F-Arby BKing Boston Evans Fazoli GSChili KFC LJSilvr McDld Pizza Prkns Schlotzsky Subwy Taco Waffle Wendy
L-Rodwy
G-Shell Spdwy
22
Tylersville Rd Hamilton
G-BP Shell Sunco
F-China PJPizza
L-Knght
21
Cin Day Rd
F-BgBoy
L-H/InnX
Cincinnati Islamic Center
West Chester
HIDDEN TREASURES - PAGE 78
SUMMER - THE MEDIAN STRIP IN THIS AREA IS SEA OF COLORFUL WILDFLOWERS
19
Union Centre Blvd
N
Butler Co.
Hamilton Co.
G-Sunco
F-Arby Bombay CaptD Knapp LJSilvr Lotus McDld Pizza Taco Texas Wendy
L-Comfrt Econo Marrtt Radsn RedRf Signtr Supr8 XStayAm
16
I-275 East & West
275
G-BP Chevn Shell Sunco
F-BgBoy Brbnk Chili Evans Waffle
L-BestW Fairfld H/Inn Hmptn Preston Woodfld
15
Sharon Rd
L-Imperial
14
Rt 126 Woodland
Shepherd Lane Lincoln Hills
F-Taco Wendy
13
RADAR
G.E. Aircraft Engines
12
Lockland Reading
YOU ARE DRIVING OVER A TROPICAL SEA BED STORY, PAGE 78
RADAR
Galbraith Rd
10B
10A
Ronald Reagan Hwy
CAUTION - THE OHIO STATE POLICE RUN VERY ACTIVE AERIAL SPEED PATROLS FROM SMALL AIRFIELDS ALONG THE I-75. ON CLEAR DAYS WATCH FOR LOW FLYING, HIGH WING SINGLE ENGINE AIRCRAFT FLYING PARALLEL TO THE INTERSTATE - SEE PAGE 142
9
Paddock Rd Seymour Ave
8
Towne Street Elmwood Place
N
7
I-71 & 562 Norwood
I-71
6
Mitchell Ave
4
Rts 52W I-74 & 27N to Indianapolis
I-74
Drive in left or center lanes
Hopple Street
3
Follow signs - "I-75 Dayton"
CINCINNATI
Pop: 1,820,000
Harrison Ave
2B
Stay in center lanes
River Rd Linn St
1G
Hamilton Co.
1A
I-71 North
I-71
KENTUCKY-OHIO BORDER
Ohio River (Brent Spence Br.)
OHIO
Hamilton County
SOUTH
-25-
-24-
-23-
-22-
-21-
-20-
-19-
-18-
-17-
-16-
-15-
-14-
-13-
-12-
-11-
-10-
-9-
-8-
-7-
-6-
-5-
-4-
-3-
-2-
-1-
-0-
1,500
1,000
500

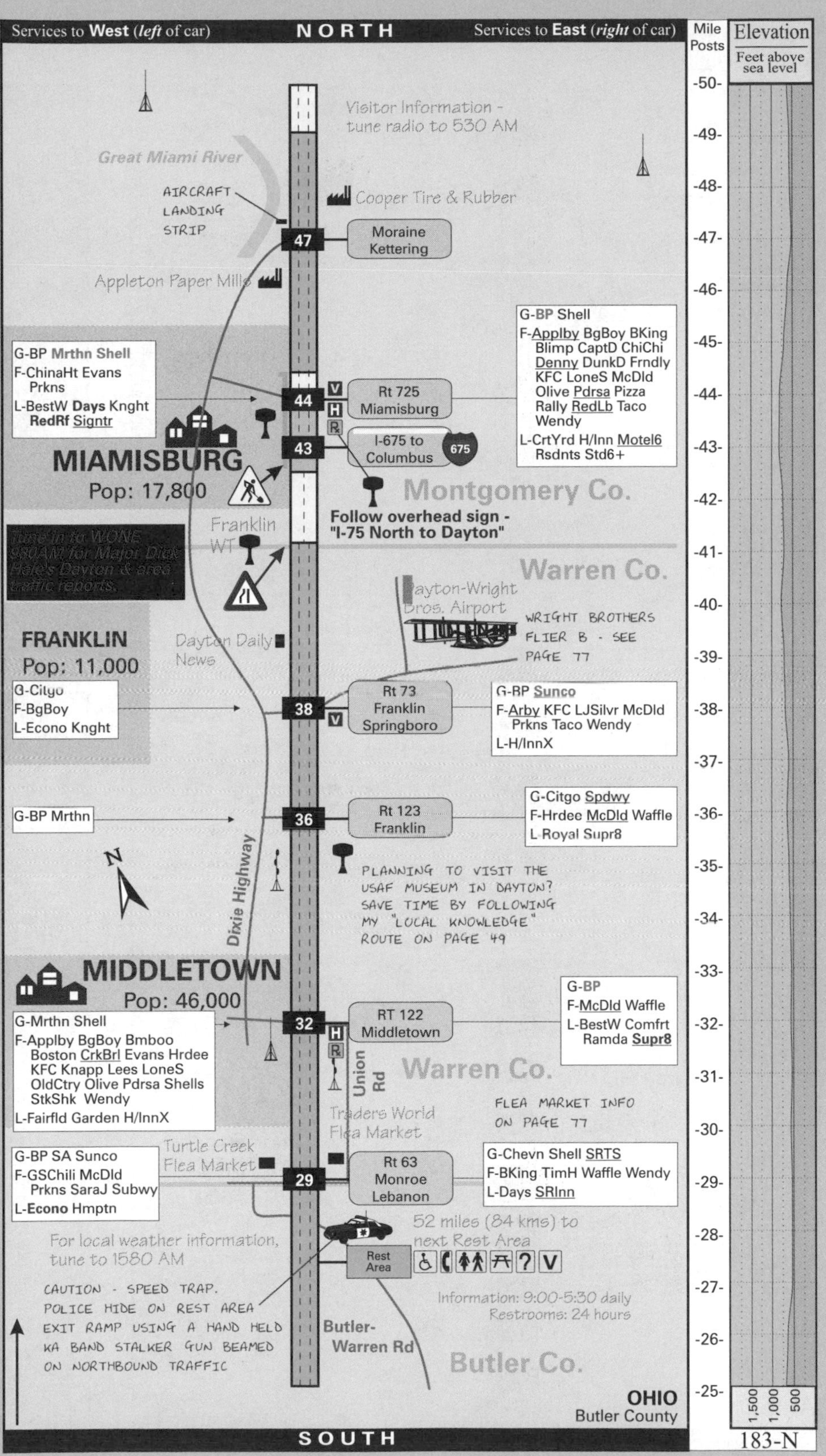

Services to West (left of car)
NORTH
Services to East (right of car)
Mile Posts
Elevation
Feet above sea level
Visitor Information - tune radio to 530 AM
Great Miami River
AIRCRAFT LANDING STRIP
Cooper Tire & Rubber
47
Moraine Kettering
Appleton Paper Mills
G-BP Shell
F-Applby BgBoy BKing Blimp CaptD ChiChi Denny DunkD Frndly KFC LoneS McDld Olive Pdrsa Pizza Rally RedLb Taco Wendy
L-CrtYrd H/Inn Motel6 Rsdnts Std6+
G-BP Mrthn Shell
F-ChinaHt Evans Prkns
L-BestW Days Knght RedRf Signtr
44
Rt 725 Miamisburg
43
I-675 to Columbus
675
MIAMISBURG
Pop: 17,800
Montgomery Co.
Follow overhead sign - "I-75 North to Dayton"
Tune in to WONE 980AM for Major Dick Hale's Dayton & area traffic reports.
Franklin WT
Warren Co.
Dayton-Wright Bros. Airport
WRIGHT BROTHERS FLIER B - SEE PAGE 77
FRANKLIN
Pop: 11,000
Dayton Daily News
G-Citgo
F-BgBoy
L-Econo Knght
38
Rt 73 Franklin Springboro
G-BP Sunco
F-Arby KFC LJSilvr McDld Prkns Taco Wendy
L-H/InnX
G-BP Mrthn
36
Rt 123 Franklin
G-Citgo Spdwy
F-Hrdee McDld Waffle
L-Royal Supr8
N
PLANNING TO VISIT THE USAF MUSEUM IN DAYTON? SAVE TIME BY FOLLOWING MY "LOCAL KNOWLEDGE" ROUTE ON PAGE 49
Dixie Highway
MIDDLETOWN
Pop: 46,000
G-Mrthn Shell
F-Applby BgBoy Bmboo Boston CrkBrl Evans Hrdee KFC Knapp Lees LoneS OldCtry Olive Pdrsa Shells StkShk Wendy
L-Fairfld Garden H/InnX
32
RT 122 Middletown
G-BP
F-McDld Waffle
L-BestW Comfrt Ramda Supr8
Union Rd
Warren Co.
Traders World Flea Market
FLEA MARKET INFO ON PAGE 77
Turtle Creek Flea Market
G-BP SA Sunco
F-GSChili McDld Prkns SaraJ Subwy
L-Econo Hmptn
29
Rt 63 Monroe Lebanon
G-Chevn Shell SRTS
F-BKing TimH Waffle Wendy
L-Days SRInn
52 miles (84 kms) to next Rest Area
Rest Area
For local weather information, tune to 1580 AM
Information: 9:00-5:30 daily
Restrooms: 24 hours
CAUTION - SPEED TRAP. POLICE HIDE ON REST AREA EXIT RAMP USING A HAND HELD KA BAND STALKER GUN BEAMED ON NORTHBOUND TRAFFIC
Butler-Warren Rd
Butler Co.
OHIO
Butler County
SOUTH
-50- -49- -48- -47- -46- -45- -44- -43- -42- -41- -40- -39- -38- -37- -36- -35- -34- -33- -32- -31- -30- -29- -28- -27- -26- -25-
1,500 1,000 500

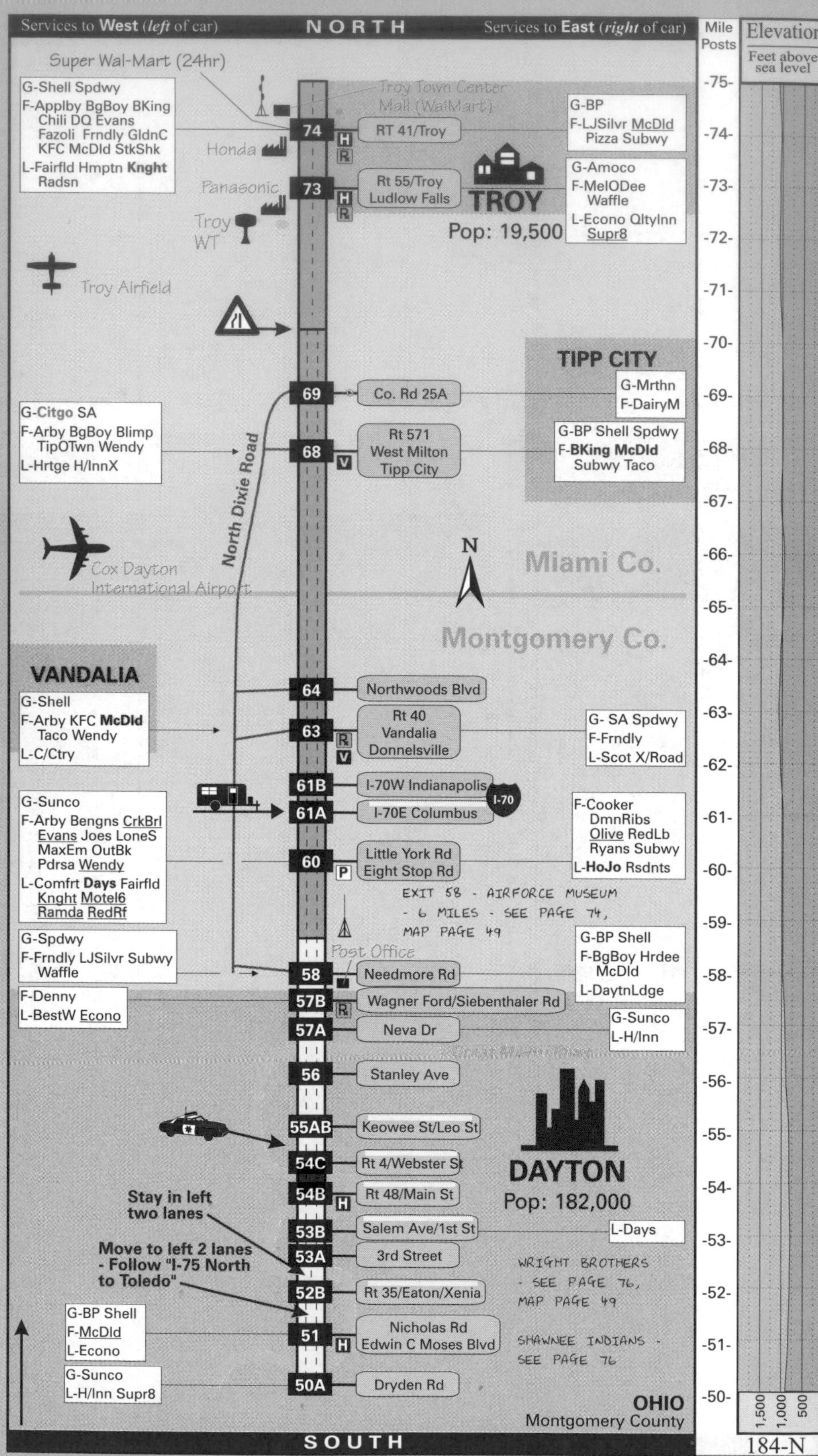

Services to West (left of car)
NORTH
Services to East (right of car)
Mile Posts
Elevation
Feet above sea level
Super Wal-Mart (24hr)
G-Shell Spdwy
F-Applby BgBoy BKing Chili DQ Evans Fazoli Frndly GldnC KFC McDld StkShk
L-Fairfld Hmptn Knght Radsn
Troy Town Center Mall (WalMart)
74
RT 41/Troy
G-BP
F-LJSilvr McDld Pizza Subwy
Honda
Panasonic
73
Rt 55/Troy Ludlow Falls
TROY
Pop: 19,500
G-Amoco
F-MelODee Waffle
L-Econo QltyInn Supr8
Troy WT
Troy Airfield
TIPP CITY
69
Co. Rd 25A
G-Mrthn
F-DairyM
G-Citgo SA
F-Arby BgBoy Blimp TipOTwn Wendy
L-Hrtge H/InnX
68
Rt 571 West Milton Tipp City
G-BP Shell Spdwy
F-BKing McDld Subwy Taco
North Dixie Road
N
Miami Co.
Cox Dayton International Airport
Montgomery Co.
VANDALIA
64
Northwoods Blvd
G-Shell
F-Arby KFC McDld Taco Wendy
L-C/Ctry
63
Rt 40 Vandalia Donnelsville
G- SA Spdwy
F-Frndly
L-Scot X/Road
61B
I-70W Indianapolis
I-70
61A
I-70E Columbus
G-Sunco
F-Arby Bengns CrkBrl Evans Joes LoneS MaxEm OutBk Pdrsa Wendy
L-Comfrt Days Fairfld Knght Motel6 Ramda RedRf
F-Cooker DmnRibs Olive RedLb Ryans Subwy
L-HoJo Rsdnts
60
Little York Rd Eight Stop Rd
EXIT 58 - AIRFORCE MUSEUM - 6 MILES - SEE PAGE 74, MAP PAGE 49
G-Spdwy
F-Frndly LJSilvr Subwy Waffle
Post Office
58
Needmore Rd
G-BP Shell
F-BgBoy Hrdee McDld
L-DaytnLdge
F-Denny
L-BestW Econo
57B
Wagner Ford/Siebenthaler Rd
57A
Neva Dr
G-Sunco
L-H/Inn
Great Miami River
56
Stanley Ave
55AB
Keowee St/Leo St
54C
Rt 4/Webster St
DAYTON
Pop: 182,000
Stay in left two lanes
54B
Rt 48/Main St
53B
Salem Ave/1st St
L-Days
Move to left 2 lanes - Follow "I-75 North to Toledo"
53A
3rd Street
WRIGHT BROTHERS - SEE PAGE 76, MAP PAGE 49
52B
Rt 35/Eaton/Xenia
G-BP Shell
F-McDld
L-Econo
51
Nicholas Rd Edwin C Moses Blvd
SHAWNEE INDIANS - SEE PAGE 76
G-Sunco
L-H/Inn Supr8
50A
Dryden Rd
OHIO
Montgomery County
SOUTH
-75- -74- -73- -72- -71- -70- -69- -68- -67- -66- -65- -64- -63- -62- -61- -60- -59- -58- -57- -56- -55- -54- -53- -52- -51- -50-
1,500 1,000 500

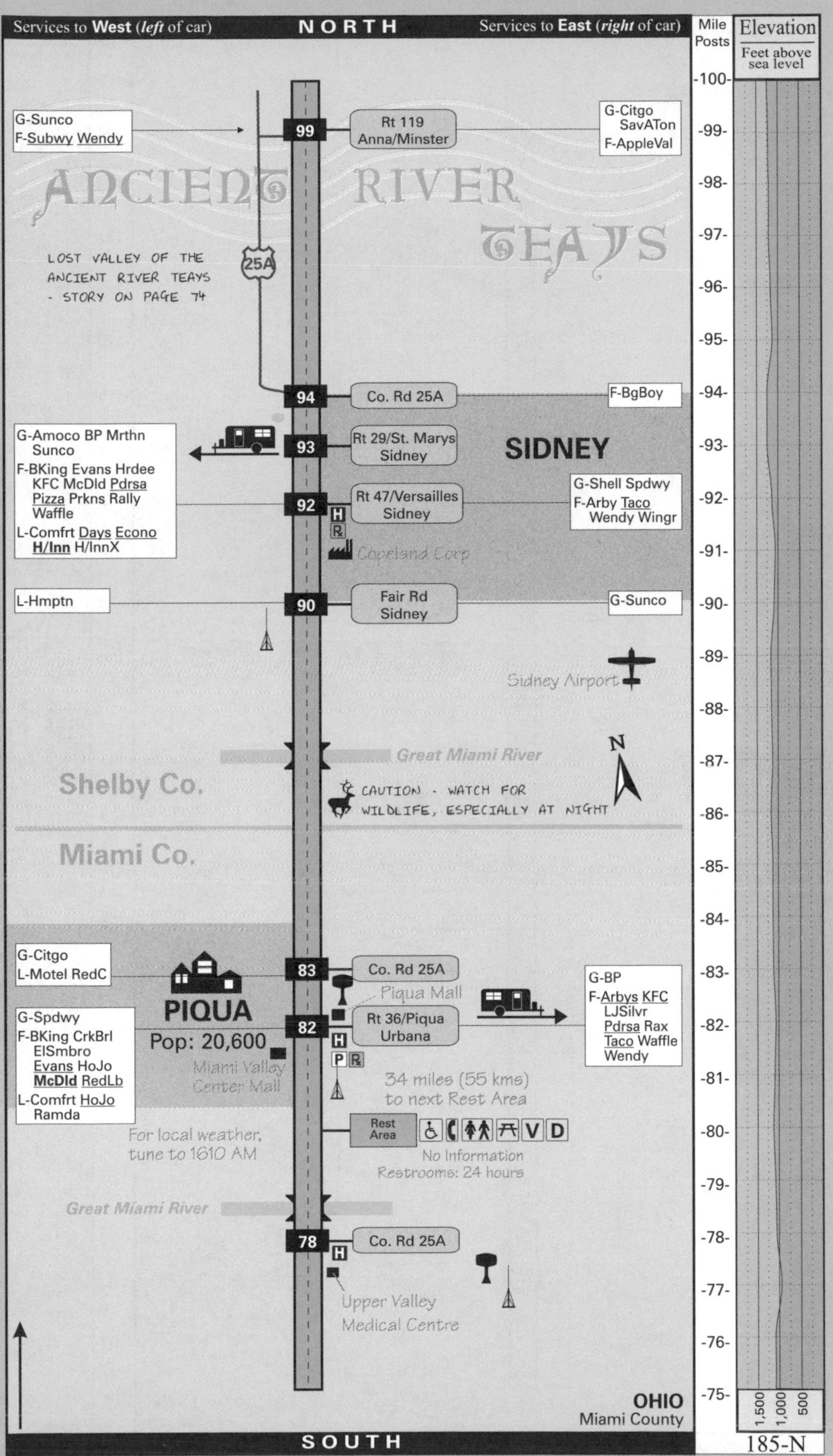

Services to West (left of car)
NORTH
Services to East (right of car)
Mile Posts
Elevation
Feet above sea level
G-Sunco
F-Subwy Wendy
99
Rt 119 Anna/Minster
G-Citgo SavATon
F-AppleVal
ANCIENT RIVER TEAYS
LOST VALLEY OF THE ANCIENT RIVER TEAYS - STORY ON PAGE 74
25A
94
Co. Rd 25A
F-BgBoy
G-Amoco BP Mrthn Sunco
F-BKing Evans Hrdee KFC McDld Pdrsa Pizza Prkns Rally Waffle
L-Comfrt Days Econo H/Inn H/InnX
93
Rt 29/St. Marys Sidney
SIDNEY
92
Rt 47/Versailles Sidney
G-Shell Spdwy
F-Arby Taco Wendy Wingr
Copeland Corp
L-Hmptn
90
Fair Rd Sidney
G-Sunco
Sidney Airport
Great Miami River
N
Shelby Co.
CAUTION - WATCH FOR WILDLIFE, ESPECIALLY AT NIGHT
Miami Co.
G-Citgo
L-Motel RedC
83
Co. Rd 25A
Piqua Mall
PIQUA
Pop: 20,600
G-Spdwy
F-BKing CrkBrl ElSmbro Evans HoJo McDld RedLb
L-Comfrt HoJo Ramda
82
Rt 36/Piqua Urbana
G-BP
F-Arbys KFC LJSilvr Pdrsa Rax Taco Waffle Wendy
Miami Valley Center Mall
34 miles (55 kms) to next Rest Area
Rest Area
V D
No Information
Restrooms: 24 hours
For local weather, tune to 1610 AM
Great Miami River
78
Co. Rd 25A
Upper Valley Medical Centre
OHIO
Miami County
SOUTH
-100- -99- -98- -97- -96- -95- -94- -93- -92- -91- -90- -89- -88- -87- -86- -85- -84- -83- -82- -81- -80- -79- -78- -77- -76- -75-
1,500 1,000 500

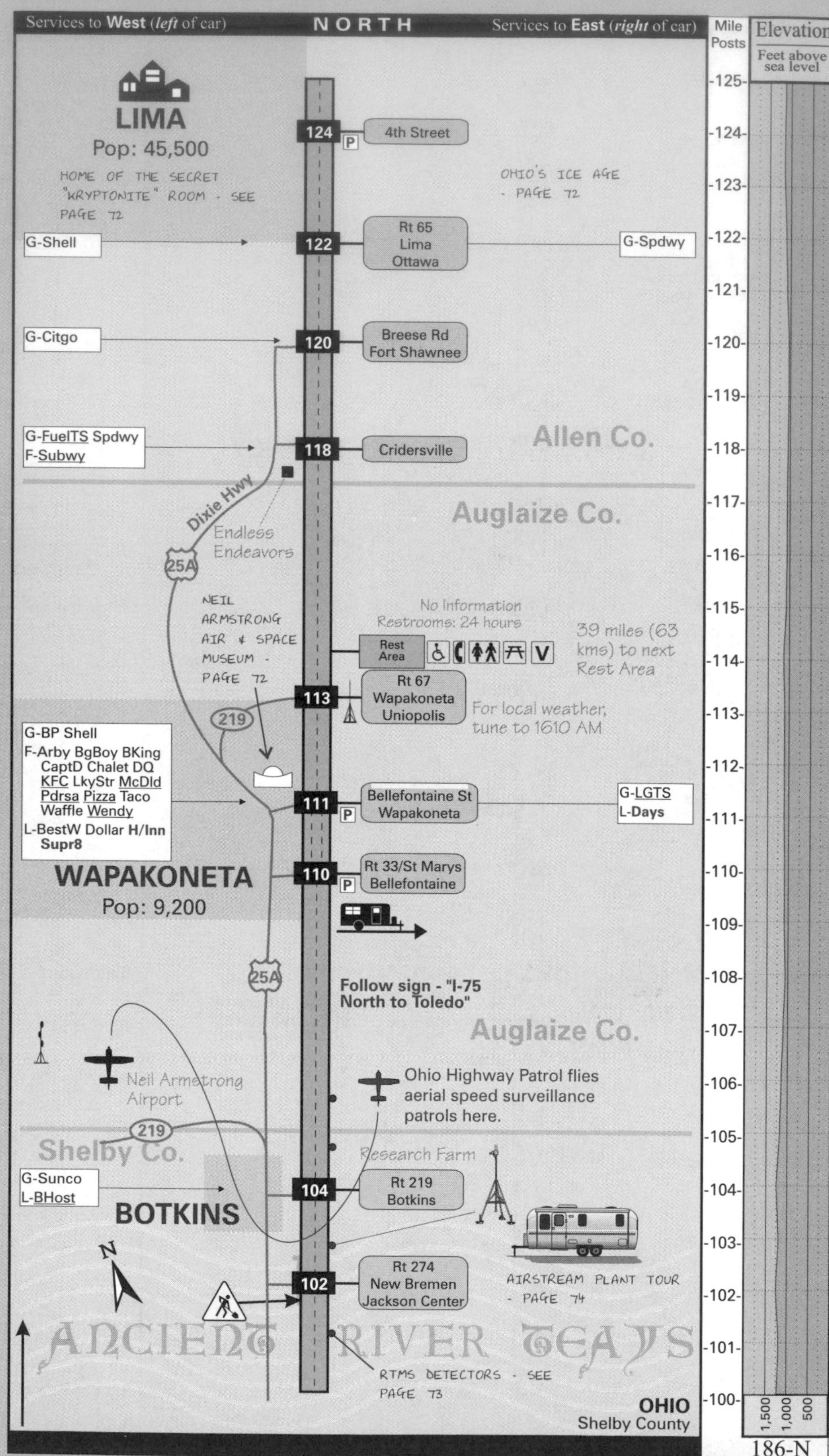

Services to West (left of car)
NORTH
Services to East (right of car)
Mile Posts
Elevation
Feet above sea level
LIMA
Pop: 45,500
HOME OF THE SECRET "KRYPTONITE" ROOM - SEE PAGE 72
OHIO'S ICE AGE - PAGE 72
124
4th Street
G-Shell
122
Rt 65 Lima Ottawa
G-Spdwy
G-Citgo
120
Breese Rd Fort Shawnee
G-FuelTS Spdwy
F-Subwy
118
Cridersville
Allen Co.
Auglaize Co.
Dixie Hwy
Endless Endeavors
25A
NEIL ARMSTRONG AIR & SPACE MUSEUM - PAGE 72
No Information
Restrooms: 24 hours
Rest Area
39 miles (63 kms) to next Rest Area
113
Rt 67 Wapakoneta Uniopolis
219
For local weather, tune to 1610 AM
G-BP Shell
F-Arby BgBoy BKing CaptD Chalet DQ KFC LkyStr McDld Pdrsa Pizza Taco Waffle Wendy
L-BestW Dollar H/Inn Supr8
111
Bellefontaine St Wapakoneta
G-LGTS
L-Days
WAPAKONETA
Pop: 9,200
110
Rt 33/St Marys Bellefontaine
25A
Follow sign - "I-75 North to Toledo"
Auglaize Co.
Neil Armstrong Airport
Ohio Highway Patrol flies aerial speed surveillance patrols here.
219
Shelby Co.
Research Farm
G-Sunco
L-BHost
104
Rt 219 Botkins
BOTKINS
AIRSTREAM PLANT TOUR - PAGE 74
102
Rt 274 New Bremen Jackson Center
ANCIENT RIVER TRAYS
RTMS DETECTORS - SEE PAGE 73
OHIO
Shelby County
-125- -124- -123- -122- -121- -120- -119- -118- -117- -116- -115- -114- -113- -112- -111- -110- -109- -108- -107- -106- -105- -104- -103- -102- -101- -100-
1,500 1,000 500

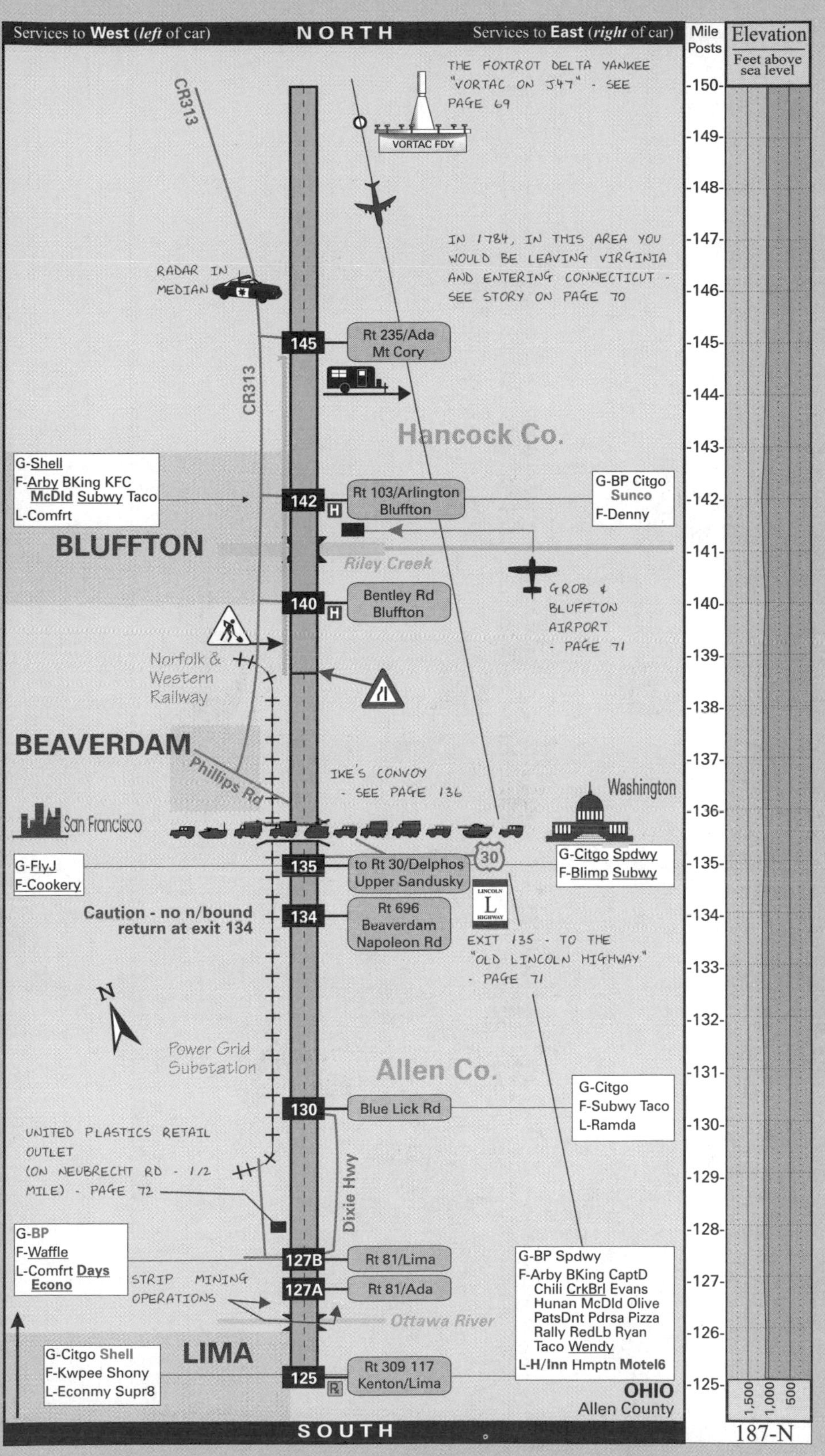
Services to West (left of car)
NORTH
Services to East (right of car)
Mile Posts
Elevation
Feet above sea level
THE FOXTROT DELTA YANKEE "VORTAC ON J47" - SEE PAGE 69
VORTAC FDY
CR313
IN 1784, IN THIS AREA YOU WOULD BE LEAVING VIRGINIA AND ENTERING CONNECTICUT - SEE STORY ON PAGE 70
RADAR IN MEDIAN
145
Rt 235/Ada
Mt Cory
Hancock Co.
G-Shell
F-Arby BKing KFC
McDld Subwy Taco
L-Comfrt
142
Rt 103/Arlington
Bluffton
G-BP Citgo
Sunco
F-Denny
BLUFFTON
Riley Creek
140
Bentley Rd
Bluffton
GROB & BLUFFTON AIRPORT - PAGE 71
Norfolk & Western Railway
BEAVERDAM
Phillips Rd
IKE'S CONVOY - SEE PAGE 136
Washington
San Francisco
G-FlyJ
F-Cookery
135
to Rt 30/Delphos
Upper Sandusky
30
G-Citgo Spdwy
F-Blimp Subwy
LINCOLN L HIGHWAY
134
Rt 696
Beaverdam
Napoleon Rd
Caution - no n/bound return at exit 134
EXIT 135 - TO THE "OLD LINCOLN HIGHWAY" - PAGE 71
N
Power Grid Substation
Allen Co.
130
Blue Lick Rd
G-Citgo
F-Subwy Taco
L-Ramda
UNITED PLASTICS RETAIL OUTLET (ON NEUBRECHT RD - 1/2 MILE) - PAGE 72
Dixie Hwy
G-BP
F-Waffle
L-Comfrt Days
Econo
127B
Rt 81/Lima
127A
Rt 81/Ada
STRIP MINING OPERATIONS
Ottawa River
G-BP Spdwy
F-Arby BKing CaptD
Chili CrkBrl Evans
Hunan McDld Olive
PatsDnt Pdrsa Pizza
Rally RedLb Ryan
Taco Wendy
L-H/Inn Hmptn Motel6
G-Citgo Shell
F-Kwpee Shony
L-Econmy Supr8
LIMA
125
Rt 309 117
Kenton/Lima
OHIO
Allen County
SOUTH
-150- -149- -148- -147- -146- -145- -144- -143- -142- -141- -140- -139- -138- -137- -136- -135- -134- -133- -132- -131- -130- -129- -128- -127- -126- -125-
1,500 1,000 500

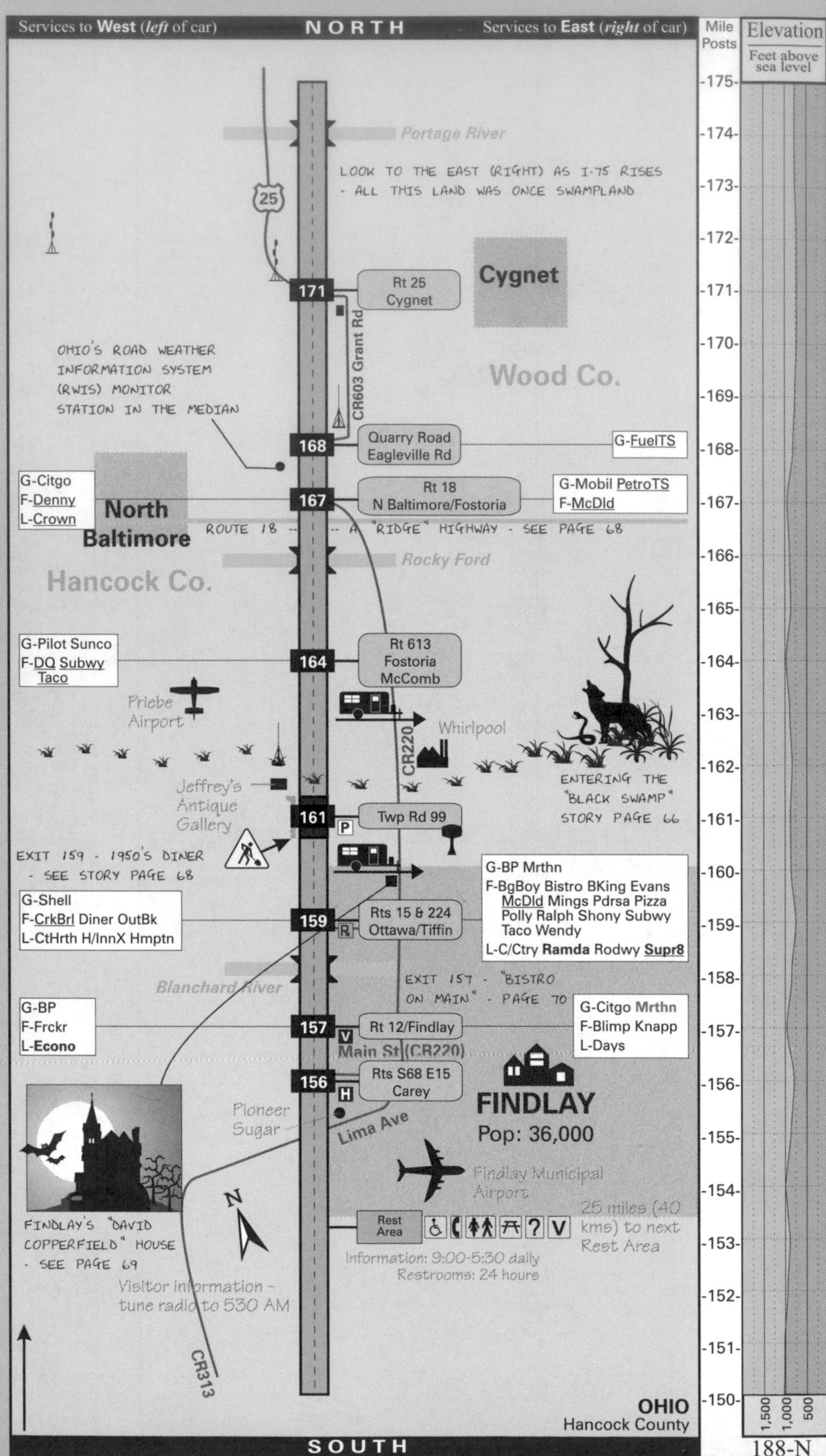

Services to West (left of car)
NORTH
Services to East (right of car)
Mile Posts
Elevation
Feet above sea level
Portage River
LOOK TO THE EAST (RIGHT) AS I-75 RISES - ALL THIS LAND WAS ONCE SWAMPLAND
25
Cygnet
171
Rt 25 Cygnet
CR603 Grant Rd
Wood Co.
OHIO'S ROAD WEATHER INFORMATION SYSTEM (RWIS) MONITOR STATION IN THE MEDIAN
168
Quarry Road Eagleville Rd
G-FuelTS
G-Citgo
F-Denny
L-Crown
North Baltimore
167
Rt 18 N Baltimore/Fostoria
G-Mobil PetroTS
F-McDld
ROUTE 18 -- A "RIDGE" HIGHWAY - SEE PAGE 68
Rocky Ford
Hancock Co.
G-Pilot Sunco
F-DQ Subwy Taco
164
Rt 613 Fostoria McComb
Priebe Airport
Whirlpool
CR220
Jeffrey's Antique Gallery
ENTERING THE "BLACK SWAMP" STORY PAGE 66
161
Twp Rd 99
EXIT 159 - 1950'S DINER - SEE STORY PAGE 68
G-BP Mrthn
F-BgBoy Bistro BKing Evans McDld Mings Pdrsa Pizza Polly Ralph Shony Subwy Taco Wendy
L-C/Ctry Ramda Rodwy Supr8
G-Shell
F-CrkBrl Diner OutBk
L-CtHrth H/InnX Hmptn
159
Rts 15 & 224 Ottawa/Tiffin
Blanchard River
EXIT 157 - "BISTRO ON MAIN" - PAGE 70
G-BP
F-Frckr
L-Econo
157
Rt 12/Findlay
G-Citgo Mrthn
F-Blimp Knapp
L-Days
Main St (CR220)
156
Rts S68 E15 Carey
FINDLAY
Pop: 36,000
Pioneer Sugar
Lima Ave
Findlay Municipal Airport
Rest Area
25 miles (40 kms) to next Rest Area
Information: 9:00-5:30 daily
Restrooms: 24 hours
FINDLAY'S "DAVID COPPERFIELD" HOUSE - SEE PAGE 69
Visitor information - tune radio to 530 AM
CR313
OHIO
Hancock County
SOUTH
-175- -174- -173- -172- -171- -170- -169- -168- -167- -166- -165- -164- -163- -162- -161- -160- -159- -158- -157- -156- -155- -154- -153- -152- -151- -150-
1,500 1,000 500
188-N

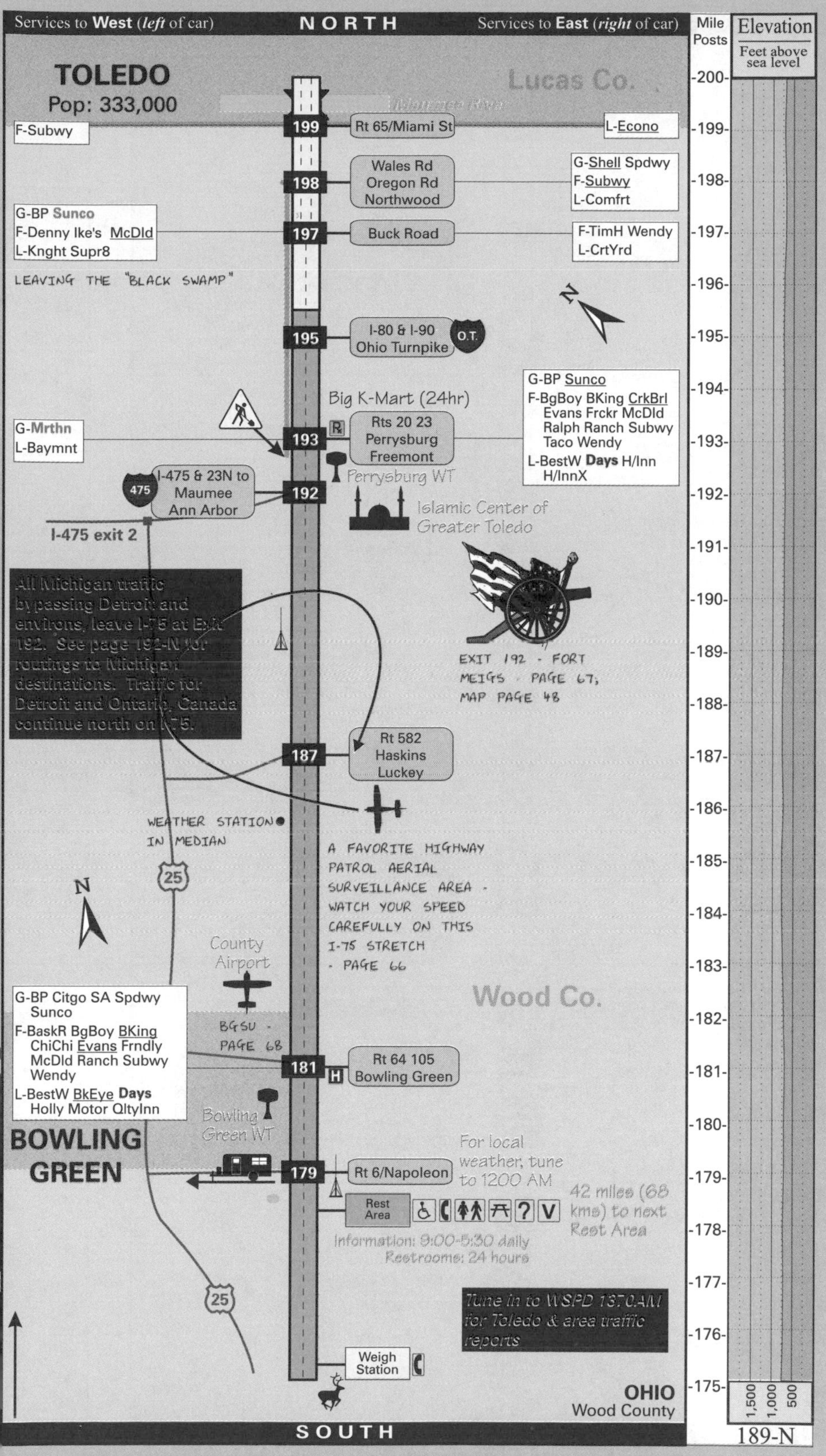

Services to West (left of car)
NORTH
Services to East (right of car)
Mile Posts
Elevation
Feet above sea level
TOLEDO
Pop: 333,000
Lucas Co.
F-Subwy
199
Rt 65/Miami St
L-Econo
198
Wales Rd
Oregon Rd
Northwood
G-Shell Spdwy
F-Subwy
L-Comfrt
G-BP Sunco
F-Denny Ike's McDld
L-Knght Supr8
197
Buck Road
F-TimH Wendy
L-CrtYrd
LEAVING THE "BLACK SWAMP"
195
I-80 & I-90
Ohio Turnpike
O.T.
G-BP Sunco
F-BgBoy BKing CrkBrl
Evans Frckr McDld
Ralph Ranch Subwy
Taco Wendy
L-BestW Days H/Inn
H/InnX
Big K-Mart (24hr)
G-Mrthn
L-Baymnt
193
Rts 20 23
Perrysburg
Freemont
Perrysburg WT
475
I-475 & 23N to
Maumee
Ann Arbor
192
Islamic Center of
Greater Toledo
I-475 exit 2
All Michigan traffic bypassing Detroit and environs, leave I-75 at Exit 192. See page 192-N for routings to Michigan destinations. Traffic for Detroit and Ontario, Canada continue north on I-75.
EXIT 192 - FORT
MEIGS - PAGE 67;
MAP PAGE 48
187
Rt 582
Haskins
Luckey
WEATHER STATION
IN MEDIAN
A FAVORITE HIGHWAY
PATROL AERIAL
SURVEILLANCE AREA -
WATCH YOUR SPEED
CAREFULLY ON THIS
I-75 STRETCH
- PAGE 66
25
N
County
Airport
Wood Co.
G-BP Citgo SA Spdwy
Sunco
F-BaskR BgBoy BKing
ChiChi Evans Frndly
McDld Ranch Subwy
Wendy
L-BestW BkEye Days
Holly Motor QltyInn
BGSU -
PAGE 68
181
H
Rt 64 105
Bowling Green
Bowling
Green WT
BOWLING
GREEN
179
Rt 6/Napoleon
For local
weather, tune
to 1200 AM
Rest
Area
V
42 miles (68 kms) to next Rest Area
Information: 9:00-5:30 daily
Restrooms: 24 hours
25
Tune in to WSPD 1370AM for Toledo & area traffic reports
Weigh
Station
OHIO
Wood County
SOUTH
-200-
-199-
-198-
-197-
-196-
-195-
-194-
-193-
-192-
-191-
-190-
-189-
-188-
-187-
-186-
-185-
-184-
-183-
-182-
-181-
-180-
-179-
-178-
-177-
-176-
-175-
1,500
1,000
500

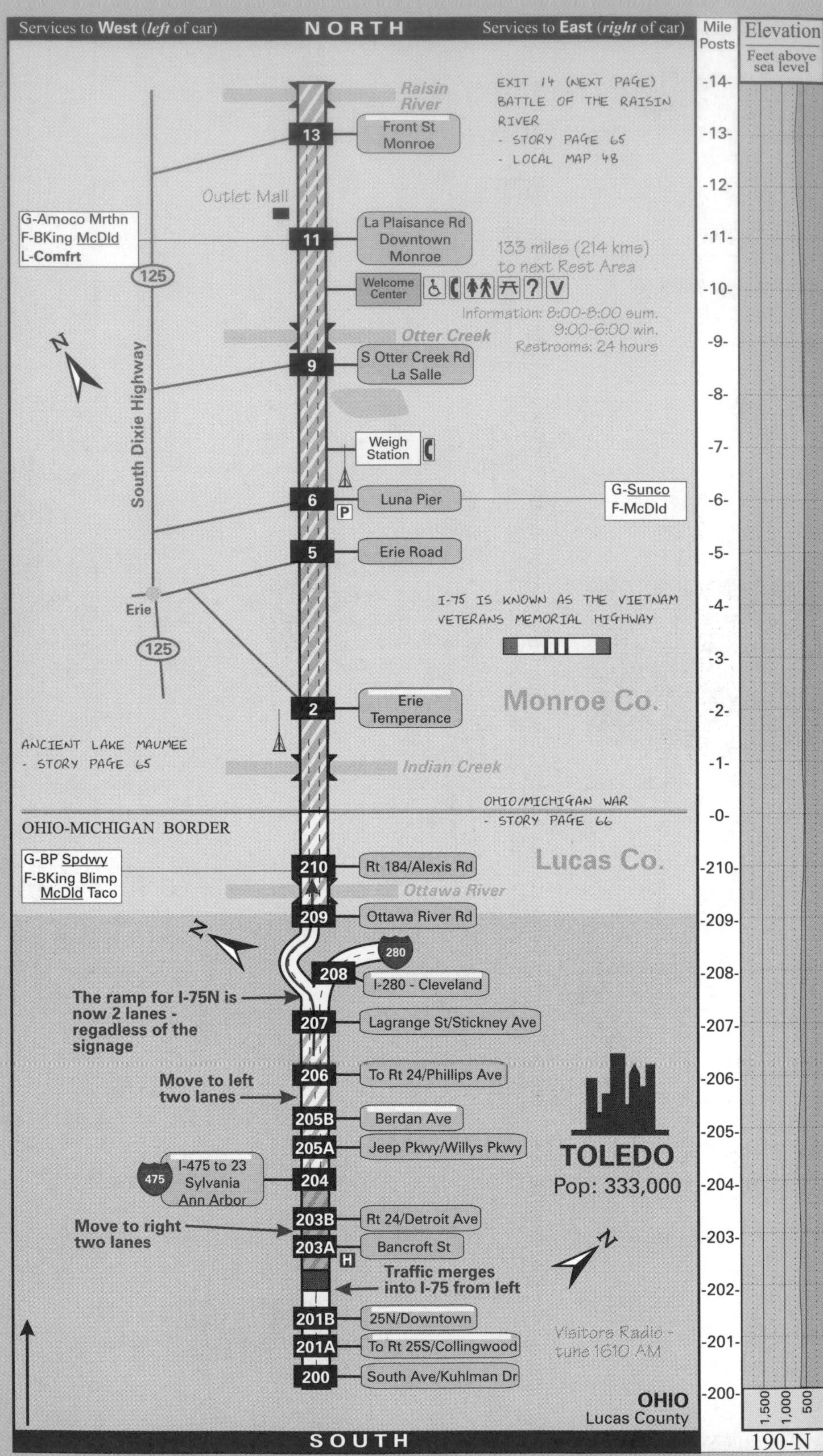

Services to West (left of car)
NORTH
Services to East (right of car)
Mile Posts
Elevation
Feet above sea level
Raisin River
EXIT 14 (NEXT PAGE) BATTLE OF THE RAISIN RIVER
- STORY PAGE 65
- LOCAL MAP 48
13
Front St Monroe
Outlet Mall
G-Amoco Mrthn
F-BKing McDld
L-Comfrt
11
La Plaisance Rd Downtown Monroe
133 miles (214 kms) to next Rest Area
125
Welcome Center
Information: 8:00-8:00 sum. 9:00-6:00 win.
Restrooms: 24 hours
Otter Creek
9
S Otter Creek Rd La Salle
South Dixie Highway
Weigh Station
6
Luna Pier
G-Sunco
F-McDld
5
Erie Road
Erie
I-75 IS KNOWN AS THE VIETNAM VETERANS MEMORIAL HIGHWAY
125
2
Erie Temperance
Monroe Co.
ANCIENT LAKE MAUMEE
- STORY PAGE 65
Indian Creek
OHIO/MICHIGAN WAR
- STORY PAGE 66
OHIO-MICHIGAN BORDER
G-BP Spdwy
F-BKing Blimp McDld Taco
210
Rt 184/Alexis Rd
Lucas Co.
Ottawa River
209
Ottawa River Rd
280
208
I-280 - Cleveland
The ramp for I-75N is now 2 lanes - regadless of the signage
207
Lagrange St/Stickney Ave
206
To Rt 24/Phillips Ave
Move to left two lanes
205B
Berdan Ave
205A
Jeep Pkwy/Willys Pkwy
TOLEDO
Pop: 333,000
475
I-475 to 23 Sylvania Ann Arbor
204
Move to right two lanes
203B
Rt 24/Detroit Ave
203A
Bancroft St
Traffic merges into I-75 from left
201B
25N/Downtown
201A
To Rt 25S/Collingwood
Visitors Radio - tune 1610 AM
200
South Ave/Kuhlman Dr
OHIO
Lucas County
SOUTH
-14- -13- -12- -11- -10- -9- -8- -7- -6- -5- -4- -3- -2- -1- -0-
-210- -209- -208- -207- -206- -205- -204- -203- -202- -201- -200-
1,500 1,000 500

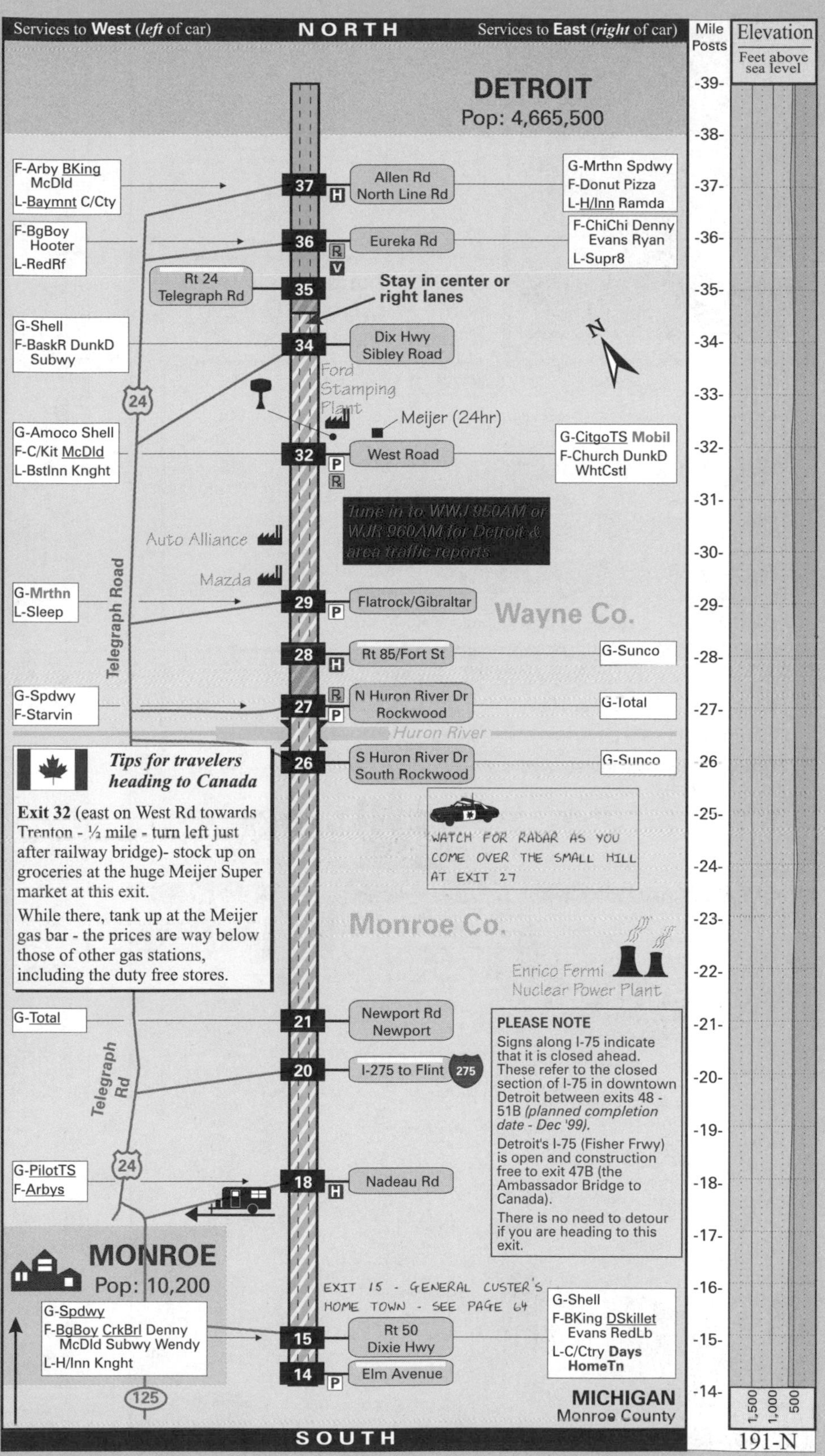

Services to West (left of car)
NORTH
Services to East (right of car)
Mile Posts
Elevation
Feet above sea level
DETROIT
Pop: 4,665,500
F-Arby BKing McDld
L-Baymnt C/Cty
37
Allen Rd North Line Rd
G-Mrthn Spdwy
F-Donut Pizza
L-H/Inn Ramda
F-BgBoy Hooter
L-RedRf
36
Eureka Rd
F-ChiChi Denny Evans Ryan
L-Supr8
Rt 24 Telegraph Rd
35
Stay in center or right lanes
G-Shell
F-BaskR DunkD Subwy
34
Dix Hwy Sibley Road
N
Ford Stamping Plant
24
Meijer (24hr)
G-Amoco Shell
F-C/Kit McDld
L-BstInn Knght
32
West Road
G-CitgoTS Mobil
F-Church DunkD WhtCstl
Tune in to WWJ 950AM or WJR 960AM for Detroit & area traffic reports
Auto Alliance
Mazda
Telegraph Road
G-Mrthn
L-Sleep
29
Flatrock/Gibraltar
Wayne Co.
28
Rt 85/Fort St
G-Sunco
G-Spdwy
F-Starvin
27
N Huron River Dr Rockwood
G-Total
Huron River
26
S Huron River Dr South Rockwood
G-Sunco
Tips for travelers heading to Canada
Exit 32 (east on West Rd towards Trenton - ½ mile - turn left just after railway bridge)- stock up on groceries at the huge Meijer Super market at this exit.
While there, tank up at the Meijer gas bar - the prices are way below those of other gas stations, including the duty free stores.
WATCH FOR RADAR AS YOU COME OVER THE SMALL HILL AT EXIT 27
Monroe Co.
Enrico Fermi Nuclear Power Plant
G-Total
21
Newport Rd Newport
PLEASE NOTE
Signs along I-75 indicate that it is closed ahead. These refer to the closed section of I-75 in downtown Detroit between exits 48 - 51B (planned completion date - Dec '99).
Detroit's I-75 (Fisher Frwy) is open and construction free to exit 47B (the Ambassador Bridge to Canada).
There is no need to detour if you are heading to this exit.
Telegraph Rd
20
I-275 to Flint
275
24
G-PilotTS
F-Arbys
18
Nadeau Rd
MONROE
Pop: 10,200
EXIT 15 - GENERAL CUSTER'S HOME TOWN - SEE PAGE 64
G-Spdwy
F-BgBoy CrkBrl Denny McDld Subwy Wendy
L-H/Inn Knght
15
Rt 50 Dixie Hwy
G-Shell
F-BKing DSkillet Evans RedLb
L-C/Ctry Days HomeTn
14
Elm Avenue
125
MICHIGAN
Monroe County
SOUTH
-39- -38- -37- -36- -35- -34- -33- -32- -31- -30- -29- -28- -27- -26- -25- -24- -23- -22- -21- -20- -19- -18- -17- -16- -15- -14-
1,500 1,000 500

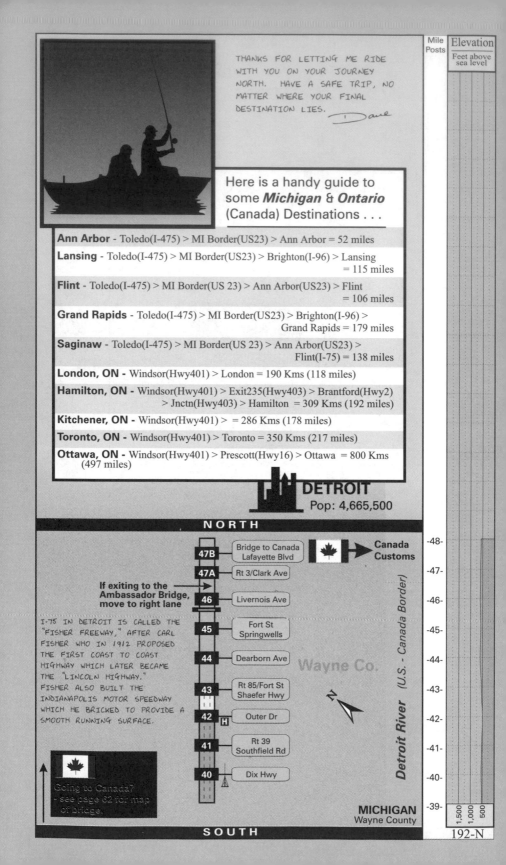

THANKS FOR LETTING ME RIDE WITH YOU ON YOUR JOURNEY NORTH. HAVE A SAFE TRIP, NO MATTER WHERE YOUR FINAL DESTINATION LIES. — Dave

Here is a handy guide to some *Michigan* & *Ontario* (Canada) Destinations . . .

Ann Arbor - Toledo(I-475) > MI Border(US23) > Ann Arbor = 52 miles

Lansing - Toledo(I-475) > MI Border(US23) > Brighton(I-96) > Lansing = 115 miles

Flint - Toledo(I-475) > MI Border(US 23) > Ann Arbor(US23) > Flint = 106 miles

Grand Rapids - Toledo(I-475) > MI Border(US23) > Brighton(I-96) > Grand Rapids = 179 miles

Saginaw - Toledo(I-475) > MI Border(US 23) > Ann Arbor(US23) > Flint(I-75) = 138 miles

London, ON - Windsor(Hwy401) > London = 190 Kms (118 miles)

Hamilton, ON - Windsor(Hwy401) > Exit235(Hwy403) > Brantford(Hwy2) > Jnctn(Hwy403) > Hamilton = 309 Kms (192 miles)

Kitchener, ON - Windsor(Hwy401) > = 286 Kms (178 miles)

Toronto, ON - Windsor(Hwy401) > Toronto = 350 Kms (217 miles)

Ottawa, ON - Windsor(Hwy401) > Prescott(Hwy16) > Ottawa = 800 Kms (497 miles)

DETROIT
Pop: 4,665,500

Mile Posts	Elevation (Feet above sea level)

NORTH

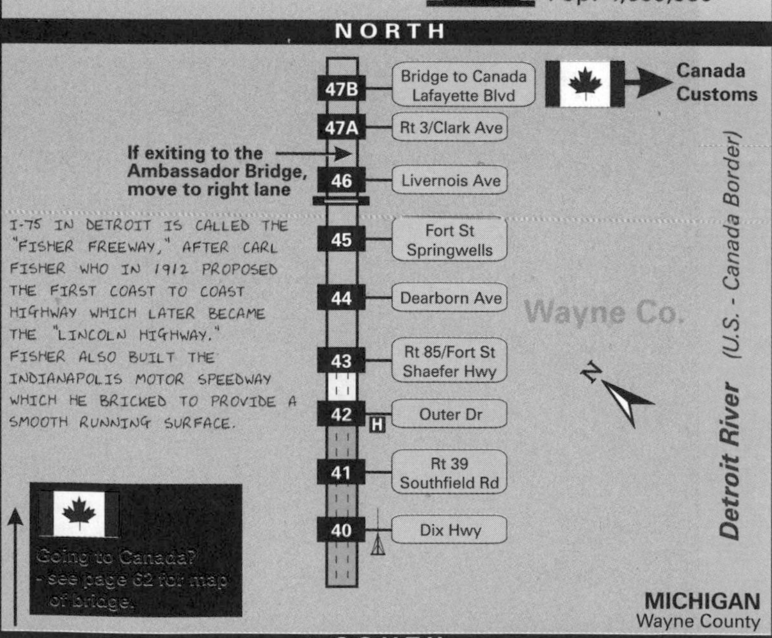

I-75 IN DETROIT IS CALLED THE "FISHER FREEWAY," AFTER CARL FISHER WHO IN 1912 PROPOSED THE FIRST COAST TO COAST HIGHWAY WHICH LATER BECAME THE "LINCOLN HIGHWAY." FISHER ALSO BUILT THE INDIANAPOLIS MOTOR SPEEDWAY WHICH HE BRICKED TO PROVIDE A SMOOTH RUNNING SURFACE.

Going to Canada?
- see page 62 for map of bridge.

SOUTH

Traffic Radio

Nobody likes rush hour traffic. Fortunately, the I-75 cities have some of the best traffic reporters in the Nation - on the ground and in the air - to speed you through the interstate cities.

To further help you on your way, the following pages provide bypass routes for Cincinnati, Atlanta and Macon. The following "rush hour" notes will help you decide whether you should take them or go through the city.

Detroit - morning rush hours are 7:00-9:00; afternoon, 4:00-6:30. For best traffic information, tune in the team of ***John Bailey*** (on the ground) and ***Tracy Gary*** (in the air) on **WWJ 950AM**, or the wider area traffic reports on **WJR 760AM**.

Toledo - morning rush hours are 7:30-9:00; afternoon, 4:30-6:00. Listen to **WSPD 1370AM**.

Dayton - morning rush hours are 7:30-9:00; afternoon, 4:30-6:00. Join ***Major Dick Hale - "The Dixter"*** on **WONE 980AM's "Airwatch Traffic."**

Cincinnati - morning rush hours are 7:00-9:00; afternoon, 3:00-6:00. Helicopter traffic reports from **WLW 700AM**'s ***John Phillips*** and ***Dave Armbruster*** will speed you through the "Queen City."

Lexington - morning rush hours are 8:00-9:00; afternoon, 4:30-5:30. ***Officer Don Evans*** on **WVLK 590AM** will help you around Lex's traffic.

Knoxville - morning rush hours are 7:00-9:00; afternoon, 4:30-6:00. Listen to ***Dave Foulk*** on **WNOX 990AM's** morning traffic and ***Ed Rupp*** in the afternoon.

Chattanooga - morning rush hours are 7:00-9:00; afternoon, 4:30-6:30 . . . but they shouldn't bother your too much unless morning I-24 traffic backs up onto I-75. Stay tuned to **WOGT 107.9FM's** Sky King ***Butch Johnson*** to check this out.

Atlanta - morning rush hours are 7:00-9:00; afternoon, 4:30-6:30. **WSB 750AM's** ***Captain Herb Emory*** is in the air in the WSB chopper - on the job all over the city.

Macon - You're on the I-475 Macon Bypass so you should be OK . . . **WAYS 99.1FM's** ***Mike Wade*** at the Traffic Center will keep an eye on thing for you, though.

Tifton/Valdosta - listen to **WTIF 1340AM.**

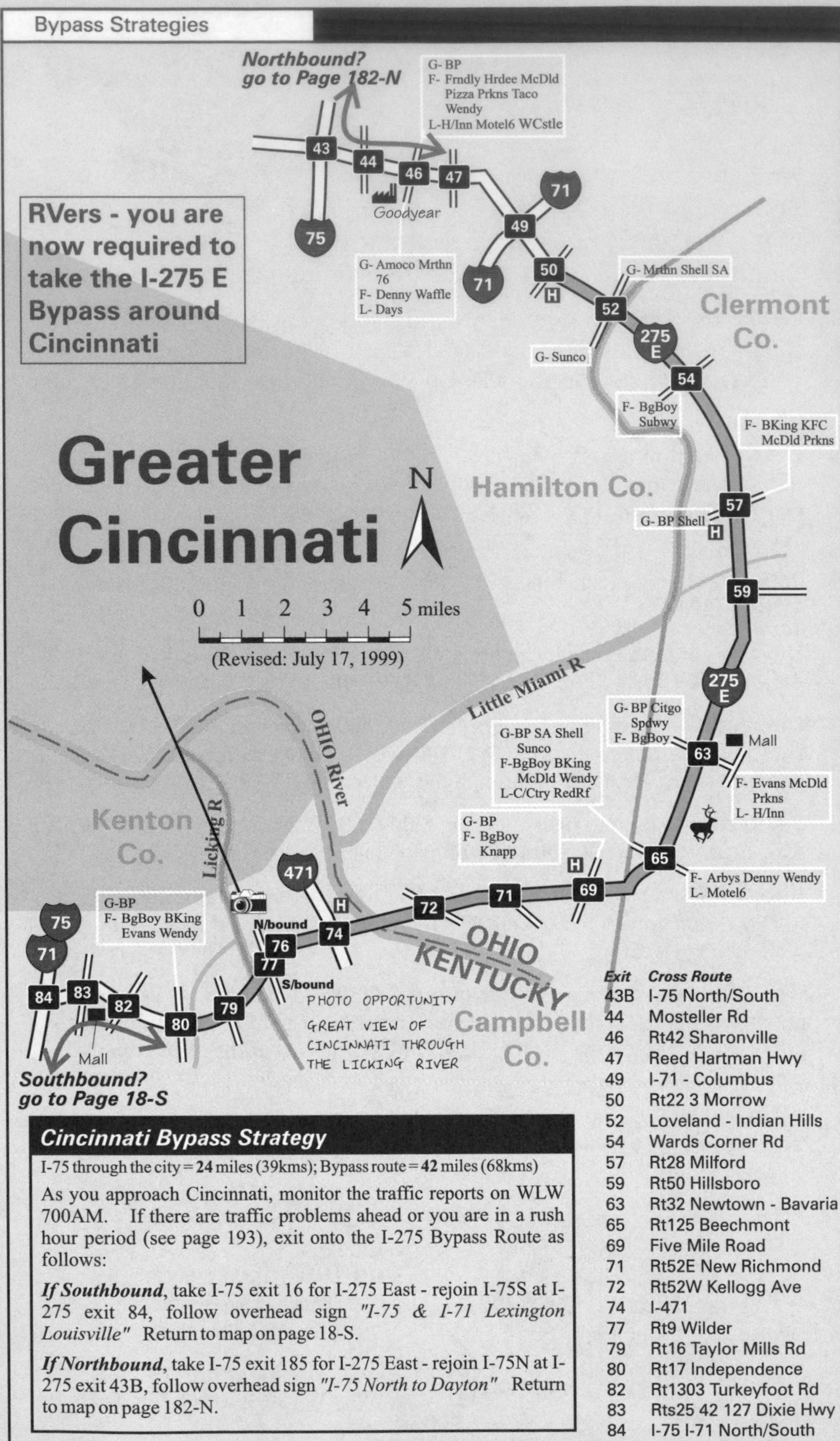

Cincinnati Bypass Strategy

I-75 through the city = **24** miles (39kms); Bypass route = **42** miles (68kms)

As you approach Cincinnati, monitor the traffic reports on WLW 700AM. If there are traffic problems ahead or you are in a rush hour period (see page 193), exit onto the I-275 Bypass Route as follows:

If Southbound, take I-75 exit 16 for I-275 East - rejoin I-75S at I-275 exit 84, follow overhead sign *"I-75 & I-71 Lexington Louisville"* Return to map on page 18-S.

If Northbound, take I-75 exit 185 for I-275 East - rejoin I-75N at I-275 exit 43B, follow overhead sign *"I-75 North to Dayton"* Return to map on page 182-N.

Exit	*Cross Route*
43B	I-75 North/South
44	Mosteller Rd
46	Rt42 Sharonville
47	Reed Hartman Hwy
49	I-71 - Columbus
50	Rt22 3 Morrow
52	Loveland - Indian Hills
54	Wards Corner Rd
57	Rt28 Milford
59	Rt50 Hillsboro
63	Rt32 Newtown - Bavaria
65	Rt125 Beechmont
69	Five Mile Road
71	Rt52E New Richmond
72	Rt52W Kellogg Ave
74	I-471
77	Rt9 Wilder
79	Rt16 Taylor Mills Rd
80	Rt17 Independence
82	Rt1303 Turkeyfoot Rd
83	Rts25 42 127 Dixie Hwy
84	I-75 I-71 North/South

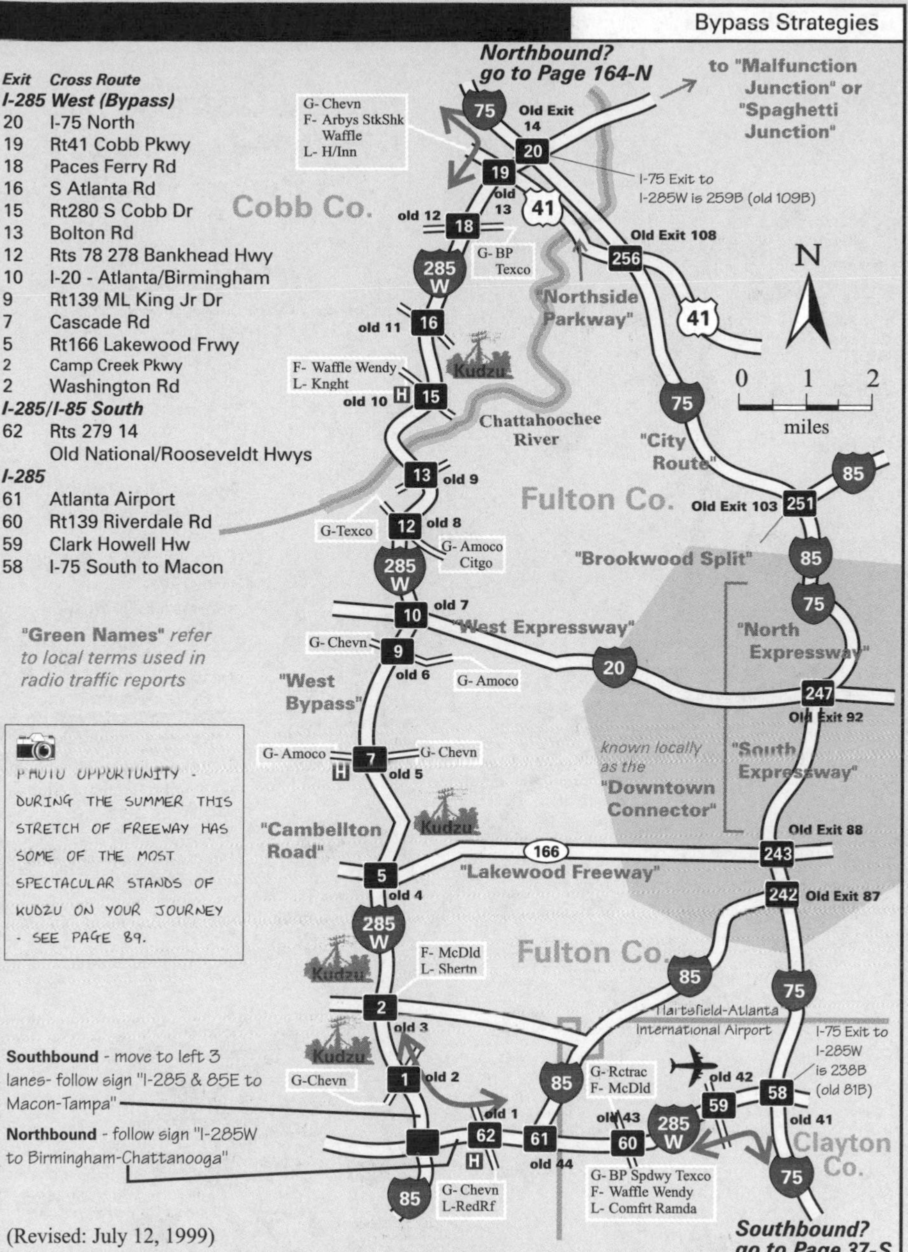

(Revised: July 12, 1999)

Atlanta Bypass Strategy

I-75 through the city = **20** miles (32kms); Bypass route = 25 miles (40kms)

As you approach Atlanta, monitor the traffic reports on WSB 750AM. If there are traffic problems ahead or you are in a rush hour period (see page 179), exit onto the I-285 Bypass Route as follows:

If Southbound, take I-75 exit 259 (old 109) for I-285 West - rejoin I-75S at I-285 exit 58 (old 41), follow overhead sign *"I-75 Macon Tampa"* **Caution** - on ramp, stay right until after split for I-75 North then move ***left quickly*** because ramp becomes single lane. Return to map on page 37-S.

If Northbound, take I-75 exit 238B (old 81B) for I-285 West - rejoin I-75N at I-285 exit 20 (old 14). On ramp, move to the left two lanes and follow overhead sign *"I-75 to Marietta/Chattanooga"* Return to map on page 164-N.

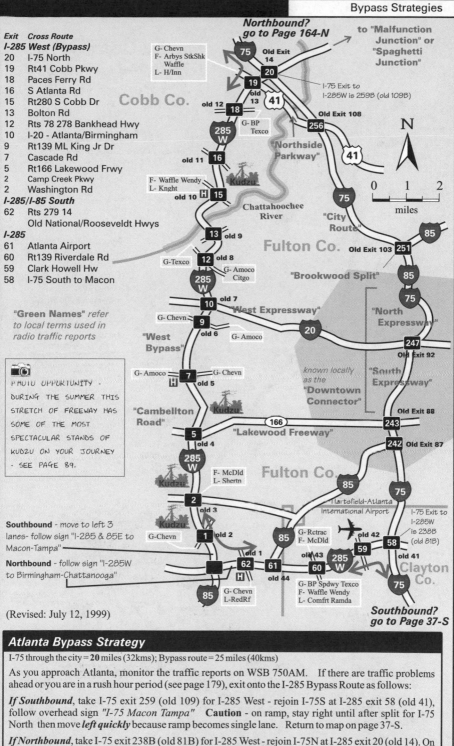

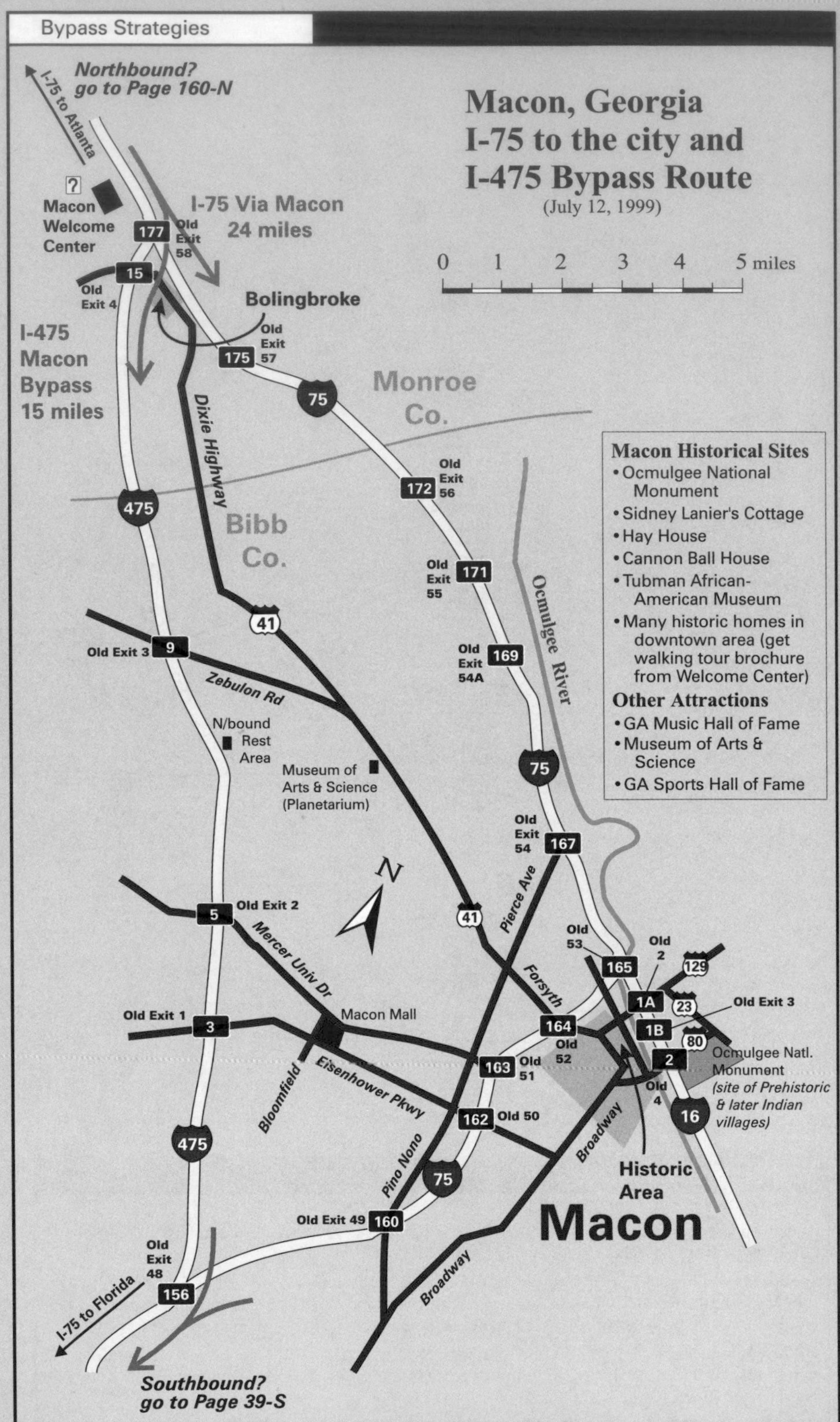
Macon, Georgia
I-75 to the city and
I-475 Bypass Route
(July 12, 1999)
0 1 2 3 4 5 miles
Northbound?
go to Page 160-N
I-75 to Atlanta
Macon
Welcome
Center
177
Old
Exit
58
I-75 Via Macon
24 miles
15
Old
Exit 4
Bolingbroke
I-475
Macon
Bypass
15 miles
Old
Exit
57
175
75
Monroe
Co.
Dixie Highway
Macon Historical Sites
• Ocmulgee National Monument
• Sidney Lanier's Cottage
• Hay House
• Cannon Ball House
• Tubman African-American Museum
• Many historic homes in downtown area (get walking tour brochure from Welcome Center)
Other Attractions
• GA Music Hall of Fame
• Museum of Arts & Science
• GA Sports Hall of Fame
Old
Exit
56
172
475
Bibb
Co.
Old
Exit
55
171
Ocmulgee River
41
Old Exit 3
9
Old
Exit
54A
169
Zebulon Rd
N/bound
Rest
Area
Museum of
Arts & Science
(Planetarium)
75
Old
Exit
54
167
N
Pierce Ave
Old Exit 2
5
41
Old
53
Old
2
Mercer Univ Dr
165
129
Forsyth
1A
Old Exit 3
23
Old Exit 1
3
Macon Mall
164
1B
80
Old
52
Ocmulgee Natl.
Monument
(site of Prehistoric
& later Indian
villages)
Bloomfield
Eisenhower Pkwy
163
Old
51
2
Old
4
162
Old 50
16
475
Broadway
Historic
Area
Pino Nono
75
Old Exit 49
160
Macon
Old
Exit
48
156
I-75 to Florida
Broadway
Southbound?
go to Page 39-S

A word about this year's listings.

Many of our readers now have access to the internet - in fact, retirees are the fastest growth group on the World Wide Web according to recent surveys. AARP has even added computer courses for "seniors" to its website. To assist you with your I-75 information needs, I have included website addresses for those information sources that have them. Don't forget, *"Along I-75"* is also now "on-line" at - **www.i75online.com**

Early next year, we plan to add updated I-75 information to this site on an ongoing basis, so purchasers of this book can obtain the most recent information such as gas prices, construction, etc., for their I-75 trip.

American Association of Retired Persons (AARP), - (www.aarp.org).
Box 199, Long Beach CA 90801. Every eligible person should belong to this organization; the annual membership is so low and the benefits broad.

American Automobile Association (AAA) - (www.aaa.com).
Check phone book for number of your local club. Emergency road number: **1-800-AAA-HELP**, (in Canada: 1-800-CAA-HELP). I would not consider traveling by car without this membership. I have had to use emergency services on several occasion and always found AAA to be responsive and solved my problems easily. Great peace of mind!

Armored Cav, by Tom Clancy,
pub: Berkley Books, NY Available at most bookstores (ISBN: 0-425-15836-5). An excellent book, jammed with facts for those who enjoy military subjects. The source of information about Lima's Kryptonite room and the Abrams M1A2 Battle Tank.

Battlefield Atlas of the Civil War,
pub: NAPCA, 8 W Madison St, Baltimore MD 21201 (phone: 301-659-0220)

Canadian Association of Retired Persons (CARP) - (www.fifty-plus.net).
27 Queen Street, Suite 1304, Toronto ON M5C 2M8

Canadian Automobile Association (CAA) - (www.caa.ca).
Check phone book for number of your local club. Emergency road number: **1-800-CAA-HELP**, (in the USA: 1-800-AAA-HELP)

Canadian Snowbird Association, - (www.snowbirds.org)
180 Lesmill Road, North York ON M3B 2T5 (phone: 1-800-265-3200). If you are Canadian, and spend your winters in the South, you should consider becoming a member of this organization. Low annual membership fees, many discounts and benefits, this 100,000+ members organization has become the "voice" of the Canadian "snowbirds."

City Behind A Fence, Oak Ridge TN 1942-1946
Indispensable source for anybody interested in the development of the atomic bomb, and the role played by Oak Ridges during the war years. Available through the Univ. of TN Press - ISBN: 0-87049-303-4

Civil War Battlefield Guide,
pub: by Houghton Mifflin (ISBN: 0-395-52282-X)

Consumer Reports Travel Buying Guide,
101 Truman Ave., Yonkers NY 10703 Available at most bookstores. Issued annually, this guide provides an insight into various aspects of the tourist industry.

Delorme Mapping Company, - (www.delorme.com).
Box 298, Freeport, MN 04032; phone: 1-800-227-1656. Available at many larger bookstores. Delorme issues an excellent set of large scale map guides, state by state. Michigan, Ohio, Tennessee and Florida are already available. We wouldn't travel Florida without our Delorme guide in the car.

EIG - Exit Information Guide Hotel Discount Travel Guides - (www.exitguide.com).
4205 NW 6th Street, Gainesville FL 32609; phone: 1-800-332-3948. Send away for your free coupon books before you travel. EIG charges $3 s&h for the first book, plus $1 for each additional. Add $5 for guides mailed to Canada.

Florida Bound, the essential Guide for Canadian Snowbirds, by Andrew Cumming - (www.floridabound.com)
An excellent book for Canadians crossing the Canada-US border and spending significant time in Florida. Available through most bookstores (ISBN: 0-7715-7584-X) or the internet world wide web site listed above.

Highway Patrol Reference Guide,
Order through Grays Electronics, 99 E Central St, Natick, MA 01760 1-800-248-5441. If you spend a lot of time on the road, this book provide a lot of interesting information. It summarizes state by state, everything you ever wanted to know about Highway Patrol speed enforcement - numbers, types of patrol cars and their markings, speed equipment used, and much more.

Long Hunter, The, (Life of Daniel Boone), by L. Elliott
May be out of print (ISBN: 0-88349-066-8), but try your local library. One of the best accounts we have read of Daniel Boone, and his travels.

MA - Market America Motel Discount Coupon Books
Box 7069, Gadsden AL 35906 (phone: 256-547-4321). Send away for your coupon books before you travel. MA charge $2 per book, to cover postage and handling ($3 to Canada).

National Motorists Association, - (www.motorists.org)
402 West 2nd St, Waunakee, WI 53597. (phone: 608-849-6000). An organization dedicated to various matters of concern to motorists, traffic and road safety. An excellent source for information about fighting unfair tickets

Traveling With Your Pet (The AAA Petbook)
Contains many pet travel tips and 466 pages listing "pet friendly" motels. An excellent resource book for people traveling with pets - available from any AAA (or CAA) office.

Traffic Radar Handbook, by Donald Sawicki
The definitive work on police radar. No longer in print but complete text is available online at http://user.aol.com/copradar/index.html

Trailer Life (Good Sam) RV Park & Services Directory, - (www.goodsamclub.com).
Box 11097, Des Moines IA 50336 phone: 1-800-234-3450. One of the two essential campground and RV services guides to have aboard your RV (see also, "Woodall's")

Unofficial Guide to Walt Disney World, by Bob Sehlinger
pub: Prentice Hall. Order through most bookstores (ISBN 0-02-862616-8). Don't consider a visit to WDW without this book. Far superior to any of the other guides ("official" and "unofficial") because it is *objective*. Many money and time saving tips.

Valentine Research, - (www.valentine1.com).
10280 Alliance Road, Cincinnati OH 45242 (order: 1-800-331-3030). Annual tests conducted by major car magazines, consistently rate the Valentine One radar detector with laser warning as the best detection equipment available, by far.

War of 1812,
"The Invasion of Canada" and *"Flames Across the Border"* by Pierre Berton (Penguin) are excellent, very readable books about the War of 1812. Well researched; great detail.

Woodall's Campground Directory, - (www.woodalls.com).
306 Maplewood Dr., Greenville MI 48838 (order: 1-800-346-7572). One of the two essential campground and RV services guides to have aboard your RV (the other is "Trailer Life" - see above).

Abbreviations used in our maps

Space limitations in the maps necessitate the use of abbreviations for many of the fuel stations, restaurants and motels listed. For your convenience, the abbreviations used are listed on the next two pages.

GAS & DIESEL

49er ..... 49er Gas Co
66 .... Phillips 66
AM .... AM Best
Chevn .. Chevron USA
Conco .... Conoco
FlCity .... Fuel City
IndGas .... any independent gas stn
Mrthn ... Marathon Oil
Omga .... Omega
Penz .... Pennzoil
Pilot .... Pilot
Racwy ...... Raceway
Rctrac ...... Racetrac
SA .... SuperAmerica
Spdwy .... Speedway
Sunco .... Sunoco
Swfty ..... Swifty Gas
Texco .... Texaco
Thrntn ..... Thorntons

TRUCK STOPS (TS)

BPTS .... BP TS
DltaTS ...... Delta TS
ExnTS ..... Exxon TS
FlyJ ...... Flying J TS
FuelTS .. Fuel Mart TS
LGTS .... L & G TS
PilotTS ...... Pilot TS
SRTS .... Stoney Ridge TS
TATS ..... Truckstops of America
TexTS ..... Texaco TS

FOOD

Applby .... Appleby's
Arby .... Arbys
BaskR . Baskin-Robbins
Bengn ..... Bennigans
BgBoy .... Big Boy Family Restaurant
BKing .... Burger King
Blimp .... Blimpies
Bombay ..... Bombay Bicycle Club
Boston . Boston Market
Brangus . . Steak House
Drchrs ..... Dutcher's
BrewH ... Brew House
Buckr ...... Buckner's Family Rest
Burbnk . Burbanks BBQ
C/Kit . Country Kitchen
CaptD .... Captain D's
CBkn .... Country Bumpkin
CCbd .... Country Cupboard
Charles ..... Sea Food
Checkr ..... Checkers
ChiChi ...... Chi Chi's
ChickF .... Chick-Fil-A
ChinaHt .... China Hut
ChkW .... Chuck Wagon BBQ
ChnGd . . China Garden
Church ...... Chicken
CntryGrill .... Country Grill
CopperK ..... Copper Kettle
CPride . . Country Pride
CPtch ... Cotton Patch Restaurant
CrkBrl . . Cracker Barrel
CrzEd ...... Crazy Eds Restaurant
CtryBft . Country Buffet
D/Bell ..... Dinner Bell
Denny ...... Denny's
Diner . . Denny's Diner
DmnRibs .... Damons
Donut .... Donut Shop
DQ ...... Dairy Queen
Drthrs ...... Druther's
Duffs ..... Duff's Rest
DunkD .... Dunkin Doughnut
Dutch ... Dutch Pantry Restaurant
Evans ..... Bob Evans
Family .... Family Rest
Fazoli .... Fazzoli's
FlkSthrn Folk Southern
Frckr ... Fricker's Rest
Frndly .... Friendly Restaurant
GldnC . . Golden Corral
Goodflw . Goodfellows
Grdma .... Grandma's Kitchen
GtAmBft .... Great American Buffet
Gthouse ... Gatehouse
Hddle . . Huddle House
HickH . . Hickory House
HoJo .... Howard Johnson
Honey .... Honey Bun
Hooter ...... Hooters
Hrdee . . Hardee's Rest
IceCrm .... Ice Cream Churn
IHOP .... International House Of Pancakes
J&L . . J&L Famous Pits
Jcqlns ..... Jacqelines
Jerry's ... Jerry's Rest
KFC ... Kentucky Fried Chicken
KFrog ...... King Frog Restaurant
Knapp ... Bob Knapp's Restaurant
Krystal ... Krystal Rest
LChick . . Lee's Country Chicken
Lees . . Lees Restaurant
Lghtho .... Lighthouse
LJSilvr .... Long John Silver
LkyStr .... Lucky Steer Restaurant
LoneS ..... Lone Star Steaks
LongH ..... Longhorn Steaks
Louie's .... Louie's on the Lake
McDld .... McDonalds
McDld-I ... McDonalds . . with Inside Playarea
Morrel ...... Morrel's Restaurant
O'Char .... O'Charlies
OldCtry . . Old Country Buffet
Olive .... Olive Garden
OutBk .... Outback Steakhouse
Pantry .... Pantry Rest
PatsDnt . . . Pats Donuts
PatTS ...... Patty's TS Restaurant
Pdrsa ..... Ponderosa Steakhouse
Pekng . . Peking House
Petes .... Pestio Petes
Picdilly ...... Picadilly
Pizza .... Pizza Hut
PopE .... Popeye's
Prkns .... Perkin's Family Restaurant
Quincy ..... Quincy's Steak House
Raffty ...... Rafferty's
Rally .... Rally Drive-In
Ralph .... Ralphies
Rax . . Rax Restaurants
RedLb ... Red Lobster
RibS .... Ribeye Steakhouse
RockC ..... Rockcastle Steak
Ryan .... Ryan's Family Steakhouse
SaraJ ...... Sara Jane
Schlotzky . Schlotzky's Deli
Shony ..... Shoney's
Sonic .... 50's Drive In
Sonny . . Sonny's BBQ
Starvn . Starvin' Marvin
StkH .... Steak House
StkShk . Steak & Shake
Stones .... Stone's TS Restaurant
Stucky ..... Stuckey's
Subwy ...... Subway
Taco .... Taco Bell
TCBY . . The Country's Best Yogurt
TexSteak . . West Texas Steakhouse
TGIF ..... TGI Friday's
TimH ..... Tim Horton
Waffle . . . Waffle House
Wallys ... Wally's Rest
Wendy ...... Wendy's
WhtCstl . . White Castle
Wilson ...... Wilson's BBQ Pit
Wingr .... Wingers
Winnrs . Winner's Rest
WSizz . Western Sizzlin' Steakhouse
WStk . Western Stk Ho
WStr . . . Western Steer Steakhouse

LODGING

Ambssdr. Ambassador
AmInn . . American Inn
Baymnt . Baymont Inns & Suites
BdgInn. . Budget Inn of America
BestW . . Best Western
BgSav. . . . Big Savings Motel
BHost . . . Budget Host
BkEye . . . . . . Buckeye Budget Motor Hotel
BluGrs . . . . . Bluegrass
Brittny . Brittany Motor Inn
BstInn. . . . . . . Best Inn
C/Ctry . . Cross Country Inn
C/Rds . . . Cross Roads
ClubHs. ClubHouse Inn
Colonial . . Colonial Inn
Comfrt . . . Comfort Inn
Contntl . . . Continental Inn
Crown. . . . . Crown Inn
Crtesy . . . . . . Courtesy
CrtYrd . . . . . Courtyard by Marriot
CstlGt . . . . Castle Gate
CtryHrth . . . . . Country Hearth
CtySte. . . Country Inns & Suites
Cumberlnd . . Cumberland Inn
Days . . . . Days Inn
DBrdge. . . Drawbridge Inn
DRInn . . Dry Ridge Inn
Duffy . . . Duffy's Motel
Econmy . . . . Economy Motel
Econo. . . Econo Lodge
EmbsyS . . . . Embassy Suites
Exec. . . . Executive Inn
Fairfld . . . . Fairfield Inn
Family . . Family Inns of America
Flag . . . . Flag Inn
FShip . . Friendship Inn
Guest . . . . . . Guest Inn
H/Inn . . . . . Holiday Inn
H/InnS Holiday Inn Select
H/InnX. . . . Holiday Inn Express
Hahra . . . . . Hahira Inn
Hilton. . . Hilton Hotels
Hmptn . . Hampton Inn
Hmstd. . . . Homestead
HmWood . Homewood
HoJo. . . . . Howard Johnson
Hol/M . . Holiday Motel
Holly . . . . Holly Lodge
HomeTn . . Hometown
Hosplty. . . . Hospitality Inn
Hrtge . . Heritage Motel
Jamsn. . . Jameson Inn
Jellico . . . . . Jellico Inn
Jolly. . . . . Jolly Inn
Kings. . . . . . Kings Inn
Knght . . . . Knights Inn/Court
LaQnt . . . La Quinta Inn
Lkview . . Lakeview Inn
Marrtt . . Marriot Hotels
MicroT . . Microtel Inns
Motel. . . . . any unidentified motel
Motel6 . . . . Motel6
Motor . . . . . Motor Inn
Mstrs . . . . Masters Inn
MtnVw . . . . . Mountain View Motel
NewC. . . . . New Colony Inn
NFsyth . . New Forsyth Inn
Pssprt . . . Passport Inn
QltyInn. . . . Quality Inn
QltyMtl. . Quality Motel
Radsn . . . Radisson Inn
Ramda . . . Ramada Inn
RedC . . Red Carpet Inn
RedRf . . . Red Roof Inn
Regency . Regency Inn
Relax . . . . . . Relax Inn
Renfro . . Renfro Valley Motel
Rest. . . . . Rest Inn
RmdaSt . . . . . Ramada Suites
Rodwy . . Rodeway Inn
Rsdnts . . Residents Inn
Scot . . . . . Scottish Inn
Shertn. . . . . . Sheraton Hotels
Shony . . Shoney's Inn
Signtr. . . Signature Inn
Sleep. . . . . . Sleep Inn
SRInn. . . Stoney Ridge Inn
Std6+ . . . Studio6 Plus
Subrn . . . . . Suburban Motel
Supr8 . . . . Super 8 Motels
SwtHtl . . . Sweetwater Hotel
TravInn . . . . Travel Inn
TravL . . . . . Travelodge
TrdWd . . . Trade Winds Motel
Valley . . . . . . Valley Inn
Wavrly . . . . . . Waverly Motel
WCstle . . White Castle
WdaleLg . . Willowdale Lodge
Welcm . . Welcome Inn
WGate . . Westgate Inn
Wilburg . Williamsburg Motel
Wilsn . . . . . Wilson Inn
Wingate . . Wingate Inn
WldWd . . . . Wildwood Inn
Woodfld Woodfield
WPark . . West Park Inn
Wyndm. . . . Wyndham
XstayAm . . . Extended Stay America

A Word to our Readers . . .

Please note that we have not listed gas, food or lodging in the downtown areas of Detroit, Toledo, Dayton, Cincinnati and Atlanta. We feel that access to such facilities (and easy return to the Interstate) is often difficult for those not familiar with streets in the area. Furthermore, downtown facilities tend to be higher priced, catering more to the business traveler than vacationer - travel bargains will generally be found elsewhere. This Guide has been written with the long distance interstate traveler in mind, and accordingly we recommend staying or eating at facilities outside these areas.

Unless a facility is specifically mentioned in the "Insider Tips," ***inclusion in the Guide does not constitute a recommendation on the part of the publisher or author.*** We are however, interested in receiving your comments about facilities and other useful travel tips. If you are the first to advise us and your recommendation or tip is used in a future edition, a complimentary Guide will be sent your way.

Finally - every effort has been made to ensure the accuracy of the Guide's listings. Prior to printing this edition, two personal survey trips were made along the I-75, cross-checking information and ensuring that services were where they were supposed to be. The most recent survey was completed just a month prior to publication. We have included all major road construction projects encountered on this trip, although many may be completed before you head south. A revised edition of the Guide will be issued each October to ensure that the very latest information is always available to our Interstate traveler friends.

DATE		MILEAGE			FUEL	DAILY EXPENSE RECORD						OVERNIGHT STOP			
(M/D)	DAY	START	STOP	DIFF	(Gals)	B/FAST	LUNCH	DINNER	GAS	MISC	TOTAL	STATE	EXIT#	LOCATION	MOTEL
A	B	C	D	E	F	G	H	I	J	K	L	M	N	O	P

- Enter the **Date** (month/day), and the **Day** of the week (e.g.. Mon, Tues, etc.) in columns A & B.
- At the beginning of the first day, record your car's odometer reading in **Mileage Start** (column C). After finishing with the car each evening, record the odometer reading in **Mileage Stop** (column D). Post the same number in column C for the next day.

  To calculate the number of miles driven during the day, deduct column C from column D, and enter the result in **Difference** (column E).
- To calculate your daily **Miles per Gallon**, make sure you fill up your tank before you start your journey (do not enter these gallons on the chart).

  Keep a note of the number of fuel gallons purchased during each day.

  Each morning before you start, fill up your car and add these gallons to the fuel purchased during the previous day's run. Record this total for the previous day in column F.

  Divide the total number of miles driven during the previous day (column E) by the total number of gallons used (column F). The result will be your Miles per Gallon for the previous day.
- **Daily expenses** can be recorded in columns G to K, and totaled for the day in column L. Post your motel costs and sundry expenses in column L.
- Record details of your **Overnight Stops** in columns M to P.

Personal Log - Northbound

DATE		MILEAGE			FUEL	DAILY EXPENSE RECORD						OVERNIGHT STOP			
(M/D)	DAY	START	STOP	DIFF	(Gals)	B/FAST	LUNCH	DINNER	GAS	MISC	TOTAL	STATE	EXIT#	LOCATION	MOTEL
A	B	C	D	E	F	G	H	I	J	K	L	M	N	O	P

- Enter the **Date** (month/day), and the **Day** of the week (e.g.. Mon, Tues, etc.) in columns A & B.
- At the beginning of the first day, record your car's odometer reading in **Mileage Start** (column C). After finishing with the car each evening, record the odometer reading in **Mileage Stop** (column D). Post the same number in column C for the next day.

  To calculate the number of miles driven during the day, deduct column C from column D, and enter the result in **Difference** (column E).
- To calculate your daily **Miles per Gallon**, make sure you fill up your tank before you start your journey (do not enter these gallons on the chart).

  Keep a note of the number of fuel gallons purchased during each day.

  Each morning before you start, fill up your car and add these gallons to the fuel purchased during the previous day's run. Record this total for the previous day in column F.

  Divide the total number of miles driven during the previous day (column E) by the total number of gallons used (column F). The result will be your Miles per Gallon for the previous day.
- **Daily expenses** can be recorded in columns G to K, and totaled for the day in column L. Post your motel costs and sundry expenses in column L.
- Record details of your **Overnight Stops** in columns M to P.

Help me write the Year 2001 edition of . . .
. . . "Along the Interstate-75"

Please help me continue to make this ***your*** book. Each year, I receive many interesting letters from our readers. Before going to press, we review *every* suggestion and try and incorporate as many of them as possible into next year's edition. This way, I am able to make sure that the guide continues to meet *your needs*.

Please use the space below to record your recommendations or changes to the book's information. Use the other side for your comments and other suggestions. Tell me what you like about the guide, or what you don't like — we are constantly trying to improve it for you. To be considered for the 2001 guide though, we must have your submission by May 31, 2000. — Dave

---

To: *Dave Hunter, c/o Mile Oak Publishing Inc.,*
Suite 81, 20 Mineola Road East,
Mississauga ON Canada L5G 4N9

From:

☐ ✔ Please add my name to your mailing list for future books.

Name: ______________________ Phone: ______________

Address: ______________________________________

____

City: ______________ State/Prov: ______________ Zip/PC ______________

My recommendation or change in information:

(If recommending a facility, please include as much information as possible:)

State: ______ Exit #: ______ Facility Name: ______________________

East or West of Interstate: ______ Owner/Mngr's Name: ______________________

Their Phone #: ______________________ Gas ☐ Food ☐ Lodging ☐ Other ☐

Recommendation or Information to be changed:

____

____

____

____

____

____

Please use the other side for your comments or suggestions:

My comments and suggestions for the Year 2001 edition:

(Offer expires December, 2000)

I-75 in Florida Map

Ontario's Hwy 401

☐ Check (✔) box to left; fill in your name & address in the space below, mail this form to Mile Oak Publishing (see address below) - we will send you a free copy of Dave Hunter's black & white panel strip-map of the ***Interstate-75 to Tampa, Florida***.

☐ Check (✔) this box if you would also like to receive a copy of Dave Hunter's ***Ontario Highway 401**** map.

* Hwy 401 is the major freeway in Ontario, Canada, between the Detroit/Windsor area, and Toronto.

Name: ....

Address: ....

....

City: .... State/Prov.: ....

ZIP/Postal Code: .... Phone: ....

Need another copy of Along Interstate-75?
. . . check your local bookstore, or use this handy Order Form

Please send me____ copies of Along Interstate-75, 2000 edition, to the address shown above. I enclose my check as follows:

Orders shipped to US addresses: # of books x $19.95 + shipping ($3.00 first book/$1.25 each additional). Amount payable in US funds.

Orders shipped to Canadian Addresses: # of books x $24.95 + shipping ($4.50 first book/$1.00 each additional). Add 7% GST calculated on cost of total order. Amount payable in Canadian

Mail this form to: Mile Oak Publishing Inc.,
Suite 81, 20 Mineola Road East,
Mississauga, ON Canada L5G 4N9

If ordering a book, please make your check payable to - Mile Oak Publishing.

Questions? Please phone us at **905-274-4356**
(fax: 905-274-8656; e.mail: mile_oak@compuserve.com)